The Fitch Gazetteer

An Annotated Index to Dr. Asa Fitch's Manuscript History of Washington County New York

Volume 2

Compiled by Kenneth A. Perry

HERITAGE BOOKS
2007

HERITAGE BOOKS

AN IMPRINT OF HERITAGE BOOKS, INC.

Books, CDs, and more—Worldwide

For our listing of thousands of titles see our website
at
www.HeritageBooks.com

Published 2007 by
HERITAGE BOOKS, INC.
Publishing Division
65 East Main Street
Westminster, Maryland 21157-5026

Other Heritage Books by the author:

*The Fitch Gazetteer of Washington County, New York
Volumes 1, 2, 3, and 4*

*We Are In A Fight Today: The Civil War Diaries
of Horace P. Mathews and King S. Hammond*

International Standard Book Number: 978-0-7884-1113-7

The contents of this index have been derived from
an original manuscript owned by

The NEW YORK GENEALOGICAL and BIOGRAPHICAL SOCIETY

155 East 58th Street
New York, New York
10022- 1939

with my sincerest thanks for
their permission.

The supplemental contents in this volume
were derived from a copy of
Dr. Fitch's original Manuscript History
found in the research collection of the

SARATOGA NATIONAL HISTORICAL PARK

Site of the decisive defeats of the allied forces of Gen. John Burgoyne
at the battles of Freeman's Farm, Sept. 19th, and Bemis Heights, Oct. 7th, 1777.
The Turning Point of the American Revolution.

Stillwater, N. Y.

and used by their permission, with my thanks.

VOLUME TWO

Articles 701- 1100

Compiled from
February 1850- September 1862

CONTENTS

THEY MIGHT BE HEROES

A staggering one third of the articles comprising the Manuscript History were compiled by Dr. Fitch during the first few years of his project. These articles were principally the first- person versions and eye witness accounts of events that occurred during the early settling of the region and the Revolutionary War, as retold by the participants, or the children and grandchildren of those families directly involved in the course of events during the early history of Washington County.

Considering the ambitious pace of his professional career, it is remarkable that Dr. Fitch gathered such an extensive body of material in so little time. By 1847, when the original project began, four of Dr. Fitch's six children had been born, and ranged in age from their early teens, to infancy. In 1848, not only was he elected as President of the Washington County Agricultural Society, but he had also determined to revise the taxonomy of the Order Homoptera in New York (p. 49, Jeffrey K. Barnes, *Asa Fitch and the Emergence of American Entomology*, NYS Museum Bulletin No. 421, Albany, N. Y., 1988; hereinafter, *Barnes*). While his plate was already decidedly full, Dr. Fitch's pace did not slow, in either his private life, the enterprise of the Manuscript History, or in his professional life.

During the first five years of his investigations, over one hundred articles were collected by Dr. Fitch per year, and an incredible 350 articles in 1849 alone. On May 4, 1854, Dr. Fitch was appointed the first government- funded Entomologist for New York state, and here, the early passion driving the manuscript project plummets. Only a dozen articles in the Manuscript History may be attributed to this year, leaving the results of his first few months of interviews and study, which catalogued the nearly two hundred items found in Volume One, unequalled in the remainder of his text.

From 1855 to 1857, there were no additions to his manuscript, reflecting the prominence of Dr. Fitch's new capacity in his use of time. Following this gap, a few items were incorporated into the Manuscript History at a rate of just over a dozen per year, until 1861, when the entries again plummet, with the advent of the Civil War.

The Rebellion years seem to coincide with several mid- points- in Dr. Fitch's career, his family life, and in the contents of the Manuscript History. At this pivotal time, filled with uncertainties, Dr. Fitch had the vantage point, with his collection of the past achievements and exploits of the Revolution, the War of 1812, and the tales of the adversity in this area's early settlement, of interpreting the region's role in the ensuing conflict.

In consequence, much of the mid portion of the Manuscript History has an underlying heroic element in it. Although items pertaining to the Civil War pervade the remainder of the manuscript, the blend of past and future intermingles most poignantly near the close of the entries contained in this volume, during the accounts of the final organization and departure of the 123rd NYSV for Virginia, alarming rumors connected with the 2nd battle of Bull Run, and the anniversary meeting of the Washington County Bible Society.

Occurring within sight of Camp Washington, the organizing ground for the Washington County regiment, and held in the Old White Meeting House, the 50th anniversary of the Bible Society, attended by Deacon John McMurray, deaf with age, and the sole surviving member of the Society's first meeting, powerfully illustrates the passing of the old order. The anxiety and the theater of the moment is almost palpable, and the juxtaposition of these events, with their requisite images of God and Country, create in the imagination a prologue to that "last full measure of devotion" asked of a new generation. From this point, Dr. Fitch's perspective seems to be one in which he sees the area as a whole, rather than an amalgamation of patents or towns, and places them in the context of one cohesive Union.

While many of the earliest manuscript articles were abbreviated, the items in this central portion of the manuscript are lengthier, and more complex. This seems to characterize the remainder of the Manuscript History. The predominant character of this middle part of the manuscript is a divergence away from direct source material, as the population of potential witnessses were, understandably, dying out, or suspect in terms of the reliability of their recollections. Where transcriptions from early newspapers had been previously utilized, Dr. Fitch now expands the scope into more contemporary newspaper accounts, always with an eye for records of early events, but more inclined to view contemporary affairs with regards to their preservation.

However, in terms of time frame, there is nothing easily divisible with Dr. Fitch's work. Incidents related to the massacre of the Allen family are noticeably relegated to the attention of his first volume, with muted attention here, but Jane McCrea's massacre, and events of the Burgoyne Campaign continue to be of perennial interest, fading only at the manuscript's end. In this respect, there is an ebb and flow of information throughout the entire text of the Manuscript History in connection with certain subjects, but the ultimate impression is that some topics have simply been set aside momentarily.

Despite an overlapping character in its subjects, the mid- portion of the manuscript divides into two dominant themes of potential- that the individuals involved in events here might be heroes, and realization- that the individuals recognized here have become lions. As a result, the Manuscript History reveals its primary nature as HIS- story, in the tradition of so many of the histories and genealogies written during the 19th century. Nevertheless, it does diverge from the substance of other works by its personable, topical qualities, which can be attributed largely to the use of interview, and contemporary newspaper accounts.

During this section of the material, the issue lies largely in the balance, and uncetainty is high over the outcome, as the horrific returns trickle in from the raging conflict. It is only afterwards, that the floodgates are opened, and a deluge of material pertaining to the Civil War comes forward, if not triumphant, at least celebratory and grateful. Here, in retrospect, the contents appear as prelude to the more expansive items of growth and development that lay ahead.

& c.= and company, etc.
abstr.= abstract(ed)
abt.= about
acc.= according (to)
accomp.= accompany
acct.= account
acq.= acquire(d)
adj.= adjacent (to)
adjoin.= adjoin(ing)
adm.= admit(ted) to
admin.= administrator
affil.= affiliate(d)
afterw.= afterwards
agreem.= agreement
Amer.= American
amt.= amount
ano.= another
a/o= and/ or
appl.= applied, et al.
approx.= approximate
appt.= appoint(ed)
arr.= arrived
ascert.= ascertain(ed)
Assoc.= Associate
assoc.= associate(d)
attrib.= attribute(d)
Atty., atty.= attorney
b.= born
bapt., bp.= baptized
bef.= before
betw.= between
bro.= brother (of)
bur.= burial, buried
bur. grd.= burial ground
c., ca.= circa
Capt.= Captain
capt.= captive, capture(d)
Cav.= Cavalry
cert.= certain

certif.= certificate, certify
C. H.= Court House
char.= character
circ.= circulation, et. al.
clergym.= clergyman
Co.= company, county
Col.= Colonel
collab.= collaborate(d)
comm.= committee
consid.= consider(ed)
cont'd.= continued
cor.- corner (of)
Corp.= Corporal,
   corporation
d.= died
D. A.= District Attorney
dau.= daughter (of)
D. D.= Doctor of Divinity
Deac.= Deacon
desc.= descandant(s) of,
   descended (from)
detachm.= detachment
diff.= differed, different
d. inf.= died as infant
disch.= discharge(d)
distrib.= distribute(d),
   distribution
doc.= document
ds.= days
d. y.= died young
ea.= each
educ.= educate(d),
   education
emb.= embark(ed)
emig.= emigrate(d), et al.
Eng.= England, English
engagem.= engagement
enl.= enlist(ed), et al.
Ens.= Ensign

Esq.= Esquire
Est.= Estate
establ.= establish(ed)
establm.= establishment
estim.= estimate(d),
   estimation
evac.= evacuate(d),
   evacuation
evid.= evident(ly), et al.
Exec'r.= Executor
fn.= footnote
foll.= follow(ing), et al.
Fr.= French
freq= frequent(ly)
Gen.= General
gr.= grant, grave, great
grd.= grand, ground
grdau.= grand daughter (of)
grdf.= grandfather (of)
grdm.= grandmother (of)
grds.= grandson (of)
H. Art.= Heavy Artillery
Hon.= Honorable
HQ= Headquarters
hr., hrs.= hour, hours
husb.= husband
immed.= immediate(ly)
immig.= immigrant,
   immigrate, immigration
incl.= include(d), includes
Ind.= Independence, Indian
Inf., inf.= Infantry, infant
influ.= influence
inhab.= inhabitant, et al.
Inv.= Inventory
insuffic.= insufficient
intro.= introduce, et al.
iss.= issue(d)
knowl.= knowledge

loc.= locate(d), location (of)
Lt.= Lieutenant
m.= married
Maj., maj.= Major, majority
ment.= mention(ed)
merch.= merchant
mo., mos.= month(s)
mtn.= mountain
n. d.= no date
N. E.= New England
neighborh.= neighborhood
no.= number(s) of
nomin.= nominate(d)
nr.= near
N. S.= New School, Presbyterian
N. S.= New Style, calendar
obit.= obituary
obt.= obtain(ed)
opp.= opposite
ord.= ordained, ordination
org.= organized
orig.= original(ly)
O. S.= Old School, Presbyterian
O. S.= Old Style, calendar
partitn.= partition(ed)
pd.= paid

pens.= pension
perf.= perfect, perform(ed)
perh.= perhaps
pert.= pertains (to)
petitn.= petition(ed)
petitn'r.= petitioner
poss., possib.= possible, possibly
preced.= precedent, et al
Pres.= President
Presbyt.= Presbyterian
prev.= previous(ly)
Priv., priv.= private
prob.= probable, probably
propri.= proprietor
publ.= publish(ed), publication (of)
purch.= purchased
qtrs., qtr'd.= quarters, quartered
rec.= record(ed)
rec'd.= received
recoll.= recollect(s), recollect(ed), et al.
Ref.= Reformed
rem.= remove(d) to
Rens.= Rensselaer (Co.)
res.= resides
resid.= residence, residence

Rev.= Reverend, Revolutionary
s.= son (of)
sd.= said
settl.= settle(d), settler
settlm.= settlement
simult.= simultaneous(ly)
sist.= sister (of)
specul.= speculation
sq.=
sugg.= suggest(ed)
suppos.= suppose(s), supposed(ly)
suppl.= supply, supplied, supplies
testif.= testified, testifies
testim.= testimony
tradit.= tradition(ally)
transf.= transfer(red)
twp.= township
unattrib.= unattributed
unm.= unmarried
var.= variation (of), variety, various(ly)
w.= with
wf., wid.= wife, widow (of)
witn.= witness
w/o= without
wnd(s).= wound(s)
yr., yrs.= year(s)

INDEXED SUBJECTS

THE INSIGHT OUT ON THE MANUSCRIPT HISTORY

In whatever source that I have consulted, or whatever area I have explored while investigating the background of the Manuscript History and its creation, strong evidence exists of earlier attempts to edit or compile Dr. Fitch's manuscript into a more accessible form. Even if it were not undertaken as a project by the authors of these other sources, each of them has recognized the Manuscript History's value, and given an urgent admonition that its contents ought to be published.

This awareness, and acknowledgment of the manuscript's importance, seems to have begun from the very time of Dr. Fitch's death. In his obituary, in the *Salem Weekly- Review*, April 12, 1879, these considerations were noted in the following comments- "During his whole life Dr. FITCH carefully treasured everything, coming to his knowledge, relating to the early history of Washington County, ... he accumulated a mass of facts and incidents appertaining to its early history that we hope to see in print at no distant day".

Yet even before his demise, Dr. Fitch was already personally attempting to consolidate and present a synthesized version of his collected material into a structure appropriate to his immediate, local audience. Most of the material indicating this direction in his endeavors appear in the incomplete manuscripts and published newspaper clippings found in Judge Gibson's Ledger Copy of the Manuscript History. Another form of this direction may be found in a post- humus publication, "Early History of the Town of Salem, From Its First Settlement in 1761 to the Close of the Revolutionary War, Together with Incidents of Pioneer Days in Other Towns of Washington County, N. Y." This latter example of his work was serialized in the October and November 1927 issues of the *Salem Press*, and then reprinted in the same year as a 20 page pamphlet.

Of the printed articles found in Judge Gibson's Ledger, their period of publication was largely during 1873 and 1874, shortly after he resigned from his position as Entomologist of the State Agricultural Society (*Barnes*, p. 72). These six articles, all appearing in the *Salem Press*. were-

1. "For Our Posterity", September 8, 1869;
2. "The Quackenbush Family. The Horrid Indian Atrocity at Sandy Hill", March 14, 1873;
3. "The Quackenbush Family", February/ March 1873;
4. "The Proudfit Family", July/ August 1873;
5. "The Parker Family", July 27, 1874;
6. "Obituary- In the death of Mr. William McAllister, of this town...", June 28, 1877.

The first of these items was a simple compilation of the contents of a capsule inserted into the wall of the new Court House in Salem, N. Y., and also appears as a newspaper clipping (§ 1804) within the contents of the Manuscript History. The remaining articles fall into two categories- the recapitulation of information found in manuscript articles, and the reworking of various manuscript articles into a composite form.

Of these articles, the second and third items, pertaining to the Quackenbush family, amount to direct copies of articles from the Manuscript History. In the first of these items, the retelling of John Quackenbush's capture by the Indians varies from § 464 only by an introductory paragraph, and the rearrangement of two paragraphs at the end of the article. The second Quackenbush article was written at approximately the same time as the first, as a response/ correction to a February 21, 1873 article, written by the Tyashoke reporter of the *Washington County Post*. This same material appears as § 1983 in the Manuscript History, with little alteration of the contents, remarking that the material was collected, in part, as a result of the errors in the reporter's article.

In the remaining items, Dr. Fitch has, on two occasions, taken the obituaries of William McAllister and Mrs. Mary (Proudfit) Reid, both previous sources of manuscript material, as the pretext for providing genealogical information on earlier generations of their respective families. "The Parker Family", however, represents a detailed and expanded genealogical article that contains material not found in any other area of the Manuscript History, except for a small entry on that family in § 759.

It is with the incomplete essays in Judge Gibson's Ledger where a more thorough reworking of Dr. Fitch's previous manuscript articles may be found. An early lecture, given October 27, 1847, concerning the massacre of the Allen family (§ 100), exemplifies the standard technique applied by Dr. Fitch in these incomplete efforts, along with its requisite Victorian embellishments in oratory. This same approach was repeated in an undated paper "Jane McCrea's murder. Gates's swaggering letter" (§ 583s), found among the loose items in Judge Gibson's Ledger. The text that appears here remains consistent with his earlier lecture, with fewer florishes, noting that he has been "much occupied for twenty years in gathering up all the information extant, respecting the early history of this county,...", which would place the approximate time of this essay at ca. 1867.

While Dr. Fitch's remarks clearly suggest that the time period of his essay on the McCrea murder was ca. 1867, its contents have more in common with other incomplete essays that were evidently written, ca. 1873. An item concerning Salem militia units and their activities during the Revolutionary War (§ 2148½) was also found in Gibson's Ledger, written on a printed page from the program of proceedings for the annual meeting of the Washington County Sabbath School Union, 1873- 74, where Dr. Fitch appears listed as a Secretary of the proceedings. This entry has a similar style and content as another incomplete item concerning Rev. Dr. Thomas Clark's ambiguous position during the Revolutionary War (§2148½c) found on the reverse side of a partial letter, or article, intended "For the Salem Press, July 21, 1867" (§ 2160s). Another loose item, § 2157, "Festus and the

White House", contains composite information from § 246 and § 768, which falls into the same context as the previously mentioned articles.

According to William H. Hill, in the introductory remarks to his manuscript for *The Gibson Papers*, "a manuscript still in the hands of Dr. Fitch's descendants" was discovered by Harry E. Cole, of Salem, N. Y., and published by him. The contents of this manuscript first appeared in serial form in the *Salem Press*, and was the *Early History of the Town of Salem..* mentioned here previously. The notes in the introduction to the pamphlet published following this serialization state that "as nearly as can be determined it was written some years previous to 1850", a seemingly plausible conclusion, since most of the material was derived from items collected in articles in the earliest portion of the Manuscript History. However, the textual qualities of this essay have a great deal more in common with these incomplete manuscripts, with some hints of a connection to them in their plain, unembellished prose.

In a note at the conclusion of this historical pamphlet, the *Salem Press* notes that Mr. Cole copied the foregoing essay from Dr. Fitch's manuscript, in contradiction of the introduction, which stated that his permission to publish the material was given by Mrs. May A. Johnson, a great granddaughter of Dr. Fitch. This postscript notes further that Mr. Cole informs the *Press* that "in the vaults of the New York Genealogical and Historical Society, New York city [sic], are 1500 pages of manuscript written by Dr. Asa Fitch between the years 1830 and 1875- historic material that the doctor had gathered at first hand...". The actual historic record, found in the statements in Dr. Fitch's manuscript, also contradicts this peculiar statement, clearly indicating that 1847- 1878 was the time frame in which the Manuscript History was assembled.

During the same time period as Mr. Cole was publishing this post- humus article, William H. Hill, a local historian residing in Ft. Edward, N. Y., was publishing *Old Fort Edward- Before 1800* (1929). This volume was followed shortly thereafter by *History of Washington County, N. Y.* (1932), the first of his volumes known collectively as *The Gibson Papers*. Included in this first volume were three titles- "History of Washington County", "Bench and Bar of Washington County for a Century", and, "History of Washington Academy". While the first of these titles was an abbreviated hodge- podge of material pertaining to early items of Washington County history, the latter two items were among the original titles serialized by Judge James Gibson in the *Salem Weekly- Review*.

This first of Mr. Hill's compilations was privately printed by The Argus Press, Albany, for the Honeywood Press, of Ft. Edward, N. Y., with a run of 125 copies. According to the *Compiler's Note* at the beginning of Hill's second collection, this first publication was "too expensive for general circulation". A second series, in three volumes, appeared between 1954- 1956, published under the auspices of the Washington County Historical Society. The reprinted material of the seven titles of Judge Gibson's articles from the *Salem Weekly- Review*, as collected by William H. Hill, were as follows-

1. *History of Washington County, N. Y.*, 1932, which included the titles "Bench and Bar of Washington County...", originally published February 4, 1887- May 25, 1888; and, "Washington Academy", originally published April 27, 1888- May 5, 1893.

2. *Old Families*, 1954; originally published May 31, 1889- April 27, 1894.

3. *Old Families* (cont'd.); and, *Graves and Graveyards of Washington County*, 1955; the latter title originally published April 15, 1887- December 13, 1889.

4. *Graves and Graveyards of Washington County* (cont'd.), 1956, along with a comprehensive index to the three most recent volumes.

Of Judge Gibson's original seven titles, those not reprinted in Hill's series were-

1. *History of the Town of Salem*, published August 4, 1893- January 19, 1894;

2. *Noted Locations*, published November 7, 1890- November 27, 1891;

3. *Fires in Town*, published February 20, 1891- March 20, 1891.

According to Hill, these last three titles were not reprinted because their contents had already been published in some form "in town or county histories", or the author (Gibson) had "supplied the editors with material before his articles were published or the person responsible for these books, published at a later date, drew upon Gibson's papers to a considerable extent". Here, is another uncanny similarity between the use of Dr. Fitch's and Judge Gibson's creative efforts, both of them having provided some of their material for other publications. In Dr. Fitch's case, some of his data was included in Crisfield Johnson's *History of Washington County, N. Y.*, 1878 (p. 73, *Barnes*), and also in the Washington County chapter of J. H. French's *Gazetteer of New York State*, 1860 (see fn. 4, p. 677; and, fn. 6, p. 679). But what may be doubly ironic, is the possibility that material contributed to other publications by Gibson may originally have been borrowed by Gibson from Dr. Fitch's manuscript.

While in many instances unavoidable, a closer examination of the contents of *The Gibson Papers* will indicate that Dr. Fitch and Judge Gibson followed many of the same avenues of research and had overlapping, shared, material. Of the seventeen families discussed in the contents of *Old Families*, the Fowler, Carswell, Tomb, Doty, Turner, McCracken, McCrea, Atwood, McKellip, McCleary, and McClaughry families also figured prominently in the Manuscript History. The same instance of overlapping also applies to *Graves and Graveyards of Washington County*, a point which is especially applicable to the material connected with the burying ground at the head of Cossayuna Lake (§ 2024). What distinguishes any of the duplication or borrowing of material by Judge Gibson is that Gibson supplemented these items with additional research that Dr. Fitch did not pursue either because he did not have access to the references, or these references became available only after Dr. Fitch's death.

This same propensity for borrowing, sharing, or embellishing the record did not cease with Dr. Fitch and Judge Gibson for, in connection with the series on which Hill based his work, he notes that only "one or two complete files [are] known to exist", so that, in the introductory comments of his manuscript, Hill states-

"My satisfaction may be easily imagined when a book dealer one day brought to my office a complete file of this journal for the years 1887 to 1897, inclusive. I immediately set to work clipping and arranging the various articles into looseleaf books as well as miscellaneous sketches and obituaries. I had previously collected several volumes of clippings on similar subjects from other local papers and it thus became possible to publish this work".

In effect, William H. Hill became for Judge Gibson what Gibson had, in essence, become for Dr. Fitch, while both were attempting to provide some continuity to the fragmentary elements of the information they had available to them by supplementing the material. Working with Judge Gibson's material, Hill notes (again, in his *Introduction*) some of the same idiosyncrasies that were applicable to Dr. Fitch- "Mr. Gibson, to be perfectly frank, was quite inconsistent in his use of capital letters and punctuation; moreover he wrote in an involved style that often left some question as to the actual meaning of a sentence". Whether these parallel traits were the result of being contemporaries, or simply an unavoidable part of the nature of historical and genealogical research is debatable.

During the fledgling years of the Rensselaer School (later Rensselaer Polytechnic Institute), Professor Amos Eaton and others were engaged in a geological and agricultural survey of Albany, and later, Rensselaer county, New York. In this latter project, "surveyors used a system of neighborhood interviews to collect information for an agricultural calendar based on the experience of working farmers" (*Barnes*, p. 7). The methodology used in compiling this survey must have been something that Dr. Fitch was familiar with during his academic years at the Rensselaer School (1826- 27), when Prof. Eaton was his mentor, and the survey was certainly fresh in memory as a unique and pioneering venture for the acquisition of practical scientific data. Dr. Fitch must have had many opportunities to examine these surveys as a student, and participate in similar projects while at the Rensselaer School, as a striking resemblance exists between the outline of the survey techniques, and the earliest oral entries in the Manuscript History.

Barnes observes further, that Dr. Fitch, in his historical efforts, visited "octogenarians in the county who had lived there in childhood. While gathering information on agricultural history, he found that many of the people he interviewed remembered details of the Revolutionary War, and he deemed it his 'paramount duty to carefully rescue from oblivion and preserve to the world, such precious mementos of those pangs which attend a nation's birth' ", (*Ibid.*, p. 49). In this capacity, Dr. Fitch seems to have been unique in his powers of observation, or we might have heard of similar manuscript histories being spawned from other agricultural surveys conducted at an early date in other counties of the state.

Nevertheless, the oral accounts collected by Dr. Fitch constituted only a portion of the total number of articles found in the Manuscript History, perhaps only a quarter of the entire contents. The overwhelming bulk of the material collected in Dr. Fitch's manuscript was derived from Dr. Fitch's own independent pursuit of information, and was taken from three other principal areas- primary references, newspapers, and lists.

The heaviest infusion of oral accounts found in the Manuscript History appear in the first portion of the manuscript, which includes over one hundred individuals. These articles consist of the accounts that Dr. Fitch became most renowned for, as described above by Barnes- those records of the individuals who were participants or witnessses to events occurring during the early settlement and Revolutionary War years. Another differentiating characteristic of these early interviews was that the individuals were sought out by Dr. Fitch, while in the later interviews, a majority of the witness accounts were people who approached Dr. Fitch.

In consequence, earlier interviews often had a highly specific agenda pertaining to historical detail, and genealogical material was coincidental. In later years, the reverse was often true about the content of interviews, and details of historical instance were of a secondary, or tertiary nature. A specific example might be mentioned in this instance, in connection with § 1002, an account of the death of Gen. Simon Frazier, taken from a story given by John McDonald, Dr. Fitch's neighbor, who heard the story from his son, to whom it was related by a Baptist clergyman from Massachusetts, who knew Gen. Frazier's waiter. The description related in this case, conflicts with other known information concerning the event, and on inspection, appears to be the description of the death of Lt. Don, of the 21st Regt., during the battle at Freeman's Farm, as found in Anburey's *Travels*. And, as often became the case, Dr. Fitch became increasingly less satisfied with the reliability of accounts, as he notes during his series of interviews (§ 997- 999) with Mrs. Isabel, the widow of Duncan MacIntyre, September 14, 1853, when, in the midst of his second interview, he notes "I was much disappointed in not getting more information from Mrs. MacIntyre. She seemed unable to think of anything, except as I questioned her directly on one point and another".

Of his witnesses, a handful- Robert Blake, Jacob Biteley, Donald McDonald, Deacon John McDonald, and Eunice Campbell Reid, account for a dozen, or more, articles apiece in the early manuscript entries, but the number of individuals who provide these repeat entries dwindles as the years progress. Even with Robert Blake, who was the most extensively consulted of the earliest witnesses, with over 30 accounts, the question of accuracy changes over the space of two years. In October 1847, when Blake gives his record of the McCrea massacre (§ 51), and Dr. Fitch observes his probable efforts at the concealment of his role in the event, his details were considered more accurate than another discussion (§ 583) on September 10, 1849. At this point, Blake's recollections were considered more obscure and less reliable, his "impressionist statements" considered "derived from subsequent hearsay information, in wove with his original knowledge" to such an extent, that Dr. Fitch considers consulting Jacob Biteley for verification of the material, and corroboration of the information he obtained from Timothy Eddy.

With over half of the earliest witnesses, Dr. Fitch allotted only a single interview, and gave repeat visits to only fourteen, or else divided the contents of a single account into two parts. Thirteen individuals contributed four articles each, but the number of multiple interviews were relegated to only a few- Rev. John Dunlap, and William McCollister and his wife, each gave eleven; Hon. John Savage and Dr. Fitch's uncle, John Pattison, both contributed nine articles. Three people- Isaac Dickison, Jonathan Jacquay, and John McEachron, gave accounts for eight articles. The largest number of individuals giving multiple accounts in the first portion of the Manuscript History was six- Jacob Quackenboss, Hon. Edward Savage, Belus Hard, Charlotte Leslie, and Ann McArthur, who each gave seven accounts.

Although some individual names may overlap through the portions of the Manuscript History that have been arbitrarily divided into volumes here, and some repeat articles were obviously portioning out of more extensive interviews, a significant drop in witness numbers occurs following the first third (Volume One) of Dr. Fitch's manuscript. From this point on, the number of witnesses remains relatively consistent from volume to volume, amounting to just over sixty per volume. Most of the later multiple accounts derive themselves primarily from contributed manuscripts that were subdivided, rather than first person interviews. The majority of witnesses continue to be consulted once, and sometimes twice, by Dr. Fitch. The number of multiple interviews per witness decreases over time, and the primary characteristics for repeat interviews seem to be that the witnesses are relatives, neighbors and individuals close at hand, persons with extensive personal knowledge, or individuals who were deliberately sought out at some distance, with whom Dr. Fitch had a specific agenda.

The highest number of primary source references copied into the Manuscript History by Dr. Fitch occur at the beginning of the manuscript and, like witness accounts, significantly declines and becomes more evenly distributed through the remainder of the text. At the beginning, newspaper items were derived mostly from early issues of *The Northern Centinel* and *The Northern Post*. However, as time progresses, the newspaper entries increase, and it seems to become both more expedient and acceptable to enter articles from newspapers of a more contemporary date. On some occasions, where newsclippings were utilized, the material was either lost, as with the biographical sketch (§ 1096) of Capt. Miller of Fort Edward, or pasted onto the pages almost beyond recognition, as mentioned in Abbie M. Fitch- Andrews' initial remarks. In the very last half of the manuscript, the number of newspaper entries swells, and in the final volume, exceeds in frequency the number of primary references consulted.

The use of lists for article information appears most frequent at the beginning and at the end of the Manuscript History, although the last portion of the manuscript relies on more than twice as many lists as the first portion. The majority of the extra lists found at the end of the manuscript pertains mostly to Civil War enlistment data, and a more spirited contribution of early lists connected with Salem's Presbyterian church and its centennial. Throughout the manuscript, many of the lists seem to arrive in an almost serendipitous fashion, just as a number of

Dr. Fitch's articles of independent research consist of "found" items, rather than reference material taken from libraries or archives.

The manner of change in the composition of sources utilized by Dr. Fitch to construct the Manuscript History reflects the way in which Dr. Fitch's work habits changed over time. At the beginning, witness accounts and primary source material were pre-eminent, but by the end of the manuscript, these sources had been superceded by lists, newspaper entries, and items of individual research, such as collections of cemetery data. The middle portion of the manuscript, on the other hand, was very homogeneous in blending all of these elements to comprise the Manuscript History.

These observations are based solely upon the raw count of article numbers rather than the depth of their content. For example, the Civil War diary of Horace P. Mathews was entered as a single article (§ 1295), while the diary of King S. Hammond was parceled out (§ 1298- 1312). This same circumstance was followed in the instance of Esq. Munro's affidavit (§ 638- 653), which was followed by Smith's report, another extensive entry on the Vermont boundary dispute (§ 654), that was curtailed in content because the closing of an office prevented further copying. While there was no indication in the text that the latter subject was ever taken up again, a series of articles (§ 883- 912) deals with many of the same issues at a slightly later point in the manuscript, and the material here was broken into smaller, more manageable chunks.

This apparently arbitrary way that Dr. Fitch had in proportioning the size of his articles seems to have had more to do with his energy, enthusiam, or time constraints in gathering the material. At the onset, each entry into the manuscript was enumerated, but following the records entered from the Hebron burying ground, Dr. Fitch appears to realize the folly of such detail and broadens the scope of each article so that later cemetery entries are treated as lists, and except where a topic consumes his attention, he serves smaller portions.

Perhaps the most disturbing problem connected with the Manuscript History pertains to the number of missing articles, and a concern over their contents. According to Abbie M. Fitch- Andrews' statement at the beginning of the manuscript, the majority of missing items were lost either when Tobias A. Wright had Mr. Blanchard rebind the volumes, or because Judge Gibson may have forgotten and mislaid some borrowed articles. In Mrs. Andrews' eyes, these items were important, to the extent that she must have been familiar with them as the keeper of the collection. However, she gives no clue as to their content, and except for the absence, or brief attention, to certain familiar subjects in the latter half of the manuscript, there is no way to determine their content.

In the extant Manuscript History, of the 2,141 enumerated articles, the missing items fall into three categories- articles Dr. Fitch never enumerated, articles that shared the same enumeration, and items that were missing outright. Only seven items were missing from the first third of the manuscript for any of the above reasons, and most were omitted because an enumeration was accidentally skipped, or repeated. Two items were missing in the portion of the manuscript appearing in this volume, both of them specifically described by Mrs. Andrews, and both of them described in Judge Gibson's Ledger, with enough detail to identify them as missing newspaper clippings.

A majority of the missing manuscript articles may be attributed to the second half of the Manuscript History, a total of 152 items, with 30 articles missing from the portion found in Volume Three, and the remaining 122 articles missing in Volume Four. These items were also missing from Judge Gibson's Ledger, and it may therefore be inferred that the Ledger's contents were probably compiled at about the same time that Mr. Blanchard was rebinding the Manuscript History.

It appears from the divisions made by Mrs. Andrews that the entire manuscript was intended to contain 2500 articles, ending with the Crozier family (§ 2500) referred to in § 1448. Whether any of the articles between 2141 and 2500 were ever compiled is debatable, as only § 2500 was ever referred to in any of the articles prior to § 2141. From all of the loose articles found in Judge Gibson's Ledger, it is clear that any articles prior to § 2141, and § 2500, were enumerated by Dr. Fitch. In fact, two copies of § 2500 may be found in the Ledger, one in Dr. Fitch's signature, and the other in Judge Gibson's signature, making it clear that of the articles enumerated beyond § 2141 that were found in the Ledger, these enumerations were added by Judge Gibson, while the text was written by Dr. Fitch.

Finally, in the introductory remarks (December 25, 1931) to his first volume of *The Gibson Papers*, William H. Hill notes that while compiling *Fort Edward- Before 1800*, he "necessarily examined as many as possible of the historical works which described the country surrounding Fort Edward and, as the work progressed, it became increasingly evident that there were three real local sources of Washington county history, outside of such material as had been preserved in public archives". These sources were listed by Mr. Hill as-

1. the Williams papers;
2. "the published and unpublished writings of Dr. Asa Fitch";
3. "the Honorable James Gibson's papers", and all three of these sources were described in Hill's *Introduction*.

The Williams papers consisted of correspondence and documents preserved by the descendants of Dr./ Gen. John Williams (1753- 1806) of Salem, N. Y., and were considered by Hill to be "the first of these, both in importance and chronology". These papers were apparently discovered in the summer of 1872, as Dr. Fitch copied several items from them (§ 1920- 1930) into the Manuscript History at that time. In the first of these copied articles, Dr. Fitch notes the discovery in the Williams family mansion of this "mass" of papers, by Miss Hattie Williams, a great granddaughter of Gen. Williams, and a Mr. Hall, of Troy, N. Y., "by whom they have been collated and arranged for fastening into portfolios for permanent preservation". The entries in the Manuscript History appearing prior to, and following after these articles, refer to events on July 3, 1872, and to newspaper information from the August 2, 1872, *Washington County Post*, respectively, which fixes the approximate date of their discovery. Hill states further that the Williams papers "were bound, I understand, in six volumes and not so many years ago given into the keeping of Mr. T. A. Wright with the request that they be presented to some historical society where they would be appreciated and preserved. Mr. Harry Cole of Albany, and formerly of Salem, advises me that Mr. Wright presented the papers to the New York Genealogical and Biographical Society and I hope in the near future that an arrangement can be made with the society to permit the publishing of these vital records".

The third source, *The Gibson Papers*, was Mr. Hill's personal contribution to the genealogical and historical sources in Washington county, and his assessment of Judge Gibson is significant both in comparison, and in contrast to Dr. Fitch and the Manuscript History. In part, Hill states that "Mr. Gibson, in my estimation, is our outstanding authority on local history, nor is his position ever likely to be occupied by anyone of present day or later generations. He lived partly, as did Dr. Fitch, at a time when survivors of the Revolution could still be interviewed to say nothing of the numberless people only one generation removed from that great conflict. ... to his indefatigable industry, legal training and apt mind we owe the preservation of invaluable information".

It is ironic that Dr. Fitch's endeavors were supplanted in importance by Judge Gibson's works and later publications that were at least partially derived from the Manuscript History. The principal reason appears to be its massive size, described by Hill as "some 1500 pages written in a microscopic hand", which prevented Dr. Fitch from fully articulating its contents in an accessible form. In consequence, some parts of the Manuscript History have been superceded over ensuing years by other authors plowing the same furrows as Dr. Fitch, or through publications offering condensed versions of certain portions of the manuscript's contents. Despite these inroads, the Manuscript History still remains the fountainhead of information, both familiar and obscure, pertaining to Washington County.

Albany, N. Y.- Proceedings of the Albany Committee of Correspondence, 1775
Alden, Timothy- A Collection of American Epitahs and Inscriptions, 1814
(Alden's Epitahs)
Allen, William- Allen's Biographical Dictionary: William Hilliard, Cambridge, &
Farrand, Mallory & Co., Boston, 1869 (Allen's Biographical Dictionary)
Barber, John Warner- The History & Antiquities of New England, New York, &
New Jersey; Worcester Mass., 1841
Burgoyne, Lt. Gen. John- Orderly Book, London, 1860; or, Orderly Book of, ...,
from his Entry into the State of New York until his Surrender at Saratoga 16th
Oct. 1777; ed., E. B. O'Callaghan; J. Munsell, Albany, 1860.
Charlesworth's Magazine of Natural History; London, 1837
Christian Magazine, Vol. 4, 1835; & Mar. 1839; Geneva, N. Y.
Croswell, Harry- Balance & State Journal
Danby, Vt.- Book of Deeds
Dowling, Rev. John- Life & Writings of Dow, Part 1,"Exemplified Experience", or
Lorenzo's Journal; New York, 1850
Duer, William Alexander- Life of William Alexander, Earl of Stirling, Major
General in the army of the United States During the Revolution (Duer's Life of
Stirling)
Ellet, Elizabeth Fries Lumis- Women of the Revolution
Gentleman's Magazine, Vol. 61, Apr. 1791; London
Hall, Edwin- The Ancient Historical Records of Norwalk, Conn., w. a Plan of the
Ancient Settlement and of the Town in 1847
Hinman, Royal R.- A Catalogue of the names of the 1st Puritan settlers of the
colony of Connecticut; Hartford, Conn., 1846
Holden's Magazine
Hollister, Gideon Hiram- History of Pawlet, Vt.
Hooker, Sir William Jackson- Hooker's Icones Plantarium, 1829- 31
Kettell, Samuel- Specimens of American Verse, 1829
Lindley, John- London Gardener's Chronicle; London, 1854
Merchants of New York
Mitchell, Nahum- History of the Early Settlement of Bridgewater, in Plymouth
County, Massachusetts; Boston, Mass., 1840
Munsell, Joel- Munsell's Albany Register, 1849; Annals of Albany; Munsell &
Rowland, Printers, Albany, 1859 (Munsell's Annals); Munsell's Typographical
Miscellany, July 1850
New York- Military Patents
O' Callaghan, Edmund Bailey, M. D., LL. D.- Documentary History of New York;
Weed, Parsons and Company, Public Printers, Albany, 1849, 1850
Parton, James- The Legend & Times of Aaron Burr, 1857

Sabine, Lorenzo- The American Loyalists: or, Biographical Sketches of Adherence to the British Crown in the War of the Rebellion; Charles C. Little & James Brown, Boston, 1847; or, Biographical Sketches of Loyalists of the American Revolution, 1864

Smith, William, Jr.- History of the Province of New York, from its Discovery to the year 1736

Sparks, Jared- The Library of American Biography, 1st series, 1834- 38; Writings of George Washington, 1834- 37; Letters to George Washington

Stone,William L.- Life of Joseph Brant- Thayendanegea, including the Indian Wars of the American Revolution, New York, 1838 (Stone's Life of Brant)

Sullivan, James, Ph. D.- Minutes of the Albany Committee of Correspondence, 1775- 1778; The University of the State of New York, Albany, 1923 (derived from the orig. bound manuscripts- Proceedings of the Albany Comm. of Corresp., above)

Thatcher, James A.- A Military Journal during the American Revolutionary War from 1775 to 1783; Richardson & Lord, Boston 1823, 1827; reprinted, 1854, as Military Journal; & 1862, as The American Revolution

Thompson, Zadock- History of Vermont, Natural, Civil, and Statistical; Chauncey Goodrich, 1842, Burlington, Vt. (Thompson's Gazetteer of Vermont)

Washburn, Emory- Sketches of the Judicial History of Massachusetts from 1630- 1775; 1840

Washington County, N. Y.- Deeds; Mortgages; Miscellanies

Weed, Thurlow- Journal of the Provincial Congress, Provincial Convention, Committee of Safety & Council of Safety of the State of New York, 1775- 76- 77; Albany, 1842

Sources identified only in the form used by Dr. Fitch

Boston City Directory, 1835
The Present State of Great Britain; printed 1710
Territory Rights

NEWSPAPERS

The Adviser (Glens Falls, N. Y.)- 721
Cambridge Valley News- 1095
Connecticut Courant- 973
Farmer's Gazette- 1078
N. Y. Express- 1035, 1076
N. Y. Herald- 920
N. Y. Leader- 1075b
N. Y. Observer- 799, 961, 971, 1008, 1024, 1056, 1067, 1072b, 1091
N. Y. Times- 988
N. Y. Tribune- 799, 1094

LISTS

Angel, Wid. Augustus (Triphena Martin)- 847- 856; 857, w. Betsey Taylor; 858- 870

Bain, Mrs. Casparus (Mary Gillespie)- 976, 977; 983, w. Mrs. Livingston; 984- 986

Barnett, Nathaniel, Esq.- 762, 762b; 763, w. Dr. Fitch; 764, 1022

Barton, Mrs. Ann- 1093

Blanchard, Judge Anthony I.- 914- 919

Boyd, Thomas- 729

Brayton, Deac. William- 745; 746, w. Dr. Fitch

Brownell, Isaac- 1006, 1007

Campbell, Caty- 1060- 1065

Campbell, Roger- 802

Clark, Reubin- 765- 767; 768, w. an addition by Richard Powell

Cleveland, Aaron- 1073

Cook, Ransom, Esq.- 1054- 1057

Cooley, Mrs. Seth- 1024

Coon, Rufus- 1033, 1034

Cornell, Paul- 806, 807

Dobbin, Samuel- 732

Doty, Isaac- 748

Emmons, Mrs. William L.- 1069

Farnsworth, Ebenezer- 750

Fitch, Almira Martin- 730, w. Dr. Fitch & Mrs. Wm. Fitch; 1049a, 1049b, w. Mary (Fitch) McFarland

Fitch, Dr. Asa- 702- 726; 730, w. Mrs. William Fitch, & Almira Martin Fitch; 731, 731½n, 735, 736; 745, w. Deac. Wm. Brayton; 747- 756, w. Esq. John C. Parker; 757, w. Samuel Standish; 759s, 760, w. Chauncey K. Williams; 761; 763, w. Nathaniel Barnett, Esq.; 772- 798; 799, w. Mrs. Sturgis & Mrs. Weed; 808- 811, 813- 838, 874- 913, 920, 928- 932, 934- 938, 944- 949b, 953- 957, 960, 961, 968b, 971, 972, 975, 987- 990, 992, 993, 996, 1003, 1005, 1008- 1017, 1019- 1021, 1023- 1030, 1035; 1037-1046, w. Charles L. Martin; 1047b, 1051, 1052, 1059, 1066- 1068, 1070, 1072, 1074, 1075; 1076, w. Mrs. Alva Freeman; 1077, 1079- 1082, 1087, 1088; 1089, w. Lambert Martin; 1090frag, 1090b, 1091, 1092, 1094- 1095b, 1097- 1099; 1100, w. Aaron Martin, Jr.

Fitch, John- 943

Fitch, Capt. Richard H.- 939, 940; 941, w. his wf.; 942

Fitch, Mrs. William- 730, w. Dr. Asa Fitch & Almira Martin Fitch

Getty, Deac. Isaac- 744, 803

Gibson, Judge James- 734s; 845, w. Sidney Wells; 1047½s

Hanna, Robert- 701

A LIST OF ARTICLES

1077. Dr. Asa Fitch of Vienna, N. Y.

1078. David Rumsey printer- Dec. 24, 1861- John B. Stevenson

1079. Maj. Menzies

1080. Washington county volunteers in the rebellion 1861

1081. Soldiers interred in Evergreen Cemetery, Salem

1082. Books printed in Washington county, pamphlets, & c.

1083. Robert Armstrong- Jan. 1862- Deac. John McMurray (1083- 1086)

1084. John Livingston- Jan. 12, 1862

1085. Reuben Turner

1086. Alexander Turner

1087. Rev. Dr. Dwight's death

1088. Gen. Orville Clark

1089. Fort Randall, Dacota- Lambert Martin, Journal, Oct. 31- Dec. 7, 1861

1090. Descendants of James Turner- Feb. 4, 1852- William & Gideon Turner

1090b*. 93d Regiment N. Y. S. V. Morgan Rifles

1090frag.* A Down- East Juryman †

1091. Hutton's Bush, former name of Putnam

1092. Putnam, Lot 23; Geo. Willey

1093. Samuel Glover's descendants- Apr. 2, 1862- Mrs. Ann Barber

1094. Slavery rebellion, 1861, '62 Washington Co. volunteers. 93d Regiment

1095. Slavery Rebellion, 1861, '62. Natives of Washington Co., in the War

1095½.* (as 1095b.)The 22d Regt. N. Y. S. V. in the 2nd battle at Bull Run

1096. Capt. Miller (Ft. Edward) Biographical Sketch- newsclipping, missing

1097. Wash. Co. Bible Society; semicentennial anniversary

1098. Departure of Regiment 123, from Salem

1099. Shinplaster currency

1100. Elizabeth Burrows

Supplemental Titles

The following items appear as articles, or notations, in the Facsimile, or Ledger copy, of the Manuscript History. Except for § 1047½, the enumerations have an "s" added, to indicate supplemental material to the articles they pertain to. In the instances of § 1048s, and 1050s, missing from the original manuscript, and only notated in the Facsimile Manuscript, the contents have been derived from "Trial of Martin Wallace for the Murder of Barney McEntee", Oct. 5, 12, & 19, 1858, *Salem Press*, & from "Execution of Martin Wallace", Dec. 7, 1858, *Salem Press*, respectively.

734s. Mack family- Judge Gibson

759s. The Parker Family- Dr. Fitch

1047½. Alvah Wright's Family Bible- Judge Gibson

1048s. Conviction of Wallace for Murder

1050s. Execution of Wallace

A

ABBOT,
Mary- of Whitehall, N. Y.; m. Robert H., s. Elijah & Martha (McAllister) Mack-
734

ABEEL,
Jacobus- def., in a case brought by Peter T. Curtenius- **878**
James- pl., Jan. 16, 1775, vs. Rev. Thomas Clark- **878**; of New Perth (Salem,
N. Y.) mortgages Jan. 15, 1774, Lot 86, Turner's Patent, 88 acres & all edifices
therein, to Rev. Dr. Thomas Clark, for £ 150- **938**
P. D.- (Abel) 1st Farrier & Blacksmith, Co. A, 2nd N. Y., Northern Black Horse,
Cav., 1861- 2- **1080**

ABERCROMBIE,
_____- merch., Pelham, Mass.; m. Sarah, only sist. Joshua & Silas Conkey, both of
Salem, N. Y.- **730**
Gen. James- (1706- 1781) prob. some time foll. his defeat at Ft. Ticonderoga
(July 8, 1758) a train of military stores was ambushed by Indians abt. 2 mi. below
Ft. Edward on the W. side of the Hudson, killing one teamster, who was bur. on
the site; incident attrib. to this time period by Dr. Fitch as "the Indians so much
infested this vicinity, & murdered so many teamsters betw. Ft. Edward & Ft.
George" during that period- **958**; c. 1798/9, the Royal Highland 'Black Watch' regt.
was reportedly under his command in Egypt, '& gained the red feather as a
peculiar mark of distinction for its gallantry there'- **990**

ABERNETHY,
Lavinia- of New Haven, Vt.; m.William Harrison, s. Newell & Charity (Blackman)
Angel- **848**

Accolent- definition; "one who dwells on or nr. the border of a country"; prob. a
reference to Isaac Brownell, who res. on the last farm on the road up White creek,
Rensselaer co., N. Y., & accomp. Dr. Fitch "walking over the ground, over which
Baume & Breyman marched their troops to the battle of Bennington"; (Dr. Fitch
would prob. have appreciated this more succinct phrase for its vernacular qualities-
'Dwelling hard by.'-Oxford English Dictionary; see Down Country)- **1006**

ACKLAND,
Lady Harriet- (Christian Henrieta Caroline, 1750- 1815, wf. Maj. John Dyke
Acland, or Ackland, who d. 1778) foll. the mortal wnd. of Gen. Simon Frazier at
the battle of Bemis Heights, Oct. 7, 1777, he was carried on a litter to a house then
occ. by her & later d. there- **1002**

ACKLIN,
Francis- def., in a case brought by Wm. Duer, Esq.- **878**

ADAMS,
Erastus- printer; publ. *Whitehall Emporium*; d. Apr. 15, 1825, at 25, Whitehall, N. Y.- **1029**
Pres. John- (1735- 1826) proposed a tax on windows & c., that was agitating the country; in anticipation of its passage, Hugh Pebbles directed John Pattison to count the windows & panes of the Duer Mansion, Ft. Miller, N. Y., leading to the latter's familiarity w. the structure's appearance- **1031**
Dr. Samuel- his Arlington, Vt. scout party suspected by Dr. Fitch as being the tory party that capt. George Hundertmark, the Hessian deserter, Aug. 1777- **740**; Ethan Allen was overheard by Benjamin Hough as saying that he should have given him 500 lashes when the Bennington mob had him 'instead of hoisting him up & exposing him upon landlord Fay's sign- post, where was fixed a dead catamount'; see Vol. 1- **881**
Rev. Dr.- officiated, Jan. 30, 1862, at the funeral of Rev. Harrison G. Otis Dwight, Presbyterian church, at Madison Ave. & 24th St., NYC; additional eulogies delivered by Revs. Anderson, Wood, & Skinner- **1007**
Walter- shoemaker; res. Younge, Leeds co., Ont., Canada; m. Freelove, dau. Thomas Golden & Wid. Catherine Patterson- **812**

ADGATE,
Asa- (1767- 1832; N. Y. Assembly, 1798; 14th Congress, 1815- 17) he & John Williams identified by Gen. Schuyler as politicians assisting Aaron Burr in intrigues leading to Schuyler's defeat for re- election as U. S. Senator- **920**

AFRICA- Cape Palmas (Liberia)- 839; Gaboon (Ogoobé) river- 1082

AKIN,
Charles H.- (Aikens) oath of alleg.; Co. D, 22nd N. Y. Inf.- **(L)- 1074**; Sgt., Co. D; promoted to 2nd Lt., Aug. 30, 1862, replacing Wm. T. Beattie- **1096b**
John- (Aikins) Co. A, 2nd N. Y., Northern Black Horse, Cav., 1861- 2- **1080**

ALABAMA- 799; Mobile- 759s; Montgomery- 799

Albany- Bennington road, the old- c. 1777, passed thru Walloomsac & Sancoick, N. Y., & down the valley of the Hoosic river, crossing it at Fonda's bridge, 2 mi. above Eagle bridge- **766**

Albany, N. Y.-
Cemeteries- "The foll. names & dates I [Dr. Fitch] gathered from the monuments
in Albany cemetery"; loc. not given, ano. textual note suggests the Van Schaik
cemetery, loc. on Court St.; the remains of Gen. Gose Van Schaik rem. to this
cemetery from Court St. on Dec. 1, 1808- **(L)- 932**;
   Committee of Correspondence- a series of entries extracted from Proceedings of
Albany Comm. of Correspondence, 1775- **817- 833**; Godliel Switzer, the British
Commissary at Ft. Ticonderoga, presents petitn., July 9, 1775, seeking a position
that would enable him to support his family; Comm. furnished him w. provisions
from the provincial stores, & advised him to go to NYC- **817**; Capt. Wells appears
bef. Comm., July 13th, & seeks payment for the services of a 25 man co. raised by
him & marched to Ticonderoga; he also responded to earlier requests for officers of
the Battalion; Comm. referred wage request to N. Y. Prov. Congress, & informed
Wells that all officer positions had been filled; Dr. Fitch notes numerous letters to
& from Gen. Philip Schuyler, & also from Tryon Co., during 1775- **818**; a letter
rec'd. July 17th, from Capt. John Graham, noting David Jones declined a position
as 2nd Lt., & requests ano. appt. in his stead; appl. rec'd. Aug. 9th, by Peter B.
Tearse, for 40 guns to outfit a grenadier co. being raised by him in Albany; loan
granted- **819**; Aug. 22nd- information rec'd. from John McCrea, Esq., saying that
he had obt. word of John Munroe, Esq. receiving comm. as Capt. in the King's
service under Col. Allen McLean; a letter drafted & sent to Cambridge Comm.
requesting that they discreetly investigate Esq. Munroe to conclude the truth of the
issue 'w. as little violence & as much secresy as you can, & the nature of the case
will admit of'- **820**; Comm. of Bennington gives notice that all militia in their
district have formed into companies; Dr. Fitch notes that all of the districts within
Albany Co. have also been ordered to do so- **821**; correspondence, Aug. 29, 1775,
from Daniel B. Bratt, Comm. of Hoosic, & rec'd. Sept. 4th, describing efforts
behind the investigation of John Monroe, Esq., concluding 'we cannot think he is
in the least guilty, & have entirely disch. him on that acct.'- **822**; Oct. 3rd- list of
recommendations for names appt. as officers in Saratoga district; additional names
for Comm. members of Saratoga district- **823**; new Committees of Correspondence
elected in all districts, Nov. 10th; new members of Cambridge & Saratoga districts
listed- **824**; Jan. 18, 1776- a no. of men from Cambridge, N. Y., in consequence of
an order to visit Sir John Johnson & disarm tories, are now in Albany; as main
body had already left, they remain uncert. over their own course, resolve to remain
in Albany, & request provisions; Comm. grants a day's provision for 21 men, & the
foll. day, they resolve to return home; see Johnstown, & Stillwater, N. Y.; Vol. 4-
825; return of Cambridge district, Feb. 4th, listing new Comm. members; Feb.
27th, James Parrot refuses his post, & ano. ordered to fill the vacancy; Gen.
Schuyler recommends Peter B. Tearse to fill the post of Adjutant; militia of the
district & corporation of Cambridge unite to form one regt., known as No. 18- **826**;
Isaac & John Man examined in 2 separate cases of a similar nature, & are ordered
disarmed for opposing, denying the authority of, & speaking disrespectfully of the
Continental Congress; ea. ordered to pay court costs; also, Archibald McNeil

refuses appt. as Adjutant, Col. John McCrea's regt., & John Vernor appt. in his place- **827**; Apr. 11- list of field officers recommended for appt. by Comm. of Cambridge district- **828**; Apr. 20- list of prices resolved to be publ. in handbills due to rise in costs of West Indies produce & Bohea teas- **829**; a servant of Gov. Skene appl. for pass to Conn., & searched for possible correspondence; Apr. 30th, resolved that Hazard Wilcox enter into secure bond to ensure his good behavior; John Monroe, Esq. brought bef. Comm. & entered into a parole agreem.- **830**; this Comm.'s 1st meeting occurred Jan. 24, 1775; Albany Co. Comm. meeting 1st occurred May 10, 1775, in its Chambers, City Hall, Albany, N. Y.; those present, from Albany- 19; Manor of Livingston- 5; Schagtekoeke (Schaghticoke)- number, or names, not given; list of names for Sinkaick (Sancoick) & Hoosick; Bennington; corporation of Cambridge; & Saratoga- **831**; May 26, 1776, John Visscher offers to raise a co. & rec'd. approval to raise 100 men & immed. go to Ticonderoga; his Lts. appt.- **832**; correspondence from Peter Yates, June 14, 1775, NYC, concerning the arr. & arrest of Maj. Skene, in Philadelphia, Pa.- **833**;

Committee of Safety- Col Benedict Arnold corresponds, May 23, 1775, from Crown Point, to Gov. Trumbull of Conn., noting his repeated written efforts to secure dry powder from Albany w/o success; N. Y. Prov. Congress communicates to the comm. that it should raise detachments for service at Crown Point & Ft. Ticonderoga, foll. word from the General Assembly of Conn. that it was supplying troops, at Arnold's request, until the militia of N. Y. "could occupy the posts & ward off the danger"- **774**; communicates to the Provincial Congress the raising of two 50 man companies to go to Ft. Ticonderoga, but lacking in ammunition & having only 250 lbs. of powder beyond that already sent N.; they further "request blankets, nails, gin, & c.", in addition to a request by Col. Arnold for seamen- **776**; letter of William Duer, Esq., June 14, 1775, read bef. Comm., complaining of insinuations against his conduct, circulated so deeply as to endanger his person & property, ending w. a request for appt. of a comm. to examine into his conduct- **777**; Albany co. militia org. Aug. 22, 1775, along w. Tryon co, as a single brigade instate militia- **782**; complaint of John Younglove, May 23, 1776, that Peter Miller, of Cambridge, N. Y., has declared that he has taken an oath obliging him to join the King's troops whenever called upon by any of his officers; resolved that Cambridge Comm. apprehend & disarm him, & bind him to his further good behavior- **888**; June 4, 1776, an order to be sent to Col. Van Schaik, requesting that Capt. McAlpin, Lt. Swords, & John Munro be rem. from their place of confinement to 'the room prepared for them in the fort', placing such guards as deemed necessary; resolved, June 5th, that the Post Master of Albany bring bef. the Comm. all letters directed 'to any persons whose name has a Mc for its completion', to be examined, found of a private nature, & then returned- **889**; a payroll submitted, June 8th, consisting of men employed in the taking of Ticonderoga, & consisting of members in Capt. Joseph McCracken's co., w. £ 69 13s 11¼d balance, along w. an acct. of expenses & disbursements totaling £ 15 4s 4d; recommended pd.; Dr. John Williams appl. for 12 lbs. of powder, & a proportional amt. of ball, June 13, 1776; he rec'd. powder & 20 lbs. of ball, being required £ 12 in lieu of the return of the same amt.; a record of powder distrib. from Albany magazine- Cambridge- 50 lbs.; Saratoga- 100 lbs.; the remaining 1,247 lbs. to be distrib. to the other districts; payroll of Capt. Ebenezer Allen's co., presented June 17th, to the amt. of £ 45 12s, for men employed in taking Crown Point & Ticonderoga; Francis A. Fister (§ 768) & John Macombe sent from Hoosic, N. Y., to be imprisoned here; refers Doc. Hist., iv, 868- **890**; Corporation of- deeded one city block, Oct. 1768, to 6 Trustees, incl. John Munro, Esq., for org. a Presbyterian church here; refers p. 180, Munsell's Albany Register, 1849- **812**; c. Nov. 1862, began issuing 25¢ & 50¢ bills, called shinplaisters, as the circulation of silver decreased- **1099**

Albany Co., N. Y.- Justices of Peace, Aug. 1771- Philip Skene, John Munro, Patrick Smith, & John McComb, Esqs.; an acct. directed to them, Aug. 24th, concerning a riot nr. Argyle on June 11th, in which Donald McIntyre & others were dispossessed by Cochran & ors.; after full inquiry, they were directed by the Provincial govt. to give as much relief as statutes of forcible entry, et. al., may permit to those who were dispossessed- **901**

ALDEN,
Hon. *John-* (1599?- 1687) of the *Mayflower*, 1620; dau. Sarah, m. Alexander, s. Capt. Miles Standish, as his 1st wf.- **757**
Timothy- a letter of Feb. 28, 1803, from Rev. Ebenezer Fitch, D. D., & found in Alden's biog. of Rev. James Fitch, conveys the essentials of the Fitch family origins- **834**; his Hist. of the Religiuos Societies of Portsmouth, N. H., Vol. 10, pg. 68, 1st series , Mass. Hist. Coll., refers to the genealogy of Rev. Jabez Fitch- **835**

ALEXANDER,
James- dau. Mary, m. Peter, s. Philip Van Brugh Livingston, as his 1st wf.; his s. William, became titled as Lord Stirling- **961**
Peter- of Greenwich, N. Y.; ments. sons E. L., & William, both stat. Cairo, Illinois, c. 1861, units not given- **1080**

ALGER,
James F.- res. Fitch's Point, Salem, N. Y., abt. ¼ mi. from Milton Seeley, & ½ mi. from James Harvey Fitch; the evening of Feb. 6, 1855, the occupants of all 3 houses reported earthquake- like shaking of their houses; see Weather, Frost Heaves- **1026**

ALLEN,
_____ - of Little White Creek, N. Y.; m. Leonard, s. Daniel Wells- **841**
_____ - formerly of Salem, N. Y.; c. 1861, soldier, 11th Illinois Inf.- **1080**
Dr. Abram- offered a voluntary toast, Nov. 29, 1814, at a public banquet in Salem, N. Y., honoring Commodore Macdonough- "The Fair of Columbia- May their

arms afford warm & serene winter quarters for the heroes of Lake Champlain"-709; attended to Harrison G. Blake, c. 1824, foll. the amputation of both Blake's feet- 733; (s. Jacob, Jr., & Lucy Howard) b. Dec. 1764, Sturbridge, Mass.; m. 1. Hannah, dau. Gen. Newell; 2. ___; ments. sons Ephriam & Newell, who both d. as minors; no daus.; & he d. Mar. 20, 1845, at 80, Salem, N. Y.- 758

Charles- acc. Hiram Sisson, was among the men gathered at Pratt's store the evening of Feb. 16, 1858, when Barney McEntee was murdered- 1048s

Judge Cornelius L.- Presiding Judge, Oct. 1- 7, 1858, People vs. Martin Wallace, for the murder of Barney McEntee- 1048s; feeble health & inclement weather combined to prevent him from attending Wallace's execution, Dec. 1, 1858- 1050s; res. Salem, N. Y.; m. dau. David Russell- 1053

Dr.- selected as one of the attending physicians, Dec. 1, 1858, at the execution of Martin Wallace- 1048s

Ebenezer- plaintiff, May 19, 1774, vs. Josiah Tirrell- 878

Capt. Ebenezer- the payroll for his co., which was employed in the taking of Crown Point & Ticonderoga, presented to Albany Comm. of Correspondence, June 17, 1776; refers Doc. Hist., iv, 868- 890

Dr. Ephriam- (s. Jacob, Jr., & Lucy Howard) m. dau. Gen. Newell, of Sturbridge, Mass.; children-

1. Timothy Newell
2. Jacob, clothier, S. Hartford, N. Y.
3. Henry, d. 1849, Whitehall, N. Y.
4. Dr. George, m. Caroline Harvey
5. William Pitt, clothier, S. Hartford, N. Y.
6. dau., m. Dr. Archibald McCollister, of Salem, N. .Y.; & he d. Mar. 3, 1815, at 48, Salem, N. Y.- 758

Gen. Ethan- (1738- 1789) ment. here as Col.; lead a mob that drove Thomas Brayton from his land in Clarendon, Vt., during the Grants controversy- 746; officer witn. by Ebenezer Farnsworth during his service, Apr. 1776- Feb. 1777, acc. his pension appl.- 750; commanded at Castleton, Vt., fall 1779; commanded units sent from here to Hubbardton, & thence to Ticonderoga, Mar. 1780, attempting to attack the enemy from its rear, when Skenesborough was capt. by the British- 752; (Col.) along w. 80- 100 men, was proceeding to St. John's, May 18, 1775, when he was met by Col. Arnold's forces, who had just taken possession of a British sloop there; unable to dissuade him from what he reported as "their rash purpose", Arnold supplied Allen & his men w. provisions to continue their march, & the party arr. within 2 mi. of St. John's by that evening; learning that a detachm. of men lay in ambush on the road from Montreal, they crossed Lake Champlain, but at dawn the foll. day, his co. was "saluted w. a disch. of grapeshot from 6 field pieces & a disch. of small arms from abt. 200 regulars"; he then made a "precipitous retreat", leaving 3 of his men behind, & returned to Ticonderoga- 774; his encounter w. Col. Arnold's co. reportedly occurred 5 leagues this side of St. John's, having left Crown Point shortly after Arnold, along w. 150 men; Arnold notes that Allen's men were in nr. starving condition when he supplied them w.

provisions, & Allen expressed his intentions to proceed w. 80- 100 men to take possession of St. John's; Col. Arnold attempted to dissuade him, relating his opinion to Gov. Trumbull that the plan "appeared to me a wild, impracticable scheme... of no consequence, so long as we are masters of the lake..."- **775**; an indirect censure of his northern activities made when the Continental Congress resolved, June 1, 1775, that no expeditions or incursions be undertaken by any colony, or body of colonies, into Canada- **776**; 2 of his letters from Crown Point, one dated June 2, 1775, read & ordered filed into records of N. Y. Provincial Congress; the 2nd, apparently a copy of one addressed to the people of Canada, & also signed by James Easton- **777**; by vote of 18 to 9, he & Seth Warner were adm. to an audience w. N. Y. Provincial Congress, July 4, 1775, after which the Congress ordered a regt. of Green Mtn. boys to be raised, distinct & independent of the N. Y. troops; by recommendation of Gen. Schuyler, £ 30 advanced to Allen & Warner by the Congress- **778**; on July 31, 1775, Gen. Schuyler notes the election of officers within his Green Mtn. regt., expressing surprise that a contest would ever occur betw. Allen & Warner over rank within the regt.- **781b**; further notice from Gen. Schuyler that the controversy betw. Allen & Warner has been carried to such lengths as to frustrate recruiting within their regt.- **782**; he & Seth Warner described by Benjamin Hough as 'two of the principal leaders of the Bennington mob'; as both of them were in Bennington at the time of Hough's capture, his trial was delayed until Jan. 30, 1775; Allen served as principal prosecutor of the court, laying bef. Hough the accusations against him, & pronouncing his sentence; it was during Hough's captivity that Allen was heard to remark that they (the Bennington mob) would prob. be obliged to drive off all the 'damned Durhamites', i. e., inhabitants of Durham, Charlotte co., N. Y. (Rutland, Vt.) & taking Daniel Walker & Thomas Braten (Brayton), 2 of Hough's constables, if they could be found above ground; Allen further pledged to be more severe w. the 'damned Yorkers', w/o troubling w. the expense of trials, but punishing them immed.; his expectation was that a fight would soon occur w. the Yorkers, due to the abuse of their Magistrates, but he believed them damned cowards, as they had not already come forth- **881**; acc. Judge Blanchard, "has been honored far beyond his merits. The taking of Ticonderoga, from which he acq. such fame, was in reality nothing entitling him to such eclat as he rec'd. He was a man of gigantic frame & herculean strength. I remember his looks well"; bef. the Vt. controversy was resolved by an adjusted payment to N. Y., Allen came to Cornelius Bogert's law offices in NYC, where Blanchard was a clerk, in order to purch. a claim to some land along the Onion river, which was of little use to Bogert; until his employer arr., Blanchard was afforded a lengthy conversation w. Allen; "He was such a Goliath in stature, & had such a restless air, & such a piercing look, that I [Blanchard] almost fancied myself unsafe in his company- not knowing but he might be some pirate or bandit"; prob. detecting some unease, Allen inquired of him whether or not he had ever heard of Ethan Allen, or of his 'Bible' (*Reason, the Only Oracle of Men*, 1784)- **917**; acc. Jacob Marsh, "The name of Ethan Allen stands high in history & he had many fine traits of character- but blended w. others, that if known to the world would detract

much from his fame... It is more than probable that he & his party, were as great land- sharks as the country ever saw"; see Vermonters- 967; harassment of settlers within Socialborough township attrib. to the interest of Allen or his associates in obt. the lands in their own right; when unable to achieve their ends by accusing them of being in N. Y.'s interest, they later called them tories, even though Allen & his friends were in correspondence w. the British & at any time, ready to join them- 968; from a passage in Macaulay's Hist. of England, v. ii, pgs. 332- 333, Dr. Fitch notes that Charles Blount's book, *Oracles of Reason*, was perh. the source of the title & ideas behind Allen's 'Bible', noting that Blount was also in the same habit of wholesale copying from other authors w/o attrib. them, & was thus served in kind by Allen- 1030; bur. Burlington, Vt.; the Vt. legislature's efforts to honor him by erecting a monument at Montpelier were thrown awry by an inability to recover his remains; "it was concluded his skeleton had been disinterred & was now ornamenting the museum of some physician of the adj. country"; Dr. Jonathan R. Chandler notes to Dr. Fitch that he & a no. of his fellow students at Castleton went to Burlington & dug up a no. of skeletons of men killed during the battle of Plattsburgh- "they procured them to sell, to defray the expenses of their medical studies"; Allen was perh. interred somewhere nr. this loc., & "was of such herculean size & a person of such notoriety", that his skeleton would have been more valuable than the others, & his relatives living within the vicinity did not seem to "care a straw abt. them"; also refers Dwight's Travels, ii, 406; a man in Allen's neighborh. informed Dr. Fitch that no bones were found under Allen's slab, but that in digging around, a skeleton was found that was regarded as his; acc. Dr. Fitch, "what they got was abt. as authentic as what the Athenians honored as the remains of Theseus"; a dau., Frances, entered a Convent of the Black Nuns, Mar. 1811, at Montreal, Canada- 1052; brief ments.- 959, 963, 997, 999
Rev. Ethan, D. D.- Apr. 1867, elected rector, Episcopal Church of the Messiah, Baltimore, Maryland- 1030
Family- conjecture by Elvira Allen, wf. Samuel Standish, to have been desc. from Samuel Allen, of Braintree, Mass., based upon family tradit. of English origins & an early settlm. in New England; res. Medfield, then rem. Sturbridge, Mass., w. family of 9 children, 8 boys & 1 girl; s. Jacob, m. Lucy Howard- 758
Frances- (b. Nov. 13, 1784, Sunderland, Vt.; d. Sept. 10, 1819, Montreal, Canada) dau. Gen. Ethan; after a novitiate of 3 yrs., "took the viel", Mar. 1811, entering a Convent of the Black Nuns, Montreal, Canada; refers Croswell's Balance & State Journal, p. 152- 1052
George- (s. Dr. Ephriam & ____ Newell) res. Salem, N. Y.; m. Caroline, dau. Maj. James Harvey- 758
Ira- bro. Gen. Ethan; w. Remember Baker & 5 ors., Sept. 29, 1772, lead an unprovoked attack upon a N. Y. survey party on the Onion river- 906
Jacob- dau. Elvira, m. Samuel, s. Samuel & Lois (Curtis) Standish- 757; res. Medfield, & then, at age 8, rem. Sturbridge, Mass., along w. his father's family; m. Lucy Howard, of Warren, Mass.; had 3 sons, but no daus. who survived to maturity-

1. Jacob, eldest, m. Mary Corbin
2. Dr. Abram, b. 1764, Sturbridge, Mass.
3. Dr. Ephriam- **758**
Jacob, Jr.- (s. Jacob & Lucy Howard) res. Sturbridge, Mass., on the family
homestead; m. Mary Corbin; children, in birth order-
  1. Dr. Amasa, d. abt. 1830, Whitehall, N. Y.
  2. Lucy, m. Phineas Walker
  3. Electa, m. Charles Hobbs
  4. Maria, m. Samuel D. Phelphs
  5. Elvira, m. Samuel Standish
  6. Mary, m. Dr. Benjamin Utter- **758**
James- Quaker; b. England; prob. emig. Bedford, or Dartmouth, Mass.; dau. m.
David Cornell; & his s. John, settl. Lot No. 16, Walloomsac Patent- **806**
James Lane- (1849- 1925; author) inspirations for his articles "White Cowl", &
"Sister Dolorosa", attrib. to Gethsemane Abbey, a Trappist monastery built prior
1818, nr. Bardstown, Kentucky, & several assoc. convents within the region- **949b**
John- s. James; settl. Lot No. 16, Walloomsac Patent, prior to Rev. war; when news
of the Allen Massacre (Vol. 1) reached Mass., it was feared by his relatives that his
was the murdered family- **806**
John- res. S. Argyle, N. Y.; c. 1777, his family & Jane McCrea, were the only ones
in the region known to be murdered by the Indians during the Burgoyne
Campaign- **982**; his family was killed on a Saturday (July 26, 1777) & the news of
the massacre 1st came to the area settlers on the foll.day; see Vol. 1; Abe, one of
Gerry Kilmer's negroes, went to Allen's house & 1st discovered the scene; David
Maxwell became infamous among his neighbors, & even w. his son, for the
dubious distinction of being the 1st person to plow over the bur. site of the family-
983; massacre, brief ment.- **1049**; acc. to one report, when the scalps of the family
were 1st brought into Burgoyne's camp, the General "was so affected he cried like a
child"; (however, the description of Burgoyne, as a "thick set man, not tall",
suggests the witn. may have mistook Col. Skene for Gen. Burgoyne)- **1062**
Justice- defendant, Nov. 3, 1784, in a case brought by Robert Cochran, Esq.- **878½**
Capt. Parmlee- commanded militia co., Col. Walbridge's regt., stat. May- Nov.
1781, at Skenesborough (Whitehall, N. Y.)- **749**; July 1777, Ebenezer Farnsworth,
in his pension appl., attrib. his co. to Col. Herrick's regt.; stat. Granville, N. Y.,
marched to Pawlet, Manchester, & then Bennington, Vt., & participated in the
battle there; returning via the same route, the co. was sent across through the
woods to Lake George to destroy Burgoyne's transports, collecting abt. 600
prisoners from var. loc. along the way; afterw., they were sent down lake George to
Dimon (Diamond) Island, & were defeated by the enemy in an engagem. there;
retreated to Pawlet, Vt., & acted as scouts on Lake Champlain to Lake George,
until Burgoyne's surrender, escorting tories from Saratoga to Lake George- **750**;
officer, May 1781, along w. Lt. Jonathan Wright & Lt. Stewart, Col. Walbridge's
regt.; marched from Granville, N. Y., to Skenesborough, & stat. there until Nov.-
754

Samuel- of Braintree, Mass.; dau. Sarah, m. Ens. Josiah, s. Capt. Miles Standish, as his 2nd wf.- **757**; suppos. by Mrs. Samuel (Elvira Allen) Standish to be anc. of her grdf., Jacob Allen, by family tradit.- **758**

ALMY,
Miss- her garden was loc. nr. Joice's store, Buskirk's Bridge, N. Y.; acc. testim., when Martin Wallace & Barney McEntee left the store, they went as far as her garden's loc. bef. returning, at which point Patrick Joice suggested McEntee go on w. Wallace- **1048s**

ALYEA,
John- Dutch; res. Pompton?, nr. NYC; daus. Hannah, b. 1776, Pompton, N. Y., m. John; & Polly, m. Samuel, both sons of John & Catherine (Reid) Munroe; rem. Canada foll. Rev. war- **812**

American Philosophical Society- c. 1785, John Fitch, the steamboat inventor, contrib. his steamboat drawings, models, & tube boilers to their collection- **949b**

AMHERST,
Gen. Sir Jeffrey- (1717- 1797) Col. Philip Skene served under him in Canada- **760**; (Lord) governership of Ft. Edward assumed by him, 1756, from John Henry Lydius- **930**; the 42nd regt., or Royal Highland 'Black Watch' regt., was under his command, c. 1758/9, during his expedition on the "N. American lakes'- **990**; Col. Skene's service under him was a total of 6 yrs.- **1059**

ANDERSON,
Sir John William- Baronet, Lord Mayor of London & c.; c. 1779, attests to papers executed by Barent Bleeck & John Richard Bleecker, conveying Lake Champlain properties of Col. John Godwin to Alexander Ellice- **880**

ANDREWS,
Gen. George Leonard- (1828- 1899; Gen. Banks' Chief of Staff, 1863) c. 1862, was part of Gen. Williams' division, Gen. Banks' corps- **1098**
Luther- Assoc. Justice, People vs. Martin Wallace- **1048s**; Justice of the Peace; ment. in the warrant of authority for the execution, Dec. 1, 1858, of Martin Wallace- **1050s**
Margaret- (Andrew) m. William Dobbin, in Ireland, prior 1798- **732**
Thankful- m. Amasa, s. Thomas & Abigail (Dutton) Parker-**759s**
William H.- m. Adeline E., dau. Edward, Esq., & Hannah (Frost) Fitch, of Saratoga Springs, N. Y.- **799**

ANGEL,
Augustus- res. Essex co., N. Y.; m. Triphena, dau. Moses, Sr., & Lydia (More) Martin; he d. abt. 1849, at Ticonderoga, N. Y., leaving a son, Newell- **731**;

carpenter, millwright; b. "Chocksett (Hooksett?)", prob. Cohasset, & rem.
Norwich, Mass., as a child, & res. there during the Rev. war; arr. Bennington, Vt.,
1 or 2 days foll. the battle there, Aug. 1777, & went to Bemis Heights; was in the
Fri. (Freeman's Farm) & Tues. (Bemis Heights) battles there, & at Burgoyne's
surrender; foll. the war, he settl. Hoosick, N. Y.; m. 1790, Triphena, dau. Moses
Martin, Sr.; much employed in putting up mills, building Carter's sawmill on
Cossayuna creek (see Vol. 4) & Conkey's fulling mill at Fitch's Point, 1 or 2 yrs.
later; he arranged w. Moses Martin to build a dam & sawmill at E. Greenwich, w.
the mill on the Jackson side; the bridge above the dam, also constructed by him,
long known as Angel's bridge; purch. his land from _____ Bunker, of NYC, & res.
there for 8- 10 yrs., until he became "embarassed" & had to give it up; rem. West
Haven, Vt., & res. there for 25 yrs.; rem. Chestertown, N. Y. (then called Chester)
& res. there for 24 yrs.; rem., c. 1850, to live w. a grdau. at Ticonderoga, N. Y.,
sickened & d. within a fortnight of arr. there- **847**; his only child, Newell, m. 1.
Charity Blackman; 2. Polly Ransom, both of West Haven, Vt.; 6 children, by ea.
wf., survived to adulthood- **848**; his wid. recounts different whig songs of the Rev.
war, incl. lyrics (44 lines) to one called "Granny O'Wale"; see Whigs, Songs of the
Rev., & Granny O'Wale- **857**; his wid. Triphena corroborates the story of Tucker
being whipped for his wf.'s crime as being "true to its very letter"; see Vol. 1- **863**;
an anecdote concerning Gen. Horatio Gates, reportedly heard by him on the day of
Burgoyne's surrender- **869**; an incident concerning a horse walking an unplanked
bridge at night (see Adams, Mr.; § 28; Vol. 1) may have had its origins from a
"performance" by him while traveling in the country below Hoosick, N. Y.; he arr.
at a bridge where the planking had been stripped up for repair, & the nearest other
bridge was 6 mi. away; his horse being sure- footed, he took off its saddle, carried
it on his back, & lead the horse across- to the astonishment of onlookers; a similar
incident occurred at Great Barrington, Mass.; refers p. 228, Hist. of Berkshire Co.;
& Dwight's Travels, ii, 380- **870**; m. Triphena, dau. Moses & Lydia (More)
Martin- **1041**

Chester Fitch- (s. Newell & Charity Blackman) unm.; summer 1849, worked in
Essex co., N. Y., at the MacIntyre Ironworks- **848**

George Newell- (s. Newell & Charity Blackman) res. Ticonderoga falls, N. Y.; m.
Palmira Warren; his wf. d., leaving one child- **848**

Newell- (s. Augustus & Triphena Martin) m. 1. Charity Blackman; 2. Polly
Ransom, both of West Haven, Vt.; 6 children, by ea. wf., survived to adulthood-
  1. Augustus, res. Malone, Michigan; 3 or 4 children
  2. William Harrison, m. Lavinia Abernethy
  3. Sarah Eliza, m. Franklin Prouty
  4. Chester Fitch
  5. Lydia Almira, m. Austin Skinner
  6. George Newell, m. Palmira Warren
  7. Harriet, d. Chestertown, N. Y.
  8. Ransom, d. Chestertown, N. Y.
  9. Charles, in Wisc., w. his father

10. Rowland Mallory, res. Chestertown, N. Y.
11. Caroline, res. Chestertown, N.Y.; m. Lyman Duel
12. Franklin
13. Frederick
14. Ransom; the last 3 children also res. in Wisc., w. their father- **848**
William Harrison- (s. Newell & Charity Blackman) res. Sunprarie, Dade co.,
Wisc.; 2 children- **848**

APPAREL, descriptions of-
English gentleman's- c. 1770's; John Ashton, of Stillwater, N. Y., was described
by a grds. as 'a fine old English gentleman, all of the olden time', a staunch
Episcopalian in his habits, whose Sabbath dress incl. "his small cloths, silver
kneebuckles & c."; his garment, on special occasions, featured an English suit, w.
"long velvet vest of scarlet, powdered wig & c."- **952b**;
summer pants- (n. d.) "mostly made from unbleached towcloth"- **1608**

APPLETON,
Col. John- of Ipswich, Mass.; children- dau. Elizabeth, m. Rev. Jabez Fitch; & son,
Rev. Dr. Nathaniel, of Cambridge, Mass.- **835**

APTHORPE,
Charles Ward- by Nov. 26, 1773 deed description, owned Lot 35, Kingsbury,
N. Y.- **(L)- 936**; July 5, 1773, owns Lot 54, Kingsbury, bounded on E. by Lot 55,
belonging to Daniel Jones- **938**

Argyle, N. Y.- towards the close of the Rev. war, whigs, especially those from the
vicinity of Salem, N. Y., would rob the inhabitants here of their cattle & sheep, in
order to pay the 3 & 6 mos. draft soldiers guarding the frontier; in this manner, the
Salem whigs made themselves rich at the expense of the Argyle people, by not
giving them any restitution- **977**; news of the Allen massacre (July 26, 1777) 1st
arr. at Duncan Taylor's, & then spread through that part of town; everybody feared
that the Indians "were still lurking in the woods ready to fall upon & cut off other
families"; on the Sun. afterw., John McDougall's, & other families, gathered at
Neal Gillespie's, w. men stat. at secret places outside the house to keep watch; the
lights were all kept out, & their guns remained out of sight; "stillness was enjoined
upon everyone- but one & ano. of the children were crying all the time-it being
impossible to hush them- & not an eye was closed in sleep the live long night"; ea.
family had brought along their dogs, & a violent fight broke out among them in the
night's stillness- "we in the house knew not but it was a pack of Indians w. whom
the dogs were fighting. Suddenly they tumbled forcibly against the door, causing it
to creak upon its wooden hinges, as though it was coming down"; one Hannah
Tinkey became so frightened, that she leapt out the back window w. a gun in her
hand, wholly unconscious of her act; as no sleep was obt. by those gathered there,
it was concluded to immed. go to Burgoyne's camp at Ft. Edward for protection;

"the cavalcade, more still than a funeral procession, in that darkness which precedes the dawn of day" began, & arr. at the little broad valley along Still creek (now called Dead creek) as light began to appear; "the dense grove of towering hemlocks... shut out every ray of light, & the swampy ground over which they had here to wade, rendered this the most gloomy & doleful part of their journey", as they went to Alexander McDougall's, abt. a mi. E. of Ft. Edward; here, they took up shelter while Burgoyne's army was in the vicinity, later moving their cattle here, & selling what milk they could spare to the soldiers; Dr. Fitch notes that their 1st night was prob. spent at Gillespie's, & the 2nd night (§ 678) at Capt. Beaty's, bef. they arr. at McDougall's, making a note to clarify this point w. Mrs. Livingston; see Vol. 1- **983**

Argyle Patent- none of the orig. lots owned by loyalists were confiscated during the Rev. war- **802**

Arlington, Vt.- its inhabitants, from a Return of persons on N. H. Grants, Dec. 18, 1765- Capt. Jehiel Hawley, Ebenezer Wallis, Isaac Wallis, E. G. Wallis, Jr., ____ Wallis, David Williams, John Searl, Samuel Adams, Zacheus malary, Gideon Searl, ____ Pindle, ____ Hail, Moses Peck, John Pray, ____ Ames, Wm. Searl, Remembrance Baker, Dr. Buton, '& many more whose name we cannot recollect'; see Vol. 1- **893**

ARMITAGE,
Mary Ann- m. John Miller- **1081**

ARMSTRONG,
____ - res. Lisbon, N. Y.; m. Elizabeth, dau. Robert, Jr., & Esther (Lytle) Lytle- **737**
____ - of Greenwich, N. Y.; c. 1861, member, 11th Illinois Inf.- **1080**
Dr.- res. Salem, N. Y.; m. 1. Hannah, dau. William & Lucinda (Conkey) Fitch; 2. Mary, his 1st wf.'s sister- **730**
Family- of Salem, N. Y.; unaware that his son had obt. work w. old Mr. Bell, Daniel McDonald's father struck a bargain w. them for his son's employment; see Vol. 1- **927**
George- of Salem, N. Y.; juror, People vs. Martin Wallace, Oct. 1- 7, 1858- **1048s**
James- either he, or James Stewart, was Capt., c. 1786, Salem militia co., when it was ordered out to quell the tax rebellion in Granville, N. Y.- **701**; (s. Robert & Margaret)- **1083**
John- of Hebron, N. Y.; m. Hannah, dau. William & Mary (Hanna) Lytle; children- Samuel, John, Robert, Margaret, & Nancy- **1069**
Capt. John- his militia co. during the Rev. war, was comprised of people from the N. part of Salem, N. Y.- **729**; (s. Robert & Margaret)- **1083**
Miss- m. John, s. James & Elizabeth (Lytle) Rowan, at Lisbon, N. Y.- **737**

Robert- member, Dr. Clark's colony; m. Margaret ____; his children settl. on farms along the turnpike N. of Salem, & all rem., c. 1800/1, Lisbon, N. Y., when a co. from Salem settl. there; children-
  1. Thomas, m. 1. ____; 2. Wid. Byrnes
  2. James
  3. Capt. John
  4. Robert
  5. Jane, m. Reubin Turner
  6. Margaret, m. Robert Qua
  7. Mary, m. Robert Huggins
  8. Elizabeth, m. Thomas Armstrong- **1083**
Thomas- (s. Robert & Margaret) had no children by his 1st wf., & m. 2. Wid. Byrnes- **1083**
Thomas- m. Elizabeth, dau. Robert & Margaret Armstrong; a distant relativeof his wf., he emig. some time after their family- **1083**

ARNOLD,
Gen. Benedict- (1741- 1801) Capt. McKinstry & other Americans taken prisoner during the St. Lawrence campaign, May- June 1776, were released into his command, & retreated to Crown Point & Mt. Independence for the summer- **748**; officer witn., Apr. 1776- Feb. 1777, acc. the pension. appl. of Ebenzer Farnsworth- **750**; (Col.) of Mass.; acc. to a communication of Conn. colony to N. Y., he was one of the "adventurers" taking Ft. Ticonderoga- **773**; his letter written from Crown Point, May 23, 1775, to Gov. Trumbull, of Conn., refers to his last communication, May 19th, delivered by Capt. Oswald, & then describes his capt. of a British sloop at St. John's; on his return, he encountered Ethan Allen's forces, intent on taking St. John's, & attempted to dissuade him from the project; acc. Arnold, Col. Allen returned w/o accomplishing his object, after learning on the evening of the 18th that a detachm. lay in ambush on the road to Montreal; Allen's retreat was further encouraged the foll. morning by an assault from 6 cannon & abt. 200 regular troops; in the meantime, Col. Arnold had returned to Crown Point w. the sloop, & a schooner, & 80 men, making the total 150 men now stat. there; intending to make a stand here & secure the capt. cannon, he notes a lack of powder & repeated but unsuccessful requests for supplies of such from Albany; his P. S. notes Capt Phelps as the bearer of his letter, & requests that Conn. send at least 1,500 men w. good arms & ammunition, & c.; a 2nd letter, to the Gen. Assembly of Conn., n. d.; notes escape & return of one of Allen's men capt. at St. John's, & his information that the 400 men stat. there are all preparing to cross the lake & be joined w. Indians, to retake Crown Point & Ticonderoga; as a defensive measure, he has sent alarms for men from as far as 50 mi. below Skenesborough & Lake George- **774**; his letter to Comm. of Safety, Cambridge, Mass., May 19, 1775, noting his last communication on May 14th; reports arr. of Capt. Jonathan Brown & Capt. Oswald, along w. 50 men enl. on the road, & a small schooner capt. at Skenesborough; all of his force proceeded to St. John's, May 17th, & arr. within 30

mi. by 8:00 PM; the weather being calm, 2 bateaux w. 30 men were manned out, & arr. at the garrison at 6:00 AM the foll. morning; surprising a Sgt. & his 12 man command, he capt. the king's sloop, of abt. 70 tons, w. 2 brass 6 pounders, & a 7 man crew, w/o loss on either side; their Capt., gone to Montreal, was expected hourly, w. a large detachm. for Ticonderoga & a number of guns & carriages for the sloop, which had just been fitted for sailing; ano. Capt., w. a 40 man co., was loc. 12 mi. away at Chamblee (Chambly); his party took on board such stores as valuable & left after 2 hrs., under a favorable wind, taking 4 of the king's bateaux, & destroying the remaining 5; reports his encounter w. Col. Allen's force, abt. 5 leagues this side of St. John's, stating his belief that so long as American forces controlled Lake Champlain, capt. of St. John's was of no consequence; remarks his intention to arm the sloop & schooner; noting that the old fort at Ticonderoga was next to impossible to repair, & lacking the qualifications to build a new one, he expresses that he would be "extremely glad to be superceded in my command here"; reports that Gen. Gage has 717 soldiers in Canada, incl. the 70 men capt. by him, & gives the no. of cannon & howitzers capt. at Crown Point & Ticonderoga- 775; (Col.) sends request to Albany Comm. of Safety, May 1775, & passed on to N. Y. Provincial Congress, for "2 mates, 2 gunners, 2 gunners mates, 2 boatswains & 18 seamen to man the sloop & schooner" then stat. at Crown Point & Ticonderoga- 776; at his request, Capt. Wells raised a 25 man co., that served a day less than one month at Ticonderoga, 1775- 818; ment. by James McDonald as being more significant in the capt. of Gen. Burgoyne than the actions of Gen. Gates; 'Arnold fought like a tiger. Mounted on an enormous glossy black charger, whose mane & tail could be seen glancing through the smoke of the fight, he seemed to be everywhere present & the life of the battle. At one time a small party of British had wheeled a large cannon up on a little emminence... One murderous charge had told but too well upon the American division, when Arnold gave the word to *Charge!* Leading on his men... Arnold reached the piece just as the match was being applied. Springing his enormous charger completely over the gun lengthwise & striking off the hand of the gunner at a blow, he sprang from his horse, & seizing the gun w. a giant grasp, wheeled it around, & applying the match, sent its death volley into the ranks of the retreating British' (these incidents prob. occurred during the 2nd battle, Oct. 7th, but the last acct. may have been an embellishment upon an incident involving Col. Joseph Cilley, & not Arnold)- **1010**
Edward- of Socialborough, Charlotte co. N. Y. (Vt.); for £ 4, quit claim Lot No. 5, Mar. 25, 1773, to Thomas Brayton, of Socialborough; bounded W- E. bank of Otter creek, N- Amos Marsh, E- highway, & S- Jacob Marsh; witns.- Benjamin Spencer & Thomas Greene- **745**; (Mr.) as an annoyance, he was once required by the Comm. of Safety to convey supplies to Skenesborough, N. Y., for the American troops; while absent, his premises were plundered & all his stock driven away, although he later recovered all of them- **968**
John- oath of alleg.; Co. D, 22nd N. Y. Inf.- **(L)- 1074**

Artillery Patent- acc. June 30, 1774 deed transaction, its survey map was drawn by Walter Mitchelson- **(L)- 936**

ASBURY,
Francis- (1745- 1816; elected Dec. 24, 1784, as superintendant of the Methodist church in America) Lorenzo Dow rec'd. his written license from him at their annual conference, 1798- **815**

ASHLEY,
Col. John- of Berkshire co. (South) regt.; Aug. 1777, Capt. Enoch Noble's co. of his regt. arr. at Bennington shortly after the battle there, & was sent to Arlington, Vt. for a short time, acting as scouts- **755**
Gen. John- of Sheffield, Mass.; eldest dau. Louisa, m. Samuel B. Sheldon- **947**
Samuel- along w. Samuel Robinson, John Horfort, & Isaac Charles, he was apprehended & detained, summer 1764, by the High Sheriff of Albany co., for forcibly ejecting Peter Voss & Bastian Deal from their lands in the Grants- **885**; when apprehended by Harmanus Schuyler, he claimed to be a Deputy Sheriff- **892**; James Van Cortlandt, a member of Schuyler's posse, noted that he & 2 others (Horfort & Charles) were brought to Albany jail, but were never indicted, gave bail, or stood trial- **897**

ASHTON,
Elizabeth- wf. Maj. James; d. Nov. 1, 1809, at 81- **(L)- 975**
Family- of England; their chiildren were all b. Lincolnshire, England; of them, John was the only one who emig. to America-
1. Samuel, b. July 13, 1730; or Sept. 5, 1738, by ano. manuscript
2. John, b. Nov. 6, 1735; d. Aug. 11, 1816, Malta, N. Y.
3. Edward, b. Nov. 19, 1741
4. Joseph, b. Nov. 29, 1744
5. Benjamin, b. Dec. 12, 1749; the above dates obt. by Dr. Fitch from John Ashton's family Bible- **960**
James- whig; c. 1775, res. Ash Grove, White Creek, N. Y.; he was among some guests invited that yr. to a Thanksgiving dinner at Edmund Wells', Cambridge, N. Y.; seated across from him was Hugh More, "whose sympathies were strongly upon the tory side in politics"; one of them made a poitical remark, which lead to a response "so severe & cutting" that the other launched the main course of the dinner, a huge chicken pie, onto the other's head; a battle of fisticuffs then ensued in the yard of the premises, & Ashton, having a "stout, atheletic & Herculean frame", prevailed over More, to the general approval of the other guests; see Holidays- **840**
Maj. James- d. Oct. 9, 1802, at 73- **(L)- 975**
John- res. N. of Stillwater, N. Y. (c. 1770; see Vol. 4); he sold out, rem. towards Ballston Spa, & d. there, & was "bur. at 'the Ridge' as it is called" (prob. Malta Ridge); during his last yrs., he m. a 2nd time; he was a mild, even tempered man,

fond of reading & intelligent beyond his neighbors, & was often employed to write deeds, wills, & c., & much esteemed by his neighbors; for an anecdote concerning an unwelcome assoc. w. a pretentious individual in his neighborh., see Collamer, Theodocia; dau. Elizabeth, m. Thomas Pattison; (& dau. Polly, m. Rev. Bradley Sillick; see Vol. 1)- **952**; his grds., Elias Pattison, described him as 'a fine old English gentleman, of the olden time'; his only labor consisted in directing & overseeing his hired help, spending most of his time in reading; "a strong Episcopalian, revering his Bible & Prayer Book", he regularly went through the service w. his family members, despite the fact that there was no meeting place they could attend in the immed. area; on the Sabbath, he dressed neatly, "in his small cloths, silver kneebuckles & c.", & on other special occasions, wore an English suit, w. "long velvet vest of scarlet, powdered wig & c."- **952b**; b. Nov. 6, 1735, Lincolnshire, England; he was the only member of his family to emig. to America, in 1768; m. Elizabeth Hargrave; their dau. Elizabeth, b. Jan. 28, 1756, m. June 1776, Thomas Pattison; & he d. Aug. 11, 1816, Malta, N. Y.- **960**

ASKEY,
William C.- oath of alleg.; Co. D, 22nd N. Y. Inf.- **(L)- 1074**

ASTRONOMY, Events of-
  Comets- Donati's- its appearance, Sept. & Oct. 1858, noted by Dr. Fitch in the western sky at evening, & the eastern sky in the morning; its greatest brilliancy occurred Sat. evening, Oct. 9th; its appearance & relationship to other stars illust. in a hand sketch by Dr. Fitch; "The dots represent the stars nearest to it, above the western horizon", (the "Dog Star- Canis Major" being the only one labeled); its appearance, on 3 separate occasions; "c̱ being a very bright star nr. the horizon, N. of due W., or nearly NW"; the comet noted as abt. 2 ft. from this star in the night sky on Tues., abt. 2 yds. from it on Wed., & abt. 2 rods distant on Sat., & its size, changing respectively, from abt. 2 ft. in length, to the point, "at ḇ, the tail extending to the 3 stars in a triangle, directly above c̱", & last- "its S. side well defined, its opp. edge dim & indefinite. It goes down below the horizon a little after 8 o'clock, at a pt. abt. due W.- its tail being visible some time longer"; visible abt. 2 wks. (prob. as viewed from Dr. Fitch's office, at Fitch's Point, Salem, N. Y.), it finally disappeared 3- 4 evenings later (Oct. 13th);
  Unnamed- acc. newspaper reports, 1st seen small, abt. July 1, 1861, & 1st observed by Dr. Fitch on July 3rd, at abt. 20° above the horizon, at 11:00 PM, & a little W. of due N.; "very brilliant, in a straight train of light, less broad than in the above [Donati's], extending up, perceptible faintly to the zenith or beyond, becoming lost in the milky way"; July 4th- abt. 40° above the horizon, & abt. the same size; July 5th- smaller & higher up, gradually diminishing in size, though remaining perfectly visible for several more nights- **1051**;
  Eclipses- June 1806, total eclipse of the sun, visible from Salem, N. Y. **1047b**

17

ATKINSON,
James F.- formerly of Brooklyn, N. Y., but now of Appleton, Wisc.; m. Apr. 18, 1867, Louise M., dau. J. M. Fitch, Esq.; by Rev. C. G. Finney- **799**
Theodore- (1697- 1779) Secretary, Province of N. H.; signed recording of a description of the colony's boundaries, Nov. 17, 1749, Portsmouth, N. H.; refers pgs. 3 & 4, Territorial Rights- **883**

ATWATER,
Benjamin & Jesse- gr. by Capt. David Blakslee, Nov. 2, 1785, 100 acres, E. end of Lot 6, Fisher's Patent- **(L)- 936**
Jesse- of Granville, N. Y.; deeds part of Lot 5, June 5, 1786, to Benjamin Atwater, as in the survey bill of Fisher's Patent- **(L)- 936**

ATWOOD,
_____- of Salem, N. Y.; c. 1861, member, 11th Illinois Inf.- **1080**
Deac. Gregory- m. Jane Pike, as his 2nd wf.- **731**
Samuel- for £ 328, Dec. 7, 1784, purch. Lot 8, Skenesborough, containing 172 acres- **(L)- 875**
Samuel- Co. A, 2nd N. Y., Northern Black Horse, Cav., 1861- 2- **1080**
Zaccheus- it was arranged that he would operate Fitch's Woolen Factory, in return for 1/3rd ownership, but when he failed to do so, it was contracted, Dec. 15, 1813, to Luther Finel- **799**; of Salem, N. Y.; dau. Eliza, m. Gideon S., s. James & Matilda (Safford) Turner- **1090**

AUSTIN,
Alexander- Co. A, 2nd N. Y., Northern Black Horse, Cav., 1861- 2- **1080**
Edmund- m. Abiah, dau. Joseph Wells, Jr.- **842**
George- s. Lewis; Co. I, 93rd N. Y. Inf.; d. Feb. 21, 1862, from congestion of lungs, Camp Bliss (Ryker's Island, NYC); bur. Feb. 23, gr. 14, soldier's plot, Evergreen Cemetery, Salem, N. Y.- **1081**
Gideon- of Castile, N. Y.; m. dau. Joseph Wells- **842**
Lewis- of Salem, N. Y.; his s. George, enl. Co. I, 93rd N. Y. Inf.- **1081**
William- Corp., Co. A, 2nd N. Y., Northern Black Horse, Cav., 1861- 2- **1080**

AYLESWORTH,
Edward- tavern keeper & Justice of Peace, E. Arlington, Vt.; m. Sarah, dau. Aaron & Elizabeth (Fitch) Martin; children- "Franklin & 2 or 3 more"- **731**
Philip- (Aylworth) of Coventry, R. I.; the S. part of "the old west farm" (prob. in Clarendon, Vt., boundaries not given) was made over to him, July 19, 1762, by Joseph Condon, of Beekman's Patent, Dutchess co., N. Y.- **745**

AYRES,
____ - m. Sarah, dau. John & Elizabeth (Hargraves) Ashton- **960**
Robert- c. 1850's, res. 2- 3 mi. N. of Ballston Spa, on the road to Saratoga Springs,
N. Y.; he was an orphan, & c. 1777, res. w. a tory family in Kingsbury, N. Y.;
when a letter from David Jones was brought from Burgoyne's army, his master
required him to take it to Jane McCrea, "w. many instructions & cautions as to the
manner he was to proceed in carrying the letter & delivering it into her hand"; he
was afterw. bound out to the tanning & currying business operated by ____
Dickison, of Stillwater, but he ran away along w. 5 other apprentices & enl. in Col.
Marinus Willet's regt., because Dickison was so severe w. his apprentices; served 3
yrs., returned to Stillwater, & m. dau. John & Elizabeth (Hargrave) Ashton; her
father was violently opposed to the match, & he courted her at Thomas &
Elizabeth (Ashton) Pattison's house, as her elder sist. & husb. favored them; her
father later gave his consent, knowing he would not heed a refusal, & was later
reconciled to the choice by his display of respectability & industry; their dau. m.
Ransom Cook, Esq.- **1054**

B

BABCOCK,
Capt.- commanded Conn. co. during Rev. war; stat. Roxbury, Mass. during the seige of Boston, 1775; co. later marched to Long Island, 1776, & then Harlem, during British occ. of N. Y.- **728**
James- res., c. 1770, Walloomsac Patent; he warned his neighbor, Samuel Gardenier, that he had better flee his lands, as the returning mob was so violent & enraged that he would be unsafe in giving them his reply, w. regards to its title- **902**
Phineas- pl., Oct. 19, 1773, vs. Jonathan Baker- **878**
Sherman- one of 16 guards raised, mid- June 1782, at Bennington, Vt., to guard the would- be abductors of Esq. Bleecker- **747**

BACKUS,
Abigail- m. Samuel, s. Samuel & Deborah (Gates) Standish; see Vol. 1- **757**

BACON,
Ebenezer- shoemaker; walked lame, w. a club foot; the naming of Bacon's Hill, N. Y. attrib. to him; he bought out a store within his neighborh. & kept it in conjunction w. his own trade, accumul. a handsome property; whenever he went to NYC to purch. goods, along w. the Paynes & Crockers, he wore ordinary clothes & cared for his own boots, while his co. dressed in the best of style & had their boots blacked at every hotel they lodged in, despite the fact he was more capable of affording the expense than they were- **933**

Bacon Hill, N. Y.- loc. N. of Ft. Miller bridge, town of Northumberland, Saratoga co.; its name attrib. to Ebenezer Bacon- **933**

BADER,
John- provided an affidavit concerning the violent Sept. 13, 1773 assault & beating of Jonathan Eckert- **911**

BAILEY,
Col.- Oct. 1777, Capt. Hatch's co., Green Mtn. rangers, placed in his regt. & sent to Stillwater, N. Y.; they arr. on E. side of the Hudson, but did not cross until after the 2nd battle of Saratoga, but were at Burgoyne's surrender- **756**
Francis- (Baily) oath of alleg.; Co. D, 22nd N. Y. Inf.- **(L)- 1074**
Francis S.- 2nd Lt., Co. G, 93rd N. Y. Inf.- **1090b**
Lt. John- Co. F, 93rd N. Y. Inf.- **1090b**

BAIN,
Mrs. Casparus- (Mary, dau. Neal Gillespie) informs concerning her father's witn.
of the execution of George Hundertmark, the Hessian deserter (§ 740), in
Burgoyne's camp at Ft. Miller, N. Y.- **976**
Catharine- m. Daniel, s. John & Betsey (Beaty) McDougall- **978**
Family- res. S. Argyle, N. Y., c. 1789, E. of Roger Reid- **802**

BAKER,
___- res. Whitetown, N. Y.; m. Mary, dau. Sidney Wells; their children-
Margaret, Charles Comstock, & Ichabod Comstock- **839**
Albert- yeoman, of Kingsbury, N. Y.; Feb. 1, 1774, for £ 900, purch. Kingsbury
Patent Lots 25, 47, & 92, from Peter & Sarah Vandervoort; (given as Backer) on
Apr. 15, 1775, conveyed to Henry Franklin, for £ 150, Lot 92, the N. half of Lot
47, & the S. half of Lot 25, & Lot 5 of the town plot; 242½ acres total- **(L)- 936**
Ben- acc. testim., Martin Wallace had threatened to kill him & was suppos.
carrying a pistol in his pocket for that purpose- **1048s**
Family- ments s. William; dau. Sarah Ann, m. Feb. 20, 1849, Pliny F., s. Adam &
Almira (Fitch) Martin; & ano. dau., who m. James H. Fitch- **731**
Jonathan- of Black Creek (Hebron, N. Y.); Jan. 25, 1776, rec'd. recommendation
for appt. as Adjutant, Charlotte co. militia- **784**
Jonathan- defendant, in cases brought by Morris Austin, Phineas Babcock, Robert
Snell, & Thomas Stone- **878**
Miss- ment. as a member of Maj. Van Tuyl's family, Cambridge, N. Y.;
"precipitously terminated her existence", spring 1815, at the family home, "as was
suppos. in a fit of anger", by fixing a skein of yarn to a beam in her chamber &
swinging from a stool- **712**
Remember- (c. 1737/40- 1775) he & Robert Cockran, acc. Wm. Duer's letter, June
28, 1775, were assembled 'w. an intent to protect the court' at Ft. Edward, N. Y.-
779; along w. Ira Allen & 5 others, lead an unprovoked attack on a N. Y. survey
party that was working along the Onion river, Sept. 29, 1772- **906**; w. Samuel
Bulsby & 2 others, charged w. the violent Sept. 13, 1773 assault & beating of
Jonathan Eckert- **911**

BALDRICH,
Mrs.- c. 1777, res. along the Indian river, in Vt.; when other inhabitants of the area
fled to Manchester, Vt., fearing the approach of Hessians & Indians, she fled on
foot, carrying one child on her back & leading the other by the hand- **728**

BALDWIN,
___- c. 1798, his tavern was one of 3 buildings in Ft. Edward, N. Y.- **804**; his
wf.'s death by fire alluded to as one of the incidents that occurred when Lorenzo
Dow was preaching in Ft. Edward, Mar. 1798; see Vol. 1- **815**

BALL,
William Burke- (n. d.); s. L. Chandler & Marcia Ann- **(L)- 772**

BALLARD,
____- Methodist; ment. as 'a young preacher rejected by the conference', c. 1798; his expulsion was promoted by T. Dewey, & it was Lorenzo Dow's anticipation that his own conduct within the conference would be pronounced upon in a similar manner- **813**
____- m. Cynthia, dau. William & Hannah (Warren) Ives- **1038**

BANKS,
Gen. *Nathaniel Prentiss-* (1816- 1894) his Red River expediton, Apr. 20, 1864, marched 40 mi., from Grand Encore, La., to the Caine river, in a single day; Dr. Fitch notes that by this feat's example, Gen. Burgoyne's army could have, by forced march, reached Albany, N. Y. within a day's time once it had crossed the Hudson river into Saratoga co.- **1072**; c. 1862, his corps incl. 123rd NYSV- **1098**

BANYARD,
William, Esq.- sold parcels in his Patent, Lot 3- 10 acres, 3 rods; & 13 acres, 3 rods; & Lot 4- 170 acres, to William Duer, Esq., July 24, 1768; 1/6 of all his tracts & falls, were also purch. by Duer, & then mortgaged, Sept. 22, 1774- **935**; was orig. gr. Lot 2 of 2nd Allotment, Ft. Edward Patent- **(L)- 936**

Banyard's Patent- or Stephen Banyard's Patent; adjoins. Schuyler's Patent, along the Hudson river, S. of Ft. Edward, N. Y.- **935**

BANYER,
____- of NYC; c. 1790's, Augustus Angel purch. lands from him, loc. at Fitch's Point, Salem, N. Y.- **847**
Goldsbrow- affidavits sent to him by John Munro, May 30, 1771, concerning conduct of inhabitants within the co., that he might do something speedily to prevent their riotous behavior; notes the danger to life & property to anyone who is a 'friend' to N. Y. govt., describing damages done to the property of Yorkers- **899**

BARBER,
Deac. *George-* d. June 14, 1832, at 79- **(L)- 975**
Family- of NYC; c. 1859, their s. James, res. on 5th Ave.; dau. Mary, prob. m. 1. ____ Cook; 2. Maj. James Harvey; this family was, in some manner, connected w. a Moore family, of NYC- **1035**

BARBOUR,
O. L.- res. Saratoga Springs, N. Y.; reporter, formerly of the Chancery, & now (1850) at the N. Y. Supreme Court; m. Elizabeth, dau. Lewis Berry; 5 or 6 children; refers Hyde Genealogy- **839**

BARD,

Dr. Samuel- he & Dr. John Jones appt. to examine Samuel Cook, Ebenezer Howland, & John Williams, for positions as Surgeons, Green Mtn. Regt.- **778**

Bardstown, Kentucky- or Bairdstown; loc. Nelson co.; newspaper article, Jan. 14, perh. late 1850's, *The Recorder*, noting that one of the state's earliest bur. grds. loc. here, containing the grave of John Fitch, the steamboat inventor, who obt. 1,000 acres nr. here; his holdings were reduced over time to 300 acres, after which he bargained half the remainder for his board & a pint a day; the old Co. prison, where the inventor d. in the keeper's house, was also loc. here; ments. that materials relating to John Fitch's life are loc. in the archives of the Co. Clerk's office; the obscurity & neglect of Fitch's grave attrib. to the celebrity of 7 local citizens bur. there, who had served as Governors in 7 states, & that the community was 'the abiding place' of the composer, Stephen Foster; in 1818, the 1st Catholic cathedral of the west, & the 2nd in the U. S., was built here; prior to that date, Gethsemane Abbey, a Trappist monastery, was erected here, 1 of 3 such institutions in the country; the loc. of other religious orders within the vicinity given as an inspiration for the writings of James Lane Allen- **949b**

BARDWELL,

Family- c. 1853, res. along the Indian river, below Mark's corners, Vt., betw. the Tamarack swamp & the Church family- **1003**

BARNARD,

John- witn., along w. Susanna Bennet, Feb. 8, 1789, to a deed by Ezra Jones to Thomas Brayton, for part of Lot No. 4, Provincial Patent- **745**

BARNES,

Capt.- (Barns) Oct. 1779, commanded co. from Lanesborough, Mass.- **749**

Family- (Barns) c. 1798, res. on the W. side of the Hudson opp. Ft. Miller, N. Y., betw. the Nevins & Craig families- **804**

Harrison- m. 1851, Mary, dau. Harvey & Sarah (Conkey) Stevens; they have lost 4 children- **730**

Capt. John- (Barns) of Salem, N. Y.; see Vol. 1; after Burgoyne's surrender, he commenced a suit against Alexander Wright for pilfering sheep from his neighbor's flock & selling them in Burgoyne's camp- **977**; some members of his scout co. were John McDonald, of Munro's Meadows; & John Dick, & Hugh Randles, of Hebron, N. Y.; much of his duties scouting nr. the end of the Rev. war were to see if Indians had come down over Lake Champlain from Canada, the countryside often being alarmed by this prospect- **1000**

Laommi- drowned, Nov. 10, 1792, from a raft in the Battenkill; inquest at the home of Isaac Clapp; Hamilton McCollister, Coroner- **(L)- 876**

BARNETT,

Nathaniel- "old Mr. Barnet"; c. 1812, his sons were digging post holes for a fence, when they unearthed some skulls believed to be of the dead bur. foll. the battle of Bennington; knowing that their father was expected back within the hr., they "set the post, & jammed the skulls in beside it, & covered them up speedily", fearing that their father would detail them to make a proper reburial- **762**; res. Plainfield, Conn.; mustered, Capt. Eaton's light horse co., to go & repel Burgoyne's invasion, along w. the militia; his part of the co. remained w. Lt. Stewart at Bennington, Vt., to ride on express & as scouts; he once escorted Gen. Benjamin Lincoln to a general council of officers at Van Schaik's Island, opp. Stillwater, N. Y.; also, ments. details of an urgent express, made w. 4 others, to Van Schaik's Island, at the time Gen. Gates assumed command (Vol. 4) & rem. the army to Stillwater; never rec'd. a pension for his service; Feb. 1792, rem. Rensselaer co., N. Y., & purch. his land from ____ Ten Eyck, of Albany, N. Y.; he d. ca. 1847- **763**

Nathaniel, Esq.- his brick house loc. SE of the heights where the Hessian fort was constructed bef. battle of Bennington, & lies W. of the Walloomsac river, & SW of the point where the road to Walloomsac, N. Y. crosses the river- **761**; member, N. Y. Legislature, 1829; owned land containing the Bennington battlesite, & went over the ground, Aug. 22, 1850, along w. Dr. Fitch, relating its features, & anecdotes concerning the battle; his house loc. S. of the heights, on the road to Walloomsac, nr. the 110 ft. long covered bridge over the river; c. 1812, while digging post holes for a fence in front of his house, drew out 3 skulls from a single hole; Eldridge, the clock cleaner, later informed him that the skulls were orig. discovered when other sons of "old Mr. Barnet" were performing the same task as he was, & hurriedly set the post, in order to avoid giving the remains a reburial, if their father should discover them- **762**; c. 1840, while plowing abt. 40 rods N. of the Hessian fort, he unearthed a lead bullet sd. to be indicative of the direction of Gen. Stark's advance; the bullet donated by Dr. Fitch, Aug. 22, 1850, to the State Antiquarian Society- **762b**; s. Nathaniel; b. ca. Feb. 1792, & was only 2 wks. old when the family rem. from Conn. to N. Y.; his farm became so badly cut up by the railroad that he later sold it to Naaman Burgess, & rem. White Creek, N. Y.- **763**; attests to having no recoll. or knowl. concerning Majors Samuel Safford & Gilbert Bradley at the battle of Bennington, or the killing of 2 Indian chiefs during the battle there- **764**; ano. breastwork, defended by tories, loc. down river from his brick house, evac. when 1st attacked by American forces- **771**; of Hoosick, N. Y.; revisited by Dr. Fitch, prob. Dec. 7?, 1853, "in the R. Road cars", noting that he was so vexed by the manner in which his farm was cut up by the R. R. that he sold it, w/o knowing where he'd relocate, & later settl. N. White Creek, N. Y.; provides additional information here abt. the Matthews house, & the bur. of Col. Baum- **1022**

BARRET,
Walter- author, "Recollections of Old Merchants of NYC", a newspaper article (n. d.) orig. written for the *N. Y. Leader* & reprinted, perh. *N. Y. Express*, c. 1860, & pert., in part, to a hist. of the Bininger family- **1075b**

BARRINGER,
F. A.- oath of alleg.; Co. D, 22nd N. Y. Inf.- **(L)**- **1074**

BARRON,
William- oath of alleg.; Co. D, 22nd N. Y. Inf.- **(L)**- **1074**

BARTHOLOMEW,
_____- res. New Haven, Conn.; m. summer 1849, Henry Martin, s. Sidney Wells-
839
Capt.- c. 1781, commanded militia co. stat. at Skenesborough (Whitehall, N. Y.)-
749

BARTLETT,
_____- m. Martha, dau. Aaron & Olive (Harding) Martin, as her 2nd husb.- **1040**
Jonathan- Salem, N. Y.; Mar. 1, 1787, killed by tree falling on him; Joshua Conkey, Coroner- **(L)**- **876**
Moses- purch. Lots 259 & 260, Turner's Patent, Mar. 24, 1779, for £ 1400, from Robert Hopkins- **(L)**- **936**

BARTON,
D. Nelson- (s. Daniel & Ann Glover) temperance hotelkeeper, res. Galesburg, Illinois; m. Aurilla, sist. Arvilla Sibley; no children- **1093**
Daniel- s. Timothy; clothier; m. Ann Glover; he worked in the factory (perh. Silas Conkey's) at Fitch's Point when he 1st met his wf., they 1st res. for 5 yrs. at Oneida Corners, Queensbury, N. Y.; 1830, rem. Moriah, N. Y.; c. 1862, owns 100 acres of land, & the only carding machine betw. Ticonderoga & Jay, N. Y.; children-
1. D. Nelson, m. Aurilla Sibley
2. Louisa, unm.
3. Wm. King, m. Arvilla Sibley
4. Hollis Gilbert, unm.; c. 1852- 62, dentist, NYC
5. Heman Ferris, m. Mary Curtis
6. Marvin Francis, unm.
7. Earl Glover, unm.- **1093**
Earl Glover- (s. Daniel & Ann Glover) res. Galesburg, Illinois, w. his bros. Nelson & King- **1093**
Eli- storekeeper, Eagle Bridge, N. Y.; acc. Marvin Wallis' testim., Martin Wallace borrowed $10 from him to pay on his acct. w. Barton, & a few days later sd. that he pd. Barton $8 & still owed him $6; he testif. that he had traded w. Wallace prev. to

& within a few days of Barney McEntee's murder, & was pd. $8 by Wallace, Aug. 5, 1857, on an acct. of $14, saying that he had obt. the money from Marvin Wallis- **1048s**

Heman Ferris- (s. Daniel & Ann Glover) res. & works on the family farm, c. 1860-62, has been operating a brick kiln here; m. Mary Curtis; a son, Homer Dovier, b. ca. 1859- **1093**

Louisa- (dau. Daniel & Ann Glover) teacher; grad. State Normal School; c. 1862, boards w. Dr. C. Hunter, & has taught for 10 yrs. in Public Schools, NYC- **1093**

Marvin Francis- (s. Daniel & Ann Glover) res. on the family farm; has phistic- the West did not agree w. his health, & he went to New Orleans, La., & then on a sea voyage to Europe, w/o improving- **1093**

Timothy- res. Bolton, N. Y.; s. Daniel, m. Ann Glover- **1093**

Wales M.- Co. A, 2nd N. Y., Northern Black Horse, Cav., 1861- 2- **1080**

William King- (s. Daniel & Ann Glover) res. Galesburg, Illinois, w. his bro. Nelson; m. Arvilla, sist. Aurilla Sibley- **1093**

BASSET,
Hannah- m. John, s. Edward & Wid. Elizabeth (Potter) Parker- **759s**

Battenkill- a popular ballad (n. d.) in Saratoga co., N. Y., concerns the drowning of 4 persons in this stream- **1057**

BAUM,
___- (Baume) Commodore Macdonough's sailing master; he stood in the bow of the *Saratoga* during the battle of Plattsburgh (Sept. 11, 1814) & superintended the turning of the ship to bring the guns of its opp. side to bear upon the enemy, "when a chain shot struck the front of his belly, tearing off his panteloons & shirt, and, as he suspected tearing open his abdomen"; feeling nothing of the wnd. in the excitement of the battle, he clasped his arms upon the spot, & finding he could rem. one arm, continued his instructions until the maneuver was completed; "on examining, he found the chain shot had only torn away his clothing & reddened his skin, w/o any serious injury to him"- **1056**

Lt. Col. Friedrich- (?- 1777) the detachm. lead by Lt. Col. Heinrich Breyman for his reinforcement reportedly arr. at the Bennington battlesite via Castleton, Vt., at the point of Col. Baum's defeat, creating a 2nd battle w. Gen. Stark- **728**; loc. his 2 cannon on a rise NW of the bridge over the Walloomsac, & below his "fort" on the heights; he suppos. that Gen. Stark would come down the road from Bennington & attack the tory breastwork 1st- **762**; the 1st hostile act against his advance appears to be when the planks were taken off the bridge at Sancoick, N. Y., & his forces were fired upon "from bushes & other coverts around", as they attempted to repair the bridge- **766**; evidently, acc. Dr. Fitch, when he encountered resistance at the Sancoick bridge, he sent a party of 15 British soldiers to old 'Festus', of Hoosick, N. Y., to recruit volunteers from among the local tory population- **768**; was carried from the battlefield by Wm. Robb & 3 others; he was placed on a litter of blankets

w. 2 poles tied to the sides, & the men who carried him had no suspicions that his wnds. were mortal, or even serious; Dr. Fitch notes that acc. Glick, he had been shot through the body; he spoke English while being carried from the field & talked w. his bearers along the way;"the men felt a strong sympathy & attachment for the wnd. Col., in consequence of his affable manners & discourse; ... he was dressed in a most costly uniform, w. a sword heavily mounted w. gold; & they deposited him in the house, w. all his accoutrements upon him"; the foll. morning, he was found dead & stripped of anything valuable; the men who carried him from the field heard of this "w. surprise & the deepest indignation", & were ever after open in expressing their belief he had been most foully dealt w. & murdered for the sake of his clothes, sword, & c.; Dr. Fitch doubts his bur. nr. the Mathews house, reasoning that the exact spot would be known & visited (however, a Vt. state marker abt. ¼ mi. frrom the N. Y. line notes his bur. somewhere along the N. bank of the Walloomsac, & states that he d. 2 days foll. the battle)- **801**; the frontal fire experienced by his expedition along their route to Bennington was attrib. to James More, mounted on his horse- **925**; brief ment.- **1005**; his expedition arr. at the Sancoick bridge almost immed. after its planking had been torn off; a convenient ford was loc. for the cannon to pass over & a small party detailed to repair the bridge, causing a 2- 3 hr. delay of the advance- **1006**; after being wnd. in battle, he was carried to the James Mathews house, some 40? rods E. of the brick Mathews House (constructed later) & d. there, "& was bur. (across the road from the house, if I understand Mr. Barnett aright, and) betw. the house & Walloomsac river- several others that were mortally wnd. in the battle being bur. at the same spot"; no stone was ever put on the spot, but it is quite nr. The Stone Paper Mill, "the grave being abt. 30 or 40 ft. W. of the W. end of sd. papermill"- **1022**; brief ment.- **1072**

BAXTER,
Nathan- Rev. war pensioner, prob. res. Ontario, Canada; dau. Electa, m. John, s. John & Hannah (Alyea) Munroe- **812**

BAY,
John- licensed in Albany co., N. Y. bef. its division, & adm. to practice in Charlotte co. court, Oct. 19, 1773- **878**

BAYLEY,
Jacob- of Newbury, Vt.; delegate, from Gloucester co., to N. Y. Provincial Congress; writes June 29, 1775, announcing his selection to the position & his inability to appear in person because of present fears from Canada; relates further information concerning the mood in Canada & notes his ability to raise a co. of 300 men in his vicinity- **780**

BEACH,
Rev. Alfred B., D. D.- officiated, June 5, 1867, at the marriage of Augustus D. Fitch to Julia Kellogg Lombard- **799**

BEALY,
Mrs.- her alleged identity; res. Whitestown, N. Y., aged abt. 21 yrs.; arr. Sept. 16, 1815, at Lytle's Tavern, Salem, N. Y., "Being evid. in perilous condition, she was hospitably adm. into a house, & within an hr. after her arrival, was delivered of a female child"; her lack of gratitude concerning the attentions given her were such that "she secretly left the roof that benevolence had provided" on the Sun. night foll. her arrival, leaving the baby behind; a female attendant, abt. 4 yrs. younger than her, came & left w. her; the general physical description of Mrs. Bealy, her attire, & that of her attendant briefly given, along w. a $30.00 reward, offered Sept. 26th, by notice of Abner Stone & Alex. McNish, Overseers of the Poor- **718**

BEARDSELL,
Hon. John- m. Ann, dau. Oliver & Susan (Pendergrass) Whiteside; their s. John, c. 1849, res. Mayville, N. Y.- **805**

BEATTIE/ BEATY,
____- m. ____ Tinkey, who later m. Miller Dobbin, as his 2nd wf.- **732**
Capt. James- res. Argyle, N. Y.; he & Neil Gillespie witn. the execution, c. 1777, of a Hessian deserter (§ 740) by Burgoyne's troops, when the army was encamped at Ft. Miller, N. Y.- **976**; b. Monaghan, Ireland; distantly connected w. the Beaty familes of Salem, he emig. at age 9, & res. for a few yrs. at Kaykett, nr. NYC, & then rem. here, c. 1772; settl. the farm adjoin. Judge Ebenezer Clark's, on the S. side, now (1853) occ. by James Shaw; he res. & d. there, at age 66, & was bur. w. a headstone, in the old Argyle bur. grd.; 2 children- Betsey, m. John, s. Alexander McDougall; & John; he was militia Capt., & an intimate friend of Neal Gillespie- **979**; acc. Dr. Fitch's notes, the Argyle settlers who went to Neal Gillespie's foll. the Allen massacre prob. spent a 2nd night here bef. reaching Burgoyne's camp at Ft. Edward; refers § 678; see Vol. 1- **983**
John- s. Capt. James; rem. Stirling, N. Y., & there d. Dec. 13, 1838; an obit., Mar. 1839, Christian Magazine; most of his children are now (1852) dec'd.- "2 sons named James- also John, Peter, Daniel, Samuel & c."- **979**
Deac. John- res. Salem, N. Y.; dau. Jane, m. Josephus Fitch- **730**
Thomas- res. Salem, N. Y.; called 'wee Tommy Beaty'; his present (1850) house occ. the same loc. as Charles Hutchinson did during the Rev. war- **729**
Thomas, Jr.- fined £ 40, plus court costs, Oct. 1780, in the assault of Alex. McNees, & confined until pd.- **877**
William J.- (Beattie) oath of alleg.; Co. D, 22nd N. Y. Inf.- **(L)- 1074**; also given as Wm. T.; 2nd Lt., Co. D; killed at 2nd Bull Run, Aug. 29- 30, 1862; Sgt. Charles H. Akin promoted to his post, Aug. 30th- **1095b**

BEAUMONT,
Carlisle D.- (C. D.) 1st Lt., 22nd N. Y. Inf.; killed, perh. at 2nd Bull Run, & replaced, Feb. 1, 1863, by Sgt. Wm. H. Hoystrant (2nd Lt., Co. C, mustered as 1st Lt.; killed Aug. 29, 1862, at Groveton, Va., acc. Phisterer)- **1095b**

BECKER,
John P.- res. Easton, N. Y.; his slave Prince, accidentally drowned, late Dec. 1801, along w. a slave of Simon DeRidder; see Negroes- **(L)- 876**

BECKWITH,
Butler- c. 1820's, was a leading citizen of N. Granville, N. Y., & served along w. Zebulon R. Shipherd & Peter Parker on committees of its Presbyt. church- **759s**
Mary- of Whitehall, N. Y.; Dec. 11, 1801, "verdict came to her death by the act of God"; Benajah Hill, Coroner- **(L)- 876**

Bedlam, N. Y.- orig. name of the section of Salem that became W. Hebron, N. Y.- **737**

BEEBE,
_____- m. Mary, dau. Aaron & Olive (Harding) Martin- **1040**
Andrew- Co. A, 2nd N. Y., Northern Black Horse, Cav., 1861- 2- **1080**
C. L.- Co. A, 2nd N. Y., Northern Black Horse, Cav., 1861- 2- **1080**
Justin E.- merch., E. Greenwich, N. Y.; m. Minerva, dau. Aaron, Jr., & Artemisia (Lynn) Martin- **731**; c. 1858, employed Francis Pro to cut wood for him- **974**

BEEKMAN,
Eve- consort of Abraham Schuyler; d. July 17, 1803, at 69- **(L)- 932**

BEERS,
Uriah- of Ballstown, N. Y.; dau. m. Thomas, s. Hugh & Mary (McWhorter) Harsha- **973**

BELDEN,
Azer- of Wilton, Conn.; m. Hannah, dau. Timothy & Esther (Platt) Fitch- **799**

BELGIUM- Bruges (Burgos)- 990; Neuiport- 990; Nes (Nive)- 990; Nivelle- 990; Quatre Bras (Quaire Bras)- 990; Waterloo- 990

BELL,
Capt.- commanded militia co., Stamford, Conn., Aug. 1776, called out in defense of NYC, until its capt. by the British- **753**
Family- c. 1798, res. on the E. side of the Hudson above Moses kill, nr. the loc. of the Black House, Ft. Edward, N. Y.- **804**
Family- Scotch; c. 1790's, res. Salem, N. Y., in the loc. Robert Shaw occ. in 1851; as a young man, Capt. John McDonald 1st obt. work w. this family, assiting them in cutting up trees blown down by a hurricane passing through a small piece of his land; however, a prior bargain by his father brought McDonald to work w. the Armstrongs, w. harder fare, instead; see Vol. 1- **927**

Robert- bro.- in- law, Wm. Gutherie; described by Robert Hanna as "an unmarried man, but a 'whoring dog' "; was among the militia killed at the capt. of Ft. Ann, 1780- **701**

BEMIS,
William?- of Bemis Heights, Stillwater, N. Y.; m.Triphena, dau. Ephriam? More; acc. Wid. Angel, he was prob. the one who gave his name to the Heights; Dr. Fitch observes that despite the fact that he res. on the next farm over from him, Neilson did not even know Bemis' 1st name; refers p. 116, Burgoyne's Campaign; children-
1. William, res. Pittstown, N. Y.; several children
2. Jonathan, rem. Red Post, Holland Purchase, in western N. Y.
3. John, res. 2 mi. W. of Saratoga Springs, N. Y. foll. Rev. war, & d. there w/o issue
4. Triphena, m. ____ Crawford- **851**

BENHAM,
Theodicia- (Theodoria) of Lowville, N. Y., who was orig. from Springfield, Mass.; m. Charles Lee, s. Walter & Sarah (Turner) Martin- **730**; her full name & marriage given, w/o additional information- **1046**

BENNET,
Phineas- (Benet) part of Lot No. 281, Turner's Patent, deeded to him, Jan. 10, 1785, by Ephriam Wheeler; 2nd entry notes purch. for £ 200, Lots No. 282, 283, & part of 281, Turner's Patent, from Ephriam Wheeler- **(L)- 936**
Susanna- witn., along w. John Barnard, Feb. 8, 1789, to deed of Ezra Jones to Thomas Brayton, for part of Lot No. 4, Provincial Patent (Hartford, N. Y.)- **745**

Bennington, Vt.- its Committee of Safety joined w. those of Cambridge & Hoosic, N. Y., Aug. 3, 1775, at a meeting held in Walloomsac, N. Y.- **783**; remarking upon the 'toryism' within the region, Gen. Schuyler notes to Gen. Washington, July 17, 1777, the possibility that Gen. Burgoyne might attempt to march as far as here in order to obt. cattle & carriages- **794**; its Comm. of Correspondence informed Albany Comm., Aug. 24, 1775, that they had formed their militia into companies; present- James Ashton, Moses Robinson, Simon Hathaway "& c."- **821**; Moses, or Samuel Robinson, Ebenezer Wood, Nathan Clark, & Nathan Brush, members of Comm. of Correspondence, joined w. Daniel B. Bratt at St. Croix (Sancoick, N. Y.) to proceed to Esq. Munro's & investigate the charges against him, late Aug. 1775- **822**; return of its Comm. members, compiled by Clark & Dewey, present at Albany, N. Y., May 10, 1775- Simon Hathaway, Ebenezer Wood, Nathan Clark, Elijah Dewey, Nathan Brush, Moses Robinson, Benjamin Wemple, & Samuel Robinson- **831**; late July 1777, Salem militia was ordered down here, in a co. commanded by Gen. John Williams, at abt. the time of the Allen & McCrea massacres; refers Slade's Vt. State Papers; in early Aug., men w. teams were directed to Salem to evac. the town to this loc.- **1049**

Bennington, battle of - (Aug. 16, 1777) acc. Moses Billings, Col. Breyman's detachm. arr. at the battlefield from Castleton, Vt., at the point of Col. Baum's defeat, forming a 2nd battle w. Gen. Stark- **728**; many squads & companies of militia passed through Williamstown, Mass. on their way to the battlesite- **744**; hand sketch by Dr. Fitch, showing plan of the battlesite, w. Hessian fort on the heights & tory breastworks on ridge SE of heights on opp. side of Walloomsac river- **761**; sketch by Dr. Fitch drawn Aug. 23, 1850, the day foll. a walk over the field w. Esq. Barnet, the current owner of the land; description of terrain in conjunction w. map- a cleared field of clay or hardpan soil, loc. across Walloomsac river & SE of Hessian works, on the height of a ridge line continuing across river & running S. of road leading to Walloomsac, N. Y.; at the time of the battle, a crop of flax, pulled & standing in stooks, was on the ground, & the tory breastworks were fashioned from the stooks, filling the interstices of rails from fences in the adj. fields, that were laid up in 2 parallel tiers; acc. Austin Wells, 17 tory dead, coll. from this breastworks, were bur. in the remains of a small outdoor cellar nearby,"thrown, in a promiscuous heap, & the dirt thrown over them"; the site was loc. when it was noticed that a freshly dug woodchuck hole had small bones thrown out of it along w. the gravel; afterw., "the plow man... struck his plow as deep as possible into the hole", thus unearthing a larger & more evidently human pile of bones; the bridge across the Walloomsac, currently (1850) a 110 ft. long covered bridge, occ. the same loc. as the bridge that stood there in 1777; the old bridge rotted down & the river for many yrs. was forded at this site until the new bridge was built; Col. Baum's 2 cannon were loc. NW of the bridgesite, on an abrupt rise of slate rock, nearly a precipice, 60 or 100 ft. above the river, on a "flattish level of small extent, above the steep rise"; it was suppos. by Col. Baum that Gen. Stark would attack the tory breastworks 1st, & the cannon would give a raking fire upon him as he came; however, Gen. Stark remained on the N. side of the stream, & foll. up the hollow where the brook runs, attacking the Hessians directly & w. full force; tory breastworks was attacked from the E., & to its rear, preventing use of the cannon on its attackers w/o also killing tories; acc. Austin Wells, 2 potato holes betw. Esq. Barnet's house & river served as graves for 30 bodies drawn from this part of the ground; a tory found in this loc.was bur. halfway betw.; see also, Vegetation, Terrain- **762**; summit was completely forested, & Hessians constructed enclosed timber breastworks here on a small, level spot, 12 rods by abt. a 3rd as wide, running in NW- SE direction; soil was too thin to make ditch or enbankment, & a single oak tree was left within the enclosure, perh. to suspend their colors; in 1777, a house was loc. some rods SW of Esq. Barnet's present (1850) brick house & several log huts were in the same neighborh.; since lands were held on 21 yr. leases, no permanent houses were built- **762b**; 3 days foll. the battle, when Nathaniel Barnet was at its site as a soldier, there were hundreds of visitors from the surrounding countryside walking over the grounds- **763**; Capt. Jacob Safford, of the Bennington militia, given as the source of Esq. Barnet's knowl. of the battle; Col. Seth Warner did not participate in the 1st battle, & it was reported that w. his arr. on the field, Gen. Stark complained to him for not being there sooner; notes (prob. Dr. Fitch) "accts. of this battle, both oral & written, differ so much that no one knows what to believe respecting it"- **764**; acct. of 2nd battle, foll. defeat of Col. Baum on the heights; "the fugitives that escaped from being capt. fled back & were pursued by the Americans, in an irregular manner, & w/o any order", passing through the settlm. of Walloomsac, N. Y., abt. 1½ mi. E. of Esq. Barnet's house; the retreating Hessians gained the top of a ridge abt. on the W. line of Walloomsac Patent, just as Col. Breyman's forces arr. on the flats beyond; as they ran to join Breyman, the Americans gained the same ridge, paused to observe the fresh troops, & then fired upon them until Col. Breyman had arranged them for advancing; the 2 Hessian cannons fired w. grapeshot, & the Americans forsook the ridge for the ravines & bushes; being an irregular force, w/o order in the ranks or a general officer to direct their movements, they soon retired as Breyman advanced & passed over the ridge, w. a "desultory firing" continued by the Americans; the Hessian force proceeded abt. a mi. & was midway betw. the point of their 1st advance & where Esq. Barnet's house was later loc., where the road leaves the river flats & ascends the hill, when it was met by Col. Warner's fresh troops, "who capt. some of the advance parties, & opposed his further advance w. such spirit, that he was eventually compelled to retire"- **766**; the wnd. Col. Baum was carried from the field by 4 American soldiers & deposited in a house nr. the present loc. of the Matthews house (which was noted for being inside the boundaries of both Vt. & N. Y.); his body was found the next day, stripped of all valuables; such crowd & confusion was abt. this house & neighborh. on the night foll. the battle that it was impossible to obt. a clue to what occurred, & no formal investigation was pursued, though the soldiers who had borne him from the field suspected he had been foully dealt w. & murdered for his uniform, sword, purse, & c.- **801**; James More, mounted on a horse, "was incessantly hovering upon the front of the force, riding up as nr. as prudent, taking aim & disch. his gun at the enemy & instantly flying off beyond their reach"; by the reputation of his "unerring aim", it was believed he prob. killed several of Col. Baum's force as they made their way to Bennington- **915**; the 3 Indians who killed a sheep (§ 333) at the Welch's house, Salem, N. Y., were reportedly refugees from the battlefield; they appeared on a Sun., when the town was evac., & were 1st seen lying in the shade of the meeting house, there being no service- **926**; prior to the battle, Gen. Stark & several officers purportedly stopped to obt. refreshment from the house of Mr. Munro, a loyalist; being absent, an officer inquired of his wf. where he might be; on replying that she didn't know, the officer drew his sword, endeavoring to intimidate her; Gen. Stark, on discovering the commotion, severely reprimanded the officer; foll. the battle, Mrs. Munro & her sist. suppos. went to the battlefield, carrying pails of milk & water to offer among the wnd.; towards noon, wagons were sent to convey the wnd. to hospitals & haul the dead away for burial- **953**; as Col. Baum advanced from Cambridge to Sancoick, the American scouts & stragglers fled bef. him to Bennington; Wm. Gilmore & 2 other men ventured to linger at Van Rensselaer's mill long enough to strip the planking from the bridge, retreat to a knoll S. of the creek & disch. their pieces as the enemy came within their sight; Col. Baum's co. halted & made a reconnaissance of the area, going some 25 rods downstream from the bridge; the 2 cannon were then passed over a convenient ford & prob. a small party came up the opp. side & repaired the bridge, causing a 2- 3 hr. delay in the advance- **1006**; a neighborh. tradit. in N. Hoosick, N. Y. was that the last man killed in the battle was a Hessian, his corpse found at the base of a hill, abt. on the old line of the Hoosic & Walloomsac Patents- **1007**; the Indian, Thomas DeRouger- Williams, sent w. Col. Baum's forces, did but little for the services he was engaged in, & almost came to confrontation w. some of the British officers involved for that reason- **1016**; rain during the day, Aug. 15, 1777, had an important effect upon the battle's outcome; Col. Warner's regt., marching from Manchester, Vt., became so wet that they excused themselves from the morning attack in order to dry & clean themselves; the proposed attack by Gen. Stark on that day was prevented by the rain, enabling the Berkshire co. militia to join his force; Col. Baum's Hessians, in attempting to throw up defensive entrenchments, were hindered "the pouring rain, such as (the acct. says) they had never known to occur in Germany, washed down the shovelfuls of earth as fast as they essayed to pile them up" & they could only fortify their positions imperfectly; Col. Breyman, marching the 24 mi. from Galesville at 8:00 AM, Aug. 15th, was impeded & delayed by the rains of that day & the muddy roads of the next, & arr. at 4:00 PM the foll. day; his loss by cannon breakdown was abt. 2 hrs.; refers Burgoyne's Orderly Book- **1072**

the Bennington Mob- (a name prob. used by its members, their principal leaders being Ethan Allen & Seth Warner; their main purpose was to intimidate or eject settlers a/o magistrates favoring the govt. of N. Y. over N. H. in the contested land titles of the Grant lands) referred to by Benjamin Hough in statements concerning his seizure, Jan. 26, 1775; among those members of the 'mob' confining Hough were Sylvanus Brown, James Meed, Samuel Campbell, ____ Daniels, ____ Powers, Stephen Meed, ____ Booley, & ____ Lyman; its members appt. as a court in Hough's trial were Ethan Allen, Seth Warner, Robert Cochran, Peleg Sunderland, James Meed, Gideon Warren, & Jesse Sawyer; acc. Hough, Cochran declared himself 'Adjutant of the rioters' & Benjamin Hoyt, one of Hough's orig. captors, professed himself to be their Drum Major; the sentence carried out on Hough was performed by William Hoyt, Abel Benedict, John Sawyer, & one other- **881**; (referred to as the Bennington people) the neighbors of Samuel Gardenier, c. 1771, Walloomsac Patent, declined to assist him in rebuilding his fences for fear of offending them; an active interest was taken by them in returning to Ichabod Cross the lands that he had relinquished to Gardenier under a mutually agreed arbitration; see Grants, N. H. Controversy- **902**

BENSON,
____ - tavernkeeper (n. d.) Easton, N. Y.; his house stood on the E. side of the main Troy road through town, where the Valley- bridge road forked from the main road; Dr. Philip Smith 1st res. here, c. 1795, at the time Asa Fitch, Sr., studied medicine w. him- **861**
Egbert- (1746- 1833; NYS Senate, 1771- 87; 1st & 2nd Congress, 1789- 93) along w. King & Lawrence, associates that Gen. Schuyler confided in concerning the reasons behind his re- election defeat, 1791, as U. S. Senator; his name was offered in the state Assembly to "obliterate" Burr's, Jan. 18, 1791, but failed 24- 34, & Burr's name was then carried to the state Senate, where he was elected to Gen. Schuyler's expired post as U. S. Senator- **920**

BENZEL,
Adolphus- c. 1773, Justice of Peace, Charlotte co., N. Y.- **911**

BERRY,
Family- from N. J.; bros. Lewis, m. Elizabeth Wells, & Thomas, who kept the Salem jail; prob. also, acc. Dr. Fitch, Sidney, of Ft. Edward, N. Y.?; John, Polly?, & ano., who m. Maj. Van Tuyl- **839**
Lewis- m. Elizabeth, dau. Edmund, Jr., & Wealthy Ann (Goodrich) Wells; rem. Whitestown, N. Y., & kept tavern there; d. abt. 15 mos. ago (Sept.- Oct. 1848) leaving his wid. & foll. children-
  1. Gerrit Wendell, d. Mayville, N. Y., w/o children
  2. Mary, res. Whitestown, N. Y., at the family homestead
  3. Morris Miller, res. Saratoga Springs, N. Y.
  4. Cornelia, at home
  5. Jane, dec'd.
  6. Wealthy, at home; d. Sept. 19, 1853, at 44?, of Ague & fever
  7. Elizabeth, m. O. L. Barbour
  8. Miriam, m. Rev. Mr. Whicker
  9. Lewis, res. Whitestown, N. Y.
  10. Catharine, res. at home
  11. John, res. at home; machinist, d. June 1852,"intemperate; but a genius"- **839**
Lewis, Jr.- (s. Lewis & Elizabeth Wells) factory superintendent at the factory village, Whitestown, N. Y.; he now (1850) "follows white washing & c. for a livelihood"; has 3 children- **839**
Samuel- c. 1798, res. on E. side of the Hudson, nr. Moses kill; kept a tavern here, his place, now (1850) occ. by Marshall Hall, was loc. N. of the Ephriam Crocker's bro.- **804**
Thomas- kept tavern, 1795, in part of the dwelling of Asa Fitch, Sr., at Fitch's Point, Salem, N. Y.- **799**; bro. Lewis; kept his tavern in the N. room of Asa Fitch, Sr.'s house "till, there being a great squirrel hunt, ending in a drunken carose in the bar room, keeping the family awake all night, father Fitch in the morning tore down the sign, sent the revellers away, & shut up his house from further use as an

inn"; rem. Whitestown, N. Y., & afterw. res. & d. Vernon, N. Y., where he had m. & left children- **839**

BETHUNE,
Divie- his s. George W., m. Mary Williams- **1045**
Dr.- c. 1817, attended Salem Academy, boarding at Dr. Proudfit's; see Vol. 1- **1053**
George W.- s. Divie; of Brooklyn, N. Y.; m. Nov. 4, 1825, Mary, dau. Col. John & Ann (Roy) Williams, by Dr. Proudfit; no children; his wf. d. Mar. 29, 1869, at La Tour, Switzerland, & her remains returned home; see Wray, George, Esq., Vol. 4- **1045**

BEVERIDGE,
Alexander, Jr.- of Hebron, N. Y.; Co. E, 123rd NYSV; d. Dec. 19, 1862, at 31, in hospital, Alexandria, Va.; bur. Dec. 29, soldier's plot, gr. 15, Evergreen Cemetery, Salem, N. Y.- **1081**; same material; see also, Vol. 4- **1098**

BEWELL,
Timothy- rec'd. recommendation, Jan. 25, 1776, for appt. as Maj., Charlotte co. militia- **784**

BIGELOW,
Samuel- 2nd U. S. Sharpshooters; mortally wnd. in the Wilderness battle (May 5-7, 1864) & d. at 17; remains rec'd. June 24, & bur. the foll. day, soldier's plot, gr. 21, Evergreen Cemetery, Salem, N. Y.- **1081**

BILLINGS,
Charles- of Salem, N. Y.; Co. H, 123rd NYSV; d. Dec. 14, 1862, Harper's Ferry?, Va.; bur. Jan. 5, 1863, soldier's plot, gr. 7, Evergreen Cemetery, Salem, N. Y.- **1081**; same material; see also, Vol. 4- **1098**
Christopher- of Stonington, Conn.; enl. Capt. Babcock's co., 1775, & was stat. at Roxbury, Mass., qtr.'d in the town's church during the siege of Boston; marched to Long Island, & then Harlem, during the British occ. of NYC; rem. Hoosick, N. Y. foll. the Rev. war & res. there 10 yrs.; rem. Indian river, in Vt., 2 mi. S. of Mark's corners; d. 1819, Algiers, Pawlet, Vt.; ments. s. Moses- **728**
George- oath of alleg.; Co. D, 22nd N. Y. Inf.- **(L)- 1074**
Moses- s. Christopher; b. 1794; c.1850, res. E. Greenwich, N. Y.; he res. Pawlet, Vt., as a boy & gives an acct. of his knowl. of Capt. Wm. Fitch & family of that region; studied medicine for 2 yrs. w. Dr. Sargent of Pawlet, but "pecuniary means prevented my completing the study of medicine"- **727**

BININGER,
Abraham- s. Rev. Abraham; b. 1740; was dispatched to NYC as an apprentice in the tanning & leather dressing trade, loc. 'in the swamp'; served 7 yrs. & afterw. expressed his distaste for the trade, & commenced work as a day laborer; m. abt.

1767, Kate Embury, niece of Rev. Philip; they set up a stand on old Augusta St., the site of City Hall, NYC, which became the foundation of the Bininger grocery houses; he later went to Camden valley, Salem, N. Y., in partnership w. his bro. Isaac, leaving his wf. to operate the NYC stand, but later returned & opened a small store on Maiden Lane, opp. the old Oswego Market; res. 164 Willow St., betw. Beekman & Ann Sts.; d. 1836, leaving 2 sons- Jacob, d. 1840; & Abraham- **1075b**

Rev. Abraham- s. Christian; arr. Savannah, Ga., c. Feb. 1736, orphaned at sea; he was raised at the Methodist Whitfield Orphan School, & emig. from Savannah to Philadelphia, Pa., along w. a large co. of Moravians; was educ. for clergy acc. Moravian tenets & settl. at Cold Spring, Pa.; went to St. Thomas, West Indies, as a missionary; informed that 'none but slaves were allowed to preach to slaves', he petitn. the Gov. that he might become one, in order to save their souls; his petitn. went to the King of Denmark, who gave his consent to preach to any class; foll. his return, went w. Rev. Whitfield as a missionary to the Indians; returned to NYC the yr. Philip Embury arr., & contrib. to the creation of his Society, & the John St. church; emig., c. 1760, to Camden valley, Wash. co., along w. Philip Embury; sons- Abraham, eldest, b. 1740; Isaac, Christian, & Joseph- **1075b**

Abraham Merrit- (A. M.) s. Isaac, & grds. Rev. Abraham; c. 1860, claims hereditary ownership of the old family mansion,'Castle Bininger', in Camden valley, Salem, N. Y., the same as it was in 1760, having the orig. papers & artifacts of his grdf., Rev. Abraham, & claiming lineal precedence as the oldest grds.; began his mercantile business in Salem, c. 1774, & establ. an agency in NYC, 1776; rem. his Salem store, 1778, which now (c. 1860's)operates as A. M. Bininger & Co., No. 19 Broad St., NYC- **1075b**

Christian- b. Zurich, Switzerland; c. 1735, emig. w. his wf. & s. Abraham, on the same vessel bringing the celebrated John Wesley to Savannah, Ga.; he & his wf. d. when 2 days from port, & their s. was educ. & cared for at the Methodist Whitfield Orphan School in Savannah- **1075b**

Isaac- s. Rev. Abraham; res. Camden valley, Salem, N. Y., foll. the Rev. war; establ. the most extensive store betw. Albany & Montreal, 'the wonder of the primitive inhabitants'; he afterw. brought his bro. into the business, but they later dissolved their partnership, & he returned to NYC- **1075b**; his wf. was reported to have come over to the house of John Priest, & on several occasions, stayed overnight, "the old man, Isaac being so drunk & tyrannical she durst not remain in the house w. him"; it was also a neighborh. report that 'Castle Bininger' was haunted w. ghosts, that Isaac had once killed a man there who had a quantity of money on him; "many similar things were reported to his discredit by his neighbors"- **1076**

Jacob- (s. Abraham & Kate Embury) had wretched health, traveled to Europe many yrs. attempting to cure himself, & d. 1840, Charleston, S. C., leaving a son- **1705b**

BIRCH,
____ - (or perh. Burch) res. Easton, N. Y.; a son, m. Lucinda C., dau. Aaron, Jr., & Artemisia (Lynn) Martin, as her 2nd husb., & they res. Hebron, N. Y.- **731**

BIRMINGHAM,
J. G.- oath of alleg.; Co. D, 22nd N. Y. Inf.- **(L)- 1074**

BISHOP,
____ - perh. res. Nova Scotia; m. dau. Moses & Desire (Burrows) Gore- **1100**
Nathaniel, Esq.- "one of the Revolutionary officers"; d. Nov. 3, 1811, at 72- **(L)- 772**
Capt. Nathaniel- d. Oct. 23, 1823, at 59- **(L)- 772**

BITELEY,
Family- c. 1798, res. on the E. side of the Hudson, above Moses kill, nr. the loc. of the Black House, Ft. Edward, N. Y.; see Vol. 1- **804**
John- "an old man since dead, ... the oracle of our neighborh. in all such matters"; informed the Thompson family of Moreau, N. Y., concerning an Indian skirmish during the French war where a teamster was killed & bur. beside the road; this incident offered in explanation of the family's discovery of a skeleton discovered, c. 1850's, while the Thompsons were repairing a road in the area- **958**

The Black House- loc. N. of Moses kill, on the E. side of the Hudson; its site was nr. the Bell & Biteley family farms; see Vol. 1- **804**

BLACKMAN,
Charity- of West Haven, Vt.; m. Newell, s. Augustus & Triphena (Martin) Angel, as his 1st wf.- **847**

BLAIR,
Hon. Bernard- c. 1850's, purch. Deac. John Steele's farm, N. of Salem, N. Y., from his s., Col. John; it is being worked by Gideon Safford- **1047**

BLAKE,
Harrison G.- from E. of the Green Mtns.; perh. res. prev. in Marlboro, Vt.; res. for 5 or 6 yrs. in Salem, N. Y., & was in indigent circumstances; he worked in the brickyard, & helped make the bricks for Washington Salem Academy; had 4 sons, incl. Harrison Otis Gray, & at least one dau. c. 1824, he was working the farm on Lot No. 55, N. of Salem village, the present (June 1850) McFarland farm; he & his wf. planned to visit his wf.'s friends from their prev. residence, & departed on a Dec. morning, foll. a light 4 in. snowfall, expecting to reach their destination by nightfall; stopping at a tavern in Arlington, Vt., they fed their horse & obt. some crackers & a pint of liquor; as the road ascended, the snow became thicker until no track was seen, & the weather became intensely cold (acc. Lemuel Lakin, this road

was the one where Roaring brook came down, acc. Dr. Fitch, it was perh. the road N. of that one); their horse became "so jaded out" that he progressed slowly, delaying their arrival so that nightfall overtook them 2- 3 mi. from their destination; their earlier provisions were inadequate for enduring the night outdoors, & their horse gave out as they reached the summit, so that Mr. Blake chose to go ahead on foot; unharnessing his horse, & putting his wf. & infant child on its back, he soon outdistanced them, & accidentally sunk into a brook crossing the path, but bur. by the snow; his boots & feet became frozen, & at length, he became completely exhausted wading through the snow; a woman in the house ahead thought she heard the noise of his calling, & sent out a man to search the area; he was discovered alive, but "chilled & senseless", & unable to speak until nr. daylight, when he informed his rescuers that his wf. & child were foll. behind him; the night had been still & no snow had drifted (as some poems on the subj. suggested) & a search discovered his wf., bur. in the snow, & stiff as a statue; she had taken off her shawl & wrapped it around her baby, who was clapsed in her arms; parting the shawl, the child awoke & smiled at its rescuers, untouched by the frost; both of Mr. Blake's feet were amputated, & he remained in Salem for ano. 2- 3 yrs., supporting himself by peddling; he rem. 1st to Ft. Edward, & from there, took his family to Ohio; his wf. was bur. where she was found, on Stratton Mtn.; the dau. who was saved, m. a Lake Eire steamboat captain, to which the widespread awareness of the story was attrib.; refers Mar. 23, 1847, *Wash. Co. Post*, concerning poetry upon the subj.; & refers Jan. 11, 1862, *N. Y. Observer*, regarding ano. acct., varying in cert. points from the above, "more accurate acct."-
733
Harrison Otis Gray- (1818- 1876; 36th- 37th Congress, 1859- 63) s. Harrison G.; was once hired, or bound out, to Jesse Rhodes, who often whipped him; now (1850) an Ohio State Senator, elected by the Whigs as their presiding officer; "but the locos were exasperated" on his election, questioning its fairness, so that he resigned & refused to serve, forcing ano. election; see Vol. 4- **733**

BLAKELEY,
Capt.- summer 1780, commanded a militia co. stat. at Granville, or Skenesborough, & sent on an alarm to Argyle, N. Y.; was also in command of a co. at the same stat., 1782- **754**

BLAKESBY,
Emily- m. Willard Cheney, Jr., s. Willard Cheney, Sr., & Mary (Faxon) Conkey-
730

BLAKSLEE,
Capt. David- of Granville, N. Y.; deeds 100 acres, on E. end of Lot 6, Fisher's Patent, Nov. 2, 10th yr. of Independence (1785), to Benjamin & Jesse Atwater-
(L)- 936

BLANCHARD,

_____- of Sturbridge, Mass.; m. Fatima, dau. Nathan & Lovinia (Shumway)
Cheney- **1038**

Alexander Hamilton- (Hamilton) s. Hon. Anthony I.; m. dau. "Landlord Wells"; d.
in Michigan, dissipated- **914**; (s. Hon. Anthony I. & Maria Williams) d. unm.-
1045; (A. H.) oath of alleg.; Co. D, 22nd N. Y. Inf.- **(L)- 1074**

Anthony- (s. Anthony I. & Maria Williams) res. Albany, N. Y.; Surrogate, Albany
co.- **914**; m. 1. Elizabeth McGill; 2. Jane, sist. Henry Martin; several children; he
d. May 1, 1861- **1045**

Hon. Anthony I.- offered a voluntary toast to the U. S. Navy, Nov. 29, 1814, at a
public banquet in Salem, N. Y., honoring Commodore Macdonough- **709**; s. John
Francis; b. Aug. 21, 1768; "his father d. when he was a small boy, & his mother
deprived herself of many comforts to give him an educ."; see Vol. 4; he rec'd. an
academic, but not a college educ., as they were generally closed during the Rev.
war; studied law w. Cornelius I. Bogert, NYC; c. 1789, arr. Ft. Edward, N. Y., foll.
completion of his legal studies, & "became an inmate in Tearse's family", the
Blanchards being in some manner connected w. Wid. McNeil, whose grdau. m.
Peter B. Tearse; c. 1791/2, rem. Salem, N. Y.; appt. 1st Wash. co. Dist. Attorney,
the office then called Assist. Attorney General, receiving his appt. from Gov. John
Jay; was Justice of the Peace, & held other minor offices; 1810- appt. 1st Judge,
Wash. co., serving 12 yrs. or more; m. dau. Gen. John Williams; children-
1. Anthony
2. John
3. dau., m. Judge Ross, of Essex co., N. Y.
4. dau., m. John McLean, Salem, N. Y.
5. Hamilton, m. dau. "Landlord Wells"
6. Williams, d. Salem, N. Y., "very dissipated"
7. Ann Eliza
8. James- **914**; observes that Gen. Williams' medical skills were "chiefly derived
from experience & his own judgment & observation, as his educ. was quite limited.
He was however skillful & active in his profession"; also notes that Williams'
presence in Salem was prob. by "mere accident, he being an adventurer in search
of some spot to make his fortune"; he also gives some other observations &
anecdotes concerning Williams' medical practice- **915**; delivers some opinions
upon the characters of personalities involved in the Vt. disturbances- Pendergrass,
Col. Robert Cochran, & his encounter w. Ethan Allen, when he was a clerk in
Boget's law office- **917**; an Orrery constructed for him, by Rev. Thomas Goss, &
_____ Griswold, the goldsmith, c. 1800's, was of considerable interest within the
town of Salem,"it being a greast curiosity in them [sic] days"- **994**; b. NYC; d. June
14, 1853, Salem, N. Y.; desc. from a Huguenot father & a Scotch mother; his obit.
notes him as 'one of the last of the oldest inhabitants of the county'; served 1811-
1822, as 1st Judge, Wash. co.; member, N. Y. Legislature, & Dist. Atty. for
Northern N. Y.- **1012**; m. Maria, dau. Gen. John & Susannah (Thomas) Williams;
children (compare w. § 914, above)-

1. Maria, m. Hon. John McLean
2. John, m. Susan Wright
3. Susannah, m. Gen. Henry H. Ross
4. Anthony, m. 1. Elizabeth McGill; 2. Jane Martin
5. Alexander Hamilton
6. Williams, m. Minerva Warren
7. Ann Eliza, m. F. L. C. Sailly
8. James, res. in the N., w. his sisters- **1045**
John- Ulster co., 1689; refers Doc. Hist., i, 281- **914**
John- s. Hon. Anthony I.; d. Salem, N. Y., dissipated; a dau. m. Archibald L.
McDougall, of Salem- **914**; m. Susan Wright; children- daus. Maria (§ 914) &
Ann Eliza; & s. James; his wid. m. again, but separated from that husb.- **1045**
John Francis- French Huguenot; "driven from their native land by religious
persecution", he was brought to America by his father when he was 9 yrs. old, &
the family settl. nr. NYC; see Vol. 4; ments. a son, Anthony I.- **914**
Matthews- from Artois, farmer, w. wf. & 3 children, arr. 1660; refers Doc. Hist.,
iii, 57- **914**
Williams- (s. Hon. Anthony I. & Maria Williams) m. Minerva Williams; c. 1858,
"he [was] dissipated, like all his bros.; dead many yrs."- **1045**

BLASHFIELD,
____- of Chatham, N. Y.; m. Mary Eliza, dau. Josephus & Lucy (Palen) Martin, as
his 2nd wf.- **731**

BLEECK,
Barent- merch., NYC; he & John Richard Bleecker, the younger, appt. by Col.
Wm. Godwin, Esq., as attorneys to execute a conveyance to Alexander Ellice- **880**

BLEECKER,
____- adm. to practice, Charlotte co.court, Oct. 19, 1773- **878**
Ann Eliza- wf. John James; d. Nov. 23, 1783, at 31- **(L)- 932**
Barent- s. John, Sr.; he & his bro. John, Jr., purch., along w. Hugh Pebbles, all of
Wm. Duer, Esq.'s property at Ft. Miller, N. Y.- **1032**
Esq.- he was at his oat farm in Pittstown, N. Y., in mid- june 1782, & was capt.,
along w. his hired hand & a negro, by a party of 4 tories & 4 British soldiers, who
had come down from Canada; the party started for the Green Mtns., came off from
the mtn. nr. Bennington, Vt., & then steered towards the eastern Green Mtns.; they
were discovered & overtaken in the woods the foll. morning, & their captives
released; the would- be abductors were then confined in Bennington until Oct.,
when they were taken to Skenesborough for exchange; refers Kettell's American
Poetry, v. 1, p. 212; & Stone's Life of Brant, ii, 178- **747**
John- ments. sons Barent & John, Jr.- **1032**
John, Jr.- s. John; res. N. of Stillwater, N. Y., nearly on Bemis Heights; m. 1.
____; 2. Wid., Bradstreet Schuyler; he & his bro. Barent, along w. Hugh Pebbles,

purch. all of Wm. Duer, Esq.'s properties at Ft. Miller, N. Y., during the Sheriff's sale; c. 1854, they still maintain the water priviledge- **1032**
John James- plaintiff, May 19, 1774, in separate cases, vs. Micah Veal, vs. Thomas Rowlee, vs. Andrew Spencer, vs. James Palmer, vs. Jeremiah Spencer, vs. Thomas Green, & vs. Josiah Tirrell- **878**
John R.- ment. as surveyor, c. 1770's, Schuyler Patent- **935**
John Richard- the younger; merch., NYC; he & Barent Bleeck appt. by Col. Wm. Godwin, Esq., as attorneys to execute a conveyance to Alexander Ellice- **880**
Justice- of Albany, N. Y.; he & the Mayor of Albany were among those referring Samuel Gardenier to higher govt. authorities for protection from the Bennington people- **902**

Blind Staggers- a toxic condition attrib. to a horse purch. (n. d.) by Moses Martin, Sr., due to its actions; "He was unable to walk straight, or even at times to stand. At length, although he was unable to walk on the ground, he was seen to be walking upon the top of a log fence"- **870**

BLINN,
Elisha- (Blin) of Whitehall, N. Y.; ments. s. Melancton O.; c. 1825, Edward W. Parker became a clerk in his store, & afterw. a partner, until 1836, when he went into business w. his s. Melancton, & Judge Wheeler- **759s**
Harriet- m. Hon. William H., s. Peter & Esther (Clark) Parker, as his 1st wf.; she d. Sept. 8, 1834, at 38, Whitehall, N. Y.- **759**; (Blin) m. Wm. H. Parker as his 1st wf.- **759s**

BLISS,
____ - res. Troy, N. Y.; bookseller, of the firm of Parker & Bliss; m. dau. Capt. Richard Hall & Theodocia (Conklin) Fitch; a dau. & 2 sons- **799**
Aaron- s. Henry; he was in partnership w. his bro.- in- law, Rodney Jayner, in a store at Union Village (Greenwich, N. Y.) & then went to California for 2 yrs., & accumul. some $8- 12,000.00, but "sank under consumption- went S. for his health, & d. in the vicinity of New Orleans, towards the close of the yr. 1852"- **1005**
Henry- very intemperate; m. Abigail, dau. Benjamin Fitch; his bro. res. Poultney, Vt., & purch. a house & lot in Galesville, N. Y., that Henry res. in for several of the last yrs. of his life; rem. w. his son to Wisc., & d. immed. after they arr. there; the remainder of his family res. in Galesville, & his wf. d. there, c. 1848/9, of consumption, "a disease entailed on all of their children"-
1. Charlotte, m. ____ Combs
2. William, m. Ann Gamble, of Argyle, N. Y.
3. Ann Eliza, m. James Brownell, of White Creek, N. Y.
4. Jane, m. Rodney Jayner
5. Elizabeth, d. unm.
6. Aaron, unm.- **1005**

Maj.- (William Wallace Smith; 1815- 1853; ca. 1845, m. Mary Elizabeth, dau. Pres. Taylor) b. Whitehall, N. Y., where he passed his youth; reportedly the natural son of Hon. Ezra Smith; he attended West Point, perh. through the influ. of his father, thus paving the way for his rank & assoc. w. Gen. Taylor, "such is the popular report in this vicinity"; m. dau. Gen./ Pres. Zachary Taylor- **845**
Peletiah- bookseller, Troy, N. Y.; m. Sarah, dau. Capt. Richard Hall & Theodocia (Conklin) Fitch; 4 children- Le Grand, James, Elizabeth, & Peletiah, who d. inf.- **940**; his dau. Elizabeth indicates to Dr. Fitch a printed facsimile of the Fitch-Rathbun shield, & a wax impression of the Fitch coat of arms taken from the ring of John Fitch; see Fitch, Genealogy- **942**
William- s. Henry; m. Ann Gamble, of Argyle, N. Y.; c. 1840's, he rem. Fall River, Wisc., along w. his father & his in- laws; no children- **1005**

BLOSSOM,
John- of Salem, N. Y.; his 'Dry house' purch. (n. d.) by Colin McFarland & built over as a dwelling place- **873**

BLOUNT,
Charles- (1654- 1693) an entry, v. ii, pgs. 332- 333, Macaulay's Hist. of England, referred to by Dr. Fitch, noting that from his acct. of Blount's book, *Oracles of Reason,* Ethan Allen "stole the title of his 'Bible' & also the leading ideas of it, from this long forgotten production"; see Paine, Thomas, Vol. 1- **1030**

BLOWERS,
William- m. Miriam, dau. Capt. Abner & Miriam (Martin) Dwelly; "moved west to Onondagua [sic] town"; she d. 1832, leaving a dau.- **731**

BLYTHE,
___- ment. as one of Daniel Shays' supporters, who settl. nr. Granville, N. Y., after being driven out of Mass.- **921**

BOCKUS,
Daniel- m. Lydia, dau. John & Hannah (Fitch) St. John- **799**

BOGERT,
Cornelius I.- lawyer, res. NYC; Judge Anthony I. Blanchard studied law in his offices during the Rev. war- **914**; he owned some land along the Onion river that was of little use to him, & at abt. the time that the Vt. controversy was resolved, Ethan Allen arr. at his offices to purch. the claim- **917**

BOGGS,
Lt.- c. 1778, ano. of the militia commanders at Skenesborough, N. Y., acc. Moses Harvey's Rev. war pens. appl.- **751**

BOVEE,
Family- tory; res. Hoosick, N. Y., during the Rev. war- **768**; along w. the Cronk family, their connections in Hoosick were numerous, & all of the men in this family were recruited by old 'Festus' to fight against the country, at the time of the Bennington battle- **769**
John- res. & d. Hoosick, N. Y.; he went into Col. Baum's camp along w. old 'Festus', & was shot during the battle of Bennington, but the musket ball was never extracted; he was in the hottest part of the battle when he rec'd. the ball, w/o being killed, & was thereafter known universally in town as 'Bullet- proof John'- **769**

BOWEN,
Dr.- res. Clarendon, Vt.; dau. Marsha, m.William D., s. Daniel & Mary (White) Marsh- **962**

BOWMAN,
Family- tory; res. S. of the McKellip farm, Jackson, N. Y., during the Rev. war; it was strongly suspected by Mrs. Moses Martin, Sr., that they were the culprits who stole whatever items were bur. by the Martins bef. retreating in front of Burgoyne's advance; they later rem. Ohio; known children- John, Samuel, Betty, & Peggy, who was a fine singer & used to work spinning flax for Moses Martin, Sr., & was encouraged by him to sing popular whig songs of the day- **856**

BOYD,
Agnes- m. Frank, prob. s. John Livingston- **1084**
Family- c. 1777, res. N. of the Rowan family, Salem, N. Y., in the remotest part of town; see Vol. 1- **1049**
Thomas- s. William; res. Salem, N. Y.; enl. for 9 mos., spring 1782, mustered at Saratoga (Schuylerville, N. Y.), remained there for 6 wks., & was then garrisoned at Ft. Williams, in Salem; c. 1850, has in his possession, the muster list of his co.; during the retreat, 1777, he returned to his family's house, along w. his bro. John & a sist., to see to affairs on the farm bef. the family returned; acc. Dr. Fitch, he "remembers but little, distinctly, being young at the time, & his memory impaired now"; attests that one of his bros. stole some of Burgoyne's horses at abt. the same time as Alex. McNish capt. a breastwork at Schuylerville; ments. an acct. in *Sexagenary* (p. 109, 1866 edition, notes that a no. of Burgoyne's horses were feeding in Gen. Schuyler's meadow, on the opp. side of the Hudson from the militia encampment; one private, name not given, obt. permission to attempt to capt. a horse, stripped & swam the river, seized & mounted one, fleeing amidst a hail of musketry; he later successfully performed the same feat, deeming it not proper that he should have a horse w/o his commander having one)- **729**
William- his family evac. Salem, N. Y. on a Mon. morning, during the retreat bef. Burgoyne's advance; they stayed overnight at McCoun's, & then at the Fonda house in Hoosick, N. Y.; his s. Thomas states that he & his bro. Thomas were taken

prisoner 5 or 6 mi. S. of the Checkered House, Cambridge, N. Y. (perh. in Aug. 1777, prior to the Bennington battle)- **729**

BOYNTON,
Capt.- (Capt. Edmund?, Co. G; succeeded by Benjamin Mosher bef. muster of regt.; p. 75, Johnson's Hist. of Wash. Co.) of Whitehall, N. Y.; May 25, 1860, commanded Co. B, 22nd N. Y. Inf.- **(L)- 1074**

BRACKETT,
____- (or Brockett) res. Galway, N. Y.; m. Matilda, dau. Adam & Abigail (Cheney) Martin; children-
1. Jared
2. Alma, d. Stillwater, N. Y., foll. a long illness attended to by Dr. Fitch
3. Matilda, m. ____ Witlock
4. dau., m. ____ Starkweather; his wf. m. 2. Dr. Potter?; & 3. Moses Scott, of Waterford, N. Y.- **730**; (Jerry Brockett) children- Abby, m. ____ Starkweather; Matilda, m.____ Whitlock; Alma, d. unm.; Jared, merch., Kenosha, Wisc.- **1038**
Jared- (s. ____ & Matilda Martin) merch., Stillwater, N. Y.; has s. Jared, & dau. Celia; c. 1850, res. Kenosha, Wisc.- **730**; (Brockett) ments. a 2nd son, dec'd.- **1038**

BRADEY,
Michael- res. Post's corners, White Creek, N. Y.; def. witn., People vs. Martin Wallace; testif. that he knew Wallace for 3- 4 yrs., & that he had res. w. him for abt. 2 wks.; he also sd. that Wallace had been sick a wk. or so bef. Feb. 16, 1858, & was not in good health on that day; at abt. 9 or 10:00 AM, the 2 of them went to Eagle Bridge, w/o stopping on the way, & went into Reynold's Tavern, where they 1st met Barney McEntee; they all drank together, & Wallace sd. he was going to look for a house; he left them there, & Wallace & McEntee went towards Buskirk's Bridge; he did not see Wallace again until he came home late that evening, when his wf. got him some supper; Wallace sd. that he had left McEntee when they had come as far as John Larmon's, as McEntee was unwilling to come home w. him; Wallace then went to bed, & abt. 1½ hrs. later, Randall & Houghton arr. at his house; they did not state their business, but searched Wallace's things; bef. this time, Wallace's behavior appeared good, as far as he could tell; on cross- exam, it was revealed that Wallace had prev. res. w. Pat Ward, who had turned him out, but he had never heard it to be because he carried a pistol; Bradey also sd. that he had never heard of Wallace's fighting or drinking, or his threatening to kill Ben Baker, or being out w. Pat Ward & trying to trip & rob him- **1048s**

BRADFORD,
Lt. William H.- Co. E, 93rd N. Y. Inf.- **1090b**

BRADLEY,
Capt.- commanded a co. of Conn. troops, Col. Waterbury's regt., Jan. 1776, sent from Stamford, Conn., to NYC- **752**
Maj. Gilbert- of Sunderland, Vt.; one of Gen. Stark's officers at the battle of Bennington; either he or Maj. Stafford attested to Gen. Stark berating Col. Warner for not arr. on the battlefield w. his forces sooner- **764**

BRADSHAW,
James- deed witn., Apr. 15, 1775, Albert Baker to Henry Franklin- **(L)- 936**
Thomas- part of Lot 49, Kingsbury, N. Y., mortgaged to him, May 19, 1798, by Joseph Fitch; disch. June 10, 1800- **938**

BRAGG,
Family- c. 1850, res. S. of Ft. Miller, N. Y., on the site orig. occ., 1798, by Solomon Smith- **804**

BRAMAN,
Lt. Waters W.- Co. C, 93rd N. Y. Inf.- **1090b**

BRANCH,
_____- c. 1752, res. Norwich, Conn.; he & _____ Standish were given £ 130 security by Dr. Peletiah Fitch, Jan. 1753, for a debt incurred by Peletiah's bro. Asa- **838**

BRANDON,
John- part of a N. Y. survey party along the Onion river, lead by Benjamin Stevenson; Sept. 29, 1772, they were attacked w/o provocation by Remember Baker, Ira Allen, & 5 others- **906**

BRANT,
Col. Joseph- (Thayendanegea; 1742- 1807) acc. Samuel Standish's Rev. war pens. appl., he was in the camp of Gen. Burgoyne's army at the time of Jane McCrea's massacre, July 1777- **747**

BRATT,
Daniel B.- member, Comm. of Correspondence, Hoosick, N. Y.; his letter, aug. 29, 1775, describes the efforts involved in investigating John Munro. Esq.; on a Sun., he & Messrs. Robinson, Wood, Clark, & Brush, of the Bennington Comm. proceeded, & early on Mon. morning, they arr. at Munro's, bringing a party of armed men; 4 of these men were sent to seize Donald Munro & return w. him; in order to acquaint Esq. Munro w. their business, 3 unarmed men were sent to him, & if he was 'refractory', it was planned to seize him & surround the house w. armed men; Bratt, John Rensselaer, & ano. waited upon Munro, & the armed men took up posts nr. every part of the house; the letter of the Albany Comm. was then read to him, & he offered to make an oath that he had never rec'd. the commission

in question & was ready to give up his papers, giving the investigators all satisfaction; Esq. Munro's bro., Donald, was brought in by the 2nd party & interviewed separately; 'it appeared on close examination his charge proceeded from a grudge he had against John Munro on acct. of a former quarrel'; it was also learned from Esq. Munro that he had been nomin. as an officer in a regt. of Highlanders that was talked of being raised, but did not know the rank; this, he had ment. to his bro., & was abt. what had been related, in turn, to John McCrea by Hugh Munro; his papers were examined & 'he opened every closet, chamber, cellar, desk, & freely showed us every private place abt. his house'; from this, & other details, the Comm. disch. him from all suspicion- **822**
John- a murder inquest, June 1802, into the shooting of John Viele, was held at his house, Cambridge, or Hoosick, N. Y.- **(L)- 876**

BRAYMER,
Henry- c. 1851, res. abt. a mi. E. of James McElherron, Hebron, N. Y.- **922**

BRAYTON,
Gideon- prob. from Providence, R. I.; rem. Dutchess co., N. Y., & afterw. settl. Durham (Rutland, Vt.); his s. Thomas, settl. Clarendon, Vt.; he later rem. White Creek, N. Y., & moved his son's family there after they were banished from the Grants; bur. in the family plot opp. the farm of his grds., Deac. William- **746**
Thomas- res. Beekman's Patent, Dutchess co., N. Y.; for £ 100 N. Y. currency, rec'd. a warrantee deed, Nov. 20, 1772, from Jacob Marsh, of Socialborough, Charlotte co., N. Y., conveying Lot No. 5, Socialborough, containing 100 acres; bounded as foll.- W- Otter creek; S- Jacob Marsh; E- highway; & N- Elisha Williams; acknowl. by Benjamin Spencer, & witn. by Ichabod Foster & Reubin Colvin (CoCuin); for £ 12, Jacob Marsh quit claimed 100 acres to him, Dec. 2, 1773, in the right of John Wilder, "he to do the duties reserved by the charter"; on Mar. 16, 1779, he res. Little White Creek, Albany co., N. Y., when Samuel Place of Socialborough gave a bond of £ 1,000 to him to deed his share, or right of land, in Durham (Rutland, Vt.), possessed by Place as an orig. proprietor of that Patent; for $38.00, John Stafford quit claimed to him, Jan. 29, 1784, a tract in Danby, Vt., beginnning at the NW corner of Lot No. 53; on Nov. 21, 1786, he res. Harwich, Vt., when a 600 acre lot in Danby was deeded to him by Andrew White; of Kingsbury, N. Y., Feb. 8, 1789, when part of Lot No. 4, Provincial Patent, was deeded to him by Ezra Jones, of Westfield, N. Y.- **745**; s. Gideon; rem. to Dutchess co., N. Y., from R. I., & then settl. Clarendon, Vt.; after res. there a few yrs., he was driven away by a mob lead by Ethan Allen; until the Vt. Controversy was settl., he res. Little White Creek, N. Y., & then purch. a farm in Danby, Vt.; he sold his farm there, & rem., 1798, Ft. Ann, N. Y.; Ethan Allen & others once came upon him & Benjamin Hough at a house w. 1 or 2 others present, but as they were armed, Allen left them alone; later, he was come upon too closely for him to effectively resist, & taken while he was working in a field, brought to Sunderland, Vt., he was sentenced to 200 lashes (this was apparently to be carried out if he was

ever found in the Grants again, & the same sentence was pronounced upon Benjamin Hough at that time as well); refers to a letter of Judge C. K. Williams; Hough later rec'd. his sentence, & wrote a letter of warning to Brayton that the Vermonters were abt. to carry out their sentence upon him as well; shortly thereafter, a mob came to his house, & he went to meet them, seeking their leader; Warner (prob. Seth Warner) was pointed out as their leader, & he sought to bargain w. him, stating his desire to settle in the Grants & do the fair thing, if any difficulty abt. the title or other matters should arise betw. them, by having the problems arbitrated by men mutually chosen by them; Warner agreed that his request was "fair & perfectly right", & Brayton thereupon requested a written "memorandum"; when Warner inquired of the name to be given in the agreem., his identity was discovered, & Baker (prob. Remember Baker), standing nearby, swore outright that instead of a writing, he should have a whipping; the mob raged for delivering sentence upon him, but Warner, pleased w. the ruse he had practiced, granted that his proposal was fair, & that he should be entitled to their protection; Brayton, a "large, athletic man", then made ano. bargain, that any of the persons who wanted him whipped might have their chance, but only if they came to him one at a time; the "pot- valient" Baker did not care to accept his challenge, nor did anyone else; he then tarried w. the mob until he had an opportunity to slip away; at a later date, c. 1777, he was taken prisoner & confined in a room w. others; as he was not assigned to care for the fireplace to defray the expense of his keep, when a brisk fire tumbled out into the room, he left it to burn, badly damaging the floor bef. it was discovered; incensed, his captors attempted to have him be a hosteler- to care for their horses, but he swore that if given the chance, he would poison some of their best horses; he became "so burthensome on their hands" that he was disch. after 3- 4 wks. of confinement; at length, it was resolved that he be banished from the Grants, but he was then so sick that he was unable to stand when ordered off; his father procured an ox cart & moved the family, which then incl. 7 children, bringing them down to Little White Creek, along w. some beds & furniture; his horse, a large stock of cattle, & the bulk of his furniture, was left w/o recompense; ments. dau. Mary, b. ca. 1777, & s. Deac. William; he d. Mar. 1810, & was bur. in a plot on the opp. side of the Champlain canal from his son's farm- **746**; (Braten) one of Benjamin Hough's constables; it was during Hough's captivity, Jan./ Feb. 1775, that Ethan Allen was overheard saying that the Bennington mob should take him, & Daniel Walker, if they could be found above ground- **881**
Deac.William- s. Thomas; res. 2 mi. S. of Ft. Ann village, town of Kingsbury, N. Y.- **746**

BRECKENRIDGE,
___- of Bennington, Vt.; prob. m. Mrs. Cown, dau. Hon. John Younglove, as her 2nd husb.- **843**
David- bro. Col. James; res. 4 mi. from Brockville, Ont., Canada; became a Methodist preacher; ments. one s., David, who was also a Methodist minister; both dec'd. prior 1853- **991**

James- (Breakenridge; 1721- 1783) the night foll. the Sheriff & his posse's attempt to eject him, prob. Aug. 1771, rioters in Walloomsac Patent tore up 200 panels of Samuel Gardenier's fence, & burnt the fence in a heap, along w. one of Gardenier's large haystacks- **902**; when a writ of ejection was served on him (§ 357), few of the Sheriff's posse were armed, & they remained back from his house, as there was an armed force lying in ambush; Robert Yates, Esq., was compelled to read the writ to him from in front of his closed door; see Grants, N. H. Controversy- **903**; along w. Jehiel Hawley, appt. Oct. 1772, to act as an agent to go to England & seek compensations for the Grants people- **907**

Col. James- (Breakenridge) a U. S. refugee of the Rev. war, res. 8 mi. NW of Brockville, Ont., Canada; he "stood so high in royal favor that he was created a nobleman, w. the title of Duke of Leeds. He was an awful proud, wicked, blasphemous wretch"; in one instance, he was offended by the behavior of his horse, & asked it if he did not know that he was Jesus Christ; m. ____ McLean; children not recoll.; he may have been James Breakenridge of Bennington, Vt., or his son- **991**

BREMNER,
George- private, 42nd Highland regt;. gr. 50 acres, town of Hebron, N. Y.; refers p. 74, Catalogue of Maps- **990**

BREWER,
Capt.- c. 1777, commander, Hoosick, N. Y. militia co.; on 1st news of Col. Baum's advance, a decision was made for his co. to proceed from his house & join w. the American forces at Bennington; however, Col. Fister determined that the militia's resolve was not firm, & enl. its. Sgt., Orra Cronk, to invite Capt. Brewer to join w. the tories; hearing Cronk's proposal, Brewer chastised him for how it would appear if his Sgt. had gone over to the tories, disclosing to him that the decision had already been made to go to Bennington; Sgt. Cronk, distressed over what he should do, sought out Col. Fister, who again enl. Cronk w. the tories, & discovered Brewer's intentions; Col. Fister then decided to have Capt. Brewer arrested, & sent a party of 3 tories & 2 British soldiers, who surprised him early the foll. morning; Brewer was in his barn, dressing a sheep he had slaughtered for his family to subsist on while he was away; w. loaded muskets pointed at him, the party ordered his surrender, pinioned & guarded him, until Fister's co. of tories joined them & marched him into the British camp as a prisoner; during the battle, he was placed under a Sgt.'s guard, "w. a file of men, somewhere in the outskirts of the camp, w. a slight knoll to the rear of them"; bef. long, the bullets began to strike nr. them, & he attempted to persuade the Sgt., who was "all absorbed in watching the progress of the engagem.", to move them over the knoll to safety; the Sgt. then shook his pistol at him, "sternly & passionately vociferating 'You d- d rebel, hold your tongue or I'll blow you through!' "; but within a minute, a bullet went through the Sgt.'s head, & "w/o groan or convulsion, he dropped lifeless to the ground", & a corp.

took command of the file & prisoners, having them retire behind the knoll until the battle's outcome was known; ments. Richard Powell as his grds.- **770**

BREWSTER,
Abel- c. 1752, res. Norwich, Conn.; a note of £ 170.2.6 was given to him, Jan. 1753, by Dr. Peletiah Fitch, for debt incurred by his bro. Asa- **838**

BREYMAN,
Lt. Col. Heinrich- (?- 1777) reported (perh. erroneously) that his detachm., sent to reinforce Col. Baum, marched from Castleton, Vt., to the Bennington battlesite; he arr. at the point in the battle where Baum was defeated (erroneous, his defeat had already been achieved) & created a 2nd battle w. Gen. Stark's forces- **728**; when his forces arr. at Bennington, Gen. Stark's men were so fatigued & overcome by the heat of the day that they were unable to fight & "push" him from the field- **764**; his force arr. at a flat beyond the ridge along the W. line of Walloomsac Patent, just as Col. Baum's forces were retreating in that direction; until he had arranged his force for advance, they were fired upon from the ridge in an irregular fashion by the Americans who had been pursuing the retreating Hessians; the ridge was abandoned by the Americans when the 2 cannons in his relief column fired w. grapeshot as his force advanced; Joshua Munro, who res. on the S. side of the Walloomsac river, observed his entire movement, & recalled "their brass kettle-drums glittering in the sunshine being a most striking feature of the scene"; his combined force advanced over the ridge & abt. a mi. further, to the point where the road ascends from the river, when Col. Warner's fresh troops arr. & caused him to retire from the field by the force of his resistance- **766**; brief ment.- **1005**; left his loc. at Galesville, N. Y., at 8:00 AM, Aug. 15, 1777, to reinforce Col. Baum; heavy rains & road conditions impeded the 24 mi. march, preventing his arr. until 4:00 PM the foll. day, after Col. Baum had already surrendered his force- **1072**

Brick Houses- the 1st in Wash. co. were those of Edmund Wells, Jr., of Cambridge, & Noah Payne, of Ft. Miller, N. Y.; both were constructed in 1787, prob. by the same mason; the old style brick pattern used in them referred to (§ 249; Vol. 1); Wickwive, or Wickwire house, recently (1850) pulled down, also constructed in 1787, on the turnpike N. of Lansingburgh, N. Y.; for many yrs., these were the only brick buildings N. of that city- **840**

BRIDGE,
Col. Ebenezer- (1742- 1823) c. 1775, commanded regt. of Mass. troops- **799**

BRIGGS,
Abraham- c. 1824, kept an inn, Salem, N. Y.- **808**

BRINKERHOEF,
____- c. 1781, kept a store, a mi. above Bedlam (W. Hebron, N. Y.) & owned the only wagon then known in Hebron & Salem; see Wagons; & Transportation, Vol. 1- **738**

BRISBANE,
Brig. Gen.- commanded a division of the invading British army, Sept. 1814, at Plattsburgh, N. Y.- **706**

BROCKETT,
Jared- (s. Jerry & Matilda Cheney) merch., res. Kenosha, Wisc.; ments. s. Jared, a dau., & ano. son, dec'd. prior 1858- **1038**
Jerry- (see also, Brackett) of Galway, N. Y.; m. Matilda, dau. Reuben & Olive (Day) Cheney; children- Abby, m. ____ Starkweather; Matilda, m. ____ Whitlock; Alma, d. unm., Stillwater, N. Y.; & Jared; his wf. m. 2. Dr. ____, of Galway; & 3. Moses Scott, of Waterford, N. Y.- **1038**

BROOKS,
Erastus- (1815- 1886; N. Y. Senate, 1856) Know- Nothing candidate for Gov. of N. Y., 1856, vs. John A. King & Amasa J. Parker- **759s**
Lt. Col. John- (1752- 1825) his regt. suffered severely at the battle of White Plains, N. Y., Oct. 28, 1776, acc. Samuel Standish's Rev. war pens. appl.- **747**

BROPHEY,
Joseph- oath of alleg.; Co. D, 22nd N. Y. Inf.- **(L)- 1074**

BROUGHTON,
J. R.- druggist; res. Whitehall, N. Y.; his business was destroyed by a fire in the Myers block, Jan. 30, 1854, w. loss of $3,500; insured for $1,800- **1023**

BROWN,
____- commanded a regt. in Gen. Fellow's brigade, July 8, 1777, at the battle of Ft. Ann- **747**
____- of Salem, N. Y.; Quartermaster, c. 1861, 7th Illinois Inf.- **1080**
____- of Salem, N. Y.; stonecutter; spring & summer 1861, employed James Fenton, bef. he enl. in the service- **1081**
Capt.- officer, Aug. 1777, Col. Seth Warner's regt.- **755**
Daniel- res. a mi. E. of Stevenson's corners, in the N. part of Argyle, N. Y.; m. Catharine, dau. Alexander McDougall- **978**
Delbert- Co. A, 2nd N. Y., Northern Black Horse, Cav., 1861- 2- **1080**
Edward- oath of alleg.; Co. D, 22nd N. Y. Inf.- **(L)- 1074**
Family- c. 1771, res. Hoosick, N. Y.; Moses Martin, Sr., evac. his family to their farm during the Burgoyne Campaign- **853**
H. V. D.- oath of alleg.; Co. D, 22nd N. Y. Inf.- **(L)- 1074**

Hiram- m. Apr. 1826, Esther Hall, dau. Luther & Martha (Curtis) Parker; his wf.
d. June 12, 1843, at 34- **759s**
Isabella- m. John Mack, in Ireland, bef. emig., 1732, to Londonderry, N. H.- **734s**
Lt. Col. John- attacked the garrison at Ft. Ticonderoga, Sept. 18, 1777; it was prob.
in this assault that Isaac & William Lytle, who were among the American
prisoners confined there, were released; refers Hemenway's Vt. Gazetteer, ii, 936-
742; killed at Stone Arabia, fall 1779- 752; his death at Stone Arabia, noted by Dr.
Fitch, occurred in an ambush where abt. 30 men were killed; he was pursuing the
enemy, Oct. 1781, foll. the burning of Schoharie, N. Y., & had been scalped; "the
Indian who had his scalp being killed by a rifleman the scalp was obt. & put on his
head & bur. w. him"; among his coffin bearers at the funeral was Reuben Smalley,
of Granville, N. Y.- **756**
Capt. Jonathan- along w. Capt. Oswald, joined Col. Benedict Arnold at Crown
Point, May 19, 1775, w. 50 men enl. on the road, & a small schooner (prob.Maj.
Skene's) capt. at Skenesborough- **775**
Lt.- Apr. 1775, commanded a co. of Col. Walbridge's regt.; his co. was sent to
NYC, Albany, & then to Ticonderoga; under the command of Gen. Richard
Montgomery, his co. proceeded from Ticonderoga to Canada- **753**
Milo H.- Co. H, 123rd NYSV; d. Nov. 27, 1862, at 21; see Vol. 4- **1098**
Dr. Seth- res. (n. d.) Lot 189, Salem, N. Y.- **1049**

BROWNELL,

Elisha- c. 1853, his grist & sawmill was loc. in approx. the same loc. as Van
Rensselaer's mill, c. 1777, on the Little White creek, nr. N. Hoosick, N. Y., abt. 50
rods from its mouth, or entrance, into the Walloomsac river- **1006**
Isaac- res. up White creek; July 1853, he accomp. Dr. Fitch over the grounds of the
Bennington battlefield, relating to him incidents that he was aware of concerning
the battle- **1006**
James- of White Creek, N. Y.; m. Ann Eliza, dau. Henry Bliss; had 2 children by
his 1st wf. who d.; his 1st wf. d. of consumption, & he m. 2. ____- **1005**
John H.- res. Hoosick, N. Y.; acc. his testim., was acquainted w. Martin Wallace
for 6 yrs., employing him for 5 mos. in 1852 or 1853; Wallace's nearest employer
after that was Nathan Cottrell, who res. 3 mi. away from him- **1048s**

BRUNEL,

Iscambert, Sr.- (Marc Isambard; 1769- 1849; &/ or, his s. Isambard Kingdom,
1806- 1859) fled France during the Reign of Terror; an early explorer of western
N. Y., & 1st surveyor of the Champlain canal; remnants of the canal, visible at
Stillwater, N. Y., were prob. marked out by him, & the canal locks nr. Little Falls,
N. Y., were prob. also constructed under his supervision; he also built the Old Park
Theatre, NYC, & was responsible for constructing the defenses of N. Y. Harbor;
refers Feb. 22, 1861, semi- wkly. *N. Y. Times*; Dr. Fitch suppos. that he was prob.
employed by the Inland Lock Navigation Co.; see Vol. 1- **1070**

BRYANT,
Dr.- of Fairfield, N. Y.; m. Phebe, dau. William & Louis (Freeman) Whiteside; 3 children- Minerva, m. Mr. North; Martha, & Orlando- **805**

BUCK,
James A.- oath of alleg.; Co. D, 22nd N. Y. Inf.- **(L)- 1074**

BUEL,
Ichabod- res. Cambridge, N. Y.; dau. Hepzibah, m. Edmund Henry Wells- **839**
Samuel- defendant, May 19, 1774, in a case brought by Hon. Charles Wapthorp-
878

BULL,
Amy- wf. Isaac; d. Jan. 8, 1835, at 87- **(L)- 772**
Michael- et. al.; defendant, May 19, 1774, in a case brought by Charity French-
878

BULLARD,
____- m. Charlotte, dau. John & Hannah (Fitch) St. John- **799**
Alpheus- of Northumberland, N. Y.; m. Hannah, dau. Ebenezer & Sarah (Hobby) Fitch; several children- **799**

BULLEN,
Charles- res. Princetown (Manchester, Vt.); he & Martin Powel were noted by Samuel Willoughby as rioters on the highway, May 16, 1771, who threatened his life if he did not withdraw the writ of ejection he had given to the wf. of Thomas French- **899**

BULLIONS,
Rev. Dr.- c. 1836, President, Wash. Co. Bible Soc.- **1097**

Bull Run (Manassas), 2nd battle of- Aug. 29- 30, 1862; during the battle, the 22nd N. Y. Inf. "was in a most exposed position, on the last day of the fight"; 2/3rds of its officers were killed or wnd., Maj. McKie being the only officer to escape unscathed- **1095b**

BULSBY,
Samuel- he & Remember Baker, along w. 5 others, were charged w. the violent assault & beating, Sept. 13, 1773, of Jonathan Eckert- **911**

BUNEL,
Col.- Apr. 1776, commanded a regt. under Maj. Sedgewick, at Granville, N. Y.- **750**

BUNGEY,
Daniel- 1st Lt., 22nd N. Y. Inf.; promoted to Capt., Sept. 3, 1862, replacing C. Clendon, Jr.- **1095b**

Bunker Hill, battle of- 12 lines recoll. from a song, favored by tories, pert. to the battle; its substance expresses surprise at the stength of American resistance, but notes that they took flight in the face of continued assault by Howe's troops- **980**

BURDEN,
Margaret- m. Ebenezer, s. Ebenezer & Betsey(Blanchard) Proudfit- **1045**

BURGESS,
Naaman- purch. Nathaniel Barnet, Esq.'s farm (n. d.), which incl. within its bounds the site of the Bennington battle- **763**

BURGOYNE,
Lt. Gen. Sir John- (1722- 1792) in correspondence w. Gen. Washington, July 17, 1777, Gen. Schuyler specul. that 'Gen. B' may attempt 'to march as far as Bennington in order to procure cattle & carriages', because of the 'toryism' prevalent within the region; a copy of one of his publications sent, along w. a copy of Schuyler's counter order that anyone taking protection from Burgoyne will be seized & put in jail- **794**; a proclamation by him from his HQ at Skenesborough House, July 10, 1777, as commander of the army & fleet of Great Britain 'against the revolted Provinces of America', directs the sending of 10 or more persons from ea. township to meet w. Col. Skene at 10:00 AM, Wed., July 15th, at Castleton, Vt.; Col. Skene was appt. to give further instructions to those complying w. an earlier 'manifesto', & to describe the means by which 'the disobedient may yet be spared'; his priviso warns- 'This fail not to obey, under pain of military execution'- **795**; acc. Morris & Yates, July 23, 1777, 'Burgoyne can not fly', & provided cert. actions that they describe are foll., 'we may laugh at Mr. Howe & Mr. Burgoyne' when the defeat of their designs is realized- **797**; his army encamped on the flats at Ft. Miller, N. Y., for several days after leaving Ft. Edward, & his HQ was in the Duer Mansion- **800**; his army was at Skenesborough when Salem, N. Y. was evac.; it was sd. that at the time he "had 100,000 soldiers w. him- British, Hessians, & Indians- & was coming down through this place, & would kill every enemy of the king"- **853**; acc. Dr. Fitch, the workof Lorenzo Sabine gives no acct. of either Col. Philip, or Maj. Andrew P. Skene, ever having accomp. his campaign- **957**; acc. James McDonald, the efforts of Benedict Arnold were more prominent in enabling Burgoyne's capt. than those of Gen. Gates- **1010**; when the scalps of John Allen's family were brought into the army's Ft. Edward camp, acc. Caty Campbell, "he was so affected he cried like a child", & then immed. sent out scouts to call in all the Indians to prevent further depredations; word was also sent out for the settlers to come into the army's camp for protection; his appearance ment. as "a thick set man, not tall" (as he was reported to have been speaking w. 'black Dunk', Caty

Campbell's father, this was perh. Col. Skene, mistaken by her for Burgoyne; see Vol. 1)- **1062**

BURGOYNE'S CAMPAIGN-

alarm- 855; *army-* 728, 739, 740, 794, 796, 797, 800, 804, 991, 998, 1050, 1050s, 1054;

bridge of boats- his 1st across the Hudson into Saratoga co., completed Aug. 14th, & the whole army was ordered to cross on the 16th, but the rains of the foll. day had caused the river to rise, & the bridge of boats & rafts, 'by the increase & rapidity of the water', gave way; refers p. 77, Burgoyne's Orderly Book; the army was not able to cross on a newly constructed bridge until Sept. 12th; but for these rains, the 36 mi. to Albany, N. Y. could have been accomplished in a day's time by forced march- **1072**;

camp- 739, 740, 742, 963, 976, 981, 1000, 1016, 1050s, 1060, 1062, 1063; at Ft. Edward- soldiers would regularly come w. canteens & pails abt. a mi. E., to Alexander McDougall's, to obt. milk from the Argyle settlers who had fled to there foll. the Allen massacre; on one of the 1st mornings at McDougall's, Mrs. ____ measured out the milk, taking the pay, but refusing to divide the money, saying that she had sold it & the money was hers; for her meanness, she was not allowed to sell any but her own from then on- **983**; betw. Sandy Hill & Ft. Edward, N. Y., the army's camp was reportedly on the land of John Jones- **991**;

campaign- the 1st printing of Neilson's *Burgoyne's Campaign* was 2,000 copies, printed by Mr. Munsell, & pd. entirely by the author- **731½n**; 851, 923;

expedition- **1072**;

general ments.- 739, 748, 794, 797, 957, 963, 981, 997, 998; *headquarters-* 800; *horses-* 729;

Indians- they reportedly had not joined w. his expedition when the army had 1st reached Skenesborough (July 6, 1777)- **997**; rebuked by Burgoyne- **1016**; there were perh. 800 w. the army, & all were dismissed by him foll. the Allen massacre, to return only when called; acc. Dr. Fitch, prob. a report circulated to allay the settler's fears, as some were w. Col. Baum at Bennington- **1062**;

invasion- 763; a dispatch from Gen. St. Clair at Ticonderoga arr. evening, June 28, 1777, at Saratoga (Schuylerville, N. Y.), giving Gen. Schuyler the 1st notice of his invasion force, when a part of the army was sighted encamped at Gilliland's creek, abt. 45 mi. from Ticonderoga, w. some of their shipping- **787**;

manifesto, publications- 794; *Orderly book-* 1072; *proclamation-* 795; *the retreat, or evac. bef.-* 739, 856, 860; 701, 744, 750, 755, 756, 847, 853, 869, 1002, 1010, 1063, 1064; *in Burgoyne's time-* 853, 986; *transports-* 750

BURKE,

Asa- Wagoner, Co. A, 2nd N. Y., Northern Black Horse, Cav., 1861- 2- **1080**
Colonel M.- Co. A, 2nd N. Y., Northern Black Horse, Cav., 1861- 2- **1080**
George- oath of alleg.; Co. D, 22nd N. Y. Inf.- **(L)- 1074**
Richard- (Birke) Co. A, 2nd N. Y., Northern Black Horse, Cav., 1861- 2- **1080**

The Fitch Gazetteer

BURNETT,
____- his mills (n. d.) on Black creek were later owned by Joseph Dobbin- **732**
Capt. James- b. Salem, N. Y.; Co. G, 30th Illinois Inf.; wnd. at Ft. Donelson,
Tenn.; d. Aug. 19, 1863, killed by a sharpshooter at the beginning of the battle of
Champion Hills, Big Black river, nr. Vicksburg, Miss.; bur. Candor churchyard,
Aledo, Mercer co., Illinois- **1095**
John- c. 1848, res. on the W. side of Black creek, Salem, N. Y., in the place orig.
occ. by Richard Hoy- **873**; juror, Oct.1- 7, 1858, People vs. Martin Wallace- **1048s**

BURR,
____- his map of Wash. co., N. Y., prior 1850, referred to for the N. boundary line
of the Duer estate at Ft. Miller, N. Y.- **800**
Col. Aaron- (1756- 1836) Atty. General of N. Y., 1791; 'a man of pleasing &
fascinating address, & at that period of his life was considered a most persuasive &
eloquent orator, & an able advocate at the bar'; contended against Gen. Philip
Schuyler in his re- election bid as U. S. Senator; he defeated Schuyler, Jan. 18,
1791, by the same 32- 27 vote that was the margin rejecting Schuyler's nomin.;
considered of the 'median party', i. e., not conspicuous on either side in adopting
the U. S. Constitution, but principally connected w. anti- Federalists politically; his
term expired Mar. 1797, no effort was made for his re- election, & Gen. Schuyler
was again returned, as his successor, Jan. 24, 1797- **920**
Belinda- m. Van Renselaer, s. John & Maria (Conkey) Waters- **730**
Jerusha- of Fairfield, Conn.; m. Hezekiah, s. Gov. Thomas Fitch- **799**
John- 1673, appt. Lt. of dragoons, Fairfield, Conn., w. Thomas Fitch as Capt.- **948**

BURRELL,
Sally- wf. Samuel; b. May 30, 1777; d. Sept. 1, 1843- **(L)- 772**
Samuel- b. June 20, 1771; d. Oct. 2, 1847- **(L)- 772**
Thomas- convicted of petit larceny, Jan. 7, 1789, & sentenced to 39 lashes on his
bare back- **877**

BURRESS,
Jeremiah- plaintiff, Oct. 19, 1773, vs. David Hunter- **878**

BURROWS,
Jeremiah- defendant, May 19, 1774, in a case brought by Henry O. Hana; & Jan.
16, 1775, in a case brought by Andrew P. Skene- **878**
Col. Jeremiah- 1779, commanded a militia regt. stat. as guards & scouts at
Skenesborough, N. Y.- **751**
Lemuel- s. Samuel; res. Groton, Conn.; rec'd. 'full consideration' on all properties
prev. deeded to him, as expressed in his father's Will, Feb. 2, 1756- **1100**
Samuel- of Easthampton, Suffolk co., N. Y.; his Will, Feb. 2, 1756, ments. sons
Samuel & Lemuel, of Groton, Conn.; daus. Phebe More, Desire Gore; Elizabeth
Fitch, wf. Dr. Peletiah; & Abigail Burrows; also, James & Brucilla, youngest sons

of Sibel & Esther Church; gr. 1½ acres of land to Daniel Lathem & his heirs, on W. side of land loc. on the S. side of the road to Mamoraneck, N. Y.; all housing, buildings, & lands not prev. disposed of gr. to Sarah, dau. Sarah Latham, his housekeeper; if any of his daus. should d. w/o issue, her share to be equally divided among the other daus.; appt. exec'rs.- James Chatfield, Esq., & Josiah Parsons; witns.- Jabe Parsons, Sarah Parsons, Esther Malford; his lands partially comprised the village of Sag Harbor, N. Y.; abt. 1833, a report came to his Salem heirs that they were entitled to a port. of this, now valuable, land; Aaron Martin, Jr., was appt. to investigate this, making a memorandum of the heirs at that time- **1100**
Samuel- s. Samuel; res. Groton, Conn.; rec'd. 'full consideration' on all properties prev. deeded to him, as expressed in his father's Will, Feb. 2, 1756- **1100**

BURT,
____- of Northumberland, N. Y.; m. Lewis Berry, s. Samuel & Miriam (Henry) Wells- **839**
Family- c. 1798, 1st family that res. above the Vandenburgh sawmills, on the W. side of the Hudson, opp. Ft. Miller, N. Y.- **804**
Mary- m. 1854, Allen, s. Harvey & Sarah (Conkey) Stevens- **730**

BURTIS,
____- bro. Evander; res. NYC, Presbyterian clergym.- **1098**
Evander- m. dau. Deac. David Cleveland; enl. Sept. 4, 1862, Co. H, 123rd NYSV; he was the 1st casualty of the regt., took sick while the regt. was in NYC, Sept. 5th, & d. Sept. 6, 1862, of cholera morbus, Philadelphia, Pa.; his remains were returned for bur. in Salem- **1098**

BURTON,
Col.- 'of Upper Brook St.', London (?); m. Catherine, dau. John Henry Lydius, the Baron de Quade; she d. ca. 1790, & their dau. m. Capt. Napier Christie, who assumed the family's name- **930**
James- res. 4 mi. from Greenbush, in E. Greenbush, N. Y.; dau. Lavinna, m. John R., s. Adam & Sabra (Russell) Martin- **731**

BUSH,
Paul- defendant, May 17, 1774, along w. Joseph Ingall, in a case brought by John Roff- **878**

BUSHNELL,
Rev. Mr.- missionary, from Gaboon river (Ogooué river, Gabon); Sept. 4, 1862, gave the opening prayer at the 50th annual meeting of the Wash. Co. Bible Soc., Salem, N. Y.- **1097**

BUTLER,
Lt. Col. Benjamin C.- field officer, 93rd N. Y. (Morgan Rifles) Inf.- **1090b**
Walter N.- (?- 1781) tory marauder; "of cruel memory"; he was killed prob. July 1782, in an engagem. at W. Canada creek (the actual date was Oct. 24, 1781, & may have been confused w. other events occurring within that vicinity & time period; see p. 411, French's Gazetteer)- **748**

BUTOLPH,
Elihu- of Jessup's Patent; c. 1853, res. Lisbon, N. Y.; m. Jane, dau. John & Nancy (McCoy) Duncan; 2 sons- Noah & John- **997**

BUTTERFIELD,
Maj.- stat. at the Cedars, St. Lawrence river valley; Dr. Fitch presumes that Capt. McKinstry's co. was among other forces sent from NYC in late May 1776, to reinforce his troops- **748**

BUTTON,
Charles- defendant, May 19, 1774, in a case brought by John Thurman, Jr.- **878**
Family- ments. 2 bros.- Deac. Ira, m. Phebe F., dau. Daniel & Mary (White) Marsh; & Franklin, c. 1852, merch., Brandon, Vt.- **962**
Deac. Frederick- a dau. m. William Gurley Marsh- **962**

BYRNES,
____- emig. 1774, in the same vessel as Deac. Robert McMurray; he d. at sea, & his wid. m. Thomas, s. Robert & Margaret Armstrong, as his 2nd wf.; their only dau., Jane Agnes, m. Robert Livingston- **1083**

C

CABOT,
Francis, Esq.- of Salem, Mass.; m. Mary, dau. Rev. Jabez & Elizabeth (Appleton) Fitch- **835**

CADWELL,
Capt.- (prob. Capt. Miles P. S., Co. K, acc. Phisterer; see Bibliography); of Moriah, N. Y.; May 25, 1861, commanded Co. J, 22nd N. Y. Inf.- **(L)- 1074**

CAGE,
Ann- m. Deac. Willis Hall, of Sutton, Mass.- **759s**

CALDWELL,
Edwin S.- of Martinsburgh, N. Y.; m. Abigail, dau. Nathan & Lovinia (Shumway) Cheney- **1038**
George- oath of alleg.; Co. D, 22nd N. Y. Inf.- **(L)- 1074**
Joseph- along w. John Williams, provides bail for Edward Savage's bond as loan officer, Oct. 20, 1785- **(L)- 936**; (Calwell) he, John Williams, & Edward Savage became security for Savage as loan officer, for putting out £ 200,000 in bills of credit- **(L)- 936b**

CALIFORNIA- 730, 799, 839, 971, 1005;
  Cities & Towns- San Diego- 971; San Luis Obispo- 971; Saw Mill Flat- 972;
  Institutions- Constitutional Convention- 971; 2nd Judicial District- 971;
  Railroads- Western Pacific- 799;
  John Telfair, "having gone tither w. one of the 1st companies from the district'" (prob. Wash. co.), arr. here c. 1849- **972**

Cambridge, Mass.- Committee of Safety- letter of Col. Benedict Arnold, May 19, 1775, Crown Point, N. Y., notes his prev. letter dated May 14th; describes arr. of Capts. Brown & Oswald, w. additional troops, & departure for St. John's, w. their combined forces; they arr. 8 PM, May 17th; surprising the garrison the foll. morning at 6 AM, he notes capt. of a British sloop & an encounter w. Ethan Allen's forces during his return to Ticonderoga; notes disrepair of the fort here, & his own lack of skills to repair or construct a new one, suggesting the suitability of giving the task to ano.; reports on size of Gen. Gage's forces at Montreal, & no. of cannon capt. at Crown Point & Ticonderoga- **775**

Cambridge, N. Y.- an appl. made to N. Y. legislature, by Democrats of the township, for its division into 3 parts; a "weighty" counter petitn. also presented by other townspeople; Mar. 7, 1816, a petitn. presented to legislature by a large body of Cambridge citizenry for repealing the act of division & referred to Wash. co.

members of the Assembly; Mar. 21- repeal of the bill of division passed in the House of Assembly, ayes- 63, nays- 44; Apr. 11- bill of repeal defeated by Senate, leaving division intact- **722**; noted that the bill for its division was intro. by Mr. Gale & advocated by both Gale & Sargent, despite opposition of a large maj. of the population; vote of taxable resid. favoring & opposing the division- Jackson- 57 vs. 117; Cambridge- 49 vs. 138; White Creek- 1 vs. 139; total in favor- 107, & those opposing division- 394- **726**; Aug. 1777, a fine mare stolen from its owner by Indians when Col. Baum's expedition passed through here to Bennington; the horse was later seen w. an Indian rider by a neighbor of its owner, who shot the Indian dead & returned the horse to its rightful owner; this incident offered by Esq. Barnet as an explanation of the story that two Indian chiefs were killed during the Bennington battle- **764**; Committees of Safety for Cambridge, Hosac, & Bennington met at Mr. Wait's in "Wallumscock", Aug. 3, 1775; an agreem. made to maintain the civil laws & assist its officers, & adjournment was made to John Rensselaer's for their next meeting- **783**; Convention held here, May 9- 15, 1781, w. representatives from the towns of Hoosic, Schaghticoke, Cambridge, Saratoga, Upper White Creek, Black Creek (Hebron), Granville, Skenesborough (Whitehall), Kingsbury, Ft. Edward, & Little Hoosic, for the purpose of drafting articles of union w. the state of Vermont- **816**; a no. of militia sent from here to Albany, N. Y., in consequence of an order to visit Sir John Johnson & disarm tories; see Johnstown, & Stillwater, N. Y.; Vol. 3; they arr. in Albany, Jan. 18, 1776, after the main body of militia had left, & uncert. whether to go on, stay, or return home, resolve to remain in Albany; Capt. Hodges, of White Creek, appl. to the Comm. for provisions & rec'd. a day's supply for 21 men; on the foll. day, the co. resolved to return to Cambridge- **825**; prob. c. 1776, the militia of the Corporation, & of the District, combine into one regt., to be known as No. 18- **826**; return of district field officers, recommended to N. Y. Provincial Congress for commissions- Col. Lewis Van Voort; Lt. Col. Gershom Woodworth; 1st Maj. James Wells; 2nd Maj. Cornelius Doty; Adjutant Ebenezer Allen; Quartermaster James Ashton- **828**; c. 1813, an epidemic of spotted fever occurred here- **839**; Dr. John Thompson began his medical practice here at abt. the time of the spotted fever epidemic; great consternation was caused by the raising of a large gristmill on the Owl kill by members of the Wells family, nr. Norman Morrison's old site, it being thought that the flooding of the land made the area unhealthy; a "dam war" developed, touting the rem. of the Wells' mill dam, because the family had not reserved additional lands to compensate for the flooding when they sold parcels along the stream- **844**; abt. 1795, a no. of families, incl. Simpson Cowden, Peleg Havens, Phineas Bell, Rodrick Morrison, Amos Potter, & _____ Bessey, rem. from here to Westmoreland, N. Y.- **846**; its library incorp., & Trustees chosen Mar. 13, 1798, at the house of Silas Peat, to service this town & Salem, N. Y.; see Independent Library- **879**; Albany Comm. resolves, June 13, 1776, to supply the town w. 50 lbs. of powder from its magazine- **890**; the 'Old White Meeting House' was its 1st Presbyterian church; see Church/ Clergy- **1024**; printed article, dated May 25, 1861, Camp Rathbone, Troy, N. Y., giving the 78 persons who took the oath of allegiance,

The Fitch Gazetteer

Co. D, 22nd N. Y. Inf., commanded by Capt. H. S. Milliman; acc. report, soon to be mustered into service- (L)- **1074**

Cambridge, N. Y., Committee of Correspondence- elected Nov. 10, 1775, as a new comm.- Joseph Wells, John McClung, Thomas Morrison, Phineas Whiteside, & Gershom Woodworth- **824**; return of its elected members, Feb. 4, 1776- Ebenezer Allen, James Parrot, Jabush Mosher, & Asa Flint; Feb. 27th- James Parrot refuses to serve, & ano. ordered elected to the vacancy- **826**; return of those members present at a meeting in Albany, N. Y., May 10, 1775, given by Thomas Morrison, moderator, & Edmund Wells, clerk- Thomas Morrison, Joseph Wells, John Blair, John Younglove, Edward Rigg, James Ashton, Joseph Younglove, Phineas Whiteside- **831**; ordered by Albany Comm. to apprehend & disarm Peter Miller, binding him to future good behavior, & reporting back to their board on actions taken- **888**; Committee of Safety- members elected, May 28, 1776- Comfort Curtis, David Preston, Phineas Whiteside, John Younglove, James Ashton, Samuel Hodges, John Blair, & Henry Smith- **889**; additional comm. members, June 13, 1776- Edward Rigg, James Green, Lewis Preston, Gershom Woodworth, Cornelius Doty, & Capt. Edmund Wells- **890**; Sidney Wells recounts the family records of two of its members, John & Joseph Younglove- **843**

Camden, Salem, N. Y.- Christ's Church parish, org. Oct. 15, 1797; w. Revs. James Nichols & Robert G. Whitmore, pastors; see Church/ Clergy- **879**

CAMP,
Isreal- acc. Nov. 26, 1773 deed description, he or his assignees owned Lot No. 31, Kingsbury, N. Y.- (L)- **936**

CAMPBELL,
Alexander- of Argyle, N. Y.; selected along w. Dr. John Williams, Jan. 25, 1775, as delegate, N. Y. Provincial Congress; also recommended on same date for appt. as Lt. Col. Charlotte co. militia- **784**
Allan- Maj., 2nd battalion, 42nd Royal Highland regt.; gr. 5,000 acres, Crown Point, Essex co., N. Y.; refers pg. 72, Catalogue of Maps- **990**
Archibald- (Archy) res. Jackson, N. Y., on opp. side of the Battenkill from James Campbell; a party of families who evac. from Salem during the retreat bef. Burgoyne's army, Aug. 1777, passed by his homsite & into the woods for shelter- **701**; (Esq.) chairman of a meeting held by Charlotte co. inhabitants at Ft. Edward, N. Y., June 29, 1775, to elect additional delegates to N. Y. Provincial Congress; elected as a delegate- **780**; res. a mi. below "black" Duncan Campbell, on the opp. side of the Battenkill; the whigs burnt "black Dunk's" house during sugaring time, when he was away, tending Archy's trees- **1064**
Archibald- surveyor; 1767, he marked out a line of trees used as the N. bounds of a Vt. township called Clarendon, & also known as Durham (Rutland, Vt.), erected under authority of N. H.; this same boundary was used by William Cockburn &

61

John Wigram, 1771, when they laid out lots for the S. part of Socialborough, Charlotte co., N. Y.- **745**; acc. Ebenezer Cole, Feb. 27, 1771, he offered to survey the lines of all the Grants settlers for his returns, if shown the boundaries by them, but only Cole & abt. a dozen others accepting, the remainder refusing on the basis that they would not pay quit rents for N. Y. grants- **896**
Archibald- defendant, Oct. 1775, in a case brought by Hugh Munro- **878**
Archibald- s. "black" Duncan; testif. to the amiable relationship betw. his father & his neighbor, "white" Duncan Campbell-**1060**
Archibald, Esq.- along w. wf. Ann, Jan. 2, 1776, conveys to Benjamin Griffin, for £ 375, Lot No. 138, Argyle Patent, containing 500 acres; deed witn., Nov. 26, 1773, Daniel Jones to John Jones- **(L)- 936**; his wf. d. Aug. 1777, while they were taking protection in Burgoyne's camp at Ft. Edward, N. Y.; see Vol. 1- **1062**
Lt. Col. Archibald- (1739- 1791) he was capt., June 16, 1776, along w. 300 other Scottish soldiers, when they arr. in Boston harbor; refers Thatcher's Military Journal; (exchanged, 1778, for Ethan Allen)- **1079**
Caty- dau. "black" Duncan; c. 1853, res. Taberg, N. Y.; served as a nurse in Dr. Asa Fitch, Sr.'s household, & during a visit w. her, Dr. Fitch "took some pencil notes" from his former nurse that he transcribed, c. 1859/60, as witn. accts.- **1060-1065**
Dr.- c. 1852, res. in the N. part of Rutland, Vt.- **966**
Duncan- "white" Dunk"; either he, or Col. Laughlin, was the ancestor of Maj. James Campbell; see Vol. 1- **706**; the gentleman; defendant, in a case brought by Alex. McNitt- **878½**; of Argyle, N. Y.; tory, went to Canada during Rev. war; a son, m. the wid. of St. John Honeywood, as her 3rd husb.- **1033**; 1st Supervisor, town of Argyle; he & "black" Duncan Campbell 1st became acquainted w. ea. other in the N. Y. Highlands, & maintained a "perfect friendship & confidence in ea. other" for 50 yrs.; see Vol. 1- **1060**; his wf. d. Aug. 1777, in Burgoyne's camp at Ft. Edward, at abt. the same time as "black" Duncan's wf.- **1062**; a dau. m. Duncan McArthur; his neighbor, "black Dunk", & Wid. Campbell (of Ft. Edward) were the only persons at his home the night that the whigs arr. to tar & feather his s. James, who was visiting from Canada foll. the Rev. war; Peter McQueen arr. at his door, bringing the news of their intentions from Capt. Martin; on hearing this, James ran to his sist. McArthur's; the party arr., & searched the house, saying that they had business w. him, but left when they were unable to discover him- **1065**
Duncan- his farm, orig. loc. Argyle Patent, but now loc. within the town of Greenwich, was purch. (n. d.) by Abner Dwelly- **731**; "black Dunk"; from Argyleshire, Scotland; he went to visit relatives in Ireland when he was 14 yrs. old, & along w. 2 other boys & 3 girls, they were amusing themselves on the seashore, when "they saw a ship hoisting her sails, as they understood to make a short cruise around in the harbor; thinking it would be a pleasant excursion, they got on board her. But she stood directly out to sea, & night coming on, they lost sight of their native land forever- crying bitterly, but their tears of no avail"; they arr. in Maryland, where the Capt. bound them out to var. places for 4 yrs.; foll. release from his indenture, hearing that labor was scarce & greatly needed at harvest time

in the N. Y. Highlands, he came there & became acquainted w. ano. Duncan Campbell, long known as "white Dunk"; he attached himself to him, & for 50 yrs., they res. as neighbors in Argyle Patent w. "such perfect friendship & confidence in ea. other, that there was never the scratch of a pen betw. them in their business transactions, in all that time"; m. 2nd, Wid. Morrison; he & his 2nd wf., along w. her son, Norman Morrison, were all bur. in the old Argyle bur. grd.; among those children by his 1st wf. were Archibald & Caty- **1060**; David Jones' denial of the existence of Jane McCrea's ghost was orig. conveyed to him by her bro., Col. John McCrea- **1061**; foll. the Allen massacre, he went to Ft. Edward along w. his family, in co. w. others of his neigborh.; as they passed Allen's house, some members of the party went inside to examine the scene for themselves, & found it so affecting that they came out of the house screaming & crying; they soon passed a party of Indians that had killed & hung up a hog to dress, & when the Indians 1st saw the settlers, "they flew for their guns, which they snatched up, ready to attack us"; but seeing a British officer & scouts accompanying the party for their protection, they fled into the woods; his 1st wf. d. Aug. 10, 1777, of jaundice, while in the camp at Ft. Edward, as did "white Dunk's" wf., & Mrs. Ann Campbell, wf. Archibald, Esq.- **1062**; he took his 2 horses w. him to Burgoyne's camp & sold them for silver; while in the British camp, the whigs tore down his fences & let his cattle get into his grain, nearly destroying the field; soon after returning, 'Mad' More & other whigs from Sodom (Shushan, N. Y.) came to drive off his cows; "they threw down the fence & went to driving them out of the field, when father got around them & drove them back"; but More came up to him, "& putting the muzzle of his loaded gun to father's breast, sd. 'Stand still, you d- d tory, or I'll shoot you through'. And the other men then drove the cattle away"; lots were cast for his cattle, & one fell to Bill Smith, who returned it to Campbell the foll. day- **1063**; his house was loc. at the head of the valley, below Wid. McDougall's, where Livingston's brook enters into the Battenkill, at the descent of the hill to the flat below; an old apple tree in the meadow nr. the kill marks where his house once stood; spring 1778, a few days foll. the burning of the school house at E. Greenwich, N. Y., his log house by the kill was burnt by the whigs; it was known to be deliberately set, as the fire began on the opp. end from the fireplace; it was sugaring time, & he was abt. a mi. below, on the opp. side of the kill, at Archy Campbell's, tapping trees; his practice was to stay overnight at the sugar camp, keeping the kettle fires going, leaving his children alone at night, & returning the foll. day; but that night, he had a "presentament", although not of danger, & returned to the house in time to snatch his children out- **1064**

Duncan- advises John McKesson, Esq., in a letter dated Dec. 12, 1777, Argyle, N. Y., that 'some fiery men' have expressed their intentions of driving all the Scots & Irish out of Argyle & New Perth (Salem, N. Y.) as tories, & requests assistance on their behalf, for 'unless the good legislature interposes & help, then Canada & the depths of poverty will be our final doom'- **791**

Duncan- (s. Roger & ____ Clark) attended Salem Academy, then taught school, 1830- 31, at Ft. Miller, N. Y.; grad. Union College, rem. Cattaraugus co., & continued teaching- **802**

Maj. Duncan- (his marker loc. Union Cemetery, Ft. Edward, N. Y.) acc. Dr. Fitch, he prob. belonged to the 42nd Royal Highland regt.; see Vol. 1- **990**

James- Aug. 1777, the party of Salem, N. Y. families seeking shelter in the town of Jackson during the evac. bef. Burgoyne's army, passed by his homesite along the Battenkill- **701**

James- s. "white" Duncan; he withdrew to Canada during the Rev. war, & returned at its close; some of the more violent whigs, on hearing of his return, resolved to tar & feather him; they assembled & went to Capt. Aaron Martin's tavern, at Fitch's Point, for a drink prior to their errand, & disclosed their purpose to Martin; while keeping them entertained, Capt. Martin had the Campbells alerted, & James left his father's house for Duncan McArthur's; some yrs. later, he went to England, & stopped at Martin's tavern while en route back to Canada; he asked to have his horse fed & watered, & as there were no men around to do this, Zerniah Martin gave him a pail & told him where the water & grain was; he "haughtily" took affront to this, & she tended the horse for him, but he later apologized profusely when he discovered that Zerniah was a member of Martin's family- **1065**

Maj. James- member, Gen. Brisbane's division, Sept. 1814; acc. Dr. Fitch, he was likely a desc. of Duncan, or Laughlin Campbell- **706**

Col. Laughlin- either he, or Duncan were probably the anc. of Maj. James Campbell- **706**; (Capt.) emig. from Argyleshire, Scotland- **802**

Moses- Sgt., 42nd Royal Highland regt.; gr. 200 acres in Vt.; refers p. 78, Catalogue of Maps- **990**

Roger- (s. William & Catharine Reid) b. 1776, in S. part of Salem, N. Y.; c. 1789, his parents rem. S. Argyle; he m. a sist. Dr. Robert Clark, & had a son, Duncan- **802**

Samuel- among those involved in the arrest & flogging (§ 881) of Benjamin Hough; acc. John L. Marsh, his surname was among those few to res. in the Clarendon, Vt. area, & involved in Hough's flogging; Marsh also ments. that an old Dr. Campbell res. in the N. part of Rutland- **966**

Wid. Sarah- (Sarah Frazer, Wid. McNeal/ McNeil) brief ment.- **1060**; she & "black" Duncan Campbell were the only ones at "white" Duncan's house the night whigs came searching for the latter's visiting s., James, in order to tar & feather him- **1065**

William- m. Catharine, dau. Roger & ____ (McDougall) Reid; their only child, Roger, b. 1776; they rem., c. 1789, from Salem to S. Argyle, N. Y.- **802**

CANADA- 703, 741, 747, 753, 759s, 760, 775- 778, 780, 784, 789, 791, 792, 805, 820, 923, 928, 961, 964, 974, 977, 985, 988, 1000, 1007, 1033, 1053, 1055, 1059-1062, 1065, 1073, 1075;
Provinces & Regions- Bay of Quinte- 802; Canada West- 962; the Cedars- 748; Isle- Aux- Noix- 719; Nova Scotia- 730, 858, 1018, 1100; Three Rivers- 750; the Sorel- 858; Upper Canada- 812;
Counties- Leeds- 812, 991;
Cities & Towns- Brockville- 991; Chambly- 750, 775, 936; Cobourg- 1075; Darlington- 812; Flanders- 760, 1059; Goodrich (Goderich)- 812; Halifax- 944; Kingston- 964; Landsdowne- 812; Montreal- 708, 774, 775, 802, 990, 1014, 1046, 1052, 1075, 1075b; as a district- 936; Ontario city- 1075; Prescott- 1075; Quebec-750, 780, 812, 922, 928, 1015, 1046; St. John's- 719, 750, 773- 775; Sorrel- 750; Streetsville- 812; Toronto- 812; Younge- 812;
Institutions- Chief Justice- 961

CANADY,
Benjamin- plaintiff, May 19, 1774, vs. John Gutry- **878**

CARI,
Benjamin- drowned in Hudson river, Easton, N. Y., "May 9th, 17th yr. of Independence" (1782)- **(L)- 876**

CARLETON,
Gov. Sir Guy- (1724- 1808) Gov.- General of Canada (1766- 1778); when the American assault on Quebec failed (Dec. 31, 1775), he sent word to the Americans scattered in the woods that if they came back to the city, they would be made "perfectly comfortable" & receive all the hospitality & leniency that could be bestowed on them- **922**

CARPENTER,
Comfort- plaintiff, May 19, 1774, vs. Josiah Tirrell- **878**
Comfort- res. Shaftsbury, Vt.; he & John Searls were arrested by John Munro for counterfeiting, but acc. Munro's letter, Nov. 24, 1772, to N .Y. Council, he escaped from the constables while in transit to jail- **912**
Isaiah- ment. Feb. 27, 1771, by Ebenezer Cole, as a Grants settler who refused the offer of a survey of his lands by Archibald Campbell, N. Y. surveyor; see Vol. 1- **896**
Mary B.- b. Nov. 9, 1815; m. Edward William, s. John C. & Susan (Mason) Parker, as his 1st wf.- **759s**
Orson- of Granville, N. Y.; juror, People vs. Martin Wallace, Oct. 1-7, 1858- **1048s**

CARRIBEAN- as West Indies- 829, 1075b; Dominica- 781; Guadeloupe- 990; Havana- 990; Jamaica- 829; Martinique- 990; St. Lucia- 990; St. Vincent- 990; St. Thomas- 1075b

CARSWELL,
David- capt. by the British at the surrender of Ft. Ann, 1780- **701**; recoll. by Wid. Angel as one of five prisoners she names as capt. at Ft. Ann & Ft. George; see Vol. 1- **858**
Family- noted as among the more violent whigs in the Salem area; along w. the McNishes, were prob. among those who went to tar & feather James Campbell when he returned from Canada foll. the Rev. war- **1065**
Nathaniel- c. Mar. 1854/5, he & Morgan Wright were standing in a roadway in the town of Greenwich, when Priest Quigley, who had just been attending Patrick Walls, accosted them & began relating his displeasure over his treatment by Archibald Hay while he was attending Walls; however, the acct. notes that Quigley's objections met w. no approval from either Carswell or Wright, concerning the manner in which Hay ejected Quigley from his house- **1058**

CARTER,
_____- his sawmill, c. early 1800's, was put up by Augustus Angel, on Cossayuna creek, below McNab's (Cossayuna) Lake- **847**
Joseph- "lives west", in Hannibal, N. Y.; m. Polly, dau. Moses, Jr., & Eunice (Clark) Martin; his wf. "is the likeliest of any of the family except the 2 youngest"; had 3 children, Eunice being the only one ment. by name- **731**

CARY,
Gen.- temperance lecturer, c. 1867; informs Dr. Fitch concerning ano. Dr. Asa Fitch- **1077**

CASE,
Elisha- res. Saratoga Springs, N. Y.; m. Horatia, dau. Charles & Hannah (Lytle) Nelson; no children- **1069**

CASSIDY,
Maj. Ambrose J.- field officer, 93rd N. Y.(Morgan Rifles) Inf.- **1090b**; he & Maj. John S. Crocker passed by their outer pickets & were capt. by the enemy, Apr. 26, 1862; both were exchanged the foll. summer; cowardice, rather than desertion, stands as the prevailing sentiment for their leave taking, as an expected bloody battle was in the offing- **1094**

Castleton, Vt.- detachm. sent here from Burgoyne's army (prob. July 7, 1777, foll. battle of Hubbardton) was presumed to be the same one that marched through Pawlet, Vt. to the Bennington battlesite, under Col. Breyman- **728**; American forces evac. from Ft. Ticonderoga under Gen. St. Clair passed through here on way to Manchester, Vt., prob. July 9, 1777- **738b**; inhabitants of the surrounding townships ordered by Gen. Burgoyne's proclamation, July 10, 1777, to convene here 10:00 AM, Wed., July 15th, to obt. from Col. Skene the conditions under which 'the persons & properties of the disobedient may yet be spared'- **795**

CAULKINS,
Miss- her information referred to by Dr. Fitch concerning the Fitch genealogy-
945b

CAVANAUGH,
Edward- res. White Creek, N. Y.; he was at Barney Giblin's house the night of McEntee's murder, bef. Martin Wallace came in; he testif. that Wallace was there for 15- 20 min., & showed nothing unusual in his manner, but asked him if he was going home, & sd. he would not have stayed so long if he didn't think that he (Cavanaugh) was going home; he left w. Lyons, to go to the tavern, & he saw Wallace leave, heading towards the R. R.; ments. that he has known Wallace since his arr. in the country, & has heard nothing bad abt. him; on cross- exam, Wallace spoke of going home some time bef. they started, & wanted to go w. him, but gave no reason & never spoke of McEntee; testif. that he never heard of his fighting or carrying a pistol to kill Ben Baker until after the murder, but has heard abt. his drinking too much- **1048s**

CHAMBERLAIN,
Samuel- was the 1st settler's child b. Thetford, Vt.- **(L)- 772**

CHAMBERS,
Cornelius- R. R. brakeman; killed instantly, Jan. 3, 1854, when the 9:00 AM train, approaching the Hoosick bridge nr. Schaghticoke, N. Y., lost a flange from a wheel, causing an accident- **1021**
John- chairman, Comm. of N. Y. Council, presenting a report, June 6, 1753, that recites to that date, the correspondences betw. N. Y. & N. H. govts. concerning boundaries; notes that a promised copy, from N. H., of Gov. Wentworth's communications on boundaries was not rec'd. prior to his forwarding of this information to England- **928**

Chambly, Quebec, Canada- loc. 12 mi. from St. John's; a garrison of 40 men stat. here, May 18, 1775, when Col. Benedict Arnold capt. a schooner at St. John's- **775**

CHANDLER,
Dr. Jonathan R.- grad. Castleton Medical College, prob. early 1820's; relates to Dr. Fitch that he & a no. of fellow students went to Burlington, Vt., & dug up a no. of skeletons of soldiers who had been killed in the battle of Plattsburgh, bleaching them on the roof a shed, & selling them to defray the expenses of their studies; they began their digging at night, continuing into the next day, w/o anyone opposing

them except a woman living nearby; the proximity of these skeltons to the bur. site of Ethan Allen suggests that his remains may have been among those retrieved- **1052**

CHAPMAN,

Robert- church sexton; res. Lot 178, Salem, N. Y.; m. Matilda, wid. James Turner, Jr.; they had a large family, & 2 of his sons res. St. Lawrence co., N. Y., where he rem. after selling his farm to James Smart- **1090**
Rev. Robert H.- c. 1804- 12, pastor, 1st Presbyterian church, Cambridge, N. Y.; he rem. to the Presidency, Chapel Hill College, N. C.- **1024**

CHARLES,

Isaac- he was apprehended, along w. Samuel Ashley, Samuel Robinson, & John Horfort, summer 1764, by the High Sheriff of Albany co., for forcibly ejecting Peter Voss & Bastian Deal from their lands in the Grants- **885**; when apprehended by Harmanus Schuyler, he & John Horfort pretended to be the owners of Voss & Deal's lands- **892**; he & John Horfort were the unnamed others ment. by James Van Cortlandt's affidavit, which stated that they were all brought to Albany jail, but never indicted, gave bail, or tried- **897**
Robert, Esq.- London Agent, Colony of N. Y.; Dec. 22, 1752, a copy of Gov. Wentworth's letter to the Board of Trade was sent by him to the N. Y. Gov., "showing Gov. Wentworth to be grossly ignorant or willfully false in his representation of the N. Y. boundaries"- **928**

CHARLOTTE COUNTY, N. Y.- selected John Williams & William Marsh as representatives to N. Y. Provincial Congress; seated May 24, 1775; an accompanying certif., design. their appt., signed by 14 gentlemen of the respective Committees of Safety for the co.; in N. Y.- White Creek, Cambden (Camden); & now, Vt.- Arlington, Manchester, Dorset, Rupert, Pawlet, & Wells- **773**; June 15, 1775, Mr. Marsh obt. leave of absence, & June 23rd, Mr. Williams given leave to go home, & left June 26th, missing the afternoon session- **777**; in correspondence from Ft. Miller, N. Y., July 5, 1775, Judge William Duer informs N. Y. Comm. of Safety concerning information he has obt. abt. a party of citizens, N. H. Grants people, 'strengthened by some persons of desparate fortunes & bad character in the Western Districts', & resolved to march to Ft. Edward for the purpose of closing the courts there; Capt. Edward Motte's co., detained from their march to Ticonderoga, in order to protect the bench; on hearing this, the 'rioters party... desisted from their attempt'; by report of Wm. Marsh, Esq. & Samuel Rose, June 28th, men of diff. parts of the co., & some from Albany co., were forming a mob to close the courts; on hearing of Capt. Motte's co., & that Remember Baker & Robert Cockran were also present, 'all w. intent to protect the court', they gave over their design; many had been alarmed on news that the cannon were ordered rem. from Ticonderoga, believing it 'laid us open' from attack in the north, & a man was appt. from their meeting to present this concern to the Continental Congress- **779**; David

Watkins, Archibald Campbell, Esq., & Dr. George Smith elected June 29, 1775, at Ft. Edward, N. Y., as additional delegates to Provincial Congress- **780**; David Watkins repesented the co. at the resumption of the Provincial Congress, July 26, 1775- **781**; org. Aug. 22, 1775, as a state militia brigade, along w. Cumberland & Gloucester counties- **782**; its delegates only appeared on the 1st day of the new Provincial Congress, Nov. 4, 1775, as the members, having no salary, or the co., pd. their expenses- **783**; by unanimous agreem. at a general meeting held Jan. 25, 1776, Dr. John Williams appt. Provincial Congress delegate, along w. Alexander Campbell, to serve until 2nd Tues. of May; on same day, recommendations for appt. by Comm. of Safety- 1st battalion, Co. militia- Col.- Dr. Williams; Lt. Col.- Alex. Campbell; Majors, Adjutant, & Quartermaster; also, Capts. & Lts. for Granville & Black Creek (Hebron); Col. Williams' appt. approved Feb. 19, 1776, & on the same day, he appl. for & obt. orders for 3 minuteman companies in the co.- **784**; May 14, 1776, 3rd Provincial Congress convenes, w. Mr. Webster attending w. certif. from Charlotte co. Comm., John Williams, chair; Edward Savage, clerk; signed May 1st, certif. states that Col. John Williams, Maj. Alex. Webster, & Maj. Wm. Malcom were legally chosen, they or either of them, to represent the co. as delegates to 3rd Congress; rangers to be raised for guarding the northern counties, July 24th, incl. 120 men in Charlotte co.; Aug. 1, 1776, militia reorganized, w. one brigade formed by Charlotte co., & ano. formed by Cumberland & Gloucester counties; Dec. 2nd- £ 464 transmitted her to pay rangers; Jan. 4, 1777- £ 524 sent for rangers' pay & bounty- **785**; notice sent to N. Y. Comm. of Safety, Feb. 17th, that a co. of rangers ordered to Ft. Ticonderoga on apprehension that the enemy might cross the lake on the ice; also informs N. Y. Comm. of Safety, June 25, 1777, that sheriff has posted election notices in E. part of co., but no election was held there; further inquiry made concerning whether election was valid if only held in W. part of co.; receiving assent, Alex. Webster, Wm. Duer, & John Williams were returned as Senators from the Eastern District- **787**; by John Williams' report, June 23, 1777, the recent Convention & declarations from the Grants that they should become an independent state, has thrown this co. into great confusion on how to proceed (the Grants then containing an Eastern port. of the co.)- **789**; renamed as Washington co., 1784, foll. the 7th session of the N. Y. Legislature- **992**

Charlotte Co., N. Y., Courts of- Oct. 19, 1773, Liber Memorabilis, by Patt Smith, clerk, noting opening of Court of Common Pleas, in the house of Patrick Smith, at Ft. Edward, N. Y.; present- William Duer, Judge; Patrick Smith & Ebenezer Clark, Esqs., Assistants; Memorandum, Apr. 19, 1775, noting the beginning of "Bellum Civile"; presiding officials, cases, given for 1st six terms-
1st- Oct. 19, 1773- Judge Wm. Duer, Esq.; Assistants- Ebenezer Clark, Benjamin Spencer; 5 cases described;
2nd- May 17- 19, 1774- Judge Philip Schuyler; Assistants- Patrick Smyth, Ebenezer Clark, John Griffith; 48 cases described;
3rd- Oct. 18, 1774- present- Schuyler, Smith, & Clark; 63 cases, 6 described;

4th- Jan. 16, 1775- present- same; 55 cases called & orders issued; 4 described;

5th- Mar. 22 & 24, 1775- Judge Duer; Smyth & Clark; 60 cases, 2 described;

6th- June 20- 22, 1775- present- same; 29 cases- **878**; temporary suspension of judicial proceedings due to outbreak of Rev. war in Apr. 1775; loss of all records & papers relating to same, unrecovered until Aug. 11, 1786; records of the Common Pleas of Charlotte & Wash. co. preserved in cert. other books in the clerk's office; Nov. 1786 term commenced at Salem, N. Y., w. Judges Webster, Russell, & Hopkins; 51 cases, 2 described; the "other book" begins- 'At the Court of Common Pleas held in & for the co. of Charlotte at the house of John Williams in New Perth on Tues., Apr. 13, 1779'; terms noted to Feb. 1786-

7th- Apr. 13, 1779- Judge Alex. Webster; Assist. Justices- Ebenezer Rustle [sic], David Hopkins, Moses Martin, Albert Baker, Esqs.; no cases entered;

8th- Oct. 13, 1779- present- Webster, Hopkins, & Martin; no cases entered;

9th- Apr. 11, 1780- present- Webster, Baker, & Rustle [sic]; 8 cases;

10th- Oct. 10, 1780- present- Webster, Baker, & Martin; (notation of term # ends here);

Apr. 1781, 2nd Tues.- present- Webster, Russell, Brinton Paine, & Martin; 3 cases;

Nov. 5, 1781- present- same, along w. Samuel Crosset;

Feb. 25, 1781, last Tues.- present- Martin; Hopkins & Crosset; 15 cases;

Nov. 5, 1783- present- Webster, Russell; Hopkins, Martin, & Aaron Fuller; 28 cases;

Feb. 24, 1784- present- Webster; Martin, Fuller, Crosset, Albert Baker, & Adiel Sherwood; 6 cases;

Nov. 3, 1784- present- Russell; Martin, John McCollister; 80 cases, 6 given;

May 1785, last Tues.- present- Webster; Hopkins, Martin, McAllister [sic]; 53 cases;

Nov. 1785, 2nd Tues.- present- Webster, Russell, Hopkins; Martin, Fuller, Baker, & Robert Cochran; 50 cases;

Feb. 1786, 2nd Tues.- present- same; Martin, McAllister [sic], &Cochran; 53 cases-878½; Apr. 7, 1772, Col. John Reid recommends to Gov. that Crown Point be chosen as Court House loc.; Apr. 8- proprietors & others of Socialborough (Rutland, Vt.) petitn. that the Court House be loc. there- **904**; ordered by the Gov., Sept. 8, 1773, w. Council's advice, that an ordinance be iss. to establ. Court of Common Pleas & Court of Gen. Sessions of the Peace, to be held annually at the house of Patrick Smith, Esq., nr. Ft. Edward, N. Y., on 3rd Tues. of May & Oct.-
910

Charlotte Co., N. Y., Justices of Peace- Oct. 15, 1773- Adolphus Benzel, Lachlan McIntosh, & Thomas Sparburn; a letter sent by them & read in N. Y. Council on above date, containing affidavits concerning the violent assault & beating of Jonathan Eckert, on Sept. 13th, at Eckert's home along Lake Champlain- **911**

CHASE,
Elijah- res. abt. ¼ mi. from Pratt's store, on the river road from Buskirk's Bridge to Eagle Bridge, N. Y.; his woodlot was abt. ¾ mi. from Ira Sisson's house, & stretched from the old turnpike road to the river road, except for abt. 15 rods of clearing; Hiram Sisson arr. at his house during the evening of Feb. 16, 1858, to spread the news of Barney McEntee's murder, & seek assistance in retrieving his body; on Feb. 19th, he & Uriah Colony found the other piece of a broken fence stake that was used in the murder; he rem. the stake from the frozen ground, measured some of the tracks in the area, & later measured tracks made by Wallace in the backyard of Randall's Tavern, in the presence of Mr. Randall, the Deputy Sheriff, & Norman Fowler- **1048s**
George- brief ment.- **1048s**
Mary M.- publ. an 8 stanza poem, "The Bloody Morning Scout", pgs. 27 & 28, *Holden's Magazine,* inspired by a reading of Dr. Fitch's History of Wash. Co. (prob. those items appearing in *Transactions of the N. Y. State Agricultural Society, 1848)-***989**
Morris- m. Miriam, dau. Adam & Polly (Granger) Martin- **1046**

CHATFIELD,
James, Esq.- he & Josiah Parsons appt. exec'rs., Samuel Burrow's Will, Feb. 2, 1756- **1100**

The Checkered House- (loc. S. of Cambridge, N. Y., its front painted in distinctive checkerboard pattern) owned, c. 1850, by Mr. Long; William Boyd & his bro. Thomas were taken prisoner 5 or 6 mi. S. of here, prob. Aug. 1777, by Col. Baum's forces- **729**

CHEEVER,
Mr.- c. 1850, Judge, Stillwater, N. Y.; offered voluntary toast, Nov. 29, 1814, at a public banquet, Salem, N. Y., honoring Commodore Macdonough- **709**

CHENEY,
Abigail- m. Adam, s. Aaron & Sarah (Newell) Martin; she d. Dec. 20, 1820, at 80, Martinsburgh, N. Y.- **1037**
Family- its "full" genealogy & that of the Martin family in possession of Charles L. Martin, of Martinsburgh, N. Y.- **730**
Joesph- m. Abigail, dau. Ephriam Warren, of Killingworth, Mass.; 8 children-
1. Hannah, m. William Ives, of Brimfield, Mass.
2. Abigail, b. July 26, 1740; m. Adam Martin
3. Joseph, m. 1. ____ ; 2. Priscilla Rice; 3. ____
4. Reuben, m. Olive Day
5. Pennel, m. Jerusha Mann; no children
6. Mary, m. Elizabeth Plympton, of Sturbridge, Mass.
7. Elizabeth, m. Samuel Freeman, of Sturbridge, Mass.

8. Nathan, m. Lovinia Shumway- **1038**
Joseph- (s. Joseph & Abigail Warren) m. 1. ____; 2. Priscilla Rice; 3. ____;
children, all by 1st wf.- Mary, who d. childless; Alpheus, m. ____ West; & Chloe-
1038
Joseph?- or Nathan?; from Sturbridge, Mass.; bro. Reuben; taught school (c.
1800's) for abt. a yr. at Fitch's Point, Salem, N. Y.- **859**
Nathan- s. Dr. Walter?; rem. directly from Sturbridge, Mass. to Martinsburgh,
N. Y., res. & d. there- **730**
Nathan- (s. Joseph & Abigail Warren) m. Louisa Shumway; children- Fatima, m.
____ Blanchard; Pennel, m. Fanny Tarbell; Walter; Amarillus, m. Edward
Johnson; Abigail, m. Edwin S. Caldwell; Warren, m. ____ Chipman; his wf. d.
Aug. 9, 1826, at 67- **1038**
Dr. Peneuil- s. Dr. Walter?; res. Scotland, Windham co., Conn.; no children; he
gave his property to an adopted child; refers American Archives, ii, 1737- **730**
Reuben- he rem. Salem, N. Y., & orig. res. on Harvey Fitch's place, towards the
creek, abt. ¼ mi. NW of Harvey's house, where his well in the meadow is still
visible, c. 1850; his s. Willard built the plank house nr. bro. Harvey's, that was torn
down when Harvey built his house in 1838; he built the dam & sawmill loc. on
Harvey Fitch's property, & later rem. Galway, N. Y., where his dau. Matilda, who
m. ____ Brackett, had prev. rem.- **730**; occ. the place at Fitch's Point that orig.
belonged to Timothy Titus; put up (n. d.) the dam & sawmill there; his s. was once
bur. in their well; see Vol. 1- **803**; from Sturbridge, Mass.; res. S. of Black creek;
bef. he came, his place also had been occ. by the Taller bros.; his bro. Joseph? or
Nathan? taught school for a yr. at Fitch's Point, & his s.Willard, afterw.
constructed a house on the present (1850) site of Harvey Fitch's house- **859**; (s.
Joseph & Abigail Warren) m. Olive Day; children- Sarah, Willard; Lucretia, m.
____ Thompson; Matilda, m. 1. Jerry Brockett; 2. Dr. ____; 3. Moses Scott- **1038**.
Thomas- res. E. Greenwich, N. Y.; evening, Feb. 6, 1855, his house shook hard
enough to rattle the dishes, & a large crack was found in the earth in front of his
house the foll. morning; see Weather, Frost Heaves- **1026**
Dr. Walter?- of Sturbridge, Mass.; 3 sons Nathan, Reubin, & Dr. Peneuil; & 3
daus., m. ____ Lyon; m. ____ Plimpton?; & Abigail, m. Adam Martin- **730**

CHERRY,
Amos- formerly of E. Greenwich, N. Y.; c. 1861, Co. B, 14th Iowa Inf., along w.
Lambert Martin, of Salem, N. Y.- **1089**
James- res. Lot No. 64, Argyle Patent, loc. E. Greenwich, N. Y.; his orig.
homestead taken down, c. 1848, by his son, who constructed a new one a few rods
W. of the old site; Wm. Tosh called his wf.over to his house that night that his wf.
Jennett d., & along w. Mrs. Wm. Taylor & Miss Murdock, she prepared Mrs.
Tosh's body for burial- **871**; res. at the "lower end" E. Greenwich; he & other area
inhabitants note their houses shaking in an earthquake- like manner bef. they
retired to bed, Feb. 6, 1855; see Weather, Frost Heaves- **1026**

Thomas- c. 1850, res. E. Greenwich, N. Y.; George & Eleanor (Dobbin) Walker res. w. him- **732**

CHILD,
Capt.- commanded militia co., Col. Williams' regt., June 1777, which marched to Ft. Ticonderoga & was in the retreat from there in July, retreating 3- 4 days to Castleton, Vt., & then retreating to Ft. Ann & Ft. Edward- **750**; ordered out & directed militia companies on scouts to Skenesborough, Ft. Ann, Lake George, East Bay, & Kingsbury, N. Y. during summer, 1780; on one occasion, he commanded a co. of 30 men to Kingsbury, when some buildings were burned there- **754**

CHILLUS,
S. B.- 1st Sgt., Co. A, 2nd N. Y., Northern Black Horse, Cav., 1861- 2- **1080**

CHINA- 1097

CHIPMAN,
____- of Canandaigua, N. Y.; m. Warren, s. Nathan & Lovinia (Shumway) Cheney- **1038**

CHOATE,
Rufus- (1799- 1859; Dartmouth, 1819; Mass. House of Reps., 1825, & Senate, 1826; 22nd & 23rd Congress, 1831- 34; U. S. Senate, 1841- 45) his emminence in the legal profession used as a comparison for the stature of Hon. Jeremiah Mason- **759s**

CHRISTIE,
Capt. Napier- m. dau. Col. Burton & Catharine Lydius, taking their family name- **930**
Elizabeth- m. Samuel, s. William & Margaret (Andrew) Dobbin- **732**
Family- early residents of Fitch's Point, Salem, N. Y.; occ. the house at the top of the hill, betw. the Point bridge & the Red House; the bacon stolen by Mrs. Tucker was hung in the chimney of this house- **867**

CHUBB,
Mrs.- her identification of Eldridge as an early resident of the Ft. Miller, N. Y. area was prob. the Matthews referred to by John Pattison as a resident in 1798; see Vol. 1- **804**

CHURCH,
Family- c. 1853, res. below Tamarack swamp, along the Indian river, nr. Mark's corners, Vt., on the opp. side of the river from the Dillingham family- **1003**

Sibel- m. Esther, perh. dau., or grdau., Samuel Burrows; their youngest sons, James & Burcilla, ea. rec'd. £ 30 in Burrow's Will, Feb. 2, 1756- **1100**

CHURCH/ CLERGY-
American Bible Society- 799; American Board (Missionary)- 839, 1087; American Tract Society- 973, 1024; Antiburgher- 732; Associate Congregational- 975; Awakenings, Revivals- 811, 813- 815;
Baptist- 730, 772, 805, 815, 879, 1058;
Cameronian- 805; Catholic- 744, 949b, 1002, 1027, 1050s, 1058, 1097; Convent of the Black Nuns, Montreal- 1052; Church of England- 759s; as the 'Establ.
Church'- 894; Church of Scotland- 1082; Congregational- 723, 799, 835, 836, 994, 1024;
Episcopal- 730, 799, 839, 952b, 1016, 1030, 1054; Fairfield West Consociation, Conn.- 1008; the 'Free Church'- 799; Oberlin sect- 799; French Huguenot- 914, 1012; Friends, Quakers- 806, 921, 1075b; Judaism- as "Jewry"- 1090frag;
Mass. Sabbath School Society- 799; Methodist- 804, 806, 813, 815, 851, 950, 991, 1005, 1058, 1075b, 1077, 1094; Millerite- 799; Moravian- 1075b; Mormon- 1058;
Presbyterian- 701, 732, 744, 759s, 812, 815, 839, 961, 1024, 1027, 1034, 1058, 1081, 1082, 1086, 1097, 1098; Associate- 732, 1097; Assoc. Congregation- 1082; Assoc. Reformed- 742, 810, 839, 973, 1045, 1047b; General Assembly- 759s, 810; Presbyterys- of Troy- 759s; of Londonderry, N. H.- 811; Assoc. Ref., of N. Y.- 811; Protestant Union- 1097;
Soc. for Propagation of the Gospel- 895; Tract Society- 799; Trappists- 949b;

Albany, N. Y.- 6 trustees, incl. John Munro, Esq., deeded a city block, Oct. 1768, for org. of a Presbyterian church here; refers p. 180, Munsell's Albany Register, 1849- **812**;

Anti- Semitism- fragm. of a newspaper article, c. Feb. 1862, prob. *Salem Press*, in which the term juryman is expressly coined 'jewryman' in a disparaging context, along w. some racial prejudices, intended as a humorous story- **1090frag**;

Awakenings, or Revivals- incidents & anecdotes concerning Lorenzo Dow, extracted from Dowling's *Life & Writings of Lorenzo Dow*, 1850, who had resolved, Dec. 1797, to either bring abt. a revival within the Cambridge District, or break up the circuit- **813- 815**;

Bardstown, Kentucky- a no. of religious centers noted inits vicinity- Gethsemane Abbey, a Trappist monastery, then one of 3 such institutions in the country; 1818- 1st Catholic cathedral of the W. built here, & 2nd in the U. S.; also, a no. of convents; their presence given as an inspirational source for some writings of James Lane Allen- the "White Cowl", & "Sister Dolorosa" ment.; article source undated, prob. late 1850's- **949b**;

Camden, Salem, N. Y.- Christ's Church parish, org. Oct. 15, 1797; Rev. James Nichols & Rev. Robert G. Whitmore in the chair; church wardens- Abraham Bininger, Abijah Hubbell; vestry- Levy Bonny, Elijah Horton, Isaac Bininger,

David Bristol, James Archer, George Alexander, Edward Gaynor, Edward Harris; recorded Apr. 15, 1799; refers p. 10, Miscellanies- **879**;

Cambridge, N. Y.- the 'Old White Meeting House', its 1st Presbyterian church; c. 1804- 1812, Rev. Robert H. Chapman, D. D., pastor; succeeded, July 1813- Feb. 1828, by Rev. Nathaniel S. Prime, D. D.- **1024**;

Catholics- Priest Quigley, who res. several yrs. (prob. 1840's- 1850's) at Schaghticoke, N. Y., had charge of the Catholics in the S. part of Wash. co.; his book, "The Cross & The Shamrock", publ. 1853, under the pseudonym, Patrick Donahue, ostensibly was an allegorical tale concerning the anti- Catholic & anti-Irish sentiments found within an area resembling the Wash. co. region, noting 'the kidnapping of Irish Catholic children from their parents or natural guardians' to be raised in regions "wholly secluded from all Catholic society" as a common means of eroding the practice of their faith; see also, O'Cleary family- **1027**; ano. incident concerning Priest Quigley, c. Mar. 1854/5, occurring over his right to perform the sacraments for Patrick Walls, a sick laborer who was being tended in the household of Archibald Hay, who objected to var. tenets of Catholicism, as he understood them, & contended that the priest had no rights or priviledges taking pre- eminence over the sanctity of his household & his own private beliefs; the very lengthy description of the controversy betw. Quigley & Hay typifies the common prejudices & suspicions betw. Catholics & Protestantsof the time period- **1058**;

Dutch church, Hoosick, N. Y.- loc. below N. Hoosick, in the area of the Van Ess house; its yard contained the graves of the earliest inhabitants; the society became disorganized, & the fence around the bur. grd. & the church dilapidated; when the new proprietor of the adj. land hired someone to tear the church down, they could not obt. any redress because the deed had been lost; the bur. grd. was later plowed & its tombstones rem., or broken up- **(L)**- **722**;

the 'Free Church'- founded c. 1835/6, Boston, Mass., "on reformatory principles, composed of those persons who thought the old churches too corrupt for them to remain in them, & who separated to form a pure church"; splitting afterw. on the issue of perfectionism, the Oberlin section became defunct bef. 1852; its ministry began w. Rev. Charles Fitch, s. Pres. Ebenezer Fitch, of Williams College; his successor was Rev. Amos A. Phelps, editor, *The Emancipator*, & was foll. by 3 others, who were also dismissed- **799**;

Methodists- their annual Conference held Dec. 1797, Buckland. Mass.; Lorenzo Dow was given over into the supervision of S. Hutchison, who was appt. to the Cambridge District circuit- **813**; quarterly meeting, held June 20, 1798, Pittstown, N. Y.; Solomon Moon, of Kingsbury, or Queensbury, N. Y., traveled over 40 mi. to be present, saying 'I bless the day that ever I saw the face of brother Dow'; annual conference of this yr. adm. Lorenzo Dow on a trial basis, his certif. signed by Francis Asbury- **815**; the celebrated John Wesley (arr. Feb. 5, 1736, Savannah, Ga.) emig. on the same vessel as the Christian Bininger family; Rev. Philip Embury arr. NYC the same yr. as Rev. Abraham, s. Christian Bininger, who had returned from his missionary work among the Indians w. Rev. George Whitfield;

w. Rev. Bininger's assitance, Rev. Embury establ. the Methodist society in NYC, & erected the John St. church- **1075b**;

Moravians- c. 1730's, a large no. settl. Savannah, Ga., & afterw. rem. Philadelphia. Pa.; they purch. abt. 5,000 acres from Abraham Bininger, in Nazareth, Pa., & rem. there- **1075b**;

New York City- Dr. John Roger's Presbyterian church, org. 1716; its lay officers, from "City Clergy in 1775", Nov. 6, 1851, *N. Y. Observer*; Elders- William Smith, Peter Van Brugh Livingston, John Smith, Garret Noel, Thomas Jackson, & Nathaniel McKinley; Deacons- John Stephens, Peter Ryker; Trustees- Thomas Smith, Whitehead Hicks, William Smith, Jr., John Lasher, Joseph Hallet, John Dunlap, Peter R. Livingston, & John Morin Scott- **961**; a no. of old locs. referred to in a newspaper article, c. 1860's, concerning NYC merchants, specifically the Bininger family; the old Brick Church (n. d.) stood opp. the corners of Beekman & Nassau Sts., where the Times Building now (1860's?) stands; Garden St. Church, on Exchange St., where Dr. Matthews preached, burnt in 1835; the old Quaker Church, c. 1830's, stood at mid- block, Liberty St.; also ments. the orig. John St. Methodist Church- **1075b**; the Presbyterian Church, loc. corner of Madison Ave. & 24th St., was site of the funeral, Jan. 30, 1862, of Rev. Harrison G. Otis Dwight, w. Rev. Dr. Adams officiating, & eulogies by Revs. Anderson, Wood, Adams, & Skinner- **1087**;

N. Granville, N. Y.- its Presbyterian church, orig. called the Union Religious Society of W. Granville, & afterw., the Fair Vale Religious Society- **759s**;

Presbyterian, or New England Church- c. 1777, Salem, N. Y.; burnt in late Aug., abt. a fortnight foll. "the Retreat", by tories & Indians, because it had been fortified & surrounded by pickets; see Pickets, Vol. 1; it was a framed building w. roof, but w/o clapboards on it; the floor was of loose boards, & the pews, or benches, were also loose (this church is differentiated from Dr. Clark's congregation in being comprised of the Salem settlers primarily from Mass., & later was recognized as the Brick church, while the membership of Dr. Clark's congregation later establ. the White church)- **744**;

Quakers- acc. Paul Cornell, Esq., several families res. bef. the Rev. war in Walloomsac Patent, holding meetings there; among this group, Isaac Wood was a prominent figure; during the Rev. war, none of the early Quakers rem. from the area when Burgoyne's army came down; their meetinghouse was built in 1801, w. those of the Baptists & Methodists built soon after; refers p. 132, Corey's Gazetteer; see Vol. 4- **806**;

Salem, N. Y.- Gen. Assembly Presbyterian (the Brick church), Rev. Samuel Tomb, pastor; 1824- 'the Lord, in the riches of his grace, visited the churches in this town w. an abundant effusion of his Spirit', & during the summer & autumn, Rev. Tomb rec'd. large numbers into communion w. the church; 1831- 'a liberal shower of divine influ., when many trees which had stood barren, presented their blossoms & fruits' within the jurisdiction of Rev. Tomb's church- **811**; the 1st framed church, c. 1853, "still standing", was loc. E. of where Dr. Clark's log meetinghouse stood (this was prob. the N. E. church); for a description of Dr. Clark's church, see Log

Cabins- **1001**; the White Church, its "window sashes, pew doors & c."constructed
(n. d.) by Deac. John Steele- **1047**; the 50th annual meeting of the Wash. Co. Bible
Scoiety held here, Sept. 4, 1862- **1097**;

Schaghticoke, N. Y.- its 1st settl. minister, c. 1773, was Rev. Elias Van Ben
Schoten; once, when going to marry a couple, he discovered that the waters of the
Hoosick had risen too high to ford, & he called upon a man on the opp. side to
bring the couple to the riverbank; standing on opp. sides of the stream, he married
them (§ 17) & appt. ano. as his deputy to kiss the bride in his stead, & also act as
his atty. for coll. the bridegroom's fee; after being shown a letter written by
Harmon Knickerbocker when he was attending Salem Academy (§ 16), he became
so impressed w. the ability displayed in the letter that he read it from his pulpit,
thus causing a sensation in the community over Knickerbocker's abilities; ano.
letter was requested, w/o anyone knowing that the 1st had been copied after
corrections by the Preceptor of the Academy; instead of presenting a 2nd letter,
Knickerbocker made ano. copy of the 1st letter; see Vol. 1- **953b**;

Washington Co. Bible Society- its 50th annual meeting held at the White Church,
Sept. 4, 1862, Salem, N. Y.; held foll. the 2nd battle of Bull Run, & during the
final days of the org. of the 123rd NYSV on the nearby fairgrounds of the Co.
Argrcultural Soc., the breadth & content of Dr. Fitch's notes as a participant in the
proceedings, serves as a poignant milestone, noting the religious roots of the early
settlm. of Salem, & the historical similarity betw. the period when the society was
org. (the country again at war w. Britain, & Napoleon "in the midst of his career")
& the country now "grappling w. the great rebellion"; the passing, or aging, of the
society's earliest members & the scattering of their desc. to other areas further
underlines the sense of urgency & transition- **1097**

CHURCHILL,
Maj.- c. 1817, he & Col. House commanded Co. D, 1st regt. of Artillery, U. S.
Army- **974**

THE CIVIL WAR- referred to as "the rebellion of 1861"; newspaper article, May
20, 1861, Camp Rathbone, Troy, N. Y.; notes the combining of the volunteer co. of
Cambridge, N. Y., w. others, to comprise the 22nd N. Y. Inf., & their impending
muster into service; a list of Capts., Co. A- J, & the loc. represented by ea.; list of
78 names from Co. D, taking the oath of allegiance- **(L)- 1074**; commanding
officers & loc. of recruitment, 22nd & 93rd N. Y. Inf., 123rd NYSV, & 2nd N. Y.
Cav.; a newspaper article, listing members, Co. A, Northern Black Horse Cav.,
recruited from Salem, N. Y.; notice by Dr. Fitch, of several individuals in Illinois
regts., principally from Greenwich, N. Y.- **1080**; record of the 14 earliest burials,
soldier's plot, Evergreen Cemetery, Salem, w. brief histories or biogs. of the
interred- **1081**; journal of Lambert Martin, Co. B, 14th Iowa Inf., Oct. 31- Dec. 7,
1861, describing the nearly 500 mi. march of Co. A- C, from Iowa City, to Ft.
Randall, S. Dakota, via Des Moines, to relieve the federal troops garrisoned at Ft.
Randall- **1089**; newsclipping, Feb. 1, 1862, Camp Rathbone, Albany, N. Y., listing

field, staff, & line officers, Co. A- I, & K, 93rd N. Y. Inf.- **1090b**; referred to as the "Slavery Rebellion, 1861, '62"; notes capt. of Col. John S. Crocker & Maj. Ambrose L. Cassidy, Apr. 26, 1862, commanders of 93rd N. Y. Inf.; notice of regt.'s loc., Nov. 8- 12, 1862, & the return & disbanding of the regt., Jan. 1864- **1094**; deaths, or activities, of 10 Wash. co. area soldiers- **1095** an acct. of the 22nd N. Y. Inf., Aug. 30, 1862, at 2nd Bull Run; notes deaths of var. officers & replacement, or promotion, of officers- **1095b**; reception of news concerning defeat of Gen. Pope at 2nd Bull Run, Sept. 4, 1862, Salem, N. Y., & rumor of Gen. Jackson crossing the Potomac, rec'd. during the final org. of 123rd NYSV; some ment. of civilian apprehensions pert. to the vices & temptations of camp life that recruits may be subj. to; the current call for troops totals 600,000, the Wash. co. quota being "some 1400"; enl. bounties- $50.00- State a/o County, & some towns giving an additional $25- 50.00- **1097**; departure of 123rd NYSV from Salem, N. Y., Sept. 5, 1862, & notice of its passage into service at Wash., D. C., & Harper's Ferry, Va.; record of its 1st deaths, & eventual encampment at Stafford's Court House, Va.- **1098**

CLAPP,
Isaac- res. Salem, N. Y.; coroner's inquest held at his house, Nov. 1792, concerning the drowning of Laommi Barnes- **(L)- 876**
Stephen- c. 1850, res. S. of Robert Getty, Hebron, N. Y.; during the Rev. war, the villagers of Salem fled for safety to the hill S. of his homestead- **744**
Maj. Stephen- rem. from nr. Dorchester, Mass., to Salem, N. Y., along w. Capt. Abner Dwelle (or Dwelly)- **731**
Pres. Thomas- (1703- 1767; Pres., Yale Univ., 1745- 66) his grdau. Sarah Saltonstall, m. Jonathan Fitch- **799**

CLARK,
Benjamin- deed witn., Nov. 1, 1783, Dr. Thomas Clark to Jedidiah Gilbert- **(L)- 936**
Qtr.Master Sgt. C. H.- (rank given as C. Q. M.) Co. A, 2nd N. Y., Northern Black Horse, Cav., 1861- 2- **1080**
Judge Ebenezer- s. Rev. Dr. Thomas Clark; res. Salem, N. Y., on a lot that his father purch. from Hamilton McCollister; he sold his lot to Gen. Williams & during the Rev. war, rem. N. Y. Highlands, returning to Argyle, N. Y. foll. peace- **744**; appt. Clerk, Charlotte co., May 8, 1777, by N. Y. Provincial Convention- **787**; the S. side of his farm in Argyle adjoins the farm orig. settl., c. 1772, by Capt. James Beaty- **978**
Eunice- m. Moses, Jr., s. Moses & Lydia (More) Martin- **731**; same material- **1041**
George- Co. A, 2nd N. Y., Northern Black Horse, Cav., 1861- 2- **1080**
Henry- s. Jeremiah, Jr.; b. ca. 1763; ments. his s. Reubin- **765**
Henry- s. Elder Joseph; "a dissipated youth"; m. dau. Alva Wright- **1047b**
James- a neighbor & employee of Benjamin Hough; foll. Hough's release by the Bennington mob, Feb. 1775, he reported to Hough that he & 2 of his neighbors-

John Lord & Joseph Randle, had been abused & insulted by the mob during the time Hough had been imprisoned- **881**

James- c. 1861, res. on the Hopkins farm, Salem, N. Y.; summer 1860, he tore down the house orig. occ. by Nathan & Samuel Hopkins- **1073**

Jeremiah- from Groton, or Preston, Conn.; had s. Jeremiah, Jr., & dau., who m. Amos Galusha; along w. his s. Jeremiah, & his son- in- law, Amos Galusha, he participated in the battle of Bennington- **765**

Jeremiah, Jr.- s. Jeremiah; ments. a son, Henry- **765**

John- of Chatham, Conn.; dau. Esther, m. Peter, s. Thomas & Abigail (Dutton) Parker- **759**; their dau. Esther, b. Oct. 2, 1754- **759s**

Deac. Joseph- his wid. res., c. 1850, on the prev. site of Abraham Turner's house- **863**; (Elder Joseph) his s. Henry, m. dau. Alva Wright- **1047b**

Nathan- chairman of a meeting, July 27, 1775, at Dorset, Vt., to select officers of the Green Mtn. regt.- **781b**

Nathan- chairman, Aug. 3, 1775, for a meeting of the Committees of Safety of Cambridge & Hoosick, N. Y., & Bennington, Vt.- **783**

Gen. Orville- b. Sandy Hill, N. Y.; d. Mar. 19, 1862, at 61, from congestion of lungs, at Des Moines, Iowa- **1088**

Reubin- res. Walloomsac, N. Y.; b. ca. 1788, Lot No. 1, Walloomsac Patent; he owned a large brick house, loc. abt. 20 rods E. of the W. line of the Patent, w. the word 'Walloomsac' cut in a marble slab over the door; gives an acct. of the Galusha family, of Shaftsbury, Vt.; d. summer 1852- **765**; gives an acct. of the 2nd half of the battle of Bennington- **766**; acc. to his acct., old 'Festus' was killed at Bennington, contradicting an earlier acct. (§ 246) given by Dr. McAllister; see Festus, Vol. 1- **768**; the remains of the last person presumed killed during the battle of Bennington were found abt. 25 rods E. of the W. line of his farm- **1007**

Robert- Lot No. 237, Turner's Patent, conveyed to him, Sept. 6, 1775, by Rev. Dr. Thomas Clark- **(L)- 936**; same transaction noted- **(L)- 936b**

Dr. Robert- m. Catharine, dau. Duncan Reid; rem. Marshall, or Munroe, Mich.; he d. there, but his wid. still res. there, c. 1850- **802**

Rev. Dr. Thomas- during "the Retreat" from Salem, 1777, he gathered the refugee families encamped nr. Wait's corners, Cambridge, N. Y., for a Sabbath service; the loc. was on a rise of ground overlooking the valley of the Owl kill, & Psalm 137 was given out for singing- 'By Babel's streams we sat & wept,/ when Zion we thought on,/ In midst thereof we hanged our lamps/ the willow- trees upon./ Oh how the Lord's song shall we sing/ within a foreign land?'- **739**; purch. Hamilton McCollister's lot during the Rev. war, & his s. Ebenezer res. on it bef. selling out to Gen. Williams- **744**; along w. Dr. Williams & Mr. Sessions, sent correspondences to Gouverneur Morris in late July 1777, concerning recent resolutions of the Provincial Congress regarding the Grants- **796**; Rev. James Proudfit was his successor at the Assoc. Ref. church, Salem, N. Y.- **810**; acc. Wid. Angel, "used to hold meetings in var. houses around through Salem & Argyle"; he bapt. Aaron, Moses, & Triphena (Wid. Angel) Martin all at the same time- **867**; defendant, Mar. 22 or 24, 1775, in a case brought by James Abeel- **878**; Lot No. 191, New

Perth (Salem, N. Y.), conveyed to him for 5 Shillings, Sterling, May 1, 1766, by Andrew Lytle; recorded July 5, 1774; Lot 237, Turner's Patent, conveyed to him by Joseph Rugg, Apr. 20, 1770, & he conveys the same, Sept. 6, 1775, to Robert Clark; for £ 23 2s; May 8, 1781, deeds 44 acres, Lot No. 38, to William Hamilton; "Late of New Perth"; Nov. 1, 1783, conveys Lot 277 to Jedidiah Gilbert, amt. not given- **(L)- 936**; his purch. & resale of Lot No. 237, Turner's Patent, ment. again- **(L)- 936b**; Lot No. 86, Turner's Patent, mortgaged to him, Jan. 15, 1774, by James Abeel- **938**; during the early settlm. of Munro's Meadows, Hebron, N. Y., he used to come up & do baptizings, & the settlers would travel 17 mi. to the meetings in Salem- **997**; A Pastoral & Farewell Letter, to the Assoc. Congregation of Presbyterians, in Ballibay; publ. 1811, by Dodd & Rumsey, Salem, N. Y.; see Vol. 3- **1082**

Dr. Clark's colony- Moses Martin, Sr., rem. to Salem, N. Y. at abt. the same time as his colony left Stillwater, & settl. at Fitch's Point, just beyond the boundary of Turner's Patent- **731**; emig. to America in 1764- **737**; acc. Dr. Proudfit's 1832 address, 'Exhausted w. oppression, evil & ecclesiastical in the old world, they left the land of their fathers in the summer of 1764'; a port. of the colony emig. 1762, 1763, & also, 1765, as noted by Dr. Fitch, but the majority came w. Dr. Clark in 1764; recognized by Dr. Proudfit as the 1st settlers of Salem, he attrib. their unique temperament & suitability for the task of settling the wilderness to their early hardships in their natvie Ireland, thus illust. 'convincing proof of a superintending providence controlling the destinies of our world'; William McFarland, who d. 1819, noted as 'the last member of the old session'- **809**; James Harsha (Hershaw) & John Thompson ment. as members of his colony who remained settl. in Stillwater after the majority had rem. Salem, N. Y.; p. 36 of Dr. Clark's Farewell letter notes that Harsha d. 6 mos. after they arr. in Stillwater, but Harsha's grds., Deac. George, & Dr. Fitch, disagree, the former stating that he d. nearly a yr. afterw.- **973**; c. 1853, their log meeting house, Salem, N. Y., was "still standing", W. of where the 1st framed church was built- **1001**

CLARY,
Dr. Isaac Baldwin- he was indicted & plead guilty, Dec. 1811, for disinterring a black woman named Peggy from the Argyle bur. grd., & dissecting her body; 3 others plead guilty in the same case; see Criminal Offenders- **874**

CLASSICAL, Biblical, Literary, & Topical Allusions-
Athenians- 1052; Babel- 739; Caesar- 709, 1082; John Calvin- 1027; Canaan-1089; Cavalier- 962; Charles I- 962; Columbia- 709; Columbus, Newton, Morse, & Stephenson- 949b; Cornelius- 809; Oliver Cromwell- 962; the Cross- 709, 1027; Crucifix- 1050s;
David- 1082; Devil- 1063; Devil- like- 902; dudgeon- 1058; Elijah- 709, 809; Elisha- 709, 809; Gethsemane- 949b; Goliath- 917; Hapsburg- 1075b; Herculean-840, 917, 1052; Hood, Thomas- 1050s;

Isreal- 709; Jenkins- 930; Jesus- 759s, 1050s; Jesus Christ- 809, 991, 1024, 1082; Latin- 834, 878, 1058; Leonidas- 709; Lord of Hosts- 811; Messiah- 1030; Moses- 953b; Mount Parnassus- 799; Munchausen- 930; Napoleon- 1097; Nebuchadnezer- 709; Pirate, bandit- 917; Pharoah- 1027; Plutarch- 1052; Purgatory- 1058; Redeeming Angel- 809; rosary- 1050s; St. Patrick- 1027; the Shamrock- 1027; Sparta- 709; Tennyson- 1052; Theseus- 1052; Zaccheus- 1050s; Zion- 739

Ethan Allen- described by Judge Blanchard as "such a Goliath in stature, & had such a restless air, & such a piercing look, that I almost fancied myself unsafe in his company- not knowing but he might be some pirate or bandit"- 917;

John Fitch, steamboat inventor- an undated newsclipping, equates his achievement w. the 'superior intellectual faculties' of Columbus, Newton, Morse, & Stephenson, in having 'revolutionized this globe'- 949b;

John Henry Lydius- his obit. notice, *Gentleman's Magazine,* 1791, notes he stated that he expected to live as long as Jenkins- 930;

George Washington- referred to as a 'political Elijah', for whom some 'Elisha' was longed for by the speaker, 'to snatch as it falls' his mantle- 709

CLEMENT,
____- of NYC; m. Mary, dau. Sidney Wells, as her 2nd husb.; children- Merion & Florence- 839

CLENDON,
Capt. George, Jr.- (Capt. C., Jr.) of Glens Falls, N. Y.; May 25, 1861, commanded Co. E, 22nd N. Y. Inf.- **(L)**- 1074; promoted, Sept. 3, 1862, rank not given- 1095b

CLEVELAND,
Aaron- c. 1861, res. Salem, N. Y.; the cellar hole from the log house of Gibson, the tory, was still visible at the foot of a hill some 50 rods distant from the back of Cleveland's house- 1073
Abel- of Salem, N. Y.; ments. sons David & James; he "was by common consent, something more than a friend in the household" of James Dobbin, one of the orig. emig. bros.- 732
Family- from R. I.; rem. a few yrs. bef. the Rev. war, & res. on the S. side of White (Ondawa) creek, Salem, N. Y.; ments. sons Aaron & Daniel R.; they constructed a house now (1861) occ. by Isaac Sherman- 1073
Newcomb- purch. Lot No. 99, Turner's Patent, the farm of Deac. Abram Savage, from his heirs, & resold it, c. 1863, to David Tefft- 971

CLINTON,
Gov. Dewitt- (1769- 1828; Gov., 1817- 22; 1825- 28) was accostumed to consulting Capt. Richard Kimball "in all matters in practical difficulty in relation to the canals"- 1067; brief ment.- 1075b

Gov. George- (1739- 1812; Gov., 1777- 95; 1801- 04) his selection as Lt. Gov. by voters of Charlotte co. noted as "pretty unanimous", by a June 23, 1777 correspondence, despite few votes within the county- **789**; presented to the Board of Trade, Nov. 30, 1745, the contents of an Express from Albany, N. Y., noting the breaking up of the Saraghtoga settlm. (Schuylerville, N. Y.) by the French & Indians; refers Land Doc., xxvii, 187, 235- **1013**; signed the commission of Dr. Peletiah Fitch, Aug. 18, 1778, as 1st Judge, Cumberland co.- **838**; he & Gen. Woodhull were among the patriots in the N. Y. Assembly that Col. Philip Schuyler co- operated w. in the struggle of the colonies' rights against the British govt.- **920**; his letter to Gen. Washington, Oct. 18, 1780, notes Gen. Schuyler's erroneous report that the settlm. of White Creek (Salem, N. Y.) had been burnt on Oct. 17th; refers Sparks' Letters to Washington, v. ii, 121- **1066**

Col. James- (1733- 1812; later Gen.) as of Feb. 28, 1776, commanded 4 regts. of N. Y. troops in Canada, that had been raised during the prev. yr.- **784**

Clinton co., N. Y.- incl. w. Wash. co. as a N. Y. Assembly district foll. its 15th session, 1792- **992**

CLOUGH,

Luther- of Black Creek district (Hebron, N. Y.); for 10 Shillings, Jan. 10, 1786, conveys an undesign. port. of land to Benjamin Ward; p. 34, Liber A, Book of Deeds, Wash. co.- **(L)- 936**

CLOUGHIN,

John- res. Salem, N. Y.; he & John Todd stole John Lytle's yoke of oxen & drove them to Burgoyne's camp, offering Lytle a receipt (which he refused) so that he might obt. recompense for them- **739**; (Cloughkin) "was the worst tory in town"- **744**

COBB,

____-"who was a pompous man, & d. a pauper"; m. Hannah Wells, wid. Moses Younglove, as her 2nd husb.; had 4 children- 3 sons- Marcus Brutus, of Westchester co.; & Brutus Marcus, & Cassius, who both res. Cleveland, Ohio; & dau., who m. E. P. Fenton; his wf. d. Mar. 30, 1876, at 85, Cleveland, Ohio- **841**

George- oath of alleg.; Co. D, 22nd N. Y. Inf.- **(L)- 1074**

Marcus Brutus- (s. ____ & Hannah Wells) lawyer, Westchester co., N. Y.- **841**

COCHRAN, see also, COCKRAN,

John- m. Ann, dau. Phineas & Ann (Cooper) Whiteside; 4 children- Mary, m. Hugh Guilford; Ann; Susan, m. John McKernon; & Margaret, d. unm.- **805**

John- of NYC; along w. wf. Gertrude, for £ 60, June 17, 1786, deeds Lot 2 of the 2nd Allottment, Ft. Edward Patent, containing 13¾ acres, to Adiel Sherwood- **(L)- 936**

Robert- court member, at the trial of Benjamin Hough, & self described as the 'Adjutant of the rioters', directing the punishment, Jan. 30, 1775, that was meted out to Hough- **881**; he & ors. noted for dispossessing Donald McIntyre & ors., June 11, 1771, from their homes nr. Argyle, N. Y.; after full inquiry, the Justices of Peace for Albany co. directed to give such relief as statutes of forcible entry may permit; see Vol. 1- **901**

Robert, Esq.- plaintiff, in separate cases, Nov. 3, 1784, vs. Justice Allen, vs. Noah Paine (Payne); also, defendant, same date, in a case brought by Dr. John Williams, where Sheriff returns on writ of fi fa. that he was levied on goods, chattels, lands & tenements of defendant the possession on which he now lives, 2 horses- one black, one roan; 2 yoke of oxen & 5 cows, which remain on hand for want of buyers- **878½**

COCKBURN,

Alexander- of Kingston, N. Y.; surviving administrator of William Cockburn; Aug. 26, 1831, assigns mortgage of Lot 23, Hutton's Bush, Westfield, N. Y., to John Williams of Salem, N. Y.- **1092**

William- surveyor; along w. John Wigram, c. 1771, laid out Lots No. 1 & 26, in the S. part of Socialborough, Charlotte co., N. Y. (Rutland, Vt.)- **745**

William- res. Kingston, N. Y.; Feb. 24, 1804, George Willey mortgaged Lot 23, Hutton's Bush, Westfield, N. Y., to him for $393.50- **1092**

COCKRAN, see also, COCHRAN,

Col.- from Colrain, Mass.; an intimate acquaintance of Archibald McNeil, & much at his house nr. Ft. Miller ferry; he was also a cousin of Thomas Pattison; had one son, & a no. of daus.; refers pgs. 198, 202, Neilson's Burgoyne- **804**

Robert- Vermonter; suppos. by Dr. Fitch to have res. Ft. Edward, N. Y., foll. his presumed involvement in the ejections from Vt. of Thomas Brayton & Benjamin Hough- **746**; he & Remember Baker, along w. Capt. Motte's co., assembled at Ft. Edward, June 28, 1775, 'w. an intent to protect the court'- **779**; (Col.) one of those persons figuring largely in the controversy w.Vt.; he was, acc. Judge Blanchard, "a rude boisterous man, but had many fine qualities"; a dau. m. Matthias Ogden- **917**

Capt. Robert- of Col. Eason's regt., Mass. line; stat. at Crown Point, N. Y., late May 1775- **750**

COFFIN,

_____ - m. Jerusha, dau. Hezekiah & Jerusha (Burr) Fitch- **799**

COGGSHALL/ COGSHALL,

Family- of Salem, N. Y.; ments. sons Thomas, William, & Joseph- **737**

George- (Coggshall) d. Sept. 30, 1824, Salem, N. Y., from a wnd. to the abdomen, inflicted Sept. 5th, by the sword of William Gordon; see Criminal Offenders- **808**

Joseph- of Salem, N. Y.; "dissipated"; m. Sarah, dau. James & Rebecca (Lytle) Mills- **737**

COGSEL,

Giles- drowned in Hudson river, "May 9th, 19th yr. of Independence" (1794), in Easton, N. Y.- **(L)**- **876**

COIT,

Charles- acc. Hiram Sisson, was among the men gathered at Pratt's store during the evening of Feb. 16, 1858, when Barney McEntee was murdered- **1048s**
Roger- of Norwich, Conn.; m. Elizabeth F., dau. Andrew & Ann (Marsh) Rowland- **799**

COLDEN,

____- res. Pittstown, N. Y.; an imported English bull purch. from him, 1820, by Asa Fitch, Sr., & provided services at $1.00 per cow- **799**
Lt. Gov. Cadwallader- (1688- 1776; Acting Gov., Lt. Gov., 1760, 1761- 63, 1769, 1776) a letter to him from Sir Wm. Johnson, Nov. 25, 1769, notes the formation of several regts. in his domain w/o prior notice to him, incl. one formed "abt. Ft. Edward, South Bay & its environs", commanded by Maj. (Philip) Skene; in a 2nd letter, Jan. 5, 1770, Sir Wm. Johnson notes that Col. (Philip) Schuyler's zeal, as well as ignorance, in making out officer's commissions, is to blame for "some of the egregious blunders" lately incurred during the creating of militia units- **735**; c. 1774, Benjamin Hough appl. to him for a gr. of land, claiming the loss of an arm in his country's service- **746**; issued a proclamation, Dec. 28, 1763, referred to by Harmanus Schuyler as the directive he pursued in making arrests of Samuel Ashley, Samuel Robinson, John Horfort, & Isaac Charles- **885**; his letter, Jan. 20, 1764, to Board of Trade, concerns actions & practices connected w. grant lands contested by N. Y. & N. H. since the cessation of the most recent Indian incursions into the Province prior to the end of the late war- **887**; a letter to the Board of Trade, Feb. 3, 1764, referring to his prev. letter (§ 887) & giving further details regarding the size of recent N. H. grants & their method of selling titles, suggesting an inquiry into the benefactors of these apparently fraudulent grants; see Grants, N. H. Controversy- **891**; an undated letter to him from Harmanus Schuyler, Sheriff of Albany co., concerning the ejection of Hans Jerry Creiger from his property in the Hoosick Patent, by N. H. people, late July 1764, & their intention to eject Peter Voss & Bastian Deale from their lands; describes his efforts to intervene w. a posse, & his arrest (§ 885) of Ashley, Robinson, Horfort, & Charles- **892**; his papers & those of James Duane, replying to the 1st six paragraphs of Samuel Robinson's petitn., annexed to Gov. Moore's June 9, 1767 letter to Lord Shelburne- **894**; issued a proclamation, Dec. 28, 1763, warning settlers not to take titles from N. H., & directing civil officers of N. Y. 'to continue to exercise jurisdiction in their respective functions as far as the banks of the Conn. river, the undoubted eastern limits of that part of the Province of N. Y.'; his letter to the Board of Trade, Apr. 12, 1764, encloses Gov. Wentworth's proclamation, & urges a speedy decision to the Grants question- 'How low it is to give N. J. as an instance that the patent of the Duke of York is obsolete! This can only be designed

for ignorant people who know not that the Proprietors of N. J. hold under the Patent to the Duke of York!'; a letter to him from Gov. Wentworth, Aug. 17, 1764, requesting the release of 4 individuals (prob. Ashley, Robinson, Horfort, & Charles) jailed by the Albany Sheriff, citing it as cruel to punish these persons as a result of a dispute betw. govts.- **928**

Richard Nichols- of NYC; deeded Lot No. 83, Cambridge Patent, May 9, 1775, to Phineas Whiteside- **805**

COLE,

____- Gov. Moore notes that he & Samuel Robinson, along w. 7 or 8 others, held lands incl. in other Patents, & that the N. Y.Council, determined to protect such . settlers, ordered these properties secured for them; Cole, in thanking the Council, requested the adding of one good deed to ano., by allowing the lands w/o fees of office, which was assured by the Gov. in front of the Board- **894**

B. F.- Orderly Sgt.; Co. A, 2nd N. Y., Northern Black Horse, Cav., 1861- 2- **1080**

Ebenezer- extracts from his affidavit, Feb. 27, 1771, marked as foll. by Dr. Fitch- (F)- notes that N. H. settlers say they have tied up & whipped ____ Moore, who came to settle in Princetown (Manchester, Vt.) under the proprietorship of N. Y., threatening to serve any others coming on the same errand, in the same way; (H)- that he & abt. a dozen others were the only persons agreeing to Archibald Campbell's offer to survey their lands for his returns, the others refusing to show their boundaries, due to an unwillingness to pay quit rents on N. Y. grants; (O)- of all settlers known to him, not one was in regular service, but a few were in provincial forces during the late war; (P)- Gov. (John) Wentworth's arr. (prob. in office) revived hope of annexation to N. H., & petitns. to the King, for that end, were circulated, reportedly upon his advice- **896**

Ebenezer, Esq.- Justice of Peace, Albany co.; res. nr. Bennington, Vt.; Benjamin Hough conferred w. him & Bliss Willoughby, Feb. 1775, foll. his release by the Bennington mob, & reported to him that he found Cole & Willoughby, w. armed people in their homes, ready for defense against the rioters- **881**

John- of Boston, Mass.?; an American prisoner at Ft. Ticonderoga, who escaped Aug. 1777, along w. Samuel Standish & 2 others, making their way to Arlington, Vt.- **747**

Laura- wf. Nathaniel, Jr.; d. Jan.1, 1811, at 23- **(L)- 772**

COLEMAN,

Capt.- undesign. co. commander, 123rd NYSV, at its org., Aug./ Sept. 1862 (perh. Capt. Warren B., 169th N. Y. Inf.; see Vol. 4)- **1097**

COLLAMER,

Theodocia- res. at 'the Ridge' (prob. Malta Ridge), Ballston, N. Y.; "an old, proud & not very bright man", who made himself an intimate of John Ashton; he pretended to be of noble descent, & was searching a great deal for, & talking abt. a family coat of arms; impressed by Ashton's talents & abilities, he once beset him to honor the Collamer family w. some poetry; at length, tired of his importunity, Ashton told him that he "would give him a verse extempore" that he might write down, if he desired, describing from all he could learn, what he presumed was the Collamer coat of arms- 'Two post rampant, one beam passant,/ one rope pendant,/ with a rogue at the end on't', which, for Ashton's peace of mind, effectively silenced his allusions to the subj. while in his presence (a similar verse may be found in the works of William Blake)- **952**

COLLINS,
Sarah- of Whitestown, N. Y.; m. James Duane, s. Chillus & Sarah (Martin) Doty- **730**
Deac. Thomas- m. Mary McCrea, perh. dau. Wid. McCrea, the lacemaker- **866**

COLONY,
Uriah- bootmaker, res. Buskirk's Bridge, N. Y.; acc. Dr. Morris, he & Andrew Houghton, & Ira & Hiram Sisson, went along w. him to the scene of Barney McEntee's murder, Feb. 16, 1858, foll. the discovery of his body; he states that a club used in the murder was found while they were there, & the Coroner's Inquest was held at his house the foll. day; a fence stake was found Feb. 19th, 48 rods & 11 ft. W. of the body, on the S. side of the road & N. side of the fence, at its corner; he & Elijah Chase observed the tracks in the area, which he measured as abt. No. 7 size boot, 4½ in. wide; there had not been many others on the road in that area since the murder, & the tracks were similar to ones made by Wallace in the backyard of Randall's Tavern- **1048s**

COLT,
Lt.- of Richmond, Mass.; succeeded Lt. Hart, in commanding a co. of 2 months' men in a Mass. brigade that marched to Fairfield, Conn., Sept. 1776- **747**

COLUMBIA- Carthegena (Cartagena)- **760, 1059**

COLVIN,
Family- res. Cambridge, or White Creek, N. Y.; their farm purch. by Dr. Sanford Smith, & later occ. by the Wilcox family- **844**
Capt. Orville L.- Co. A, 93rd N. Y. Inf.- **1090b**
Reuben- or CoCuin; witn., Nov. 20, 1772, along w. Ichabod Foster, to a warrantee deed from Jacob Marsh to Thomas Brayton, for Lot No. 5, Socialborough, Vt.- **745**

COMBS,
____- Methodist minister; m. 1. Charlotte, dau. Henry Bliss; she d. Galesville, N. Y., & he m. 2. ____, & res. Ft. Ann, N. Y., "working at some mechanical trade"- **1005**

COMSTOCK,
Samuel- his wf. Elizabeth, d. Nov. 3, 1823, at 98; & he d. Sept. 3, 1817, at 90- **(L)**-
772
Theodore F.- of Wilton, N. Y.; m. Mary, dau. Ebenezer & Sarah (Hobby) Fitch;
several children- **799**

CONDON,
Joseph- "of Bakeman's Precink" (Beekman's Patent, Dutchess co., N. Y.); makes,
sets over, & delivers, July 19, 1762, to Philip Aylworth, of Coventry, Kent co.,
R. I., the S. part of the old west farm (prob. Clarendon, Vt., no boundary
description)- **745**

CONKEY,
Adam- (s. Silas & Zerniah Martin) m. Betsey Lee, who d. ca. 1847; he rem.
Mattison, Ohio, where most of his children now live- Oscar, Amanda; Elizabeth,
m. ____ McCormick; Mary Ann, William Fitch, & Cornelia- **730**
Charles Grandison- (s. Silas & Zerniah Martin) canal collector, Rome, N. Y.; m.
Paulina Pitcher, at Martinsburgh, N. Y.; a dau., Miriam- **730**
Family- res. Pelham, Mass.; had 2 sons who were among the 1st settlers of Salem,
N. Y.- Joshua, an orig. settler, c. 1761- 3; & Silas, who arr. ca. 1780; the other
family members remained in Pelham- John, Alexander; Isaac, rem. & d. Nova
Scotia; James; & Sarah, who m. ____ Abercrombie, of Pelham- **730**
J. A.- 2nd Farrier & Blacksmith, Co. A, 2nd N. Y., Northern Black Horse, Cav.,
1861- 2- **1080**
John- bro. Joshua & Silas; had 2 sons, Isaac & ____, who were once merchs.,
Troy, N. Y.- **730**
Joshua- bro. Silas; orig. settler, Salem, N. Y.; see Vol. 1- **730**; acc. Mrs. Vance
(Susan Lytle), his house in Turner's Patent had not yet been built by 1767, & only
James Turner & David Webb then had inhabited structures- **738**; (Capt.) was the
courier of John Williams' corespondence, June 23, 1777, to John McKesson, Esq.,
of the N. Y. Provincial Congress- **789**; his sureties given, along w. Moses Martin
& Hamilton McCollister, May 9, 1786, for Martin as loan officer- **(L)**- **936b**
Mary- m. Alexander Turner, Sr., acc. V. R., Worcester & Pelham, Mass.
(manuscript does not give date)- **1085b**
Silas- bro. Joshua; came from Pelham, Mass., ca. 1780, arr. Salem, N. Y.; m. June
27, 1781, Zerniah, dau. Col. Adam & Abigail (Cheney) Martin; 8 children-
  1. Willard Cheney, m. Mary Faxon
  2. Maria, m. John Waters
  3. Lucinda, b. Aug. 29, 1788, Salem, N. Y.; m. William Fitch
  4. Adam, m. Betsey Lee
  5. Sarah, m. Harvey Stevens
  6. Silas, m. Lydia Spears
  7. Charles Grandison, m. Paulina Pitcher

8. Walter Martin, b. 1805; m. Frances Randle; he purch. Lot No. 67, Argyle Patent, from William Reid, & res. on the SW corner of the lot; purch. 10 acres on the N. side of White (Ondawa) creek from Moses Martin, Sr., & put up a clothing works; built a large house, long occ. as a tavern, & sold out bef. 1803, to William Fitch; rem. Martinsburgh, N. Y., & d. Apr. 6, 1813, at 54- **730**; his fulling mill, at Fitch's Point, constructed by Augustus Angel, 1 or 2 yrs. after Carter's sawmill- **847**; he was only the 2nd person to build N. of the creek, foll. MacQueen (prob. Peter McQueen); constructed a small framed house where the present (1850) tavern stands; his house built on 2 levels, the upper room occ. by the family, & the lower, 1 or 2 steps below, used for dressing & finishing off cloth- **867**; his wf., & the wf. of Chillus Doty, convey var. particulars of the Martin genealogy, for Charles L. Martin's manuscript- **1037**; his wf. d. Oct. 16, 1849, Martinsburgh, N. Y.- **1039**

Silas, Jr.- (s. Silas & Zerniah Martin) m. Lydia Spears, of New Berlin, N. Y, where his wid. & children now (1850) res.- Arnold; Anson, or Lansing; Silas, William Fitch, & Martin; they had 2 daus. who d.- **730**

Walter Martin, Esq.- (s. Silas & Zerniah Martin) b. 1805; m. Francis Randle, of Norwich, N. Y.; cashier, 1833, Bank of Chenango, & President, 1854; children- John, Frances; d. Dec. 29, 1872; see Vol. 4- **730**; his wf.'s niece, Ernestine R., the only surviving child of Charles P. & Ernestine (Randall) Freeman, has res. w. her aunt since infancy, foll. the death of both her parents- **1046**

Willard Cheney- (s. Silas & Zerniah Martin) m. Mary Faxon, of Whitesboro, in Martinsburgh, N. Y.; children-
1. Willard Cheney, Jr.; res. Watertown, N. Y.; m. Emily Blakesby; 4 or 5 children
2. Legrand, d. a minor, Martinsburgh, N. Y.
3. Abigail, m. Dr. Lewis, at Utica, N. Y.; res. Wisc. or Illinois
4. Mary, rem. Wisc., where her mother & sist. Abigail rem. foll. their father's death
5. John, now (1850) studying divinity
6. Lucinda, rem. Wisc., w. her sist. & mother- **730**

CONKLIN,
James H.- Co. A, 2nd N. Y., Northern Black Horse, Cav., 1861- 2- **1080**
John- dau. Theodocia, m. Capt. Richard Hall, s. Thomas & ____ (Hill) Fitch- **799**; of Norwalk, Conn.; dau. Theodocia, m. Capt. Richard Hall Fitch, of Troy, N. Y.- **940**

CONNECTICUT- 779, 793, 797, 799, 830, 836, 839, 840, 860, 887, 894, 1078;
Counties- Fairfield- 936; Litchfield- 756, 759s; Trumbull- 955; Windham- 763; Cities & Towns- Bethlehem- 759; Brookfield- 759, 759s; Canfield- 955; Canterbury- 799; Chatham- 759, 759s; Chestnut Hill- 943; Cornwall- 756; Coventry- 813;
Danbury- 752, 936, 950; E. Windsor- 949;

Fairfield- 747, 799, 940, 948; Farmigton- 752, 855; Fitchville- 945; Goshen- 936; Greenwich- 799, 950, 955; Groton- 765, 799, 838, 1100; Noank- 838; Guilford- 799, 834;
Hartford- 754, 759s, 799, 945b, 946, 957; Hebron- 772; Horseneck- 747, 752, 950; Killingly- 1037; Killingworth- 731; Lebanon- 799, 945b, 968b; Litchfield- 759, 951, 960; Litchfield farms- 759. 759s;
Mansfield- 962, 967; Marlboro?- 1039; New Canaan- 799, 1008; Naugatuck- 799; New Haven- 759s, 799, 839; New London- 730; Norwalk- 753, 799, 812, 834, 939- 941, 943, 945b, 946, 949b, 955, 1036; Norwich- 727, 747, 757, 759s, 799, 834, 838, 945b, 947; Plainfield- 763; Preston- 757, 765; Roxbury- 1052;
Salisbury- 759, 759s, 799, 939, 947; Saybrook- 759s, 945b, 946; Scotland- 730; Sharon- 759s; Simsbury- 850; Stamford- 752, 753, 799, 955; Stonington- 728, 799, 962; Thompson- 729; Torrington- 759, 759s;
Wallingford- 752,759s; Washington- 759s; Westford- 799; Wilton- 799; Windham- 730; Windsor- 837, 945b, 949, 949b; Woodbury- 1052; Woodstock- 758;
Features- Conn. river- 837, 858, 887, 891, 894, 896, 928;
Institutions- Colonial- General Assembly- 774; General Court- 799
Colony/ State of- communication to N. Y. Provincial Congress, adm. to record, May 30, 1775; information conveyed that Ticonderoga was not taken by their regular troops, "but by adventurers"-773; 2 letters from Col. Benedict Arnold, at Crown Point; the 1st, May 23, 1775, to Gov. Trumbull, sends a request for 4- 500 wt. of powder, besides details of event since May 18th; the 2nd, n. d., to General Assembly of the Colony, notes the escape from St. John's, Canada, of one of Col. Allen's men, & his report that the force there is making preparations to recapt. Crown Point & Ticonderoga; requests at least 1,500 men in arms to be sent immed.; as a response to Arnold's request, 500 lbs. of powder & 4 companies, ea. containing 100 men, raised by Conn., to march to Ft. Ticonderoga; communication sent to N. Y. stating that Conn.'s troops were being sent until N. Y. might occ. these posts in their own right- 774; Col. Benjamin Hinman sent to N. Y. frontier, May 1775, w. 1,000 men until he may be relieved by N. Y. troops- 776; 1673, Grand Comm., appt. for ordering the militia foll. legislature's order to raise 500 dragoons capable of being able to march within an hr.'s warning; for Fairfield troops, appt. as Capt.- Thomas Fitch; Lt.- John Burr- **948**

Continental Congress- delegates from N. Y. chosen Apr. 20, 1775, at N. Y. Provincial Convention- **773**; passes resolution, July 1, 1775, similar to any earlier one made by N. Y., forbidding expeditions or incursions into Canada by any colony, or group of colonies; the resolution noted as an indirect censure of Ethan Allen's activities- 776; delegate James Duane, of N. Y., notes the arr. of June 30, 1777, *Connecticut Courant*, in Philadelphia, Pa., in his July 10th letter to N. Y. Council; the newspaper's contents incl. a declaration by inhabitants of the part of N. Y. 'which is attempted to be wrested out of our jurisdiction, & which is dubbed the State of Vermont, a name hatched for it in Philadelphia'; he notes, in addition, that the plan for statehoood was directed by Dr. Young, & others 'of more consequence' who have pushed the people 'to this last extremity'; Duane notes the list of complaints against N. Y. incl. within the article as an attempt to bolster their cause in the eyes of the Convention, but 'such a train of falsehoods & misrepresentations does but little credit to this mock Convention [Vt.'s], which will very prob. proceed to elect Delegates for Congress, & once more press for their admission'; Duane deems their success w. the Congress to be unlikely; refers p. 1,000, Journal of Council of Safety- **793**

CONVERSE,
Capt. Thomas- of Goshen, Conn.; deeded 1 acre, Morrison's Patent, Aug. 6, 1785, by Daniel H. White- **(L)- 936**; same material; purch. for £ 8- **(L)- 936b**

CONWAY,
Martin- occ. a house on the turnpike, Buskirk's Bridge, N. Y., nr. Elijah Chase's woodlot, abt. ½ mi. from where Barney McEntee's body was found- **1048s**
Michael- farmer, res. Oak Hill, White Creek, N. Y.; he testif. that he was acquainted w. Martin Wallace for 4 yrs., & that he had employed him during the winter, 1854, & that Wallace had a good character; acc. Patrick Joice's testim., Martin Wallace sd. that he had been invited to supper w. him, but had declined, as he was waiting for Barney McEntee to leave Joice's store w. him earlier in the evening that McEntee was murdered- **1048s**

COOK,
____ - of NYC; m. Mary Barber; their surviving s., Edward A., c. 1859, res. NYC; his wf. m. 2. Maj. James Harvey- **1035**
Asaph, Esq.- def., Nov. 1786, in a case brought by Hamilton McCollister, Sheriff- **878½**; of Granville, N. Y.; for £ 20, rec'd. quit claim, May 1, 1782, for Lot 8, Morrison's Patent, from John Williams & Joseph McCracken- **(L)- 936**; same material as prev.- **(L)- 936b**
Henry- (H. B.) oath of alleg.; Co. D, 22nd N. Y. Inf.- **(L)- 1074**; 1st Sgt.; promoted Sept. 23, 1862, to 1st Lt., replacing Thomas R. Fisk (prob. Thomas B.; see Vol. 3)- **1095b**
John- def., May 19, 1774, in a case brought by Stephen Tuttle- **878**
Lt.- officer, May 1781, Col. Walbridge's regt.- **754**
Louis- (or Col. Louis) b. abt. 1740, Saratoga (Schuylerville, N. Y.); "unquestionably the greatest man that ever flourished at St. Regis, among the native population", his father was a colored man in the sevice of one of the govt. officials at Montreal, & his mother was a St. Francis Indian; in an attack made on Saratoga towards the close of 1755, he & his parents were among the captives; refers p. 180, Hough's Hist. of St. Lawrence & Franklin co.- **1014**
Dr. Oliver- def.witn., People vs. Martin Wallace; he was present at the examinations of witns. bef. Squire Dyer, & by Col. Crocker's request, kept the minutes of the inquiries; his testim. was principally concerned w. the conversations

in Randall's parlor betw. Marvin Wallis & Col. Crocker, concerning money that Wallis had pd. to Martin Wallace- **1048s**
Ransom, Esq.- c. 1859, res. Saratoga Springs, N. Y.; m. dau. Robert Ayres; he was once the Keeper, Clinton State Prison, St. Lawrence co., N. Y., & notes that at one time, a neph. of Jane McCrea was in his employ there as an assistant, while a neph. of her lover, David Jones, was held there as a convict- **1054**; relates var. particulars to Dr. Fitch concerning the battle of Plattsburgh (Sept. 11, 1814)- **1055**
Samuel- by order of June 30, 1775, was to be appt. surgeon, Green Mtn. boys, but did not pass the qualifying exam- **778**
Col. Thaddeus- his regt. was prob. stat., Oct. 1776, at the "saw pits", Rye, N. Y.- **752**

COOLEY,
Dr.- res. W. part of Benson, Vt.; Sat., Aug. 13, 1853, a small barn on his land, filled w. hay, was struck by lightning & totally consumed- **996**
Seth- res. Hartford, N. Y.; Colporteur, American Tract Society, for Saratoga & Wash. co.; m. Mary, dau. Deac. James Ingalsbe; his wf. d. Jan. 23, 1854, at 39 yrs., 2 mos., of typhus fever- **1024**

COON,
John- c. 1850, res. Fitch's Point, Salem, N. Y.; his house loc. on Black creek, opp. Ezra Turner's- **863**
Rufus- relates some particulars to Dr. Fitch, May 25, 1858, abt. St. John Honeywood, while the 2 men were en route to the funeral of Capt. Daniel McDonald; as a boy, he was sent to Honeywood by his schoolmaster, to retrieve copies he had agreed to make for penmanship students, & he recoll. that Honeywood wrote the copies "rapidly, w/o ruling the paper- yet they were as elegant as cooper- plate engravings"- **1033**
Thomas- res. Salem, N. Y.; m. Sarah, dau. Elijah Mack- **731**; m. Jane, dau. Elijah & Martha (McCollister) Mack- **734**

COOPER,
Ann- of Pennsylvania; m. Phineas Whiteside; 6 of her 7 children were b. in Pennsylvania prior 1764, the yr. that the family rem. Cambridge Patent- **805**
Family- of Salem, N. Y.; ments. bros. George & John, rem. Sterling, N. Y.; ea. bro. had a dau. who m. a son of Hugh Harsha- **973**
George- res. Sterling, N. Y.; dau. m. Elias, s. Hugh & Mary (McWhorter) Harsha- **973**
James Fenimore- (1789- 1851) his portrayal of Ethan Allen & others of "this class of persons", observes John L. Marsh, could not so easily be appl. to the 'Neutral Ground' around N. Y., for, acc. Marsh, "they were prepared to be patriots or loyalists, & come under a republic or a monarchy, as their own self- interest might require"- **967**

John- res. Eagle Bridge, along the Hoosick river, abt. 2 mi. above Tyashoke, N. Y.; ments. s. Samuel, m. Wealthy Wells; & a dau., m. Edmund Wells- **839**

John- of Salem; res. Sterling, N. Y.; dau. m. John, s. Hugh & Mary (McWhorter) Harsha- **973**

Mr.- ment. as the murder victim, in a fragm. of a fictitious newspaper article (n. d.), entitled 'A Down- East Juryman'- **1090frag**

Samuel- s. John; m. Wealthy Wells; rem. Chatauqua, N. Y., along w. his bro.- in-law, Edmund Wells; he afterw. rem. Quincy, Illinois, "where he soon d. of the fever of the country", leaving several children- **839**

CORBETT,
Family- res. a mi. S. of Joseph Heath's house, Jackson, N. Y.- **853**

CORBIN,
Mary- m. Jacob, Jr., eldest s. Jacob & Lucy (Howard) Allen; prob. at Sturbridge, Mass.- **758**

CORNELL,
Alvin- (s. Paul & Elizabeth Soule) res. at the head of Seneca Lake; imprisoned for killing his wf.- **806**

Dr. B. F.- (Cornells) c. 1848/9, res. along the w. side of the Hudson, Moreau, N. Y.; m. sist. Martin F. Thompson; one winter, at abt. this time, 2 strangers left their teams w. him & began cutting holes in the river ice to examine the bottom w. poles, saying that a cannon being transported during the Rev. war had accidentally sunk in the area; the 2 men had been promised $250.00 by a NYC museum for the cannon's recovery, but they never returned to attempt any further salvage effort- **959**

David- Quaker; b. England; emig. w. his parents, & m. dau. James Allen, prob. at Bedford, or Dartmouth, Mass.; settl. Walloomsac Patent bef. the Rev. war; c. 1778, rem. Easton, N. Y.; ments. sons Paul, m. 1. Elizabeth Soule; 2. ____ Wells; & Thomas; he d. & was bur. in Easton, on the grounds of the Quaker meeting house- **806**

MacDonald- (s. Paul & ____ Wells; c. 1870, res. E. Greenwich, & c. 1871, res. Cambridge, N. Y.; "landlord (very popular) at White Creek some yrs."; ments. s. Walter- **806**

Matthew- Cambridge, N. Y., Mar. 4, 1807, cut his throat w. a knife- **(L)- 876**

Paul, Esq.- (s. David & ____ Allen) b. Sept. 16, 1759, Dartmouth, Mass.; res. Little White Creek, N. Y.; his memory "considerably impaired w. age", informs Dr. Fitch, Nov. 15, 1849, concerning his family origins & Quaker settlm. in the area during the Rev. war; m. 1. Elizabeth, dau. Esq. Timothy Soule, in 1779; 2. dau. Daniel Wells, & wid. Esq. Raleigh, on Dec. 2, 1804; children by 1st wf.- Mary, m. John Osborn; Hannah, m. John Stevens; Alvin; Hiram, drowned; Hiram, 2nd; by 2nd wf.- Walter R., MacDonald (prob. Thomas McDonough); Elizabeth, m. ____ Palmer; Maria, m. David Niles; 1778, he rem. Easton, N. Y., & res. there

until 1800, & then returned to Lot No. 15, subdivision Lot No. 3, Walloomsac
Patent; d. 1851, at 92; see Vol. 4- **806**; informs concerning tradit. accts. of Esq.
(John) Munro. of Shaftsbury hollow- **807**; m. Abigail, dau. Daniel Wells, as her
2nd husb.- **841**

Thomas- (s. David & ____ Allen) c. 1777, rem. from Walloomsac Patent to Easton,
N. Y.- **806**

Walter R.- (s. Paul & ____ Wells) was once Deputy Sheriff, Wash. co., N. Y.; land
agent, 1872, Chicago, Illinois- **806**

CORNWALLIS,
Maj. Gen. Lord Charles- (1738- 1805) notice of his surrender sent to the British
commander at Crown Point by a packet from Lord Striling, late fall 1781- **750**;
brief ment.- **1010**

Coroner's Inquests- in Wash. co., N. Y.; 29 cases, 1787- 1810, labeled a- z, & aa-
cc; Coroners- Benajah Hill- Hartford & Whitehall; Alex. McNish- Hartford,
Salem; Elisha Forbes- Argyle, Easton; Peter B. Tearse- Queensbury; Ozias
Colman, Jr.- Westfield; John Perigo- Skenesborough (Whitehall); Argyle- Adiel
Sherwood, Wm. Stevenson; Cambridge- Barnabus Smith, Joshua Conkey, James
Gilmore; Salem- Hamilton McCollister, Joshua Conkey, James Gilmore, Robert
Pennel; lists decedent, date of inquest, loc., statement of cause, & coroner- **(L)- 876**

COTTRELL,
____- (Cotterel) m. Martha Lucy, dau. Josephus & Lucy (Palen) Martin- **731**
John- wealthy farmer; res. 2 mi. S. of Union Village (Greenwich), Easton, N. Y.;
m. Betsey, dau. Capt. Abner & Miriam (Martin) Dwelly- **731**
Nathan-def. witn., People vs. Martin Wallace; testif. that he had known Wallace
for 4- 5 yrs., employed him, & had pd. him abt. $80 during the time he worked for
him, & had no means of knowing much abt. his general character- **1048s**

COULTER,
John T.- oath of alleg.; Co. D, 22nd N. Y. Inf.- **(L)- 1074**

Counterfeiting- letter to N. Y. council, Nov. 24, 1772, from John Munro, Esq.,
stating that he has in custody 'the stamps, moulds, mills, & several other materials
for coining of dollars (dated 1760) & one dated 1768, one crown piece dated 1752,
& one dollar dated 1766 which are all counterfeited'; these found in the possession
of John Searls, of Arlington, & Comfort Carpenter, of Shaftsbury, Vt.; both were
sent to jail by escort of 2 constables, w. Carpenter escaping on the same night they
were sent; while one constable hunted for him, the other, after being delayed 10
days on the road, released Searls; their confessions revealed a line of counterfeiters
from N. J. to Co- os (Vt., or Coos co., N. H.?) & provided him w. a list (not given)
of 17 names; he has 'sent constables to arrest them, but know it will not be done';
refers pgs. 97- 99, Duer's Life of Stirling- **912**

COUNTY OFFICIALS- for Charlotte co.; appt. by N. Y. Provincial Convention, May 8, 1777- Sheriff- Edward Savage; 1st Judge- William Duer, Esq.; Assist. Judges- John Williams, William Marsh; Clerk- Ebenezer Clark- **787**; for Wash. co., 1815; names of those appt. Mar. 3rd, incl. 9 Judges, & 11 Assist. Judges; Justices of Peace- Salem- 8; Argyle- 10; Greenwich- 7; Hebron- 7; Cambridge- 6; Hartford- 6; U. S. Dist. Atty.- Roger Skinner; see also, Charlotte co., & Wash. co., N. Y.- **711**

COUZEN,
William?- owned 10 acres, Lots 270 & 271, Turner's Patent, excepted from purch. of Asa Estee, Sept. 20, 1784, from John Law- **(L)- 936b**

Coventry, Vt.- loc. Rutland co.; name later changed to Dorset, Vt.- **964**

COVILL,
Family- U. S. refugee of Rev. war; their name incl. on U. E. loyalist list, entitling them to 200 acres of land in Canada- **991**

COWAN,
Hugh R.- of Salem, N. Y.; his s. James, d. Dec. 2, 1862- **1081**; former Wash. co. Sheriff- **1098**
James- s. Hugh R.; Co. H, 123rd NYSV; d. Dec. 2, 1862, at 20, of typhoid fever, Harper's Ferry, Va.; bur. Dec. 6, gr. 6, soldier's plot, Evergreen Cemetery, Salem, N. Y.- **1081**; same material- **1098**
Sheriff- of Wash. co.; provided the biog. material concerning Martin Wallace, in an article giving an acct. of his execution; refers Dec. 7, 1858, Salem Press- **1050s**

COWDEN,
____- c. 1851, res. Fitch's Point, Salem, N. Y., in the house orig. occ. by Ezra Turner- **863**
Maj. James- d. July 30, 1800, at 65- **(L)- 975**
Maj.- officer, 1781, Col. Walbridge's militia regt.- **749**

COWN,
____- of Union Village (Greenwich, N. Y.); m. dau. Hon. John Younglove- **843**

CRAIG,
Family- c. 1798, res. S. of Bunnel Payne, & N. of the Barns family, on the W. side of the Hudson, opp. Ft. Miller, N. Y.- **804**
Jane- m. Andrew, s. Andrew & Nancy (Stewart) Lytle- **1069**
Molly- m. John, eldest s. James Harsha, the emig.- **973**

CRAFTS,
William- m. Martha, dau. Oliver & Susan (Pendergrass) Whiteside; their only child, Willard, a merch. at Mayville, N. Y.- **805**

CRAMER,
____- of Granville, N. Y.; m. Elizabeth, dau. Hon. Nathaniel & Cynthia (Mason) Hall- **759s**
Conrad, Sr.- of Saratoga (Schuylerville, N. Y.); dau. Elizabeth, m. Thomas, s. Phineas & Ann (Cooper) Whiteside- **805**

CRANDALL,
Dr.- was called in to consult w. Dr. Mack, in the case of Patrick Walls, c. 1854/5, when his condition worsened into an inflammation of the lungs, foll. his recuperation from an accident that occurred while he was working for Archibald Hay- **1058**
Elias P.- (Crandell) Co. A, 2nd N. Y., Northern Black Horse, Cav., 1861- 2- **1080**

CRANE,
Rev. Abijah- m. Hannah E., dau. Rev. Nathaniel & Hannah (Emerson) Hall; his wf. d. June 12, 1846, at 67, Clinton, N. Y.- **759s**

CRARY,
Hon. John. Esq.- (1782- 1872) offered a voluntary toast, to the clergy of our country, Nov. 29, 1814, Salem, N. Y., at a public banquet honoring Commodore Macdonough- **709**; res. Salem; Walter Martin, Jr., studied law under his direction- **730**

CRAW,
Volney- Co. A, 2nd N. Y., Northern Black Horse, Cav., 1861- 2- **1080**

CRAWFORD,
____- m. Triphena, dau. William & Triphena (More) Bemis; res. 2 mi. W. of Saratoga Springs, N. Y., in the same area as his wf.'s bro. John; one of their sons was a Methodist minister- **851**
James M.- 2nd Lt., 93rd N. Y. Inf.- **1090b**

CREIGER,
Hans Jerry- an inhabitant under the proprietors of Hoosic Patent; turned out of his lands & tenements, prob. July 26, 1764, by the N. H. people; his cattle were driven off, a parcel of Indian corn taken, & he was compelled to pay $45 for redeeming his cattle- **892**

CRIMINAL OFFENDERS-

Nov. 24, 1772- John Munro, Esq.'s letter of this date notes the apprehension of John Searls & Comfort Carpenter, along w. the confiscation of counterfeiting devices, & the disclosure of a line of counterfeiters from N. J. to Co- os; see Counterfeiters- **912**;

Oct. 1780- Thomas Beaty, Jr., fined £ 4 for breach of peace, by assaulting Alex. McNees, & ordered to pay court costs, standing committed until pd.; Alex. McNees, sentenced to 'The like'; refers § 258, Vol. 1;

Jan. 7, 1789- John Wiser Wheeler, for knowingly & feloniously passing counterfeit bill of credit, sentenced to be 'branded on his left cheek w. the letter C w. a Red Hot Iron, & that he be committed to the bridewell of the City of N. Y. during his life; & there be confined to hard labor, under the direction of the Mayor, Alderman & commonality of the sd. City'; Thomas Burrell, for petit larceny, sentenced to be taken to the public whipping post & there receive 'thirty lashes on his bare back from the waist upwards';

Jan. 8, 1789- Edmund Hunt, for perjury, committed to custody of Wash. co. Sheriff for 6 mos., 'w/o bail or mainprize', & that he 'stand upon the pillory for the space of one hr. betw. the hrs. of 9 o'clock in the forenoon & 3 of the clock in the afternoon of the 9th day of Inst. month of Jan. at the town of Salem in the co. of Wash'.; Squire Haskins, for perjury, given 'The like Judgement in all things'- **877**; 3rd Tues., Dec. 1811- Dr. Isaac Baldwin Clary, indicted for digging up "a dec'd. black woman named Peggy", on Sept. 9, 1811, & dissecting her body; plead guilty; Robert Cook, Arnold Drake, & Benjamin Danielson, indicted & plead guilty concerning the same offense;

Jan. 14, 1812- Thomas Mitchell, of Hartford, N. Y., indicted, tried, & acquitted in the killing of Hannah Fanning by an axe blow to the side of her head- **874**;

1825, Salem, N. Y.- William Gordon sentenced to 14 yrs., Auburn state prison, for manslaughter, in the murder of George Coggshall, who d. Sept. 30, 1824; acc. *Wash. Co. Post*, on the evening of Sept. 5, 1824, in Salem, 'Gordon, Coggshall, & a number of others were assembled at the inn of Abraham Briggs. On that day, there had been a co. training in which Gordon had been engaged, & consequently he was in uniform, w. a sword suspended from his side. Gordon, being intoxicated, conducted improperly, & a number put him out of the room... He drew his sword & a scuffle ensued, during which Coggshall rec'd. a wound, in his abdomen, of which he died, Sept. 30th'; trial occurred over 2 days, Lathrop & Wendell for the prosecution, & Stevens, Russell, & Viele, for the defense- **808**; prev. to the construction of the jail, whipping & setting in stocks were the principal modes of punishment; an allusion given to one circumstance where a person, placed in the stocks, was pelted w. rotten eggs by a crowd that had gathered around; Dr. Fitch suppos. this may have been a sentence (§ 258) given out by Judge John Sloss Hobart (prob. betw. 1789- 97, for perjury- 'to stand upon the pillory for the spaceof an hr.'); besides Tucker, the only other person who res. Fitch's Point, & was ordered whipped by Moses Martin, Sr., was James Orr, for stealing- **868**

CRIPPEN,
Joseph- res. Granville, N. Y.; b. Nov. 23, 1753, Sharon, Conn.; during Rev. war, res. Alford, Berkshire co., Mass.; volunteered, late Aug. 1776, Capt. George King's Barrington militia co., Col. Fellow's regt.; sent to Dutchess, & then to Westchester co., N. Y.; stat. part of the time at Valentine's hill, & was then in the battle of White Plains; disch. & sent home foll. 4 mos. expiration; volunteered for 3½ mos. service, July/ Aug. 1777, Capt. Enoch Noble's co., Col. Ashley's regt.; arr. at Bennington a short time foll. the battle, & remained at Arlington, Vt., as a scout; rem. Stillwater, N. Y., & was present at Burgoyne's surrender; officers witn. during service- Col. Seth Warner, Capt. Brown; "was out several other times, scouting & hunting tories"- 755

CROCKER,
Ephriam- c. 1798, res. N. above the Potter family "in the old red house which he so long occ.", Ft. Miller, N. Y.; he was a bro.- in- law of ____ Seelye; see Vol. 1- **804**
Family- of Ft. Miller, N. Y.; every spring, they would go down to NYC on their rafts of lumber, along w. the Paynes, & Ebenezer Bacon; while Bacon, who was worth more than any of them, wore ordinary clothes, the Crockers & Paynes would dress all in the best style, having their boots blacked at every hotel they lodged in on the way- **933**
Col. John S.- (J. S.) def. atty., along w. James Gibson & H. K. Sharpe, People vs. Martin Wallace, Oct. 1- 7, 1858- **1048s**; commandant of the militia, he requisitioned 4 area militia companies to preserve order on Dec. 1st, the day of Wallace's execution, in Salem, N. Y.- **1050s**; commander, 93rd N. Y. (Morgan Rifles) Inf.- **1090b**; he & Maj. Cassidy passed by their outer pickets, Apr. 26, 1862, & were capt. by the enemy; cowardice, rather than desertion, stands as the prevailing sentiment for their leave taking, as an expected bloody battle was in the offing; both were exchanged the foll. summer- **1094**

CRONAN,
1st Lt. D. E.- Co. A, 2nd N. Y., Northern Black Horse, Cav., 1861- 2- **1080**

CRONK,
Family- tory; res. Hoosick, N. Y., during the Rev. war; the men of the family were recruited by old 'Festus' to go into Col. Baum's camp & fight at Bennington for the royalist cause- **768**; their connections, & those of the Bovee family, were numerous in Hoosick, & all of them were lead away by Festus to fight against the country- **769**
Orra- Sgt., Hoosic militia co., Aug. 1777; "was an irresolute man- & knew not what to do in these critical times"; Col. Fister (Festus) determined that Cronk's Capt. was not firm, & might be induced to join the British, so he persuaded Cronk to invite him to join w. the other tories; when he gave this invitation to Capt. Brewer, he was warned that the remainder of the co. had already decided to join the Americans at Bennington, & as their Sgt., he should come w. the others;

finally, he returned to Col. Fister for advice, & was persuaded to rejoin the tories, while Fister set abt. arresting & confining Capt. Brewer bef. the battle- 770; although he went into the British camp w. Col. Fister, "he was a timorous, irresolute man"; stat. at a breastwork down river below where Esq. Barnet's house was later loc., an American party advanced to attack the works, & he became horrified as the bullets flew thicker & thicker; a large tub or cask, in which bread had been brought to the soldiers, stood empty behind the breastworks, & he surreptitiously inched his way towards it during the attack, upending it over himself; when firing ceased in the area, he discovered that the works had been evac. & he was alone in it; he then made for the woods & took a straight course home, having had enough of war- 771
Solomon- res. Cambridge, N. Y.; he m. 2 sisters, & res. a wk. alternately w. ea., having 13 children by ea. wf.; their houses were not very far apart, & the sisters "maintained the utmost harmony & affection" towards ea. other concerning the arrangement; d. Nov. 1815, "of a wnd. in the hand, by the cut of a scythe, which occasioned a mortification"; his funeral was attended by both wives & all 26 children- 720

CRONKHITE,
Teunis- res. on the N. side of the Hoosick river, abt. ¾ mi. from Buskirk's Bridge on the road to Eagle Bridge, White Creek, N. Y.; betw. 8 & 9:00 PM on the night of Barney McEntee's murder, Feb. 16, 1858, Hiram Sisson arr. at his house & brought him back to the murder scene, where he testif. that they found var. bloodstained pieces of bark & wood that were retrieved by Uriah Colony as evidence; he did not remain at the scene, but went to assist in Martin Wallace's arrest on suspicion of the crime- **1048s**

CROSBY,
Edward M.- merch., Plattsburgh, N. Y.; m. Caroline H., dau. Hon. Wm. Henry & Harriet (Blin) Parker- **759s**
J. B.- witn., Dec. 1, 1858, certif. of execution for Martin Wallace- **1050s**

CROSS,
Ichabod- c. 1769, res.Walloomsac Patent; he had settl. & improved part of Samuel Gardenier's lands, under N. H. title; the two entered into an agreem. of arbitration, & it was determined that he should receive £ 25 for half of his improved land & lease the other half for 5 yrs., & then surrender it to Gardenier; while he was pd. £ 15 on the released half, he declined payment of the remainder, & Gardenier's neighbors soon sd. that he had better leave, as "no Yorker would be allowed to live there in peace"; Cross expected to retrieve all of his improved lands, & the Bennington people soon took up his cause, demanding that Gardenier give up the writings that Cross had given him, give a £ 1,000 bond to Cross until the papers were retrieved, & that he be allowed to enjoy his lands as bef. the arbitration; he often informed Gardenier that if any N. H. settlers were taken to Albany jail in

connection w. the matter, 'they would raise a mob & go in a body to Albany, break open the gaol there & take them out'; see Grants, N. H. Controversy; & Vermonters- **902**

CROWL,
Alvin- c. 1850, res. nr. the Red Bridge, Salem, N. Y., on the orig. homesite of James Dobbin- **732**

Crown Point, N. Y.- American forces retreated w. Gen. Arnold from the St. Lawrence river valley, & remained here & at Mt. Independence for the summer, 1776- **748**; the American army left the fortifications here for Canada, & the taking of St. John's, late spring, 1775; notice of Cornwallis' surrender was sent by packet from Lord Stirling to the British forces stat. here, late fall 1781- **750**; Col. Benedict Arnold sent 2 letters from here, the 1st, dated May 23, 1775, indicated nearly 70 men stat. here, & 80 more recently added, along w. a sloop & schooner, as well armed as possible; foll. news of Col. Ethan Allen's retreat from St. John's; Arnold states his intention to make a stand here against possible attempts by the enemy to recapt. it, in order to secure the cannon capt. here & at Ft. Ticonderoga; he notes plenty of ball, of var. types, but only 150 lbs. of powder, w. necessity for more, & desires 4- 500 wt., as of 26 barrels here, not one lb. is good- **774**; acc. Col. Arnold's May 19, 1775 letter to Cambridge, Mass., Comm. of Safety, "111 cannon, howitzers & c. (some bad & useless)" were capt. here- **775**; Capt. Ebenezer Allen's co. employed in its capt. during the taking of Ticonderoga; his co. payroll presented to Albany Comm., June 17, 1776- **890**; letter to Col. John Reid, Apr. 7, 1772, recommending its loc. for site of Charlotte co. Courthouse, as being centrally loc., w. access to waters & an armed garrison nearby to enforce the law- **904**; Gen. Haldimand notes to N. Y. Gov., Sept. 1, 1773, that "Crown Point is entirely destroyed & Ti in ruins", when commenting upon prospective sites for loc. regular troops to enforce order in the Grants- **909**; Sept. 29, 1773, Gen. Haldimand proposes a 200 man force be sent here & to Ticonderoga, withdrawing 150 men on Nov. 1st, "as not more than 50 can be sheltered there in a winter at present"; nevertheless, N. Y. Council deems the season too late to send the required force, & postpones the measure- **910**; report of a party seen surveying lands within the vicinity, Sept. 1762, under authority of N. H.- **928**

CROZIER,
_____- gr.20, soldier's plot, Evergreen Cemetery, Salem, N. Y.; see James A., Vol. 3- **1081**
James- c. 1850, rem. Wisc.; m. Susan, dau. James & Rebecca (Lytle) Mills- **737**
John- occ. the farm 1st settl., c. 1767, by David Webb, Turner's Patent (Salem, N. Y.)- **738**

CRUGER,

John Harris- deed of George Stuart, May 8, 1766, to William Malcom, acknowl. bef. him; also, deed of Francis Panton to Michael Hoffnagle; both recorded Jan. 3, 1776- **(L)- 936**

CULVER,

____- m. Mary, dau. Jonathan & ____ Fitch; his wid. res. w. her sist., wid. ____ Rathbun, Brooklyn, N. Y.- **799**
____- of Greenwich, N. Y.; member, c. 1861, 11th Illinois Inf.- **1080**
Hon. Erastus Dean- (1803- 1889; N. Y. Assembly, 1838- 40; 29th Congress, 1845-47; City Judge, Brooklyn, 1854- 61; appt. Minister Resident to Venezuela, 1862-66; d. Greenwich, N. Y., & bur. in Culver vault) of Brooklyn, N. Y.; lawyer; George West Parker practiced in partnership w. him bef. entering the firm of Benedict & Co.- **759s**

Cumberland Co., N. Y.- John Hazeltine, Paul Spooner, & William Williams, its delegation to N. Y. Provincial Congress, seated June 21, 1775- **777**;org. Aug. 22, 1775, along w. Charlotte & Gloucester counties, into one brigade of state militia- **782**; formed into a separate militia brigade, Aug. 1, 1776, along w. Gloucester co., foll. reorganization of militia- **785**; Dr. Peletiah Fitch, appt. 1st Judge, co. circuit, Aug. 18, 1778- **838**; Gov. Moore notes its creation, in a June 9, 1767 letter to Lord Shelburne, w. every priviledge except representation in the Legislative Assembly, which its inhabitants refused, due to expense; a 600 man militia regt. org.- **894**; its N. Y. Assembly members; 3rd session, 1779- Micah Townsend, Elkanah Day, John Sessions; 4th, 5th, & 6th sessions- William Shattuck, Joel Biglo, Elijah Proughty (Prouty)- their individual terms of service not stipulated- **993**

Currency- "shinplaisters", of "shinplasters"; partially circulated, summer 1862, when silver change began disappearing & postage were issued as replacements, "the city shopmen doing up these stamps in small envelopes, of 25 or 50 cents in a package"; by Sept., shinplasters were in considerable use in the city, but silver was still circulating in the country; in Nov., the R. R. issued 5¢ shinplasters, & Troy, Albany, & other city corporations issued 25 & 50¢ bills- **1099**

CURTENIUS,

Peter T.- appt. Commissary, N. Y. Province, June 2, 1775, by Provincial Congress; directed to purch. stores & c. in NYC, for shipment to the north- **776**; by Gen. Schuyler's request, July 31, 1775, 'directed to get coarse cloth for making 225 green coats faced w. red & tents for accomodating 225 men' for the Green Mtn. regt.- **781b**; plaintiff, Oct. 19, 1774, vs. Jacobus Abeel- **878**

CURTIS,
____- res. Ashville, N. Y.; m. Elizabeth, dau. Edmund Henry & Hepzibah (Buel) Wells; 2 or 3 children- **839**
Ashbill- deed witn., Mar. 25, 1772, James, John, & Amos McKenney, quit claim to Michael Hoffnagle- **(L)- 936**
Daniel- of Granville, N. Y.; c. 1782, purch. Lots 9 & 12, Morrison's Patent, from John Williams & Joseph McCracken, for £ 7 4s 2d- **(L)- 936b**
David- of Granville, N. Y.; Lots 9 & 12, Morrison's Patent, conveyed to him, Apr. 13, 1783, by John Williams & Joseph McCracken- **(L)- 936**
Lois- native of Woodbury, Conn.; m. Samuel, s. Samuel & Abigail (Backus) Standish, prob. in Pawlet, Vt.- **757**
Martha- m. Luther, s. Peter & Esther (Clark) Parker- **759s**
Mary- of Moriah, N. Y.; m. Heman Ferris, s. Daniel & Ann (Glover) Barton- **1093**
Sarah- m. Joseph, 2nd s. John & Hannah (Basset) Parker- **759s**

CUSHMAN,
Hon. John P.- of Troy, N. Y.; c. 1830's, Hon. John Mason Parker studied law in his office- **759s**

CUTCHET,
Duncan- Argyle, N. Y., June 22, 1802, fell from a sawmill into Moses kill & drowned; Elisha Forbes, Coroner- **(L)- 876**

CUYLER, see also, *KUYLER/ KYLER,*
Family- or Van Cuyler; res. Walloomsac Patent bef. Rev. war- **806**
Family- res. nr. Moses kill, prior 1798, in the same loc. where Samuel Berry kept tavern- **804**
Henry- res. Greenbush, N. Y.; m. Catharine ____; their s. Henry, res. Maidstone, England- **934**; his wid. sold all of the extensive remains of their property in the Ft. Miller, N. Y. area to Gerrit Pebbles; they had 3 sons- one was killed, 1812, on the Niagara frontier while in the American army (see Vol. 1), & the other two became British officers "in India & c."; one of these two sons never married, but the other had a son, "a little, insignificant, drunken, worthless fellow" who came to res. in Ft. Miller for a few yrs. recently (c. 1854) on some inherited land,"having his courtezan w. him"; his property was soon squandered & he returned to England; he used to visit his relative, Mrs. LeRoy, of NYC, until she forbid him to come anymore- **1032**
Henry- of Maidstone, Kent co., England; Sept. 15, 1818, appt. William Duer, of Albany, N. Y., as his atty., to receive his legacies by the last Will of his father, Henry, late of Greenbush, N. Y., mother Catharine, & his aunt, Elizabeth Van Courtland, of NYC; refers p. 301, Miscellanies- **934**
Henry, Esq.- his youngest dau., Elizabeth, m. John Sproull- **(L)- 932**
Capt. Ralph Burton- d. Mar. 5, 1817, at 34- **(L)- 932**

D

Dacota Territory- c. 1861, Ft. Randall, garrisoned by Federal troops; Co. A- C, 14th Iowa Inf., arr. Dec. 5th, to replace the "regulars", moved into the fort on Dec. 7th, & served there throughout the foll. yr.; c. 1863, Ft. Sally being constructed nr. Farm Island, prob. known later as Ft. Pierre; territorial capital, Vermillion; see S. Dakota- **1089**

DAHN,
J.- tobacconist; res. Whitehall, N. Y.; his business was destroyed by a fire in the Myers block, Jan. 30, 1854, at a $2,500 loss, no insurance- **1023**

Dam Wars- colloq.; controversies occurring in some area communities w. respect to probable health risks caused by the raising of dams, or flooding of land parcels beyond those reserved for the flow, w. one party favoring the raising of sd. dams & ano. urging their removal; ment (n. d.) on the Owlkill, Cambridge, N. Y., & later, c. 1850, at Ft. Miller; the death of Archibald McCollister (§ 188) attrib. to a malignant fever caused in one instance of a dam raising nr. Salem; see Vol. 1- **844**

DANA,
Rev. John F.- of Canaan, N. Y.; m. Abigail M., dau. Andrew & Elizabeth (Martin) Freeman; she d. July 17, 1849, leaving 2 children- Elizabeth & Stephen- **730**
Capt. William G.- "one of the oldest & most respected American citizens of our state" (California); eldest dau., Eliza Josefa, m. Judge Henry H., s. David & ____ (Woodard) Tefft- **971**

DANFORTH,
Jonathan E.- m. Lucinda C., dau. Aaron, Jr., & Artemsia (Lynn) Martin; he divorced her, leaving a son, Henry; & she m. 2. ____ Birch- **731**
P. H.- Co. A, 2nd N. Y., Northern Black Horse, Cav., 1861- 2- **1080**

DARROW,
Hiram- of Cambridge, N. Y.; juror, Oct. 1- 7, 1858, People vs. Martin Wallace- **1048s**
Jedidiah- of Black Creek (Hebron, N. Y.) purch. 73 acre tract from Bernard Lyntott, & May 13, 1785, deeded same to Daniel Whedon- **(L)- 936**; noted that same tract was sold to Whedon for £ 80- **(L)- 936b**

DARTMOUTH,
Lord William Legge- Colonial Secretary; a lengthy letter written to him by Gov. Tryon, July 1, 1773, in response to his proposals for settling & adjusting the dispute w. N. H.- **913**

DAVENPORT,
____- res. Illinois; m. Mary Esther, dau. Thomas & Amelia (Lewis) Fitch- **799**

DAVIS,
____- m. Sarah, dau. Hezekiah & Jerusha (Burr) Fitch; no children- **799**
James- d. Dec. 25, 1825, at 66- **(L)- 772**
John- plaintiff, May 19, 1774, vs. Samuel Hinman- **878**

DAY,
Olive- m. Reuben, s. Joseph & Abigail (Warren) Cheney- **1083**

DAYTON,
____- res. Litchfield, Conn.; m. Aurelia, dau. Jonathan & ____ (Stone) McNeil;
her bro. John's son, George, was sent to live w. them foll. his mother's death,
c. 1813; abt. 2 yrs. later, his sist. Elizabeth was also sent there; this family finally
rem. Chenango Point (Binghamton, N. Y.) but it was eventually concluded,
c. 1816/7, that Elizabeth should return & res.w. her father in Stillwater, N. Y.- **951**
Jehial- char. witn., Rev. war pens. appl., Samuel Standish of Granville, N. Y.- **747**

DEAL,
Bastian- noted by Harmanus Schuyler that he & Peter Vaſs (Voss) were focibly
turned out of possession of their lands within N. Y. Province, held by them for
upwards of 30 yrs., under the pretense the land was in N. H.; in his undated letter
to N. Y. Council, Sheriff Schuyler notes that Samuel Ashley, Samuel Robinson,
John Horfort, & Isaac Charles were apprehended by him in connection w. the
ejection of Deal & Voss from their lands- **885**; particulars of Schuyler's letter
indicate the apprehension of Ashley & others prob. occurred July 30, 1764- **892**

DEAN,
Family- c. 1850, res. Eaton co., Michigan; their s. Jonathan, m. Elizabeth Munroe;
& their s. David, who res. Wayne co., m. Catherine Munroe- **812**
Mary- by an act passed Feb. 10, 1797, the Feb. term of Wash. co. courts was moved
from Adiel Sherwood's, in Ft. Edward, to her home in Kingsbury, N. Y.; refers
Laws of N. Y., iii, 217; court convened here for the 1st time on the 2nd Tues., Feb.
1788- **874**

DEKLYN
Leonard- deed witn., Mar. 25, 1772; James, John, & Amos McKenney quit claim
to Michael Hoffnagle- **(L)- 936**

DELANCEY,
James- (the elder; 1732- 1800) c. 1767, for £ 300, sold 318 acres of Walloomsac
Patent to Samuel Gardenier- **902**

Hon. James- (1703- 1760; Lt. Gov., 1753- 55; 1757- 60) noted, c. 1753, as Lt. Gov., Province of N. Y.- **883**; iss. a proclamation, Sept. 21, 1759, inviting settlers to loc. on lands in the vicinity of Ft. Edward & Wood Creek, "as the forts now erecting there, will protect them from hostile incursions of the enemy from Canada"- **928**

DELANO,
Samuel- m. Elizabeth, dau. Alexander Standish- **757**

DELAWARE- 949b, 1056; Wilmington- 950; Delaware river- 949b

DeMOND,
____- abt. 1790, purch. Archibald McNeil's place at Ft. Miller bridge (Northumberland, N. Y.), & kept the ferry there until after the bridge was built (n. d.) by the turnpike co.; he sold out to Van Tuyl- **804**

DENMARK- 759s; King of- 1075b

DENNIS,
____- res. New London, Conn.; m. Prudence, dau. William & Lucinda (Conkey) Fitch- **730**

DENTON-
Catherine- of Orange Co., N. Y.; m. Prof. Wm. Henry, s. John C. & Susan (Mason) Parker, as his 2nd wf.- **759s**

DeRIDDER,
Brig. Gen.- his orders rec'd. Tues., Sept. 6, 1814, for the militia of Salem, N. Y. to rendezvous at Ft. Miller & proceed N.- **706**
Killian- c. 1770's, Commissioner, along w. Jan Winne & Abram Jacob Lansing, for the division of Schuyler's Patent- **935**
Simon- res. Easton, N. Y.; his slave, Pomp, accidentally drowned in late Dec. 1801, along w. a slave of John P. Becker- **(L)- 876**

DeROGUERS,
Chief- m. Eunice, dau. Rev. John Williams, who was taken captive Feb. 29, 1704, at Deerfield, Mass.; they had 3 children- Catharine, Mary, & John- **1016**
Mary- (dau. Chief DeRoguers & Eunice Williams) she d. when her s. Thomas was an inf., & he was raised by her sist. Catharine; see Williams, Thomas (DeRoguers)- **1016**

DEVENPORT,
____- res. Rock river, Illinois; m. Mary Esther, dau. Thomas & ____ (Hill) Fitch; 3 sons- Charles, Thomas, & ____; & 2 daus., names not recoll.; & he d. ca. 1841-**940**

DEWEY,
T.- Methodist; c. 1798, his expulsion of ____ Ballard from the conference lead Lorenzo Dow to suspect that he would be scolded for his own conduct in preaching, but at their meeting, Dow discovered an unexpected advocate- **813**; Apr./ May 1798, he was 'exhorting' a gathering in Easton, N. Y., when a flash of forked lightning pierced the air, & rolling thunder shook the house, leading some of those gathered to screech aloud, & others to jump from windows or run out of the door; a favorable change was then noted in the spiritual atmosphere of the vicinity; Nov. 20th, he & Lorenzo Dow visited the N. part of their circuit, traveling to Argyle, Thurman's Patent, & Queensbury, N. Y., & thence to Rutland, & Brandon, Vt., & other Vt. areas not ment. by name- **815**

DICK,
John- res. Hebron, N. Y.; member, Capt. Barns' Salem scout party-**1000**

DICKINSON,
____- (prob. Daniel Dickison; see Vol. 1) res. Stillwater, N. Y.; opearated a tanning & currying business during the Rev. war; his treatment of his apprentices was so severe that 5 of them, incl. Robert Ayres, ran away & enl., c. 1778, in Col. Marinus Willet's Regt.- **1054**
Daniel- c. 1850's, blacksmith, Stillwater, N. Y.; his sist. m., ____ Wilson, of Albany, as his 1st wf.- **1053**

DICKISON,
____- res. Busti, N. Y.; m. Pamilla, dau. Edmund Henry & Hepzibah (Buel) Wells; 3 or 4 children- **839**
____- res. Troy, N. Y.; was grds. Rev. Dickison, who preached Gov. Fitch's funeral sermon- **941**
John- of Troy, N. Y.; a perpetual rent to Phineas Whiteside's property, Cambridge Patent, was pd. to him, his heirs, or his executor, Mr. Gould- **805**
Rev.- preached the funeral sermon (c. 1775), of Gov. Thomas Fitch, of Conn.; his sermon later reprinted- **941**

DILLAWAY,
S. C.- char. witn., Rev. war pens. appl., Samuel Standish of Granville, N. Y.- **747**

DILLINGHAM,
Family- c. 1853, res. along the Indian river, on the R. R. right of way, below
Mark's corners, Vt.; their loc. was on the opp. side of the river from the Bardwell
& Church families- **1003**

DILLON,
Family- res. Fitch's Point, Salem, N. Y., & presently (1850) own the place once
occ. by Joseph Tucker- **863**

DIMMICK,
Capt.- c. 1832, stat. at Ft. Washington, nr. Wash., D. C.; he was ment. as an officer
who demoted Francis Pro for not joining a Temperance Society- **974**

DIMON,
Lt. John- of Stockbridge, Mass.; Capt. Rowley's co., Brown's regt., Gen. Fellow's
brigade; stat. at Ft. Ann, July 8, 1777- **747**

DINGBY,
John- (Dingley, acc. Savage) of Marshfield, Mass.; dau. Mary, m. abt. 1654, Ens.
Josiah, s. Capt. Miles Standish; & she d. the same yr. (acc. Savage, she "was bur. 1
July 1665... had sev. ch. by her & also by sec. w. Sarah")- **747**

DINWIDDIE,
____- English; was head clerk for Wm. Duer, Esq., at Ft. Miller, N. Y., bef. the
Rev. war; "well educ., a beautiful pen man & book- keeper"; in contrast to Pebbles
& others, his script was "as elegant as copper- plate engraving"; he continued in
his capacity until he d. unm., perh. 1787, but certainly bef. 1791, when Hugh
Pebbles rem. to a store in Half Moon, N. Y.- **1032**

District of Columbia- see WASHINGTON, D. C.

DOBBIN,
David- Irish; one of 6 bros. who fled the country foll. the rebellion of 1798; res.
2nd house on the road to Summit Lake, from the Anti- burgher church, S. Argyle,
N. Y.; m. 1. Miss Kay; 2. Miss Lowrie; had 5 children, the last 2 by his 2nd wf.-
1. John
2. Elizabeth, m. James Mains
3. Mary, m. ____ Harrison
4. Martha, unm.
5. Jane, m. ____ Telford- **732**
David- (s. William & Margaret Andrew) res. DeKalb co., Illinois; m. 1. Miss
Graham; 2. Miss French- **732**
Family- Irish; from "Bellinoany" (perh. Ballymoney), Co. Antrim; ments. 6 bros.,
who left the country in consequence of their participation in the rebellion of 1798;

they all settl. in the central part of Wash. co., N. Y.; they were members of the Anti- burgher, or Assoc. branch, of the Presbyterian church, & democrats politically-

1. William, eldest, m. Margaret Andrew
2. John, m. James McKellip
3. James
4. David, m. 1. ____ Kay; 2. ____ Lowrie
5. Miller, m. 1. Margaret Mains; 2. ____ Tinkey
6. Deac. Samuel, m. Sarah McNaughton- **732**

James- Irish; one of 6 bros. who fled the country foll. the rebellion of 1798; res. nr. the Red bridge, Salem, N. Y., the loc. presently (1850) occ. by Alvin Crowl; town constable, crier in the courts; "He was emasculated, & Abel, the father of David & James Cleveland, was by common consent, something more than a friend in the household"; d. some 20 yrs. ago, leaving wid. & several children, names & whereabouts unknown- **732**

James- (s. John & Jane McKellip) Preceptor, Salem Academy, 1849- 1854?; m. Miss L. Philips, whom he met when they were assistants in Union Village Academy; enl. 123rd NYSV (see Vol. 4) & was in the march through Georgia; served again as Preceptor, for 2 or 3 terms foll. the Civil war, & d. July 27, 1867- **732**

John- Irish; one of 6 bros. who fled the country foll. the rebellion of 1798; res. on the turnpike, nr. Collins' Tavern, Jackson, N. Y.; his farm, loc. a mi. up the Battenkill from Shushan, has the finest wooled flock of Saxony sheep to date (1850) in Wash. co.; cabinetmaker, "reputed one of the best workmen in the county"; m. Jane McKellip; children-

1. John McKellip, m. ____ Hubbard
2. David, m. & res. on his father's place
3. James, m. ____ Philips
4. Maria, m. Paschal D. More
5. Martha, m. her cousin, Joseph Dobbin
6. Sarah, unm.
7. Jane, unm.- **732**

John- (s. William & Margaret Andrew) cooper; res. several yrs. at the turnpike gate, Jackson, N. Y., & was the gatekeeper; spring 1850, rem. nr. Salem, N. Y., to become partner w. John Larkin; m. Rachel McLean- **732**

John- (s. David & ____ Kay) sawyer; res. Union Village (Greenwich, N. Y.)- **732**

John McKellip- (s. John & Jane McKellip) m. ____ Hubbard; keeps shoe shop, White Creek, N. Y.- **732**

Joseph- (s. William & Maragaret Andrew) m. his cousin, Martha Dobbin; owns Burnett's mills, on Black creek- **732**

Miller- Irish; one of 6 bros. who fled the country foll. the rebellion of 1798; res. abt. a mi. SW of Lakeville (nr. Cossayuna, N. Y.); m. 1. Margaret Mains; 2. ____ Tinkey; his children, all unm., res. at home- Samuel, Margaret, Jane, Eleanor; & by 2nd wf.- Sarah- **732**

Samuel- (s. William & Margaret Andrew) owns 140 acre farm, loc. W. end, Lot No. 33, Argyle Patent, Greenwich, N. Y.; m. Elizabeth Christie; 13 children- **732**
Deac. Samuel- Irish; youngest of 6 bros. who fled the country foll. the rebellion of 1798, & informs Dr. Fitch upon the family history; res. old Esq. McNaughton's place; m. Sarah McNaughton; children-
  1. Alexander; owns the lime kiln W. of Big Pond, Jackson, N. Y.
  2. Polly, unm.
  3. Eleanor, m. George Walker
  4. John, m. ____ Graham; res. w. his father
  5. James, res. Carter Street, i. e., the road from the Battenkill to McNab's (Cossayuna) Lake, Greenwich, N. Y.- **732**
William- Irish; eldest of 6 bros. who fled the country foll. the rebellion of 1798; res. a mi. down the Battenkill from Shushan, in Jackson, N. Y.; while res. in Ireland, m. Margaret Andrew; had 7 children who survived to maturity-
  1. Samuel, m. Elizabeth Christie
  2. John, m. Rachel McLean
  3. Joseph, m. his cousin, Martha Dobbin
  4. William, m. ____ Milliman
  5. David, m. 1. ____ Graham; 2. ____ French
  6. Jane, m. ____ McAllister
  7. Mary, m. ____ Nelson, & res. w. her father- **732**
William- (s. William & Margaret Andrew) res. NW Illinois; m. Miss Milliman, of Hoosick, N. Y.- **732**

DODD,
Henry- editor, *The Northern Post,* along w. David Rumsey; their partnership joined by James Stevenson, Jr., on June 6, 1814, who cont'd. w. Dodd foll. Jan. 1, 1815, when Rumsey left town; he then cont'd. in partnership w. Stevenson until shortly bef. his death; see Newspapers, & Vol. 1- **721**; his partnership w. Rumsey referred to- **1078**

Dodd & Rumsey- printers, Salem, N. Y.; principal writngs of Rev. Dr. Alexander Proudfit, D. D., publ. by them; on var. publications, appears 1799- 1801, as Henry Dodd; 1804- 1811, as Dodd & Rumsey; 1818, & 1825, as Dodd & Stevenson; & as Dodd & co., in 1822- **1082**

DOIG,
John- m. Margaret, dau. Deac. John & Eleanor (Webster) Steele; c. 1858, "she dead, & her children scattered"- **1047**
John S.- Co. A, 2nd N. Y., Northern Black Horse, Cav., 1861- 2- **1080**

DOLE,
James- defendant, Oct. 18, 1774, in a case brought by John McLean- **878**

DONAHUE,
Patrick- pseudonym for Priest Quigley; author, *The Cross & The Shamrock,* publ.
Boston, 1853; the full text of its sub- title- "or How to Defend the Faith, an Irish-
American Catholic tale of real life, descriptive of the temptations, sufferings, trials,
& triumphs of the children of St. Patrick in the great republic of Washington. A
book of the entertainment & special instruction of the Catholic male & female
servants of the United States"; see Priest Quigley- **1027**

DOOLITTLE,
_____- res. Burlington, Vt.; m. dau. Ephriam Fitch, of Algiers, Pawlet, Vt.- **727**

DORR,
Dr. Jonathan, Sr.- of Cambridge, N. Y.; his bro., Judge Joseph Dorr, of Hoosick,
N. Y.- **(L)**- 772; d. Apr. 22, 1825, at 65 yrs., 3 mos., & 22 ds.- **(L)**- **975**;d. White
Creek, N. Y., of palsy; his obit. notes perh. 1,000 people attended his funeral- **1029**
Joseph- b. 1760; d. 1830; was important in Hoosick, N. Y., as Co. judge "& c."-
(L)- 772

Dorset, Vt.- meeting held here at Cephas Kent's, July 9, 1775, to select officers of
the Green Mtn. regt.- **781b**; orig. named Coventry- **964**

DOTY,
Chillus- m. Feb. 6, 1790, Sarah, dau. Col. Adam & Abigail (Cheney) Martin;
children-
   1. child, b. Oct. 10, 1793, Duanesburg, N. Y.; was stillborn, or d. as inf.; refers
   Day Book, Dr. Asa Fitch, Sr.
   2. Stuben (Baron), b. Mar. 23, 1795; m. Esther, dau. Rev. James Murdock, of
   Martinsburg, N. Y.
   3. Lanada, b. June 6, 1797; d. June 8, 1798
   4. James Duane, b. Nov. 5, 1800; see Vol. 3; m. Sarah Collins, of Whitestown,
N. Y.; & their father d. Oct. 16, 1824, at 60- **730**; his wf. & Zerniah (Martin)
Conkey convey var. particulars of the Martin genealogy to Charles L. Martin for
his manuscript- **1037**; his wf. Sarah, d. Sept. 11, 1843- **1039**
Desire- (given as Doter; acc. Savage, dau. Edward, of the *Mayflower*)
m. 1. William Sherman; 2. Isreal Holms (Holmes); & 3. Alexander, s. Capt. Miles
Standish, as his 2nd wf., & d. 1723, Marshfield, Mass., having survived him; "she
named her children thus"- William Sherman, John Holmes, Isreal Holmes, Hannah
Ring, Experience Sherman, Desire Weston, & grdau. Desire Wermall; by her 3rd
husb., had Thomas, Ichabod, & Desire, b. 1698, Marshfield, Mass.- **757**
Family- ments. foll. 6 children-
   1. Chillus, m. Feb. 6, 1790, Sarah Martin
   2. John, Sheriff, Wash. co., N. Y.
   3. Philander, res. across Hudson river from Ft. Edward, N. Y.
   4. Prince, res. Duanesburg, N. Y.

5. Thuder, or Theodorus
6. Nancy, m. Nivium Frost- **730**

Isaac- b. ca. 1759; res. 2 mi. NE of N. Granville, N. Y.; an abstract of his Rev. war pension appl., sworn July 9, 1832; enl. late May 1775, Capt. McKinstry's co., Col. Pattison's regt., Mass. troops; Jan. 1776, marched to the Boston area; abt. Feb. 1st, re- enl. & marched towards Boston again; when news arr. the British had left Boston (prob. Mar.), they were marched to New London, Conn., & sailed from there to NYC; ordered to Canada a few wks. later, & arr. there the forepart of May, marched up the St. Lawrence, & engaged the enemy; his Capt. & many others taken prisoner, but soon released to Gen. Arnold; retreated to Crown Point & Mt. Independence, & remained there for the summer; Dr. Fitch suspects his co. was prob. sent to reinforce Maj. Butterfield at the Cedars; ordered S. in the fall, he took sick at Albany, N. Y., & returned home, his term expiring abt. Jan. 1, 1777, & he did not rejoin; answered militia call, July 1777, & was sent to Ft. Edward, & retreated to Stillwater, N. Y., again under Capt. McKinstry; was out w. militia at the fort, when Schoharie, N. Y. was burned by British & Indians (Oct. 16, 1780), & joined other troops on the Mohawk river, to pursue the enemy, giving 1- 2 mos. service here; in ano. yr., served 1 or 2 mos. at Cherry Valley; July- Dec. 1781, served 4 mos. w. Lt. John Spencer, Col. Willet's regt.; marched to German flats, pursuing the enemy & engaging w. them at W. Canada creek, & subsequently defeating them, "when the British Butler, of cruel memory was killed", & pursued them until nightfall; Dr. Fitch further notes that he never rec'd. a pension, & was of no relation to "old Sheriff" John Doty; ments. s. Levi- **748**

Gov. James Duane- (s. Chillus & Sarah Martin; Gov., Wisc. Territory, 1841- 44; 26th, 31st- 32nd Congress, 1839- 41, 1849- 53; Gov., Utah Territory, 1863- 65) b. Nov. 5, 1800; m. Sarah Collins, of Whitetown, N. Y.; children-

1. Charles, b. Aug. 2, 1824
2. James D., b. May 23, 1827
3. Amelia, now (c. 1850) dec'd.
4. Mary, b. Mar. 27, 1832; m. John Fitzergald; rem. Michigan, where he has been Gov.; res. Fond du Lac, Wisc.; was actively opposed in Wisc. politics by Lewis Martin, s. Walter & Sarah (Turner) Martin, but is now a member of Congress from Wisc., & later Gov., Utah; d. June 13, 1865, at Salt Lake City; see Vol. 3- **730**

Sheriff John- of Wash. co.; Dr. Fitch notes no relation betw. him & Isaac Doty of N. Granville, N. Y.- **748**

Rev. John F.- of Canaan, N. Y.; m. Abigail M., dau. Andrew & Elizabeth (Martin) Freeman; his wf. d. July 17, 1849, leaving 2 children- Elizabeth & Stephen- **730**

Levi- s. Isaac; res. 2 mi. NE of N. Granville, N. Y, & occ. his father's prev. resid.- **748**

Stuben (Baron)- (s. Chillus & Sarah Martin) b. Mar. 23, 1795; m. Esther, dau. Rev. James Murdock, of Martinsburg, N. Y.; res. Ogdensburgh, N. Y.; was once NYS Assembly member; children-

1. Sarah Ann, b. Jan. 31, 1819; m. ____ Rossel
2. Joseph, b. Apr. 23, 1820- **730**

DOUGLAS,
Capt.- "guardian" of the Stockbridge Indians, c. 1775; named in a communication
of the Conn. Colony to N. Y. Prov. Congress, as one of the "adventurers" who capt.
Ft. Ticonderoga & 'was a principal & had great merit in the success of the
enterprise'- **773**
Sen. Stephen A.- (1813- 1861) brief ment.- **1035**

DOW,
Caroline- of Madison co., N. Y.; m. Hugh, s. Hugh & Mary (McWhorter) Harsha-
973
Lorenzo- b. Oct. 16, 1777, Coventry,Conn.; Methodist evangelist; when 1st
converted, he was eager to preach & accomp. others on their circuit, but was
rejected 4 or 5 times at quarterly meetings; persevering, he was given into the
charge of S. Hutchison, in the Cambridge District, Dec. 1797; Hutchison informed
him that he had 3 mos. under his supervision to obt. a recommendation for a
circuit; on hearing this, Dow determined that, considering the low state of religion
in the circuit, that only a revival within the circuit would gain him such a
recommendation, & so he resolved to bring one abt., or else break up the circuit; he
then began visiting from house to house, regardless of denomination, beginning in
Pittstown, N. Y., where he went to abt. 100 families, some of them visited 2 or 3
times, & there became known by the settlers as "Crazy Dow"; at a qtrly. meeting
held in Welsh Hollow, Ft. Ann, N. Y., he expected to be scolded for his conduct,
but he remained firm in the defense of his efforts, & found an unexpected advocate
in the minister, Mr. T. Dewey, would had been influential in having the
Conference reject ano. candidate; he then went to Hutchison, to seek his exclusion,
so that he might go out on his own, w/o being any further trouble to him, but
Hutchison refused to release him, & compelled him to remain w. him for ano.
quarter; Dow then resolved to disappoint him in some manner, in order to be
dismissed, & made visits to Clarendon & Castleton, & then New Haven, &
Poultney, Vt.- **813**; some revival affected by him during his visit to Hampton &
Skenesborough, N. Y., & the area around Lake Champlain; he also visited
"Kingsborough & Queensborough" (Kingsbury & Queensbury, N. Y.) 'where many
were brought to a sense of themselves' & from there, went to Therman's
(Thurman's) Patent- **814**; was preaching at Ft. Edward, N. Y., c. Mar. 1798, 'where
one took fire mysteriously & was burnt to death'; see Baldwin, Capt.; § 392;Vol. 1;
he then proceeded to Easton, where T. Dewey was preaching, & converted Gideon
Draper, who became an itinerant preacher; his attempts to convert here, esp.
among the young, were aided one evening while Dewey was 'exhorting', when a
flash of lightning appeared to strike the meeting house; at the next annual
Conference, in Vt., he was adm. on a trial basis, his name printed in the minutes &
his written license rec'd. from Francis Asbury; he & Dewey then set out for the N.,
although he was so weak from a severe sickness that he could not get on or off his
horse on his own; during this circuit, he visited Argyle, Thurman's Patent, &
Queensbury, N. Y., & thence to Rutland & Brandon, Vt., & other locs.; at the Ash

Grove qtrly. meeting, Dec. 29 (prob. 1798) he 'was whipped [in words] by brother Hutchison, for jealousy', although he had brought in 600 people during his 10 month stay, & abt. as many more in Bapt. & Presbyt. congregations; he then proceeded south- **815**

Down Country- colloq.; c. 1770's, in the area of Salem, N. Y., it meant going from the area & into the area of Mass. & Conn., or having come from that area; during the retreat bef. Burgoyne, Lyon the carpenter, who res. at Fitch's Point, went "down country"- "as going into Mass. & Conn. has always been called in this neighborh." & then returned after the danger was over- **860**

DRAPER,
Nathaniel- purch. Lot 9, of Donald Fisher's tract, Nov. 10, 1783, from Jaben Williams- **(L)- 936**

DUANE,
James- (1733- 1797) reports to N. Y. Comm. of Safety, Mar. 1, 1777, on the matter of disaffection within Cumberland & Gloucester counties, noting that the majority still adhere to N. Y. govt. & that only 20 of 80 anticipated delegates actually attended their "mock convention" regarding the formation of a separate state- **786**; John Williams instructs John McKesson, Esq., to notify him & Mr. Duer of cert. pamphlets (sent by Williams June 23, 1777) being circulated in the Grants, if Duane should be in attendance at Congress- **789**; N. Y. delegate, Continental Congress; sends correspondence, July 10, 1777, & notes a June 30th issue of *Connecticut Courant* has arr. in Philadelphia on July 9th, containing a declaration from a part of N. Y. 'which is attempted to be arrested out of our jurisdiction & which is dubbed the State of Vermont, a name hatched for it in Philadelphia'; acc. Duane, the plan evidently laid here under the direction of Mr. Young, w. 'some others of more consequence & that his letters have pushed the people to this last extremity', subjoined w. a list of complaints against N. Y. meant to bolster their cause in the public eye; 'such a train of falsehoods & misrepresentations does but little credit to this mock Convention, which will porb. proceed to elect Delegates to Congress, & once more press for their admission'; he states that the N. Y. delegation remains confident that their move will be discouraged by the Congress at large, & in example, relates how one of the printers who was requested to publ. their production came to the N. Y. delegation w. the proposal that the Vt. declaration be printed w. the June 30th resolution of Congress, either preceding, or foll. it; refers p. 1,000, Journal of Council of Safety- **793**; his papers & Gov. Colden's, replying to the 1st six paragraphs of Samiuel Robinson's petitn., annexed to Gov. Moore's June 9, 1767 letter to Lord Shelburne- **894**; (Mayor of NYC, 1783-1789); proposed by NYS Assembly, July 1789, as 2nd U.S. Senator from N. Y.; carried, 35- 19, but defeated in the Senate, 9- 1 (prev. served as Senator, 1782-85)- **920**

Judge James- for 5 yrs., Asa Fitch, Sr. performed duties as his agent for coll. rents "& c.", & settl. his accts. to date w. him, June 5, 1794, making a final settlm. w. him, Jan. 15, 1795- **799**

DUEL,
Lyman- res. Chestertown, N. Y.; m. Caroline, dau. Newell & Polly (Ransom) Angel- **848**

DUER,
Henrietta- spinster, of Fulham, England; the foll. lands of Wm. Duer, Esq., deeded to her, Feb. 14, 1769, for £ 1,474- in Schuyler's Patent- Lot 3- 364 acres, & 2 acres in the upper end of the long island; Lot 22- 431 acres; Lot 12- 530 acres, & the island, containing 8 acres, loc. abt. 60 chains below Ft. Edward, opp. the place where the ferry used to be; Lot 13- 539 acres; & of lands formerly belonging to Derick Swart- 2 parcels of Lot 1- 8 acres; & 2 acres, 2 roods, & 24 perches; 2 parcels of Lot 6- 1 rood & 6 perches; & 20 acres, 1 rood, & 16 perches; Lot 5- 321 acres; in Banyard's Patent- Lot 4- 170 acres; 2 parcels of Lot 3- 10 acres, 3 rods; & 13 acres, 3 rods; to be redeemed on or bef. Feb. 15, 1770; mortgage allowed & recorded, Oct. 12, 1792; refers p. 519, Vol. A, Deeds, Wash. Co.- **935**
William- of Albany, N. Y.; appt. attorney by Henry Cuyler, Jr., Sept. 15, 1818, w. regards to legacies & c. by last Will of his father- **934**
William, Esq.- (1747- 1799) complained in a letter, June 14, 1775, to N. Y. Prov. Congress, that "sundry insinuations against his conduct" have been made w. relation to the colony's northern frontier & that these reports have been "industriously circulated as deeply to endanger his person & property"; requests that a comm. be appt. to examine into his conduct; on June 15th, a comm. concludes that they 'are fully convinced that these insinuations are entirely groundless; that they are altogether satisfied of his integrity & attachm. to American liberty'; assent to comm.'s conclusion given by entire Prov. Congress, & order & recommendation made that he & his property not be injured by any of this colony, or other inhabitants in America- **777**; corresponds from Ft. Miller, July 5, 1777, to N. Y. Comm. of Safety, addressing President, Prov. Congress, noting his apprehensions concerning the intent of some Charlotte co. citizens to close the courts were not wholly unfounded; a party of N. H. grants people, 'strengthened by some persons of desparate fortunes & bad character in the Western Districts', formed a resolution for abolishing the law & began marching to Ft. Edward for that purpose; to prevent their proceedings, he has detained Capt. Edward Motte (the deliverer of this letter) & his co. from their destination at Ticonderoga, in order to protect the bench, declaring 'should the attempt [to break up the courts] once succeed, it will not be an easy matter to restore order among a people of so turbulent a spirit...we shall not only have to oppose the incursions of an enemy on its frontier, but shall be torn to pieces by intestine anarchy & confusion'; he further pledges his intention of keeping the courts open 'even at the risk of my life'- **779**; chosen Deputy Adjutant Gen., w. rank of Col., by N. Y. Prov. Congress, July 27,

1775; in response, Aug. 15th, he requests 3 days to consider 'whether his connections w. his brothers in Dominica will admit of his accepting the commission w/o risking their fortune by his political conduct'; Aug. 23rd, a comm. appt. to confer w. him reports that due to 'his peculiar situation', he be excused-**781**; attended N. Y. Prov. Convention, July 9, 1776, along w. Col. Williams & Maj. Webster- **785**; appt. 1st Judge,Charlotte co., May 8, 1777, by Provincial Convention- **787**; John Williams instructs John McKesson, Esq., to notify him & Mr. Duane of cert. pamphlets (delivered in his June 23, 1777 letter) being circulated within the Grants, if he should be in attendance of Congress- **789**; plaintiff, in separate cases, May 19, 1774, vs. John Kenney, vs. Samuel Hinman, vs. Samuel Loadman, vs. Duncan Gilchrist, vs. Wm. Johnston, vs. Francis Acklin, & vs. Hugh Mallory, Jr.- **878**; purch. 193 acres, 6 rods, in Banyard's Patent, July 24, 1768, from William Banyard, late of NYC, & Feb. 14, 1769, of Fulham, Middlesex co., England; listed as items of property in his estate, deeded to Henrietta Duer, spinster, of Fulham, England, for £ 1,474, on above date-

1. all or part of 7 lots, Schuyler Patent, totaling 1,256 acres & 40 perches;
2. 3 lots, Banyard's Patent, totaling 293 acres; as mortgage, to be redeemed Feb. 15, 1770; mortgaged Sept. 22, 1774, to John Watts, of NYC, to secure payment of £ 1,000 on or bef. Sept. 7, 1775, the foll. lots in the Patent of John Schuyler, Jr., on the E. side of the Hudson, above "Saraghtoga"-
   1. the dwelling house, grist & sawmills;
   2. Lot No. 1, of the 1st Allotment, beginning on the river bank at the N. side of a cert. creek where there is a small island in the river; marked in chains & links, to a road running along the river- 8 acres, 3 rods, & 27 perches;
   3. Lot No. 6, of the 2nd Allotment, beginning on NE corner of Lot No. 5, described in chains & links- 9 acres, 1 rod, & 11 perches;
   4. Lot No. 1, of 3rd Allotment, beginning from SW corner of Lot No. 1, of 2nd Allotment, at an angle, described in chains & links- 2 acres, 2 rods, & 24 perches;
   5. Lot No. 5, of the 5th Allotment- 321 acres, 1 rod, & 23 perches;
   6. Stephen Banyard's Patent, adjoin. Schuyler's Patent, Lot No. 4, of the 1st Allotment- 170 acres;
   7. also, 1/6th of all tracts & falls belonging lately to William Banyard, purch. July 24, 1768, along w. the preceding;
   8. Farm Lot No. 3, Argyle township, gr. Oct. 5, 1771, to Wm. Duer by Alexander McNachten- 285 acres;
   9. part of Lot No.4, Argyle, adj. to Lot No. 3, gr. Apr. 23, 1771, to Wm. Duer by Daniel Gillespie;
   10. Schuyler's Patent, Lot No. 4- 244 acres, laid out to defray charges of Patent division by Killian DeRidder, Jan Winne, & Abram Jacob Lansing, Commissioners, & John R. Bleecker, Surveyor; Lot 4, Crown Allotment- 8 acres; Lot 3, Blue Allotment- 6 acres; released by Henry Cuyler in exchange for other lots in sd. Patent; refers p. 15, Liber A, Mortgages, Wash. Co.- **935**; deeds of Albert Baker to Henry Franklin; Archibald Campbell, Esq. to Benjamin Griffin; Daniel Jones to John Jones; James, John, & Amos McKenney to Michael Hoffnagle; &

Michael Hoffnagle to Robert Gorden, all acknowl. bef. him- **(L)- 936**; his property inventoried at £ 120,000 N. Y. currency, & his lands appraised at $2- 3.00 per acre; he undertook to possess the whole of the govt. securities proposed by Alexander Hamilton to fund the govt. debt, but "being unable to pay the money on them as it became due, he was imprisoned"; released, c. 1795, having been "in durance vile perh. 2 yrs."; & he d. 10 days after his release- **1031**; in the Sheriff's sale of his property, Hugh Pebbles, & John & Barent Bleecker purch. his Ft. Miller lands; the clerks at his store there began bef. the Rev. war w. ____ Dinwiddie, until his death, c. 1787; Hugh Pebbles, until 1791; ____ Mayhew, who failed; then ____ Wicks, until 1797; & after him, 1798, John Pattison & Gerrit Pebbles- **1032**

Duer Mansion- was the HQ of Gen. Burgoyne when the army was encamped at Ft. Miller, N. Y.; now owned by Mr. Robertson, its remains visited, Oct. 7, 1850, by Dr. Fitch & his uncle Pattison, who provides a detailed description of the ruins, terrain, & other buildings; the N. line of its grounds prob. the same as the N. line of Lot No.3, as laid down in Burr's map of Wash. co.; a highway runs E. of the property, straight for some distance, on the same line; the house, itself, stood so nr. the line, that its N. wing reached over into the next lot N., prob. Lot No. 4; the cellar of the main building, still conspicuous at this time, was a square hollow "which is never entered w. the plow, its sides are so steep"; fragm. of brick & stone profusely scattered over the site of the main building & its wings, showing abt. how far they extended; "The stone underpinning was a kind of bastard limestone which I should think had been drawed [sic] from the Bald mountain range of hills, some 2 mi. E. of here"; the well, appears to be a few rods SE of the house, which, acc. Mrs. Chubb (§ 101; Vol. 1) was filled up w. rubbish by Burgoyne's soldiers; acc. John Pattison, the barn, a smallish building, stood some rods further to the SE from the well; Duer had 2 large barns nr. the river bank, a few rods below where a woolen factory was lately built; the barn on the hill was taken down, c. 1800, & re-erected on John Pattison's lot, nr. the canal, & its timber later used for his barn & carriage house; the land here was cleared from the mansion to the river, & a large tract was made into a meadow, E. of the mansion, but its production of hay was gradually impoverished until by 1798, it produced only 4 or 5tons; the road to the mansion came off the river road at the village, & up a ravine SW of the mansion, & foll. the N. side of the ravine, & was S. of where Burgoyne's army had encamped- **800**; the estate was loc. betw. where Solomon Smith res., c. 1798, & where Ransom kept tavern, now (1850) kept by Perkins; 3 or 4 dwellings owned by Duer were loc. in the village, housing his millers & others in his employ- **804**; the execution of George Hundertmark, the Hessian deserter (§ 740) capt. nr. Salem, occurred in the big meadow E. of the mansion; the soldier was marched from the house to his grave, dug neatly in the middle of the meadow, knelt bef. the open grave, hooded, & shot by the firing squad- **976**; anticipating Pres. Adams' enactment of a proposal for a tax on windows, Hugh Pebbles instructed John Pattison to count those in the mansion, to determine the probable cost; which lead to Pattison's familiarity w. the structure's appearance- the main building 52 ft.

square, & 2 stories high,"w. a high basement in which was a cellar kitchen & c."; the interior, divided by "a hall running through its middle, w. 2 large square rooms on ea. side & a stairway (w. elegant bannisters) on one side of the hall; the lower story was 11 ft. high & the upper story was 10 ft. high, & divided "into a hall & 4 rooms, the same as below- the windows of this story were all bow windows"; its roof "was flattish & four square"; on the E., or nr. side, was a piazza "the whole length, 2 stories high, & very wide, w. turned pillars; bedrooms partitioned off at ea. end of this piazza"; a kind of alley, 4 ft. wide & 14 ft. long, & one story high, divided the main building from its wings; the wings "were 22 ft. square, & a story & a half high, the main story 11 ft. in height"; its frame was heavy oak timber; the walls were "lined w. thick two- inch plank, & filled in w. brick, over which was the lathing & plaistering"; the windows were "hung w. chains & leaden weights" & the cornices nicely carved all around; a sketch, drawn by John Pattison, lost during a major fire in Troy, N. Y., when his store was destroyed- **1031**; brief ment.- **1050s**

DUNBAR,
John- was a member of a N. Y. survey party along the Onion river, Sept. 29, 1772, when it was attacked by Remember Baker, Ira Allen, & others, who 'threw Dunbar bound, into a fire, burned him & otherwise beat & abused him in a cruel manner'- **906**

DUNCAN,
John- from Argyleshire, in the Scotish Highlands; emig., c. 1771, from Greenock, Scotland, & arr. NYC, foll. 9½ wk. passage; rem. Albany, N. Y., & res. there for 3 mos., then leased land in Rev. Harry Munroe's Hebron Patent (Munroe's Meadows); his family traveled through Salem, N. Y., by wagon, & arr. at the Meadows by Aug.; they res. in one of Rev. Munroe's houses until they had constructed their own cabin by fall; unable to clear any land & sow wheat, he 1st purch. supplies from Munroe until he was establ.; m. Nancy McCoy; 6 children- William, James, John; Isabel, b. Mar. 15, 1763, m. Duncan MacIntyre; Jane, m. Elihu Butolph; & Nancy, m. John McCall- **997**; when Burgoyne's army was at Skenesborough, he went there to obt. protection, taking his family there one morning on foot, foll. a path in the woods, & driving their cattle ahead of them; he had w. him a horse, 3 milch cows, & 2 steers; the journey of abt. 17 mi. took a day, passing only 2 or 3 houses along the way; at Skenesborough, their cattle ran at large & they sold their milk daily to the soldiers; they returned to Munroe's Meadows after being there abt. 5 wks.; his youngest dau., Nancy, was b. Sept., or Oct., 1777, at abt. the time of one of the Saratoga battles- **998**

DUNHAM,
____ - res. at the Ponds, Jackson, N. Y.; dau. Margaret, m. Lansing, s. Moses, Jr., & Eunice (Clark) Martin- **731**

Samuel- of Marblehead, Mass.; an American prisoner at Ft. Ticonderoga, he escaped along w. Samuel Standish & 2 others, late Aug. 1777, making their way to Arlington, Vt.- **747**

DUNLAP,
Rev. Mr. John- of Cambridge, N. Y.; offered the benediction during ceremonies in Salem, N. Y., Nov. 29, 1814, honoring Commodore Macdonough at a public reception here; gave a voluntary toast at the banquet foll., for 'A speedy & honorable peace- May the only emulation betw. America & Britain be to carry the banners of the cross to the ends of the earth"- **709**; dau. Mary Ann, m. Solomon Wells; see Vol. 1- **839**; his wf. Catharine, d. July 24, 1830, at 69 yrs., 6 mos., & 3 ds.; & he d. Mar. 7, 1829, at 72- **(L)- 975**; brief ment. as 1st President, Wash. Co. Bible Society, having one grdchild, now dec'd. (1862), a missionary to Africa; ano., a missionary to China; & a 3rd, a soldier, 123rd NYSV- **1097**
John J.- Co. A, 2nd N. Y., Northern Black Horse, Cav., 1861- 2- **1080**
Martin F.- prob. grds. Rev. John; bur. soldier's plot, gr. 19, Evergreen Cemetery, Salem, N. Y.; refers § 1133; Vol. 3- **1081**

DUNMORE,
Lord, 4th Earl of- (John Murray; Gov. N. Y., 1770; Gov. Va., 1771) his letter to Lord Hillsborough, Mar. 9, 1771, notes that the only remaining requisite for restoration of the peace within the Province of N. Y. appears to be revocation of the order suspending the issuing of grants; he notes that inhabitants within the contested grants amt to abt. 6- 700 families, w. 450+ having signed a petitn. requesting to be continued within N. Y.govt.; ano. petitn., sent by Gov. Wentworth, w. abt. 200 signatures, requests continuance under N. H. govt.- **898**

DURFEE,
Calvin- his sketch of the life of Ebenezer Fitch, D. D., the 1st President, Williams College, publ. 1865, by Mass. Sabbath School Society, Boston; a review of his work, July 20, 1865, *N. Y. Observer*, comments that although a small work, it 'is valuable for its careful statements', considering that scant material on the subject's life has frustrated prev. attempts, where reliable material was concerned- **799**

Durham, Vt.- orig. name, Clarendon, Vt., 1st belonging to Charlotte co., N. Y.; it was also erected as a township under the govt. of N. H., & called Clarendon; its N. bounds marked, 1767, by Archibald Campbell, & his marks later used as the boundary line for Socialborough, Charlotte co., N. Y. (Rutland, Vt.)- **745**; during his confinement, Jan. 1775, & trial at Sunderland, Vt., Benjamin Hough, a Justice of Peace for Charlotte co., reportedly overheard Ethan Allen declaring that the Bennington mob would prob. soon be obliged to drive off all the 'damned Durhamites';see Grants/ N. H.Controversy- **881**; bef. 'the quieting act', 1785, a strip of land, prob. 50 rods wide, was contested over by Silas Whitney of Durham, & Daniel Marsh of Socialborough; this situation referred to, p. 499, Slade's Vt.

State Papers; title eventually was vested in Marsh, but while contested, ea. contrived to maintain ownership by having a tenant occ. it & c.- **970**

DURKEE,
Ansel- (res. ?) "Lockhaven, Clinton co., Pa."; n. d., appears as a faint image, w. other illeg. notes perh. pert. to him, found at the end of this article- **1004**

DURYEA,
Rev. Philip- (Rev. Mr.) c. 1798, was the only minister in Schuylerville, N. Y., & the communities N. along the Hudson to Ft. Miller, N. Y.; see Vol. 3- **804**

DUTCH- 759s, 772, 812, 859, 930, 953b, 1032; Hessian, as Dutchman- 976; Holland- 920, 930; Gildermaison (Geldermaisen)- 990; Hulse (Hulst)- 990; South Seveland (South Beveland)- 990; Walcheren (Island)- 990

DUTTON,
Abigail- m. Thomas Parker, of Washington,Conn.- **759**; her husb. Thomas, s. Joseph & Sarah (Curtis) Parker- **759s**

DWELLE/ DWELLY,
Abner?- res. on North river (Hudson) at Half Moon, N. Y., or nearby; had 4 sons- Capt. Abner, eldest; Lemuel; Jedidiah, d. in Rev. war service, leaving a child; & Asa- **731**
Capt. Abner- s. Abner?; b. Scituate, Mass.; rem. here from neighborh. of Dorchester, Mass., along w. Maj. Stephen Clapp, & for some time, worked lumbering for him; purch. from old Duncan ("white Dunk") Campbell, & res. Dwelly's Hill, Greenwich, N. Y.; m. Miriam, dau. Moses, Sr., & Lydia (More) Martin; children-
  1. Lemuel, b. 1788; m. Betsey Rose
  2. Moses Martin
  3. Lydia, b. 1792; m. Joshua Dyer
  4. Jedidiah, d. inf.
  5. Jedidiah, b. 1796; m. Lydia Cross
  6. Betsey, m. John Cottrell
  7. Alphonso, m. Betsey Tefft
  8. Almira, m. Francis Robinson, Jr.
  9. Abner
  10. Miriam, m. William Blowers
  11. Horatio Nelson, d. y.
  12. Horatio Nelson, res. Bennington, Vt.; his wf. d. Oct. 23, 1825; & he d. June 28, 1826; here, & in latter part of text, given as "Dwelle"; foll. a separation of 45 yrs., a reunion was held at his homestead, Nov. 3, 1871, where his s. Alphonso res., attended by 6 surviving bros. & sists.- Moses Martin, Betsey, Alphonso,

Almira, Abner, & Horatio Nelson, ranging in age from 64- 81½ yrs. old at the time- **731**; (Dwellie) ments. children Alphonso, Miriam, & Elizabeth- **1041**
Abner, Jr.- (s. Capt. Abner & Miriam Martin) clothier; rem. Michigan & m. there; c. 1871, res. Minnesota, on a farm along the shore of Lake Pepin; 7 children- **731**
Alphonso- (s. Capt. Abner & Miriam Martin) res. Dwelly's Hill, Greenwich, N. Y.; m. Betsey Tefft; 4 daus. & 6 sons- Caroline, Elizabeth, Lydia, Miriam (dec'd.), Lemuel, Albert, Horace, & Henry- **731**; his residence ment.- **1041**
Jedidiah- (s. Capt. Abner & Miriam Martin) b. 1796; m. Lydia Cross; he d. 1832, of consumption & intemperance, leaving 2 or 3 children- **731**
Lemuel- s. Abner?; res. around Salem, N. Y., & rem. Canandaigua co.; children- Jarvis, Abner, James, William, Michael; & Lavina, who m. _____ Wilson, & res. within 3- 4 mi. of Canandaigua, N. Y.- **731**
Lemuel- (s. Capt. Abner & Miriam Martin) b. 1788; m. Betsey Rose, who d. leaving one son, Abner, now (1871) in Illinois; & he d. 1811- **731**
Moses Martin- (s. Capt. Abner & Miriam Martin) "lives out west", nr. Syracuse, or Hannibal, N. Y., town of Onondaga, & m. a wid. there; has a son & a dau., but unclear by text whether he adopted his wf.'s children; the son, c. 1873, has 3 children- 2 sons & a dau.- **731**

DWIGHT,
Rev. Harrison Gray Otis- (1803- 1862) b. Mass.; grad. Hamilton College, 1825; studied theology at Andover; missionary to the American Board, Constantinople, editing a newspaper there; author, *Christianity Revisited,* 1850 (publ. as *Christianity in Turkey,* 1854, London); his 2nd wf. d. 1860; he has 2 sons, a chaplain, & a private, in the army; d. Jan. 25, 1862, Shaftsbury, Vt., when his R. R. car was blown off the track & down an enbankment; he was en route to one of the colleges in the N.; his funeral, Jan. 30th, NYC- **1087**

DWYER,
Bridget- Irish Catholic; there was "some intimacy beginning to exist" betw. her & Patrick Walls, an Irish laborer, so that when he was injured while working for Archibald Hay at his farm in Greenwich, N. Y., she volunteered her services as his nurse; after abt. 4 wks. improvement, Walls' condition worsened, & she went for a fortnight to Mr. Smalls, in Cambridge, where it was presumed she informed Priest Quigley of Walls' condition; she had prev. been informed by Hay that he "would not have a man pretending to pardon ano.'s sins, in my house", but the priest arr. to visit Walls abt. a wk. after her return, causing a controversy betw. Hay & Quigley over religious & personal freedoms, & illust. the common predjudices of the day; foll. the controversy, she remiained at Hay's home for ano. 2 wks., attending to Walls, although acc. Hays, she was "in such a dudgeon that half the time she would not answer me when I spoke to her"- **1058**

DYER,
Joshua- res. E. of Union Village (Greenwich, N. Y.) m. Lydia, dau. Capt. Abner &
Miriam (Martin) Dwelly; they had a child, who d. a minor; his wf. d. 1813, & he d.
prior 1850- **731**
Squire- he examined var. witns. connected w. the murder of Barney McEntee, Feb.
17, 1858, the day foll. the murder, at Wait's Corners, White Creek, N. Y., Leonard
Wells taking acting for the prosecution- **1048s**

E

EARL,
Robert- purch. Lots 38, 40, & 41, Skenesborough, containing 328, 264, & 71½ acres, for £ 120, £ 115, & £ 44, respectively; all on the same date, Dec. 7, 1784- **(L)- 875**

EASON,
Col.- commanded a regt. of Mass. line, stat. Crown Point, N. Y., late May 1775- **750**

EAST INDIES- 805

EASTON,
James- co- signer, w. Ethan Allen, of a letter addressed to the people of Canada; a copy read into the record of the N. Y. Provincial Congress, June 15, 1777- **777**

Easton, N. Y.- c. 1778, then part of Saratoga co.; Quaker meeting house & bur. grd. loc. here; families of David Cornell, & his sons Thomas & Paul, rem. here from Walloomsac Patent- **806**; after preaching in Ft. Edward, Mar. 1798, Lorenzo Dow joined here w. T. Dewey, who was 'exhorting' the inhabitants; Gideon Draper, a young man here, sd. that if he could stand the crazy man (Dow), he would venture all the Methodist preachers to convert him, & he later became an itinerant preacher; observations made upon the lack of interest or low spirituality of religion here, esp. concern among the young abt. derision from their peers if they indicated an interest; anecdotal material relating to incidents occurring coincidentally to Dow's & Dewey's meetings- **815**; incl. in Saratoga Comm. of Safety; May 10, 1775, list of members in attendance at Albany, N. Y.- Col. Schuyler, John McCrea, Peter Lansingh, Cornelius Van Veghten, Har.s [Harmanus] Schuyler, Dirck Swart, John Tayler, Daniel Dickinson, John Fish, Cornelius Van Den Burgh- **831**

EATON,
Prof. Amos- d. May 10, 1842, at 66 yrs.; bur. Troy, N. Y.; he was an instructor of Dr. Fitch at the Rensselaer Institute (RPI); his 2nd wf., & sons Buckland & Dwight, bur. in same loc.- **954**
Capt.- commanded light horse co., c. 1777, prob. from Windham co., Conn.; mustered & sent to Bennington, Vt., to repel Burgoyne's invasion; he was sent N. w. a port. of his co. (here Dr. Fitch specul. he may have been sent to join Gen. Lincoln at Pawlet, Vt.) & Lt. Stewart commanded the remainder at Bennington, to ride express & scout- **763**
Charles J.- oath of alleg.; Co. D, 22nd N. Y. Inf.- **(L)- 1074**
Dwight- s. Prof. Amos; "(my old comrade in entomological pursuits when I & he were enthusiastic infants in this science)"; bur. Troy, N. Y.- **954**

Lucy- m. John, s. Duncan & Isabel (Duncan) MacIntyre- **999**

ECKERT,
Jonathan- (or Eckurt) res. along Lake Champlain, Charlotte co., N. Y., "where he had quitely lived since the fall of 1769"; he was violently assaulted & beaten, Sept. 13, 1773, by Samuel Bulsby, Remember Baker, & 2 others, who were supporters of the N. H. Grants- **911**

EDDY,
Family- ments. s. Hiram; & dau. Mary Ann, who m. 1. ____ Wheeler; 2. Hon. William H. Parker, as his 2nd wf.- **759**
Family- incl. bros. Jonathan, of Hoosick; & Seth, of Stillwater, N. Y.- **(L)- 772**
Jonathan- merch., Hoosick, N. Y.; b. Apr. 14, 1774; d. July 12, 1840; his wf., b. Dec. 20, 1779; d. Apr. 12, 1846- **(L)- 772**
Mary Ann- m. 1. ____ Wheeler; 2. Hon. Wm. Henry Parker, as his 2nd wf.- **759s**
Samuel- of Greenfield, N. Y.; m. Adeline, dau. Ebenezer & Sally (Hobby) Fitch; no children- **799**
Seth- res. Stillwater, N. Y.; "lately dec'd.", c. 1850- **772**

EDGERTON,
Christopher H.- Chaplain, 93rd N. Y. Inf.- **1090b**

EGYPT- **990**

ELDRIDGE,
____- "the clock cleaner"; see Vol. 4; described to Esq. Barnet an incident in which several skulls were unearthed from a mass grave connected w. the Bennington battlesite; these artifacts were discovered when some of Barnet's bros. were digging post holes- **762**
____- identified by Mrs. Chubb (§ 101- 103) as res., c. 1792, at Ft. Miller, N. Y.; acc. Dr. Fitch, he was prob. the same person who, c. 1798, res. along the Hudson river below Ft. Miller, & was identified, by John Pattison, as ____ Matthews- **804**

ELECTIONS-
1777- John Williams reports to N. Y. Provincial Congress, June 23rd, that the election of Gen. Scott for Gov., & Gen. Clinton for Lt. Gov., has been 'pretty unanimous' in Charlotte co., though few have voted- **789**;
1815- N. Y. Assembly- votes for Warren & Washington co.; 10 candidates & total votes for ea., the Federalists taking all seats; U. S. Congress- Elisha I. Winter, Federalist, 2,861, vs. Asa Adgate, Democrat, 2,703; incl. the vote for ea. candidate in the foll. towns- Argyle, Kingsbury, Salem, Greenwich, Hebron, Putnam, Hartford, Whitehall, Granville, Hampton, Easton, Ft. Ann, & Cambridge; total vote count for entire Congressional District, then incl. Essex, Clinton, Franklin,

Warren, & Washington counties- Adgate- 4,247, vs. Winter- 4,051; Democratic majority in N. Y. state- 3,692- **714**;

1852- President, Gov., Lt. Gov., Canal Commissioner, State Prison Inspector, Congress; County Sheriff, Clerk, & Treasurer, Superintendent of Poor; Court of Gen. Sessions, 1st & 2nd N. Y. Assembly Districts; a newspaper clipping giving the aggregate results in Wash. co., w. votes for ea. party, & majority margins; names of candidates not given; while co. offices were primarily 2- way races, state & national races also incl. Free Soil party- **1011**;

1853- N. Y. Secretary of State, Canal Commissioner, Senator, State Supreme Court Justice, District Attorneys, Superintendent of Poor; Justice, Court of Gen. Sessions; 1st & 2nd Assembly Districts; ano. newspaper clipping, giving aggregate Wash. co. results, w/o candidates names; incl. 4 parties- Maine Law, Free Soil, Whig, & Democrat (hard & soft)- **1025**;

1854- N. Y. Governor- Amasa J. Parker, Democrat; ____ King, Republican; & ____ Brooks, Know- nothing; newspaper clipping of the results, Nov. 4, 1854 election; lists Gov., Lt. Gov., Canal Commissioner, Inspector of State Prison, Superintendent of Poor; Justices, Court of Gen. Sessions; 1st & 2nd Assembly Districts; gives total votes for electoral districts in ea. town of Washington co.- **1028**

11th Illinois Infantry- c. 1862, its ranks incl. ____ Allen, & ____ Atwood, from Salem; & ____ Gilbert, ____ Culver, ____ Paxton, & ____ Armstrong, from Greenwich, N. Y.; other names ment. in context w. these, but perh. not directly attrib. to this unit, & stat. at Cairo, Illinois- Capt. Edward? McAllister, Emmet F. Hill; & also, E. L. & William Alexander, sons of Peter Alexander, prob. of E. Greenwich, N. Y.- **1080**

ELLET,
Mrs. *Elizabeth Fries Lumis*- (1818- 1877) refers to an incident in her work, *Women in the Revolution*, v. 2, p. 302, although why significant enough to publ. deemed uncert., acc. Dr. Fitch; the acct. concerns a loyalist, Mrs. Munro, & her sist., who ostensibly supplied milk & water to the wnd. on the Bennington battlefield- **953**

ELLICE,
Alexander- of London, England; c. 1779, lots nr. Lake Champlain, orig. drawn by Col. John Godwin, conveyed to Ellice by Col. Wm. Godwin, Esq., Alexander's neph. & heir at law- **880**

ELLIOT,
John- m. Rebecca, dau. James & Elizabeth (Lytle) Rowan- **737**
Zebulon- c. 1833, ment. as an heir of Desire (Burrows) Gore, of Nova Scotia- **1100**

ELLIS,
Ruben- m. Sarah, wid. Aaron Martin, Sr., to her children's "great dissatisfaction"-
730; m. ____ Newell, wid. ____ Martin, as her 2nd husb. (int., Nov. 12, 1752-
V. R., Sturbridge, Mass.); their children- Reuben, Amasa, & Moses; res.
Shaftsbury, Vt., where she d.; his wf. was very religious, but the Martin children
disliked her calling one of her Ellis children Moses, as she already had a son by
that name; she, however, insisted it was one of the prettiest names she found in the
Bible & remained firm in her belief in naming from that source- **849**; of
Southbridge, Mass.; his m. to Wid. Martin noted as above, rem. Shaftsbury, Vt., of
Stillwater, N. Y.; ments. a 4th child, Sarah- **1037**
William B.- oath of alleg.; Co. D, 22nd N. Y. Inf.- **(L)- 1074**

Ellsworth Regiment (44th N. Y. Inf.)- organized to have a representative from ea.
town in N. Y. state; Salem representative, N. Albert Wilson, d. Oct. 1861, at
Wash., D. C.- "He was the 1st martyr from this town, who perished in this wicked
war"; Ft. Edward representative- Capt. William Henry Miller, d. Apr. 30, 1862;
they were the 1st & 2nd burials, soldier's plot, Evergreen Cemetery, Salem, N. Y.,
in graves 2 & 1, respectively- **1081**

ELMER,
Maj.- officer witn. during May- Dec. 1775 service of Ebenezer Farnsworth, acc. his
Rev. war pension appl.- **750**

ELY,
William D.- witn., Dec. 1, 1858, certif. of execution for Martin Wallace- **1050s**

EMBURY,
Kate- niece, Rev. Philip; m. Abraham Bininger, Jr., abt. 1761- **1075b**
Peter- bro. Kate, & neph. Rev. Philip; res. Greenwich St., NYC; establ. a grocer at
the corner of Beekman & Nassau Sts.; d. abt. mid- 1850's- **1075b**
Rev. Philip- (1728- 1773) 1st Methodist in America; arr. NYC, & establ. the John
St. church, w. assist. of Rev. Abraham Bininger, & rem. w. him to Camden Valley,
Wash. co., N. Y.; see Vol. 1- **1075b**

EMERSON,
Daniel- of Hollis, N. H.; dau. Hannah, m. Rev. Nathaniel, s. Deac. Willis & Ann
(Cage) Hall- **759s**

EMMONS,
____ - tavernkeeper, Clarendon, Vt.; dau. m. Benjamin, s. Silas Whitney, Sr.;
ments. sons Adjoniah, & youngest, Horatio; prob. other children; he later kept
tavern (§ 240) in Ft. Edward, N. Y.; see Vol. 1- **969**; he was once sued by his
father- in- law on a charge that amounted to a flagrant dishonesty on the
tavernkeeper's part; when he went to plead w. him for consideration on the basis of

their kinship, Whitney was "insensible" to the argument, but returned to normal relations w. him foll. legal resolution of the matter- **970**
Adonijah- from Clarendon, Vt.; edited a newspaper (n. d.) at Sandy Hill, N. Y., & afterw., ano. in Essex co., N. Y.; rem. Detroit, Mich., & opened a law office there; d. Detroit, n. d.- **969**
Gen. Carlos- acc. William L. Emmons, his English heirs had become extinct, & the family in America had been holding meetins & sending an agent to England for the purpose of obt. his fortune- **969**
Horatio, Esq.- from Clarendon, Vt.; for many yrs., Justice of Peace, Union Village (Greenwich, N. Y.); youngest of his family; 'Raish' was his family nickname; "this boy used to get a whipping from his father & mother regularly every day as the day came"; one day this practice was apparently overlooked for some reason & he was sent to bed w/o one; when his father realized that he hadn't "flogged" him for the day, he asked if his wf. had done so, & discovering that she hadn't, he went upstairs & pulled him from his bed "& gave him a most severe basting"; had one son, William L.- **969**; his s., Wm. L., m. Jane Lytle- **1069**
William L.- s. Horatio; winter, 1851/2, he occ. one of Dr. Fitch's houses at Fitch's Point, Salem, N. Y.; acc. Dr. Fitch, he spoke "incessantly" of the family's efforts to obt. a fortune from their ancestor, 'Gen. Carlos Emmons', whose English heirs had become extinct- **969**; m. Jane, dau. William & Mary (Hanna) Lytle; his wf. gives record of some of the desc. of Andrew Lytle, of Salem, N. Y.; he was, acc. Dr. Fitch, "a miserable scamp, who ran himself out of money & character here, & moved to Illinois, where she soon died- an amiable woman, worthy of a better fate"; he had been a partner in a chairmaking business at Fitch's Point, w. his bro.- in- law, Wm. J. Lytle- **1069**

England- see GREAT BRITAIN

EPIDEMICS-
Cholera- c. 1832, an outbreak occurred in Quebec & Montreal, & in Albany, N. Y., alarming the whole countryside-**1038**;
Spotted Fever- an epidemic, c. 1813, Cambridge, N. Y.; one of its victims was Edmund HenryWells- **839**; Dr. John Thompson began his practice in Cambridge at abt. the time of its outbreak- **844**

ESLER,
Frank W.- Saddler, Co. A, 2nd N. Y., Northern Black Horse, Cav., 1861- 2- **1080**

Essex Co., N. Y.- May 25, 1861, its units comprising 22nd N. Y. Inf. ordered to Camp Rathbone, Troy, N. Y., for their final organization- Co. C- Keesville; Co. I- Schroon Lake; Co. J- Moriah- **1074**

ESTEE,
Asa- of Brookfield, Mass.; Sept. 20, 1784, purch. Lots 270 & 271, Turner's Patent, from John Law, for £ 500; see Vol. 4- **(L)- 936**

EVANS,
Mr.- res. Clear Creek, Iowa; Nov. 12, 1861, presented a flag to Co. A- C, 14th Iowa Inf., made by the ladies of his community, & gave an evening address, while the 3 companies were encamped at his town during their march to Ft. Randall, S. Dakota- **1089**

Evergreen Cemetery, Salem, N. Y.- partly loc. on the land of Alexander Turner, Jr., an orig. proprietor of the Patent; his land purch. by David Russell, & his house site later sold to the cemetery; the flat was smoothed over & formed the SW corner of the cemetery grounds; the branch road N. was later straightened & moved several rods W. when the bounds were agreed to w. Russell, Jan. 1862- **1034**; diagram of soldier's plot for Civil War burials, placement of graves 1- 26; ment. of interments & brief biog. data for burials 1- 4, 6, 7, 10, 11, 14, 15, & 18- 21- **(L)- 1081**

F

FAIRCHILD,
Jesse- dau. Sylvia, m. Sidney Wells, as his 1st wf.- **839**
Marinus- assist. for the prosecution, Oct. 1- 7, 1858, People vs. Martin Wallace-
1048s
Wilson- (Fairchilds) oath of alleg.; Co. D, 22nd N. Y. Inf.- **(L)- 1074**

FANNING,
Thomas- m. Hannah ____; his wf. was killed by the blow of an axe to the side of
her head & behind the ear; Jan. 14, 1812, Thomas Mitchell was indicted, tried, &
acquitted in the incident- **874**

FAREWELL,
Benjamin- Argyle, N. Y., May 18, 1805, 'did come to his death by the hand of God
& Mischance, & so did sufficate & did drown & did die'; Elisha Forbes, Coroner-
(L)- 876

FARMING, early techniques-
  flax- early farmers raised their own, making homespun linen of it for garments &
ropes; whitening was done by spreading the flax on the grass beside a stream or
spring, a watering pot was filled & water sprinkled on it as often as it dried in the
sun; see Farming, & Granger, Mrs.; Vol. 3- **1068**

FARNSWORTH,
Col.- Apr. 1780, commanded regt., prob. Albany co. militia, or N. Y. troops, which
was detailed to the Schoharie fort for the season, & incl. a co. commanded by a
Capt. Miller- **756**
Ebenezer- b. Nov. 6, 1756, Rutland, Mass.; res. Granville, N. Y.; contents of his
entire pens. appl.; enl. for 6 months, beginning end of May 1775, at Crown Point,
Capt. Robert Cockran's co., Col. Eason's regt., Mass. line; was sent from there to
Canada as a marine on a schooner, & was at the taking of St. John's; returned to
Ft. Ticonderoga & was disch. by Gen. Schuyler, abt. Dec. 1, 1775; witn. Gens.
Schuyler & Montgomery, Col. Hinman, Maj. Elmer, & Col. Ethan Allen during
his service; enl. Apr. 1776, for 1 yr., Oliver Parmley's co., Col. Bunel's regt., at
Granville, N. Y.; proceeded to Skenesborough & embarked from there to Canada,
meeting w. other troops on St. Lawrence, nr. Quebec; was in the battle of Three
Rivers, & retreated from there to "Sorrell & Chamblee", & out of Canada to Mt.
Independence, remaining there until disch., Feb. 1, 1777, by Col. Wayne; witn.
Gens. Arnold, Sullivan, & Thompson, & Cols. Maxwell & St. Clair; enl. again,
June 1777, Capt. Child's co., Col. Williams' regt., & marched to Ft. Ticonderoga;
was in the American retreat for 3- 4 days, & arr. at Castleton, Vt. during the night,
& heard the firing at Hubbardston the foll. morning; continued in the retreat to Ft.

Ann & Ft. Edward, & remained there until mid- July, serving abt. 1 month; returned to Granville, & enl. for 6 months upon arr. there, Capt. Parmlee Allen's co., Col. Herricks? regt.; marched to Pawlet, Manchester, & then Bennington, Vt., & was in the battle there; afterw. took prisoners into the meetinghouse there to guard; returned via the same route, crossing through the woods to Lake George, nr. Ft. Ticonderoga, to destroy Burgoyne's transports; his co. took 600 prisoners from different areas while performing this task, & then went down Lake George to Dimon [Diamond] Island, where they were defeated by the enemy; retreated to Ft. Ann, & then Pawlet, Vt., scouting the region surrounding Lake Champlain to Lake George from this base until the battle of Saratoga; arr. at Saratoga for the surrender, & escorted tories to Lake George; returned to Pawlet, & proceeded to Mt. Independence w. Maj. Wait, & then to Gillinus creek, Willsborough, Vt., taking a no. of horses & 40 British & tory prisoners along the way; disbanded at Pawlet, Jan. 1778; witn. Cols. Warner, Leonard, & Wells, & Gen. St. Clair during this service; afterw. stat. on frontier w. militia for the remainder of war, acting as scout; abt. Sept. 1779, was Sgt., Capt. Child's co., & rec'd. a request by Capt. Stockwell, at Whitehall, N. Y., to reinforce garrison there; was there abt. ½ month, & again abt. a wk.- 10 days foll. the burning of Skene's house; late fall 1781, went w. Capt. McCarr under flag of truce to the British commander at Crown Point, bearing packet from Lord Stirling that gave news of Cornwallis' surrender; 10- 12 days service; refers Stone's Life of Brant, ii, 202, 203; his disch. lost or destroyed, & no doc. evidence of his age; res. Granville, & abt. 1782, rem. Ft. Ann, & has lived partly in Kingsbury, Granville, & now, Ft. Ann, N. Y.- **750**
Ebenezer- purch. Lot 90, Artillery Patent, 240 acres, for £ 242, Dec. 28, 1784- **(L)- 875**

FARRAR,
John- res. Fitch's Point, Salem, N. Y., at the time that Tucker was whipped for his wf.'s crime (Vol. 1); he res. at the top of the hill, betw. the bridge & the Red House; as he had a large chimney, his neighbor, St. John Honeywood, hung some bacon in it to smoke, & one night, Mrs. Tucker "mounted" his house & stole a piece of it from the chimney- **863**

FASSET,
John- selected as Lt., July 27, 1775, at a meeting held in Dorset, Vt., to elect officers of the Green Mtn. regt.- **781b**

FAY,
____- referred to as 'landlord Fay'; Dr. Adams, of Arlington, Vt., was hoisted up by the Bennington mob (n. d.) & exposed upon his signpost, 'where was fixed a dead catamount'- **881**

FELLOWS,
Gen. *John-* (1733- 1828) of Stockbridge, Mass.; his brigade stat. at Ft. Ann, July 8, 1777, during the battle there w. Burgoyne's army- **747**; (Col.) late Aug. 1776, commanded Mass. regt. sent to Dutchess co., N. Y., & stat. on Valentine's hill; regt. later participated in battle of White Plains- **755**

FENTON,
____- he & John Todd owned the lot in Argyle Patent orig. drawn by John McDougall, & loc. a mi. S. of N. Argyle, N. Y.- **802**
Benjamin- res. White Creek, N. Y.; m. Elizabeth, dau. Joseph Wells, Sr.; of their children, ments. s. Salmon- **842**
Francis- res. Bald Mountain, N. Y.; m. Mary E. ____; their s. James E., enl. Co. F, 5th Vt. Inf., & d. Nov. 29, 1861- **1081**
James E.- (s. Francis & Mary E. ____) Co. F, 5th Vt. Inf.; he worked as a stone cutter w. ____ Brown during the spring & summer, 1861, when ano. man, while visiting, told him what a fine regt. he belonged to; he later enl. Aug. 23nd, at Middlebury, Vt., & was stat. w. his co. nr. Washington, D. C.; ordered out on picket guard along the Potomac on a Fri., his relief was forgotten until Sun. morning; he became ill shortly after being relieved, & d. Nov. 29, 1861, at 23, apparently from typhoid pneumonia; bur. Dec. 24th, grave #10, soldier's plot, Evergreen Cemetery, Salem, N. Y.- **1081**
Ruel- witn., Dec. 1, 1858, certif. for the execution of Martin Wallace- **1050s**
Dr. *Stephen Fitch-* physician & clergym.; res. Mt. Kisco, N. Y.; was perh. grds. Dr. Asa Fitch, of Vienna, N. Y.- **1077**

FERGUSON,
Charles- oath of alleg.; Co. D, 22nd N. Y. Inf.- **(L)- 1074**
Samuel- c. 1852, res. Argyle, N. Y., his loc. once occ. by Alexander McDougall, Esq.- **978**

FIJI ISLANDS- 799

FINEL,
Luther- of Poultney, Vt.; Dec. 13, 1813, for $1,200.00, purch. 1/3 of the rights of Asa Fitch, Sr., in a Woolen Factory loc. at Fitch's Point, Salem, N. Y.; the sum was to be pd. in 4 yrs., in return for his operating the mill; ano. 1/3 of the factory was sold to him, Mar. 25, 1820, for $945.00- **799**

FINNEY,
Rev. C. G.- Apr. 18, 1867, performed the marriage ceremony of James F. Atkinson & Louise M. Fitch- **799**

FISHER,

Caleb- he & Timothy Smith were killed "July 4th, 24th yr. of Independence"
(1799), at Salem, N. Y., "by the bursting of a gun disch. by Nathaniel Starns- w/o
malice"; Hamilton McCollister, Coroner; see Vol. 1- **(L)- 876**
Donald- owned 2,000 acre tract, prob. loc. Granville, N. Y.; Nov. 10, 1783, Jaben
Williams conveyed Lot 9 of his property to Nathaniel Draper- **(L)- 936**
Family- c. 1771, res. nr. Granville, N. Y.; 2 or 3 brothers who were tories, & rem.
to Canada during the Rev. war- **997**
H. K.- oath of alleg.; Co. D, 22nd N. Y. Inf.- **(L)- 1074**
John- res. Goodrich, Upper Canada (Goderich, Huron co., Ont.); m. Margaret, dau.
Samuel & Polly (Alyea) Munroe- **812**
William G.- 1st Bugler, Co. A, 2nd N. Y., Northern Black Horse, Cav., 1861- 2-
1080

FISK,

Isaac H.- of Watertown, N. Y.; m. Mary, dau. Dr. John & Susan (Martin) Safford-
730; their children-
1. John Safford, b. Jan. 18, 1838
2. Susan Martin, b. Nov. 31, 1839
3. Isaac Rockwell, b. Jan. 17, 1841
4. Mary Hubbard, b. July 14, 1844- **1046**
Thomas B.- oath of alleg.; Co. D, 22nd N. Y. Inf.- **(L)- 1074**; 1st Lt.; wnd., prob.
2nd Bull Run, & resigned; replaced Sept. 23, 1862, by Henry Cook; see Vol. 3-
1095b

FISTER,

Francis A.- notice, June 17, 1776, that he & John Macombe were sent from
Hoosick to be imprisoned at Albany, N. Y.- **890**
Col. John P.- referred to as old "Festus"; res. Hoosick, N. Y.; acc. Reubin Clark,
was killed at the battle of Bennington, which conflicts w. Dr. McAllister's earlier
(§ 246) statement; see Festus, Vol. 1; his correct surname questioned by Dr. Fitch,
as John Fester, or Foster (his actual name was Francis Pfister); he was stat. at
Niagara during the old French war, disch., & retired on half pay; he came to the
Hoosick valley & purch. the farm & house "well known of old as The White
House"; m. Sarah? McComb; a decided & active tory, he "was one of the most
important men in Hoosic"; his house was the HQ of all loyalists in the vicinity, &
in advance of the force coming to Bennington, 15 British soldiers were sent,
requesting him to rally all the area loyalists to assist Col. Baum; these soldiers
were instructed to go wherever he directed them to tories in the neighborh., to urge
& entreat them to the Royalist cause; he went into the British camp w. other tories
1- 2 days bef. the battle, & was severely wnd. during the fighting & taken prisoner;
placed on an ox cart w. other wnd. to be carried to Bennington, he d. bef. reaching
there & was bur. beside the road w. some other dead, his body placed face down, so
that his friends might distinguish it, if they wished to rem. him from there; his

body was later taken to NYC for bur., & all his property confiscated; Dr. Fitch notes that Aug. 14, 1777, when the bridge at Sancoick was taken up, was prob. the day that soldiers were sent to Festus to gather recruits; he also persists in emphasizing that Foster was his probable surname- 768; he lead away all the men of the Bovee & Cronk families in Hoosick to fight against the country at Bennington- 769; deciding that Capt. Brewer was not firm in his commitment to the patriot cause, he sent Orra Cronk, the Sgt. of Brewer's militia co., to persuade him to join w. the tories; discovering that his Capt. & the remainder of the co. had already resolved to join the Americans at Bennington, Sgt. Cronk returned to Fister w. his own indecisions, thus revealing Capt. Brewer's intentions; Col. Fister then planned to frustrate the militia by sending a party of 2 British soldiers & 3 tories to arrest their Capt.- 770; brief ment.- 771

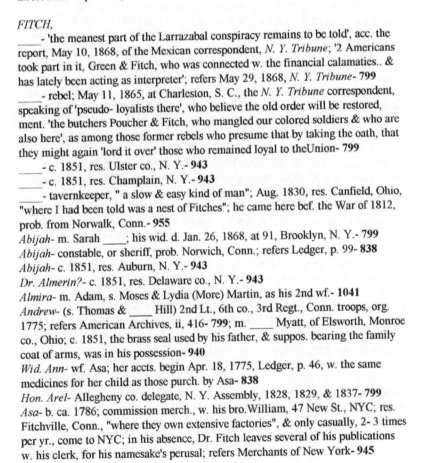

FITCH,

_____ - 'the meanest part of the Larrazabal conspiracy remains to be told', acc. the report, May 10, 1868, of the Mexican correspondent, *N. Y. Tribune*; '2 Americans took part in it, Green & Fitch, who was connected w. the financial calamaties.. & has lately been acting as interpreter'; refers May 29, 1868, *N. Y. Tribune*- 799

_____ - rebel; May 11, 1865, at Charleston, S. C., the *N. Y. Tribune* correspondent, speaking of 'pseudo- loyalists there', who believe the old order will be restored, ment. 'the butchers Poucher & Fitch, who mangled our colored soldiers & who are also here', as among those former rebels who presume that by taking the oath, that they might again 'lord it over' those who remained loyal to theUnion- 799

_____ - c. 1851, res. Ulster co., N. Y.- 943

_____ - c. 1851, res. Champlain, N. Y.- 943

_____ - tavernkeeper, " a slow & easy kind of man"; Aug. 1830, res. Canfield, Ohio, "where I had been told was a nest of Fitches"; he came here bef. the War of 1812, prob. from Norwalk, Conn.- 955

Abijah- m. Sarah _____; his wid. d. Jan. 26, 1868, at 91, Brooklyn, N. Y.- 799

Abijah- constable, or sheriff, prob. Norwich, Conn.; refers Ledger, p. 99- 838

Abijah- c. 1851, res. Auburn, N. Y.- 943

Dr. Almerin?- c. 1851, res. Delaware co., N. Y.- 943

Almira- m. Adam, s. Moses & Lydia (More) Martin, as his 2nd wf.- 1041

Andrew- (s. Thomas & _____ Hill) 2nd Lt., 6th co., 3rd Regt., Conn. troops, org. 1775; refers American Archives, ii, 416- 799; m. _____ Myatt, of Elsworth, Monroe co., Ohio; c. 1851, the brass seal used by his father, & suppos. bearing the family coat of arms, was in his possession- 940

Wid. Ann- wf. Asa; her accts. begin Apr. 18, 1775, Ledger, p. 46, w. the same medicines for her child as those purch. by Asa- 838

Hon. Arel- Allegheny co. delegate, N. Y. Assembly, 1828, 1829, & 1837- 799

Asa- b. ca. 1786; commission merch., w. his bro.William, 47 New St., NYC; res. Fitchville, Conn., "where they own extensive factories", & only casually, 2- 3 times per yr., come to NYC; in his absence, Dr. Fitch leaves several of his publications w. his clerk, for his namesake's perusal; refers Merchants of New York- 945

Dr. Asa- res.Vienna, N. Y.; his obit., c.1860, noted by Dr. Fitch, w. the remark, "I am surprised that I have never heard of this man until I saw this obit. notice", afterw. added to his genealogical material- **1077**

Dr. Asa- physician, Methodist clergym.; practiced, c. 1866, at NYC; he was thrown out of his carriage on the Harlem R. R. & rec'd. a fractured leg, which was later amputated; he d. Apr. 26, 1867, or his obit. given on that date- **1077**

Mr. Asa- of Norwich, Conn.; s. Mr. Jabez; acc. Dr. Fitch, his name was prob. given from the maternal side, as it appears 2 or 3 generations from the orig. family, & was confined to this branch; "this Asa (my father's namesake) appears to have been very dissipated in his habits A. D. 1752"; an acct. of his, from Dr. Peletiah Fitch's Ledger, note prices for var. refreshments current at that time; see Liquor, Spirits; it appears that he became so involved that his bro., Dr. Peletiah, was compelled to assume some of his property to pay off demands against him, noting- Jan. 1753- 'my note given toAbel Brewster £ 130.0' & 'my security given to Branch & Standish £ 130.0' & credit to him 'by part of his land £ 577.10.11', "which appears to have sobered & reformed him"; charges afterw. were principally for medicines, & rarely liquor; m. Ann ____; he prob. d. Apr. 1755, as his accts. end Apr. 13th, & those of his wf. begin Apr. 18th- **838**

Dr. Asa, Jr.- (1809- 1879; s. Hon. Asa, Sr., & Abigail Martin) gives hand sketch of Bennington battlesite- **761**; notes his sketch of Bennington battlesite drawn Aug. 23, 1850, after going over the ground on the prev. day w. Nathaniel Barnet, Esq., the current owner of the property- **762**; retrieved part of the oak tree stump left in the center of the Hessian stronghold at Bennington, & was given a lead bullet from Esq. Barnet, indicating the direction of Gen. Stark's attack, sending both to N. Y. State Antiquarian Collection- **762b**; newspaper clipping, July 27, 1874, *Salem Press*, "The Parker Family", authored by him; his credentials given as M. D., & corresponding member, N. Y. Hist. Soc., & honorary member, N. J. Hist. Soc.; an extensive genealogy of the Parker family, going beyond the immed. family of John C. Parker, Esq., of Granville, N. Y., as found in the original manuscript; the Editor, *Salem Press*, notes- '[The writer of the foll. article will pardon us for varying from his manuscript & placing his name & c., at its head, instead of his initials at its close, there is such an obvious propriety in having communications of this character authenticated by the author's name, instead of being ranked as dubious authority in consequence of a *quasi- anonymous* signature]'; acc. to this article, his information was obt. from Prof. Wm. H. Parker, Hon. James Gibson, B. F. Bancroft, Esq., & Esq. John C. Parker- **759s**; occ. the house, built c. 1791- 94, by Adam Martin- **852**; among his var. visits in compiling Fitch genealogical information, calls upon Asa & William Fitch, commission merchs., NYC, & finding them absent, leaves w. their clerk "copies of my pamphlets, the Wheat Fly, Hessian Fly, Winter Insects, Currant moth & Hemipterous insects, to hand to Asa Fitch when he came into the city"- **945**; a reading of his Hist. of Wash. Co. (prob. from *Transactions of the N. Y. State Agricultural Society, 1848)* prob. served for inspiration of Mary M. Chase's poem, "The Bloody Morning Scout"; pgs. 27, 28, *Holden's Magazine*, 1851- **989**; an item missing from his orig. manuscript, recorded in Judge Gibson's facsimile manuscript, as "Conviction of Wallace for Murder"; this article appears in Oct. 5, 12, & 19, 1858, issues of the *Salem Press* as 'Trial of Martin Wallace for the Murder of Barney McEntee'; orig. issued in 2 parts, the Oct. 12th issue notes that the entire transcript will be republ. in the Oct. 19th issue, in response to public demand for copies- **1048s**; his orig. manuscript contains a newspaper clipping, Dec. 7, 1858, *Salem Press*, w. the obit. of Hon. John McLean; the interior columns of this same pg. incl. an article, "Execution of Martin Wallace", which occurred on Dec. 1st, & was recorded in Judge Gibson's facsimile manuscript as 'Execution of Wallace', along w. McLean's obit.; the 2 articles were separated, & the latter apparently lost from the orig. text; Dr. Fitch was also witn., Dec. 1, 1858, certif. for the execution of Martin Wallace- **1050s**; his s. Charles, a house guest, Leonard Hurd, & Betsey Taylor, who occ. a chamber in his house, all felt earth tremors, abt. 9:15 PM, July 11, 1860, after they had retired to bed; ea. attrib. the cause to separate reasons to the event, which Dr. Fitch conveyed an acct. of to the Smithsonian Institute, noting that newspapers on July 13th indicated an earthquake in Canada- **1075**; compiles notes of the day's proceedings, Sept. 4, 1862, at the 50th annual meeting of Wash. Co. Bible Soc., Salem, N. Y., as a participant- **1097**; conveys his thoughts & observations on the departure of the 123rd NYSV from Salem, Sept. 5, 1862, to join Union forces in the Civil War- **1098**

Hon. Asa, Sr.- (1765- 1843) offered a voluntary toast, describing the U. S. Navy as our 'wooden walls', at a public banquet held Nov. 29, 1814, in Salem, N. Y., honoring Commodore Macdonough- **709**; enl. spring 1782, as a '9 months man', & was garrisoned at Saratoga (Schuylerville, N. Y.) & Salem, guarding the northern frontier- **729**; m. Jan. 27, 1791, Abigail, dau. Col. Adam & Abigail (Cheney) Martin, at Salem, N. Y.; had 8 children, & refers to their genealogy (§ 235; Vol. 1) briefly-

1. Martin, m. Sophia Harvey
2. Mary, m. Capt. William M. McFarland
3. Almira, m. 1. Adam Martin; 2. Lewis D. Alger
4. Barbara Jervis, d. y.
5. Barbara J., m. Peter C. Dunlap
6. Dr. Asa, Jr., m. Elizabeth McNeil
7. Abigail M., m. 1. Dr. William Savage; 2. Rev. Eli T. Mack
8. James Harvey, m. Catharine Baker; see further, Vol. 1; his practice succeeded at Fitch's Point by Dr. Alfred Freeman- **730**; (Dr. Peletiah- 4, Jabez- 3, Samuel- 2, Rev. James) b. Nov. 10, 1765, Groton, Conn.; excerpts of his life events- enl. 1782, as 9 months man, guarding northern frontier; mustered into service as Ensign, May 18, 1782; served as a private in his co., as it lacked a full complement & was consolidated w. ano.; by his Ledger, Oct. 1, 1788, began medical practice at Duanesburg, N. Y.; by same source, p. 30, began his practice in Salem, Feb. 7, 1795; in the same yr., on Sept. 4th, purch. the farm & mills at Fitch's Point that belonged to Walter Martin; part of his dwelling opened as a tavern, operated by Thomas Berry; studied medicine in Easton, N. Y., w. Dr. Philip Smith; rec'd.

physician's certif., Oct. 2, 1797, pursuant to statute; appt. Auctioneer, Feb. 5, 1799; Justice of Peace, 1799, 1801, 1807; Assist. Co. Judge, 1807; chosen Vice Pres., Wash. Co. Medical Soc., at it org., 1807, & served 5 yrs. in that office, 5 yrs. as its Treasurer, & 15 yrs. as its President, being 1st elected in 1812; defeated by Nathan Wilson for U. S. Congress, 1808; appt. Co. Judge, 1810, & elected to Congress over Roger Skinner; re- appt. Co. Judge, 1813, foll. his Congressional service; he & William Fitch erect a woolen factory at Fitch's Point; appt. chairman, Sept. 12, 1814, of a comm. to forward supplies to Salem militia at Plattsburgh, N. Y.; Co. Judge again, 1815- 1828; filled out Rev. war pension appl., 1818, for 15 veteran soldiers, at $3.00 ea., & again, in 1820, for an increase, size of fee & no. of appls. not given; Feb. 1819, elected Elder, Presbyterian church; President, Wash. Co. Agricultural Soc., 1820; gr. Pension Certif. #1721, for his Rev. war services, & resigned in the same yr. as Pres., Wash. Co. Medical Soc.; rec'd. honorary degree of M. D., Feb. 26, 1834, from N. Y. Regents of University; became life member, American Bible Soc., Mar. 16, 1836; d. Aug. 24, 1843, Salem, N. Y.- 799; "father's recoll. of his ancestors only extended to his grdf. [Dr. Peletiah's father] whose name he knew was Jabez & who lived & d. at Norwich"- 838; wf. Abigail, d. Mar. 26, 1840, Salem, N. Y.- 1039

Asahel- (s. Joseph) had 3 or 3 sons, one perh. named Hiram- 727

Asahel- Surgeon's mate, 5th Regt., Conn. troops, 1775; refers American Archives, ii, p. 417- 799

Hon. Asahel- delegate, N. Y. Assembly, 1824, from Cayuga Co.- 799

Augustus D.- of NYC; m. June 5, 1867, Julia Kellogg Lombard, of Yonkers, N. Y.; by Rev. Alfred B. Beach, D. D.- 799

B. Dwight- of Brooklyn, N. Y.; m. Nov. 28, 1866, Emma Walbrath, of Chittenango, N. Y.- 799

Benajah- c. 1750- 55, res. Norwich, Conn.; p. 90, Ledger, Dr. Peletiah Fitch- 838

Benjamin- d. Mar. 21, 1816, at 49, Salem, N. Y.; by a blow which fractured his "scull"; given by John Getty, of Hebron, N. Y.- 724

Benjamin- res. Salem, N. Y., in the place now (1850) occ. by Thomas Milliman- 872

Benjamin- deed witn., Dec. 16, 1791, Dr. Peletiah Fitch to James Tomb- **(L)**- 936

Benjamin- (s. John- 5) from Norwalk, Conn.; farmer, res. Schodack, N. Y.; 2 children, a dau., dec'd. prior 1851, & his s. John, lawyer, Troy, N. Y.- 943

Benjamin- dau. Abigail, m. Henry Bliss; see Vol. 1- **1005**

Benjamin, Jr.- c. 1750- 55, res. Norwich, Conn.; prob. neph., Dr. Peltiah, whose Ledger charges note only a dau., Zipporah, who once had a tooth extracted- 838

Betsey- m. Aaron, s. Moses & Lydia (More) Martin- **1041**

Calvin M.- s. John, & neph. Dr. Samuel S.; present at the latter's home, 702 Broadway, NYC, on Sept. 25, 1851, when, in the absence of his uncle, he assisted Dr. Fitch "in the object of my visit"- 947

Charles- of Montgomery, Alabama; his wf., Mary Seelye, d. Dec. 1, 1864, of Brain Fever- 799

Capt. Charles- Assist. Surgeon, U. S. A.; among those killed or wnd., Apr. 12, 1864, during the massacre at Ft. Pillow, Tennesee- **799**

Rev. Charles- s. Rev. Ebenezer, of Williams College; 1st pastor of the 'Free Church', Boston, Mass., org. c. 1835/6 "on reformatory principles, composed of those persons who thought the old churches too corrupt for them to remain in them, & who separated to form a pure church", which afterw. "split on perfectionism & the Oberlin sect is now defunct"; he later became a Millerite; refers Feb. 19, 1852, *N. Y. Observer-* **799**

Charles E.- lawyer, member of New Bern, N. C. bar; was orator, July 4, 1865, at the Independence day celebrations there- **799**

Chauncey- Sheriff,Clinton co., N. Y., Feb. 2, 1797; served 4 yrs.- **799**

Dr. Chauncey- (s. Jabez, of Hyde Park, Vt.) late of Sheldon, Vt.; m. Eliza, dau. Samuel B. & Louisa (Ashley) Sheldon; children- Jabez, Samuel S., John, Louisa, & Eliza- **947**

Rev. Chester- dismissed Mar. 3, 1852, North church society, New Marlborough, Mass.- **799**

Cordella- c. 1755, res. Norwich, Conn.; credits of several days work by him given in Dr. Peletiah Fitch's Ledger- drawing & cutting wood, mowing, harvesting, & c.; & 'to help move', Apr. 1756, indicating the date that Dr. Peletiah rem. to Groton, Conn.- **838**

Dennis W.- of NYC; formerly of Troy, N. Y.; goldsmith?; his 2nd s., Augustus Dennis, d. Feb. 10, 1869, NYC, & his remains returned to Troy- **799**

E. F.- schoolteacher,California?; had a leg fractured during a R. R. collision on the Western Pacific, Nov. 14, 1869- **799**

Ebenezer- Ensign, Col. Bridge's regt., Mass. troops, 1775; refers American Archives, ii, p. 826- **799**

Ebenezer- res. Wilton, Conn; m. Lydia Mills, of Greenwich, Conn.; 4 children-
1. Jabez, m. Amy Knapp
2. Ebenezer, m. Sarah Hobby
3. Giles, m. Dolly Betts
4. Hannah, m. John St. John- **799**

Ebenezer- (s. Ebenezer & Lydia Mills) res. Saratoga (Schuylerville, N. Y.); children-
1. Sarah, m. Jesse Viele
2. Ebenezer, m. Mary Howland
3. Lydia, m. Jacob Thorn
4. Hannah, m. Alpheus Bullard
5. David H., drowned at the mouth of Fish creek, childless
6. Edward, Esq., m. Hannah Frost
7. Adeline, m. Samuel Eddy
8. Ann H., m. Dr. John Searls
9. Mary, m. Theodore F. Comstock- **799**

Ebenezer- (s. Ebenezer & Sarah Hobby) m. Mary Howland; rem. Wayne co., N. Y., & d. there, leaving several children- **799**

Ebenezer- c. 1750- 55, res. Norwich, Conn.; Dr. Peletiah Fitch's Ledger indicates he was employed in blacksmithing & sawing- **838**

Rev. Ebenezer, D. D.- (1756- 1833) 1st President, Williams College; sketch of his life, by Calvin Durfee, publ. Boston, 1865; refers July 20, 1865, *N. Y. Observer,* for its review; notes material for his biog. scanty, due to a fire that consumed his son's house, incl. the library, & all of his father's manuscripts; several prev. attempts have been relinquished due to lack of reliable material; he was native of Canterbury, Conn.; tutor, Yale; Principal, Williamstown free school, Oct. 1791, & under his direction, it 'became so prosperous it was chartered as a college, & he its President from 1794 till 1815 when (in Sept.) he resigned & became minister of the Presbyterian church, West Bloomfield, N. Y.'; refers Hist. of Berkshire Co., pgs. 167- 170; Rev. Ebenezer also provided information found in Alden's *Epitahs,* regarding the family ancestor, James Fitch- 799; his letter to Timothy Alden, Feb. 28, 1803, conveyed the orig. family history ment. above- **834**

Edmund- (s. William & Sally Hanford) res. NYC; m. there, & rem. Ohio; d. abt. June 1851, leaving 3 children in Ohio- **939**

Lt. Edson- Co. H, 93rd N. Y. Inf.- **1090b**

Edward- (s. Timothy & Esther Platt) m. Esther, dau. Thomas & _____ (Hill) Fitch; ments. 2 daus.- Ann Jennet, m. Daniel Hall; & Adeline, d. a minor- **799**

Edward- Co. E, 88th N. Y. Inf.; wnd. in left hip, Oct. 27, 1864, at Cedar Creek, Va.- **799**

Edward, Esq.- (s. Ebenezer & Sarah Hobby) res. Stafford's bridge, Saratoga co., N. Y.; m. Hannah Frost; 4 children-
1. Adeline E., m. William H. Andrews
2. Harriet Rachel
3. Edward H.
4. Cornelia L.- **799**

Hon. Edward- N. Y. Assembly delegate, from Franklin co., 1855- **799**

Elijah- emig. along w. his bros. Samuel & Hooker, & settl. Norwich, Conn.; refers p. 394, Barber's Hist. Coll. of Conn.- **799**

Elijah- acc. Boston Directory, 1835, res. 752 Washington St., Boston, Mass.- **799**

Rev. Elijah- res. Hopkinton, Mass.; the poet; d. Dec. 16, 1788, at 42; refers Kettel's American Poetry, v. 1, p. 300- **799**; s. Capt. John, 2nd, of Conn.; ord. Jan. 18, 1772, as colleague pastor, Congregational church, Hopkinton, Mass.; his principal work, *The Beauties of Religion,* a blank verse poem; his talents ment., noting that 'the only thing that was ever objected to his character, was his taciturnity; & perh. he was a little too reserved in public & mixed companies'; refers Coll. of the Mass. Hist. Soc., 1st series, iv, p. 16- **836**

Elisha- of Salem, N. Y.; among those taken prisoner at Ft. Ann & Ft. George, 1780 (ano. acct. of his escape, see. Vol. 3); "a remarkably spry, athletic man, a capital singer of songs, a great mimic, & story- teller, readily imitating ano. person's speech & manners to the very life"; he became a favorite among the Indians & was kept w. them instead of being given over to the authorities & confined to prison; "he joined them in their hunts, their pow- wows & dances, & copied all their motions & whoops & shouts so readily, that he rose to high repute among them"; during the winter season, the Indian village was much engaged in skating & he greatly amused his captors by performances on the ice, soon discovering that he could outstrip the fleetest of them; not revealing this, he lulled their suspicions by allowing himself to be beaten in their races; one fine day, when the whole village was out on the ice, he drew 2 or 3 of the best skaters into a race, leading them quite a distance away; he finally shot ahead, exciting them, & for mile after mile, they strove to come up w. him but failed & at length, gave up; he continued w/o pause, despite their shouts that they had accepted defeat, & after great hardship, came through the wilderness; acc. Dr. Fitch, this incident may have occurred on the St. Francis river, his return being via the Conn. river & Coos co., N. H.- **858**

Esq. Elisha- of Norwich, Conn.; s. Mr. Jabez; c. 1755, Jonathan Tracy credited for labor at his home; considered by his family as something of a poet, & wrote "Vision of Happiness", or a poem of similar title (the same title attrib. to a work by Jabez, of Hyde Park, Vt., see § 1997; Vol. 4)- **838**

Elizabeth- m. Col. Jeremiah, s. Jeremiah Mason- **759s**

Wid. Elizabeth- 3rd wf. Peletiah, s. Jabez- 3; ment. as 'Aunt Elizabeth', p. 27, Dr. Peletiah Fitch's Ledger; also ment. on p. 118- **838**

Ephriam- s. Joseph; c. 1810/11, built the new gristmill at Algiers, Pawlet, Vt., nr. his old mill; 2 or 3 yrs. later, he was killed, while cutting out ice to free his overshot wheel; the wheel loosened too quickly, & the weight of ice in its buckets caused it to turn, crushing him betw. the wheel & mill wall; children, by 1st wf.- Derastus, Return, & a dau., who m. _____ Doolittle, & res. Burlington, Vt.; by 2nd wf.- 2 or 3 sons, & dau. Nancy- **727**

Ephriam- of Egremont, Mass.; Deputy to Congress of Berkshire co., July 6, 1774; refers Hist. of Berkshire co., p. 114- **799**

F. W.- Apr. 1864, was 3rd Assist. Engineer, *Pensacola*, a U. S. steam sloop of war- **799**

F. J.- c. 1851, res. Green co., N. Y.- **943**

Dr. Francis P.- of Amherst, N. H.; appt. Examining Surgeon, by the Pension Commissioner; refers Dec. 9, 1852, *N. Y. Tribune-* **799**

Dr. Frederick- s. Elisha; see Vol. 1; refers case of the People vs. Frederick Fitch, for forgery, Wendell's Reports, v. 1, p. 198- **799**

GENEALOGY- some particulars obt. from Mrs. Gershom Sturgis (Elizabeth Rowland) & Mrs. Smith Weed (Sarah Fitch), at the home of Alfred B. Street, Albany, N. Y., on Sept. 5, 1850; an acct., found in Hist. Coll. of Conn., thought to be erroneous, states that there were 3 bros. named Fitch, who orig. came to this country; this material also ment. by information "recently rec'd." from Mrs. Belden, Mrs. Fitch, & Mrs. Raymond, all grandchildren of Gov. Thomas Fitch of Conn., identifying the bros. as- Elijah, & Samuel, who settl. Norwich, Conn.; & Hooker, who settl. Stamford, Conn.; the name of Thomas Ffitch appears on a list of freeholders for Norwalk, Conn., Oct. 13, 1669, & was prob. the father of Gov. Thomas; Dr. Fitch suspects that Samuel, who emig. 1638, along w. his bro. Rev. James, was prob. grdf. of Gov. Thomas; further research indicates that Thomas was the older bro. of Rev. James, & was the father of Gov. Thomas, as suspected; refers Alden's *Epitahs*, iv, p. 139, the art. on James Fitch- the surname sd. to be spelled "Fytche", loc. Essex co., England; also refers 'The Present State of Great Britain', described by Dr. Fitch as "a kind of Blue Book or Register, printed in 1710", & part of the library coll. of Salem Academy; this source notes, p. 594- 'William Fytche, Esq.', member, House of Commons, during Queen Anne's reign, from Borough of Malden, Essex co.; & 'Thomas Fitch', created Baronet, by James, 2nd, Patent #906; in addition, Mrs. Daniel Hall (Ann Jennett Fitch), of 60 Fourth St., Troy, N. Y., "has gathered much respecting the pedigree of the Fitch family"- 799; further notice that the bros. Thomas & James, 'in the ancient way of writing the name, Fytche', emig. 1738, from Bocking, Essex co., England; Thomas settl. Norwalk, Conn., & was father of Gov. Thomas, of the colony- **834**; acc. Capt. Richard Hall Fitch, the brass seal used by his father, Col. (?) Thomas, to stamp naval shipping papers, bore the family coat of arms, & differed from the coat of arms of John Fitch, of Troy, N. Y.- **940**; the Fitch bros. were ostensibly from English nobility, bringing over a coat of arms that was conferred upon Gov. Thomas Fitch; his s. Thomas, used a seal, now possessed (1851) by his s. Andrew, which had "the device", differing from "the device" of John Fitch, of Troy, N. Y., who obt. his "at some Herald's office in the city of New York"; a similar design, the combined arms of the Fitch & Rathbun families, possessed by Miss Rathbun, of Brooklyn, N. Y., the Rathbun design "occ. the left or dexter" side, & the Fitch design "occ. the right or sinister half of the escutcheon"; the Fitch half- green crossed horizontally at the fess pt. by a bar, w. 2 leopard's heads above & 1 below the bar; a wax impression of John Fitch's ring, shows a shield green w. chevron at the fess pt., & 3 antelope heads occ. the dexter chief, sinister chief, & hombril pt. of the escutcheon, w. a sword in its mouth; see Bliss, Peletiah; & Rathbun, Genealogy- **942**; bros. Rev. James, Norwich; Thomas, Norwalk; & Joseph, Windsor, Conn.; Dr. Fitch conjectures that Thomas & Rev. James came over together, & that Joseph foll. some yrs. afterw., hence confusion over whether Joseph was the bro., or son, of Rev. James; refers Hinman's Catalogue- **945b**; Gov. Hopkins noted as the only other individual to do as much for the schools & schooling in early Conn. as was done by the Fitch family- **946**; c. 1830, acc. Fitch, the tavernkeeper, Canfield, Ohio, the family was orig. from Germany & res. for several generations in England bef. the 3 bros. emig. to America; of Gov. Thomas Fitch's sons, some of them came to Ohio & settl. upon the Reserve there- **955**

George M.- Co. L, 9th N. Y. Artillery; killed in action, Oct. 19, 1864, Cedar Creek, Va.- **1799**

George W.- housewright; c. 1835, res. 11 Washington Place, Boston, Mass.- **799**

Giles- (s. Ebenezer & Lydia Mills) m. Dolly Betts; had 6 children- Giles, res. Wayne co., N. Y.; Thaddeus, Dr. Hezekiah, Emma, Elizabeth, & John; & he d. Greenfield, N. Y.- **799**

Hon. H. S.- U. S. Dist. Atty. for Georgia; believes that the President's pardon "blots out all disenfranchisement & c."; refers July 2, 1867, *N. Y. Tribune*; ran, Apr. 1868, as Democratic (rebel) member of Congress- **799**

Wid. Hannah- c. 1750's, res. Norwich, Conn.; p. 42, Dr. Peletiah's Ledger- **838**

Harvey- s. Hon. Asa, Sr.; his house lot, Fitch's Point, Salem. N. Y., orig. occ. by Adam Martin; he built his own house on the lot, 1838; see Fitch, James Harvey- **730**

Henry- of Bergen, N. J.; m. Harriet ___; their s., Beniah Morse, d. Nov. 13, 1863, at 2 yrs., 9 mos., & 8 ds.- **799**

Henry S.- (s. Sen. Graham Newell, of Indiana, who served 1857- 1861) Dist. Atty., Chicago, Illinois; gave a keynote address, July 1858, at a 'monster meeting in Metropolitan Hall', among the National Democrats, & 'made a most capital speech last night for a Buchananeer'; acc. to editorial comments on his speech by the *Chicago Press & Tribune,* 'after giving the Republicans several severe raps, he waded into Douglas & followers, & at every crack of his whip the fur flew & the audience cheered'- **1035**

Henry W.- 1st Assistant Engineer, U. S. steam sloop of war, *Pensacola,* Apr. 1864- **799**

Hezekiah- s. Gov. Thomas; res. Salisbury, Conn.; m. Jerusha Burr of Fairfield; delegate, Conn. Assembly, 1775; refers American Archives, ii, p. 410; had 7 sons & 3 daus., most also res. Salisbury- Hezekiah, Henry, Thomas; Richard, rem. Ohio Reserve; William, refers American Archives, ii, p. 1761, lis.; Charles, Samuel; Sarah, m. ___ Davis, no children; Jerusha, m. ___ Coffin; & Elizabeth, m. ___ Lee- **799**

Hooker- suppos. emig., along w. bros. Elijah & Samuel, & settl. Stamford, Conn.- **799**

Ichabod- Sheriff, Clinton co., N. Y., Nov. 1834; served 3 yrs.- **799**

Ichabod- one of the 1st settlers, 1782, Isle of La Motte,Vt.; refers Thompson's Gazetteer of Vt.- **799**

Irwin L.- Co. A, 9th N. Y. Artillery; killed in action, Oct. 19, 1864, Cedar Creek, Va.- **799**

Lt. J. A.- 40th Regt., Mass. Vols.; killed Sept. 30, 1864, in the battle bef. Richmond, Va.- **799**

J. B.- clerk; c. 1835, res. 165 Court St., Boston, Mass.- **799**

J. M., Esq.- of Oberlin, Ohio; dau. Louise M., m. Apr. 18, 1867, James F. Atkinson- **799**

Jabez- s. Samuel; had sons Samuel & Dr. Peletiah, Sr.- **799**; grds. Rev. James, the emig.; res. & d. Norwich, Conn.; inferred by his grds., Dr. Asa, Sr., that Rev. Jabez, of Portsmouth, N. H., was his father, but concluded in the latter's biog. (§ 835) that he must have been a neph.; var. charges, meetinghouse, minister, & town rates, 1755, pd. by Dr. Peletiah; from his son's Ledger, it appears the eldest sons were Esq. Elisha, Dr. Peletiah; & Asa, who m. Anna ___, & d. Apr. 1775; Cordella & Jabez, Jr., who was "undoubtedly" the Jabez of Hyde Park, Vt., res. w. their father; prob. other children- **838**

Jabez- (s. Ebenezer & Lydia Mills) res. Greenwich, Conn.; m. Amy Knapp; 6 children-

1. Samuel, merch., NYC; d. unm.

2. Sarah, m. Smith Weed
3. Elizabeth, unm.
4. Amy, unm.
5. Amy Knapp, d. childless
6. Thomas, d. childless- **799**

Rev. Jabez- (1672- 1746; s. Rev. James & Priscilla Mason) grad. Harvard, 1694; minister, Ipswich, Mass., & later Portsmouth, N. H.; refers Alden's manuscript of the Ministers of Portsmouth, Coll. of the Mass. Hist. Soc.- **799**; was prob. author, of a biog. of his father, found in Alden's *Epitahs*- **834**; sd. to have left Ipswich in consequence of inadequate pecuniary support, & afterw., a call given for his return; 'his abilities may be inferred by being called to take charge of so significant a church as that of Portsmouth, N. H.'; m. Elizabeth, dau. Col. John Appleton ; children-
1. Elizabeth, m. John Wibird, Esq.
2. Margaret, m.____ Gibbs, of Watertown, Mass.
3. Mary, m. Francis Cabot, Esq.
4. Ann, m. Rev. Nathaniel Gookin, as his 1st wf.
5. John, grad. Harvard, 1728; he 'studied physic w. Dr. Nathaniel Sargent of Hampton, & d. in early life'; it appears to Dr. Fitch that the 2nd Jabez (§ 799) was prob. his neph., rather than his son; refers Alden's Hist. of the Religious Societies of Portsmouth, N. H., Mass. Hist. Coll., 1st series, v. 10, p. 68- **835**

Jabez, 2nd- s. Maj. Samuel, & grds. Rev. James- **838**

Jabez, Esq.- s. Samuel; b. 1740; res. Hyde Park, Vt., one of its 1st grantees; refers Thompson's Gazetteer of Vt.; served 2 campaigns in the old French war & held commission in 1st two campaigns of the Rev. war (appt. 1st Lt., 8th co., 8th Regt. Conn. troops when 1st org. at outbreak of Rev. war; refers American Archives, ii, p. 1582); capt. by British on Long Island & imprisoned 18 mos. on board several of their prison ships- kept a narrative while prisoner & a diary for nearly 40 yrs.; wrote moral & political essays for periodicals of the day '& occasionally ascended mount Parnassus'; rem. Hyde Park, spring 1788, w. his sons, & was 1st town clerk, 1791; d. Feb. 29, 1812, at 75- **799**; erroneously attrib. by Dr. Fitch as "undoubtedly" s. Mr. Jabez, of Norwich, Conn.- **838**; ments. s. Dr. Chauncey- **947**

James- (s. Benjamin & Nancy Duncan) worked at Onondaga Salt Works, & during War of 1812, enl. in U. S. Army, the govt. having taken most of their boats & property so that the works were abandoned; foll. the restoration of peace, he returned to the works & soon after 1815, or as late as1816, "fell into one of the kettles of boiling brine, & was so badly scalded that he d. in a few hrs."; he made a defective conveyance of land in Warren co., Illinois, suppos. belonging to his bro. Peletiah, having (acc. to ano. heir) no authority to draw or convey the land, if ever conveyed to him- **1004**

Capt. James, Esq.- appt. June 13, 1689, w. Maj. Nathan Gold, as delegation from Gen. Court at Hartford, Conn., to advise w. Gov. Leisler of N. Y.; refers Doc. Hist. of N. Y., ii, p. 15; their letter of advisement appears on the foll. pg.; he was also alluded to, ibid., pgs. 5, 7, 25, & 69; & also, Colonial Hist., viii, pgs. 590, 595,

598, 617, & 707; in 1690, was 2nd in command of Gen. Winthrop's army in its march to Ft. Ann; ibid., iv, pgs. 193- 195- **799**

Maj. James- of Conn.; at battle of Lake George w. his regt., 1755; in the assault on Ft. Ticonderoga, 1758; & also, at treaty of Ft. Stanwix, Oct. 28, 1768; refers Colonial Hist., vi, p. 1007; x, p. 732; & viii, p. 122, respectively- **799**

Rev. James, D. D.- b. Dec. 24, 1622, Bocking, Essex co., England; studied partly at Cambridge; emig. 1638, at age 16, w. his older bro. Thomas; settl. Congregational ministry at Saybrook, & afterw. Norwich, Conn.; m. 1. Abigail, dau. Rev. Henry Whitfield, of Guilford, Conn.; 6 children; m. 2. Priscilla, dau. Maj. John Mason, of Norwich, Conn.; 8 children- James, Abigail, Elizabeth, Hannah, Samuel, Dorothy, Daniel, John, Jeremiah, Jabez, Ann, Nathaniel, Joseph, & Eleazor- **799**; refers p. 139, Alden's *Epitahs*; his biog. there, prob. authored by Rev. Jabez Fitch, of Portsmouth, N. H.; same genealogical information, except Eleazor noted as the only one not having a family; also refers Coll. of the Mass. Hist. Soc., 1st series, v. 10, p. 68- **838**; was placed under charge of Rev. Thomas Hooker & Samuel Stone for completion of his literary & religious educ., remaining for 7 yrs., & afterw., settl. Saybrook, for abt. 14 yrs., then rem. Norwalk, Conn., 1660, w. most of his church; remainder of genealogical material, same as § 799; refers Hinman's Catalogue; ord. 1646, became acquainted w. Mohegan language & preached the gospel to Indians in the vicinity of Norwich, Conn.; refers p. 552, Barber's Hist. & Antiquities of N. E. & c.- **945b**; brief ments.- **949, 955**

James Harvey- m. sist. Sarah Ann & William Baker- **731**; res. Salem, N. Y.; his farm was occ. for some yrs. by the "boss" who rebuilt the Presbyterian, or New England, church after it was burnt by tories & Indians during the Rev. war- **744**; s. Dr. Asa, Sr.; occ. the place at Fitch's Point that was once occ. by Timothy Titus, the blacksmith- **803**; an early school in Salem township, built of logs, was loc. on the opp. side of the road from his present (1850) house- **859**; a house was prev. constructed on his homesite by Williard Cheney; the road to Salem branched off at the schoolhouse to go to the sawmill in his upper pasture- **860**; during summer 1852, & for some yrs. prev., Francis Pro, a French army deserter who served as a career soldier in the American army, res. at his home- **974**; res. ¼ mi. from Milton Seeley, & ½ mi. from James F. Alger, at Fitch's Point; during the evening of Feb. 6, 1855, the houses of all 3 men were shaken by earthquake- like motions, & the foll. morning, a crack was found in the earth betw. his house & Mr. Seeley's; see Weather, Frost Heaves- **1026**

James Hillhouse- (s. Jonathan & Sarah Saltonstall) his mother's maiden name was orig. presumed to be "Hillhouse" because of his middle name; "no sons, but some daus.", who m. ____ Galpin, & ____ Taylor; other children left no living descendants-**799**

Jeremiah- dealer in English goods; c. 1835, res. 40 Central St., Boston, Mass.- **799**

John- c. 1835, res. Portland St., Boston, Mass.- **799**

John- portrait painter; c. 1835, res. 12 Myrtle St., Boston, Mass.- **799**

John- the steamboat inventor; his anc. unknown to Capt. R. H. Fitch- **939**; b. E. Windsor, Conn.; apprenticed bef. Rev. war as watch & clockmaker; establ.

business in clock- making & engraving, & repairing muskets, at New Brunswick, N. J.; he retired into Pennsylvania & repaired arms for the American army after the British overran N. J.; in 1785, conceived of a project for propelling a vessel 'by the force of condensed vapor', & relates that when the idea came over him, he had no idea of the existence of a steam engine; built a boat in Philadelphia, 1787, which went at a rate of 8 mph; went to France at abt. this time to introduce the invention, but rec'd. little interest, due to the Rev. there; obt. a patent, 1788, for appl.. steam to navigation, & induced abt. 20 people into an interest in his plans, w. shares at $50.00; made alterations to perfect his invention, 1790, but unable to do so, or obt. the means to continue,"He became so disheartened & impoverished, 'and to drown his reflections, he had recourse to the common but deceptive remedy, strong drink, in which he indulged to excess, & retiring to Pittsburgh, he ended his days by plunging into the Alleghany' "; was prob. desc. from Joseph, of Windsor, Conn.; refers p. 552, Barber's Hist. & Antiquities of N. E. & c.- 949; newspaper clipping, prob. late 1850's, from *The Recorder*, dated Jan. 14, Lawrenceville, Ky., notes 'The Sad Story of John Fitch, the Forgotten Genius'; the reporter equates the magnitude of his achievement w. the pioneer geniuses & inventors who were his predecessors in 'revolutionizing this globe', juxtaposing his accomplishment w. the obscurity of his death; a sketch of his life obt. from materials in the Nelson Co. clerk's office, Bardstown, Ky., also traces the development of his invention; b. Jan. 21, 1743, Windsor, Conn.; learned the silversmith trade & became a brass founder & clockmaker; enl. N. J. line during Rev. war, becoming a Lt., but resigned, became a gunsmith, & sold beer, tobacco, & other items to the troops, thus amassing a fortune in depreciated Continental money; arr. Kentucky, & 'pre-empted' 1,000 acres of Nelson co. bef. 1778; appt. Deputy Surveyor, Kentucky, 1779; ascending the Ohio, his boat was fired upon at the mouth of Big Sandy, & he was capt., but soon regained his liberty; in a few wks., while on the banksof the Ohio, he was musing upon Watt's steam achievements & the possibility of applying them to water travel; Apr. 1785, he conceived of a steam carriage for roads, but after a wk., abandoned the idea as impracticable; during the same yr., he vainly petitn. Congress & several state legislatures- Virginia, Pennsylvania, Delaware, N. J., & N. Y., for aid to perfect & practically apply his idea; presented 'a drawing of the boat; models & tube boilers' to the American Philosophical Society; petitn. Congress, 1789, for gr. of a patent, after prev. disappointments in England; sought aid in France & Spain,1793, but 'compelled by his desperate circumstances to retire to lands nr. Bardstown. Here he became despondent, his mind & body gradually gave way to despair, & he sought relief in habitual intoxication'; his lands reduced to 300 acres, he bargained half of it to a tavern keeper for his board & a pint of spirits per day; d. July 1798, at 55; Will, June 20, Prob. Aug. 14, 1798; incl. bequests to William Rowan,William Thornton, & Eliza Vail; & to John Rowan & James Nourse, the remainder of his real & personal property; 1782- his steamship, a boat 60 ft. long, 1st announced as ready for trials on the Delaware river; 1785- he built steamers that ran from Philadelphia to Burlington, N. J., at 4- 7½ mph;1791- rec'd. patent, & several yrs. foll. his death, the N. Y. Legislature decided that

Livingston & Fulton's boats were, in substance, his invention; in 1813, Fulton was defeated in a N. Y. suit to enforce claim of his orig. invention, although the fame & credit of Fitch's achievement was largely given to Fulton in late yrs.; reported that he d. in the keeper's house of the old stone Co. Jail, & his grave loc. in sight of the Co. Courthouse & Jail; head & foot stones, placed there Oct. 5, 1854, by Wm. McCown, but now gone; neglect of his grave attrib. to the celebrity of other natives from the area, & it being 'the abiding place' of Stephen Foster, etc.; see Bardstown, Kentucky- **949b**

John- (s. William & Sally Hanford) lawyer; res. Toledo, Ohio; m. twice, & has 5 children; Sept. 26, 1851- "is this present evening at Daniel's Hall in Troy"- **939**

John- (s. Benjamin- 6) lawyer; res. Troy, N. Y.; politically a whig, "a youngerly man, who is thought by many to have an over estimate of his own ability & importance, & is rather officious in crowding himself forward- & is currently known by the sobriquet of '<u>Count Fitch</u>' "; recounts his Fitch ancestry, tracing it to Gov. Thomas, a point disagreed w. by Capt. R. H. Fitch & wf.; provides Dr. Fitch w. a letter of introduction to Dr. S. S. Fitch of NYC- **943**

John- (s. Theophilus- 4) it was claimed by his grds. that his father was s. Gov. Thomas, but that has been refuted by other sources- **943**

John- (s. Thomas, the emig.) m. Dec. 3, 1674, Rebecca Lindall; their s. John, b. Sept. 29, 1677; refers pgs. 189, 241, Hall's Norwalk- **943**

John- of Windsor, Conn.; d. 1676, bequeathing his estate to the support of schools there, in such a manner as to allow the Co. court & Selectm. to direct its application- **946**

John- (s. Dr. Chauncey & Eliza Ashley) farmer, Sheldon, Vt.; had s. Calvin M.- **947**

Capt. John, 2nd- of Conn.; s. Rev. Elijah, of Hopkinton, Mass.- **836**

Rev. John- minister, Congregational church, Danville, Vt., from its organization, 1739- 1816; refers Thompson's Gazetteer of Vt.- **799**

Jonathan- (s. Capt. Jonathan & Sarah Saltonstall) m. ____; had daus. Eliza, m. ____ Rathbun; & Mary, m. ____ Culver- **799**

Capt. Jonathan- s. Gov. Thomas; settl. New Haven, Conn.; Sheriff, & collector of the port; m. Sarah Saltonstall, grdau. Gov. Saltonstall, & President Clapp; refers p. 599, Hinman's Catalogue; 9 children- James Hillhouse, Jonathan; Thomas, unm.; Elizabeth, d. a minor; Samuel, d. a minor; William, res. New Haven, Conn.; 2 daus.; Henry, no children; Sarah, m. ____ Graham; & David, unm.; Capt. Jonathan Fitch, recommended for Commissary of Conn. troops, 1775; member, Conn. Assembly, 1775; refers American Archives, ii, pgs. 545; & 55 & 1579, respectively- **799**

Hon. Jonathan- Tioga co. delegate, N. Y. Assembly, 1792- **799**

Joseph- was suppos. the son of Capt. Wm. Fitch, of Pawlet, Vt.; acc. Dr. Fitch, he was s. Benjamin, & grds. Benjamin & Hannah (Read) Fitch, of Norwich, Conn.; had 4 sons- Ephriam, Benjamin, Asahel, & Silas- **727**

Joseph- of New Marlborough, Mass.; magistrate, & deac., Congregational church; rem. Geneva, Ohio; refers Hist. of Berkshire co., pgs. 296, 297- **799**

Joseph- eldest s. Dr. Peletiah; rec'd. his father's place, Noank, Groton, Conn., May 1774- **838**

Joseph- of Kingsbury, N. Y.; mortgaged part of Lot 49 to Thomas Bradshaw, May 19, 1798, for $750.00; disch. June 10, 1800- **938**

Joseph- accepted as inhabitant, Hartford, Conn., 1659; Selectm., 1661- **946**

Joseph- of Windsor, Conn.; bro. Thomas & Rev. James; Dr. Fitch suppos. that he came some time foll. his bros., hence confusion that he may have been the s., rather than the bro., Rev. James- **949b**; brief ment., noting that he res. in N. part of Conn.- **955**

Joseph- of Windsor, Conn.; marginal notation by Dr. Fitch, indicating that his s. was John Fitch, the steamboat inventor- **949b**

Lt. Joseph- officer, Capt. Vissher's co., Albany co. recruits, May 1775- **799**; recommended by Albany Comm. of Safety, May 26, 1775, to serve in John Visscher's co., which was directed to go immed. to Ticonderoga upon completion of its ranks- **832**

Josephus- (s. William & Lucinda Conkey) m. Jane, dau. Deac. John Beaty; res. N. end of the village, Salem, N. Y.- **730**

Hon. Lemuel- Otsego co. delegate, N. Y. Assembly, 1808, 1814, 1815- **799**

Lt. Leroy- Commandant, of a gun boat fleet on the Ohio river; see Vol. 3- **799**

Lucy W.- wf. John; d. Sept. 1, 1833, at 23- **(L)- 772**

Lydia- wf. Simeon; d. July 8, 1838, at 60- **(L)- 932**

Mrs. Marcia R.- d. Mar. 18, 1864, at 73, Williamsburg, N. Y.; her funeral from the house of her son- in- law, Howell Smith; notice of her decease requested to appear in newspapers of Mahoning & Trumbull co., Ohio- **799**

Mr.- refers Hooker's Icones (?) Plantarium, v. x, pt. 1"wholly occ. by figures of ferns, executed w. great skill by Mr. Fitch"; also, Gardner's Chronicle, p. 255, London, 1854; also, the 1st part of Dr. Seeman's quarto work on the flora of the Fiji Islands, recently publ., "to contain 400 pgs. letter press, & 100 colored plates" by Fitch; refers Apr. 6, 1865, *N. Y. Tribune-* **799**

Nancy- dau. Ephriam; taught school at Fitch's Point, Salem, N. Y., c. 1820; "was of embonpoint size & somewhat affected in her airs, pronouncing very precise"- **727**

Nathan- of Guilford, Vt., 1782; refers Thompson's Gazetteer of Vt.- **799**

Hon. Nathaniel- Oneida co. delegate, N. Y. Assembly, 1831, 1832- **799**

Peletiah- (s. Benjamin & Nancy Duncan) acc. Benjamin Lombard, Jr., by Warrant No. 8128, Dec. 4, 1817, he was entitled to 160 acres, in the NW quarter, Sect. No. 13, Township No. 9 North, & Range No. 1 West, apparently the SW corner of Warren co., Illinois; this tract, defectively conveyed by his bro. James, & later bid off for taxes; in order to secure a more perfect title, Lombard came to Dr. Fitch, Sept. 29, 1853, to seek out his heirs & obt. quit claims from them; his heirs, acc. Dr. Fitch, were 5 in number, who were ea. offered $5 by Lombard to quit claim; of these, only Betsey Taylor was ment. by name, & she refused to accept the offer until after the other heirs had been consulted; acc. Hon. John Savage, the warrant land was acq. by Peletiah when he served as Sgt., Capt. Lytle's co., 4th regt. of rifleman, during the War of 1812- **1004**

Dr. Peletiah- dau. Elizabeth, b. Apr. 6, 1799, m. Aaron, s. Moses, Sr., & Lydia (More) Martin- **731**; (Jabez- 3, Samuel-2, Rev. James- 1)- **799**; b. ca. 1721; his Ledger utilized by Dr. Fitch to identify relationships of cert. family members who res. Norwich & Groton, Conn.; settl. medical practice & kept tavern, 1752- 55, at Norwich, when he was betw. 30- 35 yrs. old, & afterw. rem. Groton, prob. Apr. 1756, continuing in the same occ.; May 1774, gave up his place at Noank,Groton, to his eldest s. Joseph, & rem. Halifax,Vt.; appt. 1st Judge,Cumberland co., Aug. 18, 1778, his commission signed by Gov. Clinton; rem. Salem, N. Y., & was appt. a commissioner, Apr. 12, 1782, "for detecting & defeating conspiracies against the liberties of America"; obt. deed for his subsequent residence, Lot No. 70, Turner's Patent, Nov. 21, 1782, from Commissioners of Forefeitures; d. Apr. 16, 1803, at 82- **838**; for £ 25, conveys 8 acres & 64 rods, on the E. end of Lot 70, Salem, to James Tomb, Dec. 16, 1791; recorded July 26, 1792- **(L)- 936**; m. Elizabeth, dau. Samuel Burrows; she rec'd. £ 30 in her father's Will, Feb. 2, 1756; their heirs, c. 1833, incl. dec'd. sons- Benjamin- 6 children; Peletiah, Jr.- 9 children; Chester-left no children; Elisha- 8 children; their s. Asa, still living; & dec'd. s. Joseph- 5 children; & dec'd. daus.- Lydia Henderson- 6 children; & Elizabeth Martin- 7 children- **1100**

Philo S.- d. Oct. 5, 1865, at 69, suddenly, New Canaan, Conn.- **799**

R. H.- of U. S. Navy; Chief Engineer, *Canandaigua*; detached & placed on waiting orders, Feb. 19, 1869- **799**

Rev.- Episcopal minister, 1866 & 1867, Akron, Ohio- **799**

Capt. Richard Hall- (s. Thomas & ____ Hill) b. Nov. 5, 1770, Norwalk, Conn.; m. Theodocia Conklin; had 3 daus.- Emily, m. Albert P. Heartt; ano., m. ____ Bliss; & the 3rd dau. d. y.; he was a steamboat Capt., Troy, N. Y., & d. Mar. 19, 1854- **799**; informs Sept. 26, 1851, on Fitch family origins- **939**; was always a sailor, on the Sound, & then 10 yrs. as Capt. of Troy steamboats; m. dau. John Conklin, of Norwalk, Conn.; 2 infants dec'd.; & 2 daus.- Sarah, m. Peletiah Bliss; Emily, m. Albert P. Heartt- **940**; a printed copy of Gov. Thomas Fitch's funeral sermon in his possession- **941**; he & his wf. "scout" statements made by John Fitch of Troy, claiming that Theophilus was a son of Gov. Thomas, refuting the possibility & stating that Theophilus came from Chestnut Hill, abt. 5 mi. from Norwalk, Conn.- **943**

Rossawell R.- of Coxsackie, N.Y.; m. Rettie Hasbrouck; his wf. d. Oct. 6, 1865, at 18 yrs., 11 mos., & 22 ds., of tent fever- **799**

Samuel- perh. emig. w. his bros. Elijah & Hooker; settl. Norwich, Conn.; was prob. grdf. Gov. Thomas- **799**

Samuel- (s. Rev. James & Abigail Whitfield) had s. Jabez- **799**

Samuel- worked as a hired hand, 1808, for Dr. Asa Fitch, Sr.- **799**

Samuel- rec'd. honorary degree at Cambridge, 1766; was one of 10 lawyers who res. Boston, Mass., 1768; Advocate General of Mass. Admiralty Court, 1770, until Rev. war; among those forbidden by the legislature to return to the province; refers pgs. 186, 200, & 232, Washburn's Judicial Hist. of Mass.- **799**; res. Boston, Mass.; held offices of Solicitor & Counselor at law to Board of Commissioners, 1776; noted as an Addressor of Hutchinson, 1777; went to Halifax, Nova Scotia, & in 1778, was proscribed & banished; 'like most of his offical associates, was incl. in the conspiracy act of 1779'; refers Lives of the Loyalists- **944**

Samuel- of Stonington, Conn.; settl. Richmond, Mass. bef. Rev. war; refers Hist. of Berkshire co., p. 325- **799**

Samuel- of ano. family desc. from Gov. Thomas; res. Norwalk, Conn.; m. Esther, dau. Timothy & Esther (Platt) Fitch; had 2 or 3 sons- **799**; he is the current (1851) owner of Gov. Thomas Fitch's homesite, Norwalk, Conn.; his wf. is a cousin of Capt. Richard H. Fitch, of Troy, N. Y.- **941**

Samuel- c. 1750- 55, res. Norwich, Conn.; refers pgs. 18 & 49, Ledger- **838**

Samuel- 1645, Hartford, Conn.; 1649, school teacher, for 3 yrs., at £ 15 per yr.- **946**

Dr. Samuel Sheldon- res. 702 Broadway, NYC; c. 1851, John Fitch, of Troy, N. Y., gives Dr. Fitch a letter of introduction to him- **943**; (s. Dr. Chauncey & Eliza Sheldon) visited Sept. 25, 1851, by Dr. Fitch;"is extensively known at present for his treatment of consumption. He was out of town for a wk. A neph. of his interested himself in the obj. of my visit, & placed in my hands Hinman's work...", see Vol. 4- **947**

Service- Co. B, 144th N. Y. Vols.; among those exchanged prisoners from Savannah, Ga., Dec. 1864, who arr. Annapolis, Md.- **799**

Silas- s. Joseph; was married 2 or 3 times- **727**

Simeon- of NYC; dau. Annie, m. Mar. 29, 1864, Henry B. Hyde- **799**

Simeon- d. Aug. 28, 1857, at 83, Oswego, N. Y.; refers Munsell's Annals- **(L)**- **932**; c. 1851, res. Oswego, N. Y.- **943**

Stephen- c. 1750- 55, res. Norwich, Conn.; refers p. 17, Ledger- **838**

Rev. Stephen- 'has been preferred to Gayton Rectory, in the Marsh, Lincolnshire'; refers *Gentleman's Magazine*, Aug. 1774, p. 391- **799**

Theophilus- (s. John- 3) his claim of ancestry as a son of Gov. Thomas refuted by Capt. R. H. Fitch, indicating that his probable origin was Chestnut Hill, abt. 5 mi. from Norwalk, Conn.; Dr. Fitch also refutes the lineage, noting that he was, instead, a 2nd cousin of Gov. Thomas; ments. s. John- **943**

Thomas- the emig.; came to America w. 2 bros.; had 2 sons- Gov. Thomas, & ____, unm.; hence, all of his desc. were from the former (compare w. next entry)- **941**; bro. Rev. James; early settler, Norwalk, Conn.; came along w. 13 other young men, 1638, preparing to become ministers of the gospel; refers Hinman's Catalogue- **945b**; 1673, appt. Capt. of dragoons for Fairfield, w. John Burr as Lt.- **948**; brief ments.- **946, 949, 955**

Thomas- "Ffitch"; appears as a freeholder, Norwalk, Conn., on a list taken Oct. 13, 1669; "This was prob. father of the Gov. & it must obviously have been his grandfather who came over w. his bro., Rev. James F. in 1638"- **799**

Thomas- (s. Thomas & ____ Hill) m. Amelia Lewis; 2 children- Thomas, d. w/o issue; Mary Esther, m. ____ Davenport, & res. Illinois- **799**; res. Norwalk, Conn., foll. by NYC; m. Amelia Lewis, of Huntington, Long Island, N. Y.; his s. Thomas d. at abt. 15 yrs. old; he rem. w. his dau., Rock river, Illinois, & d. there abt. 1847- **940**

Col. Thomas- s. Gov. Thomas; lawyer, res. Norwalk, Conn.; m. ____ Hill, of Fairfield, Conn.; 5 children-

1. Thomas, m. Amelia Lewis
2. Sarah, m. Stephen St. John
3. Andrew, rem. Ellsworth, Ohio
4. Capt. Richard Hall, b. Nov. 5, 1770, Norwalk, Conn.; m. Theodocia Conklin
5. Esther, m. Edward Fitch; Col. Thomas Fitch was a delegate to Conn.

Assembly, 1775; refers American Archives, ii, p. 1580- **799**; also a naval officer, & prob. many yrs. in the militia; referred to as "Col."; he stamped shipping papers w. a brass seal which was believed to have the family coat of arms on it, now in possession of his s. Andrew; this record notes 6 children, incl. Thaddeus Hill, who d. y., & unm.; he d. 1792, at 69, & his wf. d. a wk. later, at 59- **940**

Gov. Thomas- of Conn. (1700- 1774; Gov., 1754- 66); res. Norwalk, Conn.; s. Thomas, the emig.; also noted that Samuel, the emig., was his grdf.; grad. Yale; a lawyer of emminence, & long the Chief Justice; was Gov. for several yrs., being the last Royal Gov. prior Rev. war; had 6 sons & 4 daus., who all survived to maturity, & res. Conn.-

1. Thomas, m. ____ Hill; res. Norwalk
2. Jonathan, m. Sarah Saltonstall; settl. New Haven
3. Hezekiah, m. Jerusha Burr, of Fairfield, & settl. Salisbury
4. Ebenezer, m. Lydia Mills; res. Wilton
5. Timothy, m. Esther Platt; res. Norwalk
6. Giles, d. as a minor, in Norwalk
7. Hannah, d. unm.
8. Esther, d. unm.
9. Mary, m. Josiah Thatcher, of Norwalk
10. Elizabeth, m. Andrew Rowland, of Fairfield; as Gov. of Conn., he signed credentials, May 30, 1754, of the colony's delegates to the Congress at Albany, N. Y.; refers Doc. Hist., ii, p. 547; d. July 18, 1774, at 70, Norwalk, Conn.; his epitah, Barber's Hist. Coll. of Conn., p. 394, states he d. July 18, 1775, at 75- **799**; his funeral sermon preached by Rev. Dickison & later reprinted; his Wid. cont'd. to res. in his mansion, slightly outside the village, & when the British descended upon Norwalk to burn the town, word was sent to her to rem. her furniture; believing that respect for the Gov. would induce them to spare the house, she rem. only the silver plate, "& wrote conspicuously w. chalk upon the walls of the house, that it was the house of Gov. Fitch"; as the force passed into the village, "a number of them went in & Helped themselves liberally to the wine in the cellar, & then passed on"; after firing the village, some stragglers again went into the house during the withdrawal & set it to flames; when the inhabitants returned, the fire was too far advanced to extinguish, & the Gov.'s house burnt to the ground; an

elm, set out under the Gov.'s direction, stands in the orig. loc. of the mansion; ments. only 2 daus.- Esther, d. unm., of smallpox; & Hannah, also unm.- **941**

Hon. Thomas- of Boston, Mass.; was one of a court at Newport, 1723, for the trial of pirates; refers Washburn's Judicial Hist. of Mass., p. 173; one of 4 Justices, Court of Common Pleas, Suffolk co., 1732; lame w. gout, he was unable to attend court to try Swanzey vs. Byfield, as Chief Justice; ibid., p. 336; representative to the General Court of Mass., 1709- 1713; refers Mass. Hist. Coll.; his 2nd service noted, x, p. 27- **799**

Timothy- s. Gov. Thomas; farmer, res. Norwalk, Conn.; m. Esther Platt; children-
1. Hannah, m. Azer Belden, of Wilton, Conn.
2. Timothy, m. Esther Wright
3. William, m. Sally Hanford
4. Edward, m. Esther, dau. Thomas Fitch
5. Esther, m. Samuel Fitch
6. Charles
7. Joseph
8. Sarah, m. ____ Raymond- **799**

Hon. Timothy- Genesee co.delegate, N. Y. Assembly, 1830; Co. Clerk, 1831- 37; Surrogate, 1841- 45- **799**; c. 1851, res. Batavia, N. Y.- **943**

Walter- res. 1750- 55, Norwich, Conn.; p. 97, Dr. Peletiah Fitch's Ledger- **838**

*William-*c. 1803, purch. Silas Conkey's homesite & mill, bef. Conkey rem. Martinsburgh, N. Y.; m. Lucinda, dau. Silas & Zerniah (Martin) Conkey, a few yrs. after her family had rem. to Martinsburgh; children-
1. Josephus, m. Jane, dau. Deac. John Beaty
2. Abigail, m. John C. McLean
3. Sophia, m. Henry K. McCleary
4. Hannah, m. Dr. Armstrong
5. Prudence, m. ____ Dennis
6. Sarah, m. Murray D. McFarland
7. Mary, m. Dr. Armstrong, foll. her sist.'s death- **730**; he & Asa Fitch, Sr., erected a large woolen factory at the Point, c. 1813, owning 1/3rd interest, & the latter owning the other 2/3rds- **799**

William- of New Haven, Conn.; Apr. 5, 1869, was Citizen's candidate for Mayor, & elected over the Democratic contender by an 85 vote margin- **799**

William- plaintiff, Oct. 19, 1774, vs. Roger Rose, & Reuben Harmon, Sr., & Jr.- **878**

William- (s. Timothy & Esther Platt) m. Sally Hanford- **799**; res. Schodack, N. Y., & later rem.Ohio; had 2 sons & 3 daus.-
1. Edmund, res. NYC, & rem. Ohio
2. John, lawyer, res. Toledo, Ohio
3. Mary, m. & res. w. her father
4. Anna, unm., res. w. her father
5. Julia, d. w/o issue- **939**; c. 1851, res. Ohio- **943**

William- (s. Hezekiah & Jerusha Burr)- 799; res. Salisbury, Conn., prob. his life long- **939**

William- lightning struck 3 pine trees, abt. 10:00 PM, Aug. 11, 1853, in the W. corner of his pine grove at Fitch's Point, Salem, N. Y.; see Weather; also, ment. of ano. tree, c. 1848/9, struck on a hill N. of Fitch's Point, tearing strips of wood from it & breaking off the top- **996**

Capt. William- res. Pawlet, Vt.; Moses Billings suppos. that Joseph Fitch, of Salem, N. Y., was his son- incorrect, acc. Dr. Fitch- 727; elected Capt., Green Mtn. regt., July 27, 1775- **781b**; acc. Capt. R. H. Fitch, prob. cannot be desc. of Gov. Thomas, as he has no information on the Fitch family in that loc., or its relation to the family- **939**

Hon. William- Otsego co. delegate, N. Y. Assembly, 1826- **799**

William, Esq.- of Ipswich, England; mineralogist; 'had coll. many rarities from the Suffolk crag'; refers Charlesworth's Magazine of Natural History, v. 1, p. 220, London, 1837- **799**

Hon. William R.- Tompkins co. delegate, N. Y. Assembly, 1836- **799**

Rev. William T.- late of the Episcopal diocese of Georgia; accepted a call to St. Michael's, Naugatuck, Conn.; refers Apr. 20, 1865, *N. Y. Observer-* **799**

Fitch's Point, Salem, N. Y.- the 'long house', a noted landmark here, loc. Mill lot, Salem, on the site where Adam Marttin 1st res. in a log house, 1781- 89- **730**; the 'red house', ano. area landmark, orig. occ. by Moses Martin, Sr., & then by Moses, Jr.; the latter's sons, Sidney & Lansing, & their mother, occ. separate ports. of it foll. his death, & it was sold foll. their mother's death- **731**; the blacksmith shop here was operated bef. the Rev. war by Timothy Titus; the same loc. was later purch. by Reuben Cheney, who erected a dam & sawmill; c. 1850, a stone quarry was opened at the Point- **803**; c. 1774/5, bef. the arr. of Moses Martin, Sr., the principal residents were Daniel Livingston, Roger Reid, Esq. McNaughton, & William Reid- **852**; c. 1777, four houses were loc. here- Moses Martin; Daniel Livingston, by the old bridge; Germond, on the Battenkill, abt. ¼ mi. from Martin's; Asher Seward, at the top of the hill, betw. the bridge across Black creek & the Red House- **855**; acc. Wid. Angel, the orig. road from the Point ran NE upon the flat, N. to the millpond, & nearly to the N. line of the Mill lot, where it went uphill, to higher ground, & remained there, abt. where it now (1851) runs; the road's course went past Jarvis Martin's & (Wm.) Moffat's places, then branched to go up Black creek, "some ways this side of Jarvis's", running to the rear of his property for some distance, "keeping over the knolls & hillocks, up where Chester Martin now lives"; the road from Jarvis to Chester Martin, further N. along the creek, was constructed by Aaron Martin, as the town would not consent to the expense for changing it- **865**; prob. during, or shortly foll. the Rev. war, Scotch & Irish settlers would come here & construct "little huts of no consequence", & become "<u>resident citizens</u>" shortly after their arrival; due to their unceremonious arr., & hasty construction, they were generally thought of as tories; some of the earliest settlers were ____ Germond, ____ Norton, Timothy Titus, ____ Reid, &

____ MacQueen (McQueen)- **867**; a horse once owned by Moses Martin, Sr., was once seen to walk along the top of a log fence here;"it was (very sagely) concluded on all hands that he was bewitched"; see Blind Staggers; other similar incidents alluded to, see Adams, ____- § 28, Vol. 1; & Angel, Augustus- **870**; some instances & descriptions of lightning striking within its vicinity, betw. 1848- 66, w. some unusual effects & damages; see Weather- **996**

Fitch's Woolen Factory- erected 1813, at Fitch's Point, by Asa Fitch, Sr., & William Fitch; nearly $1,100.00 was advanced by Asa, Sr., for the work, materials, machinery, & stock, incl. a carding machine costing $400.00; Joseph Stout & Wm. McKellip engaged as carpenters; Zaccheus Atwood was to operate the factory in return for 1/3rd ownership, but failed to do so, & Dec. 15, 1813, Luther Finel was contracted in his stead- **799**

FITZGERALD,
John- m. Jan. 1, 1855, Mary, dau. James Duane & Sarah (Collins) Doty- **730**

FLACK,
James- of Salem, N. Y.; m. Martha, dau. James Harsha, the emig.- **973**; his wid. m. 2nd, David Hanna Lytle, as his 2nd wf.- **1069**
Robert- m. Martha, dau. William & Mary (Hanna) Lytle; she d. St. Lawrence co., N. Y., leaving children there- **1069**

FLEMMING,
Henry- Co. A, 2nd N. Y., Northern Black Horse, Cav., 1861- 2- **1080**

FLINT,
Asa- of Cambridge, N. Y.; Lot 60, "Kingsberry", N. Y., conveyed to him for £ 242, Mar. 15, 1784, by David Sprague- **(L)- 936**

FLOOD,
____- Scotch; taught school at an early date, Fitch's Point, Salem, N. Y., teaching 8- 10 "scholars" in Roger Reid's house- **859**

FLORIDA- **759s**; Appilachicola- **974**; Ft. Foster- **974**; Tampa Bay- **974**

FLOWER,
Byron L.- of Rupet, Vt.; Assist. Surgeon, 9th N. Y. H. Art.; d. in hospital, Wash., D. C.; bur. Oct. 30, 1862, gr. 4, soldier's plot, Evergreen Cemetery, Salem, N. Y.- **1081**

FOLLET,
____- of Pittstown, N. Y.; m. James Howard, s. James & Clarinda (Griffin) Wells- **839**

FONDA,
Douw- d. May 17, 1838, at 74- **(L)- 932**
Family- c. 1777, res. Hoosick, N. Y.; foll. the evac. of Salem, William Boyd's family took shelter here- **729**

FOOT,
Nivium- m. Nancy Doty; had 2 sons & a dau.; see Foot, Adoniram, Vol. 3- **730**

Forfeitures- a partial listing of lands forfeited foll. the Rev. war, 'Registered for by the direction of Alex. Webster, Esq., Commissioner of Forfeitures for theEastern District State of New York in pursuance of an Act entitled an Act for the speedy sale of confiscated & forfeitured estates within this State, & for other Purposes therein mentioned, Passed the 12th day of May 1784'; contains 50 entries, extracted from pgs. 1- 25 of the doc. ment.; tracts loc. Artillery Patent & Skenesborough (Whitehall, N. Y.) & sold 1784- 87; 1st entries incl. 484 acres, Artillery Patent, confiscated from Col. Philip & Maj. Andrew P. Skene; list gives purchaser, Lot No., loc., acres, price, & purch. date- **(L)- 875**; (or Confiscated lands) acc. Dr. Fitch's notes, a vol., c. 1853, loc. in the Surveyor General's Office, Albany, N. Y., lists all the confiscated lands within the Wash. co. vicinity foll. the Rev. war- **991**

FORT,
Col.- res. Hoosick, N. Y.; the old Van Ess homestead was the 1st house above his on the old Albany- Bennington road along the Hoosick river- **766**
Gen.- c. 1850, res. nr. the Hoosick river, where the Vrooman family res. during the Rev. war- **744**

Fort Ann, N. Y.- July 17, 1777, the blockhouse here was the advance post of the British army- **794**

Fort Ann, battle of- apparently began when 2 American companies, one lead by a Capt. Rowley, were detailed to seize a scow lying in Wood creek w. 2 field pieces on it; the companies came upon the British, Indians, & tories while in the process of completing their assignment, & drove the enemy up Battle Hill; Capt. Rowley & some of his co. later made an attack from ano. position, forcing the enemy from the hill; all of the American forces then retreated towards Ft. Edward nr. evening, halting at Sandy Hill, where a skirmish occurred; the American army, retreating from Ticonderoga, arr. at Ft. Edward the foll. morning- **747**; acc. Gouverneur Morris' correspondence to N. Y. Provincial Congress, July 14, 1777, Gen. St. Clair's rear guard was fallen upon by a force of 10 companies of grenadiers & light infantry, abt. 16- 18 mi. from Mt. Independence, or by part of the British army from Ticonderoga sent in pursuit of the "fugitive" American force there; our loss was 'from 300 to 20', & the enemy's loss was 'from 1,000 to 50'; there were 24 prisoners taken- 14 Canadians, 2 British, & 4 foreigners (Germans); the fort was attacked by the British & repulsed twice, w. considerable loss, but none occurring on the American side; foll. the last repulse, Col. Henry R. Van Rensselaer was sent out w. some militia, & fell upon the 9th Regt.; a severe conflict ensued, w. 12 Americans killed on the field, & a considerable no. of wnd., incl. Col. Van Rensselaer, & the assault was evaluated as less effective than possible; a British Capt., Dr., & 1 or 2 more, were capt.- 792; names & residences of 5 soldiers capt. here & at Ft. George, 1780, recoll.; see Prisoners, Rev. War- **858**

Fort Edward, N. Y.- Gen. Arthur St. Clair's force at Ft. Ticonderoga joined the troops stat. here under Gen. Schuyler, July 12, 1777- **738b**; no. of men stat. here, late July 1777, given as 6,000, by Samuel Standish's acct. when interrogated by Gen. Simon Frazier, who stated that he, presumably, had observed only half that number there 3 days earlier- **747**; a party of N. H. people, 'strengthened by some persons of desperate fortunes & bad character in the Western Districts', acc. Wm. Duer, Esq., July 11, 1775, & also by William Marsh & Samuel Rose, June 28th, had assembled into a mob, resolved to stop the Charlotte co. courts here; on news that Duer had detained Capt. Motte's co. to protect the courts, they desisted in their plans- **779**; Abram Yates, Jr., & Gouverneur Morris report from Moses kill, July 23, 1777, on Gen. Schuyler's retreat to here from Ft. Edward; on the morning of this report, the picket guard of their party was attacked on the Ft. Ann road at abt. noon, by British troops & 'savages', killing & scalping one of their number, killing 12 more, & wnd. 12, ano. 5 of them, mortally; by evening, the full force had arr. at Moses kill, where Gen. Schuyler would have a strong post, acc. Yates & Morris, if he had suffic. numbers; in the morning, 300 Mass. militia were disch., despite their officers' entreaties, & all the militia 'are so heartily tired & so desirous of getting home' that this report expects none will remain after 10 days, & the army will be '700 Continental troops, sick & well'- **797**; houses noted, 1798- Sherwood's (prob. Adiel), Baldwin's tavern, & Kane's store- **804**; Lorenzo Dow preached here at abt. the time Mrs. Baldwin was burned to death, late Mar. 1798- **815**; trustees,Union Library, elected Apr. 1796- Sidney Berry, Ebenezer Willoughby, John Eddy, Robert Willoby [sic], & Matthais Ogden; refers p. 7, Miscellanies- **879**; Gov. Delancey iss. a proclamation, Sept. 21, 1759, inviting settlm. on lands loc. in this vicinity & Wood creek,"as the forts now erecting there, will protect them from hostile incursions of the enemy from Canada"- **928**; the area was 1st governed by John Henry Lydius, from Albany, N. Y., & then Lord Jeffrey Amherst assumed its governorship in 1756- **930**; during the old French war, some teamsters were conducting a train of military stores from down river to this loc., on a military road along the W. side of the Hudson, in what is now the town of Moreau; abt. 2 mi. below Ft. Edward, they came upon a small run of water (perh. Snook's kill) where the bridge had been taken up; as they stopped, Indians almost instantly fired upon them from the N. side of the runlet; one teamster was shot dead & bur. on the spot by the other teamsters; acc. Dr. Fitch, the teamster was prob. killed foll. Abercrombie's defeat (at Ticonderoga, July 8, 1758) illust. the "audacity" of the Indians in boldly crossing the Hudson & attacking trains above & below Ft.

154

Edward; a strip of causeway from this old military road settl. below the river nr. Martin F. Thompson's house (c. 1851) in the town of Moreau- **958**; the highway abt. 2 mi. below here approaches the riverbank on the W. side of the Hudson, & the river is unsafe for ice transportation further S.; during the Rev. war, it was obstensibly at this point that a sleigh transporting cannon conveyed its cargo to the road, but lost the heaviest cannon in the river- **959**; Hon. John Winslow, Esq., was perh., acc. Dr. Fitch, the Gen. Winslow commanding troops here, 1758, for an expedition against Canada- **988**; having obt. intelligence from Indians sent to spy the frontier that the English were planning to push their settlm. N. to Lake George (Lac St. Sacrement), Monsig. Piquet advised sending a force to intimidate & blunt their enterprises; a force lead by Mons. Marin, & accomp. by Piquet, came down, & a detachm. burnt the fort & the "Lydius establishments", along w. "several sawmills, planks, boards & other building timber, the stock of supplies, provisions, the herds of cattle along nearly 15 leagues of settlm., & made 145 prisoners, w/o having lost a single Frenchman or w/o having any even wnd."; Dr. Fitch notes that an acct. of the destruction of Saraghtoga (Schuylerville, N. Y.) on Nov. 19, 1745, was perh. the event described (Col. Lydius' house was not burnt until 1749)- **1013**

Fort George- 2 wagons from the American force nr. here were capt. by Burgoyne's Indian scouts, July 15, 1777; foll. the incident, everything here was brought to Ft. Edward, & Col. Van Dyck 'quitted the post after seeing every part of it in flames' on the foll. day- **794**; names & residences of 5 soldiers capt. here & at Ft. Ann, 1780, recoll.; see Prisoners, Rev. War- **858**

Fort Miller, N. Y.- after leaving Ft. Edward, Gen. Burgoyne's army encamped here for several days; their tents were pitched on the flat at the base of the river hills & E. of the canal lock; a no. of bullets were recovered nr. the loc. of the Duer Mansion, particularly nr. the barn, & many were found in the highway that lead from the mansion to the village, nr. the base of the hill; this was S. of where the army suppos. camped; the bullets were so numerous here, & at Duer's barn, that apparently these locations were used for target practice- **800**; c. 1798, the families res. in the area, going from S. to N., beginning at the mouth of the Battenkill on the Hudson- Thomas & Samuel Rogers; Archibald McNeil, on the W. side of the Hudson, at the ferry, where Ft. Miller bridge was later built (Northumberland, N. Y.); Thomas Jacquay, on the E. side of the ferry; Seelye- above Jacquay, foll. by Matthews, & then Solomon Smith; a schoolhouse, & 1 or 2 small houses, then Duer Mansion; above Duer was Ransom, foll. by Noah Payne, Sr., then Noah Payne, Jr., & Daniel Payne; Potter, Ephriam Crocker, & Samuel Berry's tavern foll., nr. Moses kill; Ephriam Crocker's bro. res. just S. of the kill, & the Bell & Bitely families were the last bef. Ft. Edward, nr. the Black House; in Saratoga co., on the W. side of the Hudson, at Ft. Miller falls, were sawmills kept at the upper & lower falls by the Vandenburghs; above them, in succession, were the Burt, Lewis, Nevins, Barns, & Craig families, foll. by Bunnel Payne; the Ft. Miller bridge was not constructed until the turnpike rec'd. a charter to construct its road- **804**; a 'dam war' occurred here, c. 1850, due to health concerns that were attrib. to flooded lands- **844**

Fort Randall, Dacota Territory- (loc. on Missouri river, opp. Pickstown, S. Dakota) its garrison of Federal troops was relieved, Dec. 7, 1861, by Co. A- C, 14th Iowa Inf., who apparently remained throughout the winter & foll. yr. as their substitutes- **1089**

Fort Ticonderoga- evac. & retreat by Gen. St. Clair, July 1777, ostensibly went through Castleton, & arr. at Manchester, Vt., on July 9th; his forces left Manchester the foll. morning & arr. in Salem, N. Y., by evening, & encamped on John Lytle's farm; they rem. the foll. day, via Argyle, & on July 12th, joined Gen. Schuyler at Ft. Edward- **738b**; an attack by American forces, prob. Col. Brown's (Sept. 18, 1777), acc. Dr. Fitch, released the prisoners confined here; the magazines were broken into & boxes of valuables opened, & left for the prisoners to confiscate as recompense for their captivity- **742**; after Burgoyne's army had left Ft. Edward, the American prisoners were taken to Lake George, & then on a gunboat to here, where they were placed under a Hessian guard; Samuel Standish was imprisoned here, & was allowed to work for wages as a teamster, w. 2 horses & a carriage, hauling pork from the head of Lake George to Ft. Edward?; on his 3rd trip doing this duty, he & 3other prisoners- Samuel Dunham, John Cole, & John Mitchel, escaped & made their way to Arlington, Vt.- **747**; Gen. Schuyler commanded here, Dec. 1775, when some of the American forces returned from the Quebec Campaign- **750**; the Provincial Congress gr. Dirck Swart a leave of absence, May 30, 1775, to superintend rem. of its cannon to the head of Lake George, fearing their recapt. by invasion from Canada; on the same day, a communication from Conn. colony to N. Y., read into the record, states that the fort was not capt. by their regular troops, "but by adventurers; among them Col. Arnold of Mass. & Capt. Douglass, guardian of the Stockbridge Indians; ...almost all of the rest of the adventurers were inhabitants of N. Y. colony"- **773**; Col. Arnold was apprehensive that the regulars might visit them if they knew the American strength here; his May 23, 1775 letter from Crown Point notes his decision to make a stand at Crown Point, in order to secure the cannon from recapt.; in response to actions of Conn. colony on Col. Arnold's behalf, N. Y. Provincial Congress appts. Dirck Swart to supervise rem. of cannon (§ 773) & directs Albany Comm. of Safety to raise militia for defense of the fort- **774**; Col. Arnold's May 19, 1775 letter to Comm. of Safety, Cambridge, Mass., notes "86 cannon, howitzers & c. (some bad & useless)" capt. here; also notes that he would be "extremely glad to be superceded in my command here", the state of the fort being next to impossible to repair, & Arnold seeing himself as not qualified for the task of rebuilding it- **775**; the order to rem. its cannon given as the reason behind the assembly of a mob, June 1775, intent on closing the Charlotte co. Court at Ft. Edward- **779**; Comm. of Safety, Charlotte co., gives notice, Feb. 17, 1777, that a co. of rangers has been ordered here on apprehension the enemy might attempt to

cross the lake on the ice; betw. Jan.- Mar. 1777, Gen. Schuyler instructs Col.
Warner to send his recruits into the Green Mtn. regt. here, immed. upon enl., but
by latest returns, only 24 men have arr.- **786**; Gen. Schuyler departed here, June
26, 1777, in his view, having improved the state of affairs here, & leaving
instructions for continuing the works here & at other points along the line of
communication; a message arr. for him at Saratoga (Schuylerville, N. Y.) evening,
June 28th, from Gen. St. Clair, advising that the enemy's vanguard was 1st sighted
abt. 45 mi. from the fort, on Gilliland's creek- **788**; either part of the British army
here, in pursuit of the American "fugitives" that evac. the fort, or 10 companies of
grenadiers & light infantry, fell in w. Gen. St. Clair's rear guard, July 1777,
leading to the battle of Ft. Ann- **792**; Godliel Switzer, Commissary of British
forces here, sent to Albany, N. Y., foll. capt. of the fort; see Swisher, Vol. 1- **817**; a
co. being raised by John Visscher, May 26, 1775, at Albany, to number 100 men,
& ordered to come here immed. upon its completion- **832**; payroll presented to
Albany Comm. by Capt. Joseph McCracken, totaling £ 69 13s 11¼d, along w.
expenses & disbursements of £ 15 15s 4d, for men of his co. engaged in taking the
fort; payroll presented to Albany Comm., June 17, 1776, for Capt. Ebenezer
Allen's co., totaling £ 45 12s, for men of his co. engaged in taking this fort, &
Crown Point- **890**; when commenting on prospective loc. for regular troops to
enforce order in the Grants, Gen. Haldimand notes to the Gov., Sept. 1, 1773, that
"Crown Point is entirely destroyed & Ti is in ruins"- **909**; proposed by Gen.
Haldimand to N. Y. Council, Sept. 29, 1773, that a 200 man force be sent to Ti &
Crown Point, withdrawing 150 men on Nov. 1st, "as not more than 50 can be
sheltered there in a winter at present"; Council postpones the measure, deeming it
too late in the season to send troops this yr.- **910**; winter, c. 1848/9, two strangers
came to search the W. side of the Hudson in the town of Moreau, to loc. cannon
lost during the Rev. war; acc. Dr. Fitch, the loss was prob. from pieces capt. by
Ethan Allen at Ti & Crown Point, & sent to Albany, N. Y.; refers *Sexagenary*; an
old man had told the two that some cannon were being rem. down the Hudson on
sleighs in March, & went 2 mi. below Ft. Edward to a point where they were taken
off river & onto the highway; the heaviest cannon broke through the thawing ice
nr. the riverbank & sank; the unidentified pair had been offered $250.00 by a NYC
museum for the cannon's recovery, but they never returned to pursue any further
excavations; Dr. Fitch specul. that if the cannon was lost in only 4 ft. of water, as
the searchers suspected, then it was prob. retrieved at the time of its loss- **959**; the
Provincial retreat from here (July 6, 1777) was suppos. to have been pursued by
Thomas DeRoguers- Williams & other Indians, but on pretense of falling on their
flanks, Williams 'is sd. to have purposely led his party by a too circuitous route to
effect their object'- **1016**

Fort William Henry- "nothing so thrilling in the catalogue of painful events", as
the massacre (Aug. 9, 1757) here compares w. the Bloody Morning Scout (Sept. 8,
1755) at Lake George, acc. Mary M. Chase, in composing a poem on the latter
subject- **989**

Fort Williams- the picketed church, Salem, N. Y.; c. 1782, it & the garrison at Saratoga (Schuylerville, N. Y.) were the northernmost American outposts; a detachm. of '9 months men', enl. from the Salem vicinity, was stat. here when fair weather permitted, or else quarted in a public house- **729**

42nd Regt. British Infantry- the Royal Highlanders, or BlackWatch; printed article, Dec. 4, 1852, *N. Y. Weekly Times*, recounts its org. & hist. of engagements; a series of entries foll., indicating gr. given in Wash. co. area to its servicemen after the Fr. & Ind. wars; see Royal Highlanders- **990**

44th N. Y. Infantry- (Ellsworth Regt.) designed to be composed of one soldier from ea. town in N. Y.; the Salem representative, N. Albert Wilson, d. Oct. 1861, & was the 1st bur., gr. 2; & the Ft. Edward representative, Capt. William Henry Miller, Co. K, d. Apr. 30, 1862, was the 2nd bur., gr. 1, soldier's plot, Evergreen Cemetery, Salem, N. Y.- **1081**

FOSGATE,
Submit- or "Metty"; m. William Russell; see Vol. 1- **731**

FOSTER,
Ichabod- witn., Nov. 20, 1772, along w. Reuben Colvin, warrantee deed from Jacob Marsh to Thomas Brayton, for Lot No. 5, Socialborough, Charlotte co., N. Y.- **745**
John- deed witn., Apr. 20, 1770, along w. Mary Foster, Thomas Johnson to James Lyttle- **(L)- 936**
Lydia- Hartford, N. Y., Jan. 30, 1802, cut her throat w. a razor; Benajah Hill, Coroner- **(L)- 876**
Mary- deed witn., along w. John Foster, Apr. 20, 1770; see above- **(L)- 936**
Stephen C.- (1826- 1864) composer of "My Old Kentucky Home"; c. 1850's, Bardstown, Kentucky, given as his 'abiding place'- **949b**

14th Iowa Infantry- its Co. A- C, marched approx. 478 mi. from Iowa City, Oct. 31, 1861, to Ft. Randall, S. Dakota, & arr. Dec. 5, 1861, to replace the Federal troops stat. there; a journal of the march, kept daily by Lambert Martin, Co. B, traces the journey W. from Iowa City, through Des Moines, to Council Bluffs, N. to Souix City, & then to Vermillon, S. Dakota; the populations of var. communities along the route noted; see Iowa; their rendezvous & encampment occurred Oct. 31- Nov. 2, at Gov. Kirkwood's farm, 2 mi. fron Iowa City;
Nov.-
2- marched 10 mi., & camped nr. Clear Creek; a bonfire, music, & addresses, along w. presentation of a flag by the community's ladies;
5- serenaded by a brass band & visit by the ladies of Brooklyn;
6- 20 mi. march to Grinnell, "our provisions scanty, we every day leave ranks & call at houses toappease our hunger & it is freely given tho [sic] we offer pay"; all

present at roll, "...but marching, not 15 men of our company sometimes are remaining in the ranks. We respectfully but decidedly refuse staying in the ranks if they will not give us the rations we are entitled to.";

9- 11- camped on the outskirts of Des Moines; amember of Co. C bur. on the 11th; 12- marched 16 mi. on half rations, & Co. B refused to keep ranks, falling out at houses to procure food;

14- nr. Dalimintha, camp foll. 34 mi. march across open prarie; "Not half enough to eat today. Night cold.";

15- camp nr. Turkey creek, on the edge of timber; some go to hunt squirrels & return w. 3 pails of honey taken from a bee tree;

17- foll. 25 mi. march, "Have for dinner 2 hard crackers & plenty of water.";

18- camp 2 mi. from Council Bluffs, foll. 28 mi. march; "Our breakfast was 2 crackers, a flapjack, small piece of pork & cup of coffee. Dinner 2 crackers only. Men much enraged at this usage; much swearing.";

19- detachm. disappointed on not going upriver by boat;

21- camp 2 mi. above Crescent City; "Men had to go on on foot. Threaten to stack their arms. Night very cold.";

22- foll. 20 mi. march, soldiers supply themselves w. straw, taken from a stack, to sleep on;

23- camp in timber nr. Little Souix river;

24- camp 4 mi. from Onawa river, on left, & 10 mi. from the bluffs, on right;

25- camp on open prarie;

26- reach Souix City; almost frozen during last 5 mi. of march, w. wind & snow in faces; their commander- in- chief refused to obt. straw until after confronted by ano. Capt.'s accusation that he was pocketing the allotted travel funds for himself;

27- marched 5 mi. into Dakota territory & camped on "the ground of Gen. Harney's fight & slaughter of the Indians a few yrs. ago";

28- abt. 3 in. of snow; no timber & short of provisions; commander- in- chief places guards at the few houses along the way, & even at their wells, to prevent soldiers from rushing in, expecting them to fill their canteens only in the morning, after which they freeze during the day; "Our commander Capt. Potter is hated by all of us";

29- camp at Vermillion, territorial capital;

Dec.-

1- march 16 mi.; so cold, many froze fingers, ears, noses, & toes; "stopped at a small house where the commander could get his women in to warm, & as they didn't want to ride further we were stopped here on the open prarie, freezing, till the teams could go 3 mi. & haul some wood to us";

5- crossed to the S. side of the river, 2 mi. from Ft. Randall; the commander, having gone ahead by stage, returns to inform co. to camp 2 days & a night in the timber until the regulars leave the fort; "Not pleasant news. Had to make new tent pins, having throwed [sic] the old ones away.";

7- moved into the fort; Lambert Martin, & prob. the entire detachm., remained stat. here throughout 1862, bef. moving upriver the foll. yr.; Lambert, s. Josephus

& Lucy (Palen) Martin, d. Oct. 14, 1863, at 23 yrs., 9 mos. , & 1 day, after 2 wks. illness w. typhoid fever, nr. Farm Island, Dakota Territory- **1089**

FOWLER,
Norman- sd. he was present at Randall's tavern, White Creek, N. Y., when Martin Wallace was asked to view the body of Barney McEntee; he was afterw. called by the def. & testif.chiefly to the conversation in Randall's parlor betw. Col. Crocker & Marvin Wallis- **1048s**
Wid.- m. William Russell, as his 2nd wf.- **737**

FRANCE- 747, 759s, 780, 914, 949, 949b, 965, 989, 990, 1013;
Cities & Towns- Artois- 914; Bordeaux- 990; Fontenay (Fontenoy)- 990;
L'Orient- 949b, 990; Orthez (Orthos)- 990; Toulouse (Thoulouse)-990;
Events- the old French war- 734, 746, 768, 799, 812, 852, 958, 1007, 1091;
Reign of Terror- 1070; Revolution- 949b, 990;
Features- Pyrennes- 990

FRANKLIN,
Henry- of NYC; he & Amos Underhill, acc. Nov. 26, 1773 deed description, own Lot No. 15, Kingsbury, N. Y.; for £ 150, purch. on Apr. 15, 1775, all of Lot 92, the N. half of Lot 47, the S. half of Lot 25, & Lot 5 of the town plot, Kingsbury, from Albert Baker- **(L)- 936**

FRASER,
Lonson- witn., Dec. 1, 1858, for certif. the execution of Martin Wallace- **1050s**

FRAZIER,
James- oath of alleg.; Co. D, 22nd N. Y. Inf.- **(L)- 1074**
Brig. Gen. Simon- (Master of Lovat; 1729- 1777) interrogated Samuel Standish, prob. July 27, 1777, after he had been capt. & brought into Burgoyne's camp during the taking of Jane McCrea; he contested Standish's claim that 6,000 soldiers were stat. at Ft. Edward, saying that he had observed only half that number in the American camp 3 days prev.- **747**; (Frasier) the incident pert. to his mortal wnd., Oct. 7th, at Bemis Heights, as conveyed by his waiter to other persons during the prisoner march foll. Burgoyne's surrender; Frazier's waiter was standing next to him when he was hit by a musketball from one of Morgan's riflemen, "The General sprang 3 ft. upwards, off from the ground when the ball hit him. The waiter asked him 'What's the matter? Are you hurt?' Gen. Frasier said 'Say nothing!' & told him to call a particular officer (whose name is not remembered) instantly to him. The officer came- Frasier was placed on a litter, & conveyed to Lady Harriet Ackland's" (while the last part of this acct. conforms w. the accepted version, Gen. Frazier was suppos. shot off his horse, & the 1st port. of this acct. appears to be the death of Lt. Don, of 21st regt., on Sept. 19th, mingled w. Frazier's; see Anburey's *Travels*)- **1002**

FREEMAN,

Adam M.- (s. Andrew & Elizabeth Martin) b. Jan. 9, 1811; merch., NYC; m. Sophia Hedges, at Castleton, or Hydeville, Vt.; c. 1869, he was depot master, Dewitt, Iowa; children- Caroline, Edward, Alfred, & ___; c. 1850, one of his sons was in California- **730**

Dr. Adolphus- s. Phineas, of Kingsbury, N. Y.- **730**

Dr. Alfred- (s. Andrew & Elizabeth Martin) b. Nov. 6, 1793; homeopathist, succeeded Dr. Asa Fitch, Sr., in his practice at Fitch's Point, Salem, & now (prob. c. 1850) res NYC; m. Dec. 11, 1817, Elizabeth, dau. Aaron & Elizabeth Martin; children-
1. Elizabeth, b. June 24, 1818; d. July 10, 1818
2. Elizabeth, b. Oct. 28, 1821; m. June 23, 1846, Rev. David Irvine, or Irving
3. Charlotte Harvey, b. Mar. 24, 1826; m. June 5, 1847, William Skidmore; & he d. Feb. 1860- **730**; m. Elizabeth, dau. Aaron, Jr., & Artemisia (Lynn) Martin; after he rem. NYC, his place was occ. by Joseph Martin- **731**; (ment. as Allen, Alva, or Alvin) his wf. relates to Dr. Fitch cert. rumors from John Priest concerning the behavior in the household of Isaac Bininger, of Camden valley- **1076**

Andrew- (s. Benjamin & Abigail Tracy) landlord, for most of his life, in Salem, Easton, & Schaghticoke, N. Y.; m. Elizabeth, dau. Col. Adam & Abigail (Cheney) Martin; children-
1. Alfred, b. Dec. 23, 1792; d. Sept. 15, 1793
2. Dr. Alfred, b. Nov. 6, 1793; m. Elizabeth Martin
3. Elizabeth, or Betsey, b. May 2, 1796; m. Samuel Hitchcock
4. Pliny, b. Apr. 8, 1798; m. Sarah Mairs
5. Marvin, b. Apr. 4, 1801; m. Charlotte Harvey
6. Phineas, b. Nov. 26, 1803; merch., NYC; d. 1859, unm.
7. Abigail, b. Feb. 2, 1806; d. Aug. 3, 1807
8. Charles Cotesworth Pinchney, b. Aug. 2, 1808; m. Susan Rockwell
9. Adam M., b. Jan. 9, 1811; m. Sophia Hedges
10. Abigail M., b. Nov. 8, 1812; m. Rev. John F. Dana
11. & 12. WilliamWarren, & William Wallace, twins, b. May 23, 1815; the latter d. Apr. 26, 1817
13. William Wallace, b. June 6, 1819; m. Catharine Russell- **730**; (s. Benjamin & Abigail Tracy) b. July 19, 1763, Marlboro?, Conn.; he was a shoemaker, Lennox, Mass., joined Shays' rebellion, & afterw. escaped to Salem, N. Y.; his wf. d. Oct. 24, 1843, or Oct. 27, 1844, acc. grs.; & he d. Jan. 29, 1829, of gangrene of the foot- **1039**

Benjamin- of Lennox, Mass.; m. Abigail Tracy; they rem. (n. d.) Salem, N. Y.; children-
1. Andrew, m. Elizabeth Martin
2. Phineas?
3. Gaiger, settl. N. J.- **730**; their s. Phineas, settl. Kingsbury, N. Y.; & s. Gayger, was thought to have settl. N. J.- **1039**

Charles Cotesworth Pinchney- (s. Andrew & Elizabeth Martin) b. Aug. 2, 1808; merch., NYC; m. Susan, dau. Philo & Abby (Martin) Rockwell, & grdau. Walter Martin; his wf. d. suddenly, leaving one child, James; & he d. Dec. 3, 1852- **730**; (Charles P.) his wf. d. Jan. 1, 1848, & he m. 2. July 1849, Ernestine Randall; by 1st wf., had 2 sons- James Rockwell; & Charles, dec'd; & by 2nd wf.- Ernestine Randall, who now (1858) is their only surviving child, an inf. when both her parents died, she now res. w. her aunt, Mrs. W. Martin Conkey- **1046**
Chester- (s. Samuel & Elizabeth Cheney) m. ____ Parker- **1038**
Gaiger- (s. Benjamin & Abigail Tracy) thought to have settl. N. J.- **730**; (Gayger) the basis for specul. that he settl. in N. J. pert. to his given name being found in a number of families in the region- **1039**
Louis- dau. of a Baptist minister from R. I.; m.William, s. Phineas & Ann (Cooper) Whiteside- **805**
Marvin- (s. Andrew & Elizabeth Martin) b. Apr. 4, 1801; merch., Salem, N. Y.; m. Charlotte, dau. Maj. James & Mary Harvey; he d. June 12, 1869, & had 2 surviving children- **730**; his wf. was perh. dau. Maj. James Harvey, & Mary Barber; c. 1859, his wf. was given as one of 2 surviving children of Maj. Harvey's wid.- **1035**
Phineas- prob. s. Benjamin, & bro. Andrew; " 'Colonel' Freeman, as he was always called"; res. Kingsbury, N. Y.; had a large family, one of the sons being Dr. Adolphus Freeman- **730**; (s. Benjamin & Abigail Tracy) settl. Kingsbury, N. Y.- **1039**
Pliny- (s. Andrew & Elizabeth Martin) b. Apr. 8, 1798; "for a long time"now (prob. 1850) res. NYC; at one time a merch., Kingsbury & Argyle, N. Y.; m. Sarah, dau. Rev. James Mairs, of Galway, N. Y.; children- Henry, Elizabeth, Margaret, & "one or two more"- **730**
Samuel- m. Elizabeth, dau. Joseph & Abigail (Warren) Cheney; children- Chester, m. ____ Parker; & Samuel, d. y.- **1038**
William Wallace- (s. Andrew & Elizabeth Martin) b. June 6, 1819; merch., Salem, N. Y.; lately (c. 1850) rem. N. Adams, Mass.; m. Catharine, dau. Hon. David Russell; "has one or two small children"- **730**
William Warren- (s. Andrew & Elizabeth Martin) b. May 23, 1815, twin, w. the 1st William Wallace; merch., Macon. Georgia, & afterw. physician, NYC; m. Julia Mars- **730**

FRENCH,
Ann- m. Edward, s. Phineas & Ann (Cooper) Whiteside- **805**
Benjamin- plaintiff, May 19, 1774, vs. John McLean, for 149s debt; & vs. Jacob Marsh, for £ 1,591 9s 10d debt- **878**
Charity- plaintiff, May 19, 1774, vs. Michael Bull, et. al.; & vs. Jonas Powers, & als.; rec'd. £ 50 & £ 13, respectively- **878**
Family- res. Ft. Edward, N. Y.; late Nov. 1853, a fire consumed their house, killing 2 of their children, the oldest age 6 yrs.; "The mother locked the children in

the house during a temporary absence & when she returned found the house in ruins, & her children blackened corpses"- **731½**
Jeremiah- he & Samuel Robinson submitted 'to your excellency & honor's', a return of person res. on the N. H. grants, Dec. 18, 1765- **893**
Miss- m. David, s. William & Margaret (Andrew) Dobbin, as his 2nd wf.- **732**
Thomas- res. Princetown (Manchester, Vt.); on May 16, 1771, he & other rioters, among them Charles Bullen & Martin Powel, overtook Samuel Willoughby, an Albany co. constable, on the highway & threatened his life if he did not withdraw the writ of ejection that he had presented to French's wf. in his absence- **899**; a posse lead by Samuel Pease, incl. David Wing, arr. in Princetown on May 21st, to arrest him for rioting; a no. of rioters, all w. clubs & 2 w. guns, confronted them & a shot was fired from the woods, w/o injury; when the posse continued to his house, it was found surrounded by men who vowed against the constable & his posse, saying that they would carry no one away & that if any of them were taken to jail, the jail would not stand 3 wks.- **900**

FRISBEE,
Rev. Levi- c. 1772, under the direction of Rev. Dr. Wheelock, he was sent to Caughnawaga, N. Y., to induce the adoptive parents of Thomas DeRougers-Williams to send him to Dartmouth College- **1016**

FROOMAN, see also, *VROOMAN,*
Family- c. 1777, res. on the S. side of the Hoosic river, in the loc. now (c. 1850) occ. by Gen. Fort- **744**

FROST,
Hannah- m. Edward, Esq., s. Ebenezer & Sarah (Hobby) Fitch- **799**

FULLER,
Lt.- c. 1779, along w. Lts. Boggs, Gould, & Stewart, one of the alternating commanders of the militia stat. at Skenesborough, N. Y.- **751**
Samuel- res. Skenesborough, N. Y.; Jan. 25, 1776, rec'd. recommendation for appt. as Quartermaster, Charlotte co. militia- **784**
William B.- b. Surry co., England; d. July 21, 1839, at 55- **(L)- 772**

FULTON,
Robert- (1765- 1815) 'has a fame he did not fully earn'; a remark noted in an unlabeled & undated newspaper article from Jan. 14th, *The Recorder,* Lawrenceville, Kentucky, concerning John Fitch, the steamboat inventor; by this acct., Fitch successfully demonstrated the principle of steamboat operations 20 yrs. bef. Fulton, & yet Fulton 'got all the high reputation & renown'; the 1st voyage of the *Clermont* occurred on the Hudson, Aug. 1807, while Fitch had announced the completion of his boat & preparation for trials on the Delaware in 1782; several yrs. after Fitch's death in 1798, the N. Y. Legislature decided that the boats of Fulton & Livingston were, in substance, the invention patented by Fitch in 1791; when Fulton brought suit in N. Y., in 1813, to enforce the claim of his orig. invention, he was defeated on these grounds- **949b**

G

GAGE,
Phineas- def., Oct. 19, 1774, w. Asahel Jacques, in a case brought by Robert Snell-
878
Maj. Gen. Thomas- (1721- 1787) acc. Col. Arnold's May 19, 1775 letter to the
Cambrige, Mass. Comm. of Safety, a return of his force at Montreal contained 717
men from the 7th & 26th Regts., incl. 70 capt. as prisoners at Ticonderoga by Cols.
Allen & Arnold- **774**

GALE,
John- (Mr.) member, N. Y. Assembly (1810, 1814- 17, 1819); intro. the bill petitn.
for the division of Cambridge, N. Y. into 3 parts, c. 1816; the effort described by
the *Northern Post* as an attempt "to gratify a leading democrat & a few friends", &
therefore, the press questions the merits of his 1816 candidacy, & whether it was
deserving of the public's vote- **726**

GALLAWAY,
Thomas- d. Mar. 9, 1785, at 42- **(L)- 975**

GALPIN,
_____- m. dau. Jonathan & Sarah (Saltonstall) Fitch- **799**

GALUSHA,
Amos- m. dau. Henry Clark; res. Shaftsbury, Vt., but had no settl. resid.;
participant, battle of Bennington- **765**
*David-*res. nr. Shaftsbury meetinghouse; his home now (1850) where Cole keeps
tavern- **765**; July 27, 1775, elected 1st Lt., Green Mtn. regt.- **781b**
Family- of Shaftsbury, Vt.; incl. bros. David, Jacob, Jonas, & Amos- **765**
Jacob- res. Shaftsbury, Vt., 100 rods S. of his bro. David- **765**
Gov. Jonas- (1753- 1834) 1st Democratic Gov. of Vt., elected 1809, 1810, & 1812
(but his dates of service given elsewhere as, 1809- 1813, 1815- 20); res.
Shaftsbury, Vt., less than ½ mi. N. of his bro. David- **765**

GAMBLE,
Family- of Argyle, N. Y.; dau. Ann, m. William, s. Henry Bliss; the family rem., c.
1840's, Fall River, Col. co., Wisc., along w. their son- in- law- **1005**

GANNON,
James- was present at Joice's store, Buskirk's Bridge, N. Y., when Barney McEntee
& Martin Wallace were there, Feb. 16, 1858; acc. Ann Joice's testim., it was his
whisky that the co. there was drinking, & that he had left it there for himself, but
that she had occasion to use, or sell it- **1048s**

GANSEVOORT,
Dr. Peter- d. Mar. 17, 1809, at 84- **(L)- 932**

GARDNER,
____- m. Mary, dau. William & Jane (Lytle) Russell- **737**
George- of Troy, N. Y.; dau., m. John Pattison; dau., m. Elias Pattison; & dau.
Louisa, m. John A. Hall, as his 2nd wf.- **940**
George, Esq.- c. 1775, Justice of Peace, Pownal, Vt., for Albany co., N. Y.; he
appraised the state of danger in his town from Vt. rioters, informing Benjamin
Hough that every day he expected to be prevented by rioters from performing his
duties; furthermore, he advised that unless protection was given by the N. Y. govt.,
many of the area inhabitants would join w. the rioters- **881**
Susan- m. George, s. William & Jane (Lytle) Russell- **737**

GARDENIER,
Samuel- his farm loc. abt. 17 mi. from the Hudson, in Walloomsac Patent; m. ____
Grodt; his testim. bef. N. Y. Council, Sept. 20, 1771- that he purch. 310 acres from
James Delancey, c. 1767, for £ 300, & settl. there abt. June 1769; discovering that
Ichabod Cross had settl. & improved part of his land under N. H. title, 'they
entered into bonds to abide to an arbitration of referees mutually chosen, as to what
should be pd. Cross for his improvements'; it was decided that Cross should receive
£ 25 for half of his improved lands & lease the remainder for 5 yrs., & then
surrender the remainder; only part of the judgment has since been carried out,
Cross accepting £ 15 for half of his land, but later refusing the remainder of the
payment; since then, Gardenier's fence has been 'often pulled down, & cattle
suffered to get into his grain', as much as 3 times per wk., w. his neighbors
informing him that "no Yorker would be allowed to live there in peace"; abt. 2 hrs.
bef. daybreak, prob. Aug. 1, 1771, a no. of men on horseback arr. at his house,
inquiring of his title & insisting he do justice to Cross w. respect to it; he referred
them to Albany & insisted that he had done justice to Cross; they finally gave him
a fortnight to consider their request, & he consulted w. Esq. Munro, who referred
him to the Mayor of Albany & Justice Bleecker, who claimed they could do
nothing & he must go to a higher authority; then, they reported to him that the
rioters had come to them & stated that they "had appl. to him civilly, but if he did
not comply they would next come Devil- like"; the night after the attempt to eject
James Breakenridge, rioters tore up 200 panels of Gardenier's fence, burning them
in a heap, along w. a haystack; nr. the end of the fortnight, he fled in fear of his
life, to his bro.'s in Kinderhook, N. Y.; when the mob arr. at his house, his wf.
informed them that he was there, & they thereupon ransacked his house & tore up
the rest of his haystacks; if it were not for his bro.'s kindness, he testif., he would
now be "a suffering outcast"; see Grants/ N. H. Controversy, & Vermonters- **902**

GATES,
Deborah- m. Samuel, prob. s. Ens. Josiah Standish, perh. in Norwich, Conn. (she was perh. b. Feb. 22, 1684, dau. Thomas & Elizabeth, of Marlborough, Mass.; acc. Savage, the family rem. Norwich, 1703)- **757**
Maj. Gen. Horatio- (c. 1728- 1806) on the day of Burgoyne's surrender (Oct. 17, 1777), he was reportedly standing among a group of officers w. a cloak over his uniform, "the day being rainy or misty"; a British officer inquired who, among the assembled, was Gen. Gates, & when he was pointed out, the officer exclaimed, 'Is that Gen. Gates! Why he looks like an old granny!', that being the current design. for midwives; overhearing the comment, Gen. Gates retorted, 'My looks then do not belie me; for I have delivered King George of ten thousand full- grown men'- **869**; his advice requested, Sept. 17, 1777, concerning the disposal of John Munro, Esq., of White Creek, N. Y., by sending him over the lines to the enemy- **956**; his efforts deemed less significant, acc. James McDonald, than those of Benedict Arnold, in capt. Gen. Burgoyne- **1010**

GEORGIA- 732, 799; Macon- 730; Savannah- 799, 1075b

GERMAIN,
Judge- of Albany, N. Y.; acquired the old Cornell mansion in Walloomsac Patent after David & Maria (Cornell) Niles became indebted to him- **806**

GERMANY- 955, 1072; as 'Jarmin'- 1090frag

GERMOND,
____ - acc. Dr. Fitch, little doubt that he built the 1st log cabin along the Battenkill, but his loc. was too remote from the principal settlm. of Salem, N. Y. to be known by the other early settlers there- **738**; his house built at Fitch's Point, abt. ¼ mi. from Daniel Livingston; c. 1777, was one of only 4 houses in the area- **855**; his loc. was later purch. & occ. by Moses Martin, Sr.- **867**

GERROLD,
____ - m. Naomi, dau. William, Jr. & Molly (Highlands) Mack; children- John, killed by a wild span of horses; Polly; & Ruth, who res. many yrs. on part of Elijah Mack's place, & then rem. Richland co., Ohio- **734**
John- (s. ____ & Naomi Mack) accidentally killed, as "a grown up boy", when a wild span of horses belonging to William Webb ran away, dragging him over the rocks in the road some rods N. of Deac. McMurray's, in Salem, N. Y.- **734**

GETTY,
Charles- of Hebron, N. Y.; m. Mary, dau. David & Margaret (Lytle) Thompson- **1069**
Deac. Isaac- res. Salem, N. Y.; s. Robert; b. ca. 1770- **744**

James Mac Whorter- res. Hebron, N. Y.; cousin of Thomas Gourly Getty; m.
Lydia, dau. Moses, Jr., & Eunice (Clark) Martin- **731**
John- res. Hebron, N. Y.; on or abt. Mar. 1, 1816, he delivered a blow to the head
of Benjamin Fitch, fracturing his skull & causing his death on Mar. 21st; a jury
inquest, called by the coroner, pronounced him guilty of murder; he was arrested
foll. examiniation of witns., & committed to jail for trial at the June circuit- **724**
Robert?- res. Salem, N. Y., on the present (prob. 1850) loc. occ. by Deac. Joseph
Hawley; during "the Retreat" bef. Burgoyne's army, evac. to Esq. Morrison's,
Cambridge, N. Y., & remained 2 days, then crossed the Hoosick river opp. where
the Vrooman (Frooman) family resided, & was quartered a fortnight w. 6 or 8
families in a barn; when news arr. that tories & Indians had taken possession of
New Perth (Salem) he packed again, moving to Pownal, Vt., for one night, & then
to Williamstown, Mass.; his family remained here, in the S. part of town, until
danger was over & Burgoyne had surrendered; they returned so late in the season
that the 1st snowfall, 4 inches, came on the night foll. their return- **744**
Thomas Gourly- res. Hebron, N. Y.; cousin of James Mac Whorter Getty; m. Lucy,
dau. Moses, Jr., & Eunice (Clark) Martin- **731**

GHOSTS, Hauntings- see WITCHCRAFT, Witches, & Superstitions

GIBBS,
_____- m. Jane Maria, dau. Charles & Hannah (Lytle) Nelson- **1069**
Rev. Henry- (1688- 1723) of Watertown, Mass.; a son, m. Margaret, dau. Rev.
Jabez & Elizabeth (Appleton) Fitch- **835**

GIBLIN,
Barney- res. Eagle Bridge, N. Y.; def. witn., testif. that he knew Martin Wallace
for 2 yrs., & heard of McEntee's murder the foll. day; Wallace had come to his
house the foll. evening, abt. 9:00 PM, showed nothing unusual in his behavior, was
offered a chair, & alongw. his wf., Edward Cavanaugh, & John Lyons (who came
in while Wallace was there), were all engaged in a sociable conversation; he
remained abt. 20 or 25 min., & might have asked Cavanaugh to go home w. him,
but Cavanaugh sd. he wanted to go to the tavern; all 3 of his visitors left,
Cavanaugh & Lyons going to a tavern; on cross- exam- Wallace had not come ¼
mi. out of his way (from the direction to his home) & never ment. McEntee during
his stay there- **1048s**

GIBSON,
_____- the tory; his farm loc. N. of Salem, N. Y., was confiscated & later purch. by
Judge Webster, & afterw. sold to Deac. John Steele- **1047**; Irish; prob. s. John; m.
Janet _____; the cellar hole of his house was still visible in 1861, loc. at the foot of a
hill, some 50 rods from the house of Aaron Cleveland; he had been away from his
family for some time during the Rev. war, & when it was learned that he had
returned, six of the Salem whigs came w. their guns one evening "& fired a volley

of bullets through Gibson's door. He instantly dropped into the cellar, & his wf., uttering a shriek, crept under the bed, to escape being hit by the balls"; a keg of beer, brewed 1 or 2 days bef., rec'd. some of the balls & the warm beer dropped through the floor, falling on Gibson, who 'thought it was puir [sic] Janets bluid [sic] that was dropping on me, & that she was surely kilt [sic], there being no noise after the scream she gev [sic]'; he & his wf. soon fled to Canada, & the land was confiscated & later purch. by Capt. McCracken- **1073**

Judge James- extracts genealogical data concerning the families of John Mack & his s. William, from pgs. 680, 681, Cochrane's Hist. of Antrim, N. H., in his facsimile copy of the Manuscript History- **734s**; acc. to him, Dr. Philip, of Tyashoke, was the only son of Thomas Smith, of Buskirk's Bridge, N. Y.- **845**; def. atty., along w. J. S. Crocker & H. K. Sharpe, Oct. 1- 7, 1858, People vs. Martin Wallace; his facsimile copy of the Manuscript History notes § 1048. Conviction of Wallace for Murder, & § 1050. Execution of Wallace, the former article missing from the extant manuscript, & the latter an additional port. of material connected w. § 1047½, a newspaper obit. for Hon. John McLean; a reconstruction of their contents incl. in this vol.- **1048s, 1050s**

James B., Esq.- succeeded Timothy Hoskins as editor, *Washington Register*, maintaining his position for abt. 2 yrs., & changing its political orientation to the Clintonian perspective- **721**

John- clerk, June 28, 1776, Comm. of Safety, Charlotte co., N. Y.- **785**

John- Irish; res. Salem, N. Y.; tory during the Rev. war, he & his s. John, Jr., were indicted, Apr. 11, 1780, for adhering to the enemy; see Vol. 1; ano. s. fled to Canada, his land confiscated, & later purch. by Capt. McCracken; ano. s., Richard, helped construct Rev. Samuel Tomb's house- **1073**

GIFFORD,

Haviland- Adjutant, 93rd N. Y. Inf.- **1090b**

Miss- schoolteacher, c.1840's, Easton, N. Y.; she was accused to the State Superintendent of Schools by Priest Quigley, for allegedly whipping a Catholic child, to force it to read the Bible; the charge was apparently false, & lead to Quigley's notoriety in the region- **1027**; the controversy betw. her & Priest Quigley alluded to, c. 1854/5, by Archibald Hay, when he was embroiled in ano. incident w. Quigley- **1058**

Seneca W.- witn., Dec. 1, 1858, certif. for the execution of Martin Wallace- **1050s**

GILBERT,

_____ - of Greenwich, N. Y.; c. 1861, member, 11th Illinois Inf.- **1080**

Charles W.- oath of alleg.; Co. D, 22nd N. Y. Inf.- **(L)- 1074**

Jacob- Cambridge, N. Y.; Aug. 29, 1792, drowned in Ruff's mill- pond; Joshua Conkey, Coroner- **(L)- 876**

Jedidiah- carpenter, New Perth (Salem, N. Y.); rec'd. Lot 277, Nov. 1, 1783, from Rev. Dr. Thomas Clark, amt. not given- **(L)- 936**

Wealthy- m. William Wells- **839**

GILCHRIST,

Charles- m. Mary, dau. Jarvis & Mary (Harvey) Fitch; she & her youngest child d. Sept. 18, 1850- **731**

Duncan- defendant, May 19, 1774, in a case brought by Wm. Duer, Esq.- **878**

James- Co. A, 2nd N. Y., Northern Black Horse, Cav., 1861- 2- **1080**

John- of Argyle, N. Y.; m. Mary, dau. William & Mary (Hanna) Lytle; children-
1. William, m. Mary Jane Northup
2. James P., drowned in Mich., prob. unm.
3. Mary Ann, m. ____ Swift
4. Nancy, res. & m. in Edinburgh, N. Y.
5. Charles N.
6. Jane Eliza
7. Hannah
8. Margaret
9. Gideon, res. Argyle, N. Y.- **1069**

John- of Hebron, N. Y.; his only s., John, b. ca. 1842, & d. 1862, Fairfax Station, Va.- **1098**

William- (s. John & Mary Lytle) res. Hebron, N. Y.; m. Mary Jane Northup- **1069**

William John- s. John; Co. E, 123rd NYSV; d. 1862, at 20, Fairfax Station, Va.- **1098**

GILLESPIE,

Daniel- part of Lot 4, Argyle, N. Y., containing 108 acres, gr. by him, Aug. 23, 1771, to William Duer, Esq.- **935**

Neal- c. 1789, res. SW of Roger Reid, on the W. side of the brook & a mi. S. of the spring, S. Argyle, N. Y.; rem. (n. d.) Canada, & c. 1850, his log house still standing- **802**; while he was at Ft. Miller one day w. Capt. James Beaty, they witn. the execution of a Hessian deserter (§ 740) capt. at Salem, N. Y., sd. by him to be "the most effecting, the most awful scene, ... of anything he had ever witn."; the "Dutchman" was shot in Burgoyne's camp, in a meadow nr. the Duer mansion; see Hundertmark, George- **976**; he & others lost cattle & sheep, at least 2 or3 head having been taken at diff. times by whigs, nr. the end of the Rev. war, to pay soldiers guarding the frontier; a large flock, coll. by Alexander Wright, of Salem, was once driven past his house to Burgoyne's camp for sale; a law suit was commenced against Wright by Capt. Barns foll. Burgoyne's surrender, & Wright was often over toGillespie to find out whether he would agree to one pt. or ano., but he was only willing to swear to what he knew, as he "regarded this as a diff. thing from what it was to tell 'a smooth lie' to keep himself out of prison"- **977**; brief ment., as neighbor & intimate friend of Capt. Beaty- **978**; the Argyle families who lived nr. him gathered at his house on the Sun. (July 27, 1777, the day Jane McCrea was massacred) foll. the Allen massacre for protection; foll. a sleepless night, it was determined to head immed. for Burgoyne's Ft. Edward camp, & he tied a feather bed on one of his horses, & placed his wf. & children on it, "enjoining peremptorily upon the children that should one of them fall off, it must not make a lisp of noise, or cry- for it would draw the Indians to them, & they would all be killed"- **983**; some earlier accts. regarding his exploits (§ 285) recounted & clarified, or embellished; see Vol.1; on his hearing a whistle- he knew that a tory scout was outside seeking refreshment, & he had to devise a way to convey something to them while an American scout party was occ. his house; w. his dau. on his knee, he sd. to his wf., 'Mother, get these children something to eat; Mary says she is hungry; & they have been to the sugar camp so long, I know the poor things must be tired. Put some cakes into a pail for them (giving mother a wink- which made her at once comprehend what he wanted) & I will go back w. them & tend the fires whilst they rest themselves & eat something"; she accordingly put a liberal quantity of food, more than cakes, into the pail & he left the house w/o the suspicion of "our unwelcome quests", though not a morsel went to the children, but instead "to the party in the woods, whose whistle we had heard"; that same evening, Gillespie told the leader of the American scout that he regarded himself 'as being one of the most useful men in the country- one of the most exemplary citizens. I "love my enemies". I serve "my king" & I serve "my country" both. I feed & entertain the friends of my king out of doors, at the same time that I am feeding & entertaining the friends of my country in my house'; the Capt. laughed heartily at such a statem., not knowing it to be the literal truth- **984**; he served as a guide for a Canadian party that had come down to Cambridge to take John Younglove prisoner & burn down his house; see Vol. 1; in affecting their escape, he met them in the woods at night nr. the Battenkill; they took their breakfast at his house & had a young man w. them that they had capt.;"he appeared to be stupid & but half witted, though whether this was natural, or merely caused by the fright & dejected spirits he was in, we did not know"- **985**

GILLIS,
Family- c. 1777, res. Argyle, N. Y.; one family member came over to Salem w. news for John Lytle's family that that their s. William was sick w. measles in his confinement in the British camp at Ft. Edward- **743**
Family- acc. Wid. Angel, once res. at Fitch's Point, Salem, N. Y., "across the creek, in the Stewart house- I think bef. Stewart lived there. There was a Samuel & a Joseph among them. They moved from there up onto the hills, somewhere in the Carswell neighborh. {prob. the present Wid. Gillis place}"- **865**

GILMAN,
Benjamin B.- Corp., Co. A, 2nd N. Y., Northern Black Horse, Cav., 1861- 2- **1080**

GILMORE,
William- res. Cambridge, N. Y.; he & a few others stripped the planking off the bridge at Sancoick, Aug. 1777, but Col. Baum's forces were "too nr. upon them to enable them to cut the string- pieces & let them down into the water"- **766**; noted that there were 2 others w. him, & they paused on reaching the summit of a ridge

or knoll S. of the creek; Col. Baum's forces almost immed.came into sight, & they all disch. their pieces & fled over the knoll- **1006**
William- d. Dec. 2, 1786, at 79- **(L)- 975**
William- d. June 16, 1847, at 97- **(L)- 975**

GLASS,
Elder James- pastor, Baptist church, Hoosick, N. Y.; d. Aug. 6, 1811, at 35- **(L)- 772**

GLICK,
____- acc. Dr. Fitch, notes that Col. Baum was shot through the body during the Bennington battle- **801**

GLINES,
Abner- m. Anna, dau. Moses, Jr., & Eunice (Clark) Martin; he was dec'd. many yrs. prior to 1850, & his wf. & children res. 45 mi. from Chicago, adj. DeKalb co., Illinois; children-
1. Martin, m. a wid., at Ft. Miller bridge (Northumberland, N. Y.) & she d. soon after, w/o children
2. Hinman, unm., res. Illinois
3. Lydia, m. 1. George Oswald; 2. "Evi" Sherman- **731**; (Glinds) only Martin & Hinman given as their children- **1041**

Gloucester Co., N. Y.- selected Jacob Bayley, of Newbury,Vt., as delegate to N. Y. Provincial Congress, June 1777- **780**; org. along w. Charlotte & Cumberland co., Aug. 22, 1775, as one of the state militia brigades- **782**; along w. Cumberland co., to form a separate milia brigade, Aug. 1, 1776, distinct from Charlotte co.- **785**; petitn. laid bef. Council, Feb. 28, 1770, by 120 proprietors, or inhabitants, of lands N. of Cumberland co., requesting erection of ano. new co.; Gloucester co. so ordered erected- **886**; request for ano. co. N. of Cumberland co. noted by Gov. Moore, June 9, 1767, but declined by legislature until larger population is reached within its limits; to encourage this, he informs Lord Shelburne (on the above date) that he has obt. gr. of a township 12 mi. from the N. line of Cumberland co. & publ. that any family may have a farm there w/o rent or any charge, on condition of making a given quantity of potash & cultivating a cert. quantity of Hemp; ments. compliance of 14 families in accordance w. these terms, w. his construction of a grist & sawmill there; & notes in additon, 'have directed a church to be built all at my sole expense', w. the township 'laid out & vested for the use of ministers of the Establ. church- & a 2nd for the college in this city'- **894**

GLOVER,
Betsey- of Salem, N. Y.; m. Artemas, s. Aaron & Olive (Harding) Martin- **1040**
Col. John- (1732- 1794; later Brig. Gen.) his regt. fired artillery at the British during the battle of White Plains, Oct. 28, 1776- **747**

Family- their s. Reuben, m. ____ Clark; & dau. Ann, m. Daniel, s. Timothy
Barton; see Vol. 1- **1093**
Henry R.- s. Elder Samuel; member, firm of Manning & Glover, & co., of Boston,
Mass., dealers in feathers & curled hair; c. 1860, he resolved to loc. his father's
relatives, & traveled 1st to Howard, N. Y., where his uncles lived, & then later,
visited w. his oldest aunt, Mrs. Artemas Martin, returning the foll. yr. w. Reuben
Glover, of Providence, R. I., to visit the old homestead, overlooking McDougall's
(Cossayuna) Lake- **1093**
Reuben- youngest s. in his family; tailor, learning his trade from Mr. Glover, of
Cambridge, N. Y.; m. ____ Clark, his cousin; was head manager of a clothing
establ. in Providence, R. I., c. 1862, w. a salary of $900 per yr.; at his wf.'s
solicitation, purch. his grdf.'s old farm in Sturbridge, Mass.; all their children d. as
inf.- **1093**
Elder Samuel- had 3 children, all sons- one, who was educ. to the ministry &
called to Virginia, took sick & d. while traveling there; ano. d. in his youth; his
only surviving s. was Henry R.- **1093**
Sophia- m.1. James, s. William & Louis [sic] (Freeman) Whiteside; 2. Rev. Peter
Gordon- **805**

GODWIN,
Col. John- of the Royal Artillery; drew the foll. lands nr. Lake Champlain, on & by
Artillery Patent- Lots 1D, 2F, 3N, & 4C, containing 250 acres ea., & 1,000 acres
total- **880**
Col. William, Esq.- of the Royal Artillery; res. Abbots Bromley, Stafford co.,
England; neph. & heir at law of Col. John Godwin; for £ 1,000, conveys to
Alexander Ellice of London, those lots drawn by his uncle; Barent Bleeck & John
Richard Bleecker, the younger, merchs. of NYC, appt. attorneys to execute a
conveyance to Ellice; recorded Aug. 1, 1779; refers Miscellanies, pgs. 13- 15- **880**

GOLD,
Maj. Nathan- appt. June 13, 1769, along w. Capt. James Fitch, Esq., as delegation
from the Gen. Court at Hartford, Conn, to advise w. Gov. Leisler of N. Y.- **799**

GOLDEN,
Thomas- m. Catharine Reid, wid. John Munroe, Esq., as her 3rd husb.; their dau.
Freelove, m. Walter Adams- **812**
Good Faith- an attempt at definition a/o observation in relation to the term, noted
by Dr. Fitch foll. his entry concerning Gov. Colden's letter to the Board of Trade,
Jan. 20, 1764, in relation to the issuing of townships in the Grants lands; acc. Gov.
Colden, the recent Indian incursions (of the last French war) had lead to the
cessation of settlm. here, & it was presumed by N. Y. that further grants
(apparently by gentleman's agreem.) would perh. be tabled until a definitive ruling
could be had over the boundaries of the 2 Provinces; however, N. H. did not foll.
that course, but began issuing grants foll. the end of hostilities, that impinged upon

what appeared to be the sovereign bounds of N. Y., & at such reduced amts. as to only benefit the bureaucratic process involved in establ. these new townships; in that perspective Dr. Fitch observed that 'Good faith consists in not deceiving deceiving on occasions, where is the least obligation for seeking truth' & noted that Gov. Wentworth's transactions w. N. Y. "greatly violated 'Good faith' "- **887**

GOODRICH,
Jane Catharine- m. Edward William, s. John C. & Susan (Mason) Parker, as his 2nd wf.- **759s**

GOODWIN,
David Chase- present (1858) owner of the old Van Ess homestead, Hoosick, N. Y.- **766**

GOOKIN,
Rev. Nathaniel- (1688- 1734) of Northampton, Mass.; m. Ann, dau. Rev. Jabez & Elizabeth (Appleton) Fitch, as his 1st wf.- **835**

GORDON,
Ann- prob. Wid. of a Lt., His Majesty's 42nd Regt. of Foot; gr. 2,000 acres, town of White Creek, N. Y., along w. Lt. John Gregor, of the same regt.- **990**
Rev. Henry- of Coila, N. Y.; chaplain, 123rd NYSV; was Vice President, Wash. Co. Bible Soc., at its org., & chair at its 50th annual meeting, Sept. 4, 1862, Salem, N. Y.; addressed the society at its meeting concerning the character of the Wash. co. volunteers in the 123rd regt., & the prospective negative influ. of camp life- **1097**; he rec'd. a 15 day furlough from camp, & preached 2 sermons to his home congregation, & gave addresses, Feb. 17, at Cambridge, & Feb. 20, 1863, at Salem, N. Y., giving an acct. of the 123rd regt.'s initial services, & the 20 deaths occurring within the regt. since their service began- **1098**
Rev. Peter- m. Sophia Glover, wid. James Whiteside, as her 2nd husb.- **805**
Robert- (Gorden) of Skenesborough (Whitehall, N. Y.); Dec. 14, 1775, for £ 30, purch. N. half of Lot 75, Artillery Patent, from Michael Hoffnagle; recorded Mar. 8, 1776- **(L)- 936**
William- convicted of manslaughter, 1825, in the death of George Coggshall, Sept. 30, 1824, & sentenced to 14 yrs., Auburn state prison; see Criminal Offenders- **808**

GORE,
Abel- c. 1833, his s. Abel, res. No. 66 Prince St., NYC; & his s. John, res. Buffalo, N. Y.- **1100**
Moses- m. Desire, dau. Samuel Burrows; his wf. rec'd. £ 30 in her father's Will, Feb. 2, 1756; c. 1833, her heirs all res. Nova Scotia, except John-
  1. Moses, Jr., dec'd., leaving 3 children
  2. Desire, m. _____ Ratchford; dec'd., leaving 2 children
  3. Marcy, m. _____ Newcomb; dec'd. leaving 4 children

4. dau., m. _____ Bishop, as her 2nd husb.; dec'd., leaving a child
5. Abel, dec'd., leaving 3 children
6. Samuel, dec'd., leaving a child
7. John, res. Staten Island, NYC; still living (1860's?), an old bachelor; & also, as heirs, Zebulon Elliot & Samuel Hastings- **1100**

GORHAM,
_____- m. Sarah, dau. Jonathan & _____ Fitch; dau. Elizabeth, m. Edward Mitchell- **799**

GOSS,
Clarissa- of N. H.; m. Phineas, s. Thomas & Elizabeth (Cramer) Whiteside- **805**
Ezra Carter- (1778- 1829) s. Rev. Thomas; lawyer, Keesville, N. Y.; member, U. S. Congress, 1819- 21; member, N. Y. Legislature, 1828 & 1829; "but unfortunately gave way to habits of dissipation, & d. of delerium tremens, when in Albany"- **994**
Rev. Thomas- (Gros, or Gross, on N. Y. civil lists, acc. Dr. Fitch) from New England; grad. Dartmouth?; Congregational minister; taught for 3- 4 yrs., abt. 1806, at the Academy, or Select School, in Salem, N. Y.; "He was a very sensible man, of considerable scientific attainments. What was much talked of in town, it being a great curiosity in them [sic] days, was an Orrery which was made for Judge Anthony I. Blanchard by Goss & Griswold"; had 2 sons, Ezra C., & Horace; a 4th of July address, delivered by him in Hebron, N. Y., greatly added to his popular esteem; his wf. d. & he m. a dau. of hers by a prev. marriage; "This indiscreet step destroyed his reputation here & he left the place"- **994**

GOULD,
Lt.- along w. Lts. Fuller, Boggs, & Stewart, one of the alternating commanders of militia forces at Skenesborough, 1779- **751**
Mr.- executor (n. d.), estate of John Dickison, of Troy, N. Y.- **805**

Gould's- c. 1850, loc. Albany, N. Y.; law bookstore- **839**

GRAHAM,
Ennis- tailor, NYC; Lot 55, Kingsbury, N. Y., mortgaged to him, July 5, 1773, by Daniel Jones- **938**
John- of New Perth (Salem, N. Y.); for £ 50, purch. Lot 266, Turner's Patent, May 7, 1784, from John McFarland- **(L)- 936**
Capt. John- his letter, July 14, 1775, Ft. Miller, N. Y., rec'd. on July 17th, by Albany Comm. of Correspondence, w. an enclosed warrant directed to Mr. David Jones, for commission as 2nd Lt.; his comm. declined, w. request to appt. ano. in his place- **819**
Miss- m. David, s. William & Margaret (Andrew) Dobbin, as his 1st wf.- **732**
Miss- m. John, s. Deac. Samuel & Sarah (McNaughton) Dobbin- **732**

Theodorus Van Dyck- adm. to practice in Wash. co., Nov. 3, 1784- **878½**

GRAINER,
Rody- oath of alleg.; Co. D, 22nd N. Y. Inf.- **(L)- 1074**

GRANGER,
Polly- m. Adam, s. Walter & Sarah (Turner) Martin- **1046**

Granny- colloq.; used during Rev. war as a design. for midwives; see Midwives, Vol. 1- **869**

"Granny O'Wale"- popular whig song in Salem, N. Y. area during Rev. war; the version of its lyrics (44 lines) remembered by Betsey Taylor, & recoll. by Wid. Angel; see Whigs, Songs of the Rev.- **857**

Grants/ N. H. Controversy- publ. statem. by Benjamin Hough, Mar. 23, 11775, a Charlotte co. Justice of Peace, concerning his seizure & ejection from the Grants; on or abt. Jan. 26, 1775, at abt. 8:00 AM, his house was entered & he was barred from attempting entrance to procure his weapons by Winthrop Hoyt, of Bennington, Vt.; he was then taken into captivity by Peleg Sunderland, who was among a party of abt. 30 persons 'a no. who were armed w. firelocks, swords & hatchets'; he was then taken 50 mi. S. by sleigh, to Sunderland, Vt., & held there by Sylvanus Brown, James Meed, _____ Booley, & _____ Lyman; Ethan Allen & Seth Warner, 'two of the principal leaders of the Bennington mob', being away in Bennington, a court was not held until Jan. 30th; Allen, Warner, Robert Cochran, Peleg Sunderland, James Meed, Gideon Warren, & Jess Sawyer comprised his trial court, & Allen presented the accusations against him, that he-
1. complained to N. Y. govt. of the rioters mobbing & injuring Benjamin Spencer, Esq., & others;
2. dissuaded & discouraged the people from joining the mob in their proceedings;
3. he had taken a commission of the peace under the govt. of N. Y., exercising his office as a Magistrate for Charlotte co., though he well knew that the mob did not allow that Magistrate here; in his defense, he inquired 1st, whether he had done an injustice to anyone in executing his office, to which Warner replied negatively, in particular declaring 'that he would as willingly have him as a Magistrate as any man whatever, but they would not, under their present circumstances, suffer any Magistrate at all'; & 2nd, he asked if he had been 'busying himself & intermeddling w. respect to titles of lands?', to which Allen replied he had not; he therefore admitted that the charges were all true, & that he had felt duty- bound in his behavior; but the court concluded his plea to have been 'self- justification', which was found insufficient by them as a defense; he was then sentenced to 200 lashes & ordered banished from the Grants, to receive 500 lashes if ever discovered there again; during his confinement, Hough reportedly overheard Ethan Allen declaring that the mob would prob. soon be obliged todrive off all the 'damned

Durhamites', i. e., inhabitants of Durham, Charlotte co. (Clarendon, Vt.) & that he would seize Daniel Walker & Thomas Brayton, constables serving under Hough; in addition, Allen ment. the exposure of Dr. Adams, by hoisting him upon the sign-post of 'landlord Fay', wishing that he had inflicted 500 lashes on him instead, & expressing his intention of being more severe w. the 'damned Yorkers', & not troubling w. the expense of trials, but punishing them immed.; he further remarked that they would pob. soon have a fight w. the Yorkers for abusing their Magistrates, but believed them damned cowards, or they would have come here sooner- **881**; presentation to N. Y. Council, at Ft. George, NYC, Dec. 6, 1753, by commission & commissioners appt. to examine into E. bounds of N. Y. colony; their report, dated Nov. 14th, incl. remarks & observations made by Gov. Benning Wentworth of N. H., in his Mar. 23, 1750/1 letter to Board of Trade, proposing division line betw. his colony & N. Y.; report approved & advised to Gov. to submit 'to the Right Honorable the Lords Commissioners for Trade & Plantations'; refers p. 13, Territorial Rights- **884**; letter rec'd. by N. Y. Council, Aug. 7, 1764, w/o date, from Harmanus Schuyler, Esq., High Sheriff for city & co. of Albany, advising that in pursuance of the Lt. Gov.'s proclamation of Dec. 28, 1763, he has apprehended & will detain in custody until they give bail, Samuel Ashley, Samuel Robinson, John Horfort, & Isaac Charles; all the foregoing had recently turned out Peter Va*f*s (Voss) & Bastian Deal, forcibly, from possession of lands held by them upwards to 30 yrs. within this Province, under the pretence that the land was rightly in the grant of N. H.; refers p. 14, Ibid.- **885**; Gov. Colden's letter, Jan. 20, 1764, to the Board of Trade notes that immed. preceding the late war, incursions of the Indians put an active stop to settlm. within contested portions of the Province, & 'rendered both Govts. less solicitous to bring the controversy to an issue'; from his perspective, it was N. Y.'s belief that N. H. would not venture to make further grants until his Majesty 'should be pleased to determine the limits betw. his two Provinces' as such grants, where interfering w. N. Y., must be considered null; notes recent surprise of N. Y. to discover that since the above recited Transactions, N. H. has 'granted upwards of 30, some affirm, 160 townships'; this point, he adds, might still be concealed, had not the grantees or persons employed by them, traveled through all parts of the Provinces of N. Y. & N. J. 'publickly [sic] offering the lands to sale at such low rates as evince the claimants had no intentions of becoming settlers either from inability or conscious they could derive no title to the lands under the grants of N. Hamp.'; giving the grounds of Conn. & Mass. titles, he then states that if extended W. & N. until meeting his Majesty's other Provinces, N. H. would not interfere w. the bounds of N. Y. Province, & the lands in question 'lay much more convenient to be incl. in N. Y. than N. H.', w. Albany, N. Y. as their natural trade outlet & w. greater revenue to the Crown, the quit rent being 1/ sterling per 100 acres under N. H., & 2/6 under N. Y.; also notes, that a great no. of reduced officers have held preference for claiming their bounties here, but many loc. their spots within the N. H. claims, otherwise it would have been impossible for N. Y. to find enough lands for them clear of dispute & not reserved to the Indians; 'but they absolutely decline any appl. to N. H. for lands westward of Ct.

R.'- **887**; Gov. Colden, Feb. 3, 1764, to Board of Trade, noting the govt. of N. H.
has lately made 'most surprising & extravagant encroachments on the jurisdiction
of lands of this His Majesty's Province w/o... the least color or plausible pretence of
right', noting 160 townships, 6 sq. mi. ea., have been gr. on the W. side of the
Conn. river; 'A man in appearance no better than a Pedlar, has lately travelled thro'
[sic] N. J. & the Prov. hawking & selling his pretended rights to 30 townships, on
trifling considerations'; he further describes N. H.'s proceedings as 'shameful & a
discredit to the Kings authority... it is evident from the low prices shares are sold at
it is not for the benefit of persons who design to settle & improve'; he concludes w.
the suggestion that an inquiry be made into who is the benefactor of these
fraudulent grants- **891**; acc. Dr. Fitch's examination, Harmanus Schuyler's undated
letter to Gov. Colden (§ 885) notes an express arr. for him from Hoosick, N. Y.,
Fri., July 27, 1764, informing of the ejection of Hans Jerry Crieger from his lands
on July 26th, under the claim that his lands belonged to & were under the
jurisdiction of N. H.; Sheriff Schuyler arr. at the homes of Peter Voss & Bastian
Deal the foll. morning, only to discover that it would not be until Mon., July 30th,
that the N. H. people would arr. there to perform the same ejections on them as
they had on Crieger; early on Mon. morning, he rec'd. news of the arr. of the N. H.
people, but arr. at the houses of Voss & Deal only after they had accomp. their
designs; he foll. & overtook them abt. a mi. further, capt. Samuel Ashley, Samuel
Robinson, John Horfort, & Isaac Charles, & remanded them to Albany jail- **892**; a
return of persons inhabiting the N. H. Grants, submitted by Samuel Robinson &
Jeremiah French 'to your excellency & honor's', incl. Pownal, Bennington,
Shaftsbury, <u>Arlington</u>, Sunderland, <u>Manchester</u>, & 'In Draper seven families- In
Danby several'; names of settlers given in those towns underlined, see Arlington, &
Manchester, Vt.- **893**; Gov. Moore's letter, June 9, 1767, to Lord Shelburne,
reciting some of the prev. history connected w. N. Y. Province's management of
settlers found to be occ. the grants of others; Oct. 22, 1765, N. Y.Council advises
that a reserve be made for lands actually possessed & improved by Jacob Marsh &
his assoc. in Patents to be gr. to Capt. John Small & Mr. Napier; report of claims
for 95 townships, recounting their status- 22 within 20 mi. of Hudson river, or
South Bay & Lake Champlain, arr. within a few months foll. ruling regarding
Marsh; Gov. Moore observes these claims may have been an experiment to see how
far N. Y. would indulge the Grants settlers, as it appeared only Shaftsbury,
Bennington, & Pownal, Vt. have actually been settl. in any manner; confirmation
of these townships to actual settlers ordered by advice of N. Y. Council; concerning
21 other townships- lying waste beyond the time required for settlm., they become
reinvested in the Crown, in accordance w. conditions of their charter; on 24 other
townships- warrants of survey, required to be returned in 6 mos., have been iss. in
some cases for 18 mos., w/o return; 4 townships- having gone through all the
forms, 'their Patents have passed the Great Seal', w. 3 others awaiting signature;
the remaining 48 townships haver never taken a step beyond filing their claim w/o
prosecuting it & few, if any, have settl. these areas; along w. erection of
Cumberland co., notes request for an additional co. establ. N. of it, & his efforts to

encourage settlm. to the extent of population needed to accomplish that end; notes suspension of further issuing of grants until his Majesty's pleasure is known; w. regards to statements in Samuel Robinson's petitn., prob. not ¼ of the 1,000 families claimed by him are actually settl. W. of the Conn. river, & far from being turned out of possession, 'most of the holders of these grants live in Boston & Ct. & have never been on the lands to be turned off'; he further states that a fee of 6/ N. Y. currencey to ea. shareholder, 350 acres per share, was required for the purch. of N. Y. grants, while being sold at 30/ in neighboring provinces; the practice of Gov.Wentworth in obt. fees for his grants & the appl. of 'Riders' to such grants referred to in contrast w. N. Y. practices; the appl. of Samuel Robinson & a few others for 45 townships ment. as a proposal so large for the no. of people concerned that it was thought absurd & rejected outright- **894**; an affidavit by Ebenezer Cole, Feb. 27, 1771, the contents noting the probable whipping of ____ Moore, who attempted to settle in Princetown (Manchester, Vt.) under N. Y. proprietorship, w. the added threat to treat anyone else intending to settle in the same manner, in the same fashion; Archibald Campbell offered to incl. surveys of settler's lands in his returns if shown their lines, but most settlers refused to show their boundaries, based upon their refusal to pay quit rents for N. Y. grants; also noted, that purchasers under N. H. title have stipulated they would pay for lands only if N. H. title is valued & maintained; the arr. Gov. Wentworth in office (Gov. John, 1767, foll. Gov. Benning Wentworth) has revived hope of annexation to that Province, & petitns. to the King to that end have circulated, sd. by the advice of Wentworth; deposition of Simon Stevens, member, Gen. Assembly of the Province of N. H., sworn Mar. 2, 1771, notes that prob. not 70 families had settl. betw. the Green Mtns. & Conn. river bef. the King's order fixing the boundary was publ.- **896**; Lord Dunmore, noting to Lord Hillsborough, Mar. 9, 1771, that the only remaining requisite for restoring peace is to revoke the suspension of grants within N. Y. Province; present no. of inhabitants within the Grants noted as betw. 6- 700 families, w. 450+ signing a petitn. requesting to continue under N. Y. govt.; ano. petitn. sent by Gov. Wentworth & signed by abt. 200, requests continuance under N. H. govt.,'but how these names were obt. your Lordship will easily be able to conceive by looking into the different papers I have sent by this packet'- **898**; letter of John Munro to Goldbrow Banyer, May 30, 1771, enclosing affidavits concerning conduct of inhabitants of this co., that he might do something speedily to prevent their continued riotous behavior; warns of dangers to life & property for anyone deeming themslves a 'friend' to N. Y. govt.- 'they assemble at night, throw down all the Yorker's fences, & c., as we are called, & drive the cattle into the fields & meadows & destroy both grass & corn, & do every mischief they can think of'; ments. his house filled w. rioters, & that the felon who shot Samuel Willoughby's horse, being sent to jail, has noted in his confession that 2 others were involved, w. doubts that they will be caught- **899**; testim., Sept. 20, 1771, of Samuel Gardenier, Walloomsac Patent, who states that he purch. 310 acres from James Delancey, c. 1767, & rem. there in June 1769, finding that Ichabod Cross had settl. & improved part of his land under N. H. title; an agreem. of arbitration was made betw. them,

& it was resolved that Cross should receive £ 25 for ½ of his improved lands & lease the remainder for 5 yrs., surrendering it at the end of that time;Gardenier pd. £ 15 towards the agreem., but Cross later refused the remainder; since that time, the fences of Gardenier have freq. been pulled down & his neighbors have feared aiding him in their repair, for fear of offending the Bennington people; & he was often warned his house & possessions would all be destroyed, & he would be beaten or perh. killed; 2 hrs. bef. daybreak, abt. Aug. 1, 1771, he was alarmed by a no. of men on horseback, wanting to see him abt. the N. H. title; he instructed them to go to Albany regarding this, but was asked to come out, whereupon his wf. declared it was an unsuitable hr. to do business; the mob insisted they would come whenever that had a mind to & Gardenier then declared he was afraid to come out; the mob, consisting of 11 men in disguises, promised they would not harm him; on coming out, he was surrounded by them & asked to give up the writings given to him by Ichabod Cross & to do justice to him; he stated that he already had done so, paying him honestly, but they remained dissatisfied & insisted on the papers at once; telling them that the papers were in Albany, the mob then demanded that he give £ 1,000 bond to Cross, agreeing he would return the papers & allow him to enjoy his lands as bef. the arbitration; Gardenier declined, wishing to go for advice to his bro. in Kinderhook, N. Y.; the mob then sd. they had no business w. his bro., "& one swore he should never have any benefit from his land, or fodder of any of its produce", finally giving him a fortnight to decide; on the foll. day, he appl. to Esq. Munro, & then met w. the Mayor of Albany & Justice Bleecker, all of whom referred him to a higher authority for his protection; it was also related to him that the rioters had reported to Munro that "they had appl. to him civilly, but if he did not comply they would next come Devil- like"; he escaped nr. the end of the fortnight, & the rioters soon came "armed w. guns, swords, pistols & clubs, to the no. of 100 persons", ransacking his house & swearing they would go to Kinderhook, if necessary, to have him; they thereupon upset & tore to pieces his remaining haystacks "scattering the hay through the mud & filth; & flung down part of his fences, & they have threatened to crop, geld, & whip him, & tie him to a tree, gagged, & leave him there to starve to death'; see Breckenridge, James; & Vermonters- **902**; depositions of the posse & Sheriff, c. 1771, sent to eject James Breckenridge; an armed force was discovered lying in ambush on the ridge N. & SE of his house, & the Sheriff sought assistance from the party of 40 men found on the SE part of the ridge, who all cocked their pieces & bade him be gone; he then went to Breckenridge's house w. an axe, & was abt. breaking the door in when the armed party aimed their guns, & one of the Sheriff's party "took hold of him & made him desist, as death would follow"; few in the posse were armed, & only abt. 20 had foll. the Sheriff to Breckenridge's door, the remaining 150 keeping back quite adistance; Robert Yates, Esq. then audibly read the writ at Breckenridge's door, that he might know the consequences- **903**; letter from Gen. Haldimand, Sept. 1, 1773, read bef. N. Y. Council by the Gov. on Sept. 3rd, in response to the Gov.'s Aug. 31st request for regular troops; the employment of such troops where militia laws exist & where Magistrates may call upon trained inhabitants for assistance in performing their duties viewed by Gen. Haldimand as a dangerous tendency; "if a few lawless vagabonds can prevail so far in such a govt. as that of N. Y. as to require regular troops to supress them it carries such reflection of weakness as he fears will be of bad consequences & render the civil Magistrates contemptible in the public eye"; it is further noted by him that Crown Point & Ticonderoga are in such decrepit state as to render them unsuitable for the stationing of such troops, if provided; he notes further that if the Gov. should persist in his request, he would like to know the no. of troops needed, when, & that the Province pay for their expense- **909**; N. Y. Council, Sept. 8, 1771, advises sending 200 men to Ti as soon as possible to assist in preserving the peace, their length of service dependent upon the people's behavior; the Gov. & Council advise an ordinance for establ. courts in Charlotte co.; Sept. 29th, Gen. Haldimand proposes sending 200 men to Ti & Crown Point, withdrawing 150 on Nov. 1st; the Council deems it too late in the season for sending troops this yr., postponing the required aid- **910**; referred to here as the Vermont controversy; was resolved (n. d.) by an adjusted payment of $30,000.00, from Vt. to N. Y.- **917**; Dr. Fitch states- "The foll. notes hastily pencilled, from docs. of minor importance, in the Secretary of State's Office, Albany- relating to the controversy in N. H."- Dec. 22, 1752, Robert Charles, Esq., Agent for the Colony of N. Y. in London, sends to the N. Y. Gov. a copy of Gov. Benning Wentworth's letter to the Board of Trade, "showing Gov. Wentworth to be grossly ignorant or willfully false in his representation of N. Y. boundaries"; Comm. of N. Y. Council, June 6, 1753, presents report reciting corresp. betw. N. H. govt. & N. Y. to this date, noting that no copy has yet been rec'd. of Gov. Wentworth's communication, which he had promised to send here, bef. forwarding the same to England; Sept. 21, 1759, Gov. Delancey issues a proclamation, inviting settlers to loc. on lands in vicinity of Ft. Edward & Wood Creek; an affidavit of Alexander McClain, Mar. 16, 1763, testif. that a N. H. party was surveying lands nr. Crown Point during the prev. Sept.; Gov. Colden issues proclamation, Dec. 28, 1763, warning settlers not to take land titles from N. H. & directing civil officers of N. Y. 'to continue to exercise jurisdiction in their respective functions as far as the banks of the Conn. river, the undoubted eastern limits of that part of the Province of N. Y.'; Gov. Wentworth writes to Gov. Colden, Aug. 17, 1764, requesting release of 4 individuals of the Pownal area, arrested by the Albany Sheriff (prob. Ashley, Robinson, Charles, & Horfort; § 892) on grounds that "it would be an act of cruelty to punish individuals for disputes betw. the 2 govts., & c."; N. Y. Council advises in response that Gov. Colden inform Gov. Wentworth of the circumstances & that the offense was committed "within the undoubted jurisdiction of this province"; ano. doc. noting that the leniency of N. Y. proprietors in enforcing their claims prob. caused N. H. settlers to think that they distrusted their titles, hence emboldening settlers to more strenous resistance- **928**

Granville, N. Y.- prob. c. 1786, a minor tax revolt, "in Shays' time", reported to have been instigated from among some of Shays' men who were then in the area;

the militia ordered out from Salem, N. Y., to quell the rebellion, but the protestors abandoned their cause as soon as news arr. of the militia's impending arr., & the insurrection was settl. by the time the militia had reached there- **701**; a ceremony presented Feb. 23, 1816, by the Washington Benevolent Society of this town, in celebration of Washington's birthday, beginning at the home of J. Stiles & joined by associates from Fair Haven, Vt., who brought a frigates, drawn by 8 horses, & appropriately banned for the occasion- **723**; the tax revolt here "was so serious that the sheriff ordered out the posse comitatis", w. Sherwood's militia co. also being ordered out from the Ft. Edward area; it being such a formidable force, the rioters at once submitted- **918**; the tax revolt here attrib. to the prescence of Shays' men, & also to Quakers who were settl. here, as equally opposed to taxes to defray war expenses, as war itself- **921**; c. 1771, only a few settlers; 2 or 3 bros. named Fisher, & others from Pelham & Palmer, Mass.- **997**

GRAVES,
Capt.- commanded Hillsdale, N. Y. militia co., July 1777; called out at the time to march to Ft. Edward & Lake George- **753**
Timothy- wf. Martha, d. Feb. 19, 1844, at 83; & he d. June 20, 1848, at 93- **(L)-772**

GRAY,
Col. Charles O.- of 96th N. Y. Inf.; from Warrensburg, N. Y., s. Gen. T. S.; d. Dec. 14, 1862, at battle of Kinston, N. C.- **1095**
David D.- bro. William; res. Salem, N. Y.- **1015**
Family- of Cambridge, N. Y.; bros. David D. & William; the latter induced a large no. of his father's family to rem. St. Regis reservation foll. the end of the Rev. war; see Vol. 2- **1015**
Sally- m. Timothy, s. John, Esq., & Catharine (Reid) Munro- **812**
Capt. Walter S.- Co. G, 93rd N. Y. Inf.- **1090b**
William- b. Cambridge, N. Y.; joined the American army at age 17, & was taken by surprise along w. others at Skenesborough (Whitehall, N. Y.) & carried to Quebec (prob. Mar. 1780) & remained there until after the peace was declared; he then repaired to Caughnawaga, N. Y., & then to St. Regis, where he m. an Indian woman, & had a family; "prob. no white person has had more influ. w. the Indian tribe of St. Regis in their negotiations" than him- his name constantly found as interpreter or agent on the old treaties & other papers executed by them; he returned to Cambridge & brought a large no. of his father's family back to St. Regis, although never intermarrying, & both his parents d. on the reservation there; by his petitn., gr. 257 acres by N. Y., Apr. 4, 1801, at a place called Gray's mills; during the War of 1812, he "espoused w. zeal the American cause" & lead a party through the woods & capt. a British co. at St. Regis, fall 1812; considered a dangerous partisan, he was surprised & capt. Dec. 1813, & confined in prison at Quebec, & d. Apr. or May, 1814; refers pgs. 198- 200, Hough's Hist. of St. Lawrence & Franklin co.- **1015**

GREAT BRITAIN- 709, 795, 878½, 880, 1010, 1097;
British- 701, 703, 706, 708, 710, 719, 728, 740, 747, 748, 750, 759s, 753, 760, 767- 771, 792, 796, 797, 799, 853, 869, 916, 920, 922, 941, 949, 949b, 956, 957, 968, 983, 990, 1010, 1015, 1016, 1032, 1050s, 1055, 1056, 1062; colonies- 1059; England- 758, 759s, 783, 799, 806, 822, 834, 837, 849, 878, 880, 894, 907, 916, 923, 924, 930, 934, 935, 942, 945b, 950, 952b, 955, 957, 960, 962, 969, 990, 998, 1010, 1029, 1032, 1033, 1054, 1065, 1082, 1093; language- 740, 801, 989; Revolution, of 1688- 1082; Royalists- 768;
Cities & Towns- Abbots Bromley- 880; Bocking- 799, 834; Fulham- 935; Hedge Hill- 962; Hensington- 930; Ipswich- 799; London- 760, 799, 928, 930, 934, 1059; Dublin & London Sts.- 857; Whitehall- 883; Maidstone- 934; Malden- 799; the Marsh, Lincolnshire- 799; Old Alvesford- 880; Newport Pagnel- 961; Northtown- 1082;
Counties- Essex- 799, 834, 945b; Hants- 880; Kent- 934, 962; Lincolnshire- 799, 960; Middlesex- 935; Stafford- 880; Surry- 772;
Features- Suffolk crag- 799;
Colonial Depts.- Board of Trade- 799, 884, 887, 891, 928, 1013; Commissioners for Trade & Plantations- 884;
Institutions- Bishops of- Canterbury- 759s; Oxford- 759s; Cambridge University- 799; Hospitals, Director Gen. of- 894; House of Commons- 799; Lord Chancellor of- 759s; Magdalen College- 759s; Parliamentary party-962; St. Thomas' hospital, London- 799; Tea Act- 857;
Military units in N. America-
French & Indian war- Regts. of Foot- 42nd- 812; 44th- 931, 936; 78th- 936;
Rev. war- 7th- 775; 9th- 792; 26th- 775; German- Hessians- 728, 740, 761- 762b, 766, 792, 853, 953, 976, 998, 1007, 1072;
Scots, Highland Regts.- 42nd (Black Watch)- 990; 71st- 990; 76th- 990; 78th- 990; 91st- 990; 93rd- 990;
Royalty- Ann- 799; Charles I- 962; Elizabeth I- 759s; George II- 759s; George III- 869, 990; James II- 759s, 799; Duke of York- 928; Earl of Macclesford- 759s

GREEN/ GREENE,
_____ - he & ____ Fitch, ment. as part of the Larrazabal conspiracy; refers May 29, 1868, *N. Y. Tribune*- **799**
Christopher C.- oath of alleg.; Co. D, 22nd N. Y. Inf.- **(L)- 1074**; s. Solomon; long sick in the hospital, he returned home, & d. Mar. 27, 1863, at 21- **1095b**
Family- c. 1780's, res. Socialborough, Charlotte co., N. Y. (Vt.); he occ. a tenant house for Daniel Marsh on a disputed tract, preventing Silas Whitney from laying claim to it; one day Whitney, sore over this situation, strove to take possession by force; after finishing his Sun. breakfast, he went to Green's house, "& w/o ceremony put the occupant & his furniture out of doors"; (a similar incident occurred nr. Fitch's Point, betw. Rogers the Squatter & Mrs. Livingston; see § 179, Vol. 1); Whitney locked himself inside the house w. an axe, threatening Marsh if

he should enter; but Marsh went around the house,"opened a window & sprang in ere Whitney was aware of it"; once in peaceable & joint possession, he reinstated Green & his furniture, & having nothing of his own to put in & hold joint possession, Whitney gave up the contest; ments. sons Dr. Joel, of Rutland, Vt.; & Dr. Horace, of NYC- **970**

Fanny- m. William, s. Hon. William Henry & Harriet (Blin) Parker- **759s** *Solomon*- of Cambridge, N. Y.; his s. Christopher C., enl. Co. D, 22nd N. Y. Inf- **1095b**

Thomas- witn., Mar. 25, 1773, w. Benjamin Spencer, to quit claim by Edward Arnold to Thomas Brayton, for Lot No. 5, Socialborough, Charlotte co., N. Y. (Vt.)- **745**; defendant, May 19, 1774, in a case brought by John James Bleecker- **878**

Green Mountain Boys- N. Y. Comm. of Safety notes, Jan. 18, 1777, that 'numbers of disaffected persons in Albany & Charlotte co., called the Green Mtn. boys, w. divers persons of Cumberland & Gloucester co., have industriously made use of every equipment to induce the inhabitants to disavow the authority of N. Y. & form a new & separate state'- **786**

Green Mountain Regiment- establ. June 30, 1775, by order of N. Y. Provincial Congress, w. 4 regts. to be raised, & officers appt.; Samuel Cook, Ebenezer Haviland, & John Williams to be surgeons if found duly qualified by examination of Drs. John Jones & Samuel Bard; foll. an audience of Ethan Allen & Seth Warner w. Prov. Congress, a regt., not exceeding 500 men, was ordered, being allowed to recommend for appt. of their own field officers as well as others, distinct & independent from N. Y. troops; on Gen. Schuyler's recommendation, £ 30 advanced to Allen & Warner for expenses- **778**; meeting of W. range of Green Mtn. towns, held July 27, 1775, at Cephas Kent's, Dorset, Vt., to select its officers; Nathan Clark, chairman, & John Fasset, clerk; Lt. Col.- Seth Warner, by vote of 41 to 5; Maj.- Samuel Safford, by vote of 28 to 17; Capts.- Wright Hopkins, Oliver Potter, John Grant, Herman Allen, William Fitch, Gideon Brownson, Micha Vail; Lts.- John Fasset, Ebenezer Allen, Barnabas Blarnan, David Galusha, Jille Bleaksley, Ira Allen, Gideon Warren; 2nd Lts.- Johan Noble, James Claghorn, John Chipman, Philo Hard, Nathan Smith, Jesse Sawyer, Joshua Stanton; aside from noting election of officers, Gen. Schuyler requests of Peter T. Curtenius 'coarse cloth for making 225 green coats faced w. red- & tents for accommodating 225 men'- **781b**; Gen. Schuyler reports, Aug. 19, 1775, that the controversy betw. Allen & Warner over selection of officers had been carried to such lengths that few, if any, men will be raised & of those, few will have firearms; on Aug. 23, 1775, Col. Warner arr. in Albany, N. Y., for clothing & c., for the regt.; Gen. Schuyler notes, 'as the men would not take the field w/o some money to buy blankets & arms I advanced him £ 500', & also remarks that 'the peculiar situation' of the regt. & its relation to N. Y. renders the controversy over officers too delicate a matter for his determination; however, on Sept. 1st, the N. Y. Prov. Congress appt. Seth Warner as Col., & Samuel Safford as Maj.- **782**

Green Mountain Rangers- May/ June 1777, divided into 3 battalions under Maj. Horsington's command; Capt. Hatch's co. was detailed to Royalton, Vt., where they constructed a picket fort, & then were directed via Onion river to Mt. Independence; they were then in the retreat to Castleton, & then Bennington, Vt., foll. the evac. of Ticonderoga; Capt. Sackett's co. was stat. at Onion river; Capt. Hale's co. was stat. at the mouth of Otter creek- **756**

Greenwich, N. Y.- prev. called Whipple City, & afterw., Union Village- **862**

GREGOR,
John- late Lt., His Majesty's 42nd Regt. of Foot; along w. Ann Gordon, gr. 2,000 acres, town of White Creek, N. Y.- **990**
Rev.- (MacGregor, or McGregor, James; 1677- 1729) brief ment. of his colony, Londonderry, N. H.- **1097**
William- Adjutant, 42nd Royal Highland regt.; gr. 2,000 acres in Vt.?; refers p. 81, Catalogue of Maps- **990**

GRIFFIN,
Banjamin- for £ 375, purch. Lot No. 138, Argyle Patent, Jan. 2, 1776, from Archibald Campbell, Esq.- **(L)- 936**
Clarinda- from Conn.; schoolteacher; m. James Wells- **839**

GRIFFITH/ GRIFFITHS,
John- (J. Griffiths) Justice of Peace, Kingsbury, N. Y.; his letter to William Smith, Esq., Dec. 20, 1776, complains of the manner in which Philip Skene "traduces" him to the Gov., noting the lack of principles behind which law is practiced within his township; see Skenesborough, N. Y.- **929**
Thomas- res. Whitehall, N. Y.; b. July 29, 1763, Hartford, Conn.; res. Shaftsbury, Vt., & Granville, N. Y. during the Rev. war; served 1 wk., July 1779, called out w. Capt. Waldo's co., Shaftsbury militia, Col. Walbridge's regt.; was marched towards Castleton, Vt., but returned upon news of the enemy's retreat; vol. at Granville, N. Y., Oct. 1779, for ½ month's service, & was stat. at Whitehall; 1780, stat. at Granville, & directed by Capt. Child as a scout to Skenesborough (Whitehall), Ft. Ann, Lake George, East Bay, & Kingsbury, N. Y.; was also on alarm to Argyle, w. Capt. Blakeley; 2 services, Capt. Parmlee Allen's co., Lt. Jonathan Wright & Lt. Stewart, Col. Walbridge's regt.; marched to Skenesborough, May 1781, & served there until Nov.; refers p. 222, Duer's Life of Stirling; served abt. a month, in total, in 1782, incl. Capt. Blakeley's co., & Col. Webster's co., of Hebron, N. Y.; also, abt. ½ month, Capt. Lytle's co., & prob. Capt. Child's co.- **754**

GRISWOLD,
____- goldsmith, Salem, N. Y.; he & Rev. Thomas Goss constructed an Orrery for Judge Blanchard, he doing the mechanical part, under Goss' direction- **994**

GRODT,
Family- c. 1770's, res. Kinderhook, N. Y.; ments. s. Jacob, & dau., who m. Samuel Gardenier- **902**
Jacob- res. Kinderhook, N. Y.; his wf., children, & a negro slave, were in Walloomsac Patent, at the house of his bro.- in- law, Samuel Gardenier, Aug. 1771, when a mob of the N. H. people 1st confronted Gardenier abt. rescinding his agreem. w. Ichabod Cross; when the mob later gave him an ultimatum abt. the issue, Gardenier fled to his bro.- in- law's for protection- **902**

GROOM/ GROOME,
Francis- of NYC, shopkeeper; he & Peter Van Brugh Livingston purch., for £ 150, a 2,000 acre tract, Sept. 20, 1773, that was orig. gr. to Thomas Trickett, loc. on the E. side of Wood creek, as it runs into Lake Champlain; he purch. again, w. Livingston, Oct. 20, 1785, property, et. al., not described- **(L)- 936**

GROSBECK,
Mr.- c. 1770's, res. Schaghticoke, N. Y.; when Rev. Van Benschoten was compelled to marry a couple from the opp. side of the Hoosick river, he was appt. by him as his deputy, to kiss the bride in his stead, & appt. atty. to coll. the bridegroom's marriage fee; see § 17, Vol. 1- **953b**

GUILD,
Jeremiah- res. Younge, Ontario, Canada; m. Asenith, dau. John & Hannah (Alyea) Munroe- **812**

GUILFORD,
Hugh- m. Mary, dau. John & Ann (Whiteside) Cochran- **805**

GUTHRIE/ GUTHERIE,
George- (Guthery) Lots 286 & 287, Turner's Patent, orig. conveyed to him & John Martin, by the proprietors- **(L)- 936**

GUTRY,
John- defendant, May 19, 1774, in a case brought by Benjamin Canady- **878**

H

HAKE,
Samuel- of NYC; 100 acres, in Durham (Clarendon, Vt.) mortgaged to him, June 11, 1773, by Benjamin Spencer- **938**

HALDIMAND,
Brig. Gen./ Gov. Sir Frederick- (1718- 1791) given here as Gen.; requested by the Gov., Aug. 31, 1773, to provide regular troops to maintain order within the Grants; his reply the foll. day. presented to N. Y. Council on Sept. 3rd, observing that in a govt. where militia provide for trained inhabitants that may be called upon to assist the civil Magistrates as needed, such action would serve to undermine the civil authority in the public eye; further comments upon the poor condition of prospective barracks at Ticonderoga & Crown Point for such a force- **909**; in N. Y. Council, Sept. 29, proposes that 200 men be sent to Ticonderoga & Crown Point, withdrawing 150 of them on Nov. 1st, "as not more than 50 can be sheltered there in a winter at present"; the Council concludes it to be too late in the season to send the required aid this yr.- **910**

HALE,
Capt.- June 1777, commanded co. of Green Mtn. rangers stat. at Onion river- **756**

HALL,
Aaron- Co. A, 2nd N. Y., Northern Black Horse, Cav., 1861- 2- **1080**
Rev. Albert G., D. D.- pastor, 1st Presbyterian church, Rochester, N. Y., for 25 yrs., "where he d. abt. 2 yrs. since"- **759s**
Capt.- commanded Co. I, 123rd NYSV (Hall, Orrin S.; see Vol. 4)- **1098**
Daniel- lawyer, 60 Fourth St., Troy, N. Y.; m. Ann Jennet, dau. Edward & Esther Fitch; they have 2 sons, both now (1850) attending Harvard; "she has gathered much respecting the pedigree of the Fitch family"- **799**; noted Sept. 26, 1851, that John Fitch was a guest in his house- **939**; their eldest s., Fitz Edwin, grad. Harvard; other children- Mary, George, Benjamin, Richard, & James- **940**
David E.- (s. Rev. Nathaniel & Hannah Emerson) d. Apr. 24, 1852, at 41, Mobile, Alabama- **759s**
Edwin, D. D.- (s. Dr. Ira & Rebecca Parker) grad. Middlebury, 1826; Prof., Christian Theology, Auburn Theological Seminary; see Vol. 4- **759s**
Fitz Edwin- (or Fitzedward; 1825- 1901; s. Daniel & Ann Jennett Fitch) b. ca. 1826, grad. Harvard, & understands several languages; c. 1851, serves as Vice Pres. of a college in India (instructor, Benares, India, 1850- 53, & for Central Provinces, 1865- 57; later Prof., Kings College, London, 1862)- **940**
George- m. Anna, dau. James & Rebecca (Lytle) Mills- **737**
Dr. Ira- res. Middle Granville, N. Y.; m. Rebecca, dau. Peter & Esther (Clark) Parker; & he d. 1816, w/o Will- **759**; (s. Nathaniel & Mehitabel Storrs) b. Dec. 20,

1772, Lebanon, N. H.; grad. Dartmouth, 1793; m. Dec. 17, 1795, Rebecca Parker; 7 children- Ira, Jr.; Silas; Edwin; Horace & Lyman, both d. in early manhood; Sidney & Storrs; he studied & practiced medicine in Granville, & d. Sept. 18, 1816; his Will, May 6, Prob., Oct. 14, 1816, appts. as Exec'rs. his wf., John C. Parker, Isaac Hollister, & Clark Northup; by his Will, a port. of the SW corner of his farm was reserved as a bur. grd. for his family, & other Masons; his wf. d. July 1, 1847- **759s**

James- res. Argyle, N. Y.; m. Mary, dau. William & Jane (Lytle) Russell, as her 2nd husb.- **737**

John A.- res. Troy, N. Y.; m. 1. Henrietta, dau. Stephen & Sarah (Fitch) St. John; she had some children, who all d. y.; & he m. 2nd, Louisa, dau. George Gardner of Troy; his wid. res. Milwaukee, Wisc., foll. by Fishkill, N. Y., c. 1853- 1867- **940**

Marshall- c. 1850, occ. the place prev. occ. by the Cuyler family, where Samuel Berry kept tavern in 1798, nr. Moses kill & above Ft. Miller, N. Y.- **804**

Mary- (dau. Rev. Nathaniel & Hannah Emerson) d. July 30, 1854, at 39, Granville, N. Y.- **759s**

Matthew- m. Margaret, dau. James & Rebecca (Lytle) Mills- **737**

Nathaniel- m. Mehitabel Storrs; their 3 sons, 1st 2 b. Lebanon, N. H.- Dr. Ira, b. Dec. 20, 1772, m. Rebecca, dau. Peter & Esther (Clark) Parker; Hon. Nathaniel, b. 1775; & Orla- **759s**

Dr. Nathaniel- (s. Hon. Nathaniel & Esther Parker) settl. in practice for many yrs. at Hanford's landing, below Rochester, N. Y., on the Genesee river- **759s**

Hon. Nathaniel- of Whitehall, N. Y.; m. Esther, dau. Peter & Esther (Clark) Parker; & he d. ca. 1835, w/o Will- **759**; (s. Nathaniel & Mehitabel Storrs) b. 1775, Lebanon, N. H.; m. 1. Esther Parker, & she d. Mar. 20, 1808; 2. Cynthia, dau. David & Susanna (West) Mason; 3 children by 1st wf., & 7 by 2nd wf.-

1. Dr. Nathaniel
2. Rev. Albert G.
3. Emma Louisa, m. Edwin Hollister
4. Francis Theodore, c. 1874, suppos. res. Kansas
5. Mary, m. & rem. Michigan
6. Cynthia, m. James Noble
7. Cornelia, d. y.
8. Augustus Ferdinand, d., leaving wid. & children
9. Mason, d. y.
10. Elizabeth, m. _____ Cramer; he studied law w. Zebulon R. Shipherd; adm. Wash. Co. bar, Feb. 11, 1802, & practiced in Granville, N. Y.; rem. Whitehall, & appt. Postmaster, 1806, & Town Clerk, 1808, serving for 17 yrs.; Justice of Peace, Master in Chancery, 1814; reappt. 1814, & continued permanently; appt. Judge, Wash. Co. Courts, July 1819- **759s**

Rev. Nathaniel- (s. Deac. Willis & Ann Cage) b. Apr. 9, 1764, Sutton, Mass.; grad. Dartmouth, 1790; m. Hannah, dau. Daniel Emerson, of Hollis, N. H.; 9 children- Hannah E., m. Rev. Abijah Crane; Willis; Nathaniel E.; Eliza, Richard Baxter; David E.; David Brainard; Mary, & Edward; installed as minister, Oct. 3, 1797,

Middle Granville, N. Y., served for 23 yrs., & rec'd. 225 members into the church; he d. July 31, 1820; & his wf. d. May 22, 1832, at 58; see also, Vol. 1- **759s**
Orla- (s. Nahaniel & Mehitabel Storrs) farmer, Justice of Peace, res. Granville, N. Y.- **759s**
Storrs- (s. Dr. Ira & Rebecca Parker) grad. Middlebury, 1838; practicing (c. 1874) at Rosendale, Wisc.- **759s**
Hon. Willis- (s. Rev. Nathaniel & Hannah Emerson) N. Y. Atty. Gen., 1842- 45; d. July 14, 1866, at 67, NYC- **759s**

HALLEY,
Rev. Ebenezer, D. D.- delivered the funeral discourse, Apr. 20, 1841, at a memorial on the death of Pres. Wm. H. Harrison, Salem, N. Y.; Dr. Fitch notes it was publ. later by the Salem Printing Office as a pamphlet- **1009**

HALSTEAD,
Esther Ann- of NYC; m. John Ashton, s. Rev. Bradley & Polly (Pattison) Sillick- **950**

HAMILTON,
____- Irish; res. Salem, N. Y.; m. Daniel, s. James & Lydia (Martin) McNitt; rem. Fond du Lac, Wisc.- **731**
Alexander- (1755- 1804) m. dau. Gen. Philip Schuyler; (as Col.) when Gen. Schuyler was U. S. Senator, 1789- 1791, it was presumed by most that Schuyler was too much influ. politically by him &, in part, he was not re- elected for that reason- **920**; his measure for funding the govt. was much opposed at the time, but noted as giving immed. confidence, reputation & prosperity to the govt. & country as a whole; Wm. Duer, Esq. attempted to possess the whole of these govt. securities, but was unable to pay them as they came due, & was thus imprisoned- **1031**
John- res. Black Creek (Hebron, N. Y.) & Jan. 25, 1776, rec'd. a recommendation for appt. as Capt., Charlotte co. militia- **784**
William- of Black Creek (Hebron, N. Y.) 44 acres deeded to him, May 8, 1781, by Dr. Thomas Clark; the purch. was Lot 38, w. bounds described- **(L)- 936**
William?- m. Maria, dau. James & Lydia (Martin) McNitt, as her 2nd husb.- **731**

HAMMOND,
King S.- Co. A, 2nd N. Y., Northern Black Horse, Cav., 1861- 2; see Vol. 3- **1080**

HANES,
Peter- of White Creek, N. Y.; carpenter, farmer; b. ca. 1841; enl. troop M, 1st N. Y. Mounted Rifles; deserted while on night picket, Providence Church, (Kentucky?) to join the enemy; reward advertised for his capt., *Cambridge Valley News*, w. an additional $10 bounty- **1095**

HANFORD,
Sally- m. William, s. Timothy & Esther (Platt) Fitch- **799**; same, was from Norwalk, Conn.- **939**

HANKS,
Joseph- former innkeeper, Salem, N. Y.; a dau. m. James, s. Aaron, Jr., & Artemisia (Lynn) Martin- **731**

HANNA,
David- res. Salem, N. Y.; sons John, b. ca. 1759, & Robert, b. ca. 1770; his family & that of William Tosh were among those from Salem who sought shelter in Jackson foll. the Allen Massacre- **701**; dau. Mary, m. William, s. Andrew & Nancy (Lytle) Vance- **737**
Henry O.- (Hana) plaintiff, May 19, 1774, vs. Jeremiah Burrows- **878**
Jane- m. James, s. Robert & Susan (Lytle) Vance- **737**
John- s. David; b. ca. 1759; he drove his father's cattle to Bennington, Vt., to keep them from falling into British hands; enl. Salem militia at age 16, & went to Skenesborough on several alarms during his service; was among the militia sent to Ft. Ann to bury the dead foll. its surrender, 1780- **701**
Robert- s. David; b. ca. 1770; ordered out, at age 16, w. the Salem milita, to quell a tax revolt in Granville, N. Y., "in Shays' time"; relates some Rev. war incidents regarding the flight of Salem families into Jackson, N. Y., c. 1777, which were-acc. Dr. Fitch, "prob. confounded" w. some other childhood events; also ments. events relating to the 1780 capt. & surrender of Ft. Ann, & Daniel Shays' flight into Salem- **701**

HANSON,
Albert- of Shushan, N. Y.; m. Eleanor, dau. James & Matilda (Safford) Turner; no children- **1090**

HARDEN,
Peter Riley- s. Benjamin, of "Sand St.", E. Greenwich, N. Y.; his mother rem. Iowa, & he enl. in one of the regts. from there & d. during the Civil War- **1095**

HARDING,
Olive- m. Aaron, s. Aaron & Sarah (Newell) Martin- **1037**

HARGRAVE,
Elizabeth- b. Oct. 6, 1730, England; m. John Ashton- **960**

HARKNESS,
William B.- printer, Salem, N. Y.; purch. (n. d.) the gambrel- roofed house orig. occ. by Nathan or Samuel Hopkins- **1073**

HARMON,
Reubin, Sr.- he & his s. Reubin, Jr., were defendants, along w. Roger Rose, in a case brought by William Fitch- **878**

HARNEY,
Gen. William Selby- (1800- 1889) his "fight & slaughter of Indians" (Sept. 3, 1855 defeat of the Souix at Sand Hill, on the Platte river) was loc. abt. 5 mi. inside S. Dakota, along or nr. the Missouri river- **1089**

HARRISON,
____ - res. Schaghticoke Point, N. Y.; m. Mary, dau. David & ____ (Lowrie) Dobbin- **732**
Gen./ Pres. William Henry- (1773- 1841) newspaper notice, Salem, N. Y., regarding honors planned in memoriam, as proposed by a public meeting held Apr. 12, 1841, 'to devise & recommend suitable arrangements for Military & Civic Honors, in consequence of the death of the late President of the United States'; see Salem, N. Y.- **1009**

HARSHA,
Abner- (s. Hugh & Mary McWhorter) m. in Sterling, N. Y., but d. w/o issue- **973**
David- res. Argyle, N. Y.; connected w. the earlier family, but arr. more recently from Ireland; m. dau. John & Molly (Craig) Harsha- **973**
David A.- (s. John & ____ McDougall) author of "Thoughts on Religion", & numerous newspaper articles; see also, Vol. 4- **973**
Elias- (s. Hugh & Mary McWhorter) res. Sterling, N. Y.; m. dau. George Cooper- **973**
Deac. George- (s. Hugh & Mary McWhorter) Colporter, American Tract Society; m. 1. dau. James McClelland; had 2 sons, one who d. y., & Rev. William; 2. dau. Daniel Reid; 2 sons, who d. y.; & 2 daus., who now (1852) res. w. him; informs Dr. Fitch concerning the family history- **973**
Hugh- s. James, the emigrant; b. ca. 1758/9; was 6 yrs. old when the family emig., & kept his father's farm in Stillwater, N. Y.; sold out, c. 1802, to Josiah or Curtis Hewitt, & rem. Argyle, N. Y.; Rev. war soldier, at Bemis Heights, & c.; m. Mary, dau. Matthew McWhorter; children-
1. James, d. at 19
2. Matthew, m. dau. John Pettit, Esq.
3. John, m. dau. John Cooper
4. Hugh, m. Caroline Dow
5. Elias, m. dau. George Cooper
6. Deac. George, m. 1. dau. James McClelland; 2. dau. Daniel Reid
7. Thomas, m. dau. Uriah Beers
8. Abner, m. in Sterling, N. Y., but childless- **973**
Hugh- (s. Hugh & Mary McWhorter) m. Caroline Dow, of Madison co., N. Y.; they rem. Sycamore, Illinois, & he is now (1852) dec'd.- **973**

James- emig. from Ireland, abt. 1764, w. Rev. Dr. Thomas Clark's co., bringing his wf. & family; leased a farm abt. 2 mi. W.of Stillwater, N. Y., on the road to Gracie's corners & Saratoga Lake; he d. abt. a yr. after emig., foll. 9 months illness w. bloody flux (dysentery); refers p. 36, Dr. Clark's Farewell letter, which notes- 'James Hershaw, one of our elders,d. abt. 6 months after our arr., joyfully singing Ps. 73; 26, 27'; had 3 sons & 5 daus.-

1. Mary, m. Stephen, or Deac. John? Rowan
2. Nancy, m. Thomas McLaughery
3. dau., m. Andrew McLaughery
4. Martha, m. James Flack
5. Ester, m. Hugh Sloan
6. John, eldest, m. Molly Craig
7. Hugh, m. Mary McWhorter
8. James, d. at abt. 12 yrs., Stillwater, N. Y., by a fall from a horse- 973

James- (s. John & Molly Craig) res. on his father's homestead, Argyle, N. Y.; m. dau. Deac. David Matthews; 4 sons- David, John, James, & Henry- 973

Jane- m. Joseph, s. John & Betsey (Beaty) McDougall- 978

John- eldest s. James, the emigrant; rem. from Stillwater to Salem, N. Y., & occ. an 88 acre lot ½ mi. E. of the village; having cleared it out & made improvements, he exchanged it w. the father of Gen. John McNaughton for 300 acres of wild land in Argyle, N. Y., which has ever since been "home & headquarters of the family"; m. Molly Craig; children reaching maturity-

1. James, m. dau. Deac. David Matthews
2. John, Jr., m. dau. Andrew McDougall
3. dau., m. John McDougall
4. dau., m. David Harsha; he was an elder of the Salem church, & June 26, 1800, chosen an elder of the S. Argyle Asooc. church- 973

John- (s. John & Molly Craig) m. dau. Alexander McDougall; sons- James, Rev. John, Daniel, & David A.- 973

John- (s. Hugh & Mary McWhorter) m. dau. John Cooper; rem. Sterling, N. Y.- 973

Matthew- (s. Hugh & Mary McWhorter) m. dau. John Pettit, Esq.; rem. Sterling, N. Y., & later d. there- 973

Thomas- (s. Hugh & Mary McWhorter) m. dau. Uriah Beers; res. Washington co., Ohio; 2 daus. & no sons- 973

HART,
Lt.- of Stockbridge, Mass.; commanded a co. of 2 months men, prev. commanded by Capt. Hewin, who marched to Fairfield,Conn., Sept. 1776- 747

HARTELL,
William- oath of alleg.; Co. D, 22nd N. Y. Inf.- **(L)- 1074**

Hartford, N. Y.- a convention called here, June 7, 1815, to form "a society for the supression of Vice & Immorality"- 713

HARVEY,

____- from Ashfield, Mass.; res. Whitehall, N. Y. during the Rev. war & retreated to Mass. on news of Burgoyne's approach, prob. to nr. Montague, Mass.; foll. the surrender of Burgoyne, he returned, but rem. again, summer 1778, to Bennington, Vt., foll. freq. plunderings of Whitehall by tories & Indians- 751
Maj. James- m. Mary ____; their dau. Charlotte, m. Marvin, s. Andrew & Elizabeth (Martin) Freeman- **730**; dau. Mary, m. Jarvis, s. Aaron & Elizabeth (Fitch) Martin- **731**; dau. Caroline, m. Dr. George, s. Dr. Ephriam & ____ (Newell) Allen- **758**; b. NYC; m. Mary Barber, of NYC; his wid. d. Jan. 24, 1859, Salem, N. Y., her only surviving children were Mr. Edward Cook, of NYC, & Mrs. Marvin Freeman, of Salem; both the Harvey & Barber families were connected w. the Moore family, also of NYC, '& highly esteemed in a large circle of friends in that city'- **1035**; the old red tavern, Salem, N. Y., was loc. N. of his home- **1049**
Moses- b. Feb. 10, 1763, Ashfield, Mass.; res. Whitehall, N. Y. during the Rev. war, & until abt. 1806; betw. 1806- 20, res. Ft. Ann, & then Granville, N. Y., for the last 3 yrs.; his pension appl. states that in the forepart of July 1777, he was res. w. his father's family, & they retreated into Mass. on news of the approach of Burgoyne's army; enl. at Montague, Mass., for 3 months, as a draft substitute in Capt. Moses Harvey's co., Col. Woodbridge's regt.; the members of his regt. were instructed to proceed separately to Bennington, Vt., & he joined his regt. there on the last of Aug., or Sept. 1, 1777; he remained there under Capt. Winchester, guarding prisoners (mostly the wnd. & sick) from the battle of Bennington, while the remainder of his co. went to Saratoga, & recoll. hearing the artillery at Stillwater "quite plain"; 1778, stat. at Skenesborough (Whitehall, N. Y.) during the spring, summer, & fall, guarding the frontier, in Capt. Levi Stockwell's co. of 8 Months men; freq. plunderings by tories & Indians kept his co. on constant alarm; also served abt. 3 months under Lt. Boggs at Col. Skene's stone house, & abt. 12 wks. or more at the landing; "the militia were a part out at one time & a part at ano., relieving ea. other alternately during the season, & sometimes on alarms, which were several, all the militia were out"; Mar. 1779, tories & Indians attacked Col. Skene's house, & murdered Mr. & Mrs. McCall shortly after he had been relieved from this station; served at var. other places during the yr., at Put's rock, at "a little place below the Elbow, so called", & at their HQ, which was "at a place called the middle of the town"; he notes that the guard would serve for 24 hrs. at their HQ, & then be relieved for ano. 24 hrs.; served ano. 4 months under Lts. Fuller, Boggs, Gould, & Lt. Daniel Stewart, these officeres alternating command as the soldiers alternated their posts; also served under Capt. Thomas Lyon, & Col. Jeremiah Burrows- **751**
Capt. Moses- perh. of Montague, Mass.; July 1777, commanded his co., as part of Col. Woodbridge's regt., & sent his soldiers to Bennington, Vt., ea. of them going

independently; part of the co. remained there as guards for prisoners from the Bennington fight, & the remainder were sent to the battle of Stillwater- **751**

HASBROUCK,
Rettie- m. Rossawell R. Fitch, of Coxsackie, N. Y.; she d. Oct. 6, 1865, at 18 yrs., 11 mos., & 22 ds., of tent fever- **799**

HASFORD,
Eunice- was 1st female child b. Thetford, Vt.- **(L)- 772**
Joseph- of Hebron, Conn.; one of the 1st settlers of Thetford, Vt.; m. Mary Peters; refers Life of Hugh Peters- **(L)- 772**
Lucinda- (grdau. Joseph & Mary Peters) m. Thomas P., only s. Samuel & Rachel (Pattison) Hewit, as his 2nd wf.- **(L)- 772**

HASKINS,
Squire- convicted of perjury, Jan. 8, 1789, & given "the like Judgement in all things" as that of Edmund Hunt- **877**
William B.- Co. A, 2nd N. Y., Northern Black Horse, Cav., 1861- 2- **1080**

HASLEM,
John- Co. A, 2nd N. Y., Northern Black Horse, Cav., 1861- 2- **1080**

HASTINGS,
Abram- oath of alleg.; Co. D, 22nd N. Y. Inf.- **(L)- 1074**
Charles- res. Whitestown, N. Y., until 1849, & now (c. 1850), in Wilburn?, Lake (Green Lake?) co., Wisc.; bro. Elijah; m. Sabra, dau. Adam & Sabra (Russell) Martin; children- Martin A., Sarah, Abby, Helen, Mary, Elizabeth, & Charles Pliny (dec'd.)- **731**
Elijah- bro. Charles; butcher, grocery man, & broom maker, Salem, N. Y.- **731**

HASWELL,
____- res. Hoosick, N. Y.; m. Mary Ann, dau. Thomas P. & Mary Ann Hewit- **(L)- 772**

HATCH,
Capt. James- June 1777, commanded co. of Green Mtn. rangers, detailed to Royalton, Vt., where they constructed a picket fort, & then marched to Mt. Independence via Onion river; in the general retreat from there, to Castleton, & then Bennington, Vt., when Burgoyne's army capt. Ft. Ticonderoga- **756**

HAVILAND,
Ebenezer- appt. as Surgeon, Green Mtn. regt., June 30, 1775, by order of N. Y. Provincial Congress, & later passed qualifying examination- **778**

HAWLEY,
Jehiel- along w. James Breakenridge, appt. Oct. 1772, as agents to go to England & seek compensations for the Grants people- **907**
Deac. Joseph- c. 1850, res. ½ mi. s. of Salem, N. Y.; Elizabeth Vance, wid. John Shaw, res. here w. her sons- **737**; his house loc. next E. of Deac. Isaac Getty- **744**; part of his estate orig. occ. by John Livingston- **1084**
Miss- of Arlington, Vt.; m. Peter, s.William & Louis [sic] (Freeman) Whiteside-**805**

HAXTUN,
Andrew K.- Quarter Master, 93rd N. Y. Inf.- **1090b**

HAY/ HAYS,
Archibald- (Hay) b. ca. 1810; res. 1- 2 mi. SW of Lakeville (Cossayuna, N. Y.); his controversy w. Priest Quigley occurred 4- 5 yrs. bef. Dr. Fitch interviewed him; "on hearing of it- & from some pencil notes, then taken, I write the foll. acct., Sept. 10, 1859, bef. destroying sd. notes"; a very lengthy, involved description of the event, in which Patrick Walls, an unchurched Irish laborer, who res. in Hay's neighborh. for some 3 yrs., was injured while working for Hay & recuperated at his house; Bridget Dwyer volunteered her services in caring for him, & after abt. 4 wks. of improving health, his condition began to deteriorate, & she apparently informed Quigley, the district priest; although Hays had informed Dwyer that he wouldn't "have a man pretending to pardon ano.'s sins, in my house- no man had power to do that, I didn't believe", Priest Quigley arr. at his home one morning; discovering "what was in the wind", Hay suspected that Quigley was attempting to have Patrick leave his money to the church; he thereupon intervened against the Priest, Walls having prev. stated that he had been raised in mixed faith, attending both Protestant & Catholic meetings, & hadn't been to the latter more than twice since he arr. in America; attempting to engage Archibald's wf. on his behalf, in order to perform the sacraments, she replied to Quigley that her husb. might allow it if asked civilly, but "his wrath was too much excited against Hay, to permit him to ask as a favor what he had been demanding as a right"; the affair ended w. Priest Quigley warning Walls of the consequences of his own position concerning last rites, & his apparently banning any Catholics from visiting him further; Quigley left, denouncing var. Protestant sects, & making implications abt. Hay's motives, who declared in his defense, that he had kept a fire, obt. watchers, & provided everything Patrick had required to recover, out of charity, not knowing if he would ever receive a cent for it- **1058**
Edward- (Hays) Irish; res. Buskirk's Bridge, N. Y.; acc. Hiram Sisson, he was among those in Jesse Pratt's store the evening that Barney McEntee was murdered, & was among the 3 men who assisted McEntee out of doors; testif. he knew Martin Wallace for 6- 7 yrs., thought he was 24- 25 yrs. old, & saw him w. McEntee at Pratt's, betw. 5 & 6:00 PM; when he asked Wallace who Barney was, he told him that McEntee was a good, harmless man, introduced him, & sd. he met him at

Joice's store; when he asked Wallace why he hadn't left him there, he sd. that Barney had a considerable amt. of money on him, & he thought he wouldn't be safe there; Wallace intended to put him up at the tavern, but McEntee wouldn't go in; he then told Wallace that he shouldn't leave McEntee on his own, as it was too cold out, & he would perish if he tried to go home on his own; Wallace promised not to leave him, & along w. David Mosher, he assisted Wallace in getting him to leave Pratt's, which he did w. Wallace reluctantly; he then told McEntee that if he didn't go w. Wallace, the constable would take him up, & that Mosher was one, although this wasn't the case; after Wallace & McEntee had gone abt. 10 rods, they stopped, & he heard Wallace tell McEntee that he would help him along home if he would go w. him, but if not, he would put him up at the tavern; on cross- exam, it was disclosed that Hays & others present were making fun of McEntee (in his drunken condition) & that Wallace took his part, but the tavernkeeper most likely would not have lodged him, as he had gotten into his intoxicated state elsewhere; called by the def., he sd. that he had heard nothing bad abt. Wallace during the time that he had known him, & stated that "the reputation of the Joice family & the house they kept, was bad"- **1048s**

J. M.- (Hayes) Co. A, 2nd N. Y., Northern Black Horse, Cav., 1861- 2- **1080**

Lt. John- (Hay) E. bounds of his gr. on the E. side of Wood creek, forms part of the W. bounds of a Sept. 7, 1771 gr. to Thomas Trickett- **(L)- 936**

HAYDEN,
Rev.- officiated Jan. 3, 1862, at the funeral of Marcus E. Sherman, Salem, N. Y.- **1081**

HAYNES,
____- m. dau. Hon. John Younglove,as her 1st husb.- **843**
Elder Aaron- (Hayns) d. Mar. 25, 1827, at 81; & his wf. Mary, d. Aug. 27, 1811, at 65- **(L)- 772**

HAYWARD,
George W.- Co. A, 2nd N. Y., Northern Black Horse, Cav., 1861- 2- **1080**

HAYWOOD,
Thomas- m. Esther, dau. James & Rebecca (Lytle)Mills- **737**

HAZELTINE,
John- adm. June 21, 1775, as Cumberland co. delegate, N. Y. Provincial Congress- **777**

HEADLEY,
George- Co. A, 2nd N. Y., Northern Black Horse, Cav., 1861- 2- **1080**

HEARN,
John A.- Co. A, 2nd N. Y., Northern Black Horse, Cav., 1861- 2- **1080**

HEARTT,
Albert P.- of Troy, N. Y.; m. Emily, dau. Capt. Richard Hall & Theodocia
(Conklin) Fitch; his wf. d. 1850, leaving a dau.- **799**; he is now (1851) dec'd.,
leaving dau. Emily- **940**

HEATH,
Joseph- his tavern loc. S. of Jackson Ponds, 1 mi. this side (prob. N.) of the Corbett
family- **853**

HEDGES,
Elias S.- m. Jan. 18, 1832, Rebecca Louisa, dau. Luther & Martha (Curtis) Parker-
759s
Sophia- m. Adam M., s. Andrew & Elizabeth (Martin) Freeman, at Castleton, or
Hydeville, Vt.- **730**
Dr. William S.- physician, Jamesville, N. Y.; m. Sept. 12, 1839, Theda Clark, dau.
Luther & Martha (Curtis) Parker- **759s**

HENDERSON,
_____- m. Lydia, dau. Dr. Peletiah & Elizabeth (Burrows) Fitch; she d. prior 1833,
leaving 6 children as her heirs- **1100**
David- prob. res. Salem, N. Y.; served as Sgt., 1782, in a 9 months co. commanded
by his bro.- in- law, John Hunsdon- **799**
David- of NYC; dau. Jessie, m. Rev. John D., s. Solomon & Mary Ann (Dunlap)
Wells- **839**
Lydia- m. Nicholas, s. Duncan & Isabel (Duncan) MacIntyre- **999**
William- for £ 250, purch. Lot 264, Turner's Patent, Mar. 7, 1785, from John
Williams- **(L)- 936**

HENRY,
Family- their orchard, loc. 2 mi. N. of Esq. Barnet's brick house & 3½ mi. W. of
the Court House, Bennington, Vt., was the site of Gen. Stark's encampment prior
to the battle of Bennington- **764**
John- res. Fitch's Point, Salem, N. Y.; at Wid. Angel's 1st recoll., he was living in
William Miller's house, prob. immed. after Miller left; his wf. d. there, & after
Moses Martin purch. his property, he prob. rem. Lisbon, N. Y.; his s. Hugh, m. &
res. Fitch's Point, in a small log house where Jarvis Martin later built his brick
house- **859**
Joseph- dau. Miriam, m. Samuel Wells- **839**

HERRICK,
Col. Samuel- Capt. Parmlee Allen's co., stat. at Granville, N. Y., July 1777, attrib.
to his regt., acc. Ebenezer Farnsworth's Rev. war pension appl.- **750**

HERRINGTON,
Daniel- m. Mercy, dau. Joseph Wells; rem. Michigan- **842**
Daniel- oath of alleg.; Co. D, 22nd N. Y. Inf.- **(L)- 1074**

HERRON,
Surname- modernized form used by desc. of James McElherron- **922**

Hessians- fearing that the detachm. sent from Burgoyne's camp to Castleton, Vt.
would come down to the Indian river along w. the Indians, the settlers in this
region bur. their valuables in haste & fled to Manchester, Vt.; this same co. was
also presumed to have marched through Pawlet, Vt., under Col. Breyman, & arr. at
the Bennington battlesite at the point of Col. Baum's defeat, & formed a 2nd battle
w. Gen. Stark- **728**; deserter, who came along "w. his gun & military clothes", arr.
at John Lytle's, Salem, N. Y., shortly after their return from "the Retreat"; he
inquired of his daus., Susan & Rebecca, the direction to Bennington, claiming that
he was deserting & seeking his way back to New England; he also implied that he
had been sent in advance of the army to find this route (a conflicting claim, as "the
Retreat" occurred bef. the battle of Bennington, was a direct result of Col. Baum's
movements toward that place, & was ended foll. the battle, or foll. Burgoyne's
surrender); he & the 2 women were shortly afterw. seized by a party of secluded
tories, who returned him to Burgoyne's camp at Ft. Edward (in actuality, the camp
was then at Ft. Miller); he was later shot as a deserter (this would suggest that he
prob. deserted foll. the Bennington battle, & that the Lytle's returned to Salem after
the battle); his name given as George Hundertmark; refers Burgoyne's Orderly
Book, Aug. 24, 1777- **740**; diagram of Bennington battlesite, drawn by Dr. Fitch,
indicating "Hessian fort" on heights W of brook, at a point where it feeds into
Walloomsac river; the road from Walloomsac to Bennington crosses the river on
the S. port. of the ridge below the heights; Col. Baum's cannon placed on the SW
corner of the ridge, commanding the road & bridge, w. tory breastworks on ridge
directly opp.- **761**; acc. Esq. Barnet, he has always understood that Gen. Stark foll.
up the hollow where the brook runs, until he came directly upon the Hessian
breastworks w. all his force- **762**; description of the Hessian works at Bennington
battlesite- timbers cut from the heights, believed enclosed on all sides, w. a single
oak tree left standing within- perh. to suspend their colors from, the ground "being
nearly impossible to dig... to plant a flag- staff"; there was not enough soil for a
ditch or embankment; by 1850, not the faintest sign of the orig. works remain, only
the uprooted & far decayed stump of the oak, as evidence of its former use- **762b**;
foll. their defeat on the heights, "the fugitives that escaped from being capt. fled
back & were pursued by the Americans, in an irregular manner, & w/o any order",
passing through Walloomsac, to the W. border of the Patent; gaining a ridge nr.

this point, the Hessians saw Col. Breyman's relief column advancing on the flat below & ran to join them; the pursuing Americans gained the same ridge, paused, & then commenced firing upon the force beyond, until it had been arranged for advancing & they were fired upon by grapeshot from Breyman's 2 cannon; the combined force advanced abt. a mi. bef. they were met by Col. Warner's column, which "opposed his further advance w. such spirit, that he was eventually compelled to retire"- 766; referred to as 'foreigners' when noted that 4 were capt. at the battle at Ft. Ann, 1777- 792; brief ments.- 853, 953; referred to as a 'Dutchman', the execution of a recapt. deserter (George Hundertmark, above) recounted by Mrs. Casparus Bain from her father's (Neal Gilespie) eyewitn. acct.- 976; their troops passed through Skenesborough after Gen. Burgoyne had evac. his British forces from there to Ft. Edward- 998; a skelton discovered (n. d.) presumed to be the remains of the last man slain in the battle of Bennington, during excavations for a R. R. line E. of N. Hoosick, N. Y.; by neighborh. tradit., he was a Hessian; his corpse was found nr. the base of the hill, where the road then ran, abt. on the line of the Hoosick & Walloomsac Patents- 1007; brief ment.- 1050s; the pouring rain of Aug. 15, 1777, which they were not familiar w. in Germany, prevented them from perfecting their fortifications at the Bennington battlesite, as the rains "washed down the shovelfuls of earth as fast as they essayed to pile them up"- 1072

HEWIN,
Capt.- of Stockbridge, Mass.; c. 1776, commanded its militia co.; called by the Comm. of Safety, Canaan, N. Y., to break up & capt. tories who were disturbing their meetings there; appt. Sept. 1776, as commander of 2 months men in a brigade that was marched to Fairfield, Conn., & later commanded by Lt. Hart- 747

HEWIT/ HEWITT,
James- of Hebron, N. Y.; his s. Smith, d. Dec. 1862- 1098
Josiah- (or Curtis Hewitt) c. 1802, purch. the Stillwater, N. Y. farms of James Harsha, the emig., from his s. Hugh- 973
Samuel- m. Rachel Pattison; their only child was Thomas P.- (L)- 772
Smith- s. James; Co. E, 123rd NYSV; d. Dec. 1862, nr. Harper's Ferry, Va.- 1098
Thomas P.- (s. Samuel & Rachel Pattison) m. 1.____; 2. Lucinda Hasford; children, by 1st wf.-
1. Mary Ann, m. ____ Haswell, of Hoosick, N. Y.
2. Caroline
3. Thomas Porter; & by 2nd wf.-
4. Sarah Elizabeth
5. Emma
6. Ann Lucinda; his wf. Mary Ann, d. Nov. 24, 1830, at 28- (L)- 772

HICKS,
Whitehead- (1728- 1780) of NYC; Trustee, Dr. John Rogers' Presbyterian church; 'was for yrs., an Alderman, & for 8 yrs. Mayor of the city' (1766- 1776)- **961**

HIGHLANDS,
Molly- or Highland Molly; m. William Mack, the emig.; at Londonderry, N. H., by Rev. Mr. MacGregor- **734**; Mary Highland, or Hylands; m. William, s. John & Isabella (Brown) Mack- **734s**

HIGHSTEAD,
____- of Stillwater, N. Y.; m. Jerusha, dau. Ephriam? More; moved off to the west- **850**

HIGSON,
Giles- plaintiff, May 19, 1774, vs. Thomas Pointer; & defendant, in ano. case brought on the same date, by Pointer- **878**

HILL,
____- m. Thomas, s. Gov. Thomas Fitch, of Conn.- **799**
Abner- c. 1861/2, purch. Lot 55, Salem, N. Y., from Daniel McFarland- **1085**
Alexander- d. Mar. 7, 1813, at 86- **(L)- 975**
Emmet F.- of Wash. co., N. Y.; c. 1861, stat. Cairo, Illinois, unit not given- **1080**
Isaac- defendant, May 19, 1774, in a case brought by John Thurman, Jr.- **878**
James- of Jackson, N. Y.; juror, Oct. 1- 7, 1858, People vs. Martin Wallace- **1048s**
Richard- began working for Asa Fitch, Sr., Nov. 1815, as a hired hand- **799**
Thomas- & wf. Henuriah; among heirs of Comfort Starr listed in Mar. 25, 1772 deed transfer- **(L)- 936**
Woodard- Co. A, 2nd N. Y., Northern Black Horse, Cav., 1861- 2- **1080**

HILLHOUSE,
Surname- apparently presumed by Dr. Fitch to be the maiden name of Sarah Saltonstall, who m. Jonathan Fitch, based upon the fact that their eldest s., James, had Hillhouse as a middle name- **799**

HILLMAN,
H. M.- oath of alleg.; Co. D, 22nd N. Y. Inf.- **(L)- 1074**
John- of Greenwich, N. Y.; juror, Oct. 1- 7, 1858, People vs. Martin Wallace- **1048s**

HILLSBOROUGH,
Lord, Wills Hills, Earl of- (1718- 1793; Pres., Board of Trade) letter from Lord Dunmore, Mar. 9, 1771, notifying him of the possibility of now restoring peace within the Grants, & in the Province of N. Y., by revoking the order suspending grants; incl. petitn. of inhabitants requesting continuance under N. Y. govt.; ano.

petitn. ment., from Gov. Wentworth's office, requesting continuance under N. H. govt.; a packet of different papers incl. to indicate probable means of obt. signatures for the latter petitn.- **898**

HINCKLEY,
_____- res. Essex, N. Y.; m. dau. _____ & Martha Palen- **731**

HINMAN,
Col. Benjamin- (1720- 1820) officer witn., May- Dec. 1775 service, Ebenezer Farnsworth's Rev. war pens. appl.- **750**; sent by Conn. colony in command of 1,000 man force to N. Y. frontiers, May 1775, until its relief may be afforded by N. Y. Province- **776**
Samuel- defendant, May 19, 1774, in a case brought by Wm. Duer, Esq., & ano. by John Davis- **878**

HITCHCOCK,
_____- of Ft. Covington, N.Y.; m. Mary, dau. Alexander & Sarah (McCrea) Turner- **1044**
Mrs. Adelaide- res. West Haven, Vt.; Sun., Aug. 14, 1853, her barn was struck by lightning & consumed at a $400.00 loss- **996**
Dr. Henry- (s. Samuel & Elizabeth Freeman) res. NYC; m. Mary, dau. Rev. Eli T. Mack- **730**
Samuel- tailor; res. Reid's corners, Pittstown, N. Y.; m. Elizabeth, dau. Andrew & Elizabeth (Martin) Freeman; oldest dau. Elizabeth, now (prob. 1850) dec'd.; other children- Mary, Charles, & Dr. Henry; & he d. Nov. 1, 1865, at 63, in NYC- **730**

HOBART,
Capt. Elijah- Co. B, 93rd N. Y. Inf.- **1090b**
Judge John Sloss- (1738- 1805) presided Jan. 8, 1789, Supreme Court, Wash. co., N. Y., concerning cases against Edmund Hunt & Squire Haskins (& prob. also cases brought against John Wiser Wheeler & Thomas Burrell on prev. day)- **877**

HOBBS,
Charles- of Sturbridge, Mass.; m. Electa, dau. Jacob, Jr., & Lucy (Howard) Allen- **758**

HOBBY,
Sarah- m. Ebenezer, s. Ebenezer & Lydia (Mills) Fitch- **799**

HODGES,
Capt.- of White Creek, N. Y.; he was among a co. of Cambridge area militia ordered to Albany under a plan to go to Sir John Johnson & disarm tories; their co. arr. here after the main body had left, resolved to remain in Albany, & Jan. 18,

1776, he appl. for & was gr. provisions from the commissary for his co., until they resolved to return home- **825**

Henry- (Hodge) Co. A, 2nd N. Y., Northern Black Horse, Cav., 1861- 2- **1080**

HOFFMAN,
Gov. John Thompson- (1828- 1888; Mayor, NYC, 1865, 1867, & 1868; Gov., 1869- 72) appt. Hon. John Mason Parker to preside over the General term of the 3rd Judicial Dept. of the state- **759s**

HOFFNAGLE,
Michael- (Huffnagle) merch., Kingsbury, N. Y.; deed witn., Apr. 15, 1775, Albert Baker to Henry Franklin; (Hoofnagel) purch. Lots 40, 55, & 66, Artillery Patent, May 6, 1775, from Francis & Jane Panton; Mar. 25, 1772, James, John, & Amos McKenney quit claim to him for £ 10, to an undivided parcel in Kingsbury, acquired by them from the heirs of Comfort Starr; conveys N. half of Lot 75, Artillery Patent, Dec. 14, 1775, for £ 30, to Robert Gorden- **(L)- 936**

HOGEBOOM,
Miss- of Columbia co., N. Y.; m. John Russell; she was sist. of Gen. David Thomas' 2nd wf.- **919**

HOLDEN,
Capt. Austin W.- (Capt. A. W.) of Glens Falls, N. Y.; May 25, 1861, commanded Co. F, 22nd N. Y. Inf.; see Vol. 4- **(L)- 1074**
Nelson B.- Co. A, 2nd N. Y., Northern Black Horse, Cav., 1861- 2- **1080**

HOLIDAYS-
4th of July- (n. d.) an address delivered in Hebron, N. Y., by Rev. Thomas Goss of Salem, prob. early 1800's, "was highly meritorious & added much to his reputation in the popular estimation, whilst he was living here"- **994;**
Thanksgiving- prob. autumn, c. 1775; Edmund Wells, Jr., of Cambridge, N. Y., attempted to "give his Scotch & Irish friends & neighbors some acquaintance w. the good old custom of Conn." by inviting guests to a sumptuous dinner; his table,"occ. the whole length of the house", was spread & the guests were seated, & grace sd. "w. becoming gravity"; the main dish, "a chicken pie, baked in a large tin pan, & containing what had been a pretty heavy draft upon the stock of poultry upon the premises", occ. the center of the table, as an apparent "secure barrier" betw. 2 guests- John Ashton, a whig, & Hugh More, "whose sympathies were strongly upon the tory side in politics"; despite the setting, a political remark was dropped by one, leading to a sharp retort by the other; a reply ensued "so severe & cutting" that its recipient seized the pie & "launched it, pan & all, at the head of the other, bef. he had time to dodge away from the formidable missle"; both were immed. to their feet, stripping off their coats & proceeding outdoors, where they were engaged "in hot combat w. their fists, the whole company around them to see

the issue of the fight"; to the gratification of the majority of bystanders,"the stout, atheletic & herculean frame of Ashton ere long proved an over match for More"- **840**;

Washington's Birthday- Feb. 23, 1816, Granville, N. Y.; celebrated under the auspices of the Washington Benevolent Society, beginning at the house of J. Stiles, & joined by associates from Fair Haven, Vt., who arr. on board a frigate, the *Saratoga*, drawn by 8 horses & festooned w. banners in tribute of Washington, & Commodore Macdonough; when the float came to a halt, its occupants disembarked & formed a procession w. their hosts, proceeding to an oration, & then retiring to Stiles' for a banquet w. toasts; see Washington Benevolent Society- **723**

Holland- See DUTCH

HOLLISTER,
Edwin- of Middle Granville, N. Y.; m. Emma Louisa, dau. Hon. Nathaniel & Esther (Parker) Hall; rem. Illinois- **759s**
Isaac- appt. one of the Exec'rs., Will of Dr. Ira Hall, May 6, 1816- **759s**

HOLMES,
Benjamin- shortly after he was hung (Mar. 28, 1800) a child in Union Village (Greenwich, N. Y.) d. from burns rec'd. under questionable circumstances (see Whaley Family); however, the expense of Holmes' conviction & a lack of substantial evidence prevented further prosecution; see Criminal Offenders, Vol. 1- **862**; postponed twice, his execution ment. as the 1st instance of capital punishment in Wash. Co. by civil authority- **1050s**
Isreal- (Holms) m. Desire Doter (Doty) as her 2nd husb.; had sons John & Isreal- **757**

HONEYWOOD,
St. John- res. Fitch's Point, Salem, N. Y., in the plank house betw. John Farrar & the Red House; he had hung some bacon in Farrar's chimney to smoke because his own was too small, & one night, Mrs. Tucker came & "mounted' on the house, stealing one of the pieces; because she was nr. the time of her confinement, her husb. was whipped for her crime- **863**; witn., May 9, 1786, for security on Moses Martin as loan officer- **(L)- 936**; the poet; built the house occ., c. 1858, by William A. Russell; acc. Rufus Coon, "was one of the weakest, most effeminate men that ever lived hereabouts", adding that, although he built the house occ. by Russell, "his wrists were so weak that he was unable to turn the knobs of the doors, to open them. He never cut a slice of bread in his life- not knowing how it was done"; acc. to his wf., while he was in Albany, N. Y., studying his profession (law), he was "paying attentions" to a young lady there & asked to be excused from her table while at tea when she requested him to slice a loaf of bread; at this point, both discovered that neither knew how to do this, & she therefore told him it would not

do for them to marry, as neither could cut bread for their table (for a different, more realistic version, see Vol. 3); foll. his death, his wf. m. ano. lawyer, who squandered the little property left to her, & when he d., being utterly destitute, she wrote to his wealthy English relatives for assistance, & obt. some $5- 600.00; her 3rd husb. was a son of Duncan Campbell, of Argyle, N. Y.; she outlived her 3rd husb., & left no children by her last 2 marriages- **1033**; brief ment.- **1049**

The Hook- ano. name given for N. Argyle, N. Y.- **801**

HOOKER,
Col.- his regt., of Farmington, Conn., Feb. 1777, commanded by Gen. McDougall- **752**
Gen. Joseph- (1814- 1879) brief ment.; 22nd N. Y. Inf. was in his division at 2nd Bull Run- **1097**
Rev. Thomas- (ca. 1586- 1647) he & Samuel Stone were placed in charge of Rev. James Fitch, for the completion of Fitch's literary & religious educ.- **945b**

Hoosick, N. Y.- ment. as "rife w. traditionary stories of 'Festus' & 'The White House' " (Festus, or Fister, the retired British officer who rallied the area tories at the battle of Bennington, & his home, referred to as the White House, a local tory gathering place)- **768**; several family, as well as public bur. grds. ment.; an old Dutch church & bur. grd. was loc. below N. Hoosick, filled w. graves & tombstones of the early inhabitants; when the church went into disrepair, the new proprietor of the adj. land hired someone "for a bottle of rum, & other pay perhaps" to"tumble the old church down"; the whole ground was later plowed & tombstones rem. or broken up; a listing of 31 inscriptions, & other material, from the Union bur. grd., Hoosick Falls, N. Y.- **(L)- 772**; Aug. 3, 1775, its Comm. of Safety joined w. Comm. of Safety for Cambridge, N. Y., & Bennington, Vt., for a meeting at Mr. Wait's, in Walloomsack, N. Y.- **783**; John Van Rensselaer's return of the Comm. of Correspondence for Hoosic & 'Sinkaick' (Sancoick) Dist., present May 10, 1775, in the Chambers at City Hall, Albany, N. Y., incl.- Daniel B. Bratt, JohnWood, & Fenner Palmer- **831**; all knowl. of the burning of this place & N. Hoosick by Indians from Canada (Aug. 28, 1754; see p. 556, French's Gazetteer) noted by Dr. Fitch as "extinct among the people now living here"- **1007**

Hoosick river- c. 1850, noted by Dr. Fitch that the Walloomsac river is abt. 1/3rd larger than it at the point where the 2 rivers join- **764**

HOPKINS,
Judge David- res. Hebron, N. Y.; ments. sons Joel, who m. Jenny Mack; & Robert, who m. Polly Mack- **734**
Family- res. Salem, N. Y.; during the Rev. war, 2 of their sons, prob. Nathan & Samuel, or R. Hopkins, joined w. the sons of Capt. McCracken & others, & one evening fired a volley into the door of Gibson, the tory; refers 1795 Salem

Assessment Roll (§ 1689, Vol. 4); Nathan & Samuel res. below Aaron Cleveland, in a gambrel- roofed house later purch. by Wm. B. Harkness; the family res. in town long after the Rev. war, & rem. Hannibal, N. Y., after Rev. Tomb's home was built; c. 1860, or later, their farm was owned by James Clark- **1073**

George- c. 1861, res. above Aaron Cleveland, opp. Seely Sherman, Salem, N. Y.; was related to the same family whose sons drove Gibson, the tory, from town- **1073**

Joel- s. Judge David; m. Jenny, dau. William, Jr., & Molly (Highlands) Mack; children- Nancy, Polly; Levi, res. Argyle, N. Y.; Hannah, David, William, James, & Margaret- **734**

Judge- of Rupert, Vt.; "a well known whig", he was capt. on the road by a tory scout party, Aug. 1777, that later capt. a Hessian deserter (George Hundertmark) nr. Salem, N. Y.- **740**

R., Jr.- witn., Dec. 1, 1858, certif. for the execution of Martin Wallace- **1050s**

Robert- s. Judge David; res. Brutus, N. Y.; m. Polly, dau. William, Jr., & Molly (Highlands) Mack; children- Esther, Mary, Emeline, Morrison, & Moses- **734**

Robert- for £ 1400, Mar. 24, 1779, deeds Lots 259 & 260, Turner's Patent, to Moses Bartlett- **(L)- 936**

William- (s. Joel & Jenny Mack) c. 1850, Preceptor of the Academy at Auburn, N. Y.- **734**

HORFORT,

John- was apprehended & detained, July 30, 1764, along w. Samuel Ashley, Samuel Robinson, & Isaac Charles, by the High Sheriff of Albany co., for forcibly ejecting Peter Voss & Bastian Deal from their lands in the Grants- **885**; (Horsfoot) when apprehended by Harmanus Schuyler, he & Isaac Charles pretended ownership of the lands of Voss & Deal- **892**; he & Isaac Charles were the unnamed others ment. by James Van Cortlandt's affidavit, which stated that all were brought to Albany jail, but never indicted, gave bail, or were ever brought to trial- **897**

HORSINGTON,

Maj.-commanded 3 battalions, May/ June 1777, comprising the Green Mtn. rangers- Capt. James Hatch, at Royalton, Vt.; Capt. Sackett, along the Onion river; & Capt. Hale, stat. at the mouth of Otter creek- **756**

HORSMANDER,

Daniel- (1694- 1778; Chief Justice, Province of N. Y., 1763- 78) prob. res. NYC; an affidavit of Benjamin Hough, Mar. 7, 1775, sworn bef. him- **881**; (Horsmanden) of N. Y. Council; Sept. 21, 1771, testim. of Samuel Gardenier, of Walloomsac Patent, given bef. him- **902**

HORTON,

____- Episcopal minister, res. Lowville, N. Y.; m. Elizabeth, dau. Stephen & Jane (Martin) Leonard- **730**; his name given as Levi Norton- **1046**

HOSKINS,

Timothy- succeeded John P. Reynolds, foll. Jan. 1816, as editor of the *Washington Register-* **721**

HOTCHKINS,

Capt.- his co., under Col. Thaddeus Cook, was prob. stat., Oct. 1776, at the "saw pits", Rye, N. Y.- **756**

HOUGH,

____- acc. John Munroe, of Mich., families of this name res. in the section of Ontario, Canada, where he once lived, & were perh. U. S. refugees during the Rev. war- **991**

Benjamin- res. Clarendon, Vt.; he & Ann Marsh were witns., Dec. 2, 1773, to a quit claim of Jacob Marsh to Thomas Brayton- **745**; he was a Justice of the Peace, & his father was a Constable, which was "what rendered them obnoxious" (to the Bennington mob); he "was a worthy man (wrote a very fair hand) & used to deliver lectures to the people on the Sabbath"; capt. by Ethan Allen's men while his wf. was away on a journey, he left a 6 yr. old child at his home (says his statement to N. Y. authorities) & was banished from the Grants; he went to the Gov. in Albany, or NYC, & afterw. came up to Ft. Edward, N. Y., & sent a request to be allowed to retrieve his wf. & child from his old home; if he had any other children, they were not here ment., & the record of his family & the outcome of his request was not disclosed by Dr. Fitch; refers to a letter of Judge C. K. Williams to Deac. William Brayton, "dated Feb. & Mar. 1850"; he was sentenced by the Vermonters to 200 lashes, & sent a letter to Thomas Brayton, stained w. blood from his wnds., warning him of a similar fate; c. 1774, appl. to Gov. Colden for a gr., saying he had lost an arm in the service of his country, & was little better than a helpless cripple; it appears that he was a soldier in the French war; he laid a memorial bef. N. Y. authorities regarding the ill treatment he & Thomas Brayton rec'd. from the Vermonters, but the outcome here, also remains undisclosed- **746**; Justice of the Peace, Charlotte co.; his affidavit, Mar. 7, 1775, sworn bef. D. Horsmander, was incl. in his publ. statement, 'To the worthy inhabitants of the city of New York', Mar. 23, 1775, referring to his ejection from the Grants; in the affidavit, he states that at 8:00 AM, on or abt. Jan. 26, 1775, while in view of but at a short distance from his house, 3 persons entered its door, all of his family being absent except for a 6 yr. old child; immed. afterw., he was attacked by abt. 30 persons 'a no. who were armed w. firelocks, swords & hatchets'; he attempted to secure his arms in defense, only to find his entrance barred by Winthrop Hoyt, who had his (Hough's) sword & pistol in his possession; he was then approached by Peleg Sunderland, who was holding a hatchet, & slapped him on the shoulder, stating that he was their prisoner; he was then forced into a sleigh & carried S. abt. 50 mi. to Sunderland, Vt., & kept 'in close confinement, part of the time bound & always under a strong guard, w. drawn swords', until Jan. 30th; on the date ment., a court

was appt. for his trial & Ethan Allen laid bef. him the foll. accusations, that he had-
1. complained to the N. Y. govt. of the rioters mobbing & injuring Benjamin Spencer & others;
2. dissuaded & discouraged the people from joining the mob in their proceedings;
3. taken a commission of the peace under the govt. of N. Y., exercising his office as magistrate for Charlotte co., though he knew well that the mob would not allow that magistrate here;
in his defense, he inquired whether he had done anyone an injustice in the execution of his office, & if he could be accused of 'busying himself or intermeddling w. respect to titles of lands?'; upon denial that he had ever done such things, he assented that the charges were true, & he had foll. this course as his duty; the court withdrew for 2- 3 hrs. to consider the judgment, & he was then ordered to be brought out nr. a tree where 'the sd. pretended Judges had placed themselves, encircled by a no. of armed men'; 4 men w. drawn swords brought him into this circle & Allen, 'who all along acted as the chief or principal Judge, pronounced the foll. sentence', that the deponent had pleaded 'self- justification', which was found insuffic. by their court to excuse his punishment, & he was to receive '200 lashes on the naked back' & then depart the N. H. grants as soon as able, not to return on pain of receiving 500 lashes; he then rec'd. the lashes, 'w. whips of cords', being given 10 lashes alternately, by 4 men, w. Robert Cochran 'who declared himself to be Adjutant of the rioters', standing nr. him & urging them 'to lay the blows well & strike harder'; it was often ment. during the proceedings that if any of his friends should attempt to interfere, they would share the same fate; foll. administration of his punishment, he was given into the care of Dr. Washburn, & requested, but was refused, the right to return to his home & settle his affairs & retrieve the son left there alone; relating var. threats he had heard while in captivity, he began to proceed to NYC, calling on Bliss Willoughby & Ebenezer Cole, two Albany co. Justices of the Peace who res. nr. Bennington, finding them armed & in a greatly distressed state, w. armed people in their homes, ready for defense; passing into Pownal, then part of the Manor of Rensselaerwyck, he found great commotion & uneasiness due to the rioters; he met there w. George Gardner, Esq., ano. Ablany co. Justice, who saw a great danger in the situation, expecting daily to be prevented by the rioters from performing his duties, & believing that many of the inhabitants would join w. the rioters unless given further protection by the govt.; he also conversed w. James Clark, a neighbor & constable in his employ, who informed him that he, John Lord, & Joseph Randel, had been much abused & insulted by the mob during his captivity, & that Lord was 'turned out of his possession & obliged to fly the country'; he also notes that his arms, 'a hanger & pistol', were robbed by the mob & not returned; the mob had also designed 'to put an end to law & justice in the co. of Cumberland', appt. a day for the attempt, but did not foll. through; refers American Archives, ii, pgs. 215- 218; see Grants/ N. H. Controversy; & Vermonters- **881**; brief ment.- **963**; his arrest & flogging, acc. John L. Marsh, was carried out by persons from the S. part

of Vt., as only 4 surnames of those involved- Meed, Powers, Campbell, & Sawyer, have any bearing upon family names found in the Clarendon, Vt. area- **966**

HOUGHTON,
Andrew- of Buskirk's Bridge, N. Y.; acc. Dr. Morris, he was one of the 4 men who accomp. him to the scene of Barney McEntee's murder the night of Feb. 16, 1858, & rem. the empty wallet & other contents from the pocket of the dec'd.; corroborate Dr. Morris' testim., saying that he rem. the wallet from McEntee's pocket & observed that the handkerchief that held his money was missing; he afterw. went w. Randall & others to assist in arresting Wallace, at abt. midnight; after a fashion, Mr. Brady opened the door, sd. Wallace was there, & had been there for 1- 1½ hrs.; they searched his clothes, & in a 2nd coat, found McEntee's gloves, & in ano. pocket, found the handkerchief, & in ano. pocket, found a quantity of money; he identifes one as a $10 bill from the Bank of Adams, & ano. as a $5 bill from the Bank of Brattleboro; he testif. that Wallace sd. these bills were pd. to him by Marvin Wallis & Cornelius Van Vechten at flax- pulling- time in the summer; Wallace claimed that he left McEntee at the foot of the hill nr. John Larmon's, & he was afterw. taken to Daniel Randall's; he also testif. that he had known Wallace for 5 yrs.; called again to testif. to the character of the Joice house bef. & after the murder, he notes that they "kept liquor there & sold it unlawfully. It was reported that they gambled. They had a reputation of getting drunk & fighting"- **1048s**

HOUSE,
Col.- c. 1817, he & Col. Churchill commanded Co. D, 1st Regt. of Artillery, U. S. Army- **974**

HOVER,
William- oath of alleg.; Co. D, 22nd N. Y. Inf.- **(L)- 1074**

HOW,
Amariah- for £ 4, Aug. 9, 1774, obt. quit claim to 70 acres, Clarendon, Charlotte co., N. Y. (now Vt.) from Jacob Marsh- **745**
Col.- officer witn. during Sept.- Nov. 1776 service, Samuel Standish's Rev. war pens. appl.- **747**

HOWARD,
_____- wid. Jacob Marsh; prob. m. as her 2nd husb.- **963**
Abel- c. 1860, acc. Dr. Fitch, res. "up the kill from Battenville- the last place bef. the road passes the dugway, coming to Salem"; his place orig. occ. by the Morrison family- **1060**
Lucy- of Warren, Mass.; m. Jacob Allen, of Sturbridge, Mass.- **758**

HOWDEN,
Rev. Mr.- former Assoc. Ref. minister, Cambridge, N. Y.; c. 1850, res. nr. Franklinville, N. Y.; m. Margaret, dau. Samuel & Miriam (Henry) Wells; 7 or 8 children- **839**

HOWE,
Maj. Gen. Sir William- (?- 1814) his correspondence from Boston, Mass., Feb. 2, 1776, refuses Gen. Washington's offer to exchange Maj. Philip Skene for James Lovell, foll. the discovery of a prohibited correspondence by Lovell- **760**; acc. to a report of Morris & Yates, July 23, 1777, if cert. measures they suggest are put into effect to hold Gen. Burgoyne in his present position, 'we may laugh at Mr. Howe & Mr. Burgoyne' at a later date (by the defeat of their campaign to divide & conquer the colonies)- **797**; brief ment. in the lyrics of a tory song concerning the battle of Bunker Hill- **980**; brief ment.- **1010**

HOWLAND,
Mary- m. Ebenezer, s. Ebenezer & Sarah (Hobby) Fitch- **799**

HOX,
William- c. 1811, was a hired hand on Asa Fitch, Sr.'s farm at Fitch's Point, Salem, N. Y.- **799**

HOY,
Betty- she was "a much less profitable & tidy wf." to William Tosh, & her sist. Sally came to res. w. them; when her family 1st arr. in NYC, she "came on foot, begging her way along to Salem"; she arr. on a Sun., & was informed that her uncles were at meeting & had such reverence for the Sabbath that they would dislike any visitors to their house on that day; she presented herself the foll. morning & her uncles sent at once for her mother & othe children; she m. 2nd, ____ McMillian, (prob.) of Argyle, N. Y.; she mistrusted his motives of courtship & secretly deeded her property to her sist. Sally; after convincing her to move from Salem to Argyle, he suggested selling the old place, & she inquired which one, to which he responded, 'The place I got by marrying you'; & she retorted, 'Indade! but that is my sister's place & not ours.'; she left him in a few wks. & returned to res. w. her sist.; "they were so extremely poor & slovenly, that their log house became a curiosity to the whole neighborh.", & it was visited as such by the children & young people in the neighborh., "their filth & rags being such that they scarcely appeared human; their pig & fowls occ. the house in common w. them"; abt. 1834, during a cold winter, fearing that they might freeze to death, their neighbors persuaded them to be taken into the Co. Poorhouse; & they (much later) d. there- **872**
Family- of Ireland; bros. Richard & William, emig. & settl. Salem, N. Y.; their sist. remained in Ireland & m. a cousin of the same surname; her husb. d., leaving her in extreme poverty, w. daus. Betty, who m. William Tosh, as his 2nd wf., &

Sally, & a son; some money was sent to her by her bros., & "she had such an exalted idea of how well her bros. were doing in this country, that when this money arr., she availed herself of it to procure a passage for her & her children to America"; as their funds brought them only as far as NYC, the dau. Betty was sent ahead to her uncles & they came to retrieve the family; "the son was the laziest dog ever known. He preferred begging to work, & w. a bag would crawl around & gather whatever folks would give him- pretending to be sick & unable to work"; some other young boys resolved to ascertain the truth & one day, offering to carry his bag, outdistanced him, set the bag nr. a bundle of straw & feigned setting the bag ablaze by lighting the straw; he then "ran w. agility & snatched his bag away from the fire", & seeing that his fraud was discovered, he left town & was never heard of again- **872**; their sist. m. 2. ____ Smith, who res. in the S. part of Salem, N. Y.- **1000**

Richard- res. W. side of Black creek, in a house now occ. by John Burnett; d. unm. & bequeathed his property to his neph., Richard; acc. Capt. Daniel McDonald, he raised a dau. of old John McMihels; see also, Vols. 3 & 4- **873**

Richard- s. William; sold his uncle's place & res. some yrs. nr. George Stewart's distillery, in the Greenwich part of Argyle Patent; his aunt res. w. him & d. there; he later rem. to Ohio w. his bro. William; see Vol. 3- **873**

William- bro. Richard; had 2 sons, Richard, who rec'd. his uncle's place, & William, who occ. his father's place; neither did as well as their father or uncle; a cellar hole, on the E. part of Lot No. 50, was believed to be his, & was built over by Colin McFarland; acc. George Webster, his log house was loc. a little N. of where he res.; see also, Vols. 3 & 4- **873**; reed- maker; "he used to supply the country w. reeds, for their looms- the loom then being part of the furniture of every family"- **1000**

William- s. William; eventually sold his father's place & rem. Mansfield, Ohio, along w. his bro. Richard; see Vol. 3- **873**

HOYSTRANT,
William H.- 1st Sgt., 22nd N. Y. Inf.; promoted to 1st Lt., Feb. 1, 1863, replacing C. D. Beaumont- **1095b**

HOYT,
Winthrop- of Bennington, Vt.; abt. Jan. 26, 1775, he barred the entrance of Benjamin Hough's house, brandishing Hough's own weapons, & thus facilitating his capt. by the Bennington mob- **881**

HUBBARD,
____- m. John McKellip, s. John & Jane (McKellip) Dobbin- **732**

HUBBELL,
Lt. Silas F.- Co. F, 93rd N. Y. Inf.- **1090b**

210

HUGGINS,
Betsey- m. John, s. Alexander & Sarah (McCrea) Turner- **1044**
Robert- m. Mary, dau. Robert & Margaret Armstrong- **1083**

HUGHES,
Bishop- (Hughs) ment. in an address by Mr. Welsh, Sept. 4, 1862, at the annual
meeting of the Wash. Co. Bible Soc., as one person who was able to manage
excluding the Bible from the 4th Ward schools of NYC- **1097**
James M.- mortgage, Feb. 14, 1769, of Wm. Duer, Esq., to Henrietta Duer,
acknowl., allowed, & recorded bef. him, Oct. 12, 1792, NYC- **935**
Joseph- defendant, Mar. 1775, in a case brought by Hugh McCowin- **878**
Michael- oath of alleg.; Co. D, 22nd N. Y. Inf.- **(L)- 1074**

HULETT,
Harvey- of Dresden, N. Y.; his barn & shed were struck by lightning, Sat., Aug.
13, 1853, & totally consumed, w. loss of $1,000.00, insured for $350.00- **996**
John M.- of Hampton, N. Y.; juror, Oct. 1- 7, 1858, People vs. Martin Wallace-
1048s

HUMPHREY,
Family- res. Tomhannock, N. Y., during the Rev. war; they were cousins of John
McNeil's wf., & when one, or both, of the parents d., the McNeils took a child to
raise; foll. the Allen massacre, the family moved down to Tomhannock from E.
Greenwich, N. Y., so that their adoptive child might be w. family connections- **986**

HUMSTEAD,
Jedidiah- of Shaftsbury, Vt.; May 12, 1783, purch. 50 acres, Skene's Patent, "that
takes in East bay & on 'Poultney river so called' ", from Samuel Waterhouse- **(L)-
936**

HUNDERTMARK,
George- Hessian soldier; he came along, "w. his gun & military clothes", &
discovered Susan & Rebecca Lytle pulling flax in their father's field, shortly after
the family had returned from "the Retreat"; speaking broken English, he inquired
the way to Bennington, implying that he was deserting from the British & finding
his way back to New England; he, at the same time, also suggested that he had
been sent out to find the route in advance of the army; a short time afterw., a tory
scout party capt. him & the 2 girls, but ano. Salem tory persuaded the scout party
to release the girls, & they returned Hundertmark to Burgoyne's camp, where he
was shot for desertion; refers Burgoyne's Orderly Book, Aug. 24, 1777- **740**; called
a "Dutchman", his execution occurred in Burgoyne's camp at Ft. Miller, N. Y., in a
meadow E. of the Duer mansion; Capt. James Beaty & Neal Gillespie, both of
Argyle, were eye witns.; he was marched from the mansion, "all dressed in white; a
clergym. on ea. side of him robed in thin black gowns"; the death march played as

they walked to the grave, dug neatly in the middle of the meadow, the turf arranged neatly on one side & the loose earth on the other; "the gentle, calm, demeanor of the man, as he walked to the spot & went through the sad ceremonies, excited the sympathy of the spectators strongly in his behalf. They came w. slow & solemn step to the grave, & passed around it, to the side where the turf was piled up; he quietly knelt down upon this turf, his opened grave bef. him; the cap was drawn down over his eyes; a file of soldiers, seven in number, were drawn up a short distance in front of him; they aimed their muskets, & on signal, simult. fired; the man dropped dead"; it was reported that the deserter had been taken in Salem the day bef.- **976**

HUNSDEN,

____- m. Susan, dau. James William & Eleanor (Hunsden) Turner, his cousin- **1044**
Abel- (or perh. Allen) d. Dec. 3, 1833, at 74, Shoreham, Vt., from injuries rec'd. 10 days bef. when thrown from his wagon by a frightened horse; refers Jan. 4, 1834, *N. Y. Observer-* **1090**
Allen- m. Elizabeth Savage; their s. John, m. Susan Turner- **1090**
Elenour- m. James William, s. James & Susannah (Thomas) Turner- **1044**
John- (s. Allen & Elizabeth Savage); res. Shoreham, Vt.; m. Susan, dau. James & Eleanor (Hunsden) Turner; 2 children, one dec'd., & the other, Charles, res., c. 1867, in Shoreham; both parents d. abt. 1840- **1090**
Ensign John- res. Salem, N. Y., where Deac. McLeary presently (1850) lives; c. 1782, Ensign, Salem militia; foll. the Rev. war, he rem. French Mills, N. Y.- **729**; c. 1782, appt. Lt., commanding a 9 months co.; his officers incl. Sgts.- David Henderson (his bro.- in- law) & Lewis Herman; Corps.- Henry Shepard, James King, & O. Selfridge; Ensign- Asa Fitch, Sr.; as his was not a full co., it was consolidated w. ano., & he was appt. Ensign, & all the other officers ment. here served as privates; see Militia- **799**

HUNT,

Abby- m. Phineas, s. John & Margaret (Robertson) Whiteside- **805**
Edmund- convicted of perjury, Jan. 8, 1789, & sentenced to 6 mos. jail w/o bail, & on Jan. 9th, to stand for an hr. in the pillory- **877**
Fanny- m. Col. John, s. Gen. John & Susannah (Thomas) Williams, as his 3rd wf.- **1045**
John- Co. A, 2nd N. Y., Northern Black Horse, Cav., 1861- 2- **1080**
Henry W.- of Watertown, N. Y.; m. July 7, 1843, Julia, dau. Harvey & Sarah (Conkey) Stevens, of Martinsburgh, N. Y.- **730**

HUNTER,

David- defendant, Apr. 19, 1775, in separate cases brought by Jeremiah Burres & Hugh Munro; & plaintiff, May 19, 1774, vs. Hugh Munro- **878**

HUNTINGS,
Samuel- c. 1833, ment. as an heir of Desire (Burrows) Gore, of Nova Scotia- **1100**

HURD,
_____- res. Salem, N. Y.; later rem. Illinois; dau. Mary Ann, m. Sidney, s. Moses, Jr., & Eunice (Clark) Martin- **731**
Charles- was a house guest at Dr. Fitch's family mansion, July 11, 1860, & was among those who felt tremors during the night that were caused by an earthquake in Canada- **1075**

HUTCHEN,
Susanna- deed witn., Aug. 14, 1786, Gile Wilson to James Wilson- **(L)**- **936**

HUTCHINSON,
Charles- (Hutchenson) res. Salem, N. Y., nr. the present (c. 1850) home of Thomas Beaty; Capt., 1st militia co. org. in Salem- **729**
Gov. Thomas- (1711- 1780; of Mass. Bay Colony, Acting Gov., 1760, 1769- 71; Gov., 1771- 74); c. 1777, Samuel Fitch, of Boston, noted as an "Addressor of"; refers Lives of the Loyalists- **944**

HUTCHISON,
_____- m. John, s. David Webb, of Salem, N. Y.- **738**
S.- methodist preacher; appt. Dec. 1797, to Cambridge District circuit, at the annual Conference, Buckland, Mass.; Lorenzo Dow was given into his supervision for a quarterly service, & he informed Dow that because of the talk & trouble that he had given the conference, he had that 3 month period to obt. a recommendation for a circuit; at a later point under his tutelage, Dow sought to be released from his supervision, but was compelled by Hutchison to serve under him for ano. quarter- **813**; complains of Lorenzo Dow, Dec. 29, 1798, at the quarterly meeting, Ash Grove, White Creek, N. Y.; out of jealousy, acc. Dow- **815**

HUTTON,
Peter- perh. s. William; Supervisor, 1822, 1825, Putnam, N. Y.- **1091**
Lt. Timothy- one of the officers of a '9 months' co. enl. from the vicinity of Salem, N. Y., c. 1782, & stat. at Saratoga (Schuylerville, N. Y.) & Ft. Williams, in Salem, to guard the northern frontier- **729**
William- 1st settler, & apparently the sole owner, of land loc. in Putnam, N. Y.; the district orig. called Hutton's Bush; perh. had s. Peter- **1091**

Hutton's Bush- orig. name, Putnam, N. Y.- **1091**

HYDE,
GENEALOGY- referred to concerning O. L. Barbour, of Saratoga Springs, N. Y.-
839
Henry B.- m. Mar. 29, 1864, Annie, dau. Simeon Fitch; at Trinity chapel, by Rev.
S. H. Weston, D. D.- **799**
Jedidiah- he & others, mostly residents of Norwich, Conn., gr. Aug. 27, 1787, land
later named Hyde Park, Vt.- **799**

I

ILLINOIS- 730, 731, 759s, 799, 1069, 1080, 1095;
  Counties- DeKalb- 731, 732, 973; Marshall- 1004; Mercer- 1095; Warren- 1004;
  Cities & Towns- Aledo- 1095; Cairo- 1080; Chicago- 730, 731, 806, 1035;
  Galena- 973; Galesburg- 1093; Quincy- 731, 839; Rockford- 731, 1035, 1095;
  Rock River- 940;
  Military units from, Civil War- Infantry- 7th- 1080; 11th- 1080; 30th- 1095;
  74th- 1095
    land purchases- by state law, c. 1853, it was required of those who purch. land bid
off for tax purposes to "redeem" the lands thus sold within 2 yrs., or forever after
be debarred from redeeming these lands; lands in Warren co., prob. gr. by warrant
to War of 1812 veterans- 1004; Wash. co., N. Y. residents- the foll. prob. stat.
Cairo, Ill., & attrib. to the 11th Inf. there, c. 1861- Capt. Edward? McAllister,
Emmet F. Hill, E. L. Alexander, & William Alexander; also, other members, 7th &
11th Ill. Inf. ment.- 1080

Independent Library- to service towns of Cambridge & Salem, N. Y.; incorp., &
Mar. 13, 1798, at the home of Silas Peat, Cambridge, chose as Trustees- Bethuel
Church, Philomen Allen, Solomon King, Stephen Clapp, Silas Peat; refers p. 6,
Miscellanies- 879

INDIA- 730, 940, 1031; Minagara (Minara)- 990, now Hyderabad, Pakistan (?)

INDIAN,
Jere- Cambridge, N. Y., June 20, 1802; he & his wf. Mercy were found dead in the
woods on the road to Salem- "no marks of violence- 'vis. of God' "- James Gilmore,
Coroner- (L)- 876

INDIANA- 734, 1035

Indian river, Vt.- when the British occ. the area surrounding Castleton, Vt. (prob.
July 7, 1777, foll. the battle of Hubbardton) settlers in this region, fearing Hessians
& Indians, bur. their valuables & feld to Manchester, Vt.- 728; (loc. betw.
Granville, N. Y. & Rutland co., Vt.); prior to Rev. war, "noted for the abundance
of fine large trout which it contained; many of them weighing 2 & 3 lbs.- (This
caused it to be much freq. by the aborigines when the 1st settlers arr.; from this
circumstance it is sd. to have rec'd. its name)"- 924; its "extreme source" noted as a
swamp at the summit level betw. the Battenkill & Granville (Mettawee) river
(prob. within the towns of Rupert & Dorset, Vt.) where a "small rivelet", a
tributary of White (Ondawa) creek derives- 1003

INDIANS-
Burgoyne's- the force that accomp. his expedition was reportedly not w. his army at the time it reached Skenesborough, N. Y., July 6, 1777- **997**; rebuke of- is sd. to have weakened their attachment to his career, & they afterw. left, incl. Thomas DeRougers- Williams- **1016**; dismissed by- **1062**;
Chiefs, killed at Bennington- to the question of whether two Indian chiefs were actually killed during the engagem., Esq. Barnet attests no knowl., but refers to an incident in which a fine mare was stolen by Indians as Col. Baum passed through Cambridge, N. Y.; a neighbor of its owner, later seeing the horse w. an Indian rider, presumed it was stolen, shot the Indian dead, & returned the horse to its owner; see Nelson, (§ 232) Vol. 1, for comparable incident- **764**;
General mentions- 701, 728, 740, 741, 744, 747, 748, 751, 756, 757, 759s, 764, 767, 775, 780, 853, 858, 887, 902, 923, 926, 945b, 949b, 958, 962, 981, 983, 989, 998, 1000, 1007, 1016, 1060, 1075b; as aborigines- 924; natives- 930; savages- 797, 809, 989, 1013;
Iroquois- 989; King Hendrick- 989; King Philip's war- 837;
malconents- after 1676, all known as such retreated from New England to 'Skotacook' (Schaghticoke, N. Y.) until the present (1761) war, when they committed hostilities on the English at Stockbridge, Mass.; they fled, c. 1754, abt. 12 families in all, & incorp. w. the St. Francis Indians- **837**;
McCrea, Jane- some members of the western tribes were presumably involved in the escort that lead to her death; two parties, ea. ignorant of the other's designs, & vying for the priviledge; on confronting ea. other, one party murdered her to frustrate the other's achievement; a Winnebago chief at Green Bay acknowl. (n. d.) to Rev. Eleazer DeRouger- Williams that he had been involved, while the murder has commonly been attrib. to the St. Regis tribe- **1016**;
Mohawk- 989; Mohegan, language- 945b; Narragansett- 962; North American- 990;
Pequot- 759s, 799; Podunk- res. on Conn. river betw. Easthampton, Mass. & Windsor, Conn.; abt. 2- 300 men in the tribe at the time of King Philip's war, all of whom went off to this war & never returned; refers p. 68, v. 10, 1st series, Mass. Hist. Coll.- **837**; reservation, St. Regis- 1015;
St. Francis- 837, 1014; St. Regis- 1014, 1015; scalping/ scalps- 982, 1062; Stockbridge- 773; Western tribes- 1016; Winnebago- 1016

INGALL,
Joseph- def., w. Paul Bush, in a case brought by John Roff- **878**

INGALLS,
Mr.- Preceptor, Union Village Academy, Greenwich, N. Y.; James Dobbins & Miss L. Philips were his assistants here at the same time- **732**; when at Salem Academy, c. 1790's, it was his policy to have all his scholars write home, & then to examine, correct & amend their drafts bef. a final copy was made; in the case of Harmon Knickerbocker, the "young Prince" of Schaghticoke, N. Y., his "letter" caused such

a sensation in the community for the ability that it illustrated, that his parents requested ano., although the orig. had been principally written by Ingalls; the "young Prince", finding the 1st to be perfect & w/o place for improvement, simply recopied the orig.; see Vol. 1- **953b**

INGALSBE,
Deac. James- res. Hartford, N. Y.; dau. Mary, b. Nov. 1814, m. Seth Cooley; in 1834, she professed her faith as a Congregationalist; see Vol. 1- **1024**

INGLES,
Joseph- res. Granville, N. Y.; Jan. 25, 1776, rec'd. recommendation for appt. as Capt., Charlotte co. militia- **799**

INGRAHAM,
Anson- m. Margaret- Ann, dau. Robert & Ann R. (Whiteside) McMurray- **805**

INMAN,
Duncan- Argyle, N. Y.; Apr. 6, 1792, drowned in Moses kill; Adiel Sherwood, Coroner- **(L)- 876**

INNS, Taverns, & Hotels-
Arlington, Vt.- c. 1821, a tavern was loc. nr. the stone church- **733**;
Baldwin's Tavern- c. 1798, one of 3 early buildings loc. Ft. Edward, N. Y.; see Vol. 1- **804**;
Bemis' Tavern- the noted tavern, kept by William Bemis, & loc. 3 mi. N. of the village of Stillwater, N. Y.; the name Bemis was given to the heights here, where the battles of Saratoga were fought; refers p. 116, Burgoyne's Campaign- **851**;
Benson's Tavern- loc. (n. d.) on the E. side of the main Troy road through Easton, N. Y., where the Valley- bridge road forked from the main road- **861**;
Berry's Tavern- kept by Samuel Berry, c. 1798, & prob. loc. just N. of Moses kill, along the Hudson- **804**;
Briggs' Inn- kept by Abraham Briggs, Salem, N. Y.; the evening of Sept. 5, 1824, George Coggshall rec'd. a mortal wnd. from William Gordon's sword during an altercation here- **808**;
Collins' Tavern- loc. nr. the turnpike, Jackson, N. Y., adj. John Dobbin- **732**;
Cole's Tavern- c. 1850, Shaftsbury, Vt.; loc. nr. the Meeting- house, in the prev. resid. of David Galusha- **765**;
Fenton's Hotel- c. 1854, loc. Cambridge, N. Y., opp. J. Stackhouse's clothing & merch. store; see Vols. 3 & 4- **1028**;
Fitch's Tavern- loc. Fitch's Point, Salem, N. Y.; a port. of Walter Martin's house, purch. Sept. 4, 1795, by Asa Fitch, Sr., was opened up for this purpose & kept by Thomas Berry- **799**; the tavern port. of the house was loc. in the N. front room, "till there being a great squirrel hunt, ending in a drunken carouse in the bar

room"; the revelers kept the Fitch family up all night, & Dr. Fitch's father tore the sign down the foll. morning, & banned any further use of it as an inn- **839**; Heath's Tavern- kept by Joseph Heath (n. d.), S. of the Jackson Ponds- **853**; Howard Hotel- c. 1860's, NYC; stood behind the old Oswego Market, Maiden Lane, fronting on Liberty St.- **1075b**;

Joice's store- kept by Patrick & Ann Joice, Buskirk's Bridge, N. Y.; Martin Wallace & Barney McEntee arr. here within the nr. bef. noon, Feb. 16, 1858, on the day that McEntee was murdered & spent the afternoon drinking together, bef. leaving for Jesse Pratt's store; acc. Ann Joice's testim. at Wallace's trial, she kept some liquor there that belonged to James Gannon, & from time to time had occasion to use, or sell it; other witns. sd. that the establishment's character was bad, that they "kept liquor there & sold it unlawfully. It was reported that they gambled. They had a reputation of getting drunk & fighting"- **1048s**;

Lyttle's Tavern- loc. Salem, N. Y.; a Mrs. Bealy arr. here Sept. 1815, "on the 16th inst.", & due to her pregnant state, was "hospitably admitted", giving birth to a female child within the hr.; she afterw. abandoned the child, leaving "the room that benevolence had provided" in the dead of night- **718**;

Capt. Adam Martin's Tavern- kept in the "long house", Fitch's Point, Salem, N. Y., foll. the Rev. war; some area whigs arr. here one night on their way to tar & feather James Campbell, when he returned from Canada to visit family members who had remained here during the Rev. war; Capt. Martin entertained them while a word of warning was sent to Campbell to flee, & thus avoid any incident- **1065**;

McNeil's Tavern- loc. nr. Ft. Miller bridge (Northumberland, N. Y.) on the W. side of the Hudson, & kept by Archibald McNeil, until abt. 1790, when sold it to _____ DeMond- **804**;

One Horse Tavern- loc. 5 mi. below Joice's store, in Buskirk's Bridge, on the route to Schaghticoke, N. Y.; on the day of his murder, Feb. 16, 1858, Barney McEntee talked of leaving Joice's store & traveling as far as here bef. lodging for the night- **1048s**;

The Old Red Tavern- Salem, N. Y.; loc. N. of Maj. James Harvey & once operated by Stephen Rowan; it was occ. as the R. R. passenger house until autumn 1863, when it was torn down & a new passenger house erected on its site- **1049**;

The Point Tavern- c. 1850, Fitch's Point, Salem, N. Y.; a large tavern, loc. N. of the creek, where Silas Conkey 1st constructed his house- **867**;

Jesse Pratt's store- loc. E. of the tavern on the corner of the old turnpike & river roads, Buskirk's Bridge, N. Y.; a group of men, incl. Barney McEntee & Martin Wallace, were gathered here in the evening, Feb. 16, 1858, prior to the murder of McEntee- **1048s**;

Randall's Tavern- c. 1858, prob. loc. White Creek, N. Y.; kept by Daniel Randall, Deputy Sheriff; Martin Wallace was brought here foll. his arrest & asked into the barn to view the body of Barney McEntee & say whether he knew him; as he walked in the back yard betw. the house & barn, he left boot tracks that were measured & later compared to those found nr. the crime scene, & at the spot where remnants of a fence stake used in the murder were found- **1048s**;

Ransom's Tavern- loc. N. of the Duer Mansion, Ft. Miller, N. Y.; c. 1850, was occ. & kept by Wid. Jacquay- **804**;

Reynold's Tavern- loc. Eagle Bridge, N. Y.; Michael Bradey & Martin Wallace came here in the morning, Feb. 16, 1858, where they 1st met Barney McEntee; acc. Bradey, they all drank together, & then he left; bef. leaving, Wallace sd. that he was going to look for a house, & McEntee accomp. him, both going towards Buskirk's Bridge- **1048s**;

Salem Hotel- i. e., "the Hotel", Salem, N. Y.; a meeting held here Sept. 12, 1814, to establ. a comm. for receiving & forwarding provisions, etc., to the Salem militia then stat. at Plattsburgh, N. Y.- **707**; Wash. Co. Medical Society convened here, July 4, 1815, & elected its officers- **716**;

Stearn's Hotel- loc. Troy, N. Y.; kept by Livy Stearns, foll. by his son James- **839**;

Taller & Williams- loc. Half Moon, N. Y.; kept by 2 bro.- in- laws, of those given names, who had orig. res. Fitch's Point, Salem, N. Y.- **802**;

Webster's Tavern- c. 1853, N. Hoosick, N. Y.; loc. on the E. side of the fork in the road from Cambridge to Walloomsac, opp. the road leading to Hoosick Falls, N. Y.; was abt. 10- 16 rods from the bridge over the Little White creek at Sancoick; see Vol. 1- **1006**; skeletal remains, believed the "last" fatality of the battle of Bennington, were discovered E. of here while excavating for the R. R. line; the bones were brought back to the tavern "where they were exposed to view, & thrown abt. for some months, & finally disappeared"- **1007**;

Well's Hotel- loc. Union Village (Greenwich, N. Y.); a recruiting "rendezvous" held here Aug. 29, 1814, for enl. in a rifleman regt.- **705**

INSTITUTIONS-

Education-
Academies- Auburn- 734; Emma Willard School (Mrs. Willard's seminary)- 732; Granville- 734, 759s, 1082; Salem- 721, 732, 733, 737, 799, 802, 953b, 994, 1053, 1081; Union Village (Greenwich)- 732;

Colleges, Universities- Andover (Theological Seminary)- 1087; Auburn Theological Seminary- 759s; Burlington (Univ. of Vt.)- 968b; Chapel Hill College, N. C.- 1024; Dartmouth- 759s, 994, 1016; Hamilton- 1087; Harvard- 799, 835, 940; Middlebury- 759, 759s; Princeton- 804; as College of N. J.- 961; Rensselaer Institute (RPI)- 839; Rutgers- 1045; Union- 759s, 802; Waukesha College, Wisc.- 1044; West Point- 845; Williams- 759s, 760, 799, 834; Yale- 759, 759s, 799, 961, 1008;

Government-
Colonial- Board of Trade- 884, 887, 891, 928, 1013; Commissioners for Trade & Plantations- 884; Lords of Trade- 894;

United Colonies of America- 830; Continental Congress- 760, 773, 776, 779, 781, 789, 793, 827, 920, 1072;

Connecticut- Assembly- 799; Deputy Governor- 759s; General Court- 799; Governor- 774, 799; Grand Committee- 948;

Massachusetts- Admiralty Court- 799; Berkshire co. Congress- 799; Board of Commissioners- 943; Cambridge, Comm. of Safety- 775; Court of Common Pleas- 799; Governor- 944; Legislature- 799; Suffolk co.- Justice, Court of Common Pleas- 799;

N. H.- General Assembly of the Province- 896; Governor- 786, 883, 884, 887, 894, 898, 896, 928;

N. Y.- Albany Congress, 1754- 799; Albany Postmaster- 889; Cambridge Convention- 816; Charlotte co., Royal courts- 964; Chief Justice- 961; Comm. of Correspondence, Albany co. Districts- Albany- 816- 833; Cambridge- 818, 820, 824, 826, 828, 831; Hoosick- 822, 831; Manor of Livingston- 831; Sancoick- 831; Saratoga- 823, 827, 831; Schaghticoke- 831; Comm. of Safety- 747, 773, 778- 780, 786- 789, 793, 794, 796, 797; Counties & Towns- Albany- 775- 777, 888- 890, 956; Cambridge- 783, 843, 889; Charlotte co.- 784, 787; Hoosick- 783; Salem- 925; Comm. of Sequestration- 936; Convention- 968b; Council- 884- 886, 894, 901- 913, 928, 961; Council of Safety- 797; Court of the King's Bench- 961; Cumberland co., circuit court- 838; Governor- 789, 799, 892, 894, 895, 909, 913, 928; Legislative Assembly- 894, 956; Lt. Governor- 735, 746, 789, 883, 885, 887, 891, 892, 894, 928; Provincial Convention- 711, 773, 785, 787, 968b; Provincial Congress- 773, 774, 776- 786, 789, 790, 792, 796, 798, 818, 821, 823, 828, 920; Secretary of State- 791; Office of- 812; Surveyor General- 991; Treasury- 776, 816;

Counties- Albany- High Sheriff- 885, 892, 897; jail- 897, 892; Justice of Peace- 901; loan officers of- 776; Charlotte- Assist. Judge- 711; Clerk- 711; Dist. Attorney- 711; 1st Judge- 711; Sheriff- 711, 748;

Vt.- Assembly- 816; Comm. of Correspondence- Bennington- 821, 822, 831; Comm. of Safety- 968; Bennington- 783, 1050; Manchester- 964; Convention- 786, 789, 793; Legislature- 816;

Government, U. S.- Congress- 709, 714, 725, 730, 759s, 799, 816, 915, 920, 949b, 994, 1011, 1028, 1056; Constitution- 920; Pension Commissioner- 799; Secretary of Navy- 715; Senate- 759s, 920, 1025; Treasury- 1028;

Government, State-
California- Constitutional Convention- 971; 2nd District Court- 971;

Delaware- Legislature- 949b;

Iowa- Governor- 962;

Maryland- Legislature- 949b;

Massachusetts- Court of Common Pleas- 799; Legislature- 1028, 1050;

Michigan- Governor- 730;

N. H.- Atty. Gen.- 759s;

N. J.- Legislature- 949b;

N. Y.- Assembly- 714, 722, 726, 730, 799, 920, 1011, 1025, 1028, 1045; as House of Assembly- 722; Attorney General- 759s, 902, 920; Canal Commissioner- 1011, 1025, 1028, 1067; Chancery- 839; Comptroller- 920; Constitutional Convention, 1788- 759s; 1867- 1078; Council of Appointment- 799; Governor- 759s, 789, 914; Inspector of State Prisons- 1028; Judicial Dists., 3rd- 759s;

Legislature- 722, 759s, 762, 791, 916, 920, 949b, 994, 1012, 1068, 1078; Master in Chancery- 7590s; NYC Mayor, 1783- 89- 920; NYS Library- 799, 816; Prisons-Auburn- 808; Clinton- 1054; Regents of the University- 759s; Sing Sing- 841; Secretary of State- 928, 1025; Senate- 722, 920; Schools, NYC Public- 1093; State Normal School- 1093; Superintendent of- 1027; Supreme Court- 759, 759s, 1050s 839, 877, 1025; 6th Dist.- 759s; Treasury- 816;
  Albany Co.- Surrogate- 1045;
  Delaware Co.- Surrogate- 759s;
  Rensselaer Co.- Judge- 772;
  Washington Co.- Agricultural Soiciety- 1097; Assist. Atty. General- 914; Board of Supervisors- 1028; Circuit Court- 759s, 914; Clerk- 759s, 1011; Court of Common Pleas- 808, 878, 878½, 910; Court of General Sessions of the Peace- 910, 1011, 1025, 1028, 1048s; Deputy Clerk- 1050s; Deputy Sheriff- 1048s; Dist. Atty.- 914, 1048s, 1050s; Libraries- Independent, Cambridge & Salem- 879; Union, Ft. Edward- 879; Medical Society- 1050s; Poor House- 872; Salem jail- 839, 868; Sheriff, under Sheriff- 759s; Superintendant of Poor- 1011, 1025, 1028; Surrogate-759s; Treasurer- 1011;
  Ohio- Senate- 733;
  Pennsylvania- Government Council- 949; Legislature- 949b;
  Utah- Governor- 730;
  Vermont- Governor- 962; Legislature- 949b; Lt. Gov.- 968b;
  Virginia- Legislature- 949b;

  Other- American Philosophical Society- 949b; Masons- 1075, 1082; Methodist Whitfield Orphan School, Savannah, Ga.- 1075b; N. J. Hist. Soc.- 759s; N. Y. Hist. Soc.- 759s; Smithsonian Institute- 1075; Temperance Society- 974; Troy House (perh. The Warren Free Institute)- 950; Union Volunteer Assoc.- 1098;

IOWA-
  Cities & Towns- Adel- 1089; Brooklyn- 1089; Clear Creek- 1089; Council Bluffs-1089; Crescent City- 1089; Dalmintha- 1089; Des Moines- 1088, 1089; Dewitt-730; Farmington- 962; Grinell- 1089; Iowa City- 1089; Lewis- 1089;
  Marengo- 1089; Newton- 1089; Reading- 1089; Souix City- 1089;
  Features- Bear creek- 1089; Coon river- 11089; Little Souix river- 1089; Onawa river- 1089; Turkey creek- 1089;
  Military units, Civil War- 14th Inf.- 1089; undesign.- 1095;
  Community populations, given in a soldier's diary, Nov. & Dec. 1861-Brooklyn- 2- 300; Newton- abt. 1,500; Reading- 100; Adel- 500; Dalmintha- 100; Lewis- 500- **1089**

IRELAND- 731, 732, 743, 791, 804, 840, 849, 867, 971, 872, 922, 972, 973, 975, 990, 1027, 1032, 1058, 1063, 1073, 1075b, 1097; language- 1058;
Counties- Antrim- 732; Tyrone- 805;
Cities & Towns- Ballibay- 1082; Ballymoney (Bellinoany)- 732;
Londonderry- 1097;
N. IRELAND- 972, 973; Counties- Londonderry- 734;
Monaghan- 737, 979, 1069;
Cities & Towns- Drumgenny- 737;
Features- the Boyne- 734

IRVINE,
Rev. David- (also given as Irving) m. June 23, 1846, Elizabeth, dau. Dr. Alfred & Elizabeth (Martin) Freeman; "late a missionary of the Presbyterian Board to India"; settl. c. 1858, N. Y.; children-
1. Eliza Melvil, b. June 1, & d. June 9, 1850
2. Alfred Freeman, b. Mar. 24, 1852
3. William Skidmore, b. Oct. 15, 1854
4. David Olyphant, b. Nov. 24, 1856- 730
Richard, Esq.- (Irvin) res. NYC; m. dau. Rev. Alexander, D. D., & Susan (Williams) Proudfit- 1019

IRVING,
Erwin- merch., NYC; m. Mary, dau. Rev. Alexander, D. D., & Susannah (Williams) Proudfit- 1045

IVES,
Julia- of Turin, N. Y.; m. Walter, s. Walter & Sarah (Turner) Martin- 730; same material- 1045
William- of Brimfield, Mass.; m. Hannah, dau. Ephriam Wheeler, of Killingworth, Mass.; children- William, Cheney; Cynthia, m. _____ Ballard; Hannah, Simon, & Lovinia- 1038

J

JACKSON,
Gen. Thomas J. "Stonewall"- (1824- 1863) brief ment.-**1097**

Jackson Party- families of Salem, N. Y., who fled into the area of this township (then partly in the present towns of Cambridge & Salem) foll. the Allen massacre, July 1777, for shelter; the families of David Hanna & William Tosh (or McIntosh) were incl. in this co.; acc. Robert Hanna, the party fled down across the Battenkill by James & Archy Campbell's, crossing the kill 3 times, & encamping nr. the Great falls at Galesville, & building their huts somewhere nr. Bald Mountain, N. Y.; Dr. Fitch notes this version was "prob. confounded" w. some other childhood memory, as James & Archibald Campbell res. on opp. sides of the Battenkill nr. ea. other & only one crossing was required to go betw. them (the Great falls, or Dionondeho, was loc. in the present town of Easton, N. Y., & at a far rem., & in a diff. direction through uninhabited wilderness, making it geographically implausible as an option); the party reportedly remained for 6 wks., until after Burgoyne's surrender; see Vol. 1- **701**

JACQUAY,
Thomas?- (or George?) res. 1798, on the E. side of the Hudson, nr. the loc. of Ft. Miller bridge- **804**
Widow- prob.wf. Thomas?; m. 2. ____ Perkins; kept Ransom's tavern, Ft. Miller, N. Y.- **804**

JACQUES,
Asahel- def., w. Phineas Gage, in a case brought by Robert Snell- **878**

Jane McCrea tree- (loc. Ft. Edward, N. Y., & suppos. the pine tree marking the historic site of Jane McCrea's massacre) was 'made into canes & snuff- boxes'; refers June 7, 1853, *Salem Press-* **1054**

JAY,
Gov. John- (1745- 1829; Gov., 1795- 1801) appt. Anthony I. Blanchard as 1st Wash. co. District Attorney- **914**

JAYNER,
Lyman- res., c. 1853, nr. the Red Bridge, Salem, N. Y.; his son Rodney, m. Jane, dau. Henry Bliss- **1005**
Rodney- s. Lyman; merch., Galesville, N. Y.; m. Jane, dau. Henry Bliss; children- Cornelia, Dwight, & William Aaron; at one time, he was partner w. his bro.- in- law, Aaron Bliss, at a store in Union Village (Greenwich, N. Y.); he failed, & "decamped", 1856, & rem. & resid. w. William Bliss in Wisc.- **1005**

JEFFERSON,
Pres. Thomas- (1743- 1826) c. 1816, acc. *Northern Post,* the division of the town
of Cambridge, N. Y. into 3 parts would prob. contrib. to the intro. his political
perspective into Wash. co.- **722**

JENKINS,
Atwood- adopted s. Asa & Sarah (Van Valkenburgh) Martin; c. 1850, res. nr.
Milwaukee, Wisc.- **731**

JERMAIN,
James- (or Germain?) Co. A, 2nd N. Y., Northern Black Horse, Cav., 1861- 2-
1080

JESSUP,
Family- incl. on U. E. list as refugees from Rev. war, & entitled to 200 acres of
land in Canada- **991**

JOCELYN,
Family- res. Hebron, N. Y.; dau. Maria, m. Chester, s. James & Matilda (Safford)
Turner; her parents have since rem., n. d., or loc. given- **1090**

JOHNSON,
Edward- of Martinsburgh, N. Y.; m. Amarillus, dau. Nathan & Lovinia
(Shumway) Cheney- **1038**
Sir Guy- (or Uraghquadirha; c. 1740- 1788) Adjutant Gen., militia of N. Y.
Province, foll. Sir H. Moore's division of the colony's militia- **735**
Sir John- (1742- 1830) an order given, Jan. 1776, for militia to "visit" him &
disarm tories under his protection; see Johnstown, & Stillwater, N. Y., Vol. 3- **825**
Leonard- res. Reynoldsburgh, nr. Columbus, Ohio; m. Millicent, dau. William &
Wealthy (Gilbert) Wells; 2 or 3 children- **839**
Capt. Miles- commanded a co. of Col. Hooker's regt., from Wallingford, Conn.;
late Feb. 1777, sent to Peekskill, & pursued the British as far as Bedford, N. Y.,
foll. the burning of Danbury, Conn.- **752**
Capt. Nathan J.- (Capt. N. J.) Co. I, 93rd N. Y. Inf.; Feb. 1862, stat. Camp Bliss,
Ryker's Island, NYC- **1081**; same rank & co., Feb. 1, 1862, stat. Camp Rathbone,
Albany, N. Y.- **1090b**
Thomas- farmer, White Creek (Salem), Albany co., N. Y.; Apr. 20, 1770, for £ 12,
conveyed Lot 217, Turner's Patent, to James Lyttle- **936**
Sir William- (1715- 1774) noted as a demotion in rank, he was appt. Brig. Gen. of
the N. division of the militia for N. Y. Province by Sir H. Moore; under his
direction, the ranks of Albany co., consisting of 6,000 men in 1 regt. & 2
battalions, were divided into smaller regts. of 5,000- 10,000 men, covering smaller
districts & more easily assembled; in a letter to Lt. Gov. Colden, Nov. 25, 1769, he

notes a variety of regts. formed w/o his prior notification, & Jan. 5, 1770, notes Col. Schuyler's propensity for making out officer's commissions- **735**

JOHNSTON,
Deac. Abraham- res. W. Hebron, N. Y.; c. 1851, prior to his death, Rev. Duncan Stalker committed his s. James G., over to his care- **1081**
William- defendant, 1774, in a case brought by William Duer, Esq.- **878**

JOICE,
Patrick- & wf. Ann; res. Buskirk's Bridge, N. Y., & kept a grocery there; his wf. testif. on the 1st & 2nd days of Martin Wallace's trial, saying that she had known Wallace for 4 or 5 yrs., but had never met Barney McEntee bef. Feb. 16, 1858, when the 2 arr. at their store, betw. 11:00 AM & 12 noon; McEntee called for drinks, & sd. that he was going to Schaghticoke to look for a dog & see friends, & Wallace sd. that he was looking for a house; McEntee drank 4 times while he was there, twice bef. Wallace left, & twice after he returned; Wallace left at abt. 3:00 PM, having asked McEntee prev. to this if he would help him pay for the house he was looking for; he returned abt. dusk, but only put his 2nd drink up to his lips, while McEntee continued to drink, & he asked McEntee if he would go home w. him, as he wanted supper; they left, but returned shortly, as McEntee was unwilling to leave w. Wallace; acc. her testim., her husb. advised McEntee to leave w. Wallace; on close questioning by James Gibson, she revealed that James Gannon & her husb. had drank w. McEntee & Wallace, at McEntee's request, from a pint of whisky sling, made from liquor belonging to Gannon; she sd. that she had no license to sell the liquor, but that Gannon kept it at the store, & she had occasion to use it & sell it; she sd. she had never heard anything against Wallace's character except for his fighting at Peter Lindsay's; her husb. afterw. testif. similarly, saying that someone had sd. abt. McEntee's plans that it was too late to go to Schaghticoke, whereupon he sd., at abt. mid- afternoon, that he would go as far as the One Horse Tavern, ano. 5 mi. from the store, & lodge for the night; Wallace told McEntee that he wasn't used well by him, & that they had come together, & McEntee should leave w. him; acc. Mr. Joice, Wallace left at abt. 4:00 PM, & when he returned, asked McEntee to leave w. him; Wallace then sd. that Michael Conway had invited him to dinner, but he declined, because he was waiting for McEntee to leave w. him; they left, but shortly returned, whereupon he told McEntee to leave w. Wallace; on cross- exam, Gibson gave a "rigid examination" concerning who owned the liquor, who called for & pd. for it, & the no. of times it was used, et. al.; acc. Bridget Millet's testim., Wallace arr. at her house at abt. 3:00 PM, sd. he was looking for a house, & claimed he was going to buy a cow from Joice; the character of the house kept by the Joices, acc. Andrew Houghton's testim., was bad, that they "kept liquor there & sold it unlawfully. It was reported that they gambled. They had a reputation of getting drunk & fighting"- **1048s**

JONALY,
John & William- plaintiffs, May 19, 1774, vs. James McDonald- **878**

JONES,
____- neph. David; res. Canada, opp. Ogdensburgh, N. Y.; he crossed over the St.
Lawrence & stole some iron lying on the river bank, & was arrested, & convicted,
when he returned for a 2nd load; he was confined (n. d.) at Clinton State Prison at
the same time as a neph. of Jane McCrea was a keeper's assistant there- **1053**
Daniel- of Queensbury, alias Kianderossa, Albany co., N. Y.; Nov. 26, 1773, for £
110, conveyed Lot No. 30, Kingsbury, to John Jones; bounded W- Lot 31, N- Lot
25, E- Lot 29, & S- Lot 15- **(L)- 936**; for £ 181, mortgaged Lot No. 55, Kingsbury,
to Ennis Graham; bounded W- Lot 54, N- Lot 70, & E- Lot 56- **938**
David- noted as Jane McCrea's lover; a neph. of his was, at one time, incarcerated
at the Clinton State Prison at the same time as one of her neph.'s was a keeper's
assistant there- **1053**; acting upon a popular belief held throughout Argyle, Col.
John McCrea inquired of him as to whether he had ever seen the ghost of his sist.
Jane; he denied it, saying that her image only appeared bef. him in his
imagination- **1061**
Ezra- of Westfield, Wash. co., N. Y.; Feb. 8, 1789, deeded part of Lot No. 4,
Provincial Patent, bounded N. by Artillery Patent, to Thomas Brayton of
Kingsbury, N. Y.; John Barnard & Susanna Bennet, witns.- **745**
Family- incl. on the U. E. list of refugees from the Rev. war, entitled to 200 acres
of land in Canada- **991**
John- non- commissioned officer, 44th Regt; for his services, drew 200 acres on
the W. side of Lake George; he was an uncle of David Jones, Jane McCrea's fiancé;
refers p. 25, v. 3, Military Patents- **931**
John- purch. from Daniel Jones, Nov. 26, 1773, Lot No. 30, Kingsbury, for £ 110-
(L)- 936; c. 1853, his lands betw. Sandy Hill & Ft. Edward, N. Y. were listed in a
vol. in the Surveyor General's Office, Albany, N. Y., as among those confiscated
during the Rev. war; during his 1777 campaign, Gen. Burgoyne's army reportedly
encamped on his lands- **991**
Dr. John- c. 1775, he & Dr. Samuel Bard appt. to examine Samuel Cook, Ebenezer
Haviland, & John Williams, to qualify as Surgeons, Green Mtn. Regt.- **778**
O. W.- m. Elizabeth, dau. Samuel & Sarah (Maltby) Rowland- **799**

JORDAN,
Axey- dau. Mrs. Seward, by her 1st husb.; m. James Thompson- **864**

JUDD,
William- res. Younge, Ont., Canada; m. Hannah, dau. John & Hannah (Alyea)
Munroe- **812**

K

KANE,
Charles- merch.; c. 1798, he & his bros. did a large business at a store they kept in Ft. Edward, N. Y.; he afterw. rem. NYC, & then Schenectady- **804**; his father was a Loyalist, "a public man of some note in Ft. Ann", & reportedly got a liberal renumeration from the English govt. for his losses during the Rev. war- **916**
Maj. Gen. Thomas Leiper- (1822- 1883) brief ment.; of Bank's corps, Williams's division; Sept. 1862, obt. placement of the 123rd NYSV under his command- **1098**

KANSAS- **759s**

KAY,
Miss- m. David Dobbin, of Co. Antrim, Ireland; as his 1st wf.- **732**

KEILER,
Capt.- commanded militia co., Norwalk, Conn., Apr. 1776; later sent to the defense of NYC- **753**

KELLEY,
Abigail- m. John, s. Robert & Susan (Lytle) Vance- **737**

KELLOGG,
Cynthia- m. James, s. Philo & Abby (Martin) Rockwell- **730**; same material- **1046**
Rev. L.- of Whitehall, N. Y.; a letter addressed to him, 1848, from Chauncey K. Williams, of Williams College, containing biog. items pert. to Maj. Philip Skene- **760**

KEMP,
John- Co. A, 2nd N. Y., Northern Black Horse, Cav., 1861- 2- **1080**

KENNEY,
John- def., in separate cases, brought by Robert Snell & Wm. Duer, Esq.; in both, Sheriff returns property attached, unsold for want of buyers- **878**

KENT,
Cephas- res. Dorset, Vt.; July 27, 1775, a meeting of the W. range of Green Mtn. towns held at his resid., to select officers for the Green Mtn. regt.- **781b**
Chancellor James- (1763- 1847; Chief Justice of N. Y.) quotation by him noting the ability & character of Gen. Philip Schuyler as a man of his times; along w. Bensen & Lawrence, an assoc. that Gen. Schuyler confided in concerning the reasons behind his re- election defeat as U. S. Senator, 1791; he was given one vote

in the N. Y. Assembly, Jan. 24, 1797, during the election that replaced Aaron Burr w. Gen. Schuyler, apparently as a token of esteem as Schuyler's friend- **920**

KENTUCKY- 962, 1010; Counties- Nelson- 949b;
Cities & Towns- Bardstown- 949b; Frankfort- 1095; Lawrenceville- 949b

KENYON,
E. P.- oath of alleg.; Co. D, 22nd N. Y. Inf.- **(L)- 1074**
Henry C.- Co. A, 2nd N. Y., Northern Black Horse, Cav., 1861- 2- **1080**

KETCHUM,
_____- of Hoosic, N. Y.; was among those capt. at Ft. Ann & Ft. George, 1780; "the hardships & ill treatment he experienced were so great that his hair came off his head", & he remained bald thereafter- **858**

Kianderossa- acc. Nov. 26, 17773 deed entry, an Indian name given to Queensbury, N. Y.- **(L)- 936**

KILLBURN,
Sirenus- oath of alleg.; Co. D, 22nd N. Y. Inf.- **(L)- 1074**

KILMER/ KILMORE,
_____- m. Hannah Tinkey; a son, Abram- **983**
Abe- a slave of Gerry Kilmore; he orig. discovered the scene of the Allen massacre (on the same day the Jane McCrea was murdered), Sunday, July 27, 1777, & 1st came to Duncan Taylor's house w. the alarm (§ 132; see Vol. 1) & "he was so scared they could scarcely get out of him any satisfactory acct. of the facts"- **983**
Yerry- (or Gerry) while in a party going to Ft. Edward for protection in Burgoyne's camp foll. the Allen massacre, Mrs. Alexander McNachten was unable to go further; the family was compelled to stop at Kilmore's home, where Eleanor McNachten was b. Aug. 10, 1777- **1062**

KIMBALL,
Capt. Richard- for many yrs., a consultant to Gov. Dewitt Clinton, "in all matters in practical difficulty in relation to the canals"; the Gov.'s confidence in his opinions was such that when the Canal Commissioners insisted it was impossib. to construct the Champlain canal through Ding's Swamp, Clinton countered that it could be done, as Kimball had sd. it could; & he was given the task, undertaking & completing it; d. at 92, Lebanon, N. H., 'last wk.', acc. Mar. 8,1860, *N. Y. Observer*; his son, Richard, Esq., res. NYC- **1067**

KIMBERLY,
Ann- m. Col. John, s. Deac. John & Eleanor (Webster)) Steele- **1047**

KING,
Charles B.- merch., Chicago, Illinois; m. Jane, dau. Philo & Abby (Martin) Rockwell- **730**; same material- **1046**
Capt. George- Aug. 1776, commanded Barrington, Mass. militia co., Col. Fellow's regt.; was sent to Dutchess, & then Westchester co., N. Y.; was stat. at Valentine's hill, & participated in the battle of White Plains- **755**
Gov. John Alsop- (s. Rufus; 1788- 1867; N. Y. Assembly, 1819- 21, 1832, 38, & 40; Senate, 1823- 25; 31st Congress, 1849- 51; Gov., 1857- 58) Republican candidate, 1858, for N. Y. Gov., vs. Amasa J. Parker & Erastus Brooks- **759s**
Rufus- (1755- 1827) chosen 1st U. S. Senator, by concurrent resolution of N. Y. legislature, July 16, 1789; seated July 25, drawing the long term, which expired Mar. 3, 1795, while Gen. Schuyler rec'd. the short term; see Senators, U. S.- **920**
William- merch., Martinsburg, N. Y.; m. Christine, dau. Philo & Abby (Martin) Rockwell- **730**; same material, wf.'s name given as Christina- **1046**

King Hendrick- (or Tiyahoga; c. 1680- 1755) Mohawk sachem; he & Col. Ephriam Williams were killed by the French during the ambush known as the Bloody Morning Scout (Sept. 8, 1755) during the battle of Lake George- **989**

Kingsbury, N. Y.- Trustees, 1st Baptist Society, elected Sept. 17, 1798; see Church/ Clergy, & § 1350, Vol. 3- **879**

KIRK,
David- c. 1858, res. Troy, N. Y.; brief ment.- **1048s**

KIRKWOOD,
Gov. Samuel Jordan- of Iowa (1813- 1894; Gov., 1860- 64, & 1876- 77) res. 2 mi. from Iowa City, Iowa; Co. A- C, 14th Iowa Inf., encamped on his farm Oct. 31, 1861, bef. beginning their march to the relief of the federal garrison at Ft. Randall, Dakota Territory, on Nov. 2nd- **1089**

KNAPP,
Amy- m. Jabez, s. Ebenezer & Lydia (Mills) Fitch- **799**

KNICKERBOCKER,
Harmon- (1799- 1855) when 1st sent to Salem Academy, the "young Prince" was, as a rule, required to write home to his parents, the Preceptor correcting the draft bef. the final copy was made; on seeing the finished article, Rev. Van Benschoten was so impressed, that he read it from his pulpit during meeting, which caused a sensation among the parishioners; his parents wrote back, requesting ano. letter, & deeming the orig. so perfect & w/o place for improvement, he made ano. copy of it, & was disappointed to discover that the 1st was so admired while no notice was given of the 2nd one; see Vol. 1- **953b**

John- c. 1775, a copy of a letter sent to him by the Albany Comm. of Correspondence encouraged Capt. Wells to raise a co. & seek an officer's position within the Albany militia Battalion- **818**

KUYLER/ KYLER,

Col.- m. Catherine, dau. John Henry Lydius; see also, Cuyler, or Van Cuyler- **930**

L

LADD,
William- Co. A, 2nd N. Y., Northern Black Horse, Cav., 1861- 2- **1080**

LAKE,
Family- here bef. Rev. war; prob. res. & purch. Van Cuyler's Patent, which adjoins Walloomsac Patent- **806**
John, Jr.- Westfield, N. Y.; Mar. 24, 1807, hung himself in the barn of John Lake; Ozias Colman, Jr., Coroner- **(L)- 876**

Lake George, battle of- acc. Mary M. Chase, the Bloody Morning Scout (the 1st part of the battle, Sept. 8, 1755) an ambuscade into which Col. Ephriam Williams & King Hendrick led 1,200 men, rivals the massacre at Ft. Wm. Henry (Aug. 9, 1757) "in the catalogue of painful events"; both commanders perished, 'w. numbers of their followers'; a large portion of the troops employed in the battle were from western Mass.; an 8 stanza poem by Chase, written on the subj., & inspired (acc. to its authoress) from a reading of Dr. Fitch's Hist. of Washington Co.- **989**

LAKIN,
Lemuel, Esq.- res. Salem, N. Y.; once worked for Harrison G. Blake, & relates an acct. of Blake's wf. freezing to death on a mountain top in Vt.- **733**

LAMBERT,
Rev. Amos Bordman- (Rev. A. B.) along w. Priest McDermott, attended to Martin Wallace's spiritual needs during his confinement prior to his Dec. 1, 1858 execution- **1050s**; officiated at the foll. funerals for Civil War dead, Salem, N. Y.- N. Albert Wilson, Dec. 10, 1861; James G. Stalker, Jan. 23, 1862- **1081**; elected President, Wash. Co. Bible Soc., Sept. 4, 1862, at their 50th annual meeting, & gave an address speaking of Deac. John McMurray, the sole surviving member of the society's 1st meeting- **1097**

LANE,
Lt. Derick- was stat. in winter qtrs. at Valley Forge w. his bro. Aaron, & they obt. a leave of absence, going home for a short time; their mother had made ea. of them 8 shirts because of the state of their clothing, but on their return, they found the state of the hospital "was so greatly in want, & the poor soldiers suffering so greatly for want of suitable dressings for their wnds., that they gave up every shirt, to the hospital- saving only the ruffles, which they pinned to their bosoms & the cuffs of their sleeves, in order to appear as respectable as possible on parade. And all that winter they attended to the drills & exercises, w/o a shirt to their backs"; w. his vest & pantelloons shrunk from washing & age, he also appeared w. abt. an inch of bare skin exposed to the weather- **1036**

Family- of N. J.; bros. Aaron & Derick, c. 1820's, were wealthy merch. in Troy, N. Y.; they opened a store in Lansingburgh soon after the close of the Rev. war, & "so little were their beginnings, that, if they made $5 in one day, they went to bed w. a light heart"; their frugalities & rigid economy attrib. by them to being trained to it from their army service- **1036**

LANGWORTHY,
W. R.- oath of alleg.; Co. D, 22nd N. Y. Inf.- **(L)- 1074**

LANSING,
Abram Jacob- (1720- 1791) c. 1770's, commissioner for division of Schuyler's Patent, along w. Killian DeRidder & Jan Winne- **935**
John Jacob- d. Apr. 19, 1808, at 92; m. Catharine Schuyler, who d. Mar. 31, 1797, at 73- **(L)- 932**
Philip P.- c. 1774, High Sheriff of Charlotte co., N. Y.; John Thurman & Jacob Van Voorhies acted as his assignees, Oct. 19, 1774; & Philip Schuyler, Esq., his assignee, Jan. 16, 1775, vs. Wm. Perry & Wm. Moffitt- **878**

LARABEE,
Timothy- of Hoosic, N. Y.; taught school at Fitch's Point, Salem, N. Y., for a season, & then rem. Shoreham, Vt.- **859**

LARMON,
John- res. abt. ¼- ½ mi. from Hiram Sisson, Buskirk's Bridge, N. Y.; he was away, at Hoosick Falls, the night of Barney McEntee's murder, when Sisson came to his house to get assistance; when he was arrested, Martin Wallace claimed to have left McEntee at the foot of the hill nr. Larmon's house, & Larmon testif. that on Feb. 17, 1858, the day foll. McEntee's murder, he went to Sisson's house bef. sunrise & discovered pieces of flannel from McEntee's gloves scattered in the road- **1048s**

LATHAM,
Daniel- he & his heirs rec'd. a 1½ acre tract, gr. in the Will, Feb. 2, 1756, of Samuel Burrows of East Hampton, N.Y.- **1100**
Sarah- was the housekeeper of Samuel Burrows; her dau. Sarah, rec'd. the remainder of Burrow's estate in his Will; & she perh. m. Clark Truman- **1100**

LATHROP,
Family- of Hartford, N. Y.; ments. a son, m. Elizabeth, & a dau., m. Daniel, both children of David & Susanna (West) Mason- **759s**
James- (Lathrup) d. Aug. 26, 1841, at 89- **(L)- 772**

LAUDERDALE,
Mr.- res. (n. d.) Cambridge, N. Y.; tailor, & 1st instructor of Reuben Glover in the trade- **1093**

LAW,
John- of New Perth (Salem, N. Y.) deeded Sept. 20, 1784, Lots 270 & 271,
Turner's Patent, to Asa Estee- **(L)- 936**; Lots 270 & 271, containing 88 acres ea.,
purch. for £ 500 by Asa Estee, of Brookfield, Mass., except for 10 acres sold to
Wm.? Couzen- **(L)- 936b**

LAWRENCE,
____ - res. Bennington, or Shaftsbury, Vt.; m. Triphena, dau. ____ & ____
(Newell) Martin; she d. & he rem. Monkton, Vt., w. their 3 children- Nathan,
Moses, & Triphena- **849**; gives his wf. as Martha, b. 1755, dau. Aaron & Sarah
(Newell) Martin- **1037**
____ - (prob. John Laurence, 1750- 1810) along w. Egbert Benson & Rufus King,
assoc. of Gen. Schuyler that he confided in concerning the reasons behind his re-
election defeat as U. S. Senator, 1791- **920**
Capt. John- reports to N. Y. Prov. Congress, Oct. 12, 1775, on the news of the
English viewpoint of conditions in America- **783**

LAWTON,
Willard- oath of alleg.; Co. D, 22nd N. Y. Inf.- **(L)- 1074**

LECK,
Daniel- sold land to Samuel Burrows of East Hampton, N. Y., loc. on the S. side of
the road to Mamoraneck, N. Y.; ment. in Burrow's Will, Feb. 2, 1756- **1100**

LEE,
____ - of Westfield, Mass.; rem. Martinsburgh, N. Y.; his dau. Betsey, m. Adam, s.
Silas & Zerniah (Martin) Conkey- **730**
____ - m. Elizabeth, dau. Hezekiah & Jerusha (Burr) Fitch- **799**
Betsey- m. Adam, s. Silas & Zerniah (Martin) Conkey- **730**
Lavinna- niece of Betsey, the wf. Adam Conkey; m. John, s. Walter & Sarah
(Turner) Martin, & they res. Martinsburgh, N. Y.- **730**; (Lavinia) same data,
giving husb.'s full name as John Williams Martin- **1046**
William C.- of Putnam, N.Y.; drowned, Dec. 15, 1853, while skating in Mill Bay,
leaving a wf. & 3 children- **1020**

LEEB,
John- m. Chloe, dau. Aaron & Olive (Harding) Martin- **1040**

LEISLER,
Gov. Jacob- (1640- 1691; of N. Y. Province, 1689- 91) a delegation consisting of
Capt. James Fitch, Esq., & Maj. Nathan Gold, was appt. June 13, 1689, by the
General court at Hartford, Conn., to advise w. him; refers Doc. Hist. of N. Y., ii, p.
15; their letter of advice appears on the pg. foll.- **799**

LENDRUM,
Deac. Archibald- c. 1860's, res. E. Greenwich, N. Y.- **1095b**
Deac.- c. 1852, res. Argyle, N. Y., in the loc. once occ. by John McCollum- **978**
Duncan- res. E. Greenwich, N. Y., where he operated a Window Sash & Blind factory; 1st Lt., Co. G, 22nd N. Y. Inf.; he was last heard in front of his men, at 2nd Bull Run, leading a charge & shouting, 'Give it to them boys!', when he was shot down- **1095b**
Family- of E. Greenwich, N. Y.; ments. sons Deac. Archibald & Lt. Duncan- **1095b**

LEONARD,
Col. Ephriam- (1705/6- 1786) Adam Martin enl. as a Capt. in his regt. during the Rev. war- **730**; officer witn. by Ebenezer Farnsworth, during the July 1777- Jan. 1778 period of his service- **750**
John- Co. A, 2nd N. Y., Northern Black Horse, Cav., 1861- 2- **1080**
Stephen- res. Lowville, N. Y.; m. Jane, dau. Walter & Sarah (Turner) Martin; children-
  1. Jane Maria, m. ____ Morse
  2. Cornelia
  3. Elizabeth, m. ____ Horton
  4. John
  5. & 6. twins, Charles & George, the latter married
  7. Lewis- **730**; children- Jane Ann, Christina, Martin, & Alexander- all dec'd. (they perh. d. y.); Jane Maria, m. Francis B. Morse; Cornelia; Elizabeth, m. Levi Norton; John Calhoun; Charles Pinkney, m. Sarah Tyler; George Clinton; & Lewis Martin, who d. Sept. 1855; his wf. d. 1871, & he d. 1868- **1046**
William- Co. A, 2nd N. Y., Northern Black Horse, Cav., 1861- 2- **1080**

LeROY,
Mrs.- of NYC; she was related to the family of Henry Cuyler, & c. 1850's, one of his grdsons, "a little, insignificant, drunken, worthless fellow", used to come down from Ft. Miller, N. Y. to visit her, until he was forbidden to; the grds. ment. later returned to England, after squandering all of his inherited properties- **1032**

LEWIS,
Amelia- m. Thomas, s. Thomas & ____ (Hill) Fitch- **799**; same information, her resid. given as Huntington, Long Island, N. Y.- **940**
Benjamin- his wf. Mary, d. Apr. 2, 1832, at 77; & he d. Oct. 29, 1831, at 76- **(L)- 772**
Dr.- m. Abigail, dau. Willard Cheney & Mary (Faxon) Conkey, at Utica, N. Y.; they rem. Wisc. or Illinois- **730**
Family- c. 1798, res. W. side of the Hudson, opp. Ft. Miller, N. Y., above the Burt family- **804**
Miss- m. Thomas, s. Walter & Sarah (Turner) Martin- **730**

L'HOMMEDIEU,
Ezra- (1734- 1811; N. Y. Senate, 1784- 1809) of Suffolk co.; anti- federalist; c. 1789, was rejected by the Assembly, 39- 20, as the 2nd proposed U. S. Senator from N. Y.; he was then proposed in the State Senate as a substitute for the Assembly's recommendation of James Duane, & was accepted 11- 7, but again rejected in the Assembly, 34- 24; Rufus King was then proposed in the Assembly & accepted by both houses- **920**

LINCOLN,
Maj. Gen. Benjamin- (1733- 1810) Sept. 1776, commanded Mass. brigade assembled from 2 months men, who were marched to Fairfield, Conn.; his brigade was then marched to NYC, via Horseneck, where they were joined w. the retreating American troops, & later fought at the battle of White Plains- **747**; commanded at Pawlet, Vt., 1777; he was escorted from there, prob. Aug. or Sept., by Nathaniel Barnet, for a general council of officers at Van Schaik's Island, opp. Stillwater, N. Y.- **763**

LINDSAY,
Duncan- d. Sept. 20, 1791, in his field, Argyle, N. Y., of apoplexy; Adiel Sherwood, Coroner- **(L)- 876**
Peter- perh. a tavernkeeper (?); among reports on the behavior of Martin Wallace during his trial for murder, Oct. 1- 7, 1858, were ments. of his fighting at Lindsay's- **1048s**

Liquor, Spirits- listing of prices, Apr. 20, 1776, printed on handbills, along w. other W. Indies items, by Albany Comm. of Correspondence; per gallon- W. Indies rum- 6/6; Jamaica spirits- 8/6; N. Y. rum- 4/6- **829**; c. 1752, ledger charges, Norwich, Conn., for var. tavern items, amts. not always noted- Flip- 5/3; Egg punch- 4/ , & 4/6; Syder- 2/1 per mug; 1/1 per pint; Egg rum & Syder- 5/6, & 2/6 per dram- **838**

Lisbon, N. Y.- c. 1799, settl. by a co. from Salem, N. Y.- **1083**; in 1801, Reuben Turner, & the Armstrong families of Salem, N. Y., rem. here- **1084**

LIVINGSTON,
____- res. Cambridge, N. Y.; m. Miriam, dau. Samuel & Olive (Scott) Wells- **839**; his home orig. occ. by Joseph Wells- **842**
Capt. Abraham- c. 1782, commanded co. of '9 months men' enl. from the Salem area & garrisoned partly at Saratoga (Schuylerville, N. Y.) & Ft. Williams, Salem, N. Y., guarding the northern frontier- **729**
Alexander, Esq.- alluded to for his ability to relate many anecdotes concerning old Mrs. Tosh, prob. in relation to incidents illust. her reputation as a witch; acc. Mrs. Taylor, a cat was found in his cellar lapping cream from his milk, & it was

suspected that the animal was Mrs. Tosh, transformed; see Witchcraft, Witches-
871

Col.- acc. John Williams, June 23, 1777, of the Capts. in his regt. now, 2 are
Canadians who have come down across the Green Mtns., citing the ill use of the
inhabitants by the British as the cause of their flight- **789**

Daniel- c. 1775, res. Fitch's Point, Salem, N. Y.; a tenant of Moses Martin, &
assisted his family in Aug. 1777, when they evac. the area during the retreat bef.
Burgoyne's army- **853**; res. nr. Battenkill; he desired to be perfectly neutral during
Rev. war, & did not move his family away; he afterw. rem. to the Greenwich part
of the Argyle Patent, E. of Reid's corners (N. Greenwich, N. Y.); he was given a lot
of land here in exchange for caring for the blind woman who owned it; had a large
family- John, Daniel, Simeon, & Silas; Mary Ann, m. James Maxwell; & Jenny, m.
Walter Maxwell; perh. others- **854**; c. 1777, his was one of only 4 houses then loc.
at Fitch's Point- **855**; occ. the place later occ. by Timothy Titus- **867**; c. 1852, res.
"the 2nd house N. of Rev. George Mairs, a mi. S. of Argyle village"; m. Catherine,
dau. John & Betsey (Beaty) McDougall, who recounts the McDougall family
history for Dr. Fitch- **978**

Frank- perh. s. John; m. Agnes Boyd- **1084**

James- c. 1750's, Alderman, NYC; his dau. Janet, m. William Smnith, Jr.- **961**

John- deed witn., May 1, 1766, Rev. Dr. Thomas Clark to Andrew Lyttle- **(L)**- **936**

John- called 'Paddy Wilson'; member, Dr.Clark's colony; res. on the Charles
Warford place, Salem, N. Y.; had a large family, widely scattered & gone from
town for a long time; of his sons- Robert, m. Jane Agnes Byrne; Dr. William, res.
Hebron, N. Y.; & perh. Frank, who m. Agnes Boyd- **1084**

Peter Van Brugh- (1710- 1792) chosen President, N. Y. Provincial Congress,
convened May 22, 1775- **773**; merch., res. NYC; Sept. 20, 1773, he & Francis
Groome purch. 2,000 acres along Wood creek as it runs into Lake Champlain,
Charlotte co., N. Y., for £ 150; orig. gr. to Thomas Trickett, Quartermaster, 44th
Regt. of Foot, the purch. was deeded, Oct. 20, 1785, to Francis Groom of NYC-
(L)- **936**; s. Philip; grad. Yale, 1731; one of the founders of the College of N. J.
(Princeton); elder, Dr. John Rogers' Presbyterian church, NYC; m. 1. Mary, dau.
James Alexander, Lord Stirling; acc. Dr. Fitch, she was sist., William, Lord
Stirling, & not his dau. as given in record; refers p. 6, Duer's Life of Stirling; 2.
Wid. Rocketts; a dau., Susannah, m. Baron Niemcewitz; & he d. at an advanced
age- **961**

Philip- (1718- 1778) chosen President, N. Y. Provincial Convention, convened
Apr. 20, 1775- **773**

Philip- 2nd Lord of the Manor of Livinston; his s. Peter Van Brugh, m. 1. Mary
Alexander; 2. Wid. Rocketts- **961**

Robert- Dr. Sealee & the British Capt. seized at Ft. Ann, July 1777, were quartered
on parole at his house; refers p. 1005, Journal of Council of Safety- **794**

Robert- s. John; m. Jane Agnes Byrne- **1083**

Robert R.- (given as Robert G.; the younger, 1746- 1813) appt. Deputy Adjutant
General, Aug. 23, 1775, by N. Y. Provincial Congress, in place of William Duer,

Esq.- **781**; a few yrs. foll. John Fitch's death (1798) the N. Y. legislature
determined that the steam boats built by him & Robert Fulton were, in substance,
the same invention patented in 1791 by Fitch- **949b**
William- oath of alleg.; Co. D, 22nd N. Y. Inf.- **(L)- 1074**
Dr. William- Wash. co. member, N. Y. legislature, for 4 times prev. War of 1812;
d. May 7, 1860, at 92, Lewis, Essex co., N. Y.- **1068**; was perh. s. John- **1083**

LOADMAN,
Samuel- defendant, 1774, in separate cases brought by Wm. Ducr, Esq. & Hugh
O'Harro; & along w. others, in a case brought by Patrick McDavitt- **878**

LOBDELL,
Benjamin- m. Lydia, dau. Benjamin Sillick- **950**

LOCKWOOD,
_____- m. Fances, dau. James & Clarinda (Griffin) Wells; once Steward, Rensselaer
Institute (RPI), Troy, N. Y., & later Justice of the Peace, Schaghticoke, N. Y.,
where he d., leaving no children- **839**

LOG CABINS, descriptions of-
Dr. Clark's meeting- house- c. 1765, Salem, N. Y.; loc.W. of the framed church;
acc. John McDonald, "It was a large building- for this country at this time- 40 ft.
long he would think. ...the door was at one end. It was built of round logs & had
prob. been chinked w. mud & c."; there was prob. no floor at that time, as there
was no sawmill in the town, & it was "prob., like most of the other log houses,
roofed w. black ash bark, though it might have been of oak shingles 3 or 4 ft. long,
like barrel staves"- **1001**;
John Duncan's- c. 1774, Munro's Meadows, Hebron, N. Y.; it had 'puncheons'
hewn out for the floor, door & c.- **997**;
Fitch's Point, Salem, N. Y.- foll. the Rev. war, "little huts of no consequence...
built of logs & covered w. bark, (w/o floor, door, or chimney)" were erected by new
settlers, their construction taking no more than 1 or 2 day's labor, & the settler
"would thus become resident citizens, in a house of their own, the day after their
arrival"- **867**;
Neal Gillespie's- erected prior to 1789, S. Argyle, N. Y., & still standing, c. 1850,
but its condition not given- **802**; c. 1777; constructed w. wooden hinges for its
door, & a window in the building's rear- **983**;
John Lytle's- c. 1767, Turner's Patent (Salem, N. Y.); was full of cracks & w/o
chimney or floor, "only a flat stone leaning against one side of the inclosure,
against which stone a fire could be built" provided a source of heat- **738**;
Roger Reid's- (n. d.) loc. Lot No. 53, Argyle Patent; built of square logs- **802**;
Roofing- orig. was primarily of black ash bark, although sometimes of oak
shingles "3 or 4 ft. long, like barrel staves"; see Log Cabins, Vol. 1; if made of
bark, it was placed over "poles running the length of the roof & notched into the

end timbers, which were gradually shorter, above ea. other, to run the roof up to the ridge"; to prepare the bark, it "was peeled into long strips, & flattened by being piled & pressed down w. weights upon it till it dried; & then was placed on the roof, the rough side of the bark being upper- most"- **1001**

LOMBARD,
Benjamin- c. 1853, res. Marshall co., Illinois; c. 1823, purch. land in the SW corner of Warren co., Ill., bid off to pay taxes, & possibly purch. from Peletiah Fitch- **1004**
Benjamin, Jr.- res. No. 8 Clinton St., Boston, Mass.; called on Dr. Fitch, Sept. 29, 1853, to ascert. the heirs of Peletiah Fitch, offering to pay $5 to ea. heir as a quit claim, in order to obt. a more perfect title to lands his father had purch. inWarren co., Illinois- **1004**
Julia Kellogg- of Yonkers, N. Y.; m. Augustus D. Fitch, of NYC, June 5, 1867; by Rev. Alfred B. Beach, D. D.- **799**

Londonderry, N. H.- orig. colonized by Scots- Irish Presbyterians lead by Rev. Mr. Gregor (McGregor); they, & their desc. later settl. Pelham & Colrain, Mass., & from these places, settl. Salem, N. Y.; see Vol. 1- **1097**

LONG,
Edward- c. 1850, owned the Checkered House, Cambridge, N. Y.- **729**; m. Charity, dau. William & Jane (Lytle) Russell, who res. 2 houses N. of him- **737**; m. Harriet, dau. Joseph Wells, as his 1st wf.- **842**

The 'Long House'- one of the early landmark houses at Fitch's Point, Salem, N. Y.; loc. on the Mill Lot, Turner's Patent- **730**; Roger Reid res. nr. its loc., & ano. house was loc. nr. him- **867**; Capt. Aaron Martin kept tavern here foll. the Rev. war- **1065**

LOOMIS,
Marcia- m. Peter Cannon Oakley, as his 1st wf.- **950**

LORD,
John- along w. James Clark & Joseph Randel, was a neighbor of Benjamin Hough, & was abused & insulted by the Bennington mob Jan./ Feb. 1775, during Hough's imprisonment by the Vermonters- **881**

LOTT,
Abraham- (1726- 1794) Treasurer, N. Y. Colony; £ 200 designated by him from the Treasury, May 1775, for the use of Dirck Swart- **776**

LOUIS,
Col.- see Cook, Louis- **1014**

LOUISIANA- Grand Encore- 1072; New Orleans- 1005; Cane river- 1072; Red river- 841, 1072

LOURIE,
James- Co. A, 2nd N. Y., Northern Black Horse, Cav., 1861- 2- **1080**

LOVELL,
James- (1737- 1814; 1st orator commemorating the Boston Massacre; imprisoned, 1776, at Halifax, Nova Scotia) confined by the British, prob. at Boston, Mass.; Gen. Washington proposed his exchange, Jan. 30, 1776, in return for Maj. Philip Skene, but he was refused by Gen. Howe, due to the discovery of some prohibited correspondence engaged in by Lovell- **760**; Oct. 1776, Col. Philip Skene was conveyed from Hartford,Conn., to be exchanged for him, it not being known that he was already at liberty- **957**

LOWRIE,
Eleanor- m. John Lytle, of Co. Monaghan, N. Ireland- **737**
Judge- res. Union Village (Greenwich, N. Y.); his family unconnected w. Mrs. David (Lowrie) Dobbin- **732**
Miss- m. David Dobbin, of Co. Antrim, Ireland, as his 2nd wf.- **732**

LUCE,
Lt.- apparently 2nd in command, Co. A- C, 14th Iowa Inf., on their Oct.- Dec. 1861 march to relieve Ft. Randall, S. Dakota- **1089**

LUDIS,
Catharine- m. David Thomas, s. Walter & Sarah (Turner) Martin- **1046**

LUDLOW,
George Duncan- Sept. 7, 1771, W. bounds of his gr. forms E. bounds of 2,000 acres gr. to Thomas Trickett; acknowl. deed of Thomas Trickett to Peter Van Brugh Livingston & Francis Groome, recorded Apr. 24, 1775- **(L)- 936**

LUSH,
Stephen- along w. John Taylor & John Williams, purch. the foll. forefeited lands, May 25, 1785, loc. Skenesborough (Whitehall, N. Y.)- for £ 155, Lots 15- 18, containing 1,615 acres; for £ 277, Lots 30, 32, & 46, containing 1,218½ acres- **(L)- 875**

LUTHER,
Elisha- dau. Mary, m. Randall; & dau. Sarah, m. Henry, both sons of Daniel & Phebe (Rice) Marsh- **962**

LYDIUS,
Balthasar- "was prob. a son of John Henry Lydius... & uncle of the 2 foll. named persons.." (i. e., Elizabeth Cuyler Sproull & Capt. Ralph Burton Cuyler) acc. Dr. Fitch; "He was a singular batchelor [sic], who lived in Albany, John McDonald informs me,... & was the sport of the boys in the street, who were accustomed to call the oddest looking boy among them 'Old Balt Lydius' "; he d. Nov. 19, 1815, at 78- **(L)- 932**
John Henry- (Baron de Quade; 1693- 1791, s. Johannes; see Dellius, Vol. 1) 1st settler, Ft. Edward, N. Y.; 'A most grandiloquent acct.' accomp. an obit. notice, *Gentleman's Magazine,* v. 61, p. 384, 1791; Dutch, b. 1694, Albany, N. Y.; for some yrs., res. at Albany, & served as Gov. of Ft. Edward; suceeded as its Gov., 1756, by Lord Amherst; came to England abt. 1776, to solicit considerable arrears from govt. service done, & money spent, in America; left his papers here while visiting the country of his family origin, & on his return, discovered that the papers & the man he entrusted them to, had gone; his American domain "which contains many millions of acres, reaching from sea to sea, contiguous to the Hudson & Susquehanna rivers", purch. for £ 11,000 from its natives; for writing the codicil to his Will, the author rec'd. 400 acres from one of his Ft. Edward lots (prob. Lot 4, acc. Dr. Fitch); a fall in the street hastened his end, & he 'd. lately', at Hensington, England; the author of the obit., "obviously", acc. Dr. Fitch, influ. by the "Munchausen statements" of Lydius; 4 heirs, 2 of them pre- deceasing him, & the others- dau. Catharine, 1st settler's child b. in Wash. co., m. Col. Kyler; see Cuyler, Vol. 1; & Capt. Napier Christie- **930**; acc. Dr. Fitch, Balthasar, who d. Nov. 19, 1815, was prob. one of his sons- **(L)- 932**; orig. titles of Socialborough (Rutland, Vt.) purch. from him by its settlers bef. they purch. valid deeds from N. Y. proprietors- **967**

LYNCH,
Thomas- oath of alleg.; Co. D, 22nd N. Y. Inf.- **(L)- 1074**

LYNN,
Artemisia- dau. Samuel & Lucinda; m.1. Jonathan E. Danforth; 2. ____ Birch; & 3. Joseph Wright- **732**
Samuel- res.Greenwich, N. Y.; m. Lucinda ____; dau. Artemisia, b. July 22, 1739, Killingworth, Conn.- **732**

LYNTOTT,
Bernard- sold 73 acre tract to Jedidiah Darrow of Black Creek (Hebron, N. Y.)- **(L)- 936**; date of purch. noted as June 5, 1784- **(L)- 936b**

LYON,
____- carpenter, res. N. of Black creek & 15- 20 rods opp. Reuben Cheney, Fitch's Point, Salem, N. Y.; he went "down country", into Mass. or Conn., during the retreat bef. Burgoyne's army, returned after the danger was over, & after several

yrs., rem. W.; had sons Daniel, Alexander, & Thomas- **860**; res. N. side of White (Ondawa) creek; his house later occ. by James Thompson- **864**
Abner- of Sturbridge, Mass.; m. Elizabeth, dau. ____ & ____ (Newell) Martin- **849**; his wf., dau. Aaron & Sarah (Newell) Martin- **1037**; their children- Abner, Abigail, Thomas, Lucy, Ephriam, Martin, & Sarah- **1043**
John- (Lyons) he arr. at Barney Giblin's house on the night of Barney McEntee's murder after Martin Wallace, & left there at the same time, going to a tavern w. Edward Cavanaugh, while Wallace went towards the R. R. tracks- **1048s**
Capt. Thomas- c. 1779, commanded militia co. under Col. Jeremiah Burrows, stat. in the area of Skenesborough, N. Y.; as he was suffering from wnds., he was not active in scouts & other activities- **751**

LYTLE/ LYTTLE,
____- he was at a meeting of the Salem Comm. of Safety when 'Mad' More began abusing a suspected person named Robinson while he was on trial; when he attempted to intervene on Robinson's behalf, More turned upon him, began abusing him & calling him a tory; Lytle's blood boiled, & he knocked More down "& kicked him repeatedly, bestowing lavishly upon him his wonted exclamation when in anger 'You d- d son of a whoore' [sic]- **925**
____- commanded co., 4th Regt. of riflemen, prob. War of 1812, in which Peletiah Fitch was perh. a Sgt.- **1004**
Andrew- ment. as bro. John- **737**; (Lyttle) purch. Lot No. 191, New Perth (Salem, N. Y.) from Rev. Dr. Thomas Clark, for 5 shillings, Sterling, May 1, 1766- **(L)- 936b**; b. 1718, Monaghan, N. Ireland; bound out to a blacksmith when he was a child; m. Nancy Stewart; emig. c. 1757; they had 6 children, 3 b. in Ireland-
1. James, m. Mary Simpson
2. Hannah, m. Charles Nelson
3. William, m. Mary Hanna
4. Mary, m. Dr. Andrew Proudfit; she was the 1st female b. Salem, N. Y., & the 3rd child b. among the settlers
5. Andrew, m. Jane Craig
6. Margaret, m. James McClelland; one of the 1st settlers of Salem, he d. May 18, 1796, at 77- **1069**
Andrew- m. Helen, dau. Deac. John & Eleanor (Webster) Steele; moved W.- **1047**
Andrew- (s. Andrew & Nancy Stewart) orig. res. on present (1860) David Russell place, Salem, N. Y.; m. Jane Craig; rem. & res. Milwaukee, Wisc.; 6 children- Sarah, Adams, Andrew, Polly, Jane, & Nancy- **1069**
Capt.- c. 1782, commanded Chartotte co. militia- **754**
David Hanna- (s. William & Mary Hanna) m. 1. ____ Taylor; children-
1. David T., m. Jane ____, of Hartford, N. Y.
2. Emily, m. James Mills, of Argyle, N. Y.
3. William J., m. ____; res. Binghamton, N. Y.
4. Hannah Amanda, m. George Wheaton; he m. 2. Wid. Flack, & has 2 or 3 other children- **1069**

David T.- (s. David Hanna & ____ Taylor) m. Jane ____, of Hartford, N. Y.; rem. & res. Port Jackson, Wisc.- **1069**

Isaac- (s. John & Eleanor Lowrie) res. Hebron, N. Y.; m. Betsey McCool; children- John, David, Polly, Isaac, Robert, Joseph, George, Betsey, Hannah; & Nancy, who m. John McAllister, of Salem, N. Y.- **737**; he & his bro. William were working some land in W. Hebron, nr. the vicinity of where Assoc. Ref. church was built, when they were taken prisoners by a party of tories & brought to the British camp at Ft. Edward- **742**

Isaac- (s. Robert, Jr., & Esther Lytle) m. Nancy Armstrong, Lisbon, N. Y.- **737**

Isaac, Jr.- (s. Isaac & Betsey McCool) drowned Mar. 6, 1823, in a brook nr. Bull's store, N. Hebron, N. Y.; the brook was swollen, & while driving his team over it, they stumbled & he was swept away, but the team came out safely- **737**

Isaac- for £ 882, Oct. 12, 1784, purch. Lots 68 & 69, Artillery Patent; & in Skenesborough, purch. the foll., Dec. 7, 1784 - Lot 5, 115 acres, for £ 332; Lot 6, 103 acres, for £ 270; Lot 7, 127 acres, for £ 326; Lot 10, 116 acres, for £ 120; & on May 26, 1785, purch. ½ of Lot 35, 250 acres, for £ 63; & July 1, 1785, purch. Lot 42, 295¾ acres, for £ 112; & on Sept. 1, 1786, purch. Lot 14, 487 acres, for £ 61- **(L)- 875**

James- farmer, White Creek (Salem), Albany co., N. Y.; for £ 12, purch. Lot 217, Turner's Patent, from Thomas Johnson, Apr. 20, 1770; deed witn., May 1, 1766, Rev. Dr. Thomas Clark to Andrew Lyttle- **(L)- 936**

James- of Hebron, N. Y.; dau. Margaret, m. John, s. John & Betsey (Beaty) McDougall- **978**

John- of Co. Monaghan, N. Ireland; m. Eleanor Lowrie; came her in 1764, w. Rev. Dr. Clark's colony; ments. bro. Andrew; children-

1. Elizabeth, m. James Rowan, of Salem, N. Y.
2. Isaac, m. Betsey McCool
3. William, m. Jane Wilson
4. Rebecca, m. James Mills
5. Esther, m. Robert Lytle, Jr.
6. Susan, m. Robert Vance
7. Jane, m. William Russell, of Cambridge, N. Y.- **737**; his family lived in an old barracks in Schuylerville while he constructed a small cabin nr. the S. line of Lot No. 92, Turner's Patent, where it crossed Trout brook; it was loc. abt. 30 rods from the turnpike on the road to Shushan, N. Y., & the family settl. there Apr. 1767- **738**; Gen. St. Clair's army, prob. on retreat from Ft. Ticonderoga, encamped overnight in & around his house; the family's beds were all given over to his officers, & more were encouraged to remain inside, but the other officers declined, pitching their tents & allowing only the leading officers to be quartered thus- **738b**; in "the Retreat", his goods were secreted in woods & swampy thickets, & beneath some hay in the barn; none were lost, although it was ascert. some of his goods had been discovered by tories; his yoke of oxen was stolen & driven into Burgoyne's camp by 2 Salem tories, John Tod & John Cloughin, who offered him a receipt for obt. recompense, but he refused it; he moved his family & all his other goods w.

one horse, traveling on foot to Cambridge, & the family encamped on the McCool's land, nr. Wait's corners- **739**; his family's stay at McCool's was of an "uncert. length", & he returned to Salem bef. the family to see to his grain; taking sick, he sent word to his wf., who returned w. his daus. Susan, Jane, & Rebecca- **740**; (Mrs. John) she was so anxious concerning the captivity & sickness of her s. William, that she determined to go into Burgoyne's camp at Ft. Edward to find & care for him; setting out on foot, she did not find him there & foll. the army down river, ovetaking it & reaching the camp the night foll. the 1st battle of Bemis Heights (Freeman's Farm, Sept. 19, 1777); unnoticed amid the confusion, by chance, she came upon a young man from the same part of Ireland as she, & aware of someof her relatives & acquaintances there; taking an interest on her behalf, he was unable to procure any information concerning William, & she left the foll. day w. a blanket over her head so that if noticed, she would be presumed a squaw; reaching Schuylerville, she waded the river at night, nr. Deridder's ferry, & walked 16 mi. the foll. day to William Reid's at Fitch's Point, remaining there overnight; Dr. Fitch laments the irony that William's release had occurred the day bef. she entered the enemy camp when a successful attack was made upon Ft. Ticonderoga; see Brown, Lt. Col. John- **743**

John- deed witn., Apr. 20, 1770, Thomas Johnson to James Lyttle- **(L)- 936**

John R.- c. 1858, under- Sheriff, Wash. Co.- **1050s**

Maj.- children- s. Andrew, m. Helen Steele; & dau. Nancy, m. Daniel Steele; the spouses of both these children were children of Deac. John & Eleanor (Webster) Steele- **1047**

Robert- (s. Isaac & Betsey McCool?) a son, Robert, Jr., m. Esther Lytle- **737**

Robert, Jr.- (s. Robert & ____) m. Esther, dau. John & Eleanor (Lowrie) Lytle; children- Lucy, m. William Lytle; Isaac, m. Nancy Armstrong; Robert, m. ?; Elizabeth, m. ____ Armstrong; Margaret, "& c."; all res. Lisbon, N. Y.- **737**

Susan- (dau. John & Eleanor Lowrie) m. Robert Vance- **737**; b. Apr. 7, 1767, in the old barracks, Schuylerville, N. Y.; she was brought to Turner's Patent when only abt. 4 wks. old, therefore claiming to be the 1st infant in the town of Salem- **738**; foll. her family's return from "the Retreat", she & her sist. Rebecca were pulling flax in their father's field foll. dinner , when they were approached by a lone Hessian "w. his gun & military clothes"; he inquired in broken English, the route to Bennington, stating his intention to desert, but implying that he had been assigned to find the route, & the army was close behind him; shortly afterw., a party of more than a dozen tories rushed from cover, seizing & disarming him; their intent was to return him to Burgoyne's camp as a deserter, bringing Susan & Rebecca along as his accomplices; after marching their prisoners some distance, they were approached by Wm. McNish, ano."rank tory", who was familiar w. this party & convinced them that the girls would be missed; they were released into McNish's custody under condition that he hold them until after sundown, thus preventing any alarm & providing for their escape- **740**

William- (s. John & Eleanor Lowrie) m. Jane Wilson; children- John, William, Andrew, Betsey Ann, "& c."; & he d. Lisbon, N. Y.- **737**; he & his bro. Isaac were

243

capt. by some tories while they were working in W. Hebron, N. Y., & taken into Burgoyne's camp at Ft. Edward, where he was stricken w. measles during their confinement; when the army moved S., he & his bro. were sent to Ft. Ticonderoga & confined ther w. other prisoners until American troops attacked, capt. these buildings & released the prisoners (prob. Sept. 18, 1777; see Brown, Lt. Col. John); refers Hemenway's Vt. Gazetteer, ii, 936; when released, being in a weakened condition, they contrived to drag themselves over the hills & mtns. to Skenesborough, & send word home from there; their neighbor, Charles Hutchison, mounted his horse & rode to Skenesborough, & brought ea. of them back one at a time, 1st William, & then Isaac; during this time, he had developed a large abcess on his side, but Dr. Clark dared not lance it, fearing his immed. death; leaving his condition to God, the abcess eventually broke & spontaneously healed- **742**; when one of the Gillis's from Argyle sent word to his family that he was confined & sick in Ft. Edward, his mother started there to find & care for him; this was at abt. the same time as he & his bro. were moved N., & when she could not loc. him there, she foll. the army S. to Bemis Heights, & when unable to find him there, she disguised herself w. a blanket & left the enemy camp, wading the Hudson & walking 16 mi. back to Salem- **743**

William- m. Lucy, dau. Robert, Jr., & Esther (Lytle) Lytle- **737**

William- c. 1789, he acquired a wagon which was the 1st one in Salem township; "It was much talked of, & folks were afraid to ride in it- having only been used to carts before"- **738**

William- May 26, 1785, purch. Lot 12, Skenesborough, containing 565 acres, for £ 50- **(L)- 875**

William- (s. Andrew & Nancy Stewart) b. ca. 1755; m. Mary, sist. Robert Hanna, of Salem, N. Y.; children-

1. Nancy, m. Samuel Wilson
2. Hannah, m. John Armstrong
3. David Hanna, m. _____ Taylor
4. Martha, m. Robert Flack
5. Mary, m. John Gilchrist
6. Margaret, twin, m. David Thompson
7. Elizabeth, twin, d. unm., Apr. 17, 1844, Saratoga Springs, N. Y.
8. Jane, m. William L. Emmons
9. William J., d. unm., Oct. 23, 1847, at 42- **1069**

M

MacAULEY,
Lord Thomas Babington- (1800- 1859) refers to his Hist. of England, ii, pgs. 332, 333, where an acct. of Charles Blount & his book, *Oracles of Reason*, appears; Dr. Fitch notes that from the contents, Ethan Allen prob. stole the title & principle ideas for his 'Bible' from Blount- **1030**

MacCALLUM,
More- acc. Dr. Fitch, ostensibly head of the clan that 'Mad' More & "black" Duncan Campbell belonged to, & possibly the source of an increasing animosity betw. the two because of their opposing political views- **1064**

MacDONOUGH,
Comodore Thomas- (1783- 1825) "the hero of Lake Champlain"; feted at a public dinner, Nov. 29, 1814, in Salem, N. Y.; his arr. at the appt. festivities delayed as "numbers had crowded in from different parts of the county to see the hero & participate in the festivities of the day"; toasted by Dr. Proudfit, the President of the ceremonies, as "The hero, the patriot, & the christian. He is worthy of double honor, being equally devout in peace & brave in battle. May his evening sun be as serene, as its meridian efflugent"; at the same ceremony, Macdonough toasted the militia of Wash. co.- "Their patriotism was displayed in marching w. promptitude to repel the enemy at Plattsburgh"; foll. the ceremonies, he was accomp. to Cambridge the next morning, where he was again toasted, foll. by receptions in Troy & Albany, N. Y.- **709**; the battle of Plattsburgh referred to as "McDonough's battle"- **1052**; b. ca. 1783, Delaware; foll. a naval career from his youth, & honorably distinguished himself in the Tripoli war; by 1814, ranked only a Lt.; he "was a plain, unassuming man, retiring in his habits- & the Plattsburghers thought him a perfect nobody"; his victory at Plattsburgh described as "the most brillaint affair in all our naval annals", notwithstanding that a representative was sent to Wash., D. C. by the Plattsburghers w. a petitn. for his recall, to replace him w. "a swaggering, blustering, blood- and- thunder Virginian" who was a Capt. under him; the request was ignored, & "when the British was [sic] drawing nigh, the swaggering Virginia captain, w. his vessel, left the line, & ran towards shore to get under protection of the guns of the forts- presuming the others would foll. him. But seeing none of them stirred, when halfway to shore, he cast anchor, & there remained, an idle spectator of the battle. Yet he rec'd. his sword... w. those of the other commanders"; it was the desire of the Plattsburghers that the fleet should be moored nr. shore, under the protection of the guns, but Macdonough did not heed the advice, perh. suspecting they would be overrun, & he would have enemies on 2 sides; during the battle, every gun facing the enemy on his ship, the *Saratoga*, was spent & a ketch was sent out to turn the opp. side to bear upon the enemy; observing the maneuvers from shore, spectators believed the *Saratoga* was

withdrawing, & all their expectations of the Commodore had been justified; but shortly afterw., "the *Saratoga* disch. a whole broadside, well aimed, into her antagonist- carrying her mast by the board- & speedily ending the fight"; the victory won, opinion now changed, but he was unaffected by success, & during the village's ovation in his honor, "he walked in the procession, w. his wonted modest, unassuming, downcast look, although he was now the observed of all observers-the contrast betw. him & other officers being strongly remarked. One Capt. close to him... so drunk he could only walk by being supported w. his arm interlocked w. the man at his side..."; his children, however, were described as "persons of inferior abilities. Herein he is much less favored by Providence than Perry, whose son [or sons?] inherit w. the name, their father's qualities" (here the writer prob. refers to Oliver Hazard Perry, & confuses Matthew C. Perry as a son, rather than younger bro. of the other naval hero of the period); d. Nov. 24, 1815; refers Dec. 21, 1872, & Apr. 1, 1826, *N. Y. Observer*, the latter article containing an anecdote concerning his reproving ano. officer for profanity- **1056**

MacGREGORE,
Rev. Mr.- (or McGregor; prob. David; 1710- 1777); perf. marriage ceremony of William Mack, Jr., & Molly Highlands; see Londonderry, N. H., Vols. 1 & 2; also given as Gregor- **734**

MacINTYRE,
Donald- he & others, June 11, 1771, were dispossessed of their homes nr. Argyle, N. Y., by Cochran & ors.; the Albany co. Justices of the Peace were directed, after full inquiry, to give such relief as forcible entry statutes, et al., allow; see Vol. 1-**901**; brief ment. that he was driven from lands on the Vt. line (§ 335) by Ethan Allen- **999**
Duncan- came from Scotland foll. the Rev. war; m. Isabel, dau. John & Nancy (McCoy) Duncan; 8 children-
1. Nicholas, eldest, m. Lydia Henderson
2. John, m. Lucy Eaton
3. James, m. Lucy Welch
4. Peter, m. Elizabeth McGregor
5. Daniel, res. NYC, unm.
6. Nancy, m. James White
7. Duncan, m. Martha Van Duzen
8. name not given; his Wid. res. 2 mi. N. of Ft. Edward, N. Y., w. their son Duncan; she recounts the hist. of the MacIntyre & Duncan families, & other events to Dr. Fitch, who notes- "I was much disappointed in not getting more information... She seemed unable to think of anything, except as I questioned her directly upon one pt. & ano."- **998**; his wf. briefly ment.- **1000**
Duncan, Jr.- (s. Duncan & Isabel Duncan) farmer, res. 1853, abt. 2 mi. N. of Ft. Edward, N. Y.; m. Martha Van Dusen; children- Cornelia, Isabel, Elizabeth, Mary Jane, John Duncan, James Augustus; Edward, dec'd.; & an inf., not yet named- **999**

James- (s. Duncan & Isabel Duncan) res. Ft. Edward, N. Y.; m. Lucy Welch; 5 children- James, John, William, Matilda, & Mary- **999**

Nicholas- (s. Duncan & Isabel Duncan) res. Ft. Edward, N. Y.; tailor, & c. 1853, Postmaster; m. Lydia Henderson; 6 children- Daniel, Nancy, Martha, Nicholas, Mary, & Francis- **999**

Peter- (s. Duncan & Isabel Duncan) res. Wilton, N. Y.; m. Elizabeth McGregor; one child, James- **999**

MacIntyre Iron Works- operated, c. 1849, Essex co., N. Y.- **848**

MACK,
Andrew- (s. William, Jr., & Molly Highlands) rem. from Salem to Cayuga co., N. Y., & m. there- **734**

Rev. Eli Thornton- dau. Mary, m. Dr. Henry, s. Samuel & Elizabeth (Freeman) Hitchcock- **730**; operated a school, c. 1830's, Castleton, Vt.- **731**; (s. Jesse & Mary Ann McAllister) Preceptor, Granville Academy, c. 1850's- **734**

Elijah- his 4 children-
 1. Betsey, m. Chester, s. Aaron & Elizabeth (Fitch) Martin
 2. James, res. Ft. Miller, N. Y.
 3. Dr. Robert, res. Ohio
 4. Sarah, m. Thomas Coon, of Salem, N. Y.- **731**; (s. William, Jr. & Molly Highlands) part of his place was res. on for many yrs. by ____ & Naomi (Mack) Gerrold bef. they settl. in Ohio; m. Martha, dau. Hamilton McAllister (or McCollister); children-
 1. Eli, d. inf.
 2. Betsey (above)
 3. James, m. ____ Stewart
 4. Sarah, m. ____
 5. Robert H., m. Mary Abbot, of Whitehall, N. Y.
 6. John, d. prior 1850
 7. Jane (above)- **734**

James- (s. Elijah & Martha McAllister) res. Ft. Miller, N. Y.; m. dau. Deac. Stewart- **734**

Jesse- (s. William, Jr., & Molly Highlands) res. Argyle, N. Y.; m. Mary Ann, dau. Hamilton McAllister; children- Eli Thornton, Charles, John, Thomas Dick; & he d. July 11, 1850, a suicide- **734**

John- (s. William, Jr. & Molly Highlands) res. Salem, & rem. Webster, N. Y.; m. Jane Robb; children- Betsey, Margaret, John, Esther, Jane, & William- **734**

John- blacksmith; m. Isabella Brown, in Ireland; settl. Londonderry, N. H.; had 8 children- William, m. Mary Highland; Jeanett, John, Robert, Martha, Elizabeth, Andrew, & Daniel- **734s**

Dr. John- (s. Jesse & Mary Ann McAllister) physician, at Lakeville (Cossayuna, N. Y.)- **734**; he was sent for & attended Patrick Walls, foll. an accident that occurred to Walls the Thurs. bef. New Year's, c. 1854/5- **1058**

Judge- res. Salem, Mass.; his anc. William Mack, was orig. from Leith, Scotland- **734**

Oliver- (s. William, Jr., & Molly Highlands) rem. from Salem to western N. Y.; he m. there & rem. Indiana, not far from Cincinatti, Ohio- **734**

Robert- s. William; c. 1709, emig. Londonderry, N. H.; was a bachelor until late in life, then had sons Jospeh & Orlando; his grdau. Hannah, was Mrs. Hugh Montgomery- **734**

Dr. Robert H.- (R. H.) his letter, Dec. 14, 1852, informs Dr. Fitch that Dr. Willard, of Pawlet, Vt., now res. Browhelm, Lorain co., Ohio- **727**; (s. Elijah & Martha McAllister) c. 1850, res. Parma, Ohio; m. Mary Abbot, of Whitehall, N. Y.; informs concerning the Mack family history, utilizing some particulars obt. from Mrs. Hugh Montgomery- **734**

William- res. Leith, nr. Edinburgh, Scotland; had 3 sons- Robert, John, & William, Jr., all of whom emig., c. 1709, Londonderry, N. H.- **734**

William, Jr.- s. William; res. N. Ireland, & fought for King William, at the battle of the Boyne, 1690, & emig. Londonderry, N. H.; had sons William & Robert- **734**

William, 3rd- s. William, Jr.; res. Londonderry, N. H., w. his uncle Robert, & m. Molly Highlands (or Highland Molly), Rev. Mr. MacGregore officiating; served 2 yrs. in the old French war, prob. as one of Rogers' rangers, for he was noted for his vigor & fleetness of foot; was also w. Gen. Abercrombie during the assault on Ticonderoga, 1758; rem., Londonderry, Vt., in its early settlm., & prob. gave his name to the gore of land known as 'Mack's leg'; refers Thompson's Gazetteer of Vt., Windham art.; served 5 yrs. during Rev. war, prob. Seth Warner's Regt., making it 7 yrs. fighting his country's battles; he never rec'd. a pension, nor did his children receive any pecuniary recompense; he later rem. Salem, N. Y., where he d.; children-

1. Margaret, or Peggy; m. William McCleary, of Rupert, Vt.
2. Oliver
3. Naomi, m. _____ Gerrold
4. June, or Jean; m. Jacob Morrison
5. John, m. Jane Robb
6. Elijah, m. Martha McAllister
7. Jenny, m. Joel Hopkins, of Hebron, N. Y.
8. Jesse, m. Mary Ann McAllister
9. Polly, m. Robert Hopkins, of Hebron, N. Y.
10. Andrew; in addition, had 2 daus., Ruth, & Naomi?, who d. of malignant dysentery, "& unskillful doctors", in Londonderry, Vt.- **734**; m. Mary Highlands, or Hylands; orig. settl. Amherst, N. H., & then Londonderry, Vt., & finally, Salem, N. Y.; ments. same children; refers pgs. 680, 681, Hist. of Antrim, N. H.- **734s**

MACOMB,

Maj. Gen. Alexander- (1782- 1841) toasted Nov. 29, 1814, by Rev. Samuel Tomb, at ceremonies in Salem, N. Y., held in honor of Commodore Thomas Macdonough- **709**; posted his militia N. of Plattsburgh, N. Y., on the ford of the

Saranac river, w. instructions that they retreat to a quantity of stores & defend them, or if unable to, destroy them; the only land fighting that occurred during the battle of Plattsburgh/ Lake Champlain, occurred at this ford- **1055**
John- (Macombe) notice, June 17, 1776, that he & Francis A. Fister were to be sent from Hoosick, N. Y., for later confinement in the Albany jail- **890**

MADISON,
Pres. James- (1751- 1836) a division of the town of Cambridge, N. Y. into 3 parts, acc. *Northern Post,* would prob. lead to the introduction of his political perspective into Washington co.- **722**

MAINE- Portland- **974, 1090frag**; as Down- East- **1090frag**

MAINS,
James- m. Mary McNaughton; their s. James, m. Elizabeth Dobbin; & dau. Margaret, m. Miller Dobbin, of Co. Antrim, Ireland, as his 1st wf.- **732**
James, Jr.- (s. James & Mary McNaughton) m. Elizabeth, dau. David & ____ (Kay) Dobbin- **732**

MAIRS,
Rev.George- of Argyle, N. Y.; bro. Rev. James- **730**; m. Margaret, dau. Thomas & Elizabeth (Cramer) Whiteside- **805**; c. 1852, res. S. of Argyle, N. Y., & 2 houses below Daniel Livingston- **978**
Rev. James- of Galway, N. Y.; bro. Rev. George; his dau. Sarah, m. Pliny, s. Andrew & Elizabeth (Martin) Freeman- **730**
Maria- m. John, s. Thomas & Elizabeth (Cramer) Whiteside- **805**

MALCOM,
William- merch., NYC; for £ 15, May 8, 1776, purch. 100 acres on the E. side of the Hudson, Albany co., from George Stuart; land orig. gr. to George Stuart & John McDonald- **(L)- 936**
Maj. William- although a non- resident, was legally chosen as Charlotte Co. representative at the 3rd N. Y. Provincial Congress, as noted May 1, 1776; adm. to his seat, May 20th, by vote of 16 to 5, "having respectable freeholds there'- **785**

MALFORD,
Esther- witn., Feb. 2, 1756, Will of Samuel Burrows, of East Hampton, N. Y.- **1100**

MALLORY,
Hugh, Jr.- def., 1774, in separate cases brought by Hugh Munro & William Duer, Esq.- **878**
Dr. James- d. Mar. 28, 1824, at 33- **(L)- 772**

Peter- m. Hannah Trickey; he d. & his wf. m. 2nd, Daniel, s. John, Esq. & Catherine (Reid) Munroe- **812**

MALTBY,
Sarah- m. Samuel, s. Andrew & Elizabeth (Fitch) Rowland- **799**

MAN/ MANN,
_____- m. Mary, dau. John K. & Sophia (Fitch) McCleary- **730**
Isaac- examinations & proofs, for & against him, were heard by the Albany Comm. of Correspondence, Mar. 28, 1776; foll. his defense, the Comm. was of the opinion, & resolved, that he had opposed & denied the authority of & spoken disrespectfully concerning the Conitnental Congress; for the offense, he was disarmed, & for the court costs, charged w. £ 2 8s; it was further resolved that the 'Comm. of Saraghtoga' put the decision against him into effect- **827**
Isaac- "& c."; a deed for Lot 56, Kingsbury, N. Y., July 5, 1773, notes the parcel as "late belonging" to them, & bounded W. by Lot 55, belonging to Daniel Jones- **938**
Jerusha- m. Pennel, s. Ephriam Wheeler, of Killingworth, Mass.- **1038**
John- in a decision similar to that of Isaac Man, prob. on or nr. the same date, the Comm. of Correspondence ordered him disarmed & subj. to £ 3 2s in court costs- **827**

Manchester, Vt.- when the British invested the area around Castleton, Vt. foll. the battle of Hubbardton, July 7, 1777, settlers along the Indian river fled here for safety- **728**; foll. the evac. of Ft. Ticonderoga, retreating American forces under Gen. St. Clair arr. here July 9, 1777, & left the foll. morning on their way to join Gen. Schuyler's army at Ft. Edward- **738b**; families that res. here, from Return of Persons on N. H. Grants, Dec. 18, 1765, incl. _____ Smeads?, William Marsh, '& c. & c.'- **893**; acc. Col. Philip Skene, Oct. 21, 1772, a meeting held here appt. Jehiel Hawley & James Breakenridge as agents to go to England to seek compensations (prob. for the Grants people)- **907**

MANCIUS,
Dr. Wilhelmus- d. Oct. 22, 1808, at 69- **(L)- 932**

MARIN,
Mons. Joseph- commanded a detachm. of French troops, accomp. by Monsig. Piquet, who burnt the fort & "the Lydius establishments" loc. at Ft. Edward, N. Y.; actually may have been a reference to the destruction of Saraghtoga (Schuylerville, N. Y), Nov. 19, 1745; refers Land Doc., xxxvii, 187, 235- **1013**

MARS,
Julia- m. William Harren, s. Andrew & Elizabeth (Martin) Freeman- **730**

MARSH,
Amos- acc. deed record, Mar. 25, 1773, his property was the N. boundary of Lot
No. 5, Socialborough, Charlotte co., N. Y.- **745**
Amos- prob. s. Jacob & Anna; res. (n. d.) Weybridge, Vt.- **963**
Amos- Speaker, Vt. House of Representatives, 1799, 1800, & 1801; refers p. 118,
Thompson's Vt.- **963**
Anna- she & Benjamin Hough were witns., Dec. 2, 1773, to quit claim of Jacob
Marsh to Thomas Brayton- **745**; perh. wf. Jacob, the Clarendon, Vt. Justice of
Peace under N. Y. authority; foll. his death, she prob. m. 2nd, ____ Howard- **963**
Anna- m. Andrew, s. Andrew & Elizabeth (Fitch) Rowland- **799**
Judge Charles- lawyer, Woodstock, Vt.; desc. of William, Marsh, the emig.;
ments. his s. George P.- **962**
Daniel- perh. 2nd or 3rd gen. desc. of William Marsh, the emig.; res. either
Mansfield, Conn., or Mass.; was a preacher "of a sect of peculiar principles,
holding that society should have all things in common, & be governed solely by the
rules laid down in the Bible"; emig. Wyoming, Pa., where many of his neighbors
had gone, & was killed by the Indians during the Wyoming Massacre (July 3- 4,
1778)- although prob. bef. this time, acc. Dr. Fitch; his bro. Joseph brought his
wid. & 2 sons, William & Daniel, back to Mansfield- **962**
Daniel- representative (n. d.) Vt. Legislature, from Hinesburgh, Vt.; acc. John L.
Marsh, ano. member, named Spencer, stole a sum of money from him & was
arrested for the crime, but the arresting officers prob. intentionally allowed him to
escape & flee from the country- **965**
Daniel, 2nd- bef. its 1771 survey, he had already improved 12 acres, Lot No. 1,
Socialborough, Charlotte co., N. Y.- **745**; s. Daniel; rem. from Mansfield, to
Clarendon, Vt., on its 1st settlm., spending most of his life there; m. Phebe Rice;
children-
   1. Gurley, m. ____ White, of Shrewsbury, Vt.
   2. Daniel, m. Mary White
   3. Eunice, m. James O. Walker, as his 2nd wf.
   4. Randall, m. Mary Luther
   5. Henry, m. Sarah Luther
   6. Laura, m. Johnson Marsh- **962**; he was accused of being a tory, arrested & kept
under guard, & finally sent to Portsmouth, N. H., where he was imprisoned on a
filthy old ship, little better than the British prison ships at NYC; while authorities
repeatedly sent to the Vt. Comm. of Safety for proofs in order to try his case, none
were forthcoming, & he was disch. after being detained for a winter, on want of
grounds- **968**; c. 1780's, he contested w. Silas Whitney, Sr., over a strip of land
betw. their farms; while title was eventually vested in him, until that point, he
contrived to have a tenant of his own occ. the land, as a means of more readily
ousting Whitney; on one occasion, Whitney forcibly rem. the tenant, but was
unable to maintain his own possession, as Marsh "opened a window & sprang in
ere Whitney was aware of it"; once in, Marsh was as much the occupant as
Whitney, as it was understood & admitted betw. them; "being thus peaceably

within, he had a right to take in whatever he pleased. He accordingly reinstated Green & his furniture- Whitney, having no right to resist, & having nothing of his own to put in & hold possession jointly w. Green, he went home, giving up the contest" (a similar incident ment., concerning Rogers, the Squatter's, attempt to eject Archibald Livingston's wf. from her house while her husb. was away; see § 179; Vol. 1); the disputed strip was managed in an equally curious way- at one time, "they both, w. their hired help, went & mowed the grass on this disputed tract; all working together in harmony. The grass being down, both partners went home to their dinners. Grandfather had got sufficient men & teams, to come on, whilst Whitney was at home at dinner & load up all the grass, & take it over the line of the disputed tract & upon land Whitney did not claim- spreading it out there, to dry"; when Whitney returned, he "made no attempt to recover it- knowing that acc. to the custom of the times it now belonged exclusively to grdf. In this singular way did they live, side by side, several yrs. perfectly understanding that when one got such an advantage over the other, there was no course whatever but for him to submit to it, & retaliate in some analogous way to balance the acct."; acc. Dr. Fitch, these conditions prob. occurred during the period when the courts were prohibited from entertaining cases regarding title, & cont'd. until 'the quieting act' was passed, in 1785; this act of resolution was partly attrib. to the considerable standing & influ. of Marsh; refers p. 405, Slade's Vt. State Papers- **970**

Daniel, 3rd- (s. Daniel & Phebe Rice) res. Clarendon, Vt.; State Senator; m. Mary White, sist. of his bro. Gurley's wf.; children-

1. John Lodowick; m. dau. Parley Enos
2. Phebe F., m. Deac. Ira Button
3. Rodney V., m. Eliza Sprague
4. William D., m. Marsha Bowen; he d. Jan. 29, 1857, at 80; & his wf. d. Feb. 1, 1857, at 75- **962**

E.- oath of alleg.; Co. D, 22nd N. Y. Inf.- **(L)- 1074**

Family- ments. bros. Charles & William- **962**

Family- res. Mansfield, Conn., or Mass.; ments. bros. Joseph & Daniel; the latter rem. Wyoming, Pa., & was killed there by the Indians, & his bro. brought his wid. & children back to Mansfield- **962**

GENEALOGY- orig. from Kent co., England; one family member was ostensibly a Cavalier, commanding a co. for Charles I in the civil war against Cromwell; he was capt. & beheaded at Hedge Hill, & his 2 sists., dreading the vengeance of the Parliamentary party, fled to America; a neph., William Marsh, who was a young man in college at that time, attended them in their passage to New England; acc. John L. Marsh, most of the Marsh families in New England desc. from him (a claim too over- reaching & apocryphal to be substantiated by the most primary of sources)- **962**

George- (s. Johnson & Laura Marsh) farmer, c. 1852, res. Dorset, Vt.- **962**

George Perkins- (1801- 1882; 28th- 31st Congress, 1843- 49) s. Judge Charles; American minister to Constantinople (1849- 53)- **962**

Gurley- (s. Daniel & Phebe Rice) res. for some yrs. in Virginia, Kentucky, & Pennsylvania, & then returned to Clarendon, Vt., & spent most of his life there; m. ____ White, of Shrewsbury, Vt.; children- a son, & 5 daus.- William Gurley, Zilpha, Laura, Mary Ann, Eliza, & Sarah; all of his daus., except Sarah, d. w/o iss., from consumption; he res. S. of John L. Marsh, on the old Whitney farm- **962**

Henry- (s. Daniel & Phebe Rice) res. Triangle, N. Y.; m. Sarah Luther; 3 sons & 2 daus.- Laura, Phebe, Henry, George, & Charles- **962**

Jacob- farmer; res. "Claradon", Charlotte co., N. Y.; for £ 100 N. Y. currency, gave a warrantee deed for Lot No. 5, Socialborough, Nov. 20, 1772, to Thomas Brayton, of Beekman's Patent; for £ 12; he quit claim, Dec. 2, 1773, to 100 acres, to Thomas Brayton, in the right of John Wilder, "he to do the duties reserved by the charter"; witn. by Benjamin Hough & Anna Marsh; for £ 4, he quit claim, Aug. 9, 1774, to Amariah Howe, his right to 70 undivided acres in Clarendon, orig. drawn by John Wilder; witn. by Thomas Stafford & Philip Nichols- **745**; (Esq.) res. & d. Clarendon, Vt.; his s.Garley res. "somewhere out west & is prob. now dead"; ano. s. Randall, c. 1846, res. W. of Glens Falls, N. Y., & was considering moving west- **746**; a reserve, to the amt. of 200 acres per person, advised by N. Y. Council, Oct. 22, 1765, for lands actually possessed & improved by him & others; foll. the ruling regarding his occ. of lands found to be in the gr. of Capt. John Small & Mr. Napier, claims for 22 townships, within 20 mi. of the Hudson river, or South Bay & Lake Champlain, were presented to the N. Y. Council- **894**; Justice of Peace, Clarendon, Vt., under N. Y.authority; was perh. cousin of Daniel Marsh, ano. early settler of the same loc.; "he had little taste for settling down as a farmer, like the other settlers, but was more of a speculating turn, buying & selling land & c. ...His being a N. Y. Justice rendered him particularly obnoxious to Allen & his party, but he eluded being capt. when Hough was taken"; nevertheless, his situation became so critical that he rem., or had to leave town, & res. w. his family somewhere nr. Glens Falls, N. Y., & d. there; suspicions were that he had taken protection from Burgoyne; but acc. John L. Marsh, he could not have d. in Burgoyne's camp, as Daniel Marsh, 3rd, on hearing of his death, retrieved his wid. & family, bringing them back to Clarendon during the winter; his wid. prob. m. 2nd, ____ Howard; his wf.'s name was prob. Anna, the deed witn. (§ 745); his children scattered; Amos was perh. one of his sons- **963**

Jacob- defendant, May 17, 1774, in a case brought by Benjamin French- **878**

James, D. D.- (1794- 1842) s. Daniel, & grds. Joseph, of Hartford, Vt.; President, Burlington Univ. (1826- 33); d. July 3, 1842, at 48, leaving 3 children, all sons- **968b**

John Lodowick- (s. Daniel & Mary White) res. N. Clarendon, Vt.; President, Protective Union store, Rutland, Vt.; informs Dr. Fitch, Feb. 28, 1852, concerning the origins of the Marsh (all, or most of the earliest material, must be considered suspect) & suppos. that his gr. grdf. Daniel was grds., or son, of William Marsh, the emig. ancestor; m. dau. Enos Parley, of Leicester, Vt.; children- John Enos, Phebe Lorain, Mary Almena, Daniel Parley, William Gurley, & Frank Ira; he owns abt. 2,000 acres, part of which was orig. settl. by his grdf., & part still occ. by his father- **962**

Johnson- of Dorset, Vt.; m. Laura, dau. Daniel & Phebe (Rice) Marsh, of Clarendon, Vt.; one child, George- 962; grds. William, of Dorset, Vt.- **964**

Joseph- (1726- 1811) from Lebanon, Conn.; settl. Hartford, Vt., 1772; member, Convention, Lt. Gov. & c.; refers Thompson's Gazetteer; ments. one son, Daniel- **968b**

Hon. Joseph- 1st settler, Randolph, Vt., 1778; refers Thompson's Gazetteer- **968b**

Randall- (s. Daniel & Phebe Rice) m. Mary Luther; children- Fidelia, Randall, & Elisha Luther; rem. from Vt. to Triangle, Broome co., N. Y., & abt. 15 yrs. ago, c. 1837, to Corinth, N. Y.; his wf. d. Feb. 1850, in Corinth, & he rem. Farmington, Ohio, purch. a farm there, & d. July 4, 1851- **962**

Randall- (s. Randall & Mary Luther) c. 1852, has a sawmill & other property, 20 mi. N. of Corinth, N. Y.- **962**

Rodney V.- (s. Daniel & Mary White) lawyer, res. Brandon, Vt.; member, Vt. Legislature, but principally a farmer; m. Eliza, dau. Judge Sprague; children- Clarence, Francis, Cornelia, & an inf.- **962**

Thomas- his s. was prob. William Marsh, of Dorset, Vt.- **964**

William- seated, May 24, 1775, along w. John Williams, as Charlotte co. representatives, N. Y. Provincial Congress- 773; obt. leave of absence from Prov. Congress, June 15, 1775- 777; during his absence, June 29, 1775, 3 additional delegates selected to represent Charlotte co.- 780; appt. Assist. Judge, Charlotte co., May 8, 1777, by N. Y. Prov. Convention; selected Juine 25, 1777, as a Senator from the Eastern District of Charlotte co. to Prov. Congress, foll. inquiry into validity of electoral process- 787; of Dorset, Vt.; perh. s. Thomas; member, Manchester Comm. of Safety; appt. Judge when Charlotte co. courts were re-organized foll. break up of the Royal courts; commonly referred to as Col. Marsh; rem. Canada during Rev. war, drawing land nr. Kingston, Ontario; his property in Dorset was not confiscated, & he returned, possessed it again, res. & d. there, while his children retained his Canadian gr. & remained there; he had a French wf., & her relatives res. nr. Lansingburgh, N. Y.; it was prob. through her family's influ. that he obt. his N. Y. offices- **964**

William- the emig.; acc. John L. Marsh, was a young man in college, & accomp. to New England the daus. of a relative who was a Cavalier during the English Civil war; he became a commissary in troops raised for the war against the Narraganset Indians (King Philip's War, 1675- 76) & was severely wnd.; he was taken to Stonington, Conn., where he recovered; m. Elizabeth Yemmonds, & had a no. of children "from whom most of the Marsh families settl. in N. E. descend"; see *Genealogy*, above- **962**

William- bro. Judge Charles; refers p. 214, Hollister's Hist. of Pawlet, Vt. (d. 1864, at 91)- **962**

William- bro. Daniel, of Mansfield, Conn., or Mass., & Clarendon, Vt.; acc. John L. Marsh, "was something of a wanderer. He lived long in Clarendon then moved to Canada West, where he became a preacher, & d., leaving desc. of whom I know nothing"- 962

William, Esq.- he & Samuel Rose were members, Comm. of Safety, Manchester, Vt.; he reported, June 28, 1775, that 'sundry' men from var. parts of Charlotte co., & some from Albany co., were abt. to form a mob to break up the courts at Ft. Edward, N. Y.- 779

William D.- (s. Daniel & Mary White) res. Clarendon, Vt., on the farm prev. belonging to Gurley Marsh; m. Marsha Bowen; no children- 962

William Gurley- (s. Gurley & ___ White) farmer, res. Wallingford, Vt.; m. dau. Deac. Frederick Button; no children- 962

MARTIN,
Aaron- m. Sarah ___ (Sarah Newell, m. May 10, 1734, Thompson, Conn.); children-
1. Mary, b. June 6, 1737 (Sturbridge, Mass.)
2. Adam (b. Aug. 27, 1739)
3. Aaron
4. Moses (bp. Apr. 1, 1744)
5. Miriam (or Martha, b. Apr. 28, 1751); he d. (drowned, Mar. 11, 1751) & his wf. m. 2. Ruben Ellis (int. Nov. 12, 1752)- all parentheses, V. R., Sturbridge, Mass.; (he may be the Aaron, s. Thomas, b. Jan. 21, 1712, Marlborough, Mass.; see Hudson- *Hist. of the Town of Marlborough, Mass.*)- 730; m. ___ Newell, of Sturbridge, Mass.; children- Adam, Aaron, Moses; Elizabeth, m. Mr. Lyon, of Sturbridge; Sarah, prob. m. Josiah Partridge; Triphena, m. ___ Lawrence; he d. when his s. Moses was abt. 3 or 4 yrs. old, & his wf. m. 2. ___ Ellis; children, surname Ellis- Reuben, Amasa, & Moses- 849; all children, b. Sturbridge, Mass.-
1. Adam, b. Aug. 27, 1739; m. Abigail Cheney
2. Aaron, b. 1743/4; m. Olive Harding
3. Moses, b. 1745/6; m. Lydia More
4. Sarah, b. 1747/48; m. Josiah Partridge; no children
5. Mary, b. 1750; m. Joseph Morse
6. Elizabeth, b. 1752; m. Abner Lyon
7. Martha, b. 1755; m. ___ Lawrence, of Shaftsbury, Vt.; he drowned in the Quinnebaug river, 1751, or 1755, & his wf. m. 2nd. Reuben Ellis, of Southbridge, Mass., & the family rem. Shaftsbury, Vt., or Stillwater, N. Y.- 1037

Aaron- (s. Aaron & Sarah Newell)- 730; his place at Fitch's Point, Salem, N. Y., orig. occ. by ___ Miller, & purch. from John Henry by his bro., Moses, Sr., who gave it to him; he constructed the road N. along Black creek from Jarvis to Chester Martin's, as the town would not go to the expense of altering its course- 865; b. 1743/4, Sturbridge, Mass.- 1037; m. Olive Harding; children-
1. Artemas, b. May 5, 1767; m. Betsey Glover
2. Martha, b. Nov. 5, 1768; m. 1.William Phenix; 2. ___ Bartlett
3. Moses, b. Aug. 10, 1777; unm.
4. Olive, b. Dec. 7, 1770; m. Jehiel Phelps

5. Chloe, b. May 27, 1775; m. John Leeb
6. Aaron, b. Apr. 3, 1773; d. Oct. 14, 1777
7. Sarah, b. Apr, 17, 1780; m. Daniel Taggart
8. Mary,b. Sept. 26, 1782, Cambridge, N. Y.; m. ____ Beebe
9. Aaron, 2nd, b. May 11, 1785, Cambridge, N. Y.
10. John, b. Aug. 4, 1787; unm.- **1040**
Aaron- (s. Moses, Sr., & Lydia More) b. Dec. 21, 1767; m.1. Elizabeth (Betsey), dau. Dr. Peletiah Fitch, Sr.; res. 1 mi. from the Point, where his s. Jarvis now resides; his wf. d. Sept. 2, 1834; m. 2. Wid. Martha (Patty) Palen; children, by 1st wf.-
1. Aaron, Jr., b. June 2, 1792; m. Feb. 27, 1815, Artemisia Lynn
2. Chester, m. Betsey Mack
3. Josephus, m. Lucy Palen
4. Lydia, m.1. Dr. John M. Rowan; 2. William Watson
5. Jarvis, m. Mary Harvey
6. Moses, d. a minor, abt. 1827
7. Sarah, m. Edward Aylesworth- **730**; m. Betsey Fitch- **1041**; his 1st wf., Elizabeth, was dau. Dr. Peletiah & Elizabeth (Burrows) Fitch, a grdau. & heir, of Samuel Burrows- **1100**
Aaron- (s. Josephus & Lucy Palen)- **731**; enl., Co. K, 74th Illinois Inf.; autumn 1862, stat. Nashville, Tenn.; was in the battle of Murfreesboro, Dec. 31st, in the right wing that broke & retreated; in ill health, 1863, & not at Missionary Ridge w. his unit; later, became an assist. at Nashville hospitals; furloughed home, June 1864, & disch. at close of war- **1095**
Aaron, Jr.- (s. Aaron & Elizabeth Fitch) b. June 2, 1792; m. Feb. 27, 1815, Artemisia, dau. Samuel & Lucinda Lynn, of Greenwich, N. Y.; has always res. at Fitch's Point; was Justice of Peace, & Supervisor; children-
1. Lucinda C., b. Jan. 12, 1816; m.1. Jonathan E. Danforth; 2. ____ Birch; 3. Joseph Wright
2. James, b. Nov. 15, 1817; m. dau. Joseph Hanks
3. Mary, m. 1. ____ Oatman; 2. William Walker
4. Elizabeth, m. Dr. Alfred Freeman
5. Minerva, m. Justin E. Beebe; he d. Sept. 22, 1862; & his wf. d. May 12, 1853- **731**; abt. 1833, he was sent to Long Island by the Salem, N. Y. heirs of Samuel Burrows, to investigate the validity of their rights to lands at Sag Harbor, N. Y., & compiled a memorandum of the heirs of Dr. Peletiah Fitch & Moses Gore- **1100**
Adam- (Col. Adam; s. Aaron & Sarah Newell) b. Aug. 27, 1739, Sturbridge, Mass.; m. Abigail, dau. Dr. Walter? Cheney, of Sturbridge, Mass.; children-
1. Zerniah (or Zerviah, b. May 19, 1763); m. Silas Conkey
2. Walter (b. Dec. 15, 1764); m. 1. Sarah Turner; 2. Sarah Granger
3. Sarah (b. Apr. 19, 1767); m. Feb. 6, 1790, Chillus Doty
4. Abigail, b. May 28, 1771 (or Aug. 27, 1772); m. Dr. Asa Fitch, Sr.
5. Elizabeth (b. Nov. 23, 1774); m. Andrew Freeman

6. Polly (b. May 13, 1777); d. July 18, 1794, at 17, Salem, N. Y.; (parenetheses indicate V. R., Sturbridge, Mass.); he never reconciled himself to his mother's 2nd marriage, despite her repeated efforts to bring a resolution; entered Continental service at beginning of Rev. war, & enl. for 9 mos. as Capt., Col. Leonard's regt.; refers American Archives, ii, 823; participated in several engagements, "certainly" the battle of Monmouth (1778) but others not recoll.; a ball once passed through his hat, severing a lock of his hair, which he sent back to his wf. in a letter; his dau. Elizabeth, then an infant, was alarmed & cried at his return, but when he left, it was the 1st time she was perceived to have laughed- the mother crying & the baby laughing in the doorway, as he returned to service; rem., spring 1781, to Salem, N. Y., & res. at Fitch'sPoint, ¼ mi. NW of the loc. occ. by Harvey Fitch; he purch. the Mill lot from William Read, & res. for 8 yrs. in a log house that stood nr. the present "Long House"; 1787, erected a large house later occ. by Dr. Asa Fitch, Jr.; 25 men worked on its construction during the summer, half of it boarded up by them, & the other half by his s. Walter; he sold his property to Asa Fitch, Sr., & rem. Martinsburg, N. Y., June 1802, w. his son- in- law, Chillus Doty, his s. Walter having rem. there the prev. Feb.- **730**; he notes that the Martins were of Welsh origins- **849**; his house at Fitch's Point built sometime betw. 1791- 94- **852**; Feb. 1791, Thomas McLean drowned in the raceway of his mill- **(L)- 876**; Wm. Reid deeds to him, Aug. 15, 1786- **(L)- 936**; Mill Lot, Salem, N. Y., purch. for £ 900 by him, on the above date- **(L)- 936b**; his family's vital statistics given here, corespond w. § 730, except that an alternate birthdate, Nov. 23, 1773, or Nov. 10, 1774, is given for Elizabeth, & 6th child, Polly, is not ment.- **1037**; (Capt.) kept tavern at the "Long House" foll. Rev. war; when James Campbell returned from Canada for a visit, some of the more violent Salem whigs came to his tavern for a drink bef. going to tar & feather Campbell; disclosing their intent, Martin, a well known whig, made a room available to them & provided them w. all they wanted to drink, saying that the evening was too early to go on such an enterprise; while they were thus occ., he repaired to Peter McQueen's mill & informed him of their plans; the Campbells informed, McQueen started his mill as a signal to Martin that he might allow the party to continue on their errand, w. the certainty that Campbell was now safe from harm; yrs. later, Campbell returned to the area while en route to Canada, & finding no men at the tavern, asked his dau. Zerniah to feed & water his horse; when she handed him a pail & told him where the grain & water was, he took offense, thinking her a servant girl; the truth later disclosed, Campbell profusely apologized for the slight, recalling the earlier effort of her father to provide for his safety- **1065**

Adam- (s. Moses, Sr., & Lydia More) res. Salem, N. Y.; harnessmaker & once Deputy Sheriff; lost his property by intemperance; m. 1. Sabra, dau. William & Submit (Fosgate) Russell; m. 2. Mar. 7, 1814, Almira, dau. Dr. Asa Fitch, Sr.; children, by 1st wf.-

1. William R.
2. John R., m. Lavinna Burton
3. Sabra, m. James Hastings;

children, by 2nd wf., refers § 235, Vol. 1-
4. Asa F., d. inf.
5. Martin F.
6. Abby F.- **731**; c. 1818, he & Asa Fitch, Sr., had a vault constructed in the graveyard, Salem, N. Y.; he obt. the stone & the mason, & Dr. Fitch, Sr., contrib. $20.00 to the cost of the project- **799**; his parentage & marriages noted again- **1041**
Adam- (s. Walter & Sarah Turner) b. Aug. 28, 1796, Salem, N. Y.; m. Polly Granger; children- Sarah, m. Nelson Moore; Miriam, m. Morris Chase; & he d. May 4, 1826- **1046**
Andrew- res. Salem, N. Y.; m. dau. Alexander Wright, the tory- **977**
Artemas- (s. Aaron & Olive Harding) b. May 5, 1767; m. Betsey Glover- **1040**; m. ____ Glover- **1093**
Asa- (s. Moses, Sr., & Lydia More) res. Salem, N. Y.; m. Sarah Van Valkenburgh; no children; "He [was] emasculated in his youth, in consequence of retrocession of mumps"; 2 adopted children- Atwood Jenkins & Jane Pike; "He has spent his life in doing nothing. A person having a blank book in his hand, passing along the side- walk of Salem village, was asked by one, what book it was he had in his hand. 'It is the Life of Asa Martin', was the reply"; his wf. d. July 23, 1864, at 73 yrs., 4 mos., & 9 ds., of breast cancer; & he d. Dec. 1, 1851, at 62 yrs., 6 mos., of stomach? cancer; their house & lot were left to Jane Pike, who remained there- **731**; c. 1853, his wid. res. nr. orig. loc. of Dr. Clark's log meeting house- **1001**; his wf. given as Sarah Follet; no children- **1041**
Ashbel- (s. Moses, Sr., & Lydia More) killed as a boy, by running backwards in the road; Esq. McKellip's sleigh was coming from the other direction & his horses struck & killed him- **731**
Capt.- (prob. Moses, Sr.) on his behalf, John Williams requests of John McKesson, Esq., that he secure Lot No. 68, Argyle Patent, belonging to Gen. Scott; Williams notes that others are seeking the lot, but it would prob. be Gen. Scott's desire to give Capt. Martin 1st preference- **789**
Capt.- his co. of Artillery incl. in a military escort, Apr. 20, 1841, commemorating of the death of Pres. William Henry Harrison, Salem, N. Y.- **1009**
Charles Lee- (s. Walter & Sarah Turner) res. Martinsburgh, N. Y.; acc. Dr. Fitch, has the "full" genealogy of the Cheney & Martin families; m. Theodoria ____, of Lowville, N. Y., who was orig. of Springfield, Mass.; "he lost heavily by his bro. John"- **730**; he "gathered from his aunts Doty & Conkey, shortly bef. their death, & from var. other sources, full particulars of several of the branches of his family relatives" (his aunts were wf. Chillus Doty, & wf. Silas Conkey); the chief part of his manuscript copied Sept. 29, 1858, in NYC, by Dr. Fitch- **1037**; b. Dec. 3, 1802, Martinsburgh, N. Y.; m. Theodocia Benham; one child, Lewis B., b. May 22, 1831; & d. Sept. 29, 1853- **1046**
Chester- (s. Aaron & Elizabeth Fitch) m. Betsey, dau. Elijah Mack; res. at Fitch's Point, Salem, N. Y., next to his bro. Jarvis; was vey intemperate; ments. one son, John Henry- **731**; his wf. Betsey, dau. Elijah & Martha (McCollister) Mack- **734**;

res. along Black creek, N. of Jarvis Martin; the road betw. their 2 houses was constructed by Aaron Martin- **865**

Clarence- (s. Sidney & Mary Ann Hurd)- **731**; of Rockford, Illinois; enl. Co. A, 74th Illinois Inf.; shot through the head, May 1864, while on picket duty during Gen. Sherman's advance from Chattanooga, Tenn.- **1095**

David Thomas- (s. Walter & Sarah Turner) b. Nov. 3, 1807, Martinsburgh, N. Y.; m. Catharine Ludis; 4 children- Francis, b. 1842; Alice, b. 1845; David, b. Dec. 24, 1848; & Catharine- **1046**

Elizabeth- (dau. Aaron & Elizabeth ____) m. Dec. 11, 1817, Dr. Alfred, s. Andrew & Elizabeth (Martin) Freeman- **730**

Eunice- acc. to her, a son of ____ & Triphena (More) Crawford once preached (n. d.) at the schoolhouse at Fitch's Point- **851**

GENEALOGY- acc. Col. Adam Martin, the family was of Welsh origin- **849**; full particiulars of several branches obt. by Charles L. Martin, from his aunts, Zerniah, wf. Silas Conkey; & Sarah, wf. Chillus Doty, & copied Sept. 29, 1858, by Dr. Fitch- **1037**

Harriet- of Avon, N. Y.; m. John, s. Col. John & Ann (Roy) Williams; see Williams, & Wray families, Vol. 4- **1045**

Henry- bank cashier (n. d.), Albany, N. Y.; his sist. Jane, m. Anthony Blanchard, Jr.- **1045**

James- (s. Aaron, Jr., & Artemisia Lynn) b. Nov. 15, 1817; res. Fitch's Point; m. dau. Joseph Hanks; several children- Charles, Abby, Elizabeth, Ann, James, & Julia; & he d. Feb. 1862- **731**

Jarvis- (s. Aaron & Elizabeth Fitch) res. on his father's place, Salem, N. Y.; Salem Supervisor, c. 1850; m. Mary, dau. Maj. James Harvey; his wf. d. summer 1849, leaving the foll. children-

1. Caroline, m. Thomas Milliman, Jr.
2. Mary, m. Charles Gilchrist
3. James Harvey
4. Sophia
5. Alfred Freeman; several others, d. inf.; he sold out, 1865, to Robert McDowell- **731**; the road from Fitch's Point ran NE, beyond his homesite, to Chester Martin's, branching to go up Black creek at some point this side of him, & running to the rear of his property; his brick house raised on orig. site of Hugh Henry's log house- **865**

John- (s. Walter & Sarah Turner) res. Martinsburgh, N. Y.; m. Lavinna Lee, & had 3 children- John, Cornelia, & ____; he had the family homestead foll. his father's death, "but became so involved it was sold", & now (c. 1850's) suppos. employed at the Customs House, NYC- **730**

John- Lots 286 & 287, Turner's Patent, orig. conveyed to him & George Guthery, Sept. 4, 1771, by proprietors- (L)- **936**

John R.- (s. Adam & Sabra Russell) merch., Bath & Albany, N. Y.; m. Lavinna, dau. James Burton, at Sand Lake, N. Y.; children- James Burton, & Elizabeth B.;

he d. in Albany, & was bur. E. Greenwich, N. Y.; his wid. res. Albany, "teaching public school or taking boarders"- **731**
John Williams- (s. Walter & Sarah Turner) b. Aug. 2, 1799, Salem, N. Y.; res. NYC; m. Lavinna Lee; children-
1. Cornelia, b. Apr. 15, 1828
2. George G., b. Apr. 1, 1832
3. Frederick, b. Sept. 21, 1844
4. Elizabeth, b. Jan. 1848- **1046**
Josephus- (s. Aaron & Elizabeth Fitch) res. on Dr. Freeman's old place, Fitch's Point, Salem, N. Y.; m. Lucy, dau. Martha (Patty) Palen; children-
1. Mary Eliza, m. ____ Blashfield
2. Aaron
3. William Robinson
4. Martha Lucy ("Mattie L."), m. Feb. 22, 1870, Horton, s. John & Betsey (Dwelly) Cottrell (or Cotterel)- **731**; c. 1838, David Tefft took rooms from his family in part of his house foll. the favorable sale of a farm he had purch. from Newcomb Cleveland, & he later rem. from there to Battenville, N. Y.- **971**; ano. s., Lambert, b. ca. 1840, enl. Co. B, 14th Iowa Inf., d. Oct. 14, 1863- **1089**; his s. Aaron, enl. Co. K, 74th Illinois Inf.; at home on furlough, June 1864, & disch. at close of war- **1095**
Lambert- (s. Josephus & Lucy Palen) b. ca. 1840, Salem, N. Y.; enl. Co. B, 14th Iowa Inf.; his journal records a march, approx. 478 mi. long, from Iowa City to Ft. Randall, Dakota Territory, beginning Oct. 31, & ending Dec. 5, 1861, by Co. A- C, 14th Iowa Inf., to the relief of Ft. Randall; this journal, recorded by Dr. Fitch, notes var. conditions & circumstances of weather & camp life along the course of the march, & the poplations of var. Iowa communities passed through by his detachm.; see Iowa, & 14th Iowa Inf.; he was posted at Ft. Randall throughout 1862, & then rem. upriver; foll. 2 wks. illness, he d. Oct. 14, 1863, at 23 yrs., 9 mos., & 1 day, of typhoid fever, nr. Farm Island, Dakota Territory, now S. Dakota- **1089**
Lansing- (s. Moses, Jr., & Eunice Clark) m. Margaret Dunham; she "was a very good woman. Several children"- **731**
Lewis- (s. Walter & Sarah Turner) lawyer, rem. Wisc. & m. there; has been prominent in the affairs of that state, in opposition to Doty" (Gov. James Duane Doty; see Vol. 3)- **730**
Lydia- wf. James; d. Sept. 29, 1813, at 35- **(L)**- **772**
Martin F.- (s. Adam & Almira Fitch) kept store at E. Greenwich, N. Y. for a few yrs., & failed; c. 1828, stage proprietor, Whitestown, N. Y.; m. Irene Parks, in Whitestown, & c. 1850, they res. Chicago, Illinois; their 3 eldest children d. 1861, of diptheria- **731**
Morgan Lewis- (s. Walter & Sarah Turner) b. Mar. 31, 1805, Martinsburgh, N. Y.; m. Elizabeth Smith; children-
1. Stephen L., b. Aug. 26, 1838
2. Ann, b. Mar. 20, 1846
3. Melancton Smith, b. 1848; d. Jan. 13, 1849

4. Sarah Jane
5. Lewis, b. Mar. 1852
6. Deborah, b. June 1854- **1046**

Moses- bro. Aaron & Col. Adam- 730; (s. Aaron & Sarah Newell) appears to be well educ. for his day; came to Stillwater, N. Y. when a young man, & was employed as a school teacher; here he became acquainted w. & m. Lydia More; children-

1. Aaron, b. Dec. 21, 1767; m. 1. Elizabeth (Betsey) Fitch; 2. Martha (Patty) Palen
2. Triphena, m. Augustus Angel
3. Miriam, m. Capt. Abner Dwelly
4. Moses, Jr., m. Eunice Clark
5. Anna, m. Abner Glines
6. Adam, m. 1. Sabra Russell; 2. Submit ("Metty") Fosgate
7. Ashbel, d. y.
8. Lydia, m. James McNitt; they rem. Salem, N. Y., when Dr. Clark's colony came, & settl. at Fitch's Point, Argyle Patent, just beyond the border of Turner's Patent; he appears to have been the 2nd settler at Fitch's Point, & was a prominent patriot during the Rev. war, assoc. w. Williams, Webster, Russell, & Savage in "managing the patriot cause in this district"; was afterw. Justice, Supervisor, Clerk, surveyor, "& c."; there being no need to reserve pine trees 'for Masting for the Royal Navy', as the orig. titles to Patents called for, he laid out the Pine Lands in Turner's Patent into 3 acre lots, & also surveyed all of Camden into its present lots; he was taken sick w. bilious cholic while surveying lands down on Lake Champlain & suddenly d. June 14, 1792, at 48 (at 49, acc. Aaron Martin's Bible- Dr. Fitch); & his wf. d. June 5, 1822- **731**; a dam & sawmill, on the Jackson side of the Battenkill at E. Greenwich, N. Y., was built for him by Augustus Angel- **847**; his wf. Lydia, dau. Ephriam? More- **850**; his father d. when he was only a few yrs. old, & he was raised in Sturbridge, Mass., by an uncle; served in the old French war, & on its close, came to Stillwater, where he taught school & was m.; his farm there was loc. on the E. side of the Hudson & his 2 eldest children, Aaron & Miriam, were b. there; rem. Fitch's Point, using an ox cart & an old mare to do so; his dau. Triphena, was the 1st of the family b. at the Point; he was away during the Rev. war, either w. the army, or in scout parties- **852**; when Salem was evac. bef. Burgoyne's army, Daniel Livingston, one of his tenants, helped move the family; some of their valuables were bur. & others sunk in the well, the remainder were taken on the ox cart, w. Livingston driving the cart, & Aaron & Miriam riding there; Mrs. Martin rode on the family's old mare, w. Triphena tied on behind her; they forded the Battenkill at McKellip's, passing the Jackson Ponds, & through Cambridge & Sancoick to Brown's, at Hoosick, N. Y., a site that their father may have pre- arranged; at this time, Aug. 1777, Moses, Jr. was b., & the family prob. returned foll. Burgoyne's surrender- **853**; a partial listing of the articles bur. in his garden, or sunk in the well, incl. pots, kettles, pewter plates, & an iron trammel; all these items were stolen by the tories, his wf. strongly suspecting the Bowman

family of Jackson; he purch. ____ Miller's place at Fitch's Point from John Henry, & gave it to his bro. Aaron- **865**; when he 1st arr. from Stillwater, he purch. & res. on ____ Germond's place; his children Aaron, Miriam, Moses, Jr., & Triphena, were all bapt. at the same time by Dr. Clark- **867**; dau. Triphena, wid. Augustus Angel, recalls only 2 whipping sentences given by him- to Tucker, for his wf.'s theft, & to James Orr, also for stealing- **868**; purch. May 26, 1785, Lot 13, Skenesborough, 543 acres, for £ 50- **(L)- 875**; deed witn., Apr. 15, 1782, Ephriam Wheeler to Phineas Bennet; & Dec. 16, 1791, Dr. Peletiah Fitch to James Tomb; his bond as loan officer recorded, Oct. 20, 1785, w. sureties provided by Joshua Conkey & Hamilton McCollister- **(L)- 936**; b. 1745/6, Sturbridge, Mass.- **1037**; their children, same data given as § 731, except Almira Fitch given as 2nd wf. Adam, & Sarah Follet (Van Valkenburg) given as wf. Asa- **1041**

Moses, Jr.- (s. Moses & Lydia More) res. in the 'red house', his father's old place at Fitch's Point, where his s. now lives; m. Eunice Clark; children-

1. Polly, m. Joseph Carter
2. Harriet, m. John Wells
3. Lansing, m. Margaret Durham
4. Sidney, m. Mary Ann Hurd
5. Lydia, m. James Mac Whorter Getty
6. Lucy, m. Thomas Gourly Getty; "He was the meanest of the whole family; stingiest; hated universally. Called 'Holy Moses' commonly, because, having no regard for religion, but purely out of love of making other folks trouble, he was once quite active in prosecuting those who violated the Sabbath by travelling"; his wf. d. Mar. 31, 1852, at 70; rheumatism caused one of his hips to go out of shape, & shorten his leg, making him a cripple; he d. Dec. 6, 1835, at 58, suddenly & unexpectedly, of dropsy- **731**; b. Aug. 1777, Hoosick, N. Y., foll. his family's evac. from Salem to escape from the advance of Burgoyne's army- **853**; the names of his children, most of them res. Wisc., except Sidney, who res. Rockford, Illinois; the names of their spouses not given- **1041**

Pliny F.- (s. Adam & Almira Fitch) b. Sept. 4, 1822; merch., E. Greenwich, N. Y.; m. Feb. 20, 1849, Sarah Ann Baker; children-

1. Catharine Elizabeth, named after her 2 aunts; b. Mar. 6, 1850; d. Apr. 26, 1867, of consumption
2. Pliny, d. 1861, of diptheria; he now (c. 1850) pursues school- teaching, & attends seminary at Whitesboro, N. Y.- **731**

Polly- (dau. Col. Adam & Abigail Cheney) d. July 18, 1794, at 17, "in the south front room of my present home"- Dr. Fitch; refers § 98; see Vol. 1- **730**

Sidney- (s. Moses, Jr., & Eunice Clark) m. Mary Ann Hurd; he owns the family property, his bro. Lansing "being so involved in his pecuniary affairs, that he made over the farm to Sidney"; presently (c. 1850) Lansing, Sidney, & their mother occ. different parts of the "red house", living apart; he sold out & rem. Rockford, Illinois foll. his mother's death (Mar. 31, 1852)- **731**; res. Fitch's Point, N. Y.; brief ment.- **996**; by his 1st wf., had 2 daus. & 2 sons- Clarence & Henry; he m. again, & had one dau.- **1095**

Susan- (dau. Walter & Sarah Turner) b. in the house now occ. (prob. 1850) by Dr.
Fitch; it was thought that she became deaf due to exposure to cold & damp during
her infancy; m. Dr. John Safford, & d. leaving a dau., Mary- **730**

Thomas- res. Martinsburgh, N. Y.; m. ____ Lewis; 2 children- **730**

Triphena- (dau. Moses & Elizabeth Fitch) b. Oct. 14, 1774; m. 1790, Augustus
Angel- **846**

Hon. Walter- (s. Col. Adam & Abigail Cheney) rem. Feb. 1801, Martinsburgh,
N. Y., & was a proprietor there; m. 1. Sarah Turner, who d. Aug. 4, 1815, at 45; &
2. Sarah Granger; children, by 1st wf.-
1. Jane, m. Stephen Leonard
2. Abby, m. Philo Rockwell
3. Walter, m. Miss Ives, of Turin, N. Y.
4. Adam, d. "many yrs. ago", Martinsburgh, N. Y., leaving 2 daus., names not
   recoll.
5. John, m. Lavinna Lee
6. Charles Lee, m. Theodoria ____
7. Lewis, rem. Wisc.
8. Thomas, m. Miss Lewis
9. Susan, m. Dr. John Safford; a child, by his 2nd wf.-
10. Mary, who res. Binghamton, N. Y., & m. there; his 2nd wf. d. Jan. 25, 1824,
at 35- **730**; his farm & mills at Fitch's Point purch. Sept. 4, 1795, by Dr. Asa Fitch,
Sr.- **799**; he d. Dec. 10, 1834, Martinsburgh, N. Y.- **1039**; his 1st 6 children b.
Salem, N. Y., & the remainder b. Martinsburgh, N. Y.-
1. Jane, b. Feb. 16, 1788; m. Stephen Leonard
2. Abigail, b. June 24, 1790; m. Philo Rockwell
3. Susannah, b. July 19, 1792; m. John Safford
4. Walter, b. Apr. 30, 1794; m. Julia Ives
5. Adam, b. Aug. 28, 1796; m. Polly Granger
6. John Williams, b. Aug. 2, 1799; m. Lavinia Lee
7. Charles Lee, b. Dec. 3, 1802; m. Theodocia Benham
8. Morgan Lewis, b. Mar. 31, 1805; m. Elizabeth Smith
9. David Thomas, b. Nov. 3, 1807; m. Catharine Ludis
10. Mary, b. Aug. 6, 1812; d. July 2, 1813
11. Mary, b. June 1817; m. Charles L. Robinson- **1046**

Walter, Jr.- (s. Walter & Sarah Turner) m. ____ Ives, of Turin, N. Y., & res.
Marshall, Michigan; he studied law w. Hon. John Crary, Salem, N. Y., but did not
do much business; spent enormous sums on gambling, but was never intemperate;
now (c. 1850) owns a farm, & has 6 or 7 children; their dau. Susan, dec'd.- **730**; b.
Apr. 30, 1794, Salem, N. Y.; m. Julia Ives; 9 children- Jane, Walter, John; Bolivar,
d. Aug. 1, 1828, at 2 yrs., 11 mos., & 15 ds.; Susan, dec'd.; Martha, d. 1855;
James; Charles, d. Apr. 19, 1834, at 2 yrs., 4 mos., & 6ds.; & Charles; he d. 1864-
1046

Willard Cheney- (s. Adam & Abigail Cheney) built a plank house (n. d.) at Fitch's Point, nr. Harvey Fitch, that was torn down in 1838, when Fitch constructed his house here- **730**

William H.- res. Jackson, N. Y.; while visiting at his house, Apr. 2, 1862, Mrs. Ann Barton informs Dr. Fitch concerning members of the Barton & Glover families- **1093**

William R.- (s. Adam & Sabra Russell) "a deaf mute, strayed away & suppos. to have been run over by a rail- road car, from a newspaper notice of an unknown date"- **731**

MARTIN'S JOURNAL- kept Oct. 31- Dec. 5, 1862, by Lambert Martin, Co. B, 14th Iowa Inf.; records the approx. 478 mi. march of his regt. from Iowa City, Iowa, to Ft. Randall, Dacota Territory, to relieve Federal troops stat. there; the line of march proceeded directly W. through Des Moines to Council Bluffs, & then N. to Souix City, & then to Vermillion, now S. Dakota; see Iowa, & 14th Iowa Inf.- **1089**

MARVIN,
Philander B.- 2nd Lt., Co. D, 93rd N. Y. Inf.- **1090b**

MARYLAND- 949b, 1060; Annapolis- 799; Baltimore- 1030, 1097, 1098; Blandensburgh- 722; Centreville- 1097

MASON,
Daniel- youngest s. Maj. Gen. John; his oldest s. was Daniel- **759s**
Daniel- oldest s. Daniel; his only s. was Jeremiah- **759s**
David- s. David; res. Hartford, N. Y., settl. here abt. 1795; m. Susanna West; 8 children-
  1. Wealthy
  2. Elizabeth (Betsey), m. ____ Lathrop
  3. Daniel, m. ____ Lathrop
  4. David
  5. Mary (Polly)
  6. Susan, m. John C. Parker, Esq.
  7. Nancy, m. Obadiah Noble
  8. Cynthia, m. Hon. Nathaniel Hall, as his 2nd wf.; & he d. abt. 1805- **759s**
David- (s. David & SusannaWest) lawyer; grad. Williams College, 1796; practiced in Cooperstown & Montgomery, N. Y.; ments. sons Dr. Theodore, of Brooklyn, N. Y.; & John, of Illinois-**759s**
David- s. Jeremiah; farmer, res. Norwich, Conn.; his s. David rem. Hartford, N. Y.- **759s**
Families- of Ft. Ann & Granville, N. Y.; they were orig. from R. I., & unrelated to David Mason, of Hartford, N. Y., who was from Norwich, Conn.- **759s**
Jeremiah- s. Daniel; his only adult sons were David, of Norwich, Conn.; & Col. Jeremiah- **759s**

Col. Jeremiah- s. Jeremiah; m. Elizabeth Fitch; ments. s. Hon. Jeremiah- **759s**
Hon. Jeremiah- (1768- 1848; s. Col. Jeremiah & Elizabeth Fitch) Atty. Gen. N. H.
(1802- 05); U. S. Senator (1813- 17), subsequently a lawyer, Boston, Mass.; acc.
Chancellor Walworth, 'he occ. a place in the front rank of the Bar of Mass., where
a Webster, a Choate, w. many other prominent men in the same profession, had
obt. an emminence which has prob. not been surpassed in any age'- **759s**
Maj. Gen. John- (1600- 1672) of Norwich, Conn.; emig. abt. 1630; Deputy Gov.,
Conn.; ments. youngest s. Daniel- **759s**; (Maj.) a commander during the Pequot
War; dau. Priscilla, m. Rev. James Fitch, as his 2nd wf.- **799**; same material;
referred to as 'the celebrated commander', et. al.- **834**

Masonic burial ground- loc. betw. Granville corners & Middle Granville, N. Y., on
the E. side of the highway; it was deeded by Dr. Ira Hall's Will, May 6, 1816, to
the Granville Lodge & Chapter of Masons, & consisted of the SW portion of his
farm- **759s**

MASSACHUSETTS- 701, 739, 773, 794, 797, 799, 806, 816, 834, 836, 837, 860,
887, 921, 989, 1002, 1029; New Plymouth- 988; Plymouth colony- 988; Western
Mass.- 988;
  Counties- Berkshire- 755, 797, 799, 870, 921, 989, 1072; Hampshire- 797;
Middlesex- 836; Suffolk- 799;
  Cities & Towns- Adams- 1048s; Andover- 1087; Ashfield- 751; Ashford- 755;
Barrington- 755; Bedford- 806; Boston- 728, 747, 748, 759s, 760, 799, 804, 894,
928, 944, 974, 1004, 1010, 1027, 1072, 1079, 1093; Braintree- 757; Brimfield-
1038; Brookfield- 936, 1044; Buckland- 813;
  Cambridge- 775, 799, 835; Cohasset ("Chocksett")- 847; Colrain- 1097;
Dartmouth- 806; Deerfield- 1016; Dorchester- 731; Duxbury- 757; E. Bridgewater-
757; Easthampton- 837; Egremont- 799; Fitchburg- 758; Great Barrington- 870;
Hancock- 747; Hopkinton- 799, 836; Housatonic- 989; Ipswich- 799, 835;
  Killingworth- 1038; Lenox- 730, 1039; Lexington- 857; Longmeadow- 1016;
Mansfield- 962, 967; Marblehead- 747; Marshfield- 757, 962, 967; Medfield- 758;
Montague- 751; Newbury- 759s, 811; New Marlborough- 799; N. Adams- 730;
Northampton- 835; Norwich- 847;
  Palmer- 997; Pelham- 997, 1044, 1097; Plymouth- 757; Quincy- 835;
  Richmond- 747, 799; Roxbury- 728; Rutland- 750; Salem- 734, 759s, 835;
Sheffield- 947; Stockbridge- 747, 837; Sturbridge- 730, 758, 849, 852, 860, 1037-
1039, 1093; Sutton- 759s; Warren- 758; Westfield- 730; W. Stockbridge- 747;
Williamstown- 744, 747, 799; Worcester- 1039;
  Features- Boston harbor- 1079; Bunker Hill- 1010; "Captain's Hill", Duxbury-
757; Hoosic Mtn.- 1028; Pawtucket falls- 883; Quinnebaug river- 1037

MASSER,
William- defendant, May 19, 1774, in a case brought by Robert Sinclair- **878**

MATHER,
Cotton- (1663- 1728) his *Magnalia* (Magnalis Christi Americana; or the Ecclesiastical Hist. of N. E., 1702) gives some acct. of Rev. Henry Whitfield, of Guilford, Conn.- **834**

MATHEWS,
David- his house was erected nr. the house where Col. Baum had been carried to foll. the battle of Bennington- **801**; s. James; built the brick house loc. in SE corner of Wash. co.; its loc. was not as prev. stated (Vol. 1), the line betw. Rens. co. & Wash. co. being some 70 rods N. of the house, & the town line of Bennington & Shaftsbury, in the NW corner of Bennington co., Vt., are 120- 130 rods S. of the house; the Matthews desc. have left here many yrs. ago & now res. Cortland co., N. Y.; the house is now (1853) owned by James Perry- **1022**
Deac. David- a dau. m. James, s. John & Molly (Craig) Harsha- **973**
Deac.- (Matthew) purch. (n. d.) the "sequestrated" farm of John Todd, the tory, of Salem, N. Y.- **744**
Dr.- (prob. James McFarlane, D. D., 1785- 1870) of NYC; 'aged & venerable', as a youth, res. Camden valley, Wash. co., N. Y.; he once preached, prior 1835, at the Garden St. church on Exchange St., NYC- **1075b**
Family- c. 1798, res. above the Seelye family, on the E. side of the Hudson, below Ft. Miller, N. Y.; he was a bro. of the David Matthews who built the noted house in the SE part of Wash. co., presently (1850) occ. by Esq. Mott; Dr. Fitch notes that Mrs. Chubb (§ 101- 103; Vol. 1) prob. identified him as Eldridge- **804**
Horace P.- Co. A, 2nd N. Y., Northern Black Horse, Cav., 1861- 2; see Vol. 3- **1080**
James- reportedly a tory, c. 1777, he res. some 40? rods E. of the brickhouse built by his s. David, on the present road along Walloomsac river; Col. Baum was carried to his house after being wnd. in the battle of Bennington, & d. here- **1022**

MATTISON,
J. B.- oath of alleg.; Co. D, 22nd N. Y. Inf.- **(L)- 1074**

MAXWELL,
*Col.-*acc. his pens. appl., an officer witn. during Apr. 1776- Feb. 1777 service of Ebenezer Farnsworth- **750**
David- res. S. Argyle, N. Y.; he acquired notoreity by being the 1st person to plow over the bur. site of the Allen family; his neighbors, & even his son, "were very indignant at this act"- **983**
James- m. Mary Ann, dau. Daniel Livingston- **854**
Walter- m. Jenny, dau. Daniel Livingston- **854**

MAYHEW,
____ - he traded at Wm. Duer's Ft. Miller store after Hugh Pebbles had left in 1791, failed in the business, & was foll. by Mr. Wicks, who left in 1797- **1032**

Mc- surname prefix; resolution, June 5, 1776, bef. Albany Comm. of Correspondence, directing the Postmaster of Albany to bring bef. the Comm. all letters directed 'to any persons whose name has a Mc for its completion', to be examined & returned, if found to be of a solely private nature- **889**

McALLISTER, see also, *McCOLLISTER,*
_____ - Irish; m. Jane, dau. William & Margaret (Andrew) Dobbin; they later res. DeKalb co., Illinois, in the same neighborh. as his bro.- in- law, David Dobbin- **732**
Dr. Archibald- of Salem, N. Y.; m. the only dau. Dr. Ephriam & _____ (Newell) Allen; see Vols. 3 & 4- **758**; his statement (§ 246; Vol. 1), disagrees w. Reubin Clark's acct. that old 'Festus' was killed at the battle of Bennington- **768**
Capt. Edward?- of Wash. co., N. Y.; c. 1861, stat. at Cairo, Illinois; unit not given- **1080**
John- m. Nancy, dau. Isaac & Betsy (McCool) Lytle- **737**

McALPIN,
Capt.- along w. Lt. Swords & John Munro, a June 4, 1776 order directs their rem. to ano. place of confinement, 'prepared for them in the fort' (prob. in Albany, N. Y.)- **889**

McARTHUR,
Duncan- res. on Esq. Reid's place foll. the Rev. war; m. dau. "white" Duncan Campbell; his wf.'s bro. James had come down from Canada to visit her father, & when word came to them that some whigs intended to tar & feather her bro., he fled to her house for safety; see also, Martin, Adam- **1065**

McAULEY,
William- d. Apr. 6, 1842, at 84- **(L)- 975**
William- d. Aug. 27, 1778, at 60- **(L)- 975**

McBAIN,
Seneca- Co. A, 2nd N. Y., Northern Black Horse, Cav., 1861- 2- **1080**

McCALL,
Aaron- c. 1850, kept store at S. Argyle, N. Y.- **802**
Duncan- of Munro's Meadows, Hebron, N. Y.; although unrelated to the McCalls who res. at Skenesborough, he was the bearer of the news regarding their deaths (Mar. 21, 1780, when the Indians & tories capt. & destroyed Skenesborough; § 244); acc. John McDonald, the news arr. during warmer weather, which suggests that their murders occurred at some time other than when the place was eliminated as a northern outpost of the American army- **1000**
John- of Hebron, N. Y.; m. Nancy, dau. John & Nancy (McCoy) Duncan; c. 1853, res. Roxbury, N. Y.; 3 sons- Allen, James, & John- **997**

267

Mr.- he & his wf. res. abt. 1½- 2 mi. E. of Skenes' stone house; they were both murdered, Mar. 1779 [sic], when tories & Indians attacked the American garrison here- **751**; acc. John McDonald, reports of their murder arr. in warmer weather, suggesting that they were killed some time after Skenesborough had been capt.; see Vol. 1- **1000**

McCARR,

Capt.- was sent under a flag of truce, late fall 1781, to give a packet from Lord Stirling to the British commander at Crown Point, giving the news of Cornwallis' surrender- **750**

McCARTER,

Samuel- res.Salem, N. Y.; he traded w. Daniel Shays for the horse he had fled Mass. on, & owned the horse for several yrs. afterw.- **701**

McCHESNEY,

William- Salem, N. Y.; Dec. 8, 1802, killed by an accidental fall; "[coming from Tomb's still, drunk, he fell into a pile of boards & broke his neck]"- Alex. McNish, Coroner- **(L)- 876**

McCLAIN, see also, McLEAN,

Alexander- his affidavit bef. N. Y. Council, Mar. 16, 1763, informs of a N. H. survey party seen in the area of Crown Point during the preceding Sept.- **928**

McCLEARY,

Henry K.- s. Hon. John, Sr.; merch., Chicago, Illinois; m. Sophia, dau. William & Lucinda (Conkey) Fitch; d. Sept. 17, 1867, leaving 2 sons & a dau. Mary, who m. ____ Mann- **730**
Jane- m. William, s. Robert & Susan (Lytle) Vance- **737**
Hon. John, Sr.- his s. Henry K., m. Sophia Fitch- **730**
William- of Rupert, Vt.; m. Margaret, dau.William, Jr., & Molly (Highlands) Mack; children- William, David, Margaret, Naomi; & Mary, who m. Thomas Sheldon, & occ. the old McCleary farm- **734**

McCLELLAN,

C. L.- oath of alleg.; Co. D, 22nd N. Y. Inf.- **(L)- 1074**
James- of Hebron, N. Y.; dau., m. Deac. George, s. Hugh & Mary (McWhorter) Harsha, as his 1st wf.- **973**; m. Margaret, dau. Andrew & Nancy (Stewart) Lytle; children- Betsey, William, John S., Polly, & Hannah- **1069**
James C.- Corp., Co. A, 2nd N. Y., Northern Black Horse, Cav., 1861- 2- **1080**
James R.- oath of alleg.; Co. D, 22nd N. Y. Inf.- **(L)- 1074**

McCLOUD,
Norman- early settler, c. 1770's, Munro's Meadows, Hebron, N. Y.; his wf. was the midwife of the neighborh. & for a large district around- **998**

McCOLLISTER, see also, *McALLISTER,*
Hamilton- dau. Martha, m. Elijah, s. William, Jr., & Molly (Highlands) Mack; dau. Mary Ann, m. Jesse, bro. Elijah Mack- **734**; an orig. settler (c. 1763) of Salem, N. Y., along w. James Turner, Joshua Conkey, David Webb, "& c."; sold his place to Dr. Clark during the Rev. war- **744**; May 26, 1785, purch. ½ of Lot 35, Skenesborough, containing 250 acres, for £ 63- **(L)**- **875**; Sheriff, Wash. co., & plaintiff, Nov. 1786, vs. Asaph Cook, Jr.- **878½**; he & Joshua Conkey provide sureties, Oct. 20, 1785, for Moses Martin's bond as loan officer- **(L)**- **936**; along w. Moses Martin & Joshua Conkey, May 9, 1786, gave sureties again for Martin as loan officer- **(L)**- **936b**; ments. s. William; & dau. Betsey, who m. ca. 1800, Stephen, s. Deac. John & Betsey (____) Rowan- **1049**
William- res. above Harvey (James Harvey) Fitch, at Fitch's Point, Salem, N. Y.; c. 1851, Dr. Fitch notes that a pine tree was struck by lightning in his grove (among the numerous ments. of instances of the phenomena occurring within his neighborh.)- **996**

McCOLLUM,
John- res. Argyle, N. Y.; his loc. presently (1852) occ. by Deac. Lendrum; m. Jane, dau. Alexander McDougall- **978**

McCOMB,
Sarah?- "whose connections were highly respectable"; m. Col. John P. Fister, known in the vicinity of Hoosick, N. Y., as old 'Festus'- **768**

McCONIHE,
Capt. Samuel- Co. K, 93rd N. Y. Inf.- **1090b**

McCOOL,
Betsey- m. isaac, s. John & Eleanor (Lowrie) Lytle- **737**
Family- c. 1777, res. nr. Wait's corners, Cambridge, N. Y.; a number of Salem families, incl. John Lytle's, encamped on their land during "the Retreat" bef. the advance of Burgoyne's army- **739**

McCORMICK,
____ - res. Mattison, Ohio; m. Elizabeth, dau. Adam & Betsey (Lee) Conkey- **730**

McCOUN,
Family- c. 1777, res. nr. the "white meetinghouse", Cambridge, or White Creek, N. Y.; immed. foll. the evac. of Salem, William Boyd's family took overnight accommodations here- **729**

McCOWIN,
Hugh- plaintiff, Jan. 16, 1775, vs. Joseph Hughes- **878**

McCOWN,
Alexander- res. Bardstown, Ky.; he was a friend of John Fitch, the steamboat inventor, & kept & cared for Fitch's models & other items foll. the inventor's death in 1798; in 1804, a fire at his house destroyed all of the inventor's items that had been stored by McCown; ments. s. William- **949b**
William- s. Alexander; his father would often point out to visitors the unmarked loc. of John Fitch's grave; on Oct. 5, 1854, he placed a head & foot stone at this loc., but the markers have since 'entirely disappeared'- **949b**

McCOY,
Betsey- m. Joseph, s. James & Rebecca (Lytle) Mills- **737**
Capt.- (Capt. Robert E.?, Co. B; p. 75, Johnson's Hist. of Wash. Co.) of Ft. Edward, N. Y.; May 25, 1861, commanded Co. G, 22nd N. Y. Inf.- **(L)- 1074**
James- oath of alleg.; Co. D, 22nd N. Y. Inf.- **(L)- 1074**
Nancy- c. 1760's, m. John Duncan, in Scotland, & emig. 1771- **997**

McCRACKEN,
Joseph- Oct. 12, 1784, purch. for £ 323, Lot 59, Arttillery Patent, containing 242 acres- **(L)- 875**; of New Perth (Salem, N. Y.) he & John Williams gave a quit claim for Lot 8, Morrison's Patent, Granville, N. Y., to Asaph Cook, May, 7th yr. of Independence (1782); also w. Williams, Apr. 13, 1783, deeds Lots 9 & 12, Morrison's Patent, to David Curtis; & again, along w. Williams, purch. Lot 1, Morrison's Patent, Aug. 16, 1787, from Comm. of Sequestration, & deeded it to John Stockings- **(L)- 936**; the purch. prices of above transactions noted- to Cook, for £ 20; to Curtis, for £ 7 4s 2d; to Stockings, for £ 13- **(L)- 936b**
Capt./ Col. Joseph- res. Salem, N. Y.; raised a full co. of 56 soldiers, & entered Continental service during the Rev. war- **729**; Nov. 27, 1775, rec'd. his enl. orders from Gen. Schuyler- **784**; presented a payroll & an acct. of expenses & disbursements to Albany Comm., June 8, 1776, for men in his co. employed during the taking of Ft. Ticonderoga- **890**; (Col.) lost an arm during the battle of Monmouth (June 28, 1778)- **1002**; some of his sons, along w. members of the Hopkins families, & other neighbors of Gibson, the tory, came to his door one evening & fired a volley through it; when Gibson's land was later confiscated, he purch. it- **1073**; (Col.) a dau., m. Nathan W. Wilson, of Salem, N. Y.- **1081**
William- of Salem, N. Y.; m. dau. Joseph Younglove- **843**; s. Capt. Joseph; acted as his father's servant, or waiter, while in the army, & was present w. him at the battle of Monmouth (which conflicts w. a later report; see § 2100; Vol. 4)- **1002**

McCREA,

_____ - a neph. of Jane; "had ruined himself by dissipation, & was anxious to reform"; his family res. Ballstown, N. Y., but feeling that he lacked suffic. self control, he solicited employment in St. Lawrence co., at Clinton State Prison, as the sale of liquor was prohibited within a 3 mi. radius of the prison; by an ironic twist of fate, a neph. of David Jones, his aunt's fiancé, became a prisoner here during the time of his employment- **1054**

Elizabeth- defendant, along w. Martha McCrea, Nov. 3, 1784, in a case brought by John & Susanna Williams, administrators of James Turner- **878½**

Jane- an acct. of her murder by an eyewitn., Samuel Standish, from his Rev. war pens. appl.; when assigned to relieve the guard on the hill (prob. the block house N. of the village; see § 578; Vol. 1) above Ft. Edward, he was not long at his post bef. he heard an Indian scream & was fired upon; running towards the river & fort, he was met by 3 Indians coming out from betw. the 2 locs., & fired upon, but missed by all 3; he was then taken prisoner, brought uphill nr. a spring, & stripped of his coat, hat, & handkerchief, & then pinioned; shortly afterw., a party of Indians made their way uphill to the spring w. 2 women; a quarrel seemed to occur, & one of the women was shot & scalped; he recognized the murdered woman as Jenny McCrea, who he had seen bef., & the other woman was her aunt, old Mrs. McNeil; bef. this incident, he reports that the American army had offered to take her down river, but she refused, saying that she was not afraid to stay- **747**; Samuel Standish noted again as an eyewitn. to her murder- **757**; John Jones, a non-commissioned officer of the 44th Regt., was an uncle of her fiancé- **931**; c. 1777, she & John Allen's family ment. as the only settlers murdered in this area during the Burgoyne Campaign- **982**; Thomas DeRougers- Williams was solicited as her escort into Burgoyne's camp, but refused; this service was instead, acc. Rev. Eleazer DeRougers- Williams, accepted 'by some Indians of the Western tribes, who, in 2 parties, ea. ignorant of the designs of the other, started on the expedition'; one of these parties persuaded her to come into camp, & they were met by the other party; an altercation arose betw. them, & 'in the strife that ensued, the girl was brutally tomahawked by one party, that the other might not be able [to] draw the reward which had been offered by the young lady's lover, for bringing her in'; a Winnebago chief at Green Bay had ostensibly offered this information to Rev. Williams while he was a missionary there, & acknowl. having had a hand in this murder, which some had attrib. to the St. Regis Indians- **1016**; a neph. of hers was a keeper's assist. at Clinton State Prison when a neph. of her lover, David Jones, was incarcerated there; Robert Ayres was perh. the bearer of Jones' letter to her from Burgoyne's camp, detailing the arrangements for her escort into camp; Burgoyne's army was then N. of Kingsbury, N. Y., & the letter was brought to her by Ayres, his master requiring him to take it to her "w. many strict instructions & cautions as to the manner he was to proceed in carrying the letter & delivering it into her hand"- **1054**; it was the report throughout Argyle that her ghost used to appear bef. David Jones every night; however, when her bro., Col. John McCrea, was in Canada, Jones denied that such a thing had ever occurred other than in his imagination- **1061**; brief ments.- **1049, 1060**

John- notifies Albany Comm. of Correspondence, Aug. 22, 1775, that Hugh Munroe had ment. to him that Donald Munroe had spoken to him regarding John Munroe, Esq.'s receipt of a Capt.'s commission in the King's service, under Col. Allen McLean; also, that Esq. Munroe also had commissions for 10 of the McDonalds who res. in Johnson's Bush, N. Y., & they were going to raise a regt. in Canada to serve the King; John Munroe, acc. McCrea, had also told him that he had been much injured by his neighbors, but implied that he had acquired something that would make amends & provide him w. £ 200 annually, & questions whether or not the Comm. should take note- **820**; acc. John Munroe, the message orig. conveyed to him was essentially that there had been talk of raising a regt. of Highlanders to defend the govt., & he had been nomin. as an officer, though he did not know the rank- **822**; rec'd. an appt., Oct. 3, 1775, for Col., Saratoga District militia- **823**; Archibald McNeil refuses a post as Adjutant in his regt., & was replaced by John Vernor (both had been recommended for posts, Oct. 3, 1775- McNeil as Adjutant, & Vernor as Quartermaster)- **827**

John- plaintiff's atty., Oct. 19, 1773, Charlotte co. Court of Common Pleas, in Morris Austin, vs. Jonathan Baker; Phineas Babcock, vs. Jonathan Baker; & Hugh Munro, vs. David Hunter- **878**; clerk, Wash. co., c. 1770's- 80's- **(L)- 936**; a series of deed entries, c. 1780's, taken by Dr. Fitch, from his "parchment bound book"- **(L)- 936b**

Col. John- bro. Jane; while in Canada, he asked David Jones abt. rumors of the existence of his sist.'s ghost, & Jones denied that he had ever seen her in any form other than in his imagination- **1061**

Martha- defendant, Nov. 3, 1784, along w. Elizabeth McCrea, in a case brought by John & Susanna Williams, administrators of James Turner- **878½**

Mary- m. Deac. Thomas Collins; Dr. Fitch specul. whether or not she may have been the mother of Wid. McCrea- **866**

Sarah- m. Alexander, s. James & Susannah (Thomas) Turner- **1044**

Stephen- (McCrey) appt. surgeon, Aug. 1775, Col. Van Schaik's battalion, superceding the prev. appt. of Dr. John Williams by N. Y. Provincial Congress; the change was apparently affected due to the fact that he had passed a qualifying exam that Williams was absent from & apparently unaware of as a requirement; in his letter of inquiry concerning the switch, Williams expresses his surprise, describing his preparations & experience, & portraying McCrey as 'just out of his time & w/o experience'- **790**

Thomas- Lot 281, Turner's Patent, sold to him by the proprietors, & part of it deeded by Ephriam Wheeler, Jan. 10, 1785, to Phineas Benet (Bennet)- **(L)- 936**

Wid.- res. Clapp's Mills, Salem, N. Y.; was a very fine spinner & supported herself by selling lace; she would spin & whiten threads, doing up skeins, & peddle her thread & knitted lace by herself, at Fitch's Point in Salem, & as far away as Cambridge & Sancoick, N. Y., taking flax & c. in exchange; the type of lace she made was most often used in pillowcases; ments. a dau., Betty; & perh. Mary, who m. Deac. Thomas Collins- **866**

McCULLOUGH,
Nathaniel- (McCulloch) 'late Lt. in His Majesty's 42nd Regt. of Foot'; gr. 2,000 acres, town of Hebron, N. Y.; refers p. 79, Catalogue of Maps- **990**
Thomas- oath of alleg.; Co. D, 22nd N. Y. Inf.- **(L)- 1074**
W. W.- 2nd Sgt., Co. A, 2nd N. Y., Northern Black Horse, Cav., 1861- 2- **1080**

McDAVITT,
Patrick- plaintiff, May 19, 1774, along w. Hugh O' Harro, vs. Samuel Loadman & als.- **878**

McDERMOTT,
Rev. Mr.- along w. Rev. A. B. Lambert, acted as spiritual guide toMartin Wallace during the time prior to his execution, Dec. 1, 1858, hearing his last confession on the scaffold- **1050s**

McDONALD,
____- c. 1775, there were 10 of this surname res. at Johnson's Bush, who ostensibly rec'd. commissions in the King's service, available to them through John Munroe, Esq., & were planning to raise a regt. in Canada- **820**
____- (c. 1858?) res. Salem, N. Y., on the straight road betw. Wm. McNish & Russell's bridge- **1034**
Capt. Daniel- informs concerning the loc. of Richard Hoy's homestead, & other facts concerning him- **873**; c. 1851, res. S. Granville, N. Y.; he attests to no awareness of distrurbances in Granville by Shays' sympathizers, c. 1786, but provides the names of several of Shays' men who settl. in the area- **921**; recounts the opening stanzas of a song of the Rev. war pert. to Burgoyne's Campaign- **923**; 1st obt. a place to live & means to support himself w. the Bell family, E. of Colin McFarland's, Salem, N. Y.; he notes that he would have fared well there, but his father had struck a bargain w. the Armstrongs (§ 332) for his employment, unaware that he had already found a place; see Vol. 1- **927**; ments. s. John, of Saratoga Springs, N. Y.- **1002**; his funeral, May 25, 1858, attended by Dr. Fitch & Rufus Coon, the latter relating his knowl. of St. John Honeywood while proceeding to the funeral- **1033**
James- defendant, May 19, 1774, in a case brought by John & William Jonlay- **878**
James- b. 1748, Scotland; joined the British army at age 18, & served as corporal at the outbreakof the Rev. war; he was transported to Boston under Lord Howe's command, & immed. deserted & joined the American forces; fought at Bunker Hill, & visited Boston, June 20, 1853, at age 105, the last survivor of the battle; was at the taking of Burgoyne at Saratoga, & under Benedict Arnold's command during the battle there; also participated in the battles of Princeton & Trenton, & lost an eye 'at the murderous Cowpens'; present at the surrender of Cornwallis;

served in the War of 1812, & res. Kentucky, until his wf.'s death, a few yrs. prior to his appearance in Boston; his only surviving dau. wrote & invited him to res. at Black Rock, N. Y., w. her; having been robbed of his funds, pension papers, & part of his clothes while en route to her, he entered the offices of the *Sandusky Register*, seeking assistance, & a substantive conversation occurred betw. him & a reporter; 'His forehead was deeply scarred: he had lost an eye, & his hands bore marks of former conflicts. He was tall & well formed, & straight as an arrow, which w. his military step betokened a life in the camp. His Scotch accent, high cheek bones, florid complexion & whitened locks, bordering on the red, told plainly his descent'; robbed while on board a boat bound for Cincinatti, a stranger provided him w. an overcoat & fare to Columbus; when he discovered that a fellow soldier that he had expected to meet there was dec'd., he appl. to the conductor for a free pass to Cleveland, but was unable to receive one, as he was unable to provide his pension papers, which had been stolen; he was offered a ticket to the Alm house, & indignant, he turned on his heel & remarked that he had fought too many battles in the Rev. to die in a 'Poor- House'; he returned to the depot, passed over to Shelby, & thence to Sandusky; the remainder of his conversation w. the Sandusky reporter concerned his experiences in the Rev. war, incl. his service under 'Mad' Anthony Wayne, & a 'vivid description' of the battle of Cowpens (which the reporter does not disclose in this article); he attrib. the success in capt. Gen. Burgoyne primarily to the efforts of Benedict Arnold, describing his actions during the battle; foll. his visit, he continued his trip by taking a boat to Buffalo, N. Y.; the acct. of his life, & incidents, incl. in a newsclipping entitled 'James M'Donald- A Revolutionary Hero', authored by "G."- **1010**

John- res. Salem, N. Y.; a grds. of William & Betsey (Rowan) Shaw res. w. him while attending Salem Academy- **737**; notes that while a schoolboy in Albany, N. Y., old Balthasar Lydius (d. 1815) "was the sport of the boys in the street" for his odd looks- **(L)- 932**

John- his s. Capt. Daniel attests that when his father 1st settl. Hebron, N. Y., he sent for Dr. Williams to set his broken ankle, & Williams was then res. along the Indian rvier- **924**; of Munro's Meadows, Hebron, N. Y.; he was among the 5 families inhabiting that region who started out to take protection in Burgoyne's camp at Skenesborough, but for some cause, stopped on the way & did not go; he later became a ranger in Capt. Barnes' co. of Salem, going out several times, mostly in the last yrs. of the Rev. war, to see if Indians had come down Lake Champlain from Canada- **1000**; gives a description of Dr. Clark's log meeting house, noting that while he res. at Mr. Welch's, the meeting house was being used by Welch as a barn- **1001**

John- an early school was taught W. of where he presently (c. 1850) res., although not recoll. by Wid. Angel- **859**; he once res. in the loc. prev. occ. by William Moffatt (or Moffit)- **864**

John- disbanded soldier, 78th Regt. of Foot; gr. 100 acres, May 1, 1765, along w. George Stuart, loc. on E. side of Hudson river, Albany co.- **(L)- 936**

John- s. Capt. Daniel; res. Saratoga Springs, N. Y.; acc. his father, he once came into the co. of a Bapt. clegym. who had known the waiter of Gen. Simon Frazier, & the waiter gave him his eyewitn. acct. of the moment Frazier was wnd. at Bemis Heights; McDonald denies that this ever happened, although he attests that he had no doubt that his fahter heard this acct. somewhere, but not from him- **1002**

McDOUGALL,

Alexander- from Scotland; after a few yrs., rem. to the part of Argyle township now in Ft. Edward, N. Y., a mi. E. of the village, on the road to Argyle; children- 4 sons & 3 daus.-John, Alexander, Dugald, Daniel; Jane, m. Alexander McDougall, Esq.; Catharine, m. Daniel Brown; & Nancy, m. John McCollum; he d. abt. 1790, & was. bur. in Argyle, w/o a headstone, "they not being had here at that date"- **978**; he was seized by 5 or 6 Indians one morning as he left his house, c. July or Aug. 1777, & was taken within sight of Burgoyne's camp at Ft. Edward; at this point, they made a camouflaged thicket so dense it couldn't be seen through, & hid while 3 of them went into the fort; returning in a few hrs., they brought w. them 3 freshly taken scalps, "for the blood was still fresh upon them & the skin not in the least dried or stiffened. They certainly were victims who had just been murdered by the Indians"; these victims were reportedly unknown, & prob. strangers coming to the camp, acc. Dr. Fitch, as the Allen family & Jane McCrea were the only residents of the area at that time who had been murdered; on their return, they wanted to kill McDougall, but an altercation arose, & the others opposed this, & at length, lead him away until coming in sight of his house, where one motioned & "spoke in an imperative tone the words 'Go home to your squaw!' "- **982**; his homestead was the destination of Argyle settlers who had left Neal Gillespie's foll. the Allen massacre; they stopped here & "took up their abode" while the British army was in the vicinity; they soon brought their cattle here & sold what milk they could spare to the soldiers, a number of them coming regularly w. canteens & pails- **983**

Gen. Alexander- (1732- 1786) officer witn., during Samuel Standish's Sept.- Nov. 1776 service, acc. his Rev. war pens. appl.- **747**; Feb. 1777, commanded a brigade that incl. Col. Hooker's Farmington, Conn. regt.- **752**

Alexander, Esq.- of no relation to the other Alexander; occ. the farm, Argyle, N. Y., now (1852) occ. by Samuel Ferguson- **978**

Andrew- of Argyle, N. Y.; dau. m. John, s. John & Molly (Craig) Harsha- **973**

Archibald L.- res. Salem, N. Y.; m. dau. John Blanchard- **914**; lawyer; m. Maria, dau. John & Susan (Wright) Blanchard; see Vol. 3- **1045**; Wash. Co. Dist. Atty.; prosecutor, Oct. 1- 7, 1858, People vs. Martin Wallace- **1048s**; witn., Dec. 1, 1858, for certif. of the execution of Martin Wallace- **1050s**

Lt. George- the S. & E. bounds of his gr., beginning at his SW corner, forms part of the bounds of an "L"- shaped gr. given to Thomas Trickett, & conveyed Sept. 20, 1773, to Peter Van Brugh Livingston & Francis Groome- **(L)- 936**

John- drew an orig. lot, Argyle Patent, loc. a mi. S. of The Hook (N. Argyle, N. Y.) now (1850) owned by ____ Fenton & John Todd; his sist. m. Roger Reid- **802**

John- of Argyle, N. Y.; m. dau. John & Molly (Craig) Harsha- **973**
John- s. Alexander; m. Betsey, dau. Capt. James Beaty; 10 children-
1. Alexander, m. Betsey Tomb, of Salem, N. Y.
2. James, m. Jane, dau. "old" William Robertson
3. John, m. Margaret, dau. James Lyttle, of Hebron, N. Y.
4. Daniel, m. Catharine Bain
5. Joseph, m. Jane Harsha
6. Catharine, m. Daniel Livingston; eldest, b. Nov. 7, 1779, on the present (1852) James Shaw farm
7. Elizabeth, m. Henry Tinkey
8. Anna, m. Daniel McNeil
9. Jane, m. Daniel Walker; she d. 1838, E. Greenwich, N. Y.
10. Margaret, m. Alexander McNeil- **978**; he was a milita Ensign prior to, a/o, during the Rev. war- **979**; went w. 3 or 4 of his neighbors to Ft. Edward, suppos. to get protection from Burgoyne, prob. when the army 1st arr. there & bef. anybody thought of taking their families there; foll. their business, & as they came out, "500 Indians met them- & as ea. Indian passed them he gave a yell- as much to say 'We'll take you prisoners bef. you leave the place' "; the yelling was heard by a British officer, who immed. came out among them & instructed them not to molest these men, who were friends of the king; the Indians then came to them, ea. shaking their hands, & alluttering '<u>Swago</u>, brother' "; the ceremony continued until nearly all 500 Indians had shook the settlers' hands- **981**
Esq. William- res. lower end, E. Greenwich, N. Y.; m. Eleanor, dau. Alexander McNachten, Esq.- **1062**; c. 1777, a schoolhouse stood at the top of the hill above the loc. of his house, as the road ran; spring 1778, this schoolhouse was set afire one night by the area whigs- **1064**

McDOWELL,
Robert- res. Salem, N. Y.; c. 1865, purch. the homestead of Aaron Martin, Sr., from his s. Jarvis- **731**

McDUGALD,
Angus- the SW corner of his land, loc. on the E. side of the Hudson, Albany co., adj. a 100 acre gr. given by patent, May1, 1765, to George Stuart & John McDonald- **(L)- 936**; private, 42nd Royal Highland regt.; gr. 50 acres in Vt.; refers p. 77, Catalogue of Maps- **990**

McEACHRON,
James- Co. E, 123rd NYSV; d. Dec. 4, 1862; see James A., Vol. 4- **1098**
William- 3rd Sgt., Co. A, 2nd N. Y., Northern Black Horse, Cav., 1861- 2- **1080**

McELHERRON,
James- Irish; Rev. soldier & pensioner; res. a mi. W. of Henry Braymer, Hebron, N. Y.; his desc. modernized their surname to "Herron"; he was w. Gen. Montgomery during the assault on Quebec, 1775, & was the 1st to mount the scaling ladder; the sentry gave him a sabre gash to the head, & a 2nd across his left wrist, but by the time these wnds. had been inflicted, his comrade had gained the rampart & split the sentry's head open w. a cutlass; he served directly under Montgomery's command when the Americans,"wounded & cut to pieces", were driven out of the city & scattered in the woods; the wnd. on his wrist was severe, apparently severing some chords, as he could never raise or hold up his hand w/o an unsteady, shaking motion- **922**

McENTEE,
Barney- an Irishman, betw. 50- 60 yrs. old, res. w. John C. Sweet, Hoosick Falls, N. Y, who described him as "a kind man, inoffensive in his manner; he was remarkable for kindness of disposition; he would have spells of drinking a little too much once in awhile"; the prosecution at the trial for his murder, in their opening remarks, portrayed him as industrious, saving more than he spent, his purse " always full, & still his hand was always open. No one approached Barney in need, & went away in want"; on Feb. 16, 1858, he was going to Schaghticoke, N. Y., to look for a dog & see friends, when he stopped at Reynolds Tavern in Eagle Bridge; at abt. 9 or 10:00 AM; Michael Bradey & Martin Wallace, who were strangers to him, came in, & the 3 drank together; Bradey left, & he went on w. Wallace, until they arr. at Joice's store, betw. 11:00 AM & 12 noon; they went in & stood drinks again, & when it came Wallace's turn to treat, he sd. that he had no money; he then showed Wallace his wallet, filled w. over $100 in bills; they continued to drink, & Wallace left at 3 or 4:00 PM, to look for a house, & returned abt. dusk; acc. testim. of Ann Joice, McEntee had 2 drinks bef. Wallace left, & 2 drinks after he returned; whenWallace joined him in the 2nd drink, he only pretended to drink, remained sober, & asked McEntee to come home w. him for supper; however, he was reluctant to leave w. Wallace, & spoke of going on to his destination, or at least to the One Horse Tavern, to lodge overnight; eventually they left, but returned briefly, as he was still reluctant to leave w. Wallace; nevertheless, Patrick Joice convinced him to go on his way w. Wallace, & they went to Jesse Pratt's store, where his intoxication became further pronounced; he was helped to leave by other patrons, & was last seen being taken home by Wallace; betw. 8- 8:30 PM, his body was found on the side of the highway by Hiram Sisson; he had been robbed, beaten w. a wooden club, or fence stake, & his skull fractured severely; Martin Wallace was apprehended later the same night, & tried for his murder the foll. Oct., convicted, & executed for his murder on Dec. 1st- **1048s**; brief ments.- **1050s**

McFADDEN,
Thomas- res. Argyle, N. Y.; m. Jane, dau. James & Rebecca (Lytle) Mills- **737**

McFARLAND,
Alexander- oath of alleg.; Co. D, 22nd N. Y. Inf.- **(L)- 1074**
Colin- purch. the 'Dry House' of John Blossom, moving it & building it over as a dwelling; he set it down upon a cellar where a log house, perh. William Hoy's, had prev. stood, in the E. part of Lot No. 50, Turner's Patent- **873**; c. 1851, res. Salem, N. Y.; the Bell farm, later part of the Shaw farm, was loc. E. of him- **927**
Daniel- d. June 22, 1808, prob. Salem, N. Y., "in the house of Stephen Rowan 'died by the inordinate use of spiritous liquors'} Thus written"; Robert Pennel, Coroner- **(L)- 876**
Daniel- s. Capt. James; res. S. of his father- in- law, Salem, N. Y., until "becoming involved by the failure of his bro., Esq. James A.", sold out abt. 1848, & rem. Hebron; m. Polly, dau. Deac. John Steele; children-
1. James, m. ____ Munson
2. John, m. Sarah Wheeler
3. Eleanor, m. ____ Munson
4. Thomas, m. ____ Munson
5. William, unm.- **1047**; c. 1861/2, sold Lot No. 55, orig. occ. by Reuben Turner, to Abner Hill- **1085**
Family- c. 1858, their farm loc. N. of the village, Salem, N. Y., was prev. owned by Judge Edward Savage; c. 1824, this farm was being worked by Harrison G. Blake- **733**
James- (s. Daniel & Polly Steele) m. ____ Munson; they had a boy & a girl; his wf. d., & he is now (1858) in the last stages of consumption- **1047**
Capt. James- had sons Esq. James A., & Daniel- **1047**
Esq. James A.- of Salem, N. Y.; m. Mary, dau. Ebenezer & Betsey (Blanchard) Proudfit- **1045**; s. Capt. James, & bro. Daniel- **1047**
John- of New Perth (Salem, N. Y.); for £ 80, May 7, 1784, conveys Lot No. 266, Turner's Patent, to John Graham- **(L)- 936**
John- (s. Daniel & Polly Steele) merch., Hebron, N. Y.; m. Sarah, dau. Paul Wheeler- **1047**
Murray D.- m. Sarah, dau. William & Lucinda (Conkey) Fitch- **730**
William- 'the last member of the old session' (the orig. church of Dr. Clark's colony); d. Aug. 1819- **809**
Col. William- Marshall of the Day, Apr. 20, 1841, Salem, N. Y., during a memorial service on the death of President Harrison- **1009**

McGEOCH,
James- Co. A, 2nd N. Y., Northern Black Horse, Cav., 1861- 2- **1080**

McGILL,
Elizabeth- m. Anthony, s. Hon. Anthony I. & Maria (Williams) Blanchard, as his 1st wf.- **1045**

McGILVRY,
____- an early inhabitant at Fitch's Point, Salem, N. Y., acc. Wid. Angel, "One Muckle- bray as he was called (MacGilvery)- a very old man, w. his wf.- from Scotland"; his home was loc. on the road that branched off from the road from the Point, & ran up along Black creek, somewhere behind Jarvis Martin's; "He had a little log hut, covered w. bark (as most of the huts orig. were)- he lived there for several yrs.; & finally moved west somewhere among the Scotch in Argyle"- **865**

McGOWAN,
Michael- oath of alleg.; Co. D, 22nd N. Y. Inf.- **(L)- 1074**

McGREGOR,
Elizabeth- m. Peter, s. Duncan & Isabel (Duncan) MacIntyre- **999**

McINTOSH,
Lachlan- c. 1773, Justice of Peace,Charlotte co., N. Y.- **911**
William- (or Tosh) his family was among those from Salem who took shelter in Jackson, N. Y. foll. the Allen massacre- **701**

McINTYRE,
Thomas- Co. A, 2nd N. Y., Northern Black Horse, Cav., 1861- 2- **1080**

McKELLIP,
____- m. David, s. David Webb, of Salem, N. Y.- **738**
Esq.- the horses drawing his sleigh (n. d.) struck Ashbel Martin, who was running backwards in the road, killing him- **731**
Family- res. Jackson, N. Y.; ments. 3 children- sons Simpson & David; & dau. Jane, who m. John Dobbin, of Co. Antrim, Ireland- **732**; c. 1775, res. S. of Fitch's Point, on the banks of the Battenkill- **853**; their farm was loc. N. of the Bowman family- **856**
William- c. 1813, he & Joseph Stout were engaged as carpenters for constructing Fitch's Woolen Factory- **799**

McKENNEY,
____- of Kingsbury, N. Y.; James, John, & Amos, yeoman, rec'd. a deed, Jan. 17, 1767, to undivided land in Kingsbury, from John & Daniel Starr, & Thomas & Henuriah Hill, heirs of Comfort Starr; also, for £ 10, quit claim, Mar. 25, 1772, to Michael Hoffnagle; no indication of family relationship of the 3 abovement.- **(L)- 936**

McKERNON,
John- m. Susan, dau. John & Ann (Whiteside) Cochran; 2 children- Margaret-Ann, & Edward- **805**

McKESSON,
John, Esq.- of N. Y. Provincial Congress; rec'd. correspondence, June 23, 1777, from John Williams, noting the circulation of cert. enclosed pamphlets within the Grants in response to some of the latest proceedings in N. Y., referring to their intention to form a separate & independent state named New Vermont; other business incl., such as the situation & conditions in Canada- **789**; from John Williams, Aug. 10, 1775, prob. addressed to him, seeking an explanation & redress for his unexpected replacement by Stephen McCrey as surgeon in Col. Van Schaik's battalion- **790**; N. Y. Secretary of State; rec'd. some correspondence from Duncan Campbell, dated Dec. 12, 1777, Argyle, relating the intent of 'some fiery men... to drive all the Scots & Irish as tories from Argyle & New Perth...', & seeks the assistance of the Legislature in preventing this- **791**

McKIBBIN,
William D.- Co. A, 2nd N. Y., Northern Black Horse, Cav., 1861- 2- **1080**

McKIE,
G. W.- witn., Dec. 1, 1858, for certif. of the execution of Martin Wallace- **1050s**
George- m. 1. Catharine, & 2. Sophia, both daus. Peter & Ann (Robertson) Whiteside; children, by 1st wf.- Neal, Edwin J.; by 2nd wf.- George Wilson, Catharine, Henry Matthews, James, & Peter- **805**
James- in order to escape from the Indians during the assault on Skenesborough (§ 244), he started across Wood creek when it was full of ice, & hid among some ice & logs, laying 2 hrs. or more in the water, w. only his head above water, which gave him rheumatism for the remainder of his life; acc. John McDonald, his escape occurred at a diff. time than the murder of the McCalls, as they were killed during warmer weather- this point refuted & corrected by Dr. Fitch, acc. earlier testim. of James Rogers; see Vol. 1 (it may have been that the news of the McCall's deaths arr. in the area when the weather was warmer)- **1000**
John- m. Catharine, dau. John & Margaret (Robertson) Whiteside; 3 sons- John, James, & William- **805**
John- oath of alleg.; Co. D, 22nd N. Y. Inf.- **(L)- 1074**
Maj. John- b. Dec. 19, 1824; ment. as the only officer, 22nd N. Y. Inf., not wnd. or killed at 2nd Bull Run, Aug. 29- 30, 1862; (later, as Lt. Col.) his health became so impaired that he was unable to continue serving, resigned, & returned to Cambridge, N. Y., Mar. 1863; he d. Sept. 1, 1864, in an accident- **1095b**

McKINLY,
Samuel & William- along w. Joseph Stringham & John Williams, Feb. 27, 1787, purch. for £ 2,750, Lot 23, Skenesborough (Whitehall, N. Y.), containing 500 acres- **(L)- 875**

McKINSTRY,
Capt. John- May 1775, commanded a co. of Mass. troops, Col. Pattison's regt.; his co. was sent to Boston, Jan. 1776, & afterw. marched to New London, Conn., then sailed to NYC; the co. was later ordered from NYC to Canada, & marched up the St. Lawrence river valley, engaging w. the British; he was capt., but released shortly thereafter, to Gen. Arnold, & retreated w. the army to Crown Point & Mt. Independence for the summer; July 1777, & afterw. they retreated from there to Ft. Edward, & thence to Stillwater, N. Y.- **748**

McKISTY,
Nial- oath of alleg.; Co. D, 22nd N. Y. Inf.- **(L)- 1074**

McKNIGHT,
*George-*res. Black Creek (Hebron, N. Y.); rec'd. recommendation, Jan. 25, 1776, for appt. as 2nd Lt., Charlotte co. militia- **784**

McLAUGHERY/ McLAUGHRY,
Andrew- bro. Thomas; rem. Kortright, N. Y.; m. dau. James Harsha, the emig.; "he had several singularities, was very squeamish abt. his health & diet, would never take a drink of water until he had warmed it by the fire or poured boiling water into it 'to take the chill off' "- **973**
Deac.- (McLaughery) res. Salem, N. Y.; m. gradau. old Capt. McNitt; c. 1814, during the War of 1812, a party of Salem men were finally able to detain his father- in- law at his house, to prevent him from proceeding to take an imaginary party of tories to Nova Scotia, the memories of his Rev. war experiences having been rekindled by the current conflict; he was later persuaded to return to his own home- **1018**
Family- of Salem, N. Y.; bros. Andrew & Thomas, both m. daus. of James Harsha, the emig.- **973**
Rev. T. C.- his statement referred to, p. 111, Corey's Gazetteer, concerning Phineas Whiteside's ord. as an Elder when he res. in Pennsylvania- **805**; grds. Thomas; minister, c. 1852, Assoc. Ref. Presbyterian church, Cambridge, N. Y.- **973**
Thomas- m. Nancy, dau. James Harsha, the emig., & rem. Kortright, N. Y.- **973**

McLEAN,
_____- m. Col. James Breakenridge, the Duke of Leeds, in Canada- **991**
Alexander- plaintiff, May 19, 1774, vs. Neal Shaw- **878**
Col. Allen- c. 1775, John Munroe, Esq. had ostensibly rec'd. a Capt's commission under his command- **820**; during his interrogation, Esq. Munroe stated that he had seen him in NYC, spring 1775, but had not seen or heard from him since- **822**
John- defendant, May 19, 1774, in a case brought by Benjamin French, for debt of 149s; & plaintiff, Oct. 18, 1774, vs. James Dole- **878**
Hon. John- res. Salem, N. Y.; m. dau. Anthony I. Blanchard; had 2 daus., one m. Alexander M. Proudfit- **914**; m. Maria, dau. Hon. Anthony I. & Maria (Williams)

Blanchard; children- Maria, m. Alexander Proudfit; Kate, & Susanna, both unm.-
1045; s. Judge John; d. Dec. 5, 1858, at 65, Salem, N. Y., 'after a brief illness of 6
days, commencing w. a severe cold & ending in congestion of the lungs'- **1050**
Judge John- had sons King, Lewis, Henry, Dr. William, & Hon. John, who m.
Maria Blanchard- **1045**; noted as one of the most distinguished citizens of Wash.
co., holding the office of Judge, & representative, N. Y. Legislature- **1050**
John C.- s. Thomas; res. Battenville, N. Y.; m. Abigail, dau.William & Lucinda
(Fitch) Conkey- **730**
Rachel- m. John, s. William & Margaret (Andrew) Dobbin- **732**
Thomas- ments. s. John C., who m. Abigail Conkey- **730**; Salem, N. Y.; Feb. 23,
1791, drowned in raceway of Adam Martin's mill; Joshua Conkey,Coroner- **(L)-**
876

McLEARY,
Deac.- res. Salem, N. Y., on the site orig. occ. by John Hunsden during the Rev.
war- **729**

McMIHELS,
John- a dau. of his was raised by Richard Hoy, of Salem, N. Y.- **873**

McMILLAN,
____- of Argyle, N. Y.; m. Betty Hoy, as her 2nd husb.; she mistrusted his motive
in courting her & secretly deeded her property to her sist. Sally; after res. there for
a short while, her husb. convinced her to move to Argyle, & then after a few wks.,
proposed selling her Salem lot; it was then that he discovered her ploy, & after a
wk. or two of turbulence, she returned to live w. her sist. for the remainder of her
life- **872**
____- c. 1861, res. on the Merrill farm, N. of Salem, N. Y.- **1078**
John- deed witn., Nov.1, 1783, Dr. Thomas Clark to Jedidiah Gilbert- **(L)- 936**

McMULLEN,
William- (McMillin) R. R. engineer; he had only been married a few months, &
was killed, Dec. 2 or 3, 1853, when his freight train derailed at Whitehall, N. Y.,
as a result of striking a cow, or horse, that had fallen betw. the bridge timbers; he
"was caught betw. the boiler & tender, & carried down w. the wreck", but replied
to inquires that he was all right; however, it was discovered "that his legs were
literally crushed to pieces & nearly torn from his body & his breast severely burned
from contact w. the boiler"; he survived for abt. an hr. after he was rem. & his
remains were taken to Saratoga (Schuylerville, N. Y.) the foll. morning- **1017**

McMURRAY,
E.- witn., Dec. 1, 1858, certif. for the execution of Martin Wallace- **1050s**
Deac. John- corroborates Robet Hanna's acct. that the Salem militia was ordered
out, c. 1786, to quell a tax revolt in Granville, N. Y., & the rebellion was settl. bef.

the militia had arr. there- **701**; res. Salem, N. Y.; John Gerrold was dragged to his death (n. d.) some rods N. of his house- **734**; attests that Phineas Whiteside's theological studies were for pastoral service in the Cameronian church- **805**; ment. in Dr. Lambert's address to the Wash. Co. Bible Soc., Sept. 4, 1862, as the sole surviving member of its 1st meeting 50 yrs. ago- **1097**

Robert- of Salem, N. Y.; m. Ann R., dau. John & Margaret (Robertson) Whiteside; children- Margaret- Ann, m. Anson Ingraham; & Robert; his wf. d. Jan. 6, 1876, at 88, W. Cambridge, N. Y.- **805**

Deac. Robert- res. Salem, N. Y.; emig. 1774, coming over in the same vessel as _____ Byrnes; see § 489; Vol. 1- **1083**

McNACHTEN,

Alexander- Oct. 5, 1771, gr. 285 acres, farm lot No. 3, Argyle township, to William Duer, Esq.- **935**

Eleanor- dau. Alexander, Esq.; b. Aug. 10, 1777, when the family was en route to Burgoyne's camp at Ft. Edward foll. the Allen massacre; her mother, being unable to go any further, they stopped at Yerry Kilmer's in Argyle, & she was b. there; m. Esq. William McDougall- **1062**

McNAUGHTON,

Alexander- was grdf. James Mains, Jr.- **732**

Esq.- his old homestead was occ. by Deac. Samuel Dobbin, who m. one of his gr. grdaus.- **732**

Gen. John- (s. Malcom; see Vol. 1) res. ½ mi. E. of Salem, N. Y., on 88 acres purch. by his father from John Harsha, after he had cleared & improved it, exchanging the lot for 300 acres of wildland in Argyle Patent- **973**

Malcom- foll. the Rev. war, Daniel Livingston res. E. of N. Greenwich, N. Y., & 3- 4 mi. beyond his place- **854**

Mary- dau. Alexander; m. James Mains- **732**

McNEIL,

Alexander- m. Margaret, dau. John & Betsey (Beaty) McDougall- **978**

Archibald- perh. Irish; b. Boston, Mass.; res. on the W. side of the Hudson, nr. the site of Ft. Miller bridge, & kept the ferry, & a tavern there, bef. the bridge was built; abt. 1790, sold out to _____ DeMond & rem. Bacon's Hill, N. Y.; he later returned to the river & purch. a farm at Saratoga (Schuylerville) nr. the guard gates to the Champlain canal; abt. 1809, sold his property & rem. Troy, N. Y.- **804**; recommended for appt., Oct. 3, 1775, as Adjutant, Saratoga District militia- **823**; refused his appt. as Adjutant, Col. John McCrea's regt., & John Vernor appt. in his place- **827**

Archibald- bro. John, of E. Greenwich, N. Y.; he was among the Argyle families who went into Burgoyne's camp at Ft. Edward foll. the Allen massacre- **986**

Daniel- m. Anna, dau. John & Betsey (Beaty) McDougall- **978**

Elizabeth- (dau. John & Sarah Pattison) b. ca. 1812; when she was abt. 13 months old, her mother died; "she was a very delicate, puny child, & we never expected her to live to womanhood"; when she was abt. 3 yrs. old, her grdf. came to visit from Litchfield, Conn., & insisted on bringing her back there w. him; the family later rem. Chenango Point (Binghamton, N. Y.) & finally, after 2 yrs. absence, decided to return her to her family; her handwriting appears in additions & corrections to the contents of this article, & briefly, in other articles adj. to it, incl. the notation that she had rem. her grdm.'s tombstone from one cemetery into a family bur. grd. elsewhere- **951**; b. Apr. 5, 1812; m. Nov. 5, 1832, Dr. Asa Fitch, Jr.- **960**

Family- c. 1789, res. S. of Roger Reid, S. Argyle, N. Y.- **802**

Family- bros. Archibald & John; res. Argyle Patent prior Rev. war- **986**

George- (s. John & ____ Stone) was subj. to epileptic fits, which impaired his bodily & mental faculties; "finally in one of them, he fell into some burning brush in a field, & was so severely burned hereby, that he d. within 24 hrs. after, A. D. 1832?"- **951**

John- (s. Jonathan & ____ Stone); b. Litchfield, Conn.; tailor, res. Stillwater, N. Y.; m. 1. ____, & had one son, Charles; 2. Sarah Pattison; had s. George, & dau. Elizabeth, who m. Dr. Asa Fitch, Jr.; his wf. Sarah d. ca. May 1813, of consumption, abt. 13 months after her dau.'s birth; their s. George was sent to res. w. relatives in Litchfield, Conn., & their dau. 1st res. w. her grdf. Pattison, & was afterw. sent to Litchfield; c. 1817, she was returned to res. w. her father, who d. shortly after her return- **951**; b. June 1780; m. Apr. 7, 1808, dau. Thomas & Elizabeth (Ashton) Pattison; children-

1. Sarah, b. July 13, 1785; d. Sept. 4, 1818
2. James, d. inf., of rickets
3. George P., b. Jan. 26, 1809; d. May 4, 1834
4. Elizabeth, b. Apr. 5, 1812; m. Nov. 5, 1832, Dr. Asa Fitch, Jr.- **960**

John- bro. Archibald; res. E. Greenwich, N. Y.; the party of tories that had come from Canada to seize John Younglove & burn his house (§ 250) passed by his house during their escape through Argyle- **985**; instead of going to Ft. Edward w. the other Argyle families foll. the Allen massacre, he moved down to Tomhennick (Tomhannock, N. Y.), at his wf.'s insistence, as a cousin of hers res. there; when her cousin died, she had taken charge of one of the children to raise, & insisted on taking the child there to be w. its Humphrey connections during the of danger- **986**

Jonathan- res. Litchfield, Conn.; m. ____ Stone; had sons Truman, Elias, & John; & 2. Sarah Pattison; of his daus., Aurelia m. ____ Dayton- **951**

Mrs./ Wid. Sarah- acc. Samuel Standish's Rev. war pens. appl., she was the aunt of Jane McCrea; see also, Campbell, Mrs./ Wid Sarah- **747**; of Ft. Edward, N. Y.; the Blanchard family was, in some way, connected w. her & her grdau., the wf. of Peter B. Tearse; see Blanchard, Vol. 4; acc. Dr. Fitch, "this seemed to open the way for Judge Blanchard to settle in this country w. a prospect of success"- **914**

McNeil's ferry- loc. 2 mi. above Saratoga (Schuylerville, N. Y.); acc. Gen. Schuyler's letter, Aug. 19, 1775, Col. Ritzma's 4 companies were marching to

Saratoga from this loc. on that very morning- **782**; loc. at the site of Ft. Miller bridge, & operated by Archibald McNeil, who sold the property to ____ DeMond, abt. 1790- **804**

McNISH,
____- c. 1817- 19, Preceptor, Salem Academy- **1053**
Alexander- along w. Abner Stone, Overseer of the Poor, Salem, N. Y.; on Sept. 26, 1815, McNish & Stone offered a $30.00 reward concerning a Mrs. Bealy, who abandoned her newborn child in town- **718**; c. 1777, commanded a co. of volunteers, Schuylerville, N. Y., who took a breast- work & made prisoners of a Lt. & some privates- **729**
Andrew- bro. William; res. Salem, N. Y., & left desc. there- **740**
Family- ments. 3 children- William; Betsey, m. Alexander, & Sally, m. Thomas, both sons of Deac. John & Eleanor (Webster) Steele- **1047**; noted as among the more violent whigs in the Salem area; along w. the Carswells, they were prob. members of the party intent on tarring & feathering James Campbell when he returned from Canada to visit his family- **1065**
John- s. James, & his heir at law; defendant, Jan. 16, 1775, in a case brought by Philip Schuyler, Esq.- **878**
Joseph- former owner, Lot No. 264, Turner's Patent; purch. from John Williams, Mar. 7, 1785, by William Henderson- **(L)- 936**
William- a "rank tory"; Aug. 1777, he was returning from Burgoyne's camp when he met a tory scout party that had capt. George Hundertmark, a Hessian deserter, & Susan & Rebecca Lytle, nr. Salem, N. Y.; being familiar w. the party, he inquired abt. the girls, & convinced them that their absence would be noticed; he then affected their release into his custody on the condition that he detain them until after sundown, thus allowing the scout party to effectively make their escape from the area- **740**
William- c. 1858, res. N. of Deac. Alexander Turner, Jr.'s property, which is now a part of Evergreen Cemetery, Salem, N. Y.- **1034**

McNITT,
Alexander- plaintiff, Nov. 1786, vs. Duncan Campbell, the gentleman- **878½**
Capt. Alexander- res. Salem, N. Y.; during the War of 1812, Betsey Taylor was working for his s. Deac. Daniel, & recoll. how Capt. McNitt, "then living, but very old & his mind much broken" had the experiences of his earlier days revived by hearing talk of the war; he spoke continually abt. killing tories, but he was "so decrepid & feeble that he only went out into the yard, but never farther", until early one morning he got up & dressed, saying that he had "to take a co. of tories to Nova Scotia"; he bid her & the others at the house goodbye, & went off down the road; "the men here foll. after him, but could not persuade him to come back"; eventually, he stopped at his grdau. McLaughery's house, & in the afternoon, they were able to get him to consent to ride back to his home- **1018**
Capt. Andrew J.- (McNett) Co. E, 93rd N. Y. Inf.- **1090b**

Daniel- (s. James & Lydia Martin) m. ____ Hamilton; res. Salem, N. Y., & later rem. Fond du Lac, Wisc.- **731**

Capt. Daniel- his s. James, m. Lydia Martin- **731**

Deac. Daniel- s. Capt. Alexander; in 1814, when the Salem militia went on alarm to Plattsburgh, N. Y., he went w. his horse & wagon to carry some baggage; his father laughed at him & sd. that he was a coward & would soon run away, describing some similar occasion during the Rev. war when he hid himself in a potato hole on the instance of an alarm or skirmish- **1018**

James- s. Capt. Daniel; res. NW part of Salem, N. Y.; m. Lydia, dau. Moses, Sr., & Lydia (More) Martin; children-

1. Martin, res. Quincy, Illinois; m. Elvira ____
2. Ann Eliza, unm., res. at home
3. Asa M.; m. Maria M. Sherman, Rupert, Vt.; he d. Sept. 20, 1864, at 49
4. Maria, married twice
5. James, m. Eliza Wilson
6. Miriam, m. Daniel Woodward
7. Daniel, m. ____ Hamilton- **731**; c. 1830- 48, the upper port. of his farm was occ. by the Telfair family- **972**; his grdf., Capt. Alexander, passed his home early one morning, c. 1814, intent upon taking a party of tories to Nova Scotia, his memories of the Rev. war having been revived by news concerning the War of 1812- **1018**; brief ment.- **1041**

Maria- (dau. James & Lydia Martin) m. 1. a hired hand of the McNitt's; "It was a run- away match, & the family never after had any intercourse w. her"; 2. Wm.? Hamilton; she d. somewhere nr. her bro. Martin's, in Illinois, where her children now (c. 1850) res.- **731**

McPHERSON,
Farquher- deed witn., May 6, 1775, Francis Panton to Michael Hoffnagle- **(L)- 936**

McQUEEN,
Peter- miller; early settler at Fitch's Point, Salem, N. Y.; he was the only one loc. N. of the creek until Silas Conkey built there; see Vol. 1- **867**; Capt. Adam Martin informed him that the more violent Salem whigs intended to go & tar & feather James Campbell when he came to visit his family foll. the Rev. war; after he conveyed a warning to the Campbells, he started his mill as a signal to Martin that it was safe to allow them to leave his tavern & go on their errand w/o any prospect of harming Campbell- **1065**

McWHORTER,
Matthew- of Salem, N. Y.; dau. Mary, m. Hugh, s. James Harsha, the emig.; his farm adjoins John Harsha's on the N. side- **973**; m. Polly (Mary), dau. Deac. Alexander Turner, Jr.; now dec'd., c. 1862, his wid. res. Waukesha, Wisc.- **1086**

Samuel- of Hebron, N. Y.; May 9, 1786, deeds Lots 30 & 31, Scott & Kemp Patent, ea. containing 238 acres, to Jonas Woodell- **(L)- 936**; (McWhurter) sold above ment. lots for £ 340- **(L)- 936b**

MEED,
Abner- res. W. Rutland, Vt.; c. 1852, Constable & Collector for Rutland, Vt.- **966**
James- among those involved in the arrest & flogging (§ 881) of Benjamin Hough; his surname (var. Mead) noted by John L. Marsh as among the few found in the Clarendon, Vt. area even remotely connected w. the event- **966**

Menstruation- suspected example of an erratic cycle ment. by Dr. Fitch, based upon symptoms described pert. to Jennet Tosh, of E. Greenwich, N. Y.; she was habitually subj. to nosebleeds, & Dr. Fitch regarded that symptom as an indication of an abnormality, although the circumstances of her death (Nov. 19, 1801; Vol. 1) suggest some other cause, perh. then not identified; see Von Willebrand's disease- **871**

MENZIES,
Maj.- d. June 16, 1776; killed at the mouth of Boston Harbor, when over 300 soldiers from Scotland were capt.; refers Thatcher's Military Journal; (this was prob. the same event in which Lt. Col. Archibald Campbell was capt., & later exchanged for Ethan Allen); Dr. Fitch queries whether he may have been one of the patentees; see Vol. 1- **1079**

Menzies Patent- its gr. extended across the middle of town of Granville, N. Y.- **1079**

MERRIAM,
_____- m. dau. _____ & Martha Palen, in NYC; shortly afterw. rem. Louisville, Kentucky- **731**
Capt. Abel- c. 1779, commanded a militia co., Wells, Vt.; called out several times to Castleton, 1779 & 1780- **752**
Hannah- m. Sidney Wells, as his 2nd wf.- **839**

MERRILL,
Family- res. N. of Salem, N. Y.; their farm was occ. at diff. times by _____ Stevenson, Wm. Proudfit, & c. 1861, by _____ McMillan- **1078**

MERRY,
Jane- m. Walter M., s. Philo & Abigail (Martin) Rockwell- **1046**
Wid. Jane- m. Martin, s. Philo & Abby (Martin) Rockwell, in NYC- **730**

MEXICO- **799, 972**

MICHIGAN- 730, 731, 799, 842, 845, 914, 991, 1045, 1069, 1090; canal- 845;
Counties- Eaton- 812; Malone- 848; Washtenaw- 812; Wayne- 812;
Cities & Towns- Ann Arbor- 812; Detroit- 812, 969; Marshall- 730, 802;
Munroe- 802, 848; Tecumseh- 975

MIDDLECOT,
Richard- (Middlecoat, or Middlecote) m. Sarah Winslow, wid. Miles Standish, Jr.,
& Tobias Payne, as her 3rd husb.- **757**

Middle Granville, N. Y.- a bur. grd. loc. S. of here, on the E. side of the highway
& equidistant betw. here & Granville corners, reserved for members of the Hall,
Parker, & other Masonic families; orig. a SW port. of Dr. Ira Hall's farm, it was
deeded to the Granville Lodge & Chapter of Masons, on instruction of Dr. Ira
Hall's Will, May 6, Prob., Oct. 14, 1816- **759s**

Midwives- during the colonial & Rev. war era, "granny" was their colloq.
designation- **869**

MILITIA- a "rendezvous" held Aug. 29, 1814, at Well's Hotel, Union Village
(Greenwich, N. Y.) for recruiting a rifleman regt.; terms of service incl. $8.00 per
month pay; $50.00 bounty for enl., $50.00 when mustered, & $24.00 when disch.;
160 acres "surveyed at public expense" & gr. foll. service- **705**; requisition law
made by Maj. Gen. Moore upon his division, due to "alarming situation of our
northern frontier"; on orders rec'd. by Brig. Gen. DeRidder, militia marched to
rendezvous point at Ft. Miller, N. Y., Sept. 8, 1814, for further advance to northern
frontier- **706**; an extract from a Salem, N. Y. militia officer's letter notes their arr.
at Burlington, Vt., on the morning of Sept. 13, 1814, w. a general desire within the
co. to pursue the British to Montreal, but uncert. regarding orders for further
advance- **708**; c. 1782, a co. of '9 months men' enl. from Salem & its vicinity,
garrisoned at Saratoga (Schuylerville, N. Y.) for 6 wks. during the spring, then
divided & stat. there & at Ft. Williams, Salem, N. Y., as the northernmost
American outposts guarding the frontier- **729**; Province of N. Y. divided into 2
brigades by Sir H. Moore; northern brigade extended from the Highlands to the W.
bounds of the Province; Sir Wm. Johnson appt. Brig. Gen., & divided Albany co.
ranks, from a regt. & 2 battalions, into several regts. covering smaller districts;
Adjutant Gen.- Sir Guy Johnson; formation of new regts. required prior notice to
Sir Wm. Johnson, but some formed w/o notice, as Johnson noted- "in partical [sic]
a Regiment formed abt. Ft. Edward, South Bay, & its environs, by which I hear
Maj. Skene is Colonel"; other regts. formed at Ranslaerwyck (Rensselaerwyck),
Livingston's manor, Claverack, "& c."; Sir Wm. was uncert. whether Cumberland
co. militia had yet reached regimental level; refers Nov. 25, 1759 letter of Sir Wm.
Johnson to Lt. Gov. Colden; orig. Albany co. force of 6,000 men was divided into
several regts. of 5- 10,000 men ea.- **735**; Apr. 1776, Capt. Hewin's co., of
Stockbridge, Mass., called upon by Comm. of Safety, New Canaan, N. Y., to assist

in capt. tories who were disturbing & breaking up their meetings; some members of militia from Richmond, Mass., also participated; w. news of Burgoyne coming down Lake Champlain, 1777, regional militia were called out; a co. from Stockbridge, Mass. marched to Ft. Ann via Richmond, Hancock, & Williamstown, Mass., to Pownal & Bennington, Vt., & thence through Cambridge, Ft. Miller, & Ft. Edward, N. Y., to arr. at Ft. Ann abt. July 8th- 747; c. 1778, the frontier around Skenesborough, N. Y. was in a constant state of alarm against tories & Indians; "the militia were a part out at one time & a part at ano., relieving ea. other alternately during the season, & sometimes on alarms, which were several, all the militia were out"; during all of the foll. yr., the militia was constantly called out, being stat. at Put's rock, the Elbow, & at an HQ loc. "at a place called the middle of the town" (in Skenesborough, or Skene's Patent); officers & privates both commanded & served, or were on relief, alternately at ea. place; HQ guards served alternate 24 hr. shifts; regt. commanders were Col Jeremiah Burrows, Capt. Thos. Lyon, & Lts. Fuller, Boggs, Gould, & Lt. Daniel Stewart- 751; Aug. 1776, prob. referring only to Conn., the militia were "called out in mass, to defend N. Y. from the British"- 753; c. 1780, Granville, N. Y., some militia called out on scouts constantly through the summer, w. abt. 3 men sent out in ea. scout, one going out as ano. came in, "the place being frontier; were under no officer except a corporal"; ordered out & directed by Capt. Child, scouts were sent to Skenesborough, Ft. Ann, Lake George, East bay, & Kingsbury, N. Y.; on one occasion, Capt. Child commanded a co. of 30 men when some buildings were burnt at Kingsbury- 754; directed Aug. 22, 1775, by N. Y. Prov. Congress, to be divided into 6 brigades; Charlotte, Cumberland, & Gloucester counties to comprise one brigade, & Albany & Tryon counties to comprise ano.- 782; c. 1775, a list of officers accepting comm. in Van Schaik's regt.; see Van Schaik, Col.; recommendations, Jan. 25, 1776, by Charlotte co. Comm. of Safety, for appt. of its militia officers- Col., Lt. Col., Majs., Adjutant, Qtrmaster, Capts., 1st & 2nd Lts.; presented to N. Y. Prov. Congress & positions filled, Feb. 19, 1776; on the same day, Col. John Williams obt. blank commissions for 3 companies of minutemen in the co.; on Feb. 28th, four N. Y. battalions were stat. in Canada, under Col. James Clinton's command- 784; July 24, 1776, rangers to be raised to guard northern couinties; 120 men designated for Charlotte co., divided into 2 companies, ea. containing a Capt., Lt., 3 Sgts., 3 Corps., & 42 privates; & one party, to consist of Lt., Sgt., Corp., & 17 privates; by order, Aug. 1, 1776, Charlotte co. to form into one militia brigade, & Cumberland & Gloucester counties to form ano.; Dec. 2nd- £ 464 transmitted to pay rangers; Jan. 4, 1777- £ 524 transmitted for rangers pay & bounty- 785; a co. of 9 mos. men mustered into service May 18, 1782, from the vicinity of Salem, N. Y.; its officers were Lt. John Hunsdon; Ens. Asa Fitch, Sr.; Sgts. David Henderson, & Lewis Herman; Corps. Henry Shepard, James King, & O. Selfridge; consolidated into ano. co., Hunsdon became its Ens., & all others served as privates; orig. privates- Robert Armstrong, John Ramge, Thomas Boid, Andrew McNitt, Ben Searls, John Baker, Benjamin Ward?, Asa Fetine?, Dan Rude, Howe Gibs, ____Baker, ____ Cook, ____ Bemus, ____ Morison, ____ Dun?, ____ West, ____ Wilson, ____

Mighel, ____ McDonald, & ____ Lane- 799; Gen. Schuyler notes to Gen. Washington, July 17, 1777, that part of the Mass. & all of the N. H. militia at Ft. Edward 'are so heartily tired & so desirous of getting home' that prob. none will remain after 10 days (Dr. Fitch noting that attention to their family's safety & gathering the harvest was prob. behind their desire to leave); half of the militia was disch. here on July 21st, to silence their clamors, & the remainder- officers excepted, 'will soon disch. themselves' leaving the army here at a strength of '700 Continental troops, sick & well'; Gen. Schuyler also notes from his retreat to Moses creek that half of the militia at Ft. Edward have been disch., provided the remainder agree to stay ano. 3 wks., listing their numbers as- N. Y.- 1,046; Mass.- Berkshire co.- 300 out of the orig. 1,200; Hampshire co.- only 29 officers & 34 privates out of 500, 'the rest having infamously deserted'; Conn.- few, if any of the orig. 100 remain, foll. the example of the Hampshire co. men; & there are now abt. 1,300 militia encamped w. the army at Moses creek, w/o prosepect of detaining half of them for more than 5- 6 days- 797; c. 1775, the Committees of Correspondence within every district ordered to form their militia into companies- 821; militia of Cambridge corporation & Cambridge district unite, prob. 1776, to form one regt., known as No. 18- 826; during the last yrs. of the Rev. war, the whigs enl. 3 & 6 months men to guard the frontier, "& to pay these men, they would take cattle & sheep from the Argyle folks" (who were all regarded as tories by the whigs)- 977; Apr. 20, 1841, the foll. units incl. in a procession at Salem, N. Y., commemorating the death of Pres. Wm. H. Harrison- Capt. Martin's Artillery co.; officers of the 10th Division & 16th Brigade; commiss. officers of Col. Shaw's 50th Regt.; officers & soldiers who had served under Gen. Harrison, & soldiers of the Rev. war- 1009; at the time of the Allen family & McCrea massacres (July 26 & 27, 1777), most of the men of the town of Salem, N. Y. were down & abt. Bennington, Vt., in a volunteer co. commanded by Dr. John Williams; refers Slade's Vt. State Papers, "one of the 1st papers"; in a few days, teams were sent to Salem to evac. the town- 1049; 4 area companies, 2 from White Creek, & one ea. from Cambridge & Union Village (Greenwich, N. Y.), were requisitioned by Col. John S. Crocker, commandant of militia, to attend the execution of Martin Wallace, Dec. 1, 1858, at Salem, N. Y.; they were paraded & marched through the streets "to occupy the attention of the populace", & were positioned for the day along the sidewalk at the front of the Court House, & at the fences around the yard to its rear, at 10:00 AM; their behavior while in attendance became prominent as "a topic of public complaint & censure", as the companies succumbed to "drunkenness & rowdyism", which was partially excused by the inclemency of weather, "but such gross excess & debauchery in men who were pd. for their attendance, on an occasion of such solemnity was felt on all hands to be an outrage on public morality & decency"- 1050s; at the battle of Plattsburgh, Sept. 1814, the militia were instructed by Gen. Alex. Macomb to defend the Saranac river ford at Pike's Cantonment, & if unable to, to retreat S. to a quantity of stores & defend, or destroy them; on the morning of the battle, Gov. Provost sent a detachm. of regulars in pursuit of them, suspecting that they would retreat to their forts, & he might assault them simult.; however, the militia drew the detachm. towards these stores, & onto a wood- road "close on their heels, determined to rush into the forts pell mell w. them"; bef. realizing their error, they had been lead away 4 mi. towards the American stores, when it was discovered that the British fleet had already surrendered- **1055**

MILLER,
Capt.- commanded a co., prob. Albany co. militia, Col. Farnsworth's regt.; sent to Schoharie, Apr. 1780, & stat. there until the end of the campaign season in Dec.- **756**
John- d. Dec. 30, 1811, at 72- **(L)- 975**
John- res. a mi. W. of Reid's spring, Ft. Edward, N. Y.; m. Mary Ann Armitage; ments. s. Capt. Wm. Henry- **1081**
Peter- of Cambridge, N. Y.; John Younglove reported to the Albany Comm., May 23, 1776, that he had declared his taking of an oath obliging him to join the King's troops when called by any of its officers, "& to kill his best friends if they were in opposition to him"; it was resolved by the Comm. that the Cambridge Comm. should apprehend, disarm, & bind him to future good behavior- **888**
William- res. Fitch's Point, Salem, N. Y.; at Wid. Angel's 1st recoll., his house was occ. by John Henry, & his mills were then down, but she had no recoll. of them ever having been burned; see Vol. 1- **859**; ano. ment. that John Henry occ. his place- **865**
Capt. William Henry- (s. John & Mary Ann Armitage) Co. K, 44th N. Y. Inf.; d. Apr. 30, (1862?), at 23½ yrs., of typhus fever, in camp hospital bef. Yorktown, Va.; bur. May 12th, gr. 1, soldier's plot, Evergreen Cemetery, Salem, N. Y.- **1081**; a newsclipping (n. d.), giving biog. sketch, *Salem Press*, perh. written by Dr. Fitch; entire text missing, except for a corner of the masthead- **1096**

MILLET,
Bridget- testif. that Martin Wallace came to her house abt. 3:00 PM on the day of Barney McEntee's murder, sd. that he was looking for a house, & that he was going to buy a cow from Patrick Joice, & left abt. 4:30 PM- **1048s**
Daniel- res. betw. Michael Conway's & Buskirk's Bridge, N. Y.; during the early evening, Feb. 16, 1858, bef. Hiram Sisson went to Pratt's store, he was seen by Sisson, loading cord wood abt. 15 rods from where Barney McEntee's body was later discovered; he & Dennis Murphy appeared to be drawing wood to the depot, under Mr. Chase's direction; by Oct. 1858, he was employed by Sisson & his father; acc. Ann Joice's testim. at Martin Wallace's trial, when he returned to their store, Wallace claimed to have been to see him- **1048s**

MILLIMAN,
Capt. Henry S.- of Cambridge, N. Y.; May 25, 1861, commanded Co. D, 22nd N. Y. Inf.- **(L)- 1074**; commanded same co., Jan. 1862- **1081**; wnd. at 2nd Bull Run, Aug. 29- 30, 1862, & later d. of wnds.- **1095b**

Miss- of Hoosick, N. Y.; m. Wm., s. William & Margaret (Andrew) Dobbin- **732**
Thomas, Jr.- res. nr. Milliman's corners, Salem, N. Y.; m. Caroline, dau. Jarvis &
Mary (Harvey) Martin; she d. & left children Jarvis & Mary- **731**; his loc., c. 1850,
prev. occ. by Benjamin Fitch- **872**

MILLS,
James- m. Rebecca, dau. John & Eleanor (Lowrie) Lytle; they res. on the 1st farm
in Argyle, N. Y., on the road from W. Hebron to Argyle corners; children-
1. Joseph, m. Betsey McCoy
2. Anna, m. George Hall
3. Eleanor, m. David Rogers
4. Susan, m. James Crozier
5. Margaret, m. Mathew Hall
6. Jane, m. 1. Robert Stewart; 2. Thomas McFadden
7. Esther, m. Thomas Haywood
8. Sarah, m. Joseph Cogshall- **737**
James- of Argyle, N. Y.; m. Emily, dau. David Hanna & ____ (Taylor) Lytle; c.
1860's, res. Illinois- **1069**
Lydia- of Greenwich, Conn.; m. Ebenezer, s. Gov. Thomas Fitch- **799**

MINNESOTA- Lake Pepin- 731

MISSISSIPPI- Vicksburg- 759s, 1095; Big Black river- 1095; Champion Hills-
1095

MISSOURI- Ft. Rolla- 1081

MITCHELL,
____- m. Austin Henry, s. Samuel & Olive (Scott) Wells- **839**
Edward- of New Haven, Conn.; m. Elizabeth, dau. ____ & Sarah (Fitch) Gorham-
799
Ensign- Dec. 28, 1784, purch. 150 acres, Whitehall, N. Y., for £ 97 10s- **(L)- 875**
Isaac- c. 1786, Sgt., militia co., Salem, N. Y.; ordered out to quell a tax rebellion
in Granville, N. Y.- **701**
John- (Mitchel) an American prisoner at Ft. Ticonderoga; he escaped along w.
Samuel Standish & 2 others, Aug. 1777, & they made their way to safety in
Arlington, Vt.- **747**
Rev. L.- c. 1785, a call given to him, to preside over the church, Salem, N. Y.; see
Vol. 4- **844**
Thomas- of Hartford, N. Y.; he struck & killed Hannah Fanning by the blow of an
axe to the side of her head & behind her ear; was indicted, tried, & acquitted,
Jan. 14, 1812- **874**

MITCHELSON,
Walter- noted in a deed transaction, recorded June 30, 1774, that the survey map of Artillery Patent was drawn by him- **(L)- 936**

MOERS,
Judge- of Champlain, N. Y.; dau. Sophia, m. Thomas I., s. John & Margaret (Robertson) Whiteside- **805**

MOFFAT,
Robert, Sr.- res. Troy, N. Y.; printer & proprietor, the *Northern Budget*; d. May 4, 1850, a Mon. evening, at 34; 'few in number are those who have been afflicted w. more pains in life; & still less the number who have endured them w. so much fortitude'- **736**
William- the loc. of his house was later occ. for several yrs. by James Thompson, & then by John McDonald- **864**; res. N. of Jarvis Martin, Fitch's Point, Salem, N. Y.; the orig. road from Fitch's Point ran N. past his house to Black creek- **865**
William- (Moffitt) defendant, Jan. 16, 1775, along w. Wm. Perry, in a case brought by Philip Schuyler, Esq., assignee of Philip P. Lansing- **878**

MOLES,
William- oath of alleg.; Co. D, 22nd N. Y. Inf.- **(L)- 1074**

MONTGOMERY,
Capt.- British; was wnd. at the battle of Ft. Ann, July 1777, & capt. by member's of Capt. Rowley's co.- **747**
Hugh- m. Hannah, dau. ____ Mack?- **734**
Mrs. Hugh- b. ca. 1760, was grdau. Robert Mack, the emig.; she res. Manchester, Vt., & now (c. 1850) Akron, Ohio- **734**
Mr.- "the delegate from Dutchess co."; appt. to a comm. of N. Y. Provincial Congress, June 14, 1775, to investigate the conduct of William Duer, Esq.- **777**
Gen. Richard- (1738- 1775) officer witn., May- Dec. 1775 service of Ebenzer Farnsworth, acc. his Rev. war pens. appl.,- **750**; some units from Col. Waterbury's Conn. regt. went under his command from Ticonderoga to Canada, 1775- **753**; nomin. as Brig. Gen., June 7, 1775, by N. Y. Provincial Congress- **776**; along w. Col. Van Schaik, Aug. 1775, expresses surprise on the disclosure that John Williams had been "superceded" by Stephen McCrey in appt. as surgeon in Col. Van Schaik's battalion- **790**; commanded American assault on Quebec (Dec. 31, 1775)- **922**

MOON,
Solomon- res. either Kingsbury, or Queensbury, N. Y.; he was among those 'brought to a sense of themselves' during Lorenzo Dow's visit to the area in early 1798- **814**; he came to the Methodist quarterly meeting, June 20, 1798, Pittstown, N. Y., a journey of over 40 mi., to say at the meeting, 'I bless the day that ever

I saw the face of brother Dow', as a witn. in support of Dow's effectiveness & continuance in the circuit- **815**

MOONEY,
John- d. July 9, 1782, at 66- **(L)- 975**

MOORE,
____- by Ebenezer Cole's affidavit, Feb. 27, 1771, he attempted to settle in Princetown (Manchester, Vt.) under N. Y. proporietorship, & was sd. to have been tied up & whipped by the N. H. settlers because of his intentions- **896**
Family- of NYC; noted in the obit. of Mrs. Mary, wid. Maj. James Harvey, that both the Harvey & Barber families of NYC, were in some manner connected w. this family- **1035**
Gurdon G.- 2nd Lt., 93rd N. Y. Inf.- **1090b**
Gov. Sir Henry- (1713- 1769; acting Gov., 1756- 62; Gov., 1765- 69) given as "Sir H. Moore"; divided Province of N. Y. into 2 military brigades, w. N. Y. Highlands as the boundary betw. divisions; refers Doc. Hist. of N. Y., v. 2, p. 958- **735**; his letter to Lord Shelburne, June 9, 1767, reacting to 2 petitns. & other material enclosed in Shelburne's Apr. 11th letter; remarking upon the manner of addressing the crown, cites that much liberty is taken in common conversation in America, but his personal belief was that no assertion of facts not incontestable, would be presented; he, therefore, refers to the strictest of inquiries concerning charges within the enclosed petitn., beginning w. recitation of proceedings of N. Y. govt., Oct. 22, 1765, relating to the occ. & improvement by Jacob Marsh, of lands gr. to Capt. John Small & Mr. Napier; relates hist. of provisions made to settlers found to be occ. lands gr. to others by N. Y. Province, particularly reduced officers; ments. numerous claims for townships made within N. Y. jurisdiction, noting occ. primarily of Shaftsbury, Bennington, & Pownal, Vt., suspecting this to be merely an experiment to discover the extent of N. Y.'s willingness to accomodate; he observes the current status of townships passing through the Patent process, noting establ. of Cumberland co.; refers to question of Samuel Robinson's petitn., remarking upon its falsities, & upon Robinson's character, annexing the replies of Messrs. Colden & James Duane to the 1st six paragraphs of sd. petitn., & giving his own counterpoints to the remainder; remarks that 'of his one thousand grantees' perh. less than half were settled there & many inhabitants of this town & adjacent Provinces have signed Robinson's petitn. w/o intentions of ever being on the lands; points out that he has never demanded a fee of Robinson, or from anyone else, having signed only 6 Patents since coming to the Province, 'giving my fees in all cases where I supposed the payment would distress the person'; the whole table of his fees, lately sent to England, referred to as an indication of Robinson's gross misrepresentations & his presumptive character for assuming the leadership role he engaged in; see Grants/ N. H. Controversy- **894**; ano. letter to Lord Shelburne, June 10, 1767, replying to petitn. of Soc. for Propagation of the Gospel, a petitn. presumed to be authored by Samuel Robinson; notes the petitn., in itself, had so

little intent to serve anyone other than its signers, containing a request to divide the public shares among them w/o the least attention to the purpose they were designed for, & w/o the least scruple of defrauding the Soc. of its rights; of the proceedings by this govt. in 28 townships, the rights of the Soc. & all gr. of public uses have been expressly reserved in 24 for the uses intended- **895**

Gen. Sir John- (1761- 1809) British; it was reported that the 42nd Royal Highland regt. was in his campaign in Portugal & Spain, & in the disastrous retreat to Corrona, & the fight there, 1808- 9- **990**

John D.- oath of alleg.; Co. D, 22nd N. Y. Inf.- **1074**

Maj. Gen.- enforced the requisition law upon his division's militia, & marched by Brig. Gen. DeRidder's orders to rendezvous Sept. 8, 1814, at Ft. Miller, N. Y.- **706**

Martin- Co. A, 2nd N. Y., Northern Black Horse, Cav., 1861- 2- **1080**

Nelson- m. Sarah, dau. Adam & Polly (Granger) Martin- **1046**

Paschal D.- res. S. Salem, N. Y.; m. Maria, dau. John & Jane (McKellip) Dobbin- **732**

MORE,

____ - m. Phebe, dau. Samuel Burrows; his wf. rec'd. clear title to lands prev. deeded to her, & £ 20 'N. England money in old tenor', by her father's Will, Feb. 2, 1756- **1100**

Ephriam?- of Simsbury, Conn.; he worked in the mines there, & his eyes were burnt by an explosion, leading to partial & later, total blindness; rem. Stillwater, N. Y.; children- sons Ephriam, Gideon, Charles, Alpheus, Phineas, & Reuben; daus. Anna, m. Job Wright; Phebe, m. Silas Wright; Anner (Hannah?), m. Ephriam Woodworth; Jerusha, m. ____ Highstead; Lydia, m. Moses Martin; & Triphena, m. William? Bemis, of Bemis Heights, Stillwater, N. Y.- **850**

Hugh- "whose sympathies were strongly upon the tory side in politics", c. 1775, res. S. Salem, N. Y.; he was a guest at a Thanksgiving dinner givenby Edmund Wells, Jr., & was seated across from James Ashton, his political opposite; a remark was passed from one to the other, which escalated into more heated remarks, until one of them became the wearer of the dinner's main course; a fistfight then ensued outside the cabin, in which Ashton prevailed over More; see Holidays- **840**

James- 'Mad More'; see Vol. 1; res. S. part of Salem, N. Y.; he "had a long musket, w. which he took unerring aim. He could kill a deer at a distance of from 25 to 30 rods"- a feat of some measure, but not uncommon among hunters of the period, acc. Dr. Fitch; he also had a fine, well trained horse, & when Col. Baum's expedition was en route to Bennington, he was mounted on the horse, "incessantly hovering upon the front of the force, riding up as nr. as was prudent, taking aim & disch. his gun at the enemy & instantly flying off beyond their reach"; this he did repeatedly, & it was believed that w. his aim, he must have killed several of the enemy; he was once at the trial of a suspected person & became abusive towards him; ____ Lytle, "who was a good whig", interfered, & he became abusive towards him as well, calling him a tory; Lytle thereupon knocked him down, swearing & kicking him repeatedly- **925**; he res. nr. ____ Smith, who had m. the sist. of

Richard & Wm. Hoy- **1000**; he & some other men of Sodom (Shushan, N. Y.) came over to drive off the cows of "black" Duncan Campbell shortly after his family had returned from Burgoyne's camp at Ft. Edward; "they threw down the fence & went to driving them out of the field"; when Campbell attempted to drive them back, More came up to him "& putting the muzzle of his loaded gun to father's breast, sd. 'Stand still, you d- d tory, or I'll shoot you through!' And the other men drove the cattle away"; More foddered 3 of these cows over the winter, at a stack he kept on the Salem side of the Battenkill; as he res. on the opp. side of the stream, when high water came & ran over the top of the ice, he could not get over to feed them; towards night, the cattle became hungry, started on the path to his house, & fell into the kill as they attempted to cross the ice, & drowned; More lost all of Campbell's stock, a cow of his own, & a yoke of oxen he had stolen from someone else, "his own cow the last to fall through"; standing on the shore, looking at them, but unable to save them, when his cow went through, "he broke out, in his Irish brogue, repeating an old proverb- 'Och! weel! ye cam to me o'er the de'il's back & have now gone under his belly- but ye need na ha ta'en wi' ye my ain honestly earned cow!' "- **1063**; spring 1778, his sawmill was suppos. burned by the tories, foll. the burning of the E. Greenwich school house & "black" Duncan Campbell's house; though it was suspected that he may have been involved in the latter incident, no particular whig was accused; Dr. Fitch attrib. the animosity betw. More & the Campbells to be the result of their being desc. from the same clan, but having opp. political views- **1064**
Lydia- m. Moses, s. Aaron & Sarah (Newell) Martin- **1037**

MOREHOUSE,
Alanson- Co. I, 123rd NYSV; d. Dec. 5, 1862- **1098**

MOREY,
Gideon- c. 1851, res. Ballston, N. Y.; m. Rebecca, dau. _____ & Rebecca (Ashton) _____ - **960**
Samuel- bro. Gideon; c. 1851, res. Stillwater, N. Y.- **960**

MORGAN,
_____ - the body of Timothy Munroe, drowned in Niagara river, was orig. suspected to be his (prob. Wm. Morgan, of Batavia, N. Y.; a Free Mason, he was presumed abducted & murdered, 1826, for revealing masonic secrets)- **812**
Daniel- (1736- 1802) it was one of his riflemen (Timothy Murphy) who shot & mortally wnd. Gen. Simon Frazier, Oct. 7, 1777, during the battle of Bemis Heights- **1002**
Ephriam- "ano. excellent merch. in Troy"; politically a Federalist, he served as its Supervisor when the city was still a town, despite being in a strongly Democratic region; during the Rev. war, he res. in Conn. w. an uncle, & was enl. by him in the army at Norwalk, when he was only 17 yrs. old; he was marched to West Point, & attached to the commissary dept., assisting the Quartermaster; when he resigned in

dissatisfaction, & he undertook the post until ano. was appt., but continued to serve in the Quartermaster's capacity until the end of the war; he might instantly have rec'd. a commission, but deemed it not to be"the best utility to him", & was disch. as a private, thus drawing only $80 per annum as a pension- **1036**

MORRIS,

Gouverneur- (1752- 1816) corresponds from Albany, N. Y., July 14, 1777, to N. Y. Provincial Congress, explaining that his venture towards Ft. Ann has been delayed by continued rains, & describes the movements involved in leading to the battle there a wk. earlier; refers p. 997, Correspondence of the Provincial Congrerss- **792**; forwards from Ft. Edward to the Council of Safety, July 21st, the approving of recent resolutions 'relative to our north eastern country', & ment. the political situation within the Grants, & Col. Skene's efforts in courting their allegiance to the British cause (Dr. Fitch notes that Morris, & Abram Yates, Jr., were part of a comm. of the Council sent to HQ, prob. Schuyler's, to assess the current state of affairs in the efforts to curtail Burgoyne's advance); states that the truth being 'very many of those villains only want a New England reason, or if you like the expression better, a plausible pretext, to desert the American states, New Vermont among the rest'; observes the importance & necessity of getting as many of the neutral inhabitants, esp. their teams & provisions, as far from the vicinity of Burgoyne's army as possible; he further warns, in the delicacy of the Grants situation, not to throw the inhabitants into the arms of the enemy where they may get now what they want, when the prospects of the region achieving statehood is that 'of a mere feather' at the present time- **796**; he & Yates report from Moses creek encampment, July 23rd, on an attack made on the picket guard of their party that day on Ft. Ann road, along w. the retreat of Gen. Schuyler's army to this loc., & the disch. & departure of militia; in light of the current strategic situation, he makes the foll. prophetic statement- 'But sir, Burgoyne cannot fly. If 3,000 New England militia can be got onto the N. H. Grants somewhere; & if Gen. Washington can spare 1,500 good troops here; & if the Gov. is put at the head of 1/3rd of the militia of the state to march to Tryon co. we may laugh at Mr. Howe & Mr. Burgoyne.'- **797**

Lewis- (1726- 1798; N. Y. Senate, 1777- 81, 1784- 88) of Westchester co., N. Y.; nomin. in N. Y. Assembly, July 1789, as 2nd U. S. Senator, but rejected w/o count; when the Senate's proposal of Ezra L'Hommedieu was rejected by the Assembly, he was given as a counter proposal to Rufus King, but was again rejected, 43- 12- **920**

Dr. Philip V. N.- physician, res. Cambridge, N. Y.; testif. at the trial of Martin Wallace that he was called toexamine the body of Barney McEntee, Feb. 16, 1858; he arr. at the scene at abt. 9:00 PM, & found it lying 30- 40 rods from Ira Sisson's house, abt. ½ mi. from Buskirk's Bridge, on the highway to Eagle Bridge, N. Y.; the feet of the victim were nr. the S. track of the road, the body slanting betw. the road & fence, w. the head facing downhill & SE, seemingly fallen over, lying on his right arm, the right side of his face lying in his hat; both the head & hat were covered in blood, & a quantity had oozed out because of the downhill position of the head; his skull had been severely fractured & there were pieces of bark intermixed in his hair w. the blood; a stick was found, 4½ ft. long, abt. 1½ in. in diameter at the large end, & 1 in. at the small end; his body was stiff & freezing, w/o warmth; Uriah Colony, Ira Sisson, Andrew Houghton, & Hiram Sisson had all gone along w. him to observe the body, & there were also others there; the dec'd. had on a coat, pants, & a white felt hat, & his left pocket was open w. a wallet crushed up & stuck into it, empty; the 1st blow was to the top of his head, from behind, & rendered him unconscious, & the 2nd blow, behind his ear, had killed him; he might have survived the 1st blow, by surgery, but could only have lived 15-30 min. foll. the 2nd blow; recalled on the 3rd day of Martin Wallace's trial for the murder, he testif. that the 2nd blow was delivered either as the victim fell, or when he was half down, or kneeling- **1048s**; President, Wash. Co. Medical Soc.; selected as one of the physicians to attend the execution of Martin Wallace, Dec. 1, 1858; he did not attend, Dr. White substituting- **1050s**

MORRISON,
_____- his old mill on the Owl kill, Cambridge, N. Y., was the site of a larger gristmill constructed (n. d.) by the Wells family- **844**
Col. Andrew J.- commander, Dec. 1861, 2nd N. Y., Northern Black Horse, Cavalry (later 7th N. Y. Cavalry); its Co. A, recruited Salem, N. Y., & stat. Wash., D. C., winter 1861- 2, & afterw. disch., there being more cavalry vols. than needed- **1080**
Esq.- c. 1777, res. Cambridge, N. Y.; during the evac. of Salem, Robert Getty's family moved down on his land & remained there for 2 days bef. fleeing further S. below the Hoosick river- **744**
Family- his wid. m. 2. "black" Duncan Campbell; ments. a son, Norman; see Vol. 1- **1060**
Mr. Justice- (perh. Thomas, of Cambridge, N. Y., acc. Dr. Fitch) noted Nov. 1772, that he declined serving as Justice of the Peace in John Munro's place- **912**
Norman- acc. Caty Campbell, he undoubtedly hid in Wid. Campbell's house when Jane McCrea was taken (July 1777) & was also taken into Burgoyne's camp by the Indians- **1060**

MORSE,
Francis B.- res. Lowville, N. Y.; m. Jane Maria, dau. Stephen & Jane (Martin) Leonard- **730**; his marriage ment. again- **1046**
Joseph- m. Mary, dau. Aaron & Sarah (Newell) Martin- **1037**; their children- Amos, Eunice, Leonard, Asenith, & Martin- all moved W.- **1042**

Moses kill- (occasionally ment. as Moses creek) loc. abt. 4 mi. below Ft. Edward, N. Y.; Gen. Schuyler's army retreated to here from Ft. Edward, July 23, 1777, & reported that half the militia were disch. here foll. a full council of general officers, on condition that the other half remain ano. 3 wks.; gives remaining no. of men from N. Y.; Berkshire & Hampshire co., Mass.; & Conn.; see Militia; combined w. the Continental force, the no. w. the army then totaled 2,700- 2,800 men- **797**; by unanimous decision of general officers, July 31st, Gen. Schuyler withdrew his force from here to Saratoga (Schuylerville, N. Y.), the ground here being too extensive for the troops to occ., nor was it possible to contract them w/o exposing them to immed. ruin- **798**

MOSHER,
Daniel- along w. Martin Wallace & Edward Hays, attempted to assist Barney McEntee in leaving Jesse Pratt's store; in his testim., Hays implied to McEntee that Mosher was a constable, & would have to take him up if he did not leave, in order to encourage McEntee to go from the store; Mosher later testif. that McEntee did not have any gloves on bef. or after he left the store (the gloves in question were 1st mislaid at Joice's store, & the proprietor placed them on the mantel- piece; when Wallace & McEntee were leaving the premises, Wallace took the gloves, but Joice told him to return them to McEntee, & Wallace sd. that he"would want them worse bef. he got home")- **1048s**
Capt. George B.- Co. F, 93rd N. Y. Inf.- **1090b**

MOSS,
John- b. Apr. 19, 1756, Cheshire, Conn.; an abstr. of his Rev. war pens. appl. states that he rem., May 1779, Wells, & then to Middleton, Vt., during the last campaign of the Rev. war; res. 15 yrs., Granville, N. Y., rem. to Ohio for 10 yrs., & then returned; vol., forepart Jan. 1776, Capt. Bradley's co., Col. Waterbury's regt.; marched to Stamford, & then Horseneck, Conn., foll. by Rye & New Rochelle, N. Y., & finally, to NYC, where they remained for 2 months; served 2 drafts of 3 months ea.- abt. Oct. 1, 1776, at the saw pits "so called", at Rye, N. Y., prob. Capt. Hotchkin's co., Col. Thaddeus Cook's regt., Gen. Woorsten's brigade; & late Feb. 1777, Capt. Miles Johnson's co. of Wallingford, Conn., in Col. Hooker's regt., Farmington, Conn., Gen. McDougall's brigade, which was sent to Peekskill, N. Y., & pursued the enemy all night foll. the burning of Danbury, Conn., bef. reaching Bedford, N. Y.; returned to Peekskill & disch. there; called out on 3 militia alarms, Capt. Abel Merriam's militia co., Wells, Vt.- fall 1779, marched to Castleton, Vt., & sent out over 2 months service as scout, then dismissed & sent home; Gen. Ethan Allen commanded here, & he heard him speak to the troops; Mar. 1780- at the burning of Skenesborough, they marched to Castleton & took provisions there; marched through the woods to Hubbardton, Vt., & then to Ticonderoga, attempting to get in the enemy's rear, commanded by Ethan Allen- abt. a wk., or more; fall 1780- called on alarm when Ft. Ann was attacked, abt. 6days service, marched to Castleton & thence to Whitehall, N. Y., & finally to Poultney,Vt.; also called out at other times, dates not recoll.; enl. for 3 months, in Vt. State troops, Aug. 1782, at Arlington, Vt.; marched to Whitehall, & stat. there until Nov.; during that time, a mutiny occurred due to lack of provisions, which became general- **752**

MOTT,

Capt. Edward- (Motte) of Conn.; his co., bound for Ticonderoga, was detained by Wm. Duer, Esq., July 10, 1775, at Ft. Edward, to protect the courts from attempts to close them by var.citizens of Charlotte co.; he was also the courier of Duer's July 11th correspondence to the N. Y. Comm. of Safety describing the attempts to close the courts- **779**

Esq.- c. 1850, res. below Ft. Miller, N. Y., where the Matthews family res. in 1798- **804**

Mount Independence- (loc. in Vt., opp. Ft. Ticonderoga) American forces under Gen. Arnold retreated to here & Crown Point from the St. Lawrence river valley, & remained here during the summer, 1776- **748**; the army retreated here foll. the battle of Three Rivers, 1776- **750**

MUNRO/ MUNROE,

Charles- (s. Samuel & Polly Alyea) was suppos. to have been murdered (n. d.) in Detroit, Mich.; left 2 daus.- **812**

Daniel- (s. John, Esq. & Catharine Reid) res. Younge, Upper Canada; m. Hannah Trickey, wid. Peter Mallory; children, all married, spouses not indicated-

1. Henry, res. Clark, Upper Canada
2. Timothy, res. nr. his bro. Henry
3. George, res. Ohio
4. Randy, keeps shoe shop, Lewiston, N. Y.
5. Mary, "is married, I know not to who"; & their father d. 1810- **812**

Donald- late 1775, Albany Comm., requests of Cambridge Comm. that they inquire of him for clues regarding a fuller discovery of the matter concerning John Munro's possible comm. in the King's service- **820**; bro. John, Esq.; as he res. at some distance, 4 of the company sent to examine Esq. Munro were sent to bring him to his bro.'s house; he acknowl. that he had told John McCrea that his bro. was to have a Capt.'s comm. under Col. Reid, 'but it appeared on closer examination his charge merely proceeded from a grudge he had against John Munro on acct. of a former quarrel'- **822**

Rev. Harry- (or Monroe) to induce people to settle on his Hebron patent, he promised his availability as preacher, but was often not up to his word on that acct.; one of the early settlers on his land, c. 1771, was John Duncan, who leased his land & res. in one of Monroe's houses until he could construct one of his own- **997**

Hugh- Aug. 1775, informed Col. John McCrea that Donald Munro had sent to him news that his bro., John, Esq., had rec'd. a Capt.'s comm. in the King's service & had comm. for others who were going to raise a regt. in Canada- **820**

Hugh- plaintiff, May 19, 1774, vs. Hugh Mallory, Jr.- **878**

John- (s. John, Esq. & Catharine Reid) m. Hannah, dau. John Alyea; children-

1. John, b. Jan. 15, 1793, nr. Ogdensburg, N. Y.
2. Samuel, dec'd. prior 1850, leaving family

3. Simeon, d. at 17 yrs.

4. James, d. at 25 yrs., w/o children

5. Simon, res. Younge, Ont., Canada; one son

6. Alfred, res. Younge, Ont.; 2 sons & 2, or 3 daus.

7. Hannah, m. William Judd

8. Polly, m. Henry Polly

9. Asenith, m. Jeremiah Guild; & their father d. Jan. 1849, at 83- **812**

John- (s. John & Hannah Alyea) b. Jan. 15, 1793, on the shore of the St. Lawrence river, opp. Ogdensburg, N. Y.; c. 1835/6, rem. & res. Ann Arbor, Mich., & visited Dr. Fitch, Nov. 16, 1850, seeking information regarding lands in this vicinity once belonging to his grdf., Esq. Munro; m. Electa, dau. Nathan Baxter; his 6 children, all res. Mich.- Almon, Fanny, Amanda, Sophia, Marilla, & Charlotte- **812**; (Monroe) informs on a visit, Jan. 1, 1853, that several families who were U. S. refugees of the Rev. war, res. in the area of Canada that he prev. res. in; he notes their inclusion on the U. E. loyalist list, & ments. one named Breakenridge, who was gr. the title, Duke of Leeds- **991**

John- plaintiff, Oct. 19, 1774, vs. Jonathan Willard- **878**

John, Esq.- of Shaftsbury hollow, Vt.; not recoll. by Reubin Clark; see Vol. 1- **766**; tradit. states that he res. in Shaftsbury hollow, along the Little White creek, abt. 4 mi. above the village of White Creek, N. Y., & 2 mi. from the head of the stream by the same name; he erected a grist & sawmill on the stream; "he was a man of superior talents & acquirements for this place at that day"; a tory during the Rev. war, rem. Canada- **807**; native of Scotland; Orderly Sgt., 42nd Highland regt.; came to America during the old French war & was w. Gen. Wolfe at the taking of Quebec; was disch. & remained here foll. the war, drawing lands for his services; his gr. loc. SE corner of Salem & E. end of Jackson, N. Y., w. a considerable part in Lower Arlington, Vt.; m. Catharine Reid, at Norwalk, Conn.; taught sword exercise to a company or school, Albany, N. Y.; was one of 6 trustees that a city block of Albany was deeded to, Oct. 1768, for the org. of a Presbyterian church; refers p. 180, Munsell's Albany Register, 1849; tradit. from his desc. was "that he was a well educ., capable, enterprising man; & that, not having been in early life a farmer, but a military man, he did not make his lands so advantageous to himself as he desired"; knowl. of his office as Justice of Peace & role in the Vt. disturbances unknown to his desc.; rem. Lansingburgh, N. Y., went into the mercantile business, & later d. here, c. 1777; his old creditors offered goods to his wid. for continuing the store, but she relinquished it & c. 1783, rem. Canada; she m. 2. John Ward; & 3. Thomas Golden; children of John, Esq., & Catharine Reid-

1. John, m. Hannah Alyea

2. Samuel, m. Polly Alyea

3. Daniel, m. Hannah Trickey

4. Timothy, drowned, c. 1826, Niagara river

5. Catharine, m. Thomas Proctor- **812**; news conveyed to Albany Comm. of Correspondence, Aug. 22, 1775, that he may have rec'd. a Capt.'s comm. in the King's service, under Col. Allen McLean; an express sent to Comm. of Cambridge

District, requesting that he be examined to determine the truth of the charges- **820**; in a letter, Aug. 29, 1775, Daniel B. Bratt details his examination; approached by Bratt, John Rensselaer, & ano. attendant, his arms were secured, & some armed men took up positions in every part of his house; a letter of instructions from the Albany Comm. was read to him; he then offered to make an oath that he had never rec'd. the comm. in question, & was ready to deliver up his papers; he & his wf. were put under guard when his bro. Donald arr. & was questioned separately; it then became known that Esq. Munro was to have a Capt.'s comm. under Col. Reid, but it appeared that the charge against him 'merely proceeded from a grudge he [Donald] had against John Munro on acct. of a former quarrel'; Munro then declared that some time ago there had been talk of raising a regt. of Highlanders, & that he was nomin. as one of its officers, but did not know the rank; acc. Munro, this was abt. what he had communicated to his bro., & had eventually been divulged to McCrea; his papers were thereupon requested & he produced a large bundle, examined by 2 men in the Comm.'s presence; when asked if he had any further, he opened 2 large trunks- one w. his clothes & some papers of no consequence, & the 2nd full of pamphlets & papers of too old a date for concern in the issue at hand; he then volunteered ownership of a trunk stored in Albany, & offered its key; by further investigation of his houschold & his willingness to go through additional examinations, it was concluded 'we cannot think he is in the least guilty, & have entirely disch. him on that acct.'- **822**; he was brought bef. Albany Comm., Apr. 30, 1776, & recommended to be entered into parole 'as being a person inimical to the present measures now pursued by the United Colonies of America'; he was required to promise not to hold any manner of correspondence or conversation on political matters w. any person, or persons, inimical to measures now pursued by the United Colonies of America; & further, it is recommended to all friends of the cause to leave him to live in peace, & unmolested, so long as he observe the terms of the parole, & to be brought to Albany in consequence of his violating these terms- **830**; along w. Capt. McAlpin & Lt. Swords, directed by an order, June 4, 1776, to be rem. to ano. place of confinement 'prepared for them in the fort' (prob. at Albany, N. Y.)- **889**; Dr. Fitch notes that events ment. in Ebenezer Cole's affidavit, Feb. 27, 1771, correspond w. the times of the 1st settlm., times Esq. Munro delivered ejection suits, etc.- **896**; in a letter dated May 30, 1771, Fowlis, Albany co., he encloses affidavits concerning the conduct of inhabitants within his county, sent to Goldsbrow Banyer, suggesting that he might do something speedily to prevent their continued riotous behavior; he notes that any 'friend' to N. Y. govt. is in danger of life & property- 'they assemble at night, throw down all the Yorker's fences & c., as we are called, & drive the cattle into the fields & meadows & destroy both grass & corn, & do every mischief they can think of'; the imperfection of his presentation attrib. by him to 'being in confusion, my house being full of rioters'- **899**; acc. David Wing, rioters surrounding Thomas French's house, May 21, 1771, 'damned the rascally Yorkers, Esq. Munro, & all his authority- w. many such other expressions' when a party was sent to arrest French- **900**; referred to as "Squire Munro", the mob that confronted Samuel Gardenier on abt. Aug. 1, 1771, pd. him a visit foll. their confrontation w. Gardenier; on the foll. day, when Gardenier appl. to Munro, he was instructed by him to consult 'the Albany gentlemen', i. e., the Mayor & Justice Bleecker; on Sept. 20, 1771, Munro petitn. N. Y. Gov. for an appt. of High Sheriff, Albany, & the Gov. referred him to William Smith, Atty. General, & William Hugh Wallace, & John Reid- **902**; reports to the Gov., Mar. 28, 1772, on his efforts against one of the worst among the rioters; notes that only 2 of his constables within the posse behaved well in the effort, & that if he had 10 men in arms ready to obey his orders rather than running into the woods when they should have resisted, then the rioter would now be secure in jail; expresses his great distress on having no other assistance than his own servants to defend his person & property, his house being surrounded nightly by rioters, firing their guns & c.; 'one of the rioters ran his pistol through [a small hole in the door] & snapped it at his [Munro's] breast' & after entering the door, 'flashed it at his servant who was going upstairs after him & fired at the constable, who took him'; he requests relief from this situation as the case may require- **905**; his letter to the Gov., Aug. 22, 1773, states that 'the mob has broke loose', repeating that he has rec'd. a message that in a few days the whole of his property would be burnt to ashes; notes that a few days prior, all his Pot & Pearl ash works, w. 20 barrels of ash, was burnt down, & that a member of the mob, arrested for horse stealing, has been rescued by them & carried to Bennington- **908**; letter to N. Y. Council, Nov. 24, 1772, noting his arrest of John Searls & Comfort Carpenter, along w. confiscation of counterfeiting devices in their possession; his pot ash works, valued at £ 50, was destroyed, & on the same night, Carpenter escaped from an escort sending the counterfeiters to jail; comments that Mr. Justice Morrison has declined serving in his capacity, but seeks to be excused from his office by the Gov. despite Morrison's unwillingness to serve in his place- **912**; of White Creek; by order of Albany Comm. of Safety, was sent to Kingston, N. Y., Apr. 18, 1777, as a "disaffected & dangerous person", not withstanding having prev. satisfied the Comm. that he was not actively engaged in British interests (§ 822, 830) & his name appears on a list of those deserting from a prison ship in the Hudson; he was prob. recapt., as an order was issued Sept. 17th, that he be sent over the lines, provided Gen. Gates approve of this manner of disposing of him; acc. Dr. Fitch, this suggests proof that Munro could not have been a merch. in Albany & d. in Lansingburgh (§ 812) if he was on his way to be conveyed beyond the lines- **956**

John, Esq.- plaintiff, Jan. 16, 1775, vs. Benjamin Spencer- **878**

Johnson- (s. Samuel & Polly Alyea) c. 1850, res. 15 mi. W. of Ann Arbor, Mich., w. wf. & child- **812**

Joshua- c. 1777, res. S. side of Walloomsac river, in sight of where Col. Breyman's forces 1st formed at the battle of Bennington; he "saw the whole of their motions- their brass kettle- drums glittering in the sunshine being a most striking feature of the scene"; later rem. Shaftsbury, Vt.; his s. Wales, also res. there, & his s. Lyman res. Wisc.- **766**

Mr.- loyalist; c. 1777, res. nr. Bennington, Vt.; Gen. Stark & several of his officers reportedly stopped at his home to obt. draughts of milk & water, prior to the battle; when one of his officers discovered him missing, the officer inquired of his wf. abt. him, & when he was not satisfied that she did not know his whereabouts, he drew his sword upon her; on hearing the commotion, Gen. Stark severly reproved the offender for his behavior; foll. a sleepless night after the battle, Mrs. Munro & her sist. 'repaired w. the earliest dawn to the battlefield, carrying pails of milk & water, & wandering among heaps of slain & wnd., relieved the thirst of many sufferers, of whom some- the Hessians- were unable to express their thankfulness, save by the mute eloquence of grateful looks'; refers Ellet, Elizabeth Fries Lumis- *Women of the Revolution*, Vol. 2, p. 301- **953**

Peter- (s. Samuel & Polly Alyea) c. 1850, res. Eaton co., Mich.; m. twice, he has only one son living of several by his 1st wf.- **812**

Samuel- (s. John, Esq., & Catharine Reid) m. Polly, dau. John Alyea; rem. Washtenaw co., Mich.; children- Peter, Charles, Johnson, Walter; Catharine, m. David Dean; Elizabeth, m. Jonathan Dean; Margaret, m. John Fisher; & Gustina, m. Thomas Proctor; their father d. 1846, 15 mi. W. of Ann Arbor, Mich.- **812**

Samuel- of Walloomsac Patent; testif. in an affidavit sent to Goldsbrow Banyer, May 30, 1771, by John Munro, that he was among those present as an assistant to Samuel Willoughby when he was threatened by rioters; he was also threatened, the rioters saying that they would tie him to a tree & flog him if he didn't go off- **899**

Timothy- (s. John, Esq., & Catharine Reid) prob. res. Darlington, Upper Canada; m. Sally Gray; children recalled- Daniel, Sally, & William; he was crossing the mouth of the Niagara river (c. 1826) in a skiff loaded w. furniture, when it was upset by a wind squall, & he was drowned; the accident occurred during an Antimasonic "excitement", & when his body was discovered it was presumed to be Morgan (prob. Wm. Morgan, of Batavia, N. Y.), but his wf. clearly identified him from clothing & c.- **812**

Walter-(s. Samuel & Polly Alyea) c. 1850, res. Eaton co., Mich.; has wf. & perh. children- **812**

Munro's Meadows, Hebron, N. Y.- c. 1771, its settlers were Duncan McCall, John McDonald, & Norman & Duncan McCloud, foll. by John Duncan; some settlers would go 17 mi. to meeting in Salem, N. Y., & Dr. Clark used to come to the meadows for baptizing; as an inducement to settle here, Rev. Munroe promised to preach, but was often not up to his word in doing so; see Vol. 1- **997**; early July, 1777, families from here went to Skenesborough to obt. protection from Burgoyne when the army was there, but not for protection from the Indians, as they had not joined his forces at that time; bef. leaving, they hid their beds & other things in the bushes, leaving nothing in their houses; some returned abt. 5 wks. later, discovering their things still safe, & they remained in their homes unmolested; no scouting parties or Indians were reported to have passed through the district, nor did any of the men in the settlm. join on either side during the Rev. war, but the cannon at Saratoga, abt. 30 mi. away, were clearly heard here- **998**

MUNSELL,
Mr.- (prob. Joel, of Albany, N. Y.) printed the 1st edition (n. d.) of Neilson's
Burgoyne's Campaign, consisting of 2,000 copies- **731½n**

MUNSON,
_____ - m. James, s. Daniel & Polly (Steele) McFarland- **1047**
_____ - m. Thomas, s. Daniel & Polly (Steele) McFarland- **1047**
_____ - m. Eleanor, dau. Daniel & Polly (Steele) McFarland- **1047**

MURDOCK,
_____ - m. Robert Shaw; bef. her marriage, she was one of the attendants who
prepared old Mrs. Tosh's body for burial; as Mrs. Tosh was large & heavy, & her
room was too small to move the bed out from the wall, she rem. her shoes &
slipped into the bed behind the corpse to turn it; while doing this, Mrs. Tosh's arm
slowly slid down until its palm fell onto her foot, at which point she leaped to the
opp. side of the room, believing the dead 'witch' had come to life- **871**
Rev. James- res. Martinsburgh, N. Y.; dau. Esther, m. Stuben, s. Chillus & Sarah
(Martin) Doty- **730**

MURPHY,
Dennis- he was observed in the early evening, Feb. 16, 1858, by Hiram Sisson, as
he was driving Elijah Chase's team from Buskirk's Bridge, N. Y., suppos. to draw
wood to the depot, along w. Daniel Millet- **759s**

MYERS,
_____ - he was the leader of a party during the Rev. war that had come from Canada
to Cambridge, N. Y., to capt. John Younglove & burn his house, because he had a
grudge against him; his party's escape through Argyle was guided by Neal
Gillespie, who later gave them breakfast at his house; during their escape,as they
approached McNeil's, in E. Greenwich, N. Y., Gillespie warned them that his dog
would bark, but Myers sd. it would not, & as that was what happened, it was
believed that Myers "had some charm or spell which he threw over the dog, that
kept him quiet"- **985**
M. J.- merch., res. Whitehall, N. Y.; his business block was destroyed by fire, Jan.
30, 1854, w. $12,500 insurance on his goods & building; the value of his total loss
not known; losses of 2 other merchs., J. R. Broughton & J. Dahn, noted- **1023**
William Henry- c. 1874, res. Little Falls, N. Y.; m. Eliza, dau. Hon. Wm. Henry &
Harriet (Blin) Parker- **759s**

MYGATT,
_____ - of Elsworth, Ohio; m. Andrew, s. Thomas & _____ (Hill) Fitch- **940**

N

NAPIER,
Mr.- Director General of the Hospitals; the N. Y. Council advises, Oct. 22, 1765, that a reserve be made in his & Capt. John Small's Patent for lands occ. & improved by Jacob Marsh & his associates- **894**

NAVY, U. S.- toasted Nov. 29, 1814, in ceremonies at Salem, N. Y., honoring Comodore Thomas Macdonough, "the hero of Lake Champlain", as being "Young in years; old in deeds of glory", foll. by a performance of "Yankee Doodle", & 3 cheers; also toasted as "Our Tars on Lake Champlain- Their conduct in the bay of Plattsburgh sheds new lustre on the naval character of our country"; also toasted at the same event by Hon. Judge Anthony I. Blanchard- "The Navy of the U.S.- Its brillaint triumphs over the Mistress of the seas are glorious proofs that it is the sure defense of the nation, & of the unequalled skill & gallantry of American sailors", foll. by 6 cheers; by Hon. Asa Fitch, Sr.- "Our 'Wooden walls'- the pride of our country & the scourge of our enemies", foll. by 6cheers- **709**; advertised by order of the Sec. of the Navy, that the sloops *President, Montgomery, Preble, Chubb, & Finch,* 10 gunboats, & boats & cutters of the Lake Champlain squadron be sold June 28, 1815, at Whitehall, N. Y.; cash only terms- **715**

NEGROES-
Male- capt. along w. Esq. Bleecker & his hired hand, mid- June 1782, Pittstown, N. Y., by a band of tories & British soldiers- **747**;
Peggy- her body was disinterred from the Argyle bur. grds., Sept. 9, 1811, & dissected by Dr. Isaac Baldwin Clary, who was indicted along w. 3 others for the offense- **874**;
Pomp- a slave of Simon DeRidder; accidentally drowned, Dec. 28, 1801, Easton, N. Y., along w. John P. Becker's slave- **(L)- 876**;
Prince- a slave of John P. Becker; accidentally drowned, Dec. 28, 1801, Easton, N. Y., along w.Simon DeRidder's slave- **(L)- 876**;
Prince- res., c. 1790's, Ft. Miller, N. Y.; a slave of Hugh Pebbles; assisted Mr. Dinwiddie at Wm. Duer's store, & discovered Dinwiddie's death when, after having gone upstairs to get something requested by a costumer, he went searching for him & found him lying dead on the floor- **1032**;
Racism, Prejudices towards- in a printed art., perh. the reverse side of a clipping from the *Salem Press,* Feb. 1862, concerning the 93rd N. Y. Inf., the beginning of an article entitled 'A Down- East Juryman'; the item concerns the recoll. of the jury experiences of Ethan Spike, orig. contrib. to the *Portland Transcript;* whether real or fictitious, the story presented consists of a thinly veiled predjudice, apparently intended as humor, regarding two capital cases, 'the criminals being a German & a "nigger" respectively'; on inquiry regarding whether he had any opinion 'agin the prisoners', Ethan recoll. that he stated 'Not perticular agin the Jarmin... but I hate

niggers as a general principle, & shall go for hanging this old white wooled cuss, whether he killed Mr. Cooper or not'; bef. mercifully ending, the dialog continues in the same venacular, w. Mr. Spike being excused by the clerk, while he insists on remaining to see his foregone conclusion accomplished- **1090frag**;

Skene's Mansion- acc. J. Griffiths, of Kingsbury, N. Y., in a Dec. 20, 1766 letter , 'The sd. Skene keeps his servants to work on the Lord's Day; allows his negroes to work for one of his tenants every Sunday, in order to get money to purch. some small necessaries'- **929**;

Slave- of Jacob Grodt, Kinderhook, N. Y.; was among the Grodt household members present, abt. Aug. 1, 1771, at Samuel Gardenier's house, Walloomsac Patent, when Vt. rioters 1st confronted Gardenier concerning his land title- **902**;

Soldiers, Civil War- acc. to the Charleston, S. C., corresp., *N. Y. Tribune*, Mar. 11, 1865, 'the butchers Poucher & Fitch, who mangled our colored soldiers', were then present in the city, & prepared to take the oath, thinking that 'the old order of things will be restored'- **799**

NEILSON,
Charles, Esq.- the 1st 2,000 copy edition of his book, *Burgoyne's Campaign*, pd. for at his own expense- **731½n**; noted by Dr. Fitch that although he resid. on the farm next to Bemis, he did not recoll. his neighbor's given name; refers p. 116, *Burgoyne's Campaign-* **851**

NELSON,
____- m. Mary, dau.William & Margaret (Andrew) Dobbin- **732**
Charles- res. Lewistown, N. Y.; m. Hannah, dau. Andrew & Nancy (Stewart) Lytle; children- James; Jane Maria, m. ____ Gibbs; Sophia; & Horatia, m. Elisha Case- **1069**
Edward- Corp., Co. A, 2nd N. Y., Northern Black Horse, Cav., 1861- 2- **1080**
John- oath of alleg.; Co. D, 22nd N. Y. Inf.- **(L)- 1074**

NESBIT,
John- deed witn., May 1, 1766, Dr. Thomas Clark to Andrew Lytle- **(L)- 936**

NEVINS,
Family- res., c. 1798, on the w. side of the Hudson opp. Ft. Miller, N. Y., & above the Lewis family- **804**

New Canaan, N. Y.- tories were disturbing & breaking up the meetings of the Comm. of Safety here, & the Comm. called upon the militia in adjoin. Stockbridge, Mass., for assistance in capt. them, Apr. 1776- **747**

NEWCOMB,
____- perh. res. Nova Scotia; m. Marcy, dau. Moses & Desire (Burrows) Gore- **1100**

NEWELL,
____ - "lives out west"; m. Julia Ann, dau.Willaim & Jane (Lytle) Russell- **737**
Family- of Killingly, Conn.; sons John & Isaac; daus. Martha, & Sarah, who m.
Aaron Martin- **1037**
Sarah- m. May 10, 1734, Aaron Martin, in Thompson, Conn.- **730**; of Sturbridge,
Mass.; m. ____ Martin- **849**
Gen. Timothy- of Sturbridge, Mass.; his sist. m. ____ Martin, & he had 3 daus.
who came to Stillwater, or Saratoga, N. Y.; one, Betsey, m. Mott Van Buerin- **849**;
had the foll. children- Asa, Ebenezer; Betsey, m. ____ Van Bearin; Hannah;
Abigail, m. Ansel Pope; & Sarah- **1037**

NEW ENGLAND- 731, 740, 744, 758, 759s, 796, 797, 834, 836, 837, 860, 945b,
949, 962, 1016, 1050, 1050s, 1100

NEW HAMPSHIRE- 745, 786, 788, 794, 805, 883- 885, 887, 891, 892, 896, 902,
928, 967; claimants- 887; controversy- 887, 928; grants- 746, 779, 789, 794, 797,
881, 887, 893, 894, 997; rights, titles- 902, 903, 967;
  Counties- Coos- 858; see also, Vt.;
  Cities & Towns- Amherst- 734s, 799; Charlestown- 896; Hampton- 835; Hollis-
759s; Lebanon- 759s; Londonderry- 734s, 734, 811, 1097; Mount Lebanon- 1067;
Newmarket- 811; Peterborough- 801; Portsmouth- 799, 834, 835, 883, 974;
  Features- rivers- Merrimac- 883; Newichwannuck, Salmon falls- 883; Piscataqua
harbor- 883;
  Colonial Govt.- Council- 894; Gen. Assembly of the Province- 896;
  Province boundaries- given in the commision of office gr. to Benning Wentworth,
July 3, 1741; consisted of a similarly curved line to the course of the Merrimac
river, & at 3 mi.distance from it on the N. side, beginning at the Atlantic Ocean &
ending at a point due N. of Pawtucket falls (nr. presentday Lowell, Mass.); & also
by a straight line drawn thence due W. across river 'until it meets w. our other
govts.'; bounded SE by a line passing through Piscataqua harbor, & up the middle
of the river to the part of Newichwannuck river known as Salmon falls, & through
the middle of same to its furthest head & thence N 2° W until 120 mi. from the
mouth of Piscataqua harbor, or until it meets our govts.'; refers pgs. 3, 4.
Territorial Rights- **883**

NEW JERSEY- 730, 759s, 804, 810, 839, 887, 891, 912, 928, 945b, 949b, 1036,
1039;
  Cities & Towns- Amboy- 1098; Burlington- 949b; Elizabethtown- 961, 990;
Minisink- 953b; Monmouth- 730, 990, 1002; New Brunswick- 949, 953b, 1045;
Princeton- 1010; Trenton- 1010;
  Proprietors of- Gov. Colden of N. Y. notes in his letter to the Board of Trade,
Apr. 12, 1764, that their Patent is held under the auspices of the Duke of York, &
that Gov. Wentworth's proclamation which uses this as an instance of an

obsolescence of the Duke of York's Patent 'can only be designed for ignorant people' unaware of the distinction- **928**

New Perth (Salem, N. Y.)- on petitn. of the inhabitants, erected into a township, Mar. 2, 1774, by the N. Y. Council; its inhabitants signed a petitn. (n. d.) in support of establ. Skenesborough (Whitehall, N. Y.) as Charlotte co. seat; refers Doc. Hist., iv, 818, on latter point- **913**

NEWSPAPERS- the *Northern Post*, Salem, N. Y.; edited by Henry Dodd & David Rumsey, & joined by James Stevenson, June 6, 1814; a bookstore & drugstore operated in conjunction w. the newspaper; the bookstore, w. circulating library, soon became a large & valuable establ.; Rumsey rem. from Salem abt. Jan. 1, 1815, & publ. continued under Dodd & Stevenson until nr. the time of Henry Dodd's death; see Vol. 1;

the *Washington Register*, "the rival paper, & organ of the democratic party" in Salem; edited by John P. Reynolds, who also had a bookstore connected w. his publ. venture; after Jan. 1816, succeeded by Timothy Hoskins, foll. by James B. Gibson, Esq.; under Gibson's 2 yrs. of publ., its political viewpoint became Clintonian, bringing both the *Post* & the *Register* into the same political perspective; Beriah Stiles, a Buck- tail, became editor foll. Gibson; Mr. Patterson succeeded Stiles, & abt. 1828, rem. the paper to Union Village (Greenwich, N. Y.) & made it the Anti- masonic organ of the county;

The Advertiser, begun 1815, Glens Falls, N. Y., as a democratic paper; edited by Linus J. Reynolds, but abandoned abt. Jan. 1816- **721**; c. 1815/6, the *Northern Post* observed that a division of the town of Cambridge, N. Y., a democratic measure, will prob. result in the introduction of the political perspectives of Madison & Jefferson into Washington co.- **722**; the votes of local representatives, Adgate & Savage, concerning Congressional pay raise from $6.00 per day to $1,500.00 per yr., Apr. 25, 1816, *Northern Post*; Hon. John Savage's vote in favor of the raise criticized in view of his short tenure, noting the salary change & travel expenses afforded to Congressmen their brief (90 day) duration of service- **725**; also Apr. 25, 1816, *Northern Post*, ano. commentary concerning the division of Cambridge, noting that the local Assemblymen voted in opposition to the people's will, fostering the division; "they preferred the gratification of a friend to the gratification of the people, & sacrificed the interests of many to serve party ends & benefit a few"; concerning these representatives, Mr. Gale, who introduced the bill, & Mr. Sargent, who advocated the division, the *Post* questions whether they should be deserving the people's suffrage in the 1816 election- **726**; newsclipping, "The Parker Family", July 27, 1874, *Salem Press*; an extensive genealogical article, authored by Dr. Fitch, concerning the ancestry of John C. Parker, Esq., of Granville, N. Y.; its contents covers his immed. family in greater detail than § 759, in the original manuscript, & incl. desc. of his bros. & sists., & desc. of the prev. generations, to Edward Parker of New Haven, 1644- **759s**; a copy of the June 30, 1777, *Connecticut Courant* arr. in Philadelphia, Pa., on July 9th, & contained a declaration from a part of N. Y. identifying itself as the State of Vermont, along w. a list of complaints against N. Y., intended to bolster their cause in the public eye- **793**; semi- weekly, *N. Y. Tribune*, primarily items from the 1860's, used heavily as a source by Dr. Fitch for vital records & other notices pert. to the Fitch family- **799**; unattrib. newsclipping, c. 1825, noting the conviction of William Gordon for the murder of George Coggshall; quotes passages from *Wash. Co. Post*, describing the events surrounding the orig. incident; see Criminal Offenders- **808**; an editor, perh. in Philadelphia, Pa., spoke of the death of Washington (Dec. 14, 1799) as being "of no more consequence than the death of a dog"; see Newspapers, Vol. 1, § 532; the May 22, 1804, *Northern Post* refers to this acct. in an editorial concerning the death of Alexander Hamilton; this opinion of Washington, noted here as being parroted by John Russell, of Salem, N. Y., & acc. Dr. Fitch, was a sentiment prevalent due to "The infidel philosophy of France, ... rampant among the warm democrats at that day"- **919**; extracts from an article entitled 'The United States Senators from New York, from 1781 to 1851, w. sketches of Political & Personal History', Mar. 8, 1851, *N. Y. Herald*; describes electoral process behind selection of earliest N. Y. Senators, Gen. Philip Schuyler & Rufus King, foll. by the appt. of Aaron Burr, thus denying a 2nd term to Gen. Schuyler; also incl. career & biog. of Gen. Schuyler; see Schuyler; & Senators, U. S.- **920**; undated printed article, c. late 1850's, entitled 'The True Inventor- The Man Who Discovered the Steam Principle', from *The Recorder*, story filed Jan. 14, Lawrenceville, Ky.; inserted betw. Dr. Fitch's text, traces the personal history of John Fitch, 'the forgotten genius' who invented the steamboat, the development of his invention, & the eclipse of his fame by Fulton; also discusses Fitch's personal decline & obscure bur. in Bardstown, Ky., along w. other distinctions connected w. the Bardstown area; 3 illust. accompany text- **949b**; an article (n. d.) prematurely printed in the *N. Y. Herald*, w. Bradley S. Osborne's byline, disclosed the Wilmington expedition to the Confederates; Osborne was arrested & imprisoned, but later acquitted- **950**; 'City Clergy in 1775', Nov. 6, 1851, *N. Y. Observer*; extracts of an acct. of Dr. John Rogers & his church, w. reference to elders & trustees who became politically prominent in early N. Y. history- William Smith, Peter Van Brugh Livingston, Whitehead Hicks, & ors.- **961**; notices from Nov. 6, 1852, *N. Y. Times*, concerning cert. members of the Winslow family, perh. taken from an article pert. to the funeral of Daniel Webster- **988**; newsclipping entitled 'A Brave Old Regiment', Dec. 4, 1852, *N. Y. Weekly Times*, pert. to the origin & history of His Majesty's 42nd Regt. of Foot, known as the 'Black Watch'; see Royal Highlanders- **990**; notice from the *Whitehall Chronicle*, concerning the loss of several barns & other buildings due to lightning, over the weekend Aug. 13 & 14, 1853, in Dresden, N. Y., & Benson & West Haven, Vt.- **996**; newsclipping, Salem, N. Y., entitled 'Funeral Honors to the Late President', noting a public meeting held Apr. 12, 1841, for appt. of a comm. to recommend 'Military & Civic Honors, in consequence of the death of the late President of the United States', Gen. Wm. Henry Harrison; list of comm. members & outline of 'order of arrangements' for ceremonies; see Salem, N. Y.- **1009**; newsclipping, entitled 'James M'Donald- A Revolutionary Hero',

The Fitch Gazetteer

June/ July 1853, *Sandusky Register*; noting that McDonald had visited Boston, Mass., June 20, 1853, as the last survivor of the battle of Bunker Hill, the reporter recalls a prev. appearance of McDonald, a few yrs. earlier, at the newspaper's office in Sandusky, after being robbed while he was traveling from his home in Kentucky, to his dau.'s, in Black Rock, N. Y.; the reporter, identified only as 'G', provides McDonald's biog. & hist. of his Rev. war experiences, incl. anecdotes McDonald provided concerning Benedict Arnold & 'Mad' Anthony Wayne, as well as particulars of his journey & robbery- **1010**; newsclipping noting the obit. of Judge Anthony I. Blanchard, who d. June 14, 1853- **1012**; report of a train derailment, Sat., Dec. 3, 1853, acc. *N. Y. Weekly Times*, but given as Fri. evening, acc. *Whitehall Chronicle*; the former attrib. the cause to running over a cow, while the latter ment. a horse, fallen betw. the timbers on the track, describing the damage from the wreck, & the engineer's death, in further detail; see McMullen, William; & Transportation- **1017**; Tues., Feb. 7, 1854, *Salem Press*, reports the loss of the Myers block, Whitehall, N. Y., during a fire on Jan. 30th, listing the businesses affected, their losses & insured values- **1023**; newsclipping, Feb. 1854, *N. Y. Observer*, giving the obits. of Lauchlin Wright (Jan. 9) & Mary Cooley (Jan. 23)- **1024**; newsclipping (n. d.) giving results in Wash. co. for the 1853 election; gives an aggregate return by party only, for N. Y Secretary of State, Canal Commissioner, Senator, Justice of Supreme Court, Dist. Attys., Co. Superintendent of Poor, Justice of Sessions, & 1st & 2nd Assembly Districts- **1025**; unattrib. newsclipping, prob. shortly foll. Thanksgiving, based upon subj. material found on reverse, entitled 'Official Statement of Votes- Taken at a General Election in Washington County, Held on the Seventh Day of November, 1854'; as in the prev., notes aggregate returns by party, giving total votes in ea. electoral district, in ea. Wash. co. town, for offices of N. Y. Governor, Lt. Gov., Canal Commissioner, Inspector of State Prisons, Congress, Co. Superintendent of Poor, Justices of Sessions, & 1st & 2nd Assembly Districts; partial articles on reverse incl.- Col. 1- condition of National finances, noting that the Treasury holds ____ amt., & public debt is at $45 million; 'Board of Supervisors'; partial article noting Wash. co. Supervisors have recently been in session at an unidentified house; Col. 2- end of an article noting that an acquaintance of the editor/ reporter, who res. Whitehall, N. Y., & is rarely seen outside his own community, has been spending time here (prob. Salem) but refused a dinner invitation, excusing himself on the basis of prev. excesses from the Thanksgiving repast; notice of replenished stocks at Stackhouse's clothing & merch. store; a waggish notice of current farming practices- 'There has been a perfect rush of dead hogs past our office for a few days past, we were scarcely aware bef., that our farmers were such a *swinish* set'; Col. 3- an article taken from the *Wash. Co. Post*, reviewing a lecture delivered by Rev. C. S. Robinson; see N. White Creek & Cambridge Literary Assoc.- **1028**; Erastus Adams, publisher, *Whitehall Emporium*, d. Apr. 15, 1825- **1029**; unattrib. newsclipping, July 1858, noting the meeting of National Democrats in Metropolitan Hall, Chicago, Illinois; Henry Fitch, s. Sen. Fitch of Indiana, keynote speaker; incl. editorial comments from a sketch of his speech, publ. by *The Press &*

312

Tribune; newsclipping, Feb. 26, 1859, *N. Y. Express*; obit., Mrs. Mary, wid. Maj.
James Harvey; largely obliterated, apparently by darkening of paste or glue- **1035**;
newspaper articles, 'The Trial of Martin Wallace for the Murder of Barney
McEntee', Oct. 5, 12, & 19, 1858, *Salem Press*; the Oct. 5th & 12th issues cover
the particulars of this trial, & the Oct. 19th issue duplicates the transcript of both
issues, to accommodate public demand & interest; this article was noted by Abbie
M. Fitch Andrews as missing foll. the binding of the orig. Manuscript Hist., but its
contents were noted in Judge Gibson's Ledger copy of the manuscript; it is more
likely that Dr. Fitch utilized the condensed Oct. 19th issue as a newsclipping, to
preserve space in his volume, but despite the effort, it was lost during the binding
project- **1048s**; newsclipping, Tues., Dec. 7, 1858, *Salem Press*; obit., 'Death of
Hon. John McLean'- **1050**; 'Execution of Martin Wallace', a newspaper article,
which accomp. the prev. newsclipping, on the inner columns of the issue, the obit.
of Judge McLean being on the outside column of the pg.; these articles appear in
Judge Gibson's Ledger copy as "Execution of Wallace & death of Hon. John
McLean"; it is likely that they were separated & the larger item lost during the
binding project; the contents of the article, however, indicate the time of Wallace's
trial, & enable the retrieval of the probable source for § 1048; its contents are,
therefore, also incl. here- **1050s**; unattrib. newsclipping, 'Correspondence of the
News', May 25, 1861, Camp Rathbone, Troy, N. Y.; ments. the movement &
combining of several companies from Camp Brintnall, & others from Albany,
N. Y., to comprise the 22nd N. Y. Infantry; lists Capts., Co. A- J, & their place of
origin, & gives the members, Co. D, Cambridge, N. Y., who have taken the oath of
allegiance; see 22nd N. Y. Inf.- **1074**; 'Recollections of Old Merchants of New
York City', by Walter Barret; c. 1860's, for *N. Y. Leader*, reprinted, in *N. Y.
Express*; an extensive article on the history & development of var. grocery
enterprises in early NYC, w. particular emphasis on the enterprises of the Bininger
family, & freq. references to streets & early landmarks in NYC- **1075b**; a
thumbnail history of David Rumsey's newspaper activities since his affiliation w.
Henry Dodd, & *Northern Post*, Salem, N. Y.- **1078**; printed article, Dec. 1861,
giving a roster for Co. A, 2nd N. Y. (Northern Black Horse) Cavalry- **1080**; Mar.
25, 1862, *Sandy Hill Herald*, obit., Gen. Orville Clark- **1088**; printed article, dated
Feb. 1, 1862, Camp Rathbone, Albany, N. Y.; gives field, stafff, & line officers,
Co. A- I, & K, 93rd N. Y. (Morgan Rifles) Infantry- **1090b**; printed article, c. Feb.
1862, prob. *Salem Press*, & perh. reverse of clipping for § 1090b, "93rd Regt.
N. Y. S. V. Morgan Rifles", dated Feb.1, 1862; a partial paragraph ends the prev.
article, & ano. begins, 'A Down- East Juryman', a reprint of an article from the
Portland Transcript, 'contributed' by Ethan Spike, being a 'sketch of his experience
as a Juryman'; the story notes his 1st two cases were for capital offenses, 'the
criminals being a German & a "nigger" respectively'; when inquired of by the
'Juege' pert. to his opinions of the defendants, Spike replies- ' "Not pertticular agin
the Jarmin", says I, "but I hate niggers as a general principle, & shall go for
hanging... whether he killed Mr. Cooper or not", says I'; the story continues, w. the
clerk excusing him from jury duty, & Spike's insistence that he must serve as a

'jewryman', anxious to see retribution appl. to the murderer, but thankfully, we are spared continuation of the tale by the margins of the clipping- **1090frag**; reward advertised (n. d.) *Cambridge Valley News*, pert. to Feb. 24,1863 desertion of Peter Hanes, of White Creek, N. Y., from his unit- **1095**

NEWTON,
Rev. Ephriam Howland- (1787- 1864) Corresponding Secretary, Wash. Co. Bible Society; delivered their annual report, Sept. 4, 1862, at the society's 50th annual meeting, incl. biogs. of its 4 dec'd. Presidents & prominent founders of the society; also delivered an address noting the religious background of the early settlers of Salem, N. Y., & the legacy of their successive descendants- **1097**
Lt. Henry C.- Co. A, 93rd N. Y. Inf.- **1090b**

NEW YORK-
Regions, Features- Cherry Valley- 748, 753; Eastern District- 875; Highlands- 735, 744, 1060; Holland Purchase- 851; Long Island- 728, 799, 839, 940, 1100; as York Island- 990; Niagara frontier- 768, 1032; Northern District- 711; Northern frontier- 706, 709, 729; Sabbath Day Point, Warren Co.- 759s; Valentine's Hill- 747, 755;
Regions, Features, in Wash. Co. & vicinity- Bald Mtn. range- 800; Camden valley, Cambridge- 1075b,1076; Cobble Hill- 762b; Diamond Island, Lake George- 750; Ding's Swamp- 1067; Dwelly's Hill, Greenwich- 731; the Elbow, Lake Champlain- 751; Oak Hill, Cambridge/ White Creek- 845, 1048s; the Ponds, Jackson- 731; Put's rock- 751; Salem- Creighton's hill- 1050s; Gallow's hill- 1050s, 1097; Pine Plains- 996; Tamarack Swamp- 1003; Van Schaik's Island, Stillwater- 763; the Vlie, Cambridge- 1003; White creek valley- 1098;
Patents- Argyle- 730- 732, 802, 871, 936; as Scotch Patent- 1050s; Artillery- 745, 875, 880, 936; Banyard- 935; Beekman's- as Bakeman's Precink- 745;
Fisher's- 936; Ft. Edward- 936, 936b; Hebron- 997; Hoosick- 892, 1007; Jessup's- 997; Kingsbury- 936, 936b; Lake's (Van Cuyler's)- 806;
Menzies- 1079; Morrison's- 936; Provincial- 745; Schuyler- 935; Scott & Kemp- 936; Thurman's (Therman's)- 814, 815; Turner's- 731, 838, 936, 936b;
Walloomsac- 763, 765, 766, 806, 899, 902, 1007;
Counties- Albany- 735, 745, 756, 773, 776, 778, 779, 782, 799, 805, 831, 878, 881, 885, 887- 889, 901, 902, 914, 936, 1045, 1050s; Allegheny- 799;
Broome- 962; Cattaraugus- 802; Cayuga- 734, 799, 844, 979; Charlotte- 745, 773, 777, 779- 785, 787, 878, 878½, 881, 890, 904, 910, 911, 936, 938, 964, 992, 1066; Chatauqua- 759s, 805, 839; Chenango- 730; Clinton- 714, 992; Columbia- 730, 731, 753, 919; Cortland- 1022; Cumberland- 735, 777, 782, 785, 786, 838, 881, 886, 894, 993;
Delaware- 759, 759s, 943, 973, 997; Dutchess- 745, 746, 755, 777, 806;
Essex- 714, 731, 848, 863, 914, 1045, 1047, 1068, 1069, 1074, 1093; Franklin- 714, 799, 1013; Genesee- 799, 842; Gloucester- 780, 782, 785, 786, 886; Green- 943, 1090; Herkimer- 718;

Lewis- 730, 842, 1037; Livingston- 759, 759s; Madison- 973; Monroe- 734; New York- 778; Niagara- 812; Oneida- 799, 839, 846, 1060; Orange- 759s; Otsego- 799, 805; Rensselaer- 747, 756, 851, 1006, 1022, 1050s; Richmond- 778;

St. Lawrence- 729, 737, 865, 997, 1013, 1054, 1069, 1083, 1085, 1090; Saratoga- 730, 731, 737, 799, 804, 805, 960, 972, 973, 999, 1024, 1038, 1045, 1057, 1069; Steuben- 1078; Suffolk- 920;

Tioga- 759, 759s, 799; Tompkins- 799; Tryon- 782, 799; Ulster- 914, 943, 1092; Warren- 714, 721, 847, 992, 1050s, 1080, 1093, 1095;

Washington- 709, 713, 714, 717, 721, 722, 724, 730, 731½, 735, 745, 750, 759, 759s, 762b, 799, 800, 804, 807, 813, 816, 837, 841, 844, 848, 868, 877, 910, 914, 919, 920, 934- 936, 938, 971, 987, 989, 992, 1003, 1011- 1013, 1022, 1024, 1025, 1027, 1028, 1035, 1050, 1050s, 1067, 1072, 1075b, 1080, 1091, 1092, 1094, 1097; Wayne- 799; Westchester- 755, 841, 920, 1077;

Cities & Towns- Albany- 709, 716, 731, 736, 746, 747, 748, 753, 756, 763, 766, 773, 774, 776, 782, 786, 788, 790, 792, 799, 806, 812, 815- 833, 837, 839, 885, 897, 902, 914, 920, 928, 930, 932- 934, 951, 956, 959, 975, 991, 994, 997, 1013, 1022, 1033, 1045, 1046, 1053, 1074, 1075b, 1081, 1082, 1099; Camp Brintnall (formerly Willard's)- 1074; Camp Rathbone- 1090b; Court St.- 932; jail- 892, 897, 900, 902, 928;

Argyle- 711, 714, 725, 730, 731, 734, 737, 738b, 743, 744, 754, 784, 789, 791, 792, 805, 854, 859, 867, 872- 874, 876, 901, 935, 936, 973, 977- 979, 983- 985, 992, 1005, 1028, 1049, 1060- 1062,1064, 1069, 1081, 1082, 1095b; as corners- 732, 737, 802, 1060; Stevenson's corners- 978;

Ashville- 839; Auburn- 759s, 808, 943; Avon- 1045;

Bacon's Hill- 804, 933; Bald Mountain- 701, 1081; Ballston, Ballstown- 952, 953b, 960, 1054; spa- 952, 1054; Batavia- 734, 943; Bath- 731, 1078; Battenville- 730, 972, 1060; Bedford- 752; Bedlam (W. Hebron)- 737, 738; Bemis Heights- 743, 744, 847, 850, 973, 989, 1002, 1032; Binghamton- 730, 732, 839, 1069;

Black Creek (Hebron)- 784, 816, 936; Black Rock- 1010; Bolton- 1093; Brooklyn- 759s, 799, 942, 990, 1045; Brutus- 734; Buffalo- 841, 1010, 1100; Buskirk's Bridge- 1048s; Busti- 839;

Caldwell- 858; Cambridge- 702, 709, 711- 714, 720, 722, 725, 726, 737, 739, 744, 762b, 764, 772, 783, 795, 805, 806, 813, 816, 818, 820, 824- 826, 828, 831, 839, 841- 843, 846, 853, 866, 876, 879, 888- 890, 912, 925, 936, 973, 992, 1006, 1015, 1024, 1027- 1029, 1040, 1048s, 1059, 1069, 1074, 1082, 1093- 1095b, 1098; Camden- 773, 795, 879, 890, 1075b, 1076; Canaan- 730; Canandaigua- 730, 731, 1038; Castile- 842; Cauyanawaga- 1015, 1016; Center Falls- 731;

Champlain- 943; Chatham- 731; Chenango Point (Binghamton)- 951; Chester(town)- 847, 858; Chittenango- 799; Claverack- 735; Clinton- 759s; Coila- 1097; Cooperstown- 759s; Corinth- 962; Coxsackie- 799; Crown Point- 760, 774, 775, 777, 848, 890, 904, 909, 910, 928, 959, 990, 1016, 1059; Cumberland Head (Plattsburgh)- 1016;

Delhi- 759, 759s; Denmark- 842; Deridder's ferry- 743; Dresden- 996, 1028; Duanesburg- 730, 799;

Eagle Bridge- 766, 839, 1003, 1048s; Eagleville (S. Salem)- 737; E. Greenbush-
731; E. Greenwich- 702, 727, 731, 732, 802, 806, 847, 871, 978, 1026, 1062,
1089, 1095, 1095b; East Hampton- 1100; Easton- 714, 725, 730, 731, 799, 806,
815, 849, 861, 876, 992, 1027, 1028, 1058, 1097; Fairfield- 805; Fishkill- 940;
Fitch's Point, Salem- 727, 730, 731, 743, 799, 803, 847, 851, 852, 855, 860, 863,
865, 867, 872, 969, 972, 996, 1026, 1051, 1065, 1069, 1075, 1076, 1093, 1098;
Ft. Ann- 701, 714, 725, 728, 746, 747, 759s, 750, 751, 752, 754, 757, 792, 794,
797, 799, 858, 916, 991, 992, 998, 1005, 1028; Battle Hill- 747; Welsh Hollow-
813;
Ft. Covington- 1044; Ft. Edward- 730, 731½, 733, 735, 738b, 740, 742, 743, 746,
747, 748, 753, 779, 780, 794- 797, 804, 815, 816, 839, 874, 878, 879, 910, 914,
918, 925, 928, 930, 935, 936, 958, 959, 969, 978, 981, 983, 986, 988, 990, 992,
997, 999, 1012, 1013, 1016, 1028, 1062, 1063, 1065, 1074, 1081, 1082, 1095b,
1096;
Ft. George- 858, 958; Ft. Miller- 706, 731, 734, 747, 779, 784, 800, 804, 819,
840, 844, 878, 879, 932, 933, 960, 976, 1031, 1050s; Ft. Plain- 756; Ft. Stanwix-
751, 799; Ft.Ticonderoga- see Ticonderoga; Frankfort-737; Franklinville- 839;
French mills- 729, 1015;
Galesville- 701, 839, 848, 1005, 1072; Galway- 730, 805, 1038; Geneva- 809;
Glens Falls (Glen's Falls)- 721, 746, 963, 969, 1074, 1097;
Granville- 734, 747, 749- 752, 754, 755, 757- 759, 759s, 784, 795, 816, 918, 921,
936, 992, 997, 1003, 1028, 1048s, 1079, 1082; corners- 759s; Greenbush- 731,
934, 1032; Greenfield- 799, 954, 973; Greenwich (Union Village, Whipple City)-
711, 714, 725, 731, 746, 04a, 854, 873, 972, 992, 1028, 1041, 1048s, 1058, 1060,
1080, 1082;
Half Moon- 731, 803, 858, 1032; Hampton- 714, 725, 814, 992, 1048s; Hanford's
Landing- 759s; Hannibal- 731, 1073; Harlem- 728, 1077; Harmony- 839; Hartford-
711, 713, 714, 725, 737, 759s, 874, 876, 992, 1024, 1028, 1069, 1082, 1098;
Hebron- 711, 713, 714, 724, 725, 731, 734, 737, 738, 921, 924, 936, 978, 990,
992, 1028, 1047, 1050s, 1069, 1081, 1082, 1084, 1090, 1098; Munro's Meadows-
731, 997- 1000;
Hillsdale- 753; Hoosick (Hoosic)- 728, 729, 732, 744, 767- 770, 772, 783, 816,
822, 831, 847, 853, 858, 859, 870, 876, 890, 892, 1022, 1048s; corners- 768;
Hoosick Falls- 768, 772, 1006, 1048s; Hutton's Bush (Putnam)- 1091, 1092;
Jackson- 812, 843, 847, 856, 992, 1028, 1048s, 1082, 1091, 1093, 1098;
Jamesville- 759s; Jay- 1093; Johnson's Bush- 820; Johnsonville- 759s; Johnstown-
730; Jordan- 1045; Kayackett- 802, 979; Keesville- 994, 1074; Kinderhook- 902;
Kingsbury- 714, 725, 730, 745, 750, 754, 816, 874, 879, 929, 936, 938, 992, 1028,
1039, 1054; as Kingsborough- 814; Kingston- 956, 1092; Kortright- 973, 1034,
1086;
Lakeville (Cossayuna)- 732, 1058; Lansingburgh- 807, 812, 840, 956, 964, 1036;
Lewistown- 812, 1068, 1069; Lima- 759s; Lisbon- 737, 865, 997, 1044, 1083;
Little Falls- 759s, 1070; Little Hoosic- 816; Little White Creek- 745, 746, 806,
841, 843, 844; Livingston's Manor- 735, 831, 961; Lowville- 730; Lysander- 806;

Malta- 960, 1045; as the Ridge- 952; Mamaroneck- 1100; Martinsburgh- 730, 1037- 1039, 1046; Mattewan- 841; Mayville- 805, 839; Mechanicville- 1027; Middlebury- 1095; Middle Granville- 759, 759s, 1003; Milford- 805; Minisink- 953b; Montgomery- 759s; Moreau- 737, 958; Moriah- 1074, 1093; Morristown- 730; Mt. Kisco- 1077; Mt. Morris- 759, 759s;

New Baltimore- 1095; New Berlin- 730; Newburgh- 950; New Canaan- 747; New Perth (Salem)- 744, 789, 791, 878½, 913, 936, 938; New Rochelle- 752; New York City- 730, 731, 737, 746, 748, 753, 759, 759s, 768, 781b, 790, 799, 802, 804, 805, 812, 813, 817, 822, 839, 841, 847, 872, 877, 880, 881, 901- 914, 920, 933- 936, 938, 940, 941, 943, 945, 947, 950, 959, 961, 962, 968- 972, 975, 979, 988, 997, 999, 1007, 1012, 1019, 1032, 1035, 1037, 1044, 1046, 1049, 1050, 1050s, 1060, 1067, 1070, 1075b, 1077, 1087, 1091, 1093, 1098, 1100; City Hall- 1075b; Ft. George- 884; Ft. Washington- 990; Ryker's Island (Camp Bliss)- 1081; time- 1050s; Wall St.- 759s; Yorkville- 950;

Niagara- 731; N. Argyle (The Hook)- 802; North Castle- 747; N. Granville- 748, 756, 757, 759, 759s; N. Greenwich (Reid's corners)- 854; N. Hoosic- 766, 772, 1022, 1048s; Northumberland- 756, 799, 804, 839, 850, 933, 1053; N. White Creek- 1003, 1022, 1028, 1050s; Norwich- 730; Nyack- 731;

Ogdensburgh- 730, 812, 1045, 1054; Onondaga- 731, 1004; Oswego- 759s; 932, 943; Owego- 759; Palatine- 772; Peekskill- 752; Philmont- 1095;

Pike's Cantonment- 1055; Pittstown- 747, 813, 815, 839, 851, 917; Reid's corners- 730; Plattsburgh- 707, 709, 759s, 799, 845, 1018, 1045, 1055, 1056; Pompton- 812; Putnam- 714, 725, 992, 1020, 1028, 1091, 1092;

Quassacook (Anaquassacook)- 1003; Queensbury- 876, 936, 938; as Kiandeross- 936; Oneida (corners)- 1093;

Red Post- 851; Reid's corners (N. Greenwich)- 854; Rensselaerwyck (Ranslaerwyck), Manor of- 735, 881; the Ridge (Malta)- 952; Rochester- 727, 841, 844, 845; Rock's Ferry- 1095; Roxbury- 997; Rye- 752;

Sag Harbor- 1100; St. Regis- 1014- 1016;

Salem- 701, 703, 706- 709, 711, 713, 714, 717- 719, 721, 724, 725, 729- 734, 734s, 737- 739, 741, 743, 744, 758, 759s, 799, 802, 805, 806, 809, 810, 812, 838, 839, 843- 845, 853, 858- 860, 867, 868, 872, 874, 876, 878½, 879, 914, 915, 919, 924- 926, 936, 958, 972, 973, 976- 978, 992, 994, 995, 1000- 1005, 1009, 1012, 1015, 1018, 1019, 1023, 1028, 1033- 1035, 1039, 1040, 1044- 1047, 1048s, 1049, 1050, 1050s- 1054, 1060, 1063, 1064, 1068, 1069, 1073, 1075, 1075b, 1078, 1080- 1086, 1089, 1090, 1092, 1095, 1097- 1100; Camp Washington- 1097; Clapp's Mills- 866, 1003; jail- 877, 1050s; Milliman's corners- 731; as White Creek- 936, 1066;

Sancoick- 766, 768, 853, 866, 1006; as St. Coick- 783; as St. Croix- 822; as Sinkaick- 831; Sandy Hill (Hudson Falls)- 711, 731½, 747, 874, 991, 1074, 1082, 1088, 1097; Sand Lake- 731;

Saratoga (Schuylerville)- 723, 729, 750, 782, 788, 798, 799, 804- 806, 816, 823, 831, 849, 890, 935, 998, 1014, 1017, 1066; Saratoga Springs- 799, 839, 851, 1002, 1054, 1069, 1082;

Schaghticoke- 730, 759s, 805, 816, 839, 1021, 1027, 1048s; as Schagtekoeke-
831; as Shaticoke- 953b; as Skotocook- 837; Schaghticoke Point- 732, 1048s;
Schenectady- 756, 804, 950; Schodack- 939, 943; Schoharie- 748, 753, 756;
Schroon Lake- 1074;

Schuylerville (Saratoga)- 729, 738, 743, 804, 972, 1058, 1066, 1095; Scipio- 844;
Shushan (Sodom)- 704, 732, 738, 841, 1003, 1050, 1050s, 1064, 1090, 1098;

Skenesborough (Whitehall)- 701, 741, 742, 747, 749- 751, 754, 774, 795, 814,
816, 875, 876, 913, 967, 998, 1000; Snicker' Gap- 1095; Snickersville- 1095;
Sodom (Shushan)- 1063, 1064;

S. Argyle- 732, 802, 973; S. Easton- 1098; S. Granville- 921; S. Hartford- 758,
759s, 1024; S. Salem- 737, 840;

Stafford's Bridge- 799; Staten Island- 1100; Stephentown- 756; Stillwater- 730,
731, 748, 751, 755, 763, 772, 773, 849- 852, 858, 859, 867, 870, 950, 951, 960,
973, 1003, 1037, 1038, 1053, 1054, 1070; Gracie's corners- 973; Stone Arabia-
752, 756; Syracuse- 731, 839, 841, 845;

Taberg- 1060; Thurman- 992; Ticonderoga- 731, 734, 738b, 742, 747, 750, 752,
753, 760, 773- 776, 778, 779, 781b, 782, 784, 786- 788, 790, 792, 794, 799, 817,
833, 847, 848, 866, 890, 910, 917, 959, 990, 1016, 1059; falls- 848;

Triangle, P. O.- 962; Trenton- 730, 843; Troy- 709, 730, 732, 736, 737, 759s,
799, 804, 805, 839, 861, 876, 939- 943, 950, 954, 969, 1003, 1027, 1031, 1036,
1044, 1048s, 1082, 1099; Camp Rathbone- 1074; Turin- 730; Tyashoke- 839, 845;

Union Village (Greenwich)- 705, 721, 731, 732, 839, 843, 862, 969, 1005, 1050s,
1058, 1069, 1080; Upper White Creek- 816; Utica- 730, 737, 1046;

Vernon- 839; Vienna- 1077;

Walloomsac- 761, 765, 766, 783, 1006; Warrensburgh- 950, 1095; Waterford-
1036, 1038, 1074; Watertown- 730; Weedsport- 805; W. Bloomfield- 799; W.
Cambridge- 805, 1048s; Westfield (Ft. Ann, Hartford)- 745, 876, 1091, 1092; W.
Granville- 759s; W. Hebron (Bedlam)- 731, 737, 742, 1081; Westmoreland- 846;
West Point- 1036; Wheeler- 1078; Whipple City (Greenwich)- 862;

White Creek- 726, 763, 773, 784, 795, 807, 825, 839, 842, 843, 936, 956, 975,
990, 992, 1005, 1028, 1029, 1048s, 1095; Ash Grove- 813, 815, 840; Post's
corners- 843, 844, 1048s; Wait's corners- 739, 987, 1003, 1048s;

Whitehall- 714- 716, 719, 725, 734, 749- 752, 754, 756, 758, 759, 759s, 845,
867, 875, 876, 992, 995, 1015, 1017, 1020, 1023, 1028, 1074; White Plains- 747,
755; Whitesboro- 730; Whitestown- 718, 730, 731; factory village- 839;

Wilbur- 943; Williamsburg- 799, 839; Wilson's Hollow- 813; Wilton- 799, 999;
Yonkers- 799;

Military Units, Civil War- Artillery- 9th- 1081; Cavalry- 1st Mounted Rifles-
1095; 2nd, Northern Black Horse, or Morrison's- 1080; Infantry- 22nd (Northern
N. Y. Regt.)- 1074, 1080, 1081, 1095b; 44th (Ellsworth)- 1081, 1095; 93rd
(Morgan Rifles)- 1080, 1081, 1090b, 1094; 96th- 1095; 123rd (Wash. Co. Regt.)-
1080, 1081, 1097, 1098; 144th- 799; 2nd U. S. Sharpshooters- 1081; Militia- 10th
Division, 16th Brigade- 1009; 50th Regt.- 1009;

Railroads- Troy & Greenfield- 954;

Assembly- list of Wash. co. members, 1777- 1857, giving no. of terms, town origin of member, & noting last term served; 1779 & 1780, no returns were made, & in 1780 & 1781, journal was not extant, & names of legislature unknown; changes in area of representation noted; see Washington County- **992**;

Committee of Safety- requested Apr. 28, 1775, that all counties elect delegates to a Provincial Congress, to meet May 22nd, "to deliberate upon & direct such measures as may be expedient for the common good"- **773**; rec'd. communication from Wm. Duer, Esq., July 11th, dated Ft. Miller, July 5, 1775, describing intent of some Charlotte co. citizens to close the court here & his efforts to prevent this by detaining Capt. Motte's co. to protect the bench; the comm. replies in commendation of Duer's actions & their intent to present the matter bef. next session of Prov. Congress; June 28th correspondence of Wm. Marsh, Esq., & Samuel Rose, both of Manchester, Vt. Comm. of Safety, describing same intent to assemble & close Charlotte co. courts; implied that fear of rem. of cannon from Ticonderoga was reason behind the orig. outcry, & meeting was held among the 'mob', selecting a person to present this concern to Continental Congress- **779**; appts. committee, Jan. 18, 1777, to proceed to Cumberland & Gloucester counties to inquire of their state reports, noting that cert. disaffected persons, calling themselves 'the Green Mountian boys' have attempted to disavow the authority of N. Y. & form a new & separate state; Mar. 1st, Mr. Duane reports on the same matter, saying a large part of the 2 counties 'continue steadfast in their allegiance to this govt.', noting that only 20 of the anticipated 80 men attended their 'mock Convention'- **786**; message sent to them from Continental Congress at Philadelphia by N. Y. delegate, James Duane, July 10, 1777, noting arr. of recent issue of *Connecticut Courant*, w. declaration from a part of N. Y. 'which is dubbed the state of Vermont'; names probable persons involved in the scheme, & observations concluding that the venture will not meet w. favor by the full Congress; see Duane, James, & Vermonters- **793**; opinions of Gouverneur Morris, pert. to the Grants, relayed from Ft. Edward, July 21st, observing Col. Skene's efforts to court the inhabitants into the British camp; warns that 'but for the sake of a mere feather', the population there may desert to the enemy, it being crucial to prevent this- **796**; Morris, & Abram Yates, Jr., appt. as a comm. to go to HQ (prob. Gen. Schuyler's), inform comm., July 23rd, of the retreat from Ft. Edward to Moses kill, & the disch. of militia, which weakens what may be an otherwise strong post against the enemy; they also point out measures that may hold Burgoyne in his present position & foil his design; from Gen. Schuyler, at Moses kill, July 24th, half of militia disch. on condition that the rest will tarry ano. 3 wks.; lists remaining militia at abt. 3,300, & total force at 2,700- 2,800- **797**

Council- July 27, 1777, corresponds w. Gov. Trumbull of Conn., seeking aid, & noting 5 counties of the state are now occ. by the enemy & '3 others are disunited by malcontents, who meditate revolt, & are attempting to avail themselves of the present troubles, to advance their interested purposes, in so much that all order of govt. has ceased among them'- **797**; report dated Nov. 14th, presented Dec. 6, 1753, bef. Lt. Gov. Hon. James Delancey, concerning the E. boundary of the

colony; advised that same be forwarded 'to the Right Hon. the Lords
Commissioners for Trade & Plantations'- **884**; letter, w/o date, from Harmanus
Schuyler, High Sheriff for city & co. of Albany, presented to Lt. Gov.
Cadwallader Colden & the Council, advising of apprehension & detaining of Samuel Ashley,
Samuel Robinson, John Horfort, & Isaac Charles, in pursuance of the Lt. Gov.'s
proclamation of Dec. 28, 1763- **885**; petitn. laid bef. Council, Feb. 28, 1770,
requesting erection of a new co. N. of Cumberland co., & an order therefore
created Gloucester co.- **886**; advised, Oct. 22, 1765, that a reserve of lands occ. &
improved by Jacob Marsh & his associates be made from lands gr. in Patents to
Mr. Napier & Capt. John Small, at a rate of 200 acres per person, for lands actually
possessed & improved by them; advised gr. of townships to actual settlers of
Shaftsbury, Bennington, & Pownal, Vt.- **894**; Aug. 24, 1771, directs Philip Skene,
John Munro, Patrick Smith, & John McComb, Esqs., all Albany co. Justices of
Peace, to give full inquiry concerning June 11th riot by Cochran & ors., in which
Donald McIntyre & ors. were dispossessed from their homes, & then to give relief
(to the victims) as statutes permit- **901**; John Munro petitn., Sept. 20, 1771, for an
appt. of High Sheriff, Albany co., & was referred to Atty. Gen.Wm. Smith & ors.;
rec'd. testim. of Samuel Gardenier of Walloomsack Patent, Sept. 21, 1771,
concerning his trials w. rioters under N. H. title; see Grants, N. H. Controversy-
902; petitn. & complaint from Benjamin Stevenson, Deputy Surveyor, & John
Brandon & John Dunbar, Oct. 21, 1772, stating that while surveying on the Onion
river, Sept. 29th, Remember Baker, Ira Allen, & 5 others, came upon them w/o
provocation, taking away their property & effects, & throwing Dunbar, bound, into
a fire; reward of £ 100 offered for their apprehension- **906**; John Munro's letter to
the Gov., Aug. 22, 1773, informing that 'the mob has broken loose', noting the
impending destruction of all his property, along w. the earlier destruction of his Pot
& Pearl ash works, & the rescue by the mob of one of its members, who had been
arrested for horse stealing- **908**; the Gov. conveys to the Board, Sept. 3, 1773, a
letter from Gen. Haldimand, replying to a request for military aid in policing the
region of the Grants; & the Gen. replies that such a precedent, in his opinion,
would serve to undermine the civil authority in the public eye, citing as well the
deteriorated state of Crown Point & Ticonderoga, the prospective barracks for the
requested force- **909**; Sept. 8th- Council noted the tenor of Gen. Haldimand's reply
reflects his lack of information concerning conditions in the Grants, & advises
ordering 200 men to Ticonderoga as soon as convenient, their length of service
dependent upon the people's behavior, & no provisions made by the Province from
which their charges maybe defrayed; the Gov. & Council advise an ordinance to
establ. a Court of Common Pleas & Gen.Court of Sessions of the Peace in
Charlotte co., at the house of Patrick Smith, Esq., nr. Ft. Edward, N. Y., on the 3rd
Tues. of May & Oct.; Sept. 29th- Gen. Haldimand proposes sending 200 men to Ti
& Crown Point, withdrawing 150 on Nov. 1st, the post not now being suitable to
maintain more than 50 menduring the winter months; & the Council now deems it
too late in the season to send the required aid, postponing the action- **910**; rec'd.
letter from Justices of Charlotte co., Oct. 15, 1773, w. affidavits charging Samuel

Bulsby, Remember Baker, & 2 others w. violently assaulting & beating Jonathan Eckert at his house along Lake Champlain- **911**; Nov. 24, 1772 letter of John Munro, Esq., rec'd. & read Dec. 16th, noting the arrest of John Searls & Comfort Carpenter for counterfeiting, w. confiscation of 'the stamps, moulds, mils, & several other materials for coining dollars...'; notes Carpenter's escape from escort & destruction of Munro's potash works on the same night; see Counterfeiting- **912**; erects New Perth (Salem, N. Y.) as a township, Mar. 4, 1774, on petitn. of its inhabitants- **913**; affidavit bef. Council, Mar. 16, 1763, by Alexander McClain, informing that a N. H. survey party has been seen in the Crown Point area the prev. Sept.; in response, Gov. Colden issues proclamation, Dec. 28, 1763, warning settlers not to take titles from N. H., giving 'the undoubted eastern limits' of the Province's boundaries as the banks of the Conn. river; Council advises Gov. Colden, Aug. 1764, to inform Gov. Wentworth of the circumstances behind the arrest of the 4 men whose release he seeks, noting the circumstances, & that the offense was committed "within the undoubted jurisdiction of this province"- **928**;

Laws of- c. 1858, requirements for persons admitted to view capital punishments; forbidden to anyone under 21 yrs. of age, allowing attendance of only the foll. persons- the judge & other officers of the court; 2 physicians, & 12 citizens, selected by the Sheriff as witns. of the execution; deputies & other officers of the jail; immed. relatives of the prisoner, & 1 or 2 clergym. selected by the prisoner- **1050s**;

Northern frontier, c. 1782- guarded by '9 months men' enl. mostly in the vicinity of Salem, N. Y.; one regt. incl. Capt. Abraham Livinston, Lt. Timothy Hutton, & Ens. John Hunsden, as its officers; some privates in the same unit were Thomas Boyd & Asa Fitch, Sr.; bef. 1782, all military posts N. of Saratoga (Schuylerville, N. Y.) & Ft. Williams, Salem, N. Y., were broken up; Capt. Livingston's co. was enl. in spring, & mustered at Saratoga, remaining there 6 wks., & then a port. was sent to Ft. Williams- **729**

Provincial Convention- Philip Livingston, President; convened Apr. 20, 1775, w. seven counties represented; delegates chosen toContinental Congress, & adjourned- **773**; convened July 9, 1776; Wm. Duer, Esq., John Williams, & Alex. Webster, delegates from Charlotte co.- **785**; appts. officials for Charlotte co., May 8, 1777- **787**;

Provincial Congress- convened May 22, 1775, w. nine counties represented; elected Peter Van Brugh Livingston, President; May 24th- John Williams & William Marsh appear as Charlotte co. representatives, w. certif. signed by 14 gentlemen of respective comm. of White Creek, Cambden (Camden), Arlington, Dorset, Rupert, Pawlet, & Wells; the certif. of their appt. read & filed, & representatives seated; May 30th- Dirck Swart, representative from Stillwater, Albany co., gr. leave of absence to superintend rem. of cannon from Ticonderoga to head of Lake George; Conn. colony communicates to N. Y. that Ft. Ticonderoga was not taken by any of their regular troops, "but by adventurers"- **773**; in response to Col. Arnold's letter from Crown Point, 500 lbs. of powder & 400 men were sent to that post from Conn. colony, & a communication sent by Conn. to N. Y. noting "that they had no design of invading, but merely took this step till N. Y. could occupy the posts, & ward off the danger"; in response, Dirck Swart appt. to supervise rem. of cannon from Ft. Ticonderoga & Albany comm. designated to raise a militia force to be sent there- 774; request rec'd. May 1775, from Albany comm., conveying Col. Arnold's request for seamen to man the sloop & schooner at Crown Point; also notes they are raising 2 companies of 50 men ea., to go to Ticonderoga, but they lack ammunition & have only 250 lbs. of powder left; £ 200 from the colony's Treasury & £ 700 from loan officers of Albany co. obt. for Dirck Swart, the members pledging themselves for their several portions of sums; June 2, 1775- Peter T. Curtenius appt. Commissary, for buying & sending stores N. from NYC; also, resolution similar to, but pre- dating one passed by Continental Congress, forbidding expeditions or incursions into Canada- 776; comm. consisting of Mr. Montgomery, _____ Silvester, Abraham Yates, _____ Scott, _____ Morris, _____ Marsh, & John Williams appt. to examine, upon his request, conduct of William Duer, Esq., w. regards to defense of N. frontier; June 15, 1775, comm. concludes that insinuations against Wm. Duer, Esq., are groundless, & the full Congress agreeing, recommendation made that a notice be given for all members of the colony & other inhabitants of America not to injure his person or property; also, same date, 2 letters from Col. Ethan Allen read into record, one being a copy of a letter sent by Col. Allen & James Easton to the people of Canada; Mr. Marsh obt. leave of absence, leaving Mr. Williams as sole representative from Charlotte co.; June 21st- delegates of Cumberland co.- John Hazeltine, Paul Spooner, & William Williams, seated; June 23rd- John Williams gr. leave of absence & left June 26th; note that GeorgePalmer much confided in for services on N. frontier- 777; June 30, 1775- four companies of Green Mtn. regt. ordered to be raised & officers appt.; Drs. John Jones & Samuel Bard appt. to examine Samuel Cook, Ebenezer Haviland, & John Williams as their surgeons; also directs Gen. Schuyler to examine condition of Ft. Ticonderoga & obt. intelligence abt. feelings in Canada; July 4th- Ethan Allen & Seth Warner adm. to an audience by 18 to 9 vote; £ 30 advanced to them, & regt. of Green Mtn. boys ordered to be raised foll. their departure; State Comm. (or Council) of Safety appt. & adjournment made on July 8, 1775- 779; certif. presented July 18, 1775, by David Watkins, indicating his election at Ft. Edward, N. Y., on June 29th, along w. Dr. George Smith, & Archibald Campbell, Esq., as additional Charlotte co. delegates to serve w. John Williams & Wm. Marsh; also, July 19th, notice rec'd. from Jacob Bayley of Newbury, dated June 29th, giving notice of his selection as Gloucester co. delegate, but conveying his inability to be present because of 'such fears from Canada'; relates that an Indian has conveyed the feeling that the French & Indians 'would all join us if an army was sent there, & that Quebec might easily be taken'- 780; Congress resumed July 26, 1775, & appt. William Duer, Esq., as Deputy Adjutant Gen., w. rank of Col., July 27th; due to 'his peculiar situation' regarding his brothers' enterprises in Dominica, a comm. conferring w. him excused the appt., replacing him w. Robert G. Livingston- 781; Gen. Schuyler corresponds from Ft. Ticonderoga, July 31st, listing officers elected in the Green Mtn. regt., noting that he could not have imagined a contest over rank occurring betw. Allen & Warner, or the possibility of a 3rd party being elected for field officer in their place; states his propensity to have made the same selections if the matter were in his own hands, but for the delicate relations betw. N. Y. & the people in the Grants; requests warrants for Capts. & Lts., & directs that Peter T. Curtenius may obt. cloth for uniforms & tents to accomodate 225 men- **781b**; Aug. 22nd- directed org. of state militia into 6 brigades; officers chosen, Sept. 1st, for Green Mtn. regt.- Lt. Col. Seth Warner & Maj. Samuel Safford; adjourned the foll. day- **782**; rec'd. & approved a proclamation from Comm. of Safety for Cambridge, Hoosick, & Bennington, which directed that 'if any person is suspected of being a tory, or an enemy of this country, they are to be complained to the Comm. of this district or town...', noting that 'cert. vicious & wicked persons, to gratify their revenge of a cert. private quarrel, seduced others, under a pretence [sic] of defending the country's liberty, to join them in night walking, house breaking & assaulting men's persons in a violent manner'; recovenes Sept. 17- Oct. 3rd; news rec'd. from England, Oct. 12th, by Capt. John Lawrence, indicating the expectation there that they would soon hear of the hanging of Maj. Skene; adjourned Nov. 4th, ordering new elections; Dec. 6th, the new Congress met, sitting until Dec. 22nd- **783**; resumed Feb. 12th, its business done by comm. ad interim, & the new session closed Mar. 16, 1776- **784**; 3rd Congress began May 14, 1776, Mr. Webster attending for Charlotte co.; Col. John Williams, Maj. Alex. Webster, & Maj. Wm. Malcom selected as Charlotte co. delegates; May 20th, Wm. Malcom seated by 16 to 5 vote, being a non- resident of Charlotte co., but 'having respectable freeholds there'; session closed June 30th- **785**; John Williams corresponds to John McKesson, Esq., June 23, 1777, that he has obt. information from some Canadians at Otter creek on the prev. day, saying that there are few regulars now in Canada, but that 'they use the inhabitants very ill' & numbers flee daily down across the Green Mtns., having found a road giving them a 12 day journey- **789**

New York City, N. Y.- time- in remarks pertaining to the execution of Martin Wallace, Dec. 1, 1858, Salem, N. Y., the *Salem Press* noted that "the watches in the company [attending the execution] were found to vary materially"; those of the militia co. from Greenwich, N. Y., were found to be "more than 20 min. in advance of what we were assured was the New- York city time, which later we found to coincide w. the Rail- road time & that at the Bank"- **1050s**; ment. of var. streets & landmarks in early 19th century, from "Recollections of Old Merchants of New York City", an unattrib. newsclipping noted as orig. written for the *N. Y. Leader*; notices given of the John St. Methodist church; the Garden St. church on Exchange St.; Bininger's Market, on the corner of Beekman & Nassau Sts.; City Hall, Augusta St.; the old Oswego Market, Maiden Lane, nr. Broadway; Howard Hotel, fronting on Liberty St., & behind the Oswego Market; the old Quaker church, mid- block, Liberty St.; the Times Building, loc. opp. corner of Beekman & Nassau Sts., where the old Brick church stood; information on the history of the Bininger family, & Rev. Philip Embury also ment.-**1075b**

NICHOLS,
James- appt. to Salem comm., Sept. 12, 1814, for receiving & forwarding
provisions, et. al., to Salem militia at Plattsburgh, N. Y.; his store in Salem village
design. as site for depositing contributions- **707**
Philip- witn., along w. Thomas Stafford, Aug. 9, 1774, to Jacob Marsh's transfer of
land in Clarendon, Charlotte co., N. Y., to Amariah How- **745**

NIEMCEWITZ,
Baron- (Niemcewicz, Julian Ursyn, 1758- 1841; aide & adviser to Kosciuszko)
Polish exile; res. Elizabethtown, N. J.; m. Susannah, dau. Peter Van Brugh
Livingston- **961**

NILES,
David- m. Maria, dau. Paul & ____ (Wells) Cornell; they acquired the old Cornell
mansion in Walloomsac Patent, but became so indebted to Judge Germain that he
assumed the property from Niles- **806**

93rd N. Y. Infantry- Col. John S. Crocker commanding, 1861; recruited wholly in
Wash. co., acc. this source- **1080**; Byron L. Flower, Assist. Surgeon, bur. Oct. 30,
(1863?), Salem, N. Y.- **1081**; nicknamed "Morgan Rifles"; a list of field, staff, &
line officers, Co. A- I, & K, from an unattrib. newspaper clipping Feb. 1, 1862,
Camp Rathbone, Albany, N. Y.; Col. J. S. Crocker, Lt. Col. Benjamin C. Butler,
Maj. Ambrose L. Cassidy; Adjutant, Haviland Gifford; Qtr.Master, Andrew K.
Haxstun; Surgeon, Strobridge Smith; Assist. Surgeon, Theodore S. Wallace;
Chaplain, Christopher H. Edgerton;
     Co. A- Capt. Orville L. Colvin; Lt. Henry C. Newton; 2nd Lt. James W.
Southwick;
     Co. B- Capt. Elijah Hobart; Lt. James W. Race; 2nd Lt. William C. Swain;
     Co. C- Capt. Dennis E. Barnes; Lt. Waters W. Braman; 2nd Lt. Milo E.
Washburn;
     Co. D- Capt. George M. Voorhees; Lt. Henry P. Smith; 2nd Lt. Philander B.
Marvin;
     Co. E- Capt. Andrew J. McNett; Lt. William H. Bradford; 2nd Lt. Lyman J.
Warren;
     Co. F- Capt. George B. Mosher; Lt. John Bailey; 2nd Lt. Silas S. Hubbell;
     Co. G- Capt. Walter S. Gray; Lt. William H. Van Schaak; 2nd Lt. Francis S.
Bailey;
     Co. H- Capt. Hiram S. Wilson; Lt. Edson Fitch; 2nd Lt. Ephriam T. Weeks;
     Co. I- Capt. Nathan J. Johnson; Lt. William Randles; 2nd Lt. James M.
Crawford;
     Co. K- Capt. Samuel McConihe; Lt. Joseph L. Young; 2nd Lt. Gurdon G. Moore-
1090b; bef. Yorktown, Va., Apr. 1862; on Apr. 26th, its commanders, Col. John S.
Crocker & Maj. Ambrose L. Cassidy, passed by the outer pickets & were capt. by
the enemy; they were exchanged the foll. summer; loc. w. the advance of the army,

Nov. 8- 12th, at Warrenton, Va.; its numbers greatly reduced, returned & disbanded, early Jan. 1864; over 200 of its veterans immed. re- enl. to serve 3 yrs. or until the war's end- **1094**

NIXON,
Brig. Gen. John- (1727- 1815) acc. this source, his artillery drove back an assault of tories & Indians on the retreating American army at Sandy Hill, N. Y., the night foll. the battle of Ft. Ann, July 8, 1777- **747**

NOBLE,
Capt. Enoch- commanded a co. of Col. Ashley's regt., July/ Aug. 1777; his co. arr. at Bennington shortly after the battle there, & was sent as scouts to Arlington, Vt., & then detailed to Stillwater, N. Y., at the time of Burgoyne's surrender- **755**
James- of Tinmouth, Vt.; m. Cynthia, dau. Hon. Nathaniel & Cynthia (Mason) Hall; he was a half bro. of Rev. Dr. Noble, of Johnsonville, N. Y.- **759s**
Rev. Jonathan H., D. D.- (s. Obadiah & Nancy Mason) pastor, Presbyterian church, Schaghticoke, N. Y., for some 30 yrs.; now (1874) pastor in the "neighborh. church", Johnsonville, N. Y.- **759s**
Obadiah- of Tinmouth, Vt.; m. Nancy, dau. David & Susanna (West) Mason; ments. their s. Rev. Jonathan H.- **759s**
Thaddeus- his wf. Sarah d. Apr. 5, 1812, at 78; & he d. June 14, 1809, at 74- **(L)-772**

NORTH,
Mr.- "a missionary printer"; m. Minerva, dau. Dr. & Phebe (Whiteside) Bryant; his wf. d. in the East Indies- **805**

NORTH CAROLINA- Kinston- 1095; New Bern- 799; Raleigh- 1024; Smithfield, Ft. Gratiot- 974

Northern Ireland- See IRELAND

N. Hoosick, N. Y.- formerly called Sancoick- **1006**; c. 1777, the road through the village was essentially the same as the route was in 1853, when Dr. Fitch makes a hand sketch of the hamlet, showing Elisha Brownell's grist & sawmill, in abt. the same loc. as Van Rensselaer's mills were in 1777; in 1853, Webster's tavern, a store, Woolen factory, & a depot for the Troy & Rutland R. R. were also loc. here; the hotel & store, were loc. abt. 10- 16 rods from the bridge over the Little White creek, at the juncture of the road E. to Walloomsac, N. Y., & the road S. to Hoosick Falls, N. Y.; the Woolen factory was loc. on the S. side of the Walloomsac river, on the road to Hoosick Falls, & the R. R. depot was loc. some rods below the factory; the Little White creek "runs through a deep rock- bound chasm, across which the bridge here is thrown"; as Col. Baum advanced from Cambridge, the American scouts & stragglers fled bef. him to Bennington, & Wm. Gilmore & 2 others lingered at Van Rensselaer's long enough to strip off the planking from the bridge, to prevent the passage of the 2 cannon incl. in Col. Baum's expedition; see SanCoick, N. Y.: & Bennington, battle of- **1006**; while excavation was being done for the R. R. here, which passed in a deep cut beyond Webster's tavern, a skeleton was disinterred, presumed to be the last man slain at the Bennington battle (prob. the last corpse found), who was by neighborh. tradit., believed to be a Hessian; the bones were taken to the hotel & displayed for awhile, "thrown abt. for some months" & then lost; acc. Dr. Fitch, all knowl. of the burning of this place & Hoosick, N. Y. by Indians from Canada (Aug. 28, 1754; see p. 556, French's Gazetteer) in the old French war "has become extinct among the people now living here"- **1007**

NORTHUP,
Clark- appt.one of the Executors of the Will of Dr. Ira Hall, May 6, 1816- **759s**
Henry- his wf. Mary d. June 20, 1798, at 46; & he d. July 5, 1797, at 56- **(L)- 772**

N. White Creek & Cambridge Literary Assoc.- review of its 1st lecture in a series, from *Wash. Co. Post*, reprinted, prob. *Salem Press*; a partial article, the reverse side of a newsclipping pert. to the results of the Nov. 7, 1854 election; deliverd by Rev. C. S. Robinson, the lecture's subj. was "This Age", & defined the time period as being 'a working age', noting cert. engineering feats characteristic of the age- **1028**

NORTON,
_____ - res. early at Fitch's Point, Salem, N. Y., halfway betw. the Red House & the Battenkill; rem. & c. 1790's, res. Whitehall, N. Y.; his house was the 2nd place occ. by Moses Martin, Sr. after he brought his family to the Point- **867**
Levi- (given as Horton; § 730) m. Elizabeth, dau. Stephen & Jane (Martin) Leonard- **1046**

Norwalk, Conn.- site of Gov. Thomas Fitch's mansion; British forces descended upon the village & burnt it (July 11 & 12, 1779) & during their withdrawal, burnt the Gov.'s mansion; his Wid. had been sent word to rem. all of her furniture, but believing respect for the Gov. would induce them to spare his house, she "wrote conspicuously w. chalk upon the walls of the house, that it was the house of Gov. Fitch"; but instead of sparing it, "as the hostile force passed it, a no. of them went in & helped themselves liberally to the wine in the cellar, & then passed on"; w. the village in flames, some stragglers in the withdrawal again entered the house & fired it as well, burning it to the ground- **941**

NOURSE,
James- c. 1798, prob. res. Bardstown, Ky.; along w. John Rowan, rec'd. the remainder of the estate- real & personal, of John Fitch, the steamboat inventor, foll. his bequests; Fitch's Will, June 20; Prob. Aug. 14, 1798- **949b**

O

OAKLEY,
Peter Cannon- b. NYC, res. Yorkville; Methodist minister; m. 1. Maria Loomis, of Windsor, Conn.; 2. Harriet, dau. Rev. Bradley & Polly (Pattison) Sillick; 2 children, by 1st wf.- Wilbur Fisk, "a youth now at the book- binding trade"; & Jane Maria- **950**

OATMAN,
____- of Arlington, Vt.; m. Mary, dau. Aaron, Jr., & Artemesia (Lynn) Martin; his wf. m. 2nd, William Walker- **731**

O'BAIL,
Jacobus- res. Fitch's Point, Salem, N. Y.; his mill later operated by William Miller; no recoll. by Wid. Angel that the mill had ever been burned after Miller purch. it; see Vol. 1; surname also given as Abeel- **859**

O'BRIEN,
Patrick- Co. A, 2nd N. Y., Northern Black Horse, Cav., 1861- 2- **1080**
Sarah- c. 1850's, perh. kept a store or tavern, where it was reported that Martin Wallace had at least one fight in, prior to the murder of Barney McEntee- **1048s**

O'CALLAHAN,
Dr.- (Edmund Bailey O'Callaghan, 1797- 1880; editor, Doc. Hist. of N. Y., Doc. Relative to the Colonial Hist. of N. Y.) res. Albany, N. Y.; Sept. 17, 1851, shows Dr. Fitch some minor documents connected w. John Munro, Esq., of White Creek, N. Y.- **956**

O'CLEARY,
Family- Irish; a fictitious, allegorical emig. family appearing in Priest Quigley's book, *The Cross & Shamrock*; during their ocean passage, the father dies, but the family eventually reaches a city resembling Troy, N. Y., where the mother also dies, leaving 3 sons & a dau.; these children are then whisked off to an orphanage operated by a Poor Master named Van Stingey; in a few hrs., he remands them to "a highly respectable farmer, away off in the country, somewhere" to prevent the priest from attending to their spiritual needs; acc. to Quigley's book, this practice was widespread 'by thejealous Pharoahsof sectarianism'; acc. Dr. Fitch, the loc. of their sequestering, by its description, resembles the Owl kill valley, in the town of Cambridge, N. Y.; Paul, at age 15, the eldest son,"had been well schooled in Ireland- & now adheres to his Catholic faith, & keeps his bros. & sist. well instructed therein, though wholly secluded from all Catholic society. He manfully withstands & even gets the better of 'the fanatical Presbyterian minister...' in repeated arguments on religion"- **1027**

OGDEN,
Matthias- m. dau. Col. Robert Cockran- **917**

O'HARRO,
Hugh- pl., w. Patrick McDavitt, May 19, 1774, vs. Samuel Loadman & als.- **878**

OHIO- 731, 733, 752, 812, 856, 863, 939, 943, 955, 971; the Reserve- 799, 955;
  Counties- Cuyahoga- 1095; Eire- 734; Lorain-727; Mahoning- 799; Monroe- 940;
  Richland- 734, 873; Trumbull- 799; Washington- 973;
  Cities & Towns- Akron- 734, 799; Browhelm- 727; Cincinatti- 734, 1010;
  Cleveland- 734, 841, 1010; Columbus- 839, 1010; Ellsworth- 799, 940; Geneva-
  799; Independence- 1095; Mansfield- 873, 1010; Mattison- 730; Oberlin- 799;
  Parma- 734; Reynoldsburgh- 839; Sandusky- 1010; Shelby- 1010; Toledo- 939;
  Features- rivers- Big Sandy- 949b; Ohio- 799, 949b;
  Military units from, Civil War- 103rd Inf.- 1095

OLIN,
Gov. Henry- (1767- 1837; 18th Congress, 1824- 25; Gov., 1827- 30) of Vt.; a dau.
m. James O. Walker, of Swanton, Vt., as his 1st wf.- **962**

123rd N. Y. S. Vol. Infantry- Col. Archibald McDougall commanding, recruited
entirely from Wash. co.- **1080**; org. at Camp Washington, Salem, N. Y., late Aug.-
Sept. 1862; Col.- Archibald McDougall; Quartermaster- John King; Chaplain-
Rev. H. Gordon, of Coila, N. Y.; Surgeon- Dr. Kennedy- **1097**; departed for
Virginia by train, betw. 10- 11:00 PM, Friday, Sept. 5, 1862, Salem, N. Y;
impressions of their departure recorded by Dr. Fitch as he listens from his office at
Fitch's Point-
"After a clear warm dry day, comes a bright moon light night"; & at 10:45 PM, he
notes- "for the past 10 min. I have been listening to the roar of the long train of
cars, in the still night air, as starting from the village, they approached down the
White Creek valley, & then turning receded up betw. the wood- clad hills of the
Batten kill- the roar of the revolving car wheels ever & anon broken by the shrill
whistle at the diff. road- crossings- the shouts of the men for awhile distinctly
audible above the roar of the cars- that roar becoming more & more faint, till now
it has expired, as they are passing the base of the hills beyond Shushan; & I have
thus heard the last sound I shall hear from the thousand young men who have gone
forth from our midst to fight their country's battles"; foll. at 11:00 PM, he muses
that- "Again I recognize the faint sound of the now distant train, for a few
moments, away off in Jackson; till it is extinguished by passing wagons. Then the
report of a cannon, once & again, announces they are receiving a salute as they are
passing the Cambridge depot"; and a final thought, at 11:30 PM- "... Oh how diff.
from all this will it be, when perh. decimated in its numbers, the remaining
fragments of this regt. will return, maimed & crippled, many of them confirmed in

habits of vice & the mere wrecks of the hale & hearty young men they are now!";
betw. 1- 2:00 AM, Sat., the Regt. arr. in NYC, & embarked from Pier No. 1, for
Perth Amboy, N. J., at 3:00 AM, & thence by train to Philadelphia, Pa.; they arr.
abt. 5:00 AM, & were taken to a large refreshment saloon run on Washington St.,
by the Union Volunteer Assoc.; here, Evander Burtis d. of cholera morbus, having
taken sick while in NYC; the regt. departed again at 1:00 PM, Sept. 8th, & stopped
overnight 5 mi. beyond Baltimore, Md., & the foll. day arr. & encamped 2 mi. E.
of the Capitol, on Capitol Hill, in Wash., D. C.; they soon rem. across the Potomac
& encamped on Arlington Heights; afterw., they were marched 2 mi. below
Harper's Ferry, to Pleasant Valley, Va.; Gen. Kane selected the regt.'s camp as his
place of worship, & foll. minute questioning of the chaplain, sought to obt. the
regt. for his command; they were placed in Kane's brigade, Gen. Williams'
division, Gen. Bank's corps, & sent to picket duty on the Shenandoah, marching 30
mi., Nov. 18, 1862, & then returned to the defense of Harper's Ferry; 8 additional
deaths noticed in the regt.; rem. Wash., D. C., & then recamped at Fairfax Station,
Va., leaving their sick & invalid at Harper's Ferry; 4 additional deaths noticed; the
chaplain, Rev. Henry Gordon, rec'd. 15 days furlough & returned home, preaching
2 sermons & giving addresses on Feb. 17, & 20, 1863, at Cambridge & Salem, N.
Y., respectively; he notes 20 deaths in the regt. thus far, & 2 fatiguing marches,
one lasting 7 days, from Loudon Valley to Fairfax, Va.; & ano., in pouring rain &
deep mud, from Fairfax, through Dumfries, to their present camp at Stafford Court
House, Va.; see Mathews Diary, Vol. 3; towns of origin for some companies- Co.
E- Hebron & Hartford; Co. H- Salem; Co. I- Cambridge & S. Easton; for a full
listing, see Vol. 4- **1098**

ORMSBY,
Capt. Lyman- of Schroon Lake, N. Y.; May 25, 1861, commanded Co. I, 22nd
N. Y. Inf.- **(L)- 1074**

ORR,
James- prob. res. Fitch's Point, Salem, N. Y.; m. Dorothy Seward; acc. Wid.
Angel, he was the only resident sentenced by Moses Martin, Sr. to be whipped- for
stealing- **868**
Mr.- c. 1853, current owner, The Stone Paper Mill, loc. E. of the Bennington
battlefield, & nr. where Col. Baum & a no. of the mortally wnd. were bur.- **1022**

OSBORN,
Abiather M.- Methodist minister; res. Newburgh, N. Y.; m. Elizabeth, dau. Rev.
Bradley & Polly (Pattison) Sillick; children- Bradley S., Abiather, Elias, & John
Raynor- **950**
Bradley S.- (s. Abiather M. & Elizabeth Sillick) "a youth who has been sailing
around the world for 3 yrs. whose propensity for roving has caused his family
much disgust. In the Rebellion he became news reporter, & the *N. Y. Herald*, publ.
his report of the Wilmington expedition prematurely he was arrested &

imprisoned, but acquitted on trial.The report appraised the rebels, enabling them to defeat the 1st expediton."- **950**

John- of W. Poultney, Vt.; m. Mary, dau. Paul & Elizabeth (Soule) Cornell; rem.White Creek, N. Y., & later to W. side of Seneca Lake, where he d.- **806**

OSWALD,
Capt.- delivered Col. Benedict Arnold's May 19, 1775 letter from Crown Point to Gov. Trumbull of Conn.- **774**; along w.Capt. Jonathan Brown, arr. at Crown Point, May 19, 1775, w. 50 men enl. on the road, & a small schooner capt. at Skenesborough- **775**
George- m. Lydia, dau. Abner & Anna (Fitch) Glines; he was killed (n. d.) by the kick of a horse; 4 children, ments. James, res. Niagara, N. Y., & Ann Eliza- **731**

OUDERKIRK,
Family- tory, res. Hoosick, N.Y., during Rev. war; old 'Festus' recruited all the men of this family to go into Col. Baum's camp & fight at Bennington in the royalist cause- **768**

Owl kill- c. 1853, tracks of the Troy & Rutland R. R. cross from Rensselaer co. intoWash. co. a little above the stream's mouth, nr. Eagle Bridge, N. Y.; within a mile, these tracks cross 4 times over the stream, & in betw. the 1st two & last two crossings, its course has been turned from its orig. stream bed & confined to the W. side of the R. R. right of way- **1003**; its valley, Cambridge, N. Y., resembles the description of farming country that the O'Cleary children were taken to in Priest Quigley's book, *The Cross & the Shamrock-* **1027**

P

PALEN,
____- m. Martha (or Patty) ____; children- Maxwell; David, of Nyack, N. Y.;
Lucy,m. Josephus Fitch; Amanda, m. ____ Merriam, of NYC; & ano. dau., m.
____ Hinckley, of Essex, N. Y.; his wf. m. 2nd, Aaron, s. Moses & Lydia (More)
Martin, as his 2nd wf.- **731**

PALMER,
____- m. Elizabeth, dau. Paul & ____ (Wells) Cornell- **806**
Benjamin- orig. proprietor, 600 acre lot, Danby, Vt.; deeded to Thomas Brayton,
Nov. 21, 1786, by Andrew White- **745**
Fenner- pursuant to the directions of the Albany Comm., he & Daniel B. Bratt, of
the Comm. of Hoosick, went to interview John Munro, Esq. in late Aug. 1775; they
were joined at St. Croix (Sancoik, N. Y.) by members of the Bennington Comm.,
sent for the same purpose; they detained Esq. Munro at his house, & sought to
ascert. whether or not he had rec'd. a commission from the enemy- **822**; among
those members of the Hoosick Comm. of Correspondence present May 10, 1775, at
the Comm. meeting, Albany, N. Y.- **831**
George, Esq.- acc. June 1775 proceedings of the N. Y. Provincial Congress, he was
much confided in for services on the northen frontier- **777**
James- def., 1774, in a case brought by John Js. Bleecker; & along w. Robert
Roset, in a case brought by John Thurman, Jr. & Jacob Van Voorhies, the
assignees of Philip P. Lansing- **878**
John, Esq.- b. 1757; d. 1843; his wf. Mary, d. May 6, 1832, at 74- **(L)- 772**

Palmer, Mass.- c. 1771, a few of the earliest settlers within the vicinity of
Granville, N. Y., were from here, & Pelham, Mass.- **997**

PANAMA- Porto Bello (Portobelo)- **760, 1059**

PANTON,
Francis- of NYC; June 13, 1774, along w. wf. Jane, conveyed Lot No. 75, Artillery
Patent, containing 250 acres, to Michael Hoffnagle of Kingsbury, N. Y., for £ 60;
recorded June 30th; also, May 6, 1775, for £ 150, conveys Lots 40, 55, & 66,
Artillery Patent, to Michael Hoffnagle- **(L)- 936**

PARKER,
____- m. Chester, s. Samuel & Elizabeth (Cheney) Freeman- **1038**
Amasa- (s. Thomas & Abigail Dutton) res. & d. Litchfield, Conn.; his s. Daniel,
was clergym. & teacher, NYC- **759**; b. Feb. 28, 1751; m. Thankful Andrews;
ments. sons Col. Amasa, & Rev. Daniel- **759s**
Col. Amasa- (s. Amasa & Thankful Andrews) lawyer, Delhi, N. Y.- **759s**

Hon. Amasa Junius- (1807- 1890; N. Y. Assembly, 1833, 34; 25th Congress, 1837- 39; NYS Supreme Court, 1847- 55; founder, Albany Law School, 1851) s. Daniel; c. 1850, Judge, 3rd District, NYS Supreme Court; acc. Dr. Fitch, he was 1854 Democratic candidate for Gov. of N. Y.; his s. Amasa, also a lawyer, res. Delhi, N. Y.- **759**; s. Rev. Daniel; b. June 2, 1807, Sharon, Conn.; grad. Union College, 1825; studied law & entered partnership w. his uncle, Col. Amasa; appt. Surrogate, Delaware Co., 1832, serving until 1840; member, N. Y. legislature, 1834; elected Regent of the Univ., 1835, resigned 1844; elected U. S. Congress; appt. Mar. 6, 1844, as Circuit Judge, 3rd Judicial Dist. of N. Y.; rem. Albany, N. Y.; elected Justice, NYS Supreme Court, June 7, 1847; Democratic candidate for Gov., 1856, vs. John A. King & Erastus Brooks- **759s**

Rev. Daniel- s. Amasa; grad. Yale; was clergym. & teacher, NYC; ments. s. Amasa J.- **759**; (s. Amasa & Thankful Andrews) grad. Yale, 1798; a minister, but spent most of his life teaching; his s. Amasa J., b. June 2, 1807, Sharon, Conn.; & he d. 1834- **759s**

Edward- settl. New Haven, 1644; "I doubt not", the progenitor of the Wallingford, Conn. line; m. Elizabeth, wid. John Potter; had 4 children, among them, John, b. Oct. 8, 1648; m. Hannah Basset- **759s**

Edward William- (s. John C. & Susan Mason) b. Aug. 11, 1807, Hartford, N. Y.; at abt. 18, entered the strore of Elisha Blin, in Whitehall, as a clerk, & 5 yrs. later, became a partner w. Elisha, & his s. Melancton O., until 1836; m. 1. Oct. 1834, Mary B. Carpenter, & had 6 children- Harriet, d. at 16 mos.; Edward John; George Henry, d. at 10 mos.; Henry W., Harriet Maria, & a son, d. at 11ds.; she d. Aug. 7, 1845, & he m. 2. Jane Catharine Goodrich, & had 3 more children- Mary Goodrich, d. at 23 mos.; Cornelia Mason; & William Horace, d. at 10 mos.; after 1836, he was connected in business w. Judge Wheeler & Melancton Blin, rem. Clintonville, N. Y., & res. there 6 yrs., w. less success, then returned to Whitehall; cashier, Franklin Co. Bank, St. Albans, Vt., at its establ., & afterw. cashier, Old Nat'l. Bank, Whitehall, for 20 yrs., until he d. Mar. 20, 1872- **759s**

GENEALOGY- acc. Dr. Fitch, a surname of ancient English ancestry; refers to personages in English history- Mathew Parker (1504- 1575), Archbishop of Canterbury (1559); Samuel Parker (1640- 1688), Bishop of Oxford (1686), forcibly inducted by James II into the Presidency of Magdalen College; Sir Thomas Parker (1666?- 1732), Earl of Macclesfeld, Lord Chancellor of England (1718- 25); Admiral Sir Hyde Parker (1714- 1782), commander of the British fleets on the American coast during the Rev. war; Sir Peter Parker (1721- 1811), commander of the naval force attacking Charleston, S. C. (1776); Rev. Thomas Parker, "who had enjoyed great favors from Queen Elizabeth, but was afterw. deprived of the livings she had bestowed upon him, his offence, it is sd., being that he showed kindness to persons who thought more of King Jesus than they did of King James"; his s., Rev. Robert Parker, who settl. in the ministry at Newbury, Mass., for 42 yrs.; in Colonial history- Alice, wf. John Parker, victim of the witchcraft delusion in Salem, Mass., 1692; Col. John Parker, who commanded the N. J. quota of troops, 1757, in the expedition to Canada, & was detached w. 250 men to cross Lake

George & drive in the French outposts at Ticonderoga; after passing Sabbath Day Point, he was decoyed into an ambush, & escaped w. only 60 survivors (see p. 672, French's Gazetteer); in Wash. Co.- Jonathan Parker, Esq., 2nd Sheriff of Wash. Co., appt. Nov. 12, 1774; Ichabod Parker, an early member, N. Y. legislature, 1780, 1786, & 1787; member, Constitutional Convention, 1788; the ancestry of John C. Parker, Esq., prev. suppos. originated w. William, Hartford, 1639; however, Dr. Fitch identifies the progenitor of the Parkers from Wallingford, Conn., as Edward, New Haven, 1644- **759s**

George- part of a guard raised at Bennington, Vt., mid- June 1782, to guard the capt. would- be abductors of Esq. Bleecker- **747**

George West- (s. John C. & Susan Mason) b. Sept. 5, 1815, Granville, N. Y.; grad. Middlebury College, 1835; studied law, Jamesville, N. Y.; m. Sept. 6, 1842, Emily M. Smith, at Jamesville; 6 children- George Mason; William Smith, d. at 3; Edward Dix; Jesse Emily, d. at 19 mos.; Gilbert D., d. at 11 mos.; & Charles Francis; he practiced in partnership w. Hon. Erastus D. Culver, of Brooklyn, & now (1874) for some yrs., member of "the great law firm of Benedict & Co. in Wall St., New York; has the reputation of being a most accomplished member of the legal fraternity"- **759s**

John- (s. Edward & Wid. Elizabeth Potter) b. Oct. 8, 1648; m. abt. 1678, Hannah Basset; rem. from New Haven to Wallingford, Conn., where 5 of their 8 children were b., 5 of them sons; among them, their 2nd s., Joseph, m. Sarah Curtis- **759s**

Hon. John Clark, Esq.- (J. C.) char. witn., pens. appl. of Samuel Standish- **747**; res. N. Granville, N. Y.; Dr. Fitch notes that information from pens. declarations, § 747- 756, "copied & extracted from papers in [his] possession... being the orig. minutes from which he made out pension papers for the persons named"- **756**; (s. Peter & Esther Clark) informs Dr. Fitch that his knowl. of his family history extends only as far as his grdf., Thomas Parker, of Washington, Conn.; acc. Dr. Fitch, served as Wash. co. Surrogate, 1840?- 44; town clerk, 9 yrs.; Supervisor, 1834; several sons, "all respectable men"; ments. s. William H., professor, Middlebury College; & ano. s., lawyer, Owego, N. Y.- **759**; b. Nov. 9, 1775, Torrington, Conn.; m. Mar. 21, 1804, Susan, dau. David Mason, of Hartford, N. Y.; 5 children, 1st 3 b. Hartford, last 2 b. Granville, N. Y.-

1. Hon. John Mason, b. June 14, 1805; m. 1. Catherine Ann Pumpelly; 2. Stella A. Pumpelly
2. Edward William, b. Aug. 11, 1807; m. 1. Mary B. Carpenter; 2. Jane Catharine Goodrich
3. Prof. William Henry, b. Aug. 23, 1809; m. 1. Ruth Robinson; 2. Catherine Denton
4. Susan, b. Jan. 26, 1813; unm.
5. George West, b. Sept. 5, 1815; m. Emily M. Smith; entered Zebulon R. Shipherd's law office at N. Granville, Apr. 17, 1798, to study; adm. Wash. Co. Courts, Feb. 11, 1802, & opened his law office at S. Hartford; appt. Master in Chancery, 1810, & Justice of Peace; was in partnership w. Zebulon R. Shipherd for nearly 20 yrs. bef. Shipherd rem. from town; appt. 1813, Justice of Peace,

Granville, & town clerk, 1826- 35; appt. one of the Exec'rs., Dr. Ira Hall's Will, May 6, 1816; appt. Wash. Co. Surrogate, Jan. 15, 1841, & served until Jan. 1845; Board of Trustees, Granville Academy; Elder, Presbyterian church, & delegate, Troy Presbytery of the General Assembly; his wf. d. June 16, 1852, at 74; & he d. July 19, 1856- **759s**

Hon. John Mason- (s. John C. & Susan Mason) b. June 14, 1805, Hartford, N. Y.; educ. Granville Academy, grad. Middlebury College, 1828; studied law w. Hon. John P. Cushman, Troy, N. Y.; adm. Bar, 1833; m. 1. Sept. 1835, Catherine Ann Pumpelly, who d. 1845, leaving 4 children; 2. Mar. 1, 1854, Stella A. Pumpelly, sist. of his 1st wf.; children, all by 1st wf.- Charles Edward, Francis Henry, John Pumpelly, & Norman Pumpelly; he practiced law, Owego, N. Y., & was elected U. S. Congress, 1855 & 1857; Justice, 6th Judicial Dist., NYS Supreme Court, 1859, re- elected 1867; appt. by Gov. Hoffman to sit in the General term, 3rd Dept. of the State; d. Dec. 16, 1873, suddenly, of apoplexy, at his home in Owego, N. Y. (bur. Evergreen Cemetery, Salem, N. Y.)- **759s**

Joseph- (s. John & Hannah Basset) m. June 7, 1705, Sarah Curtis; had 4 sons & 4 daus; their 2nd s., Thomas, b. June 7, 1708, m. Abigail Dutton- **759s**

Dr. Joseph- (s. Thomas & Abigail Dutton) b. Apr. 21, 1760; practiced at Litchfield Farms, Conn.; ments. sons Frederick S.; & Joseph, of New Haven- **759s**

Hon. Joseph- c. 1874, Dist. Judge, NYS Supreme Court; he was once law partners w. Hon. Wm. Henry Parker- **759s**

Lt.- officer, Col. Walbridge's regt., May 1781- **754**

Luther- (s. Peter & Esther Clark) b. Dec. 26, 1781, Salisbury, Conn.; m. Feb. 7, 1805, Martha Curtis; abt. 1811, rem. Mount Morris, N. Y.; 4 children-

  1. Dr. Samuel Curtis, b. Dec. 19, 1806; m. Resetta Sylvester

  2. Esther Hall, b. Apr. 7, 1809; m. Hiram Brown

  3. Rebecca Louisa, b. Oct. 18, 1812; m. Elias S. Hedges

  4. Theda Clark, b. May 15, 1819; m. Dr. Wm. S. Hedges; & he d. June 22, 1824- **759s**

Peter- (s. Thomas & Abigail Dutton) prob. b. Bethelehem, Conn.; m. Esther Clark; res. Torrington, & then 1 or 2 yrs. at Salisbury, Conn.; rem. Clarendon, Vt., for 1- 2 yrs., & finally settl., c. 1786, in Granville, N. Y.; children-

  1. John C., b. Nov. 9, 1775, prob. Torrington, Conn.

  2. Rebecca, m. Dr. Ira Hall, of Middle Granville, N. Y.

  3. Esther, m. Hon. Nathaniel Hall, of Whitehall, N. Y.

  4. Luther, c. 1825, rem. Mt. Morris, N. Y., & d. there

  5. Hon. William H., m. 1. Harriet Blinn; 2. Mary Ann Eddy; & he d. Dec. 1838, at abt. 86 yrs. old- **759**; b. Mar. 10, 1753, Wallingford, Conn.; m. Nov. 24, 1774, Esther, dau. John Clark, of Chatham, Conn.; orig. settl. Torrington, & rem., 1780, Salisbury, Conn.; rem. Clarendon, Vt., & res. there 1 or 2 yrs. bef. coming to Granville, N. Y., 1786; he purch. a farm in the NE part of Hartford, 3 mi. from N. Granville, now (1874) occ. by Harvey S. Wing; 5 children, 1st 3 b. Torrington, Conn.-

  1. John Clark, Esq., b. Nov. 9, 1775

2. Rebecca, b. July 28, 1777; m. Dr. Ira Hall

3. Esther, b. Jan. 25, 1780; m. Hon. Nathaniel Hall

4. Luther, b. Dec. 26, 1781, Salisbury, Conn.; m. Martha Curtis

5. Hon. William Henry, b.July 31, 1787, Granville, N. Y.; m. 1. Harriet Blin; 2. Mrs. Mary Ann (Eddy) Wheeler; his wf. d. May 20, 1827, & he sold to Mr. Wing, Sr., & then res. N. Granville, w. his son; member, N. Granville Presbyt. church, & freq. on important committees acc. their records, along w. Zebulon R. Shipherd, Butler Beckwith, & other leading members of the community at that time; d. Dec. 28, 1838, bur. in the Masonic bur. grd. S. of Middle Granville, N. Y.- 759s

Dr. Samuel Curtis- (s. Luther & Martha Curtis) b. Dec. 19, 1806; m. Nov. 10, 1833, Resetta Sylvester; & he d. May 30, 1840- 759s

Susan- (dau. John C. & Susan Mason) b. Jan. 26, 1813, Granville, N. Y.; unm., res. w. her aunt, wid. Wm. H. Parker, in Whitehall, N. Y., foll. her father's death- 759s

Thomas- res. Washington, Conn.; m. Abigail Dutton; had 6 or more sons, named in the foll. sequence-

1. Amasa, d. Litchfield, Conn.

2. Thomas, res. Litchfield, Conn.

3. Dr. Joseph (4th s.), res. & d. Litchfield farms, Conn.

4. Abner, b. ca. 1764; c.1850, res. Brookfield, Conn.

5. David, res. & d. in western N. Y.

6. Peter (3rd s.), m. Esther Clark- 759; (s. Joseph & Sarah Curtis) b. June 7, 1708; rem., 1756, from Wallingford, to Washington, Conn.; had 10 children-

   1. Thomas, b. Apr. 3, 1749

   2. Amasa, b. Feb. 28, 1751; m. Thankful Andrews

   3. Peter

   4. Abigail, b. Apr. 28, 1755; m. David Root

   5. Justus, b. Mar. 6, 1758; prob. d. y.

   6. Dr. Joseph, b. Apr. 21, 1761

   7. Sarah, b. Oct. 10, 1762; m. Daniel Richards

   8. Abner, bp. Apr. 14, 1765

   9. Rebecca, bp. June 21, 1767; m. Joseph Smith

10. David, bp. Mar. 6, 1770- 759s

Thomas- (s. Thomas & Abigail Dutton) b. Apr. 3, 1749; res. Litchfield Co., Conn- 759s

William- orig. propri., Hartford, 1639; his s. John, of Saybrook, was suppos. the father of John, b. Oct. 8, 1648, by whom the Wallingford, Conn. line was establ.; however, acc. Dr. Fitch, John, of Saybrook, was b. Feb. 1, 1642, & therefore could not be the ancestor- 759s

William- (s. Hon. Wm. Henry & Harriet Blin) b. Mar. 4, 1822; merch., Vicksburg, Miss., for a no. of yrs.; m. Sept. 14, 1855, Fanny Green; 4 children- Henry Green, Mary, Wm. Henry, & Nellie; rem. NYC, & became a Wall St. broker, & now (1874) partners w. Roach & Co., a steamship establ., at Chester, Pa.- 759s

Hon. William Henry- (William H.; s. Peter & Esther Clark) res. Whitehall, N. Y.; m. 1. Harriet Blinn, who d. Sept. 8, 1834, at 38; 2. Mary Ann Eddy, wid. ____ Wheeler; & he d. Nov. 28, 1849, at 62; children, named in his Will- Caroline H., William, H. Elizabeth, & Fanny H.; he studied law w. Shipherd & Parker, Granville, N. Y., & was adm. by Wash. co. Court, Dec. 24, 1813, & 1st settl. in partnership w. Charles A. Wheeler of Whitehall, & then w. Joseph Potter; was Justice of Peace, 1831; Co. Judge; director & attorney, Whitehall Bank, "& c."- **759**; b. July 31, 1787, Granville, N. Y.; 4 children, 3 by 1st wf.-
1. Caroline H., m. Edward M. Crosby
2. William, b. Mar. 4, 1822; m. Fanny Green
3. Eliza, m. Wm. Henry Myers
4. Fanny H.; his appt. as Justice of Peace given as 1837; his 2nd wf. d. May 26, 1840; & he d. Nov. 28, 1849- **759s**

Prof. William Henry- (s. John C. & Susan Mason) b. Aug. 23, 1809, Hartford, N. Y.; educ. Granville Academy, grad. Middlebury College, 1830; Tutor, 1832; Prof. of Mathematics & Natural Philosophy, 1848; Treasurer of the College Corp.; m. 1. Ruth Robinson, of Bennington, Vt.; 2 children- John Edmund; & William Robinson, d. inf.; his 1st wf. d. Apr. 5, 1846, & he m. 2. Catherine Denton, of Orange Co., N. Y., & had 6 children- Ruth Robinson; Catherine Denton, dec'd.; Susan; Jessie Elizabeth, dec'd.; William Henry, dec'd.; & Edward Mason- **759s**

Parker & Bliss- bookstore, c. 1850's, Troy, N. Y.- **799**

PARKS,
____- m. Daniel Lothrup, s. Daniel Wells- **841**
Irene- res. Whitestown, N. Y.; m. Martin F., s. Adam & Almira (Fitch) Martin- **731**

PARMLEY,
Capt. Oliver- or Parmlee; of Col. Bunel's regt., under Maj. Sedgewick; Apr. 1776, stat. Granville, N. Y.- **750**

PARRIS,
Henry- Co. A, 2nd N. Y., Northern Black Horse, Cav., 1861- 2- **1080**

PARROT,
James- among those elected Feb. 4, 1776, to serve on Cambridge, N. Y. Comm. of Correspondence; Feb. 27th, refused to serve, & ano. ordered elected to servre in his place- **826**

PARSONS,
Jabe- witn., Feb. 2, 1756, Will of Samuel Burrows, of East Hampton, N. Y.- **1100**
Josiah- w. James Chatfield, Esq., appt. Exec'r., Will of Samuel Burrows- **1100**
Sarah- witn., Feb. 2, 1756, Will of Samuel Burrows- **1100**

PARTRIDGE,
Josiah- prob. m. Sarah, dau. ____ & ____ (Newell) Martin- **849**

PATCHIN,
Dr. Aaron D.- b. 1777; d. 1828- **(L)**- **772**

PATTEN,
____- c. 1850, res. Caldwell, N. Y.; was among those capt. by the British at Ft. Ann & Ft. George, 1780- **858**
Robert- b. May 15, 1754; d. July 21, 1826, at 72- **(L)**- **772**

PATTERSON,
Cruth- m. Sarah, dau. John Ward & Wid. Catharine (Reid) Munro; foll. her husb.'s death, she res. Landsdowne, Leeds co., Ontario, Canada- **810**
Mr.- succeeded Beriah Stiles as editor, *Washington Register*; abt. 1828, rem. the paper from Salem to Union Village (Greenwich, N. Y.) where it became the anti-masonic paper in the county- **721**

PATTINGELL,
Oliver- deed witn., Apr. 15, 1775; Ephriam Wheeler to Phineas Bennet- **(L)**-**936**

PATTISON,
Daniel- (s. Thomas & Elizabeth Ashton) reported by his sist. Polly (Mrs. Rev. Bradley Sillick) that he went from the Mechanicville area to Chenango Point (Binghamton, N. Y.) during "the last sleighing" & arr. there Mar. 1, c. 1816/7, taking 3 days to journey there, & ano. 3 days to return-**951**
Elias- m. dau. George Gardener, of Troy, N. Y.- **940**; informs Dr. Fitch, Sept. 26, 1851, concerning recoll. of his grdf., John Ashton- **952b**
Elizabeth- wf. Thomas; in 1888, her tombstone was rem. from the village cemetery, Stillwater, N. Y., to the Yellow- Meeting House bur. grd. "& placed beside my grdf.'s- Thomas Pattison- in the family plot", by Mrs. Elizabeth McNeil Fitch- **951**
John- res. Ft. Miller, N. Y.; an uncle of Dr. Fitch; Oct. 7, 1850, toured the area surrounding the orig. Duer Mansion w. Dr. Fitch- **800**; gives accts. of settlers loc. along the Hudson river, 1798, from the mouth of the Battenkill to Ft. Edward, N. Y.- **804**; m. dau. George Gardener, of Troy, N. Y.- **940**; (s. Thomas & Elizabeth Ashton) the family Bible of John Ashton desc. to him from his mother when she was in her old age- **960**; once drew an exact copy of the Duer Mansion, which "slid down behind the desk in my store in Troy, & when the store was burnt, rushing in & carrying out the desk, I saw the paper behind it, for the last time"; anticipating Pres. Adams' tax on windows & c., Hugh Pebbles sent word to him to count the windows & panes in the Duer Mansion to determine how much tax would be incurred if the measure was enacted, which lead to his familiarity w. the structure's appearance- **1031**

Rachel- m. Samuel Hewit- **(L)**- 772

Thomas- was father of John Pattison, & cousin of Col. Robert Cockran- **804**; of Stillwater, N. Y.; his 2nd dau. Polly, m. Rev. Bradley Sillick- **950**; m. June 1776, Elizabeth, dau. John & Elizabeth (Hargrave) Ashton; besides Polly, also had s. Daniel, & dau. Betsey, who m. ___ Robbins; their dau. Sarah, b. July 13, 1785; d. Sept. 4, 1818; his dau. Polly remarks upon var. sites where McNeil & Pattison family members were bur. in the area; & he d. Apr. 8, 1819- **960**; Robert Ayres courted ___ Ashton, the younger sist. of his wf., at their house, as her father violently opposed the match, while her sist. & husb. both favored it- **1054**

Pawlet, Vt.- foll. the battle of Bennington, Aug. 1777, Capt. Parmlee Allen's co. was stat. here to scout on Lake Champlain & to Lake George- **750**

PAXTEN,
___- of Greenwich, N. Y.; c. 1861, member, 11th Illinois Inf.- **1080**

PAYNE,
Bunnel- c. 1798, res. on W. side of the Hudson river, the last N. above Ft. Miller, bef. reaching Ft. Edward, N. Y.- **804**

Charles- s. Reubin; res. Ft. Miller, N. Y.- **804**

Daniel- bro. Noah, Sr.; c. 1798, res. Ft. Miller, N. Y.; had 3 sons, one named Reuben; his house now (1850) occ. by the Galusha family- **804**

Family- of Ft. Miller, N. Y.; they would take their rafts of lumber to NYC every spring along w. the Crockers, & Ebenezer Bacon would accompany them; while they would dress in the best of style & spend extravagantly, Bacon, who was worth more than either family, would assume only ordinary dress & a plain manner in his habits- **933**

Noah- c. 1798, res. Ft. Miller, N. Y., at the present (1850) loc. occ. by Esq. Stewart; ments. sons Noah, Jr., & Daniel- **804**; his brick house was constructed in 1787- **840**; (Paine) defendant, Nov. 3, 1784, in a case brought by Robert Cochran, Esq.- **878½**

Noah, Jr.- s. Noah; c. 1798, res. Ft. Miller, N. Y., in the brick house next N. of his father- **804**

Tobias- m. 1669, Sarah Winslow, wid. Miles Standish, Jr.- **757**

PEABODY,
Capt. Oliver D.- of Keesville, N. Y.; May 25, 1861, commander, Co. C, 22nd N. Y. Inf.- **(L)**- **1074**

PEASE,
Samuel- Constable, prob. Albany co., N. Y.; May 21, 1771, he was sent to arrest Thomas French of Princetown (Manchester, Vt.) for rioting, & found his house surrounded by a great no. of men vowing against him & his party, if he should carry out the arrest warrant- **900**

338

PEAT,
Silas- res. Cambridge, N. Y.; at a vote taken in his house, Mar. 13, 1798, he was chosen one of the trustees of the Independent Library- **879**

PEBBLES,
Gerrit- bro. Hugh; having 1st been in partnership w. his bro. at Half Moon, c. 1798, he came into partnership w. John Pattison at Wm. Duer's store in Ft. Miller, N. Y.; he purch. all of what remained of the Cuyler properties in the Ft. Miller area- **1032**
Hugh- purch. the Duer Mansion & other Ft. Miller properties belonging to Wm. Duer, Esq.; anticipating the enactment of Pres. Adams' measure for taxing windows & c., he enjoined John Pattison to count the windows & panes of the Mansion in order to determine how much tax might be incurred- **1031**; b. Half Moon, N. Y.; his father Irish, & his mother Dutch; he was clerk for Wm. Duer under _____ Dinwiddie, bef. the Rev. war; his slave, Prince, was the person who discovered Dinwiddie's death; in 1791, he rem. & built a store at Half Moon; along w. Barent & John Bleecker, purch. the portion of Wm. Duer's properties lying in Ft. Miller, during the Sheriff's sale, & afterw. sold his portion to them- **1032**

Pelham, Mass.- c. 1771, a few of the earliest settlers in the vicinity of Granville, N. Y. were from here & Palmer, Mass.- **997**

PEMBER,
Esq.- "who has recently come into this town from Vt." (c. 1851, prob. Granville, N. Y); a part of his farm was formed from the farm prev. of George? Wilcox- **921**

PENDERGRASS,
Family- res. Pittstown, N. Y.; noted as a man of some respectability, "who zealously sided w. Vermont"; N. Y. authorities arrested, or at least attempted his arrest, for his disaffection- **917**
Maria- of Mayville, N. Y.; m. Robertson, s. John & Margaret (Robertson) Whiteside- **805**
Susan- m. Oliver, s. Phineas & Ann (Cooper) Whiteside- **805**

PENNOCK,
David- of Schuylerville, N. Y.; was in The Seven Days (June 25- July 1, 1862), Richmond, Va., unit not given; after 15 months service, he returned home & drowned a wk. later, Nov. 13, 1862, at 22, at the Saratoga dam- **1095**

PENNSYLVANIA- 949, 950, 962, 1028;
  Counties- Clinton- 1004;
  Cities & Towns- Bethlehem- 1075b; Brandywine- 990; Chester- 759s; Cold Spring- 1075b; Eire- 805; Germantown- 990; Lancaster- 805, 833, 842;

Lock Haven- 1004; Mauk Chunk- 839; Nazareth- 1075b; Philadelphia- 759s, 760, 793, 833, 842, 919, 949, 949b, 1003, 1045, 1059, 1075b, 1082, 1097, 1098; Pittsburgh- 949; Valley Forge- 1036; Wyoming- 962; Features- Allegheny river- 949

PENSIONS, Revolutionary War- some of the foll. copied by Dr. Fitch & entered as manuscript articles, noting whether the entire appl. was copied, or only extracts-
Nathan Baxter- prob. res. Ontario, Canada; noted as a Rev. war pensioner- **812**;
Joseph Crippen- (S10509, Mass.) res. Granville, N. Y.; enl. 1776, Capt. King's co., Col. Fellows' Mass. militia regt.; extracts- **755**;
Isaac Doty- (S23200, Mass. & N. Y.) res. nr. Granville, N. Y.; appl. July 9, 1832; orig. enl. 1775, Col. McKinstry's Mass. regt.; extracts- **748**;
Ebenezer Farnsworth- (Farnworth; S28724, N. Y.) res. Granville, N. Y.; orig. enl. 1775, Mass. line; entire- **750**;
Dr. Asa Fitch, Sr.- (S15121, N. Y.) res. Salem, N. Y.; Pens. #1721, Nov. 8, 1832; enl. 1782, Charlotte co. militia; c. 1818, he filled out other pension appl. for 15 soldiers, at $3.00 ea.; c. 1820, he filled an unrecorded no. of appl. at a slightly higher fee than the prev. ones- **799**;
Thomas Griffith- (S23663, N. Y. & Vt.) res. Whitehall, N. Y.; orig. enl. 1779, Shaftsbury co., Col. Walbridge's Vt. militia regt.; extracts of nearly all- **754**;
Moses Harvey- (W7683, BLW #26328- 160- 55, Mass. & N. Y.) res. Granville, N. Y.; orig. enl. 1777, Capt. Moses Harvey's co., Col. Woodbridge's Mass. regt.; entire- **751**;
James McDonald- Scotch; enl. at age 18 in the British army, & deserted from Lord Howe's command at Boston, Mass., & immed. enl. in the American army, & was in the battle of Bunker Hill; June 20, 1853, at 105 yrs. of age, was the last surviving participant in the battle; served under Gens. Arnold & Wayne, & was at Saratoga, Princeton, Trenton, & Cowpens, where he was severely wnd. & lost an eye; was at Cornwallis' surrender; also enl. War of 1812; res. Kentucky foll. his service, until his wf.'s death, then rem. Black Rock, N. Y., to res. w. a dau., & lost his pension papers when robbed while in transit on a boat bound for Cincinatti, Ohio- **1010**;
James McElherron- (S28809, Cont. Line, Mass.) Irish; res. Hebron, N. Y.; rec'd. his pension for injuries incurred during the assault on Quebec, 1775, under Gen. Montgomery; he rec'd. a sabre gash to his head, & a 2nd on his left wrist, which impaired that hand; the effects of these injuries ment. further- **922**;
John Moss- (W25730, BLW #38538- 160- 55, Ct.) res. Granville, N. Y.; orig. enl. 1776, Capt. Bradley's co., Col. Waterbury's Conn. regt.; extracts- **752**;
John C. Parker, Esq.- res. N. Granville, N. Y.; character witn., Samuel Standish pens. appl.; compiled orig. minutes for pens. appls. ment. § 747- 756, copied & extracted by Dr. Fitch- **756**;
Kitchel Reed- (S28851, Ct.) res. Granville, N. Y.; orig. enl. 1775, Lt. Brown's co., Col. Waterbury's Conn. regt.; extracts- **753**;

Reubin Smalley- (S14521, Vt.) res. Whitehall, N. Y.; orig. enl. 1777, Capt. Hatch's co., Col. Horsington's Green Mtn. rangers; extracts of nearly all- 756; *Samuel Standish-* (S28899, Mass.) res. Granville, N. Y.; appl. May 8, 1832; orig. enl. 1776, Capt. Hewin's Mass. militia co.; character witns.- John C. Parker, Esq., & John Tanner; abstract of entire- 747; *John Tanner-* character witn., Samuel Standish pens. appl.- 747; (W22376, R. I., Mass., & N. Y.) res. Granville, N. Y.; appl. July 16, 1832; enl. Exeter, R. I.; enl. 1779, Lanesborough, Mass.; enl. 1781, Granville, N. Y.; extracts- 749

People vs. Martin Wallace- covened Oct. 1, 1858, Salem, N. Y., & concerned the murder of Barney McEntee, Feb. 16, 1858; one of the missing items from Dr. Fitch's orig. manuscript, it appears in Judge Gibson's facsimile copy of the Manuscript History as § 1048. Conviction of Wallace for Murder; a companion article, § 1050, notes the execution of Wallace & the death of Judge John McLean, the latter item appears in the orig. manuscript as a newspaper clipping, Dec. 7, 1858, *Salem Press*; in the newspaper, Wallace's execution appears as a companion piece to the obit., giving the date of the trial; prosecuted Oct. 1- 7, 1858, a transcript of the proceedings was publ. in the Oct. 5th & 12th issues of the *Salem Press*, and a special edition, w. extra copies, to satisfy public demand, was publ. on Oct. 19th, containing a reprinting of the transcript; all 3 articles were publ. under the title "Trial of Martin Wallace for the Murder of Barney McEntee"; while Dr. Fitch prob. rec'd. all 3 issues, he prob. featured the Oct. 19th issue in his manuscript, in an attempt to preserve space; Hon. Cornelius L. Allen, presiding; Hon. A. Dallas Wait, Co. Judge; Harvey Rice & Luther Andrews, Esqs., Justices & Associates; Dist. Atty. A. L. McDougall, assisted by Marinus Fairchild, for the prosecution; for the defense, Hon. James Gibson, & J. S. Crocker; Jurors- John M. Hulett, Abel S. Webb, George Armstrong, Jehiel Russell, Orson Carpenter, Oliver Whitcomb, John Hillman, Norman Van Kirk, James Hill, Seth Stearns, Hiram Darrow, & John Burnett; witns., as called for prosecution (21)- Dr. Philip V. N. Morris, Hiram Sisson, Ann Joice, Patrick Joice, Edward Hays, Teunis Cronkhite, Wm. I. Perry, Uriah Colony, Elijah Chase, Andrew Houghton, Marvin Wallis, Daniel Randall, Daniel Mosher, John Larmon, Cornelius Van Vechten, Henry Van Vechten, Bridget Millet, John C. Sweet, Frank Williams, Eli Barton, Amos A. Slosson; for defense (11)- Michael Bradey, Dr. Oliver Cook, Nathan Cottrell, Barney Giblin, Edward Hays, Edward Cavanaugh, Andrew Houghton, John H. Brownell, Michael Conway, Henry Van Vechten, Norman Fowler; 3 closing witns. called by the Dist. Atty.- Joseph Wallis, Patrick Ward, & George Wallis; the particulars of this crime have some similarity to the robbery of Edward Callary, Cambridge, N. Y., an acct. of that trial given Mar. 29, 1872, *Wash. Co. Post*; see People vs. James McClellan & William Wells; § 2017, Vol. 4; in substance, Martin Wallace, a 22 yr. old Irish laborer, who res. White Creek, N. Y., after borrowing from his employer to pay debts, went to a tavern in Eagle Bridge, where he 1st met Barney McEntee, of Hoosick Falls, & they began drinking together; McEntee was en route to Schaghticoke, N. Y., where he sd. he was going to look for a dog & see friends, & Wallace told him that he was going in search of a house; the two cont'd. together to a grocery store at Buskirk's Bridge, where they again drank together, & when it came Wallace's turn to treat, he sd. he had no money; at this point, McEntee opened his wallet, revealing over $100, & they cont'd. to drink at his expense; some time in the afternoon, 3 or 4:00 PM, acc. diff. testim., Wallace left to see the house he ment., & returned abt. dusk; McEntee & Wallace again drank together, but Wallace only pretended drinking, & remained sober, & proposed that McEntee come w. him to his supper; although unwilling to go, he was finally induced by the storekeeper to leave w. Wallace, & they went to Jesse Pratt's store, where McEntee's intoxication became more pronounced, & several of the men gathered there assisted him out, w. the impression that Wallace was taking him home; betw. 8- 9:00 PM, McEntee's body was found along the highway, his skull fractured by blows from a club, or fence stake; Wallace was suspected, & was apprehended at his lodgings, at abt. midnight that same evening; his clothing was searched, & a pr. of gloves from the dec'd., a handkerchief in which the dec'd. had kept his money, & money that was presumably from the dec'd., were all found in var. pockets of a coat belonging to Wallace; the foll. day, he was asked to observe McEntee's body, & he left tracks in the snow which matched others found nr. the murder scene & nr. where pieces were found from a fence stake that was involved in the murder; the jury reached a quilty verdict foll. an hr.'s deliberation, & that afternoon, Wallace was sentenced to hang, Dec. 1, 1858- **1048s**

PERKINS,
_____- m. Wid. Jacquay, of Ft. Miller, N. Y.- **804**

PERRY,
_____- he was struck on the breast w. a heavy piece of wood & killed by Hazard Wilcox, when an attempt was made to arrest him as a tory; his death was prob. 'the alarming affair that lately happened in this place' alluded to in the Aug. 7, 1775 meeting of the Sancoick, N. Y. Comm. of safety- **799**
E. S.- 2nd Bugler, Co. A, 2nd N. Y., Northern Black Horse, Cav., 1861- 2- **1080**
Family (?)- ments. Ovando, Delavan, & Elihu, who all res., c. 1850, on the Cambridge side of Little White Creek, N. Y.; acc. Sidney Wells, they may be desc. of the Perry killed by Hazard Wilcox, but Dr. Fitch gives no indication of their relationships to ea. other- **844**
James- c. 1853, current owner of the Matthews House, the brick house erected by David Matthews & known for its loc. on the N. Y. & Vt. line nr. Bennington- **1022**
Josephus- Co. A, 2nd N. Y., Northern Black Horse, Cav., 1861- 2- **1080**
Oliver Hazard- (1785- 1819) brief ment., noting that his desc. were more favored in inheriting "their father's qualities" than the desc. of Commodore Thomas Macdonough (this was perh. referring to Matthew C. Perry, his younger bro.)- **1056**

William- defendant, May 19, 1774, in a case brought by Philip Schuyler, Esq.; &
w. Wm. Moffitt, Jan. 16, 1775, in a case brought by Schuyler as assignee of Philip
P. Lansing- **878**
William I., Jr.- res. a mi. E. of Post's Corners, White Creek, N. Y.; acc. Hiram
Sisson, he was among the men gathered at Pratt's store the evening Barney
McEntee was murdered, Feb. 16, 1858; he testif. at Wallace's trial that he 1st heard
of the murder on the foll. morning, & found the shorter end of the fence stake at
abt. sunset, on the day of the Coroner's Inquest, abt. 48 rods from where the blood
was in the snow, along w. a man's tracks; he carried the piece home, & on
examination bef. Justices, he & Mr. Randall matched the 2 pieces- **1048s**

PETTIT,
John- purch. for £ 301, Lot 47, Artillery Patent, Oct. 12, 1784- **(L)- 875**
John, Esq.- of Greenfield, N. Y.; dau. m. Matthew, s. Hugh & Mary (McWhorter)
Harsha- **973**

PHELPS,
Rev. Amos A.- (Amos Augustus; 1805- 1847) editor, *The Emancipator*; succeeded
Rev. Charles Fitch as pastor, the 'Free Church', Boston, Mass.- **799**
Capt.- delivered Gen. Arnold's May 23, 1775 letter to Gov. Trumbull of Conn.,
where Arnold notes that he "has been very serviceable here", & entrusted w.
particulars of Arnold's needs at Crown Point & Ticonderoga- **774**
Judge Charles B.- of Woodbury, Conn. (Charles Bartlett; 1788- 1858; Conn.
House of Reps., 1831, 37, & 52); was giving a eulogy to Seth Warner, Dec. 23,
1858, at the laying of a cornerstone to a monument to Warner, when he took ill &
d. suddenly; refers Dec. 24, 1858, semi- wkly. *N. Y. Times*; later reports disclose
that he had been ill prev. to delivering the address, & his demise was not quite as
indicative of "an over- ruling Providence as frowning upon the attempts to do
honor to such men" (as Warner, or Ethan Allen)- **1052**
Jehiel- m. Olive, dau. Aaron & Olive (Harding) Martin- **1040**
Samuel D.- (Phelps) of Fitchburg, Mass.; m. Maria, dau. Jacob, Jr., & Lucy
(Howard) Allen- **758**

PHENIX,
William- m. Martha, dau. Aaron & Olive (Harding) Martin, as her 1st husb.- **1040**

PHILIPS,
Family- res. Binghamton, N. Y.; dau. m. James Dobbin- **732**
Henry- (Phillips) oath of alleg.; Co. D, 22nd N. Y. Inf.- **(L)- 1074**
John- deed witn., Mar. 25, 1772; James, John, & Amos McKenney quit claim to
Michael Hoffnagle- **(L)- 936**
Miss L.- she attended Mrs. Willard's Seminary (Emma Willard School, Troy,

N. Y.) & was obt. by Mr. Ingalls as an assistant at Union Village Academy, Greenwich, N. Y., where she met & m. James, s. John & Jane (McKellip) Dobbin, who was also an assistant at the Academy- **732**

PIKE,
Jane- adopted child of Asa & Sarah (Van Valkenburgh) Martin; the family house & lot was left to her when her mother d., & she m. 1868?, Deac. Gregory Atwood, as his 2nd wf.- **731**

PIQUET,
Monsignr.- (or Picquet, Francois; 1708- 1781) he obt. knowl. from a co. of Indians sent to spy the frontier, c. 1745, that the English were making preparations at Sarasota (prob. Saratoga) & pushing their settlm. up to Lake St. Sacrement (Lake Champlain); informing the General (name not given), he proposed sending a force to intimidate a/o impede their progress, & accomp. Mons. Marin, who commanded the force sent against them, which laid waste to the "Lydius establishments"; refers Hough's Hist. of St. Lawrence & Franklin co.; & Memoirs of Father Piquet, Doc. Hist. of N. Y.- **1013**

PITCHER,
Lyman- of Martinsburgh, N. Y.; m. Sophia, dau. John & Maria (Conkey) Waters; & he d. May 1842, leaving 3 children- "Sophia & c."- **730**
Paulina- m. at Martinsburgh, N. Y., Charles Grandison, s. Silas & Zerniah (Martin) Conkey- **730**

PITNEY,
Charles B.- s. Norman, of Cambridge, N. Y.; enl. (Co. E) 93rd N. Y. Inf.; bur. Apr. 24, 1863, from the Methodist church- **1094**

PLACE,
Samuel- of Socialborough, Charlotte co., N. Y.; orig. proprietor, Jan. 17, 1772, to N. Y. patent gr. loc. Durham, N. Y. (Clarendon, Vt.); on Mar. 16, 1779, he gave £ 1,000 bond to Thomas Brayton, then of Little White Creek, Albany co., deeding his share or right of land that he possessed in Durham to Brayton- **745**

PLATT,
____- res. Michigan; m. Jane, dau. James & Susannah (Thomas) Turner- **1090**
Jeremiah- m. Mary, dau. Thomas & Elizabeth (Cramer) Whiteside; they res. Eire, Pa.; 5 children- Sarah Ann, Eliza, Mary, Phineas W., & Sophia- **805**

Plattsburgh, battle of- the naval engagem. began on Sun., a little after sunrise, Sept. 11, 1814- **708**; the land fighting consisted of only a slight skirmish at Pike's Cantonment, abt. 2 mi. up the Saranac river from Plattsburgh; acc. to history, the British attempted to cross the ford here & were driven back by the miliita; "This is a great falsehood, for they did not cross", acc. Ransom Cook; the militia were posted here by Gen. Macomb to defend the ford, & if driven back, retreat 5 mi. S. to a quantity of stores & defend them, & if not able to, then to destroy them; Gov. Provost occ. the N. side of the Saranac in the village, while 3 or 4 small forts were occ. by the Americans on the S. side; the bridge betw. them had its planks rem., but the stringers were still on; having no batteries erected to fire on the forts, Gov. Provost sent a detachm. up river to dislodge the militia at the ford, as the naval battle commenced in the morning; it wass Provost's belief that the militia would retreat to the forts, & the detachm. should foll. them; on sighting the 2 forces, he would then fire on the fort & militia simult.; when the British detachm. reached the ford, the milita began "an irregular fire... every man popping at them as he loaded his gun"; however, the British pd. no attention to this, but in regular lines waded the river till they were nr. enough to give an effective fire, when the whole rank disch. their pieces as one man- This so frightened the militia, that, seeing them continue to advance in an unbroken line, they fled"; the British pursued, "close on their heels, determined to rush into the forts pell mell w. them"; not doubting that the militia were taking the shortest route to the forts nr. the river's mouth, the British were lead off amid the thick bushes on the 5 mi. road to the stores, & thinking the 2 mi. "confoundedly long", they eventually got a glimpse of the lake as they neared the American stores; they were now nr. enough to hear the word passing from one to ano. of the militia that 'The big ship has struck its flag!'; satisfied that there was some mistake, the detachm. rushed forward & capt. 2 or 3 militia, & demanded to know 'where the hell they were? where the forts were?' & discovered that they were some 4 mi. rem. from where they expected themselves to be, "& so badly blowed w. the rapid chase... that they were unable to make their return to them w. any celerity"; threatening to bayonet any American who practiced the slightest deception, they began to retrace their steps, but Gov. Provost recalled them bef. they reached the forts, having seen the fleet's surrender; his army broke camp that night, retreating to Canada "under a pelting storm"- **1055**; during the naval battle "every gun on the side of his [Macdonough's] ship towards his antagonist had given out & become dismounted- the fire from his ship gradually slackening & becoming less effective. A ketch was sent... whereby his ship, the *Saratoga*, might be turned around to bring the guns on her opp. side to bear upon the enemy- a most perilous maneuver to be performed in the midst of battle..."; the officer superintending this maneuver "his sailing master, a heroic man named Baume" was struck by a chain shot while giving commands; he continued the instructions despite injury & once the feat had been accomplished, glanced downward to discover that he had only been grazed, despite the initially mortal appearance of his wnds.; spectators on the shore, watching the action & seeing the fire from the *Saratoga* slacken, suspected it was withdrawing from the fight & their ire towards Macdonough "rose to the highest pitch. Shortly after, the *Saratoga* disch. a whole broadside, well aimed, into her antagonist- carrying her masts by the board- & speedily ending the fight"- **1056**

PLYMPTON,
Elijah- of Sturbridge, Mass.; m. Mary, dau. Ephriam Wheeler, of Killingworth, Mass.; children- Louisa, Rinaldo, Elisha, Mary, Daniel, & Cheney- **1038**

POINTER,
Thomas- plaintiff, May 19, 1774, vs. Giles Higson; & defendant, in a case brought by Giles Higson- **878**

POLAND- 961

POLITICAL AFFILIATIONS-
Colonial, Rev. war- Loyalist- 768, 802, 944, 953, 957, 967, 991; neutral- 854; patriots- 967, 988; rebel- 770, 980; tories- 739, 740, 744, 747, 751, 755, 762, 763, 783, 791, 797, 807, 854, 867, 916, 923, 925, 967, 997, 1018, 1033, 1047, 1050s, 1063, 1064; toryism- 794; whigs- 740, 767, 857, 925, 967, 977, 1063, 1064; Yankee- 980; Yorker- 783, 899, 900, 902;
Federal- Anti- federalist- 920; Anti- mason- 721, 812; Buchananeer- 1035; Buck-tail- 721; Citizen's party- 799; Clintonian- 721; Democrat- 714, 721, 725, 726, 732, 759, 759s, 799, 1011, 1035, 1036; hard- 1025; soft- 1025; Federalist- 709, 714, 723, 920, 1036; Free soil- 1011, 1025; Know- nothing- 759, 759s; Maine law- 1025; Mason- 759s; 'median party'- 920; Republican- 726, 759, 759s, 1035; Whig- 733, 943, 1011, 1025;
Civil War- Democrat (rebel)- 799; loyalist- 799; pseudo- loyalist- 799; rebel- 950, 1095b, 1097;
Rev. war- an individual's political affiliation was freq. indicated by placing above the doorway, or in the hat, a slip of white paper to indicate tory, or a sprig. of hemlock to indicate whig- 767; neutrals & tories all remained within their homes during the evac. bef. Burgoyne's army; the Scotch & Irish were generally recognized as tories by the orig. settlers- **854**

POLLY,
Henry- res. Younge, Ont., Canada; m. Polly, dau. John & Hannah (Alyea) Munroe- **812**

POPE,
Ansel- m. Abigail, dau. John Newell- **1037**
Maj. Gen. John- (1822- 1892) brief ment. of his retreat to Centreville, Md., foll. 2nd Bull Run, Aug. 29- 30, 1862, & a rumor that on Sept. 2nd, he had retreated to Wash., D. C., foll. by Gen. Stonewall Jackson, w. 40,000 rebel troops- **1097**

PORTER,
____- Lot No. 55, Salem, N. Y., orig. occ. by Reuben Turner, loc. W. of the brick house built by him- **1085**

William- lawyer, Jordan, N. Y.; m. Mary Ellen, dau. Hon. Anthony I. & Maria (Williams) Blanchard- **1045**

Judge William- res. Hebron, N. Y.; the farm long owned by Robert Vance, Sr., was loc. ½ mi. E. of him- **737**

PORTUGAL- 990

POTTER,

Capt.- commander- in- chief, Co. A- C, 14th Iowa Inf., in their march, Oct. 31- Dec. 5, 1862, from Iowa City, Iowa, to Ft. Randall, S. Dakota; the unpopularity of his practice of marching the companies on half rations or less noted by Lambert Martin in his journal of the march, along w. the foll. irregularities in his command; on Nov. 26th, ano. Capt. confronts him for refusing to procure straw for the encampment, insisting that he would purch. it himself for the men, & impuning that he is pocketing the expedition's funds for his own use; on Nov. 28th, Potter places guards at the houses & wells of settlers along the march to prevent his troops from rushing in for fare; respecting this measure, Martin's journal notes- "our commander Capt. Potter is hated by all of us"; on Dec. 1st, the company "stopped at a small house where the commander could get his women in to warm... we were stopped here on an open prarie, freezing, till the teams could go 3 mi. & haul some wood to us"; having gone ahead by stage at Ft. Randall, Capt. Potter returns on Dec. 5th, & instructs the company that they must camp in the timber for 2 days & nights until the regulars have left the fort- **1089**

Dr.- presumed to be the 2nd husb. of Matilda Martin; they had no children who reached maturity, & she m. 3rd, Moses Scott- **730**

Family?- c. 1798, res. above Daniel Payne, Ft. Miller, N. Y.- **804**

John- m. Elizabeth ____; his wid. m. Edward Parker, of New Haven, Conn., as her 2nd husb.- **759s**

John- oath of alleg.; Co. D, 22nd N. Y. Inf.- **(L)- 1074**

Hon. Joseph- lawyer, prob. res. Whitehall, N. Y.; practiced in partnership (n. d.) w. Hon. William H. Parker, foll. the latter's partnership w. Charles A. Wheeler- **759**; c. 1874, Dist. Judge, NYS Supreme Court; once law partner w. Wm. H. Parker- **759s**

POUCHER,

____- he & ____ Fitch ment. by the *N. Y. Tribune* correspondent as 'butchers', now in Charleston, S. C., May 11, 1865, 'who mangled our colored soldiers'- **799**

POWELL,

Martin- res. Princetown (Manchester, Vt.); noted by Samuel Willoughby that he & Charles Bullen were rioters who had threatened his life, May 16, 1771, if he did not withdraw a writ of ejection served upon Thomas French- **899**

Richard- c. 1850, res. Hoosick Falls, N. Y.; noted as prob. the most accurate informant concerning old 'Festus' (Col. John P., or Francis Fister), as his grdf. had once been imprisoned by him; described as an elderly, uneduc. man, "I visited him in the evening of Aug. 22, 1850 & though he was fatigued w. a hard day's labor in haying, w. much animation he told me the foll. incidents" (i. e., § 768- 771)- **768**; his grdf. was Capt. Brewer, of the Hoosick militia- **770**

POWERS,
_____- among those involved in the arrest & flogging (§ 881) of Benjamin Hough; his surname was among the few involved in the incident that John L. Marsh could connect w. names found in the Clarendon, Vt. area where Hough was living when he was arrested- **966**
Family- c. 1852, res. Rutland, Vt.- **966**
Jonas- & als.; defendant, May 19, 1774, in a case brought by Charity French- **878**

Pownal, Vt.- c. 1775, was part of the manor of "Rensellaerwyck", Albany co., N. Y.; George Gardner, Esq., its Justice of Peace, related to Benjamin Hough the great commotion & uneasiness of its inhabitants due to Vt. rioters, as settlers had agreed to take leases from the proprietors of the Manor, but feared retribution; Gardner observed further, that unless given protection by the N. Y. govt., many of the inhabitants would prob. join the rioters- **881**; in a letter to Gov. Colden, Gov. Wentworth of N. H. notes that when the Deputy Sheriff was executing a legal precept, the Albany Sheriff & more than 30 armed men on horseback set upon him & several inhabitants of this town, carrying 4 of them to jail (these 4 referred to were prob. Ashley, Robinson, Charles, & Horfort)- **928**

PRATT,
Alexander- Co. A, 2nd N. Y., Northern Black Horse, Cav., 1861- 2- **1080**
Capt.- officer, May 1781, Col. Walbridge's regt.- **754**
Hiram- oath of alleg.; Co. D, 22nd N. Y. Inf.- (**L**)- **1074**
Jesse- operated a store at Buskirk's Bridge, N. Y., w. Morris Pratt as his clerk; acc. Hiram Sisson's testim., Edward Hays, Charles Allen, Charles Coit, Daniel Mosher, Morris Pratt, & William Perry, Jr., were all present at his store, along w. Barney McEntee, the dec'd., & Martin Wallace, the prisoner, during the evening of Feb. 16, 1858; Sisson sd. he arr. at the store abt. 7:25 PM; McEntee was very intoxicated, & Hays suggested that he leave; while he was being helped up, McEntee sd. he wanted some tobacco, & stumbled ito the counter in going after it; it was then sd. that it was too cold to let him leave alone, & then others sd. that Hays, Wallace, & Mosher were helping him out & Wallace was taking him home- **1048s**

PRESIDENTS, brief mentions- Adams, John- 1031; Harrison, Wm. H.- 1009; Van Buren, Martin- 849

Prices- listings for tea & West Indies produce, printed on handbills by Albany Comm. of Correspondence, Apr. 20, 1776, due to price rises; per gallon- West Indies rum- 6/6; Jamaica spirits- 8/6; N. Y. rum- 4/6; Mollasses- 3/6; per lb.- coffee- 1/6; chocolate- 2/4; Bohea tea- 6/ ; pepper- 6/6; leaf sugar- 1/6; brown sugar- 68/ per Cwt.; & 'Good Coarse Salt- 4/ per shippel'- **829**

PRIDE,
Reuben- Lt., Mass. line, during the Rev. war; res. abt. 35 yrs. in Cambridge, N. Y.; d. Apr. 25, 1825, at 78, White Creek, N. Y.- **1029**

PRIEST,
John- res. Camden valley, & later rem. Fitch's Point, Salem, N. Y.; a neighbor of Isaac Bininger, his wf. used to come over to Priest's house on nights when her husb. was "drunk & tyrannical"- **1076**
John, Jr.- c. 1812, a hired hand of Asa Fitch, Sr., along w. ano. man named James ____ - **799**

PRIME,
Rev. Nathaniel Scudder, D. D.- (1785- 1856; Preceptor, Cambridge Academy, 1821- 30) pastor, 1st Presbyterian church, Cambridge, N. Y., July 1813- Feb. 1828- **1024**; was accustomed to celebrating the 4th of July by giving a discourse at his church & having a comm. "invite the publ. of this discourse"; his 'The Year of Jubilee, but not to Africans', prob. an Abolitionist sermon, delivered July 4, 1825, on the 49th anniversary of Independence, & publ. by Dodd & Stevenson, Salem, N. Y.- **1082**; brief ment. as early supporter of Wash. Co. Bible Soc.- **1097**

PRISONERS, Rev. War-
Ft. Ann & Ft. George- fall 1780; acc. Wid. Angel, among the Americans capt. at the surrenders were David Carswell & Elisha Fitch, of Salem; Obadiah Knapp, of Half Moon, or Stillwater; ____ Patten, who c. 1850, res. Caldwell; & ____ Ketchum, of Hoosick; most of these captives remained prisoners in Canada until the restoration of peace, being gone a yr. or two; those returning via Nova Scotia came back at abt. the same time as those coming directly across country- **858**;
Salem, N. Y.- late Aug. 1777; a party of abt. a dozen tories capt. a Hessian soldier here, along w. Susan & Rebecca Lytle, taken as accomplices to his escape; the 2 girls were marched along w. the soldier, & Judge Hopkins, of Rupert, Vt., who had been capt. by them bef. the other 3; the girls were released when the party was met by Wm. McNish, who convinced them that they would be missed, & promised to keep them in his custody until the tory party had made their escape to Burgoyne's camp- **740**;
Skenesborough, N. Y.- among those American soldiers capt. here (prob. Mar. 1780) was William Gray, of Cambridge, N. Y., who was carried to Quebec & held there until after the peace; foll. his release, he immed. went from there to

Caughnawaga, N. Y., & then to St. Regis, where he became prominent within the Indian tribe there- **1015**;

Socialborough, Vt.- Daniel Marsh, accused of being a tory, was arrested & kept guard for some time, & finally sent to Portsmouth, N. H.; he was detained there on a prison ship, as filthy as those kept by the British at NYC, while the authorities repeatedly sent to the Comm. of Safety of Vt. for proofs of his affiliation; failing to send anything against him, he was disch. for want of grounds, after being detained for a winter- **968**;

W. Hebron, N. Y.- c. July 1777; Isaac & William Lytle, capt. by tories while working here, were taken into Burgoyne's camp at Ft. Edward, & later rem. to Ticonderoga, where they were released foll. an American assault there, prob. Sept. 18, 1777- **742**

PRO,

Francis- b. Sept. 11, 1790, Bordeaux, France; deserted from the French army, changing his name to its present form; enl. Oct. 23, 1817, at Boston, Mass., Co. D, 1st Regt. of Artlllery, in the American army, & served abt. 20 yrs.; he joined his co. at Portland, Me., & was ordered to Boston; served 6 yrs., Newport, R. I.; served 8 yrs., Ft. Gratiot, Smithfield, N. C.; served 8- 9 mos., Ft. Washington, Wash., D. C., where he was broke from corporal to private, " 'because he would not join the Temperance Society'- he being too long addicted to drink, in the army, to be able, he says, to give up liquor"; ordered to Florida, 1833, to serve in the Indian war (prob. Second Seminole war, 1835- 42) & remained there until disch., Feb. 7, 1837, at Ft. Foster, abt. 20 mi. from Tampa Bay; his disch. was lost a few days later, the paper being in his hat, which was blown off when he was in the harbor at Apalachicola; "intemperate in his habits", he res. w. James H. Fitch, summer 1852, when Dr. Fitch recorded his story, & for several yrs. prev.; in 1858, he lived alone in a little hut in the woods, cutting wood for Justin E. Beebe, when he suddenly disappeared; it was suspected that he was murdered by a family of Canadians who res. in ano. hut nr. him, & they were arrested, but no proof was found to justify their detention- **974**

PROCTOR,

Thomas- res. Eaton co., Mich.; m. Gustina, dau. Samuel & Polly (Alyea) Munroe- **812**

Thomas- res. nr. Streetsville, W. of Toronto, Ont., Upper Canada; m. Catharine, dau. John, Esq., & Catharine (Reid) Munro; children- Joseph, dec'd.; John, William, Thomas, & Samuel- **812**

PROUDFIT,

Rev. Dr. Alexander- was President of the Day, Nov. 29, 1814, at a public reception honoring Commodore Thomas Macdonough, in Salem, N. Y.; he delivered the salutatory address bef. the reception & toasted the Commodore during banquet ceremonies- **709**; the text of his address honoring Commodore Macdonough occ.

nearly 2 columns of *The Northern Post*, referring to his naval victory, Sept. 11, 1814, at Plattsburgh, N. Y.; the port. ment. by Dr. Fitch incl. a description of the general gloom & overcast mood of Rev. Proudfit's congregation on the Sunday when the battle occurred, as the males were almost universally absent & on the march to Plattsburgh, rather than in attendance- "all was anxiety & alarm w. those who remained to home"; the outnumbering & overpowering array of the British army, w. its military experience, is contrasted w. the size & inexperience of the militia force sent to oppose it, evoking a comparison to "ransomed Isreal"- **710**; an address delivered by him, Mar. 1832, at the funeral of Rev. Samuel Tomb, reprinted *Christian Magazine*, Vol. iv, 1835; the port. of extracts by Dr. Fitch incl. remarks on the character of Salem's 1st settlers & the emig. of Dr. Clark's colony- **809**; a 2nd port. of extracts from his address, describing Rev. Tomb's early hist. & educ.- **810**; a 3rd port. of extracts, highlighting Rev. Tomb's 1st ministry, 1791, to the end of his services, in 1832- **811**; m. Susan, dau. Gen. John Williams, who d. Dec. 23, 1853, at the resid.of Richard Irvin, Esq., NYC, & was bur. the foll. Tues., Salem, N. Y.- **1019**; s. Rev. James; m. Susan, dau. Gen. John & Susanna (Thomas) Williams; children-

1. John, m. Abby, dau. Robert Ralston
2. Mary, m. Erwin Irving
3. James Owen, d. unm.
4. Alexander, m. Maria McLean; also noted here, that he perf. the marriage ceremony of George W. Bethune & Mary Williams, Nov. 4, 1825- **1045**; c. 1817-19, several students of Salem Academy boarded at his home, incl. ____ Wilson, "Dr. Bethune, Talmadge, & other schoolmates since distinguished"- **1053**; brief ment.- **1086**; a list & description of his books & pamphlets, publ. Salem, N. Y.- Mason's Select Remains: Janeway's Token for Children, 1801; Importance of Family Religion: A Sermon, 1799; Two Sermons, 1804; The Importance of Winning Souls to Christ, 1805; The Female Laborer in the Gospel, 1805; The Ruin & Recovery of Man, 1806, 1813; Discourses on the Leading Doctrines & Duties of Christianity, 4 vols., 1815; The One Thing Needful, n. d., in a series of short practical discourses- **1082**; the origin & conception of the Wash. co. Bible Soc. attrib. to him- **1097**

Alexander M.- m. dau. John & ____ (Blanchard) McLean- **914**; (s. Rev. Alexander & Susan Williams) merch., res. NYC; m. Maria, dau. Hon. John & Maria (Blanchard) McLean- **1045**

Rev. Alexander-(s. Ebenezer & Betsey Williams) clergym., Malta, N. Y.; m. Delia Williams; one child, Richard Irvin- **1045**

Andrew- Dec. 7, 1784, purch. in Skenesborough (Whitehall, N. Y.), Lot 22, containing 127 acres, for £ 195; & on Feb. 27, 1787, Lot 31, containing 500 acres, for £ 137 10s- **(L)**- **875**

Dr. Andrew- physician, of Hebron, N. Y.; conveyed Lot 286, & 67 acres of Lot 287, Turner's Patent, Aug. 15, 1786, to Dan Rude, of Salem, N. Y.; the lot & port. orig. conveyed by the proprietors, Sept. 4, 1771, to John Martin & George Guthery- **(L)**- **936**; (of Argyle) m. Mary, dau. Andrew & Nancy (Stewart) Lytle; children- Jane,

James, Andrew, Daniel, John, Mary, Alexander, William, Susan; Margaret, m.
Thomas C. Whiteside; Dr. Hugh; & Hannah, m. Ransom Stiles- **1069**
Ebenezer- s. Rev. James; m. Betsey, dau. Gen. John & Susannah (Thomas)
Williams; children-
1. John, lawyer, unm.; member, N. Y. Assembly
2. James, m. Jane Wells
3. Mary, m. Esq. James McFarland
4. Ebenezer, m. Margaret Burden
5. Alexander, m. Delia Williams
6. Susannah, m. George W. Shepherd; his wf. d. 1857; & he d. June 2, 1813, at
38- **1045**
Ebenezer, Jr.- (s. Ebenezer & Betsey Blanchard) merch., res. Troy, N. Y.- **1045**
James- (s. Ebenezer & Betsey Williams) m. Jane, dau. Joseph Wells; hotel keeper
in Michigan, where his wf. d.- **1045**
Rev. James- succeeded Rev. Dr. Clark as pastor, Assoc. Ref. church, Salem, N. Y.-
810; ments. sons Rev. Alexander, D. D., & Ebenezer- **1045**; arr. in America, 1754,
as Assoc. Presbyterian missionary; his influ. upon the Wash. Co. Bible Soc. noted
down through the yrs. to its 50th anniversary, Sept. 4, 1862, by representatives
from the 3rd & 4th generations of his family- **1097**
John- (s. Rev. Alexander, D. D., & Susannah Williams) Professor, Rutgers college;
m. Abby, dau. Robert Robertson; several children- **1045**
Margaret- of Argyle, N. Y.; m. Thomas C., s. Thomas & Elizabeth (Cramer)
Whiteside- **805**
Rev.- gave an address, Sept. 4, 1862, bef. the 50th annual meeting of the Wash.
Co. Bible Soc., relating some of his experiences in superintending the spiritual
welfare of sick & wnd. soldiers; the crux of his address pert. to the vices prevalent
in camp life & the effect it has in causing soldiers to soon lose all regard for
religious concerns- **1097**
William- once res. (n. d.) on the Merrill farm, N. of the village, Salem, N. Y.- **1078**

PROUTY,
____- named as one of Daniel Shays' men who settl. nr. Granville, N. Y., after
being driven from Mass. foll. Shays' revolt- **921**
Franklin- res.Galesville, N. Y.; m. Sarah Eliza, dau. Newell & Charity (Blackman)
Angel; one child- **848**

PROVOST,
Gen./ Gov. Sir George- (or Prevost; 1767- 1816) Gov. of Canada; his forces occ.
the village of Plattsburgh, N. Y., c. 1814, on the N. side of the Saranac river; as he
had no batteries erected to attack the American forts onthe S. side, he sent a
detachm. to dislodge the militia at the river ford; while his intent was to simult.
attack the militia & the forts, as the militia fled back to them, his detachm. was
instead drawn off 4 mi. out of its way by the militia, to a coll. of stores they had
been instructed to defend; the Gov. had been "on a house top, spy- glass in hand",

watching for the detachm.'s approach on the road along the S. side of the river, waiting to order the attack on the forts; however, he saw the fleet surrender, recalled the detachm., struck his camp that evening, & returned to Canada- **1055**

PUBLICATIONS- a survey of pamphlets & books publ. in Wash. co., 1799, 1801, 1804- 6, 1811, 1814- 16, 1822, & 1825; a total of 21 titles, giving descriptions of bindings, some sizes, no. of pgs. & vols., a/o prices, & printer; publ. principally in Salem, N. Y.; incl. several works by Rev. Dr. Alexander Proudfit, D. D., & the foll. works- The Psalms of David, in metre, acc. Church of Scotland, 1814; Select Essays... in Divinity, Rev. Wm. McEwen; The Child's Instructor; Dr. Watt's plain & easy Catechisms, 1815; The Hist. of England, from the invasion of Julius Caesar, to the revolution in 1688, David Humes, Esq.; American edition; A System of Speculative Masonry; A Practical Exposition on the CXXX Psalm, John Owen, D. D., 1806; The Child's Monitor: or the dying experience of Mary Jones of Northtown in England, w. remarks by Rev. John Cook, 1822; Washington's Farewell Address; The Year of Jubilee, but not to Africans, Rev. Nathaniel S. Prime, 1825; Bisset's George III; A Pastoral & Farewell Letter..., Rev. Dr. Thomas Clark, 1811; see Bestsellers, 1798, Vol. 1- **1082**

PULMAN,
Asaph, Jr.- defendant, May 19, 1774, in a case brought by Hugh Munro- **878**

PUMPELLY,
Family- ments. daus. Catherine Ann, & Stella A., who m. Hon. John Mason Parker, as his 1st & 2nd wf., respectively- **759s**

PUTNAM,
Gen. Isreal- (1718- 1790) officer witn. by Samuel Standish, Sept.- Nov. 1776, acc. his Rev. war pens. appl.- **747**; town of Putnam, N. Y., named in his honor- **1091**

Putnam, N. Y.- created from the town of Westfield (Ft. Ann & Hartford) & renamed from Hutton's Bush, honoring Gen. Isreal Putnam, who performed so many exploits within this town & its vicinity during the French war; land in this town orig. gr. to a military officer who prob. returned to Scotland, where the title was purch. by a co. of Scots, who left to settle there; some cooled to the enterprise while coming here & sold out to other co. members; after they arr. in NYC, the remainder sold out, leaving a sole owner, perh. William Hutton, who appears as the 1st settler & principal land owner; refers Corey's Gazetteer; Supervisors- Peter Hutton, 1822, 1825; Wm. Hutton, 1840, 1841; town org. 1806; 1st clerk- George Wiley, 1806- 7- **1092**

Q

QUA,
Matta- (or Martha) m. Nathaniel White, s. Samuel & Nancy (Lytle) Wilson- **1069**
Robert- m. Margaret, dau. Robert & Margaret Armstrong- **1069**
Thomas- ment. as the 2nd instance of capital punishment under civil law in Wash.
Co., Aug. 12, 1808, Salem, N. Y.; see Vol. 1- **1050s**

QUACKENBUSH,
Henry- Dec. 15, 1785, purch. Lot 37, Skenesborough (Whitehall, N. Y.), for £ 205-
(L)- 875

Quebec, American assault on- (Dec. 31, 1775) commanded by Gen. Richard
Montgomery; when the Americans were "wnd. & cut to pieces", & driven from the
city, they scattered 2- 3 mi. into the woods, nearly perishing from the intense cold,
wnds., & other privations; Gov. Carleton sent word to them that if they returned to
the city, they would be made "perfectly comfortable", & receive all the hospitality
& leniency that could be bestowed upon them, but the offer apparently was not
accepted- **922**

Queensbury, N. Y.- also called Kianderossa, acc. Nov. 26, 1773 deed- **(L)- 936**

QUIGLEY,
Priest- loc. at Schaghticoke, N. Y. for several yrs., & in charge of the Catholics in
the S. part of Wash. co.; he orig. gained notoriety in this region in connection w.
Miss Gifford, a schoolteacher in Easton, N. Y., "whom he accused to the State
Superintendent of Schools for (as he alleged, though falsely) whipping a Catholic
child to make it read the Bible"; author, under pseud. Patrick Donahue, "The Cross
& the Shamrock", 264 pgs., publ. Boston, 1853; acc. Dr. Fitch, "A more
mischievious & abominable book than this- which Quigley circ. among all the
Catholics of his circuit- could scarcely be written. Its chief object... evidently is to
produce a deep- rooted, virulent hatred in the minds of the Catholic Irish towards
Americans & everything pert. to them"; its main plot concerns an emig. family of
5, losing their father during the ocean passage, & its mother, shortly after arr. on
these shores & reaching a city resembling Troy, N. Y.; acc. Dr. Fitch, the setting &
characters of Quigley's book, are thinly disguised versions of Wash. co. & its
vicinity, & personalities within the Protestant ministry of the area; the orphaned
children are, under auspices of Van Stingey, the Poor Master, prevented from the
spiritual influ. of the priest by being given away to a respectable farmer (this was a
common practice in the Troy Orphan Asylum, incorp. Apr. 10, 1835; see p. 561,
French's Gazetteer), hinting that 'there was many an instance of the kidnapping of
Irish Catholic children from their parents or natural guardians, by the jealous
Pharoahs of sectarianism'; aside from its pretexts, the extent of Dr. Fitch's

attentions to Quigley's efforts reveals as much abt. the anti- Catholic & anti- Irish sentiments within the region, as Quigley's own prejudices- **1027**; c. Mar. 1854/5, he was prob. called by Bridget Dwyer to the house of Archibald Hay, N. of Greenwich, N. Y., to attend to the last sacraments of Patrick Walls, who had been injured the Thurs. bef. New Year's, while working for Hay; he arr. at Hay's house one morning & began attending to Walls w/o Hay's express permission, & suspecting that Quigley was attempting to obt. Patrick's money "to pay him out of purgatory, or some other flummery", refused to allow him to proceed w. his sacraments in private; Father Quigley informed Hay that he had opened himself up to arrest by preventing him from perfoming his ministrations, but Hay countered that he was prepared to come to blows w. the priest to prevent his violating the privacy of his house, & his own beliefs, by continuing; when he sought Hay's wf. as an ally in allowing him to continue & found it not forthcoming, he withdrew, excusing himself from delivering the sacraments at that time; shortly thereafter, it was disclosed that Walls was not firm in his religious beliefs anymore, & Quigley warned Walls of the consequences, giving a general condemnation of var. Protestant sects, & characterizing the Hay family as "barbarians", who only "wanted to get his money from him, & let his soul go to perdition"; the priest then left, saying that he would publ. to the world their abuse of him- **1058**

R

RACE,
Lt. James W.- Co. B, 93rd N. Y. Inf.- **1090b**

RALEIGH,
Esq.- m. dau. Daniel Wells; his wid. m. 2nd, Paul Cornell- **806**; m. Abigail Wells-
841

RALSTON,
Robert- dau. Abby, m. John, s. Rev. Alexander, D. D., & Susannah (Williams)
Proudfit- **1045**

RANDALL,
Daniel- Deputy Sheriff, res. White Creek, N. Y.; he arrested Martin Wallace at
Michael Bradey's house, abt. midnight, Feb. 16, 1858, on suspicion of the murder
of Barney McEntee; Wallace was taken to Randall's tavern, where he was later
asked to view the body & reveal whether he had any knowl. abt. the dec'd.; foll. the
conversation Randall had w. him during their walk betw. the house & the barn
where McEntee's body was, his tracks were measured & found to be similar to ones
Elijah Chase had measured at the murder scene- **1048s**

RANDLE,
Frances- of Norwich, N. Y.; m. Walter Martin, s. Silas & Zerniah (Martin)
Conkey- **730**
Hugh- (Randles) member, Capt. Barn's scout co., of Salem, N. Y.- **1000**
Joseph- (Randel) one of 3 neighbors of Benjamin Hough, who were abused &
insulted by Vt. rioters during Hough's captivity, Jan./ Feb. 1775, by the mob- **881**
William- (Randles) s. Hugh; c. 1853, res. Hebron, N. Y.- **1000**
Lt. William- Co. I, 93rd N. Y. Inf.- **1090b**

RANSOM,
_____- 1798, res. Ft. Miller, N. Y., above the loc. of the Duer Mansion, keeping a
tavern there, presently kept (1850) by Wid. Jacquay- **804**
Chauncey- res. Cleveland, Ohio; m. Ann Eliza, dau. Moses & Hannah (Wells)
Younglove; their dau., m. E. P. Fenton- **841**
Polly- of West Haven, Vt.; m. Newell, s. Augustus & Triphena (Martin) Angel, as
his 2nd wf.- **847**

RASEY,
Charles W.- Co. A, 2nd N. Y., Northern Black Horse, Cav., 1861-2- **1080**

RASIDE,
Susan- consort of William; d. Oct. 7, 1776, at 21- **(L)- 975**

RATCHFORD,
____- perh. res. Nova Scotia; m. Desire, dau. Moses & Desire (Burrows) Gore-
1100

RATHBONE,
Elmore- he & Alvin Russell were officers of the jail, Salem, N. Y., who were
assigned alternate 12 hr. shifts guarding the cell of Martin Wallace foll. his
attempt to escape on the Sun. night bef. his execution, Dec. 1, 1858- **1050s**

RATHBUN,
____- res. Brooklyn, N. Y.; m. Eliza, dau. Jonathan & ____ Fitch; several
children- **799**
GENEALOGY- their coat of arms occ. one side of an escutcheon, w. a Fitch coat of
arms on the other side; its design, shown to Dr. Fitch by Miss Bliss, grdau. Capt.
R. H. Fitch, is argent, w. 3 martlets, & the whole surmounted by a martlet; see
Fitch, Genealogy- **942**
Miss- of Brooklyn, N. Y.; possesses a ring w. a Fitch coat of arms, similar to the
device of Gov. Thomas Fitch, combined w. the Rathbun coat of arms, which "occ.
the left or dexter" side of the ring; see Bliss, Peletiah; & Fitch, Genealogy- **942**

REA,
Robert- 4th Sgt., Co. A, 2nd N. Y., Northern Black Horse, Cav., 1861- 2- **1080**

READ,
William- c. 1781, Col. Adam Martin purch. the Mill Lot, Turner's Patent, from
him; & c. 1780's, Silas Conkey purch. Lot No. 67, Argyle Patent, from him- **730**;
foll. her unsuccessful search for her son in Burgoyne's camp at Stillwater, Sept./
Oct. 1777, Mrs. John Lytle returned as far as his home at Fitch's Point, & lodged
there for the night- **743**; (Esq.) his house once occ. by Duncan McArthur- **1069**

The Red House an architectural landmark at Fitch's Point, Salem, N. Y.; orig. occ.
by Moses Martin, Sr., foll. by Moses, Jr., & then his sons Sidney & Lansing;
c. 1850, the families of Sidney & Lansing, & their wid. mother, Eunice Clark, occ.
separate portions of the building; Sidney sold the building in 1852, foll. his
mother's death- **731**; built abt. 1785/6, some 6- 8 yrs. prior to the house of Adam
Martin- **852**; c. 1777, Asher Seward's house was loc. betw. it & the bridge over
Black creek- **855**; John Farrar res. at the top of the hill, betw. it & the bridge, & St.
John Honeywood res. betw. Farrar & the Red house- **863**; the Christie family res.
betw. it & the Point bridge, & the Norton family res. halfway betw. it & the
Battenkill- **867**

REED,
Kitchel- b. Mar. 8, 1754, Norwalk, Conn.; c. 1777, rem. Columbia co., N. Y., & abt. 40 yrs. ago (c. 1780's) settl. Granville, N. Y.; enl. Apr. 1775, for 9 mos., Lt. Brown's co., Col. Waterbury's regt.; marched to NYC, & then Albany, & thence to Ft. Ticonderoga, & went to Canada under Gen. Richard Montgomery; rec'd. his disch. from Gen. Schuyler; Apr. 1776, served 1 month at NYC, Capt. Keiler's militia co., of Norwalk, Conn.; Aug. 1776, served 2 mos., Capt. Bell's militia co., of Stamford, Conn., defending NYC until its capt. by the British; Jan. 1777, served 1 month, guarding lines nr. NYC, Capt. Slosson's militia co.; Mar. 1777, drafted, & served 2 mos. guarding stores, Capt. Seymour's co., of Norwalk, Conn.; rem. Columbia co., May 1777, & in July, served 1 month, Capt. Graves' militia co., of Hillsdale, N. Y., called out & marched to Ft. Edward & Lake George; drafted, prob. Aug. 1778, & served 1 month at Cherry Valley; called out again when the British burnt Schoharie, in 1780- **753**

REID,
Andrew J.- s. Peter; Orderly Sgt., Co. G, 30th Illinois Inf.; rec'd. several bullet holes in his clothes at the battle of Ft. Donelson (Feb. 3, 1863), was Postmaster there in April, & therefore not present in the battle of Pittsburgh Landing (Shiloh)- **1095**
Col.- acc. Dr. Fitch, prob. of Otter creek falls; bef. he left for England, there was talk of raising a regt.of Highlanders to defend the govt., & acc. Donald Munro, his bro. John, Esq., was to have a Capt.'s commission under his command- **822**
Daniel- of Argyle, N. Y.; dau. m. Deac. George, s. Hugh & Mary (McWhorter) Harsha, as his 2nd wf.- **973**
Duncan- (s. Roger & ____ McDougall) loyalist, rem. Canada during Rev. war; he m. & d. nr. Montreal; several children- William, Duncan, Mary; Catharine, m. Dr. Robert Clark; & Nancy- **802**
Family- res. Norwalk, Conn.; dau. Catharine, m. John Munro, Esq.- **812**
John- prob. res. NYC; he & Wm. Wallace referred to by the Gov., along w. Atty. Gen. Smith, when John Munro petitn. for an appt. of High Sheriff for Albany, Sept. 20, 1771- **902**
Col. John- his letter, Apr. 7, 1772, to N. Y. Gov. recommends selecting Crown Point as Charlotte co. seat, 'as being most centered, most easy access by water- an armed garrison nearby to enforce the law should it be necessary, & c.'- **904**
Peter- res. E. Greenwich, N. Y.; his s. Andrew J., enl. Co. G, 30th Illinois Inf.- **1095**
Roger- b. Scotland; emig. from Argyleshire, a member, Capt. Laughlin Campbell's co.; "he tarried many yrs. at Kaykett, above N. Y."; at age 30, m. sist. John McDougall; res. Lot No. 53, Argyle Patent, & erected a house of square logs there; 2 children- Duncan, loyalist, rem. Canada; Catharine, m. William Campbell; he sold his lot to Alex. Shaw, & purch. in S. Argyle, N. Y., c. 1798; he d. there in 1806, at 86, & was. bur. w/o stone, nr. Argyle corners- **802**; res. Fitch's Point, Salem, N. Y.; the 1st school remembered by Wid. Angel was taught in his house,

when only he & his wf. occ. it- **859**; res. early at Fitch's Point, nr. where the Long House stands, w. ano. house nr. him, but w. a space betw. them wide enough for a wagon to pass- **867**

William- of Argyle, N. Y.; deeds to Adam Martin, Aug. 15, 1786- **(L)- 936**; (Read) Mill Lot, Salem, N. Y., deeded to Martin on above date, for £ 900- **(L)- 936b**

Reid's Mineral Spring- loc. S. Argyle, N. Y.; was a mi. S. of Neal Gillespie's home- **802**

RELIHAN,
Mathew- Co. A, 2nd N. Y., Northern Black Horse, Cav., 1861- 2- **1080**

RENSSELAER,
Col. Henry K.- (Henry Killian; 1743- 1816) officer witn., acc. Rev. war pension appl. of Samuel Standish; his wnd. at battle of Ft. Ann noted; see Van Rensselaer, Vol. 1- **747**
John- res. Sancoick, N. Y.; Aug. 7, 1775,Comm. of Safety held its meeting at his home- **783**
Surname- modern var. of Van Rensselaer
Rensselaerwyck, Manor of- 'Rensellaerwyck'; loc. Albany co., N. Y.; c. 1775, Pownal,Vt. was incl. as a port. of its area, & the inhabitants were agreeable to taking their leases from the proprietors, but feared retribution from the Vt. rioters- **881**

Rents- c. 1777, lands in the neighborh. of the Bennington battleground, Hoosick, Rens. co., N. Y., were held on 21 yr. leases; consequently, most structures in the vicinity were impermanent log huts- **762b**; Lot No. 83, Cambridge Patent, containing 583 acres, rented to Phineas Whiteside at £ 29 16s annually- **805**; by letter of Gov. Colden to the Board of Trade, Jan. 20, 1764, quit rents in N. Y. Province were levied at 2/6 per 100 acres, compared w. 1/ sterling per 100 acres in N. H. Province- **887**

"the Retreat"- "or the evac. of the country bef. Burgoyne", July- Sept. 1777; common phrase given by most early settlers in reference to the time period during the Burgoyne Campaign when their communities moved S. bef. the army's movements; the time varied w. communities, Salem (§ 853) & Cambridge evac. at, or bef., the time of the battle of Bennington, & other areas, such as Schaghticoke & Stillwater, retreating at the time that the combative forces encamped at Bemis Heights- **739**

REYNOLDS,
John P.- (John Parker, Sr., s. Rev. Parker; b. Sept. 21, 1782, Nine Partners, N. Y.; d. Mar. 21, 1858, Hamilton, Ohio) editor, *Washington Register*, the rival newspaper of *The Northern Post* (1812- 16), Salem, N. Y.; he rem. from here, Jan.

1816 (to Cincinatti, Ohio); see Vols. 3 & 4; parenthetical infromation from p. 169, Reynolds Genealogy- **721**; printer, c. 1814- 16; his bookstore & shop loc. next N. of the Hotel; printed Psalms of David, McEwen's Selected Essays... in Divinity; The Child's Instructor; Dr. Watt's Catechisms; & Hume's Hist. of England; see Publications- **1082**

Judge? L.- witn., Dec. 1, 1858, for the certif. of the execution of Martin Wallace- **1050s**

Linus J.- bro. John P.; abt. 1815, began publ. *The Advertiser*, Glens Falls, N. Y., as a democratic newspaper; abandoned abt. Jan. 1816- **721**

Nehemiah- orig. proprietor to a land tract, Danby, Vt., beginning at NW corner of Lot No. 53, & running E10°S, crossing the Mill creek to the leith of the 1st Hemlock ridge, & then W. on the ridge, etc.; 1st conveyed to John Stafford, & then quit claim, Jan. 29, 1784, to Thomas Brayton- **745**

RHODE ISLAND- 759s, 844, 1073;
   Counties- Kent- 745;
   Cities & Towns- Coventry- 745; Exeter- 749; Newport- 799, 974;
   Newport News- 1097; Providence- 746, 1093

RHODES,
Jesse- of Salem, N. Y.; c. 1820's, Harrison Otis Gray Blake was hired, or bound out, to him, & during his service, suffered whippings at Rhodes' hand- **733**

RICE,
Harvey- Justice of Sessions, People vs. Martin Wallace, Oct. 1- 7, 1858- **1048s**; ments. the warrant of authority for the execution of Martin Wallace during the proceedings of the execution, & was also a witn., Dec. 1, 1858, certif. his execution- **1050s**

John L.- oath of alleg.; Co. D, 22nd N. Y. Inf.- **(L)**- **1074**
Marcus D.- Co. A, 2nd N. Y., Northern Black Horse, Cav., 1861- 2- **1080**
Mr.- abt. 1809, purch. the farm of Archibald McNeil, loc. nr. the guard gates of the Champlain canal, at Saratoga (Schuylerville, N. Y.)- **804**
Patty- m. John, s. William & Jane (Lytle) Russell- **737**
Phebe- m. Daniel, s. Daniel Marsh- **962**
Priscilla- m. Joseph, s. Joseph & Abigail (Warren) Cheney, as his 2nd wf.- **1038**
Robert A.- oath of alleg.; Co. D, 22nd N. Y. Inf.- **(L)**- **1074**

RICH,
Family- of Salem, N. Y.; c. 1850, their farm was prob. orig. 1767 homesite of David Webb, in Turner's Patent- **738**

RICHARDS,
Daniel- of Milton, N. Y.; m. Sarah, dau. Thomas & Abigail (Dutton) Parker- **759s**
Dr.- c. 1830, along w. Dr. Sherwood & 1 or 2 others, unearthed the Bennington dead bur. on Esq. Barnet's house lot, finding the skeletons in nearly perfect & whole condition, although "flung in at random" when orig. bur.- **762**

RICHMOND,
Edward- d. Oct. 15, 1827, at 70- **(L)**- **772**

RIDER,
Family- c. 1853, loc. NE of Salem, N. Y., nr. Vt. line, along White (Ondawa) creek, & the right of way for the Troy & Rutland R. R.- **1051**
John- Argyle, N. Y.; Mar. 18, 1805, accident; Elisha Forbes, Coroner- **(L)**- **876**

Riders- acc. N. Y. Gov. Moore, were reservations amounting to 5- 600 acres in some townships gr. by N. H., giving particular lots to some N. H. Council members & public officers beyond the 500 acres allocated to Gov. Wentworth as a gr. fee; they were regarded as 'grievances' by the real settlers, as their owners would be at no expense in making roads & other improvements upon them- **894**

RITZMA,
Col. Rudolph- (or Ritzema) he was stat. at McNeil's (prob. McNeil's ferry) w. 4 companies, acc. Gen. Schuyler's letter, Aug. 19, 1775, & was expected to arr. at Saratoga (Schuylerville, N. Y.) the morning of this same day- **782**

ROBB,
Jane- m. John, s. William, Jr. & Molly (Highlands) Mack- **734**
Capt. William- of Peterborough, N. H.; along w. 3 others, was one of the soldiers who carried Col. Baum from the Bennington battleground; provided a minute description of the Col.'s death to Samuel T. Shipherd, when Shipherd was a child living in his neighborh.- **801**

ROBBINS,
_____- res. nr. Saratoga Lake; m. Betsey, dau. Thomas Pattison; 2 of their children were bur. nr. there- **951**
F. L.- oath of alleg.; Co. D, 22nd N. Y. Inf.- **(L)**- **1074**

ROBERTS,
William- Nov. 29, 1790, "died by Mischance"; Joshua Conkey, Coroner- **(L)**- **876**

ROBERTSON,

_____- res. Reynoldsburgh, Ohio; m. Mary Ann, dau. William & Wealthy (Gilbert) Wells- **839**

Alexander- Wash. Co. Surrogate; succeeded Jan. 15, 1841, by Hon. John C. Parker, Esq.- **759s**

Family- bros., George R., res. White Creek, N. Y.; & ano., m. Mary Ann Wells, & res. Reynoldsburgh, Ohio- **839**

Mr.- of Scotland; c. 1850, owned the property on which the Duer mansion once stood, Ft. Miller, N. Y.- **800**

Thomas- Scotchman; res. nr. Checkered House, Cambridge, N. Y.; dau. Margaret, m. John, & dau. Ann, m. Peter, both sons of Phineas & Ann (Cooper) Whiteside; was tory during Rev. war, & rem. Canada- **805**

William- dau. Jane, m. James, s. John & Betsey (Beaty) McDougall- **978**

ROBINSON,

_____- former bookseller, NYC; m. dau. _____ & Martha Palen- **731**

_____- arrested & tried (n. d.) as a suspected person, by Salem Comm. of Safety; "Mad" More was present, & became verbally abusive towards him, & when ano. whig, Mr. Lytle, interceded, More turned his abuse upon him, causing a fight betw. the 2 whigs- **925**

Charles L.- m. Mary, dau. Walter & Sarah (Turner) Martin; his wf. d. 1852- **1046**

Col.- raised a guard of 16 men at Bennington, Vt., mid- June 1782, to guard a party of tories & British soldiers who had recently attempted to abduct Esq. Bleecker from Pittstown, N. Y.- **747**

Rev. C. S.- delivered the 1st lecture in a series, Nov. 1854, presented by the N. White Creek & Cambridge Literary Assoc., entitled "This Age"; a partial newspaper acct. reviewing the lecture indicates his definition of the period as a 'working age', noting the coal mines of Pennsylvania & 'the gigantic scheme' of tunneling the Hoosic Mtn. as characteristic of the time period- **1028**

Francis, Jr.- Supervisor, "& c.", Greenwich, N. Y.; m. Almira, dau. Capt. Abner & Miriam (Martin) Dwelly; a son, Francis, Jr., & other children- **731**

Moses- clerk, Aug. 3, 1775, at Comm. of Safety meeting for Cambridge & Hoosick, N. Y., & Bennington, Vt.- **783**; chairman, Cambridge Convention Comm., May 9- 15, 1781, concerning union of Wash. co. w. Vt.- **816**

Ruth- of Bennington, Vt.; m. Prof. Wm. Henry, s. John C. & Susan (Mason) Parker, as his 1st wf.- **759s**

Samuel- (1705- 1767) along w. Samuel Ashley, John Horfort, & Isaac Charles, he was apprehended & detained by Harmanus Schuyler, High Sheriff of Albany co., N. Y., July 30, 1764, for forcibly ejecting Peter Voss & Bastian Deal from their lands in the Grants- **885**; when apprehended by Schuyler, he claimed to be a Justice of the Peace- **892**; he & Jeremiah French compiled a Return of persons on N. H. Grants, submitted 'to your excellency & honor's', Dec. 18, 1765- **893**; his activities in connection w. the Grants referred to by Gov. Moore, June 9, 1767, in a letter to Lord Shelburne, in which the Gov. replies to the contents of petitns.

submitted by Robinson; noting that Robinson's petitns. have caused obstacles to completion of Patent process for some claims, he observes that perh. not more than half the numbers ment. in Robinson's petitns. are actually inhabitants of the townships in question, & most are inhabitants of adj. Provinces who signed the petitns. w/o intending to settle the lands; his charges regarding the Gov.'s fees is denied as a gross misrepresentation, referring to his table of fees, then in transit to England; Gov. Moore remarks on his character, saying that 'Robinson can plead but little merit from his service, which I am told here was nothing more than that of driving an oxcart for the settlers'; concerning the nature of the 9 articles, or paragraphs, of his petitn., Moore considers their whole tenor & the no.of falsehoods within 'to have been the offspring of a very bad heart & I think there is the greatest reason to apprehend that the head might likewise have been impaired. How else should a man of the lowest & meanest occupation at once set up for a Statesman, & from a notion that the wheels of govt. are easily managed & conducted as those of a waggon [sic], take upon him to direct the King's Ministers in their Departments'; his only appl. to the Gov. noted as a 'humble suitor' seeking assist. in the distress brought on himself by settl. on lands he later found to be prev. gr. by the N. Y. govt. to others; his pretensions then examined by the Council, w. Gov. Moore acting as his advocate, though he didn't need one, as the Council had already determined to protect settlers in such circumstances by securing his lands, Cole's, & 7 or 8 others- **894**; presumed by Gov. Moore to be the author of a petitn. of the Soc. for the Propagation of the Gospel; in ano. letter to Lord Shelburne, it is noted that this petitn. holds so little design to serve any but its signers, w/o attention to the purpose designed for & w/o scruple for defrauding the Soc. of its rights- **895**; he, Samuel Ashley, & 2 others (Horfort & Charles) noted by James Van Cortlandt, a member of Sheriff Schuyler's posse, as having been brought to Albany jail, but never indicted, nor gave bail, nor brought to trial- **897**

ROCKETTS,
Widow- m. Peter Van Brugh Livingston, as his 2nd wf.- **961**

ROCKWELL,
Philo- merch., Utica, N. Y.; m. Abby, dau. Walter & Sarah (Turner) Martin; children-
1. Mary, m. _____ Scovil
2. Christine, m.William? King
3. Martin, m. Wid. Jane Merry
4. James, m. Cynthia Kellogg
5. Susan, m. Charles C. P. Freeman
6. Jane, m. Charles King
7. George, boat Capt., Lake Eire
8. Henry, res. Martinsburgh, N. Y.; on the alarm of cholera in the country, he packed up his furniture & intended to leave w. the 1st outbreak, but became its 1st victim, & d. 1832; his wf. d. a few days foll. the death of their dau. Susan- **730**;

ano. record of their children- Mary, m. C. P. Scovil; Christina, m. Wm. King; Walter M., m. Jane Merry; James, m. Cynthia Kellogg; Jane, d. Aug. 23, 1825, at 17 mos., 23 ds.; Susan, m. Charles P. Freeman; Jane, m. C. B. King; George, Henry Clay; & Sarah, dec'd. prior 1858; he d. Aug. 13, 1832, of cholera, in Utica; the epidemic 1st appeared in Montreal & Quebec, Canada, & in Albany, N. Y.; he intended to rem. Martinsburgh, N. Y., at the 1st outbreak in Utica, but "Lo! He himself was the 1st victim!"; his wf. d. Jan. 5, 1848, at NYC- **1046**

ROFF,
John- plaintiff, May 17, 1774, vs. Joseph Ingall & Paul Bush, concerning debt for £ 501 3s 6d & costs; to his favor- **878**

ROGERS,
A. L.- oath of alleg.; Co. D, 22nd N. Y. Inf.- **(L)**- **1074**
Daniel- Co. A, 2nd N. Y., Northern Black Horse, Cav., 1861- 2- **1080**
David- m. Eleanor, dau. James & Rebecca (Lytle) Mills- **737**
Families- bros. Samuel & Thomas, c. 1798, res. in separate houses at the mouth of the Battenkill; at that time, there was a bridge across the kill in that loc.- **804**
George E.- oath of alleg.; Co. D, 22nd N. Y. Inf.- **(L)**- **1074**
James- the validity of his statem. concerning the assault on Skenesborough, 1780, James McKie's escape, & the murder of the McCalls (§ 244) upheld by Dr. Fitch, in light of the witn. acct. given here; see Vol. 1- **1000**
John- (Rodgers) chairman, Cambridge Convention, May 9- 15, 1781, concerning union of Wash. co. w. Vt.- **816**
Rev. Dr. John- extracts taken from "City Clergy in 1775", Nov. 6, 1851, *N. Y. Observer,* noting elders,deacons, & trustees of his Presbyterian church, org. 1716, NYC, w. particular reference to those becoming prominent in N. Y. public life; see Church/ Clergy- **961**

Rogers' Rangers- William Mack, Jr. prob. served in this unit- **734**

ROORBACK,
Mr.- (prob. John Rooröback; see Vol. 1) acted on behalf of P. W. Yates, plaintiff's attorney, in Thomas Stone vs. Jonathan Baker; defense attorney, Phineas Babcock vs. Jonathan Baker, & Hugh Munro vs. David Hunter; all 1st term, Oct. 19, 1773, Charlotte co. Court of Common Pleas- **878**

ROOT,
David- m. Abigail, dau. Thomas & Abigail (Dutton) Parker- **759s**

ROSE,
Betsey- m. Lemuel, s. Capt. Abner & Miriam (Martin) Dwelly- **731**

Samuel- member, Comm. of Safety, Manchester, Vt., along w. Wm. Marsh, Esq; corresponds to N. Y. Comm. of Safety, June 28, 1775, to warn that var. people of Charlotte co. were consorting to form a mob to stop the Co. Courts at Ft. Edward, N. Y.- **779**

ROSET,
Robert- defendant, w. James Palmer, Oct. 19, 1774, in a case brought by John Thurman, Jr., & Jacob Van Voorhies, assignees of Philip P. Lansing- **878**

ROSS,
Daniel R.- Co. A, 2nd N. Y., Northern Black Horse, Cav., 1861- 2- **1080**
Gen. Henry Howard- (1790- 1862; s. Judge Daniel & Elizabeth Gilliland; 19th Congress, 1825- 27; Co. Judge, 1847- 48) of Essex co., N. Y.; m. Susannah, dau. Hon. Anthony I. & Maria (Williams) Blanchard- **1045**

ROSSEL,
____- minister; m. Sarah Ann, dau. Stuben & Esther (Murdock) Doty; had daus. Esther & Collette; "he once strangely left her for parts unknown"- **730**

ROSSITER,
Maj.- of Richmond, Mass.; officer, Mass. brigade that marched Sept. 1776, to Fairfield, Conn.- **747**

ROWAN,
Abram- oath of alleg.; Co. D, 22nd N. Y. Inf.- **(L)- 1074**
Deac. Archibald- (s. Stephen & Betsey McCollister) c. 1864, res. Argyle, N. Y.- **1049**
James- of Salem, N. Y.; m. Elizabeth, dau. John & Eleanor (Lowrie) Lytle; children-
  1. Rebecca, m. John Elliot
  2. Abraham, m. Margaret Thompson
  3. John, m. ____ Armstrong
  4. James, unm.
  5. Betsey, m. William Shaw
  6. William, m. Eleanor Wright
  7. Rev. Stephen- **737**; their farm loc. on a hill NE of Salem village, on the road to Boyd's, & "off to the E. of sd. road, by a byway of difficult passage"; (Mrs. Betty) used to relate her hardships during the Rev. war; the town was mostly absent of men, & she & her children were all alone when alarm of the Allen family & McCrea murders reached town; "it was deemed unsafe to remain in their houses overnight, lest the Indians should fall upon & massacre them", & at night, she took her 2 or 3 children, the youngest only 2 wks. old, away from the house & into the woods, hiding until morning; one night they laid out w. the rain falling all night, w/o injury, she used to boast, "except the loss of one breast- which from cold,

formed an ague- cake therein, whereby she was unable to nurse the child upon that breast"; in the mornings, she would return & occ. the house during the day, & withdraw again at night; in a few days, men w. teams were sent from Bennington w. an order to move the families down there; ea. family was allowed to pack a barrel of goods to evac. w., & she left everything else in the house, finding it all intact on returning; the remoteness of her house was prob. why the tories had left it unmolested- **1049**

John- (s. James & Elizabeth Lytle) m. ____ Armstrong, at Lisbon, N. Y.- **737**
John- deed witn., Apr. 20, 1770; Rev. Dr. Thomas Clark to Andrew Lytle- **(L)- 936**; deed witn., Sept. 6, 1775; Rev. Dr. Thomas Clark to Robert Clark- **(L)- 936b**
John- c. 1798, res. Bardstown, Kentucky; John Fitch, the steamboat inventor, in his Will, June 20, Prob. Aug. 14, 1798, leaves the remainder of his estate, real & personal, to Rowan & James Nourse- **949b**
Deac. John- perh. it was he, & not Stephen Rowan, acc. Dr. Fitch, who m. Mary, dau. James Harsha, the emig.- **973**; c. 1858, his house, loc. Lot 189, Salem, N. Y., was occ. by Dr. Seth Brown- **1049**
Dr. John M.- m. Lydia, dau. Aaron & Elizabeth (Fitch) Martin; of their children, "a girl, Sarah, an idiot, d. 8 yrs. old, a month after her father"; his wf. m. 2nd, William Watson- **731**; (s. Stephen & Betsey McCollister) dec'd. prior 1864- **1049**
Stephen- prob. res. Salem, N. Y.; late June 1808, Daniel McFarland d. in his house, from an 'inordinate use of spiritous liquors'- **(L)- 876**; m. Mary, dau. James Harsha, the emig.; or perh., it was Deac. John who m. her, acc. Dr. Fitch- **973**
Stephen- s. Deac. John; m. Betsey McCollister, c. 1800- 1803, when he was still res. at his father's place; their children Archibald & John were b. there & his wf. soon d.; he m. a 2nd time, & later became landlord of the old red tavern, Salem, N. Y.- **1049**
Rev. Stephen, D. D.- (s. James & Elizabeth Lytle) res. NYC- **737**
William- (s. James & Elizabeth Lytle) res NYC; a great horse jockey, "commonly called 'Jockey Billy' "; m. 1. Eleanor Wright; 2. ____; he d. an indigent, Jan.? 1860- **737**
William- c. 1798, res. Bardstown, Kentucky; was bequeathed a beaver hat; shoe, knee & stock buckles; & a walking stick & spectacles, by John Fitch, the steamboat inventor, in his Will, June 20, Prob. Aug. 14, 1798; it was reported that of all Fitch's bequests, he rec'd. 'the lion's share'- **949b**
William- (s. ____ & Betty ____) horse dealer, NYC; d. Jan. 21, 1867, at 76; bur. Salem, N. Y.- **1049**

ROWLAND,
Andrew- of Fairfield, Conn.; lawyer; m. Elizabeth, dau. Gov. Thomas Fitch; 5 children-
1. Samuel, m. Sarah Maltby
2. Thomas, m. Lucy Woodward
3. Andrew, m. Ann Marsh
4. Elizabeth, m. Gershom Sturgis

5. Dr. James, unm.; lost at sea- **799**

Andrew- (s. Andrew & Elizabeth Fitch) m. Anna Marsh; ments. dau. Elizabeth F.-
799

Rev. Jonathan M.- (s. Andrew & Elizabeth Fitch) lawyer; res. Fairfield, Conn.; m.
Sarah Maltby; 9 children- William, George, Samuel, Dr. Charles; Elizabeth,
m. O. W. Jones; Rev. Jonathan M., Henry, James, Andrew, & Edward S.- **799**

Thomas- (s. Andrew & Elizabeth Fitch) a farmer & judge; res. Westford, Conn.; m.
Lucy Woodward; no children- **799**

ROWLEY,

Capt.- of Richmond, Mass.; commanded co., Brown's regt., Gen. Fellows' brigade,
stat. at Ft. Ann, July 1777; along w. ano. co., he was ordered to capt. a scow lying
in Wood creek, & in the process, engaged w. enemy forces, which precipitated the
battle here; at a later point in the battle, he & a no. of his co. drove the enemy from
their position on Battle Hill, bef. the American army retreated to Ft. Edward- **747**;
Joseph Crippen was his neph.; both participated in the battle of White Plains, in
different companies- **755**

Thomas, Jr.- (Rowlee) def., May 19, 1774, in a case brought by John Js. Bleecker-
878

ROY,

Esq. W.- of Ft. Ann, N. Y.; dau. Ann, m. Col John, s. Gen. John & Susannah
(Thomas) Williams, as his 1st wf.; see Wray, George, Esq., Vol. 4- **1045**

Royal Highlanders- or His Majesty's 42nd Regt. of Foot; org. May 1740; embodied,
1730, Perthshire, Scotland, as a local corps & widely known as the "Black Watch";
even its privates were gentlemen 'by birth & fortune'; numbered 42nd, 1749, &
made 'Royal', 1758, by George II; active abroad for more than 64 yrs. (as of 1852)
& in England & Ireland for 35 yrs.; only 13 yrs. spent in Scotland; service in 29
expeditions & campaigns, w. engagem. in more than 50 battles, sieges, &
skirmishes; a list of principal campaigns participated in, beginning in France, at
Fontenoy, 1745; in the Carribean; during the French Revolution; in Egypt,
Portugal, & Spain, & the Napoleonic wars; its American engagem. incl. the attack
on Ticonderoga, 1758; expedition on the N. American lakes w. Gen. Amherst,
incl. surrender of the French at Crown Point & Ticonderoga, 1759; surrender of
Montreal, 1760; campaigns against the N. American Indians, 1763- 1765; during
the American Revolution- the battles of Brooklyn & York Island, & capt. of Ft.
Washington, 1776; Brandywine, Germantown, 1777; Monmouth, 1778;
Elizabethtown, 1779; siege of Charlestown, 1780; the oldest of all the Scots regts.
in the British army which also incl. the 71st- 76th, 78th, & 91st- 93rd regts.- **990**

RUDE,
Dan- of Salem, N. Y.; Lot No. 286, & 67 acres in the N. part, Lot No. 287,
Turner's Patent, conveyed to him, Aug. 15, 1786, by Dr. Andrew Proudfit- **(L)-**
936
Jeremiah- Salem, N. Y.; June 8, 1808, "in a canoe? on Batten kill, being subj. to
fits, fell into the stream & was drowned"; Hamilton McCollister, Coroner- **(L)- 876**

RUFF,
___- res. Cambridge, N. Y.; Aug. 1792, Jacob Gilbert drowned in his millpond-
(L)- 876

RUGG,
Joseph- of Salem, N. Y.; Lot No. 237, Turner's Patent, conveyed to him by
proprietors, & Apr. 20, 1770, conveyed by him to Rev. Dr. Thomas Clark- **(L)-**
936

RUMSEY,
David- co- editor, *The Northern Post,* Salem, N. Y., along w. Henry Dodd; their
partnership joined June 6, 1814, by James Stevenson, Jr.; he left the newspaper abt.
Jan. 1, 1815; see Newspapers, & Vol. 1- **721**; from Conn.; res. N. end of Salem; he
was in partnership for several yrs. w. Dodd, then rem. Steuben co., where he publ.
a newspaper in Bath, N. Y.; member, N. Y. Legislature, & Delegate, State
Constitutional Convention, 1867; acc. Dr. Fitch, French's Gazetteer (fn. 1, p. 620)
lists the *Farmer's Gazette,* begun 1816, by Rumsey, & also, the *Steuben
Messenger,* Apr. 17, 1828; & in 1854, the *Temperance Gem* was publ. by Jenney &
Caroline Rumsey- **1078**

RUSSELL,
Alvin- he & Elmore Rathbone were officers of the jail, Salem, N. Y., & were
assigned alternate 12 hr. shifts guarding the cell of Martin Wallace, foll. his
attempted escape on the Sun. night prev. to his execution, Dec. 1, 1858- **759s**
Benjamin- (s. William & Jane Lytle) m. ___; res. Moreau, N. Y.- **737**
David- c. 1850, res. Hebron, N. Y.; the tory scout party that capt. a Hessian
deserter, along w. Susan & Rebecca Lytle, & marched all of their prisoners from
John Lytle's house in Salem to as far as his home, bef. they were met by William
McNish, who persuaded them to release the 2 girls bef. they were missed- **470**
David- (s. William & Jane Lytle) res. Hebron, N. Y.; m. Phebe Russell- **737**
David- occ. the land orig. held by Deac. Alexander Turner, Jr., an orig. Salem
proprietor; he sold Turner's homesite to Evergreen Cemetery, forming its SW
corner; its bounds agreed upon, Jan. 1862- **1034**
David- res. Salem, N. Y., opp. the parsonage & W. of the Academy; a dau., m.
Judge Cornelius L. Allen- **1053**
Hon. David- res. Salem, N. Y.; dau. Catharine, m. William Wallace, s. Andrew &
Elizabeth (Martin) Freeman- **730**

Ebenezer- deeds acknowl. bef. him- Dr. Thomas Clark to Jedidiah Gilbert;
Ephriam Wheeler to Phineas Bennet- **(L)- 936**
George- (s. William & Jane Lytle) owns "the factory & c." at Eagleville, S. Salem,
N. Y.; m. Susan Gardner- **737**
Jehiel- of Greenwich, N. Y.; juror, People vs. Martin Wallace, Oct. 1- 7, 1858-
1048s
John- (s. William & Jane Lytle) res. Cambridge, & "recently" (prob. 1850)
Eagleville, S. Salem, N. Y.; m. Patty Rice- **737**
John- occ. orig. homesite of David Webb, Turner's Patent, foll. John Crozier- **738**
John- res. Salem, N. Y.; coming "from somewhere south", & unrelated to other
Russells in Wash. co.; "one of the most arrant democrats in the co.", he openly
concurred w. a disparaging opinion on the death of George Washington; see
Newspapers; m. ____ Hogeboom, of Col. co., & rem. there, acquiring considerable
property there through his wf.- **919**
John- emig. from Ireland w. wf. Jane, & abt. 1766, settl. White Creek, N. Y.; his
wf. d. 1770, & he d. 1777, their ages unknown; stone erected by their s. William-
(L)- 975
Joseph- (s. William & Jane Lytle) res. Hartford, N. Y.; m. Jemima Wheeler- **737**
Phebe- m. David, s. William & Jane (Lytle) Russell- **737**
Capt. S. W.- Co. A, 2nd N. Y., Northern Black Horse, Cav., 1861- 2- **1080**
William- m. Submit "Metty" Fosgate; dau. Sabra, m. Adam, s. Moses, Sr., & Lydia
(More) Martin- **731**; dau. Sabra, was Adam Martin's 1st wf.- **1041**
William- c. 1850, res. 2nd house N. of the Checkered House, Cambridge, N. Y.; m.
1. Jane, dau. John & Eleanor (Lowrie) Lytle; 2. Wid. Fowler; children-
　1. Jane, m. Solomon Smith
　2. John, m. Patty Rice
　3. Charity, m. Edward Long
　4. David, m. Phebe Russell
　5. George, m. Susan Gardner
　6. Benjamin, m. ____
　7. Joseph, m. Jemima Wheeler
　8. Julia Ann, m. ____ Newell
　9. Mary, m. 1. ____ Gardner; 2. James Hall
　10. William
　11. Morton- **737**; a rise of ground in the rear of his house, overlooking the valley
of the Owl kill, was the site of an open air Sabbath given to Salem refugees by Rev.
Dr. Clark during "the Retreat", Aug. 1777- **739**; (old Mr.) recoll. a childhood
incident connected w. Mrs. Edmund Wells, Jr.'s reputation as a cook- **840**
William, Jr.- (s. William & Jane Lytle) "an unsteady rover has been at sea, &
resides nowhere"- **737**
William A.- c. 1858, res. Salem, N. Y., in the house orig. built by St. John
Honeywood- **1033**

RUTGER,
_____ - adm. to practice, Oct. 19, 1773, Charlotte co. court- **878**

RYAN,
John, Esq.- res. S. side of the Walloomsac river; was a decided whig, "long an important man in Hoosic"; when Col. Baum's forces arr. here, he was a neighbor of Joshua Munro, & had been m. only 1 or 2 yrs.; his wf. was then in feeble health & subj. to fits, & since he could not move her, or allow his house to be disturbed, he "therefore constrained to go & take a written protection from Baum to secure himself from molestation"; while placing his protection over the door was a safeguard against entry by the Hessians & Indians, it was an invitation to plunder by the American forces, & he had to avail himself of alternately placing the white paper (tory) or the hemlock sprig (whig) over his doorway as the tide shifted during the battle of Bennington- **767**; his 1st wf. Meribah, d. May 5, 1779, at 24; & his 2nd wf. Mary, d. Dec. 8, 1795, at 37; & his 3rd wf. Patience, d. Nov. 17, 1842, at 81; & he d. Mar. 25, 1827, at 72- **(L)- 772**

S

SACKETT,
Capt.- commanded a co. of Green Mtn. rangers, June 1777, stat. at the mouth of Otter creek- **756**

SAFFORD,
Gideon- c. 1858, worked the Deac. John Steele farm, N. of Salem, N. Y., then owned by Hon. Bernard Blair- **1047**
Gideon- dau. Matilda, b. Nov. 1790, m. James, s. James & Susannah (Thomas) Turner- **1090**
Gideon F.- "lame" Gideon; res. Salem, N. Y.; m. 1873, Lucy M., dau. James & Matilda (Safford) Turner, as his 2nd wf.- **1090**
Jacob- was 'Capt. of the Bennington boys', as he used to express it, during the battle of that name, Aug. 16, 1777; referred to as the authority from whom Esq. Barnet acq. his knowl. of the battle- **764**
Dr. John- m. Susan, dau. Walter & Sarah (Turner) Martin; she d., leaving dau. Mary, who m. ____ Fisk, of Watertown, N. Y.- **730**; their children- Mary, d. Aug. 15, 1816, at 1 yr., 10 mos., & 21 ds.; Mary, b. June 8, 1816; m. Isaac H. Fisk; his wf. Susan, d. July 26, 1818; & he d. Jan. 5, 1842- **1046**
P.- res. nr. Shushan, in town of Cambridge, N. Y.; his house caught fire Thurs., June 23, 1814, betw. 11:00 & 12:00 PM, & was completely engulfed within a few minutes, the family losing its provisions, furniture, & most of their clothing- **704**
Samuel- res. nr. Bennington, Vt.; on the night of May 23, 1771, Samuel Willoughby lodged w. him, & at abt. 9 or 10 PM, the family was alarmed by gunfire; in the morning, it was discovered that Willoughby's horse had been shot dead in the barn- **899**
Maj. Samuel- of Col. Seth Warner's regt.; either he, or Maj. Gilbert Bradley, reportedly overheard Gen. John Stark finding fault w. Col. Warner for not arr. sooner on the Bennington battlefield- **764**; elected as Maj., Green Mtn. regt., June 27,1775, by a vote of 28 to 17- **781b**; foll. the controversy concerning selection of officers, was chosen as Maj. for the Green Mtn. regt., Sept. 1st, by the N. Y. Provincial Congress- **782**

SAILLY,
F. L. C.- bank cashier, Plattsburgh, N. Y.; m. Dec. 1825, Ann Eliza, dau. Hon. Anthony I. & Maria (Williams) Blanchard- **1045**

ST. CLAIR,
Gen. Arthur- (1737- 1818) his army passed through Salem, N. Y., & encamped overnight in a body, in & around John Lytle's house (prob. in retreat from Ft. Ticonderoga, through Castleton, Vt., & c., acc. Dr. Fitch); his retreat appears as foll.- July 9, 1777- arr. Manchester, Vt., & rem. the foll. morning, tracing the

Battenkill to Camden creek, & then struck across country, & arr. at Lytle's by evening; marched via Argyle the foll. day, & joined Gen. Schuyler at Ft. Edward on July 12th- **738b**; (Col.) ment. as an officer witn. by Ebenezer Farnsworth, during his pens. appl. statem. of service, Apr. 1776- Feb. 1777, & also July 1777- Feb. 1778- **750**; commanded at Ft. Ticonderoga foll. Gen. Schuyler's departure, June 26, 1777; he dispatched a notice to Schuyler, which arr. at Saratoga on the evening of June 28th, that part of Burgoyne's force had been sighted abt. 45 mi. above Ticonderoga- **788**; by Gouverneur Morris' acct., July 14, 1777, his rear guard was fallen upon abt. 16- 18 mi. from Mt. Independence, either by 10 companies of grenadiers & light infantry, or by part of the British army at Ticonderoga that had been sent in pursuit of the fleeing Americans; the ensuing action precipitated the battle of Ft. Ann- **792**; he & Gen. Schuyler advise Morris, late July 1777, on examining recent correspondences of Dr. Williams, Mr. Sessions, & Dr. Clark- **796**

ST. JOHN,
John- res. Greenfield, N. Y.; Capt., Rev. war; m. Hannah, dau. Ebenezer & Lydia (Mills) Fitch; 4 children-
  1. Dr. Samuel, rem. Alabama
  2. Charlotte, m. _____ Bullard
  3. Lydia, m. Daniel Bockus
  4. Jabez, res. at his father's old place; see Vol. 4- **799**
Stephen- m. Sarah, dau. Thomas & _____ (Hill) Fitch; had 2 daus.- **799**; res. Norwalk, Conn.; dau. Henrietta, m. John A. Hall; his wf. Sarah, has been dead "some yrs."- **940**

St. John's, Quebec, Canada- by letter, May 23, 1775, Col. Arnold notes his capt. of a British sloop here on May 18th; on his return to Crown Point, he ran into a party of 80- 100 men lead by Col. Ethan Allen, bound for St. John's, & determined to make a stand there; unable to dissaude him, Col. Arnold supplied Allen's force w. additional provisions bef. they proceeded; within 2 mi. of St. John's, Allen learned that a detachm. on the road from Montreal lay in ambush; crossing the lake to avoid the ambush, his party was greeted the foll. morning by an assault from 6 field pieces & abt. 200 regulars, & he retreated back to Ft. Ticonderoga; Col. Arnold notes, that provided w. bateaux from Montreal, the garrison here will prob. visit Crown Point & Ticonderoga, jeopardizing the cannon capt. there; in a 2nd letter, sent to the Conn. General Assembly, Col. Arnold notes that one of Allen's men, capt. at St. John's on May 19th, escaped & returned w. a report that 400 regulars are stat. there, making preparations to cross the lake, & are expected to be joined by a no. of Indians, to recapt. Crown Point & Ticonderoga- **774**; surprising the garrison here at 6 AM, May 18, 1775, Col. Arnold reports to the Cambridge, Mass. Comm. of Safety, that his forces capt. a Sgt. & his 12 man company, along w. a 70 ton sloop, w. 2 brass 6 pounders, readied to sail; their Capt. was scheduled to return from Montreal w. a large detachm. for Ticonderoga, so that such stores as were valuable were loaded, & the assault force left after 2 hrs., taking 4 of the King's bateaux & destroying the 5 remaining ones- **775**

Salem, N. Y.- the stockaded Presbyterian church, was reportedly burnt by the British & Indians when the town was evac., Aug. 1777- **701**; the area militia departed from here, Sept. 8, 1814, to march on alarm northward, w. 4 days provisions- **706**; a meeting was held "at the Hotel", Sept. 12, 1814, to organize a comm. for the receiving & forwarding of provisions, et. al., to Salem militia now being stat. w. the army at Plattsburgh, N. Y.; chairman- Ebenezer Russell; clerk- James McNish; appt. as comm.- Asa Fitch, Abram Allen, Alex. McNish, James McFarland, James Nichols, David D. Gray, & Wm. Williams; resolved that sd. comm. should go to army & ascert. items needed, mode for transporting, & provisions for rem. of sick & wnd. to their homes; also resolved that the comm. procure & convey all obtainable firearms to Salem militia at Plattsburgh; a subscription opened for defraying transportation costs, & $200.00 was immed. subscribed- **707**; when news of Commodore Macdonough's victory was rec'd. here, a unanimous resolution was made to provide the Commodore w. a public dinner; a comm. of arrangements was appt, & 10 days later rec'd. news that Macdonough was available for the honor on Nov. 29, 1814; on the appt. day, the comm., "joined by a large no. of their fellow citizens, formed a cavalcade, & rode out several miles to meet & escort their expected guest"; a delay of Macdonough's arrival lead to great anxiety, "vexation & chagrin" by dusk; the hero's eventual arrival was preceded by a signal gun, & as his "suite" reached the "summit of an adj. hill which commands a prospect of the village", an unexpected & unscheduled "blaze of a general illumination occurred", foll. by "a national salute [that] drowns in its martial roar the pacific chiming of the village bells"; a procession formed, comprised of the respective units, incl. "Military Officers in full uniform- Strangers & Citizens", & was preceded by the Salem band; the procession adjourned to the church for a prayer by Rev. Tomb, & an address by Rev. Dr. Proudfit, w. benediction by Rev. Mr. Dunlap; the public banquet foll., & "after the cloth was rem. the foll. <u>toasts</u> were drank, interspersed w. excellent music by the band"; a total of 18 toasts, foll. by 13 voluntary toasts, were given; their contents given, foll. by ment. of musical selections, a/o no. of cheers, listed; selections played to accomp. foll. toasts- 1st- "Hail Columbia"; 2nd- "Yankee Doodle"; 6th- "Federal March"; 7th- "Free Mason's March"; 8th- "Soldier's Return"; 10th- "Turkish March"; 11th- "Green's March"; 15th- "Death March" (to George Washington); 18th- "Serenade"; the proceedings noted for their political harmony; Commodore Macdonough proceeded to Cambridge, N. Y. the foll. morning, accomp. by numerous citizens of Salem, & was feted again at that place- **709**; c. 1782, a co. of '9 months men' was enl. from the vicinity & mustered that spring at Saratoga (Schuylerville, N. Y.) for 6 wks., after which a portion was returned to Ft. Williams, here in Salem; these 2 locations became the northernmost outposts of the American army; foll. the Rev. war, John Hunsden, a member of this detachm., & several others from town, emig. French Mills, St. Lawrence co.- **729**; Moses

Martin, Sr.; Dr./ Gen. John Williams, Alexander Webster, Ebenezer Russell, & Capt. John Savage, were the principal associates involved in "managing the patriot cause in this district"- 730; c. 1767, only 2 houses loc. here, James Turner's- where the Coffee House, or Union Hall, now (1850) stands; & David Webb's; John Lytle constructed a cabin nr. the S. line, Lot No. 92, where it crossed Trout brook; his dau. Susan, b. Apr. 7, 1767, came here at age 4 wks., suppos. the 1st infant (female?) in town; in 1789, Wm.Lytle acquired the 1st wagon in town, "it was much talked of, & folks were afraid to ride in it- having only been used to carts bef."; see Wagons, Vol. 1, for comparison- 738; in the Retreat, "or evac. of the country bef. Burgoyne", Aug. 1777, many Salem families stopped at the McCool's farm, nr. Wait's corners, Cambridge, N. Y., & others went on to Bennington, Vt., & Mass.; a Sabbath, held by Dr. Clark, gathered some of the refugees on a rise of ground in the rear of where William Russell now res. (1850), overlooking the valley of the Owl kill; acc. Mrs.Vance, the setting created an effective backdrop for Dr. Clark's sermon, which incl. Psalm 137- 739; a fortnight foll. "the Retreat", news arr. in the Hoosick area that a considerable force of tories & Indians had taken the town, & burnt the Presbyterian, or New England church, which had been fortified & surrounded by pickets; description of the structure given, see Church/ Clergy; afterw., they also capt. Cambridge, N. Y.; freq. alarms, later proved false, lead some of the settlers to sell their places & move to safety; others, who lived where the village is, fled their houses to the safety of a high hill S. of Robert Getty's, in Hebron- 744; acc. to an address by Rev. Dr. Alexander Proudfit, 1st settlers here were from Rev. Dr. Clark's colony; remarking that 'rarely has an assemblage of men been better fitting for marching foremost in any arduous enterprise, than the 1st settlers of Salem', he attrib. cert. factors of their experience in Ireland for their adaptability as settlers- the privations & hadrships of their youth; 'the iron rod of persecution', which lead them to find in religion 'those supports, of which the intolerances of tyrants could not deprive them'; & freq. collisions w. arbitrary civil powers, which lead them to investigate their natural rights; these, given by Dr. Proudfit as evidences of a divine control in 'the adaptation of instruments for the executions of purposes assigned them'- 809; evac. at the time when Burgoyne's army was at Whitehall, N. Y., July 1777- 853; the school taught W. of John McDonald's place was in use bef. Wid. Angel's recoll., & the 1st recalled by her was taught at Roger Reid's, in the W. part of town, w. 8- 10 "scholars"; ano. school was taught by Samuel Williams, nr. Daniel Livingston's; one was later built of logs, nr. James Harvey Fitch's house, & 1st taught by Joseph, or Nathan, Cheney, & then for a season, by Timothy Larabee, foll. for 2- 3 yrs., by Wm. Selfridge- 859; a library incorp., & its trustees elected, Mar. 13, 1798, to serve the towns of Cambridge & Salem; see Independent Library- 879; "the honesty & scrupulous integrity" of the early settlers given as a major reason behind Dr. John Williams' decision to settle here; only 2 or 3 physicians res. in the area when Dr. Williams 1st arr. here, & they "sneered much at him & his pretensions to medical skill", laying a scheme that would make him subj. to ridicule & destroy his prospects of success; "one cold, dark, disagreeable night", he was called some miles to someone who had hurt his shoulder, saying it was out of joint; upon his examination, perceiving that there was nothing out of place, "& enquiring minutely how the accident had occurred, & c. he became satisfied it was a trick they were putting upon him"; he then "directed the bystanders to pull upon the arm, for him to set it- & when the extension was made, he succeeded in slipping the shoulder out of joint- & telling the person that he had done all he could do for him, left him & returned home"; more trouble was taken by the schemers in putting the shoulder back in place than Dr.Williams had taken in dislocating it, & the story spread, contributing greatly to the success of Williams' practice- **915**; Comm. of Safety met at Dr.Williams' house; at one time, a man named Robinson was arrested & tried as a suspected person; "Mad" More was present at the proceedings, & became abusive towards the accused; Mr. Lytle, ano. whig, intervened, & became involved in a fight w. More- **925**; towards the close of the Rev. war, area whigs made themselves rich by robbing the cattle & sheep of the Argyle inhabitants, partly to pay 3 & 6 months soldiers enl. to guard the frontier- **977**; public meeting held, Apr. 12, 1841; Alexander Robinson, Chairman; John H. McFarland, Secretary; & James Gibson, Esq.; stated purpose- unanimously resolved for appt. of a comm. 'to devise & recommend suitable arrangements for Military & Civic Honors' due to the death of Pres. Wm. Henry Harrison; lists Comm., consisting of 24 members; Tues., Apr. 20th, appt. as the day for paying respects; an order of arrangements, incl. a procession w. a 'Horse caparisoned & in mourning; Hearse & Urn', flanked by guards, Salem citizens, & fronted by Pall Bearers, foll. by officers & soldiers of the Rev. war, & military officers in uniform; further listing of public officials, '& finally, Citizens & Strangers'; procession departed Court House at 11:00 AM, w. bells tolling, & the "minute" guns fired during the march through the streets to the Brick church; an order of exercise, & recessional to the place of beginning- **1009**; grounds of the SW corner, Evergreen Cemetery, was house site of orig. settler & proprietor, Alexander Turner, Jr.; property transferred to cemetery, Jan. 1862, by David Russell- **1034**; at the time of the Allen family & McCrea massacres, July 1777, the men of town were mostly absent, in a militia co. at & abt. Bennington, Vt.; it was deemed unsafe to remain overnight in the houses "lest the Indians should fall upon & massacre them"; in a few days, teams were sent to evac. the town down to the Bennington area, allowing ea. family to pack only a barrel of their goods to bring- **1049**; Co. A, 2nd N. Y., Northern Black Horse, Cavalry, commanded by Capt. Solomon W. Russell, & recruited here; winter, 1861- 2, stat. Wash., D. C., & disch., there being more cavalry vols. than needed; a printed article, Dec. 1861, listing its officers & privates; some of those listed afterw. served in other units, see Vols. 3 & 4- **1080**; a co. from here settl. Lisbon, N. Y., & incl. desc. of Robert Armstrong- **1083**; the Armstrong families rem. to Lisbon, in 1801, along w. Reubin Turner- **1085**; Camp Washington, occ. the flats betw. the R. R., machine & paint shops, & the base of Gallows Hill, "the ground which is now being fenced & pitted up for the fairs of the Co. Agricultural Soc."; for some 2 wks. volunteers have been asembling here for the org. of the 123rd NYSV; "Salem village is daily thronged w. citizens from all parts of the co., to visit their relatives in the camp"; at the same time, the Wash. Co. Bible Soc. held its 50th annual anniversary meeting, Sept. 4, 1862, at the White Church- **1097**; departure of the 123rd NYSV from Camp Washington, by train, betw. 10- 11:00 PM, on Sept. 5, 1862; foll. the train's departure, Dr. Fitch notes the passing of families by his home- "For 2 hrs., vehicles have been passing every few moments over the dusty road, & now it is an almost continous procession, rattling rapidly by, occasionally w. singing from female as well as male voices; bearing to their widely scattered homes those who have bid a last farewell, to brothers, sons, dear kinsmen, & valued friends, many of whom they may never see more"; at 11:30 PM- "The wagons now pass at longer intervals, & the scene is abt. closed"; the last sounds faded into stillness at abt. midnight- **1098**

SALTONSTALL,
Gov. Gurdon- (1666- 1724; Gov., 1707- 24) of Conn.; his grdau. Sarah, m. Jonathan Fitch- **757**

SAMPSON,
Abraham- m. Lorah, dau. Alexander Standish- **757**
Caleb- ("Ebb") m. Mary, dau. Alexander Standish- **757**
Isaac- m. Lydia, dau. Alexander Standish- **757**

Sancoick (N. Hoosick, N. Y.)- planks from the bridge were stripped off by Wm. Gilmore & others, to prevent the advance of Col. Baum; his expedition was so nr. this loc. that it was impossible "to cut the string- pieces & let them down into the water"; this appears to be the 1st hostile act against Baum, as men fired upon the repair efforts, from bushes & other coverts nearby- 766; Col. Baum reached this point in the morning, Aug. 14, 1777, & acc. Dr. Fitch, prob. sent out a party of soldiers to Col. Fister to recruit loyalist support- 768; (St. Coick) Aug. 7, 1775 meeting of area Committees of Safety was held here, at John Rensselaer's house; proclamation drafted here concerning the recent death of one man & wounding of ano. in an attempt to arrest someone on the grounds of being a tory; directs that future accusations be presented to the Committees for arbitration; a copy sent to, & approved by the State Comm.- **783**; 'Sinkaick' Comm. of Correspondence, its members incl. w. those of Hoosick in a list of those present May 10, 1775, in Albany, N. Y.- **831**; the road through the village, c. 1777, was essentially the same in 1853, Van Rensselaer's mill being loc. where Elisha Brownell's grist & sawmill stand now, along Little White creek, which "runs through a deep rock- bound chasm, across which chasm the bridge here is thrown"; as Col. Baum advanced from Cambridge to Bennington, the American scouts & stragglers fled bef. him; Wm. Gilmore, w. 2 others, ventured to linger at Van Rensselaer's mill long enough to strip the planks from the bridge; they escaped to the summit of a ridge or knoll some rods S. of the creek, when Col. Baum's forces came into sight; they disch. their pieces & fled out of sight, over the knoll; a reconnaisance was made of the spot, going downstream abt. 25 rods below the bridge, & Col. Baum passed his 2 cannon over the ford here; after 2- 3 hrs. delay, the remainder of the expedition crossed over the repaired bridge- **1006**

Sandy Hill, N. Y.- (incorp. 1810; named changed, 1910, to Hudson Falls, N. Y.) skirmish w. Indians & tories occurred here, prob. at nightfall, foll. battle of Ft. Ann, July 8, 1777; Gen. Nixon's artillery drove back the assault; 2 tentmates of Samuel Standish were among those killed here, & the American army arr. at Ft. Edward the foll. morning- **747**

Saratoga (Schuylerville, N. Y.)- c. 1782, the garrison here & at Ft.Williams, Salem, N. Y., were the northernmost outposts of the Americans; a co. of '9 months men', enl. from Salem vicinity, were mustered here in the spring & remained for abt. 6 wks.; a detachm. of this co. was then returned to the Salem garrison- **729**; Gen. Schuyler arr. here from Ticonderoga, Aug. 18, 1775, expecting Col. Ritzma & his 4 companies to cross from McNeil's (ferry) & arr. the foll. morning- **782**; retreat of American army to here from Moses kill noted by Gen. Schuyler, Aug. 1, 1777; the ground at their prev. loc. being viewed as too extensive for the size of his force, he spent the day on horseback scanning the countryside here for a suitable encampment loc. that might give a chance of stopping the enemy's career, noting an intention to move further S. if unsuccessful in his search- **798**; return of field officers, Oct. 3, 1775, recommended for appt. within the district- Col. John McCrea, Lt. Col. Cornelius Van Veghten, 1st Maj. Daniel Dickison, 2nd Maj. Jacob Van Schaik, Adjutant Archibald McNeil, & Quartermaster John Vernor- **823**; (Sarasota) an acct. by Express from Albany, N. Y., Nov. 19, 1745, that the French & their Indians had cut off a settlm. called "Saraghtoga", abt. 50 mi. from Albany, presented by Gov. Clinton to the Board of Trade, Nov. 30th; the dispatch notes 20 houses & a fort burnt to ashes, 30 persons killed & scalped, & abt. 60 prisoners taken; refers Land Doc., xxvii, 187, 235; possibly the same endeavor, acc. Dr. Fitch, in which Mons. Marin burnt "the Lydius establishments"; see Ft. Edward, N. Y.- **1013**

Saratoga, battles of- 1st battle, Fri., Sept. 19, 1777, at Freeman's Farm, known as "The Friday Battle"; the night foll. the battle, Mrs. John (Eleanor Lowrie) Lytle arr. in the British camp, searching for her son, the scene "all confusion, running to & froe [sic], blood flowing from the wnd. as they were brought to the hospital, & the groans of the dying", all too busy & anxious abt. themselves to notice her presence- **743**; cannon firing at Bemis Heights distinctly heard in Hoosick, N. Y.- **744**; the Friday (Freeman's Farm) & Tuesday (Bemis Heights) battles referred to; Augustus Angel was a participant in both battles- **847**; on the day of Burgoyne's surrender, Oct. 17, 1777, it was reportedly "rainy or misty"- **869**; the cannon here could be heard in Munro's Meadows, Hebron, N. Y., abt. 30 mi. away- **998**; at Bemis Heights, Gen. Simon Frazier was mortally wnd. by one of Daniel Morgan's rifleman, & carried from the field to a house then occ. by Lady Harriet Ackland- **1002**; the success in capt. Gen. Burgoyne attrib. by James McDonald to the efforts

of Benedict Arnold, rather than Gen. Gates; 'Arnold fought like tiger. ...he seemed
to be everywhere present & the life of the battle'; an anecdote related concerning
his actions, although seemingly embellished upon; see Arnold, Gen. Benedict-
1010

Saratoga, Comm. of Correspondence- additional members, Oct. 3, 1775- Justus
Ashman, Walter DeRidder, George Palmer, Richard Hart, & Jonathan Jones, Esq.-
823; elected as new comm., Nov. 10- Daniel Dickison, Richard Hart, Ebenezer
Marvin, Joseph Row, Philip Rodgers, Cornelius Van Den Burgh, & Samuel Bacon-
824; (incl. Easton, N. Y.) a list of those members present, May 10, 1775, Albany,
N. Y.- Col. Schuyler, John McCrea, Peter Lansingh, Cornelius Van Veghten, Har.s
(Harmanus) Schuyler, Dirck Swart, John Tayler, Daniel Dickinson, John Fish, &
Cornelius Van Den Burgh- **831**

SARGENT,
Dr. John- res. Pawlet,Vt.; a celebrated surgeon there, d. at 80 yrs. old, a few
yrs.ago (d. 1843, at 82; p. 234, Hollister's Pawlet)- **728**
Dr. Isaac-res. Ft. Ann, N. Y.; his bro. was Dr. John Sargent, of Pawlet, Vt.- **728**
Dr. Nathaniel- of Hampton, N. H.; John, s. Rev. Jabez & Elizabeth (Appleton)
Fitch, 'studied physic' w. him- **835**
Mr.- member, N. Y. Assembly, & local district candidate, 1816; advocated passage
of a bill dividing Cambridge township into 3 parts- **726**

SAUNDERS,
Esq.- m. Mary, dau. Daniel Wells, in Shushan, N. Y.; no children- **841**

SAVAGE,
Deac. Abram- his farm, Lot 99, Turner's Patent, Salem, N. Y., purch. from his
heirs by Newcomb Cleveland- **971**; his s. Rev. John, res.Waukesha, Wisc.; ano. s.,
Dr. James, res. Argyle, N. Y.- **1044**
Edward- for £ 127 6s, purch.127 acres, Skenesborough, Mar. 1, 1787- **(L)- 875**;
his bond as loan officer, recorded Oct. 20, 1785, w. John Williams & Joseph
Caldwell providing bail- **(L)- 936**; he, John Williams & Joseph Caldwell, became
security for him as loan officer (n. d.) for putting out £ 200,000 in bills of credit-
(L)- 936b
Judge Edward- owned farm, loc. Lot No. 55, N. of the village, Salem, N. Y.; c.
1824, it was worked by Harrison G. Blake, & owned, c. 1850, by one of the
McFarland families- **733**; clerk, Charlotte co. Comm. of Safety, May 1, 1776- **785**;
appt. Sheriff, Charlotte co., May 8, 1777, by N. Y. Province- **787**
Elizabeth- m. Allen Hunsden- **1090**
Dr. James- s. Deac. Abraham; res. Argyle, N. Y.- **1044**; Secretary, Wash. Co.
Bible Soc., since 1826; while reading the minutes of the society's 50th annual
meeting, Sept. 4, 1862, requested the selection of a replacement, having been
present at every meeting since the aforementioned date- **1097**

Hon. John- appt. 2nd Vice President of a public reception honoring Commodore
Macdonough, Nov. 29, 1814, Salem, N. Y.; he toasted Capt.Young, prob.
Macdonough's aide, during the ceremonies- **709**; his vote, favoring the 1816
Congressional pay raise, criticized Apr. 25, 1816, by *The Northern Post*, noting
that the salary increase amounted to an avg. of $17.00 per day, or $117.00 per wk.,
for 90 days service; his tenure began Dec.4, 1815, & the pay raise began Mar. 3,
1816; also noted that the democrats returned him to their ticket, but Mr. Adgate,
who opposed the increase, was left off- **725**; notes, Dec. 16, 1853, that Peletiah
Fitch obt. his land warrant for a tract in Warren co., Illinois, for his service as Sgt.,
Capt. Lytle's co., 4th regt. of riflemen, prob.War of 1812- **1004**
Rev. John, D. D.- s. Deac. Abraham, of Salem, N. Y.; res. Waukesha, Wisc., &
Pres. of the college there; m. Eliza, dau. James William & Elenour (Hunsden)
Turner- **1044**; same material- **1090**

SAWYER,
____- formerly res. (n. d.) Clarendon, Vt., & rem. Leicester, Vt.- **966**
Col.- res. (n. d.) Clarendon, Vt.- **966**
Jesse- one of those involved in the arrest & flogging (§ 881) of Benjamin Hough;
his surname noted by John L. Marsh as one of those found in the Clarendon, Vt.
area- **966**

SAYLES,
Frank- oath of alleg.; Co. D, 22nd N. Y. Inf.- **(L)- 1074**

SCANDALL,
William- Co. A, 2nd N. Y., Northern Black Horse, Cav., 1861- 2- **1080**

Schaghticoke, N. Y.- 'Skotacook'; loc. abt. 12 mi. N. of Albany, N. Y., on the E.
side of the Hudson river; all the 'Indian malcontents' retreated here from New
England after 1676; abt. 1754, they fled the area, incorporating w. the St. Francis
Indians, having commited hostilities on the English at Stockbridge, Mass., during
the present (1761) war- **837**; its 1st settled minister, c. 1773, was Rev. Mr. Elias
Van Benschoten- **953b**; the 9:00 AM train, on Jan. 3, 1854, lost a flange off a
forward truck wheel as the train was nearing the Hoosick Bridge; although the
seats of its passenger cars were filled, w. 10 or 15 people standing in the aisle, they
incurred no injuries, but the brakeman was killed instantly; on that afternoon, a
carpenter repairing the bridge, fell to the river below, & broke his hip & back on
the ice, dying a day or two later- **1021**

SCHAUD,
Rev. Mr.- pastor, prob. 1850, Assoc. Ref. church, W. Hebron, N. Y.- **742**

SCHOON,
William- c. 1806, was hired hand of Asa Fitch, Sr., at $12.00 per month- **799**

SCHUYLER,
Abraham- m. Eve Beekman; his wf. d. July 17, 1803, at 69- **(L)- 932**
Bradstreet- his wid., m. John Bleecker, Jr., as her 2nd husb.- **1032**
Catharine- m. John Jacob Lansing- **(L)- 932**
Elizabeth- 2nd wf., James Van Ingen; d. Feb. 28, 1801, at 29- **(L)- 932**
Harmanus- High Sheriff, for city & co. of Albany, N. Y.; an undated letter from
him presented to N. Y. Council, Aug. 7, 1764, noting his apprehension &
confinement of Samuel Ashley, Samuel Robinson, John Horfort, & Isaac Charles,
until bail can be secured by them- **885**; contents of the above letter addressed to
Gov. Colden; an express rec'd. by him Fri. last (prob. July 27, 1764, acc. Dr. Fitch)
acquainting him w. the turning out (July 26?) of Hans Jerry Creiger, an inhabitant
under the proprietors of Hoosick Patent, by the N. H. people; Creiger's cattle were
driven off, & he was forced to pay for their redemption; express discloses that the
rioters were to arr. at the houses of Peter Voss & Bastian Deal on the foll. day, for
the same purpose; in consequence, Schuyler brought along 2 Justices & 'a few good
people of this Province', & arr. at the houses of Voss & Deal on Sat. morning (July
28) only to hear that the N. H. people would not arr. until Mon. (July 30); early on
that morning, word came to him of their arr., but he did not reach their homes
until after they had already accomplished their task & had 'but just gone'; he foll. &
overtook them abt. a mi. further, apprehending Ashley, Robinson, Horfort (or
Horsford), & Charles, bringing them all to Albany jail- **892**; a correspondence
betw. the contents of his letters, & a deposition made by James Van Cortlandt,
noted by Dr. Fitch- **897**
John, Jr.- his Patent loc. on E. side of the Hudson river, above Saraghtoga
(Schuylerville, N. Y.)- **935**
Gen. Philip- (1733- 1804) (as Col.) Sir William Johnson notes of him, Jan. 5,
1770, in a letter to Lt. Gov. Colden, as one who has been making himself "busy" in
giving out officer's commissions, & in his eagerness & ignorance in these matters
"some of the egregious blunders may be attributed"- **735**; commanded the
American forces stat. at Ft. Edward, July 12, 1777, when Gen. St. Clair's forces
arr. there foll. the evac. of Ft. Ticonderoga- **738b**; stat. at Ft. Ticonderoga, Dec.
1775, as its commander, acc. Ebenezer Farnsworth's Rev. war pension appl.- **750**;
officer ment., Kitchel Reed's Rev. war pension appl.- **753**; nomin. for Maj. Gen.,
June 7, 1775, by N. Y. Provincial Congress- **776**; directed by Prov. Congress, June
30, 1775, to go to Ticonderoga & examine its condition; & also, to obt. intelligence
concerning feelings in Canada- **778**; notes to the Prov. Congress, July 31st, the
selection of officers in Green Mtn. regt., remarking that their choices coincide w.
what he would choose, if he had had the authority; requests that Peter T. Curtenius
obt. cloth for uniform & tents to accommodate 225 men of the regt.- **781b**; informs
Prov. Congress of his arr. at Saratoga from Ticonderoga, Aug. 18th, & notes on
Aug. 20th that the controversy betw. Allen & Warner over selection of their
officers has been carried to such length that few men will be raised for the regt., &
of those, very few will have arms; Aug. 23, 1775, Albany, N. Y., advances £ 500 to
Col. Warner, as his men would not take to the field w/o money for blankets &

arms; remarks that the 'peculiar situation of these people & the controversy they have had w. this colony... renders that matter [officers] too delicate for me to determine'- **782**; issues enl. orders to Capt. Joseph McCracken & others, Nov. 27, 1775; notes on Feb. 29, 1776, that 3 companies of Col. Van Schaik's regt. are nearly complete, & gives their loc.- **784**; Jan.- Mar. 1777, directs Col. Warner to send his recruits to Ticonderoga as they enl., but only 24 have come by the latest return- **786**; bound for Albany, 'to rem. the cloud of confusion which has of late enveloped our affairs in the northern dept.', he leaves Ticonderoga, June 26, 1777, giving instructions for continuing the works there & along the communications post; while at Saratoga, he writes to N. Y. Comm. that a dispatch from Gen. St. Clair was rec'd. evening, June 28th, noting that part of the enemy was sighted encamped above Ticonderoga w. some of their shipping; concerning their intentions, & 'does not imagine they mean a serious attack on Ti', but suspects the movement to be a cover for an attack on the Mohawk river, to harass the line of communication, or to penetrate into N. H.; suspecting the latter, he has 'extended my attention to guard as much as possible against either; but the slender force I have does not flatter me w. so affected an opposition as might be wished' (here, Schuyler anticipates Burgoyne's ultimate designs, but envisions their execution w. more alacrity than was forthcoming, prob. expecting Ticonderoga to be bypassed)- **788**; writing at Ft. Edward, July 17, 1777, to Gen. Washington, noting that the advance post of the British is at the Ft. Ann block- house; their Indian scouts continually lurk abt. American advance posts, & capt. 2 wagons nr. Ft. George on July 15th; this same post was abandoned & put to the flame on the foll. day; w. its force added to his own, the militia remaining, & the enemy giving a few days, he expresses certainty of holding his present post agaist the British; remarking upon the toryism in the region, he suspects that Gen. Burgoyne might attempt marching as far as Bennington to acquire cattle & carriages; part of Wood creek has been filled w. trees, & the road betw. Ft. Edward & Ft. Ann broken up to render it impassable; cattle from the area have also been brought away, or are in that process, & no forage is being left for the enemy's to subsist on; also encloses one of Burgoyne's publications, along w. a copy of his response- **794**; his reply to Burgoyne's July 10th proclamation, by an order of July 13, 1777, states that all who comply w. Burgoyne's orders will be dealt w. as traitors- **795**; along w. Gen. St. Clair, advises Gouverneur Morris to examine recent correspondences from Dr. Williams, Mr. Sessions, & Dr. Clark; his intention to write the Council of Safety on the subj. of the Grants; Morris notes that if Schuyler's opinion should agree w. his own, then an express dispatch should be sent to prevent publ. in London (apparently of cert. unfavorable articles that, if known, might turn the allegiance of the Grants inhabitants toward the enemy)- **796**; his force retreats, July 23, 1777, from Ft. Edward to Moses kill, & he corresponds from there to the Council of Safety, that a full council of general officers has resolved to disch. half of the militia on condition the other half remain; 1,046 N. Y. troops have remained, but not above 300 of the 1,200 from Berkshire co., & only 29 officers & 34 privates from the 500 men of Hampshire co., Mass., 'the rest having infamously deserted', & of

100 from Conn., few, if any, remain; abt. 1,300 militia remain, & he desires having the most distant prospect of detaining half of their no. for 5- 6 days; reports the Continental force at 2,700- 2,800 troops- 797; from Saratoga, Aug. 1st; by unanimous decision of general officers on the prev. day, the army withdrew from Moses kill, noting that the ground was too extensive for the size of their force; has been on horseback all day, searching for a suitable spot that may give chance to stopping the enemy's career, but 'I have not yet been able to find a spot that has the least prospect of answering the purpose, & I believe you will soon learn that we are retreated further south'- 798; numerous letters to & from him noted by Dr. Fitch as contained within the Proceedings of The Albany Comm. of Correspondence, 1775- 818; Peter B. Tearse recommended to him, prob. Feb. 1776, for a position as Adjutant- 826; (Esq.) plaintiff, May 19, 1774, vs. Samuel Loadman; Philip P. Lansing's assignee, Jan. 16, 1775, vs. Wm. Perry & Wm. Moffitt; plaintiff, same date, vs. James McNish- 878; of Dutch parentage, from a family 'standing conspicuous in our colonial annals'; b. 1733, Albany, N. Y.; Capt., 1755, in colonial forces, serving in several northern expeditions; as Col., 1768- 1775, co-operated w. George Clinton, Gen. Woodhull, & other patriots in the N. Y. Assembly 'in the struggle for the rights of the colonies against the British govt.'; 1775- chosen by Provincial Congress as delegate to the Continental Congress; assoc. w. Gen. Washington in comm. appt. to prepare rules & regulations for governing the army; June 19, 1775- appt. the 3rd Maj. Gen. in the Continental Army; Chancellor Kent (prob. James Kent, Chief Justice of N. Y.) says of him: 'Take him for all in all, he was one of the wisest & most efficient men, both in military & civil life, that the State or the nation has produced'; elected & served, Continental Congress, 1777- 1780; Nov. 1779- appt. to confer w. Gen. Washington on the state of the Southern Dept.; 1781- elected to N. Y. Senate, & a member there when selected U. S. Senator; 1792- again as N. Y. Senator, active in promoting inland navigation, taking a prominent interest in 2 early companies in that enterprise; created a plan for improving state revenues, adopted 1797, from which office of Comptroller was establ.; "he was an ardent & violent partisan of the federal school" & it was thought he was guided too much by the influ. of his son- in- law, Alexander Hamilton; he was therefore, not re- elected Senator; his manners being 'formed in the army, & not in courts of law, or among the people, were considered austere & aristocratic, & rendered him personally unpopular'; Jan. 18, 1791- in a blank resolution offered in the state Assembly, motion to insert his name failed, 32- 27, & Aaron Burr was chosen in his place by the same margin; in a "pleasant" letter written to his friends, Messrs. King, Lawrence, & Benson, he humorously speaks of his defeat, referring to Burr as his 'wily' opponent, attrib. the loss to the course of 2 conspicuous politicians of the time, (Asa) Adgate & John Williams, who seem to have assisted Burr in his intrigues against him; was elected Jan. 24, 1797, as Burr's successor in the by nearly unanimous vote- in the Senate by general consent, 35 present; & in the Assembly by 85 votes, except one given to his friend, James Kent; the gratifying nature of his selection was reflected by his retirement speech, "an address, liberal, conciliatory, & affecting in its style, & it

was ordered to be inserted in the journals"; however, the infirmities of old age prevented him from taking his seat, & he d. autumn 1804; see Senators, U. S.- **920**; deeds acknowl. bef. him- Thomas Johnson to James Lytle, Apr. 20, 1770; Thomas Clark to Andrew Lytle, July 4, 1774- **(L)- 936**; noted to Gov. Clinton, Oct. 17, 1780, that he observed what appeared to be the burning of White Creek (Salem, N. Y.), seeing the smoke from his mansion at Saratoga (Schuylerville, N. Y.); acc. Dr. Fitch, this was prob. erroneous, but "prob. the smoke of some new clearing in this direction, that was seen at Schuylerville, & gave the opinion to Schuyler, that it was the buildings at this settlm."- **1066**

Schuylerville, N. Y. (Old Saratoga)- a barracks here, prob. left from the French war, occ. by John Lytle's family bef. they settl. in Turner's Patent; Lytle's dau. Susan, was b. Apr. 7, 1767, while the family there, & they rem. abt. 4 wks. later; (this was perh. the same barracks occ. c. 1772 by Robert Blake's family (§ 42) when they 1st emig. here from the area of Tappan Bay, in lower N. Y.; see Vol. 1)- **738**; c. 1798, Mr. Duryea was the only minister here, & for communites along the Hudson above here, as far as Ft. Miller; he was preceded by ____ Smith, who afterw. was either the President of, or a Professor at, Princeton University- **804**

SCOTLAND- 791, 800, 802, 805, 810, 840, 849, 867, 871, 927, 1010, 1012, 1050s, 1075b, 1079, 1082, 1091, 1097; Highlands, Highlander- 812, 822;
   Argyleshire- 802, 1060; Culloden- 760, 1059; Edinburgh- 734; Greenock- 997; Leith- 734;
   Military units- c. 1852, the foll. British army regts. were design. as Scots regts.- 71st- 76th, 78th, & 91st- 93rd, w. the 42nd Royal Highlanders, the oldest, establ. 1740- **990**

SCOTT,
   ____ - one of the guard raised at Bennington, Vt., mid- June 1782, to guard the would- be abductors of Esq. Bleecker- **747**
   ____ - m. James, s. Daniel Wells- **841**
Gen.- (was prob. John Morin, below) his election as N. Y. Gov. termed 'pretty unanimous' in Charlotte co., despite few votes; his ownership of Lot No. 68, Argyle Patent, also noted in the same correspondence, June 23, 1777, w. a request that this property be secured for Capt. Martin- **789**
John Morin- (1730- 1784; Council of Safety, 1777; N. Y. Secretary of State, 1778- 84; & Senate, 1777- 82) of NYC; lawyer, 'eloquent, witty, & of great influ., was also an Alderman for 7 yrs. [1756- 61]'; Trustee, Dr. John Rogers' Presbyterian church- **961**
Moses- of Waterford, N. Y.; m. Matilda, dau. Reuben Cheney, as her 3rd husb.- **730**; merch.; was stat. at Valley Forge during Rev. war, relating that "when spring had so far advanced that the breaks started up in the fields & woods, the soldiers exalted greatly- gathering & boiling them for greens- & relishing them as great

luxury after their long confinement to salt meat"- **1036**; m. Matilda, dau. Reuben & Olive (Day) Cheney, as her 3rd husb.- **1038**
Olive- m. Samuel Wells, as his 2nd wf.; 4 children- **839**

Scott & Smith- publishers, Philadelphia, Pa.; their map of Wash. co., publ. 1853, noted by Dr. Fitch for its inaccuracies in depicting the route of the Troy & Rutland R. R. as it passes over the Owl kill, Dr. Fitch giving 5 figures indicating the correct course of the tracks- **1003**

SCOULLER,
Rev. James B.- President, 1862, Wash. Co. Bible Society; in failing health, returned to Philadelphia, Pa., to become editor of the *Christian Instructor*- **1097**

SCOVIL,
C. P.- lawyer; res. Martinsburgh, N. Y.; m. Mary, dau. Philo & Abby (Martin) Rockwell- **730**; same material- **1046**

SEALEE,
Dr.- was qtr'd. on parole at the house of Robert Livingston (prob. Albany, N. Y.) along w. a British Capt. who was capt. at the battle of Ft. Ann, July 1777- **794**

SEARLS,
John- res. Shaftsbury, Vt.; arrested w. Coimfort Carpenter for counterfeiting; in his Nov. 4, 1772 letter, John Munro, Esq. notes that Carpenter escaped from the 2 constables who were escorting the pair to jail, & while one hunted for him, 'the other went on w. Searls but stopped 10 days on the road & at last let Searls go abt. his business'- **912**
Dr. John- of N. Granville, N. Y.; m. Ann H., dau. Ebenezer & Sarah (Hobby) Fitch- **799**

SEBOR,
Jacob- merch., NYC; appt. by William Shirreff, June 18, 1796, to act as his atty. in coll. debts & transacting his affairs- **880**

2nd N. Y. Cavalry- Morrison's Black Horse, or Northern Black Horse Cavalry; Co. A, recruited Salem, N. Y.; stat. at Wash., D. C. during the winter months & disch. 1862, there being more cavalry volunteers than the govt. then needed; a Dec. 1861 newsclipping, giving the roster for Co. A; Officers- Capt. S. W. Russell, Jr.; 1st Lt., D. E. Cronan; 2nd Lt., Wm. Robertson; Orderly Sgt., B. F. Cole; Qtr. Master Sgt., C. H. Clark; 1st Sgt., S. B. Chillus; 2nd Sgt., W. W. McCullough; 3rd Sgt., Wm. McEachron; 4th Sgt., Robt. Rea; Corporals (8)- King S. Hammond (see Vol. 3), Wm. Austin, Benjamin B. Gilman, Andrew Beebe, Edward Nelson, Ira Sisson, James C. McClellan, James R. Skinner; 1st Bugler, Wm. G. Fisher; 2nd Bugler, E. S. Perry; 1st Farrier & Blacksmith, P. D. Abel; 2nd, J. A. Conkey;

Wagoner, Asa Burke; Saddler, Frank W. Esler; 70 privates; for ano. ment., see Hammond's Diary, Vol. 3- **1080**

SEELYE,
____- c. 1798, res. on the E. side of the Hudson, N. of the Jacquay family, nr. Ft. Miller, N. Y.; m. sist. Ephriam Crocker; see Vol. 1- **804**
Benjamin & Ebenezer- (Silye) conveyed Lots 25, 47, 87, & 92, Kingsbury Patent, to Peter & Sarah Vandervoort, who later sold them to Albert Baker- **(L)- 936**
Frederic- dau. Mary C., m. Leroy Fitch- **799**
Milton- (Seeley) res. Fitch's Point, Salem, N. Y.; his home was loc. betw. James F. Alger & James Harvey Fitch, & abt. ¼ mi. distant from ea. of them; evening, Feb. 6, 1855, the residents of all 3 houses reported an earthquake- like shaking of the ground, & the foll. morning, a crack was found in the earth betw. Seeley's & Fitch's homes; see Weather, Frost Heaves- **1026**
Sidney W.- oath of alleg.; Co. D, 22nd N. Y. Inf.- **(L)- 1074**

SEDGEWICK,
Maj.- Apr. 1776, his brigade was stat. at Granville, N. Y.- **750**

SELFRIDGE,
William- taught school (n. d.) at Fitch's Point, for 2- 3 yrs. foll. Timothy Larabee, & then rem. Argyle, N. Y.- **859**

SELLECK,
Surname- its other variations appear as Sellock, Sellick, & Silleck; Dr. Fitch records the name as *Sillick*, w. some uncertainty- **950**

Senators, U. S.- an article entitled "The United States Senators from New York, from 1787 to 1851, w. sketches of Political & Personal History", May 8, 1851, *N. Y. Herald*; the selection of N. Y.'s first Senators traced, w. biog. acct. of Philip Schuyler's life & career; in the process of the 1st selections, a resolution was offered in blank, June 15, 1789, w. the expectation of inserting Gen. Schuyler's name, & adopted by N. Y. Assembly; a resolution offering the insertion of Rufus King instead, was then presented & defeated, 37- 19; Gen. Schuyler's name was then sent to the N. Y. Senate for concurrence, & a 2nd resolution was offered in blank, & Lewis Morris was rejected w/o count; Ezra L'Hommedieu, rejected, 34- 21; & Rufus King, also rejected, 34- 21; a proposal for James Duane carried, 35- 19; by manuever, being nomin. & chosen by the Assembly, King's name was presented 1st in the Senate, despite Schuyler's name being sent there 1st; the Senate rejected Duane, 9- 10, & substituted L'Hommedieu, carrying him, 11- 7; a move to replace his name w. King's was rejected, 6- 12, & L'Hommedieu was returned to the Assembly for approval; Gen. Schuyler rec'd. Senate approval, 13- 6; July 16th- Assembly rejected L'Hommedieu, 34- 24; Rufus King was proposed, Lewis Morris moved as substitute & rejected, 43- 12; King was then unanimously accepted & sent to Senate, where resolution was concurred, 11- 8; Rufus King & Gen. Philip Schuyler were then approved as 1st U. S. Senators from N. Y., w. King seated July 25th, in NYC, & drawing the longer term, expiring May 3, 1795; Gen. Schuyler was seated July 27th, his term expiring Mar. 3, 1791; during the 2nd election, foll. Schuyler's short term, a blank resolution was offered, Jan. 18, 1791, & the motion to insert Schuyler's name was defeated, 32- 27, & Aaron Burr was proposed & selected by the same margin; Egbert Benson waqs then proposed in Burr's stead, but defeated, 24- 34; the foll. day, Burr was concurred in the Senate, 14- 4, w. 6 Senators absent; Aaron Burr then became the 3rd U. S. Senator from N. Y., his term expiring Jan. 24, 1797; no effort was made for his re- election, & he did not receive a single vote in the next selection process; Gen. Schuyler was elected by nearly unanimous vote as Burr's successor, by general consent in the Senate, w. 35 present, & by 85 votes in the Assembly, equal to the number present, less one vote given to Gen. Schuyler's friend, James Kent; although elected to a 2nd, non- consecutive term, Gen. Schuyler did not serve, due to the infirmities of old age- **920**

SESSIONS,
Mr.- along w. Dr. Williams & Rev. Dr. Clark, sent correspondence to Gouverneur Morris, late July 1777, concerning recent resolutions made by the N. Y. Provincial Congress on the Grants issue- **796**

7th Illinois Infantry- c. 1861, incl. as Quartermaster, ____ Brown, of Salem, N. Y.; & as Adjutant, ____ Waller, of Union Village (Greenwich, N. Y.)- **1080**

SEWARD,
Asher- of Farmington, Conn.; c. 1777, res. Fitch's Point, Salem, N. Y.; during the Burgoyne alarm, he rem. to his native place, & returned foll. the Rev. war; his sons, Dyer & Timothy, were both soldiers during the war; other children- Dorothy, John, & Lucene; the family res. here for several yrs. foll. the Rev. war, & then rem. Clarendon, Vt.- **855**
Dorothy- m. James Orr- **868**
John- res. Highgate, Vt.; killed, 1832, by a fall while working at a gristmill; his wf. Polly, b. ca. 1782, was still living, 1870; refers Hemenway's Gazetteer, ii, 262- **855**
Mrs.- her 1st husb. was ____ Jordan, & their dau. Axey, m. James Thompson- **864**

SEXTON,
Salina- m. Edward, s. Edward & Ann (French) Whiteside- **805**

SEYMOUR,
Capt.- commanded militia co., Norwalk, Conn.; his co. called out, Mar. 1776, to guard the shores- **753**
D.- President, Bank of Brattleboro, Vt., as noted on a $10 bill, dated Oct. 1, 1852, found at the scene of Barney McEntee's murder, Feb. 16, 1858- **1048s**

SHARP,
Abraham- drowned, May 15, 1787, while wading across Pawlet river at the lower
falls; Joshua Conkey, Coroner- **(L)- 876**
Herman K.- (H. K. Sharpe) def. atty., Oct. 1- 7, 1858, along w. J. S. Crocker &
James Gibson, People vs. Martin Wallace- **1048s**

SHAW,
Alexander- c. 1789, purch. Lot No. 53, Argyle Patent, from Roger Reid- **802**
Cornelius- Co. A, 2nd N. Y., Northern Black Horse, Cav., 1861- 2- **1080**
James- res. E. Greenwich, N. Y.; acc. Wid. Angel, a cat found licking cream off
the milk in his cellar, c. 1800's, was suspected of being old Mrs. Tosh, transformed
into one; see Witchcraft, Witches- **871**
James- c. 1852, res. Argyle, N. Y., in the loc. occ., c. 1779, by John McDougall-
978; his farm settl., c. 1772, by Capt. James Beaty, & adjoins the S. side of Judge
Ebenezer Clark's farm- **979**
John- m. Elizabeth, dau. Robert & Susan (Lytle) Vance; he d. prior 1850, & his
wid. & sons res. a mi. S. of Salem, N. Y., on Deac. Joseph Hawley's farm- **737**
Col. John- commanded 50th Regt.; its comm. officers incl. in a procession at
Salem, N. Y., Apr. 20, 1841, commemorating the death of Pres. Wm. H. Harrison-
1009
Neal- defendant, May 19, 1774, in a case brought by Alex. McLean- **878**
Robert- m. ____ Murdock- **871**
Robert- c. 1851, res. Salem, N. Y.; his farm was prob. orig. loc. of the Bell family-
927
William- res. Lisbon, N. Y.; m. Betsey, dau. James & Elizabeth (Lytle) Rowan; one
of their sons was a lumber merch., Troy, N. Y., & d. 1849, leaving sons, incl. one
who res. at John McDonald's (n. d.) while attending Salem Academy- **737**

SHAYS,
Daniel- (c. 1747- 1825) fled through Salem, N. Y., when driven out of Mass.; he
arr. "on a stud horse, which was so fatigued & jaded out, that he was anxious to
exchange it for a fresh one"- **701**

Shays' Rebellion- c. 1786, a tax rebellion in Granville, N. Y., reportedly began
among some of his men, who had fled there; acc. Moses Billings, many Hoosick,
N. Y. residents favored the rebellion & resisted the govt., but were finally quelled
w/o bloodshed- **728**; when driven out of Mass., a no. of his supporters settl. nr.
Granville, N. Y.- ____ Prouty, ____ Blythe; & George Wilcox, who res. in Hebron,
on the road W. of Granville, that goes to Hartford, N. Y.; there was also ano.
unnamed individual- **921**

Sheep- finest wool flock of Saxony breed in Wash. co. to date (1850) owned by
John Dobbin, of Jackson, N. Y.; see Vol. 1- **732**

SHELBURNE,

Lord, Sir William Petty- (1737- 1805; 2nd Earl of Shelburne, 1st Marquis of Lansdowne; Pres., Board of Trade, 1763; opposed Stamp Act, & govt. policies on Amer. colonies, 1768- 82, until opposed in office, 1783) letter addressed to him, June 9, 1767, from Gov. Moore, referring to Shelburne's letter of Apr. 11th, & his reaction to enclosed copies of 2 petitns. & other things; details part of the history of the Province's procedures when settlers were found to be on lands gr. to others; see Grants/ N. H. Controversy- **894**; ano. letter from Gov. Moore, June 10, 1767, in response to petitn. for the Society for the Propogation of the Gospel- **895**

SHELDON,

Samuel B.- of Salisbury, Conn.; m. Louisa, dau. Gen. John Ashley; settl. Sheldon, Vt.; 2 children- John, d. y.; & Eliza, m. Dr. Chauncey, s. Jabez Fitch of Hyde Park, Vt.- **947**

Thomas- m. Mary, dau. William & Margaret (Mack) McCleary, & occ. the old McCleary farm, Rupert, Vt.- **734**

SHEPHERD,

_____- c. 1818, was a waiter for the family of David Russell, Salem, N. Y.; "a perfect sot; one morning, when kindling a fire, his breath took fire, & his body was consumed" (this was a prevalent opinion during the time period, that excessive & habitual consumption of alcohol could enhance, or lead to accelerated consumption of the body by fire; see Alcohol, Consumption of; Alcoholism; Baldwin, Capt. Ezekiel; a/o Catacusis ebrosia; Vol. 1)- **1053**

Charles A.- (Shepard) Co. A, 2nd N. Y., Northern Black Horse, Cav., 1861- 2- **1080**

George W.- of Ogdensburg, N. Y.; m. Susannah, dau. Ebenezer & Betsey (Williams) Proudfit- **1045**

SHERMAN,

"Evi"- m. Lydia, dau. Abner & Anna (Martin) Glines, as her 2nd husb.; no children by him now (c. 1850's) now living- **731**

Family- c. 1853, loc. nr. the Vt. line, along the R. R. right of way, NE of Salem, N. Y.- **1003**

Isaac- c. 1861, res. Salem, N. Y., in a house orig. built by the Cleveland family- **1073**

Marcus E.- s. Grandison; b. ca. 1840, Salem, N. Y.; d. at 21, of typhoid fever, at Ft. Rolla, Missouri; unit not given; a student at Salem Academy, he left here Apr. 1861; his remains arr. Jan. 3rd, & he was bur. Jan. 9, 1862, gr. 3, soldier's plot, Evergreen Cemetery, Salem, N. Y.- **1081**

Maria M.- m. Asa M., s. James & Lydia (Martin) McNitt- **731**

William- m. Desire Doter (Doty) as her 1st husb.; (acc. Savage, had children Hannah, Elizabeth, William, Patience, & Experience; "& he d. perhaps, early in 1681. His wid. m. 24 Nov. of that yr. Isreal Holmes, & next, Alexander Standish");

their dau. Experience, erroneously noted in Dr. Fitch's notes as surnamed
Standish- **757**
Gen. William Tecumseh- (1820- 1891) brief ment.- **1095**

SHERWOOD,
____- his militia co. called out from the neighborh. of Ft. Edward to assist in
quelling the tax revolt, c. 1786, in Granville, N. Y.- **918**
Adiel- c. 1798, res. Ft. Edward, N. Y.; his was one of the 3 principal houses ment.
as still standing within the village at that time; see Vol. 1- **804**; Feb. terms of
Wash. co. courts held at his home; refers Laws of N. Y., 1, 461; the last session
was held here Feb. 1797, bef. courts were rem. to Mary Dean's home, Kingsbury,
N. Y.- **874**; for £ 60, June 17, 1786, gr. 13¾ acres, Lot 2 of 2nd Alottment, Ft.
Edward Patent, by Robert Cochran- **(L)**- **936**
Dr.- c. 1830, along w. Dr. Richards & 1 or 2 others, dug up the Bennington dead
found on Esq. Barnet's house lot, finding the skeletons "still so perfect that they
could take out the whole bones of ea. individual body" w. only the softer parts
decayed, & took them home w. them; the remains had been bur. "lying across & on
top of ea. other, flung in at random"- **762**
Seth- Oct. 12, 1784, purch. for £ 420, Lot 39, Artillery Patent, containing 242
acres- **(L)**- **875**

SHIELL,
William- c. 1862, res. Jackson, N. Y.; prev. a church elder & longtime resid. of
Putnam, informing Dr. Fitch concerning its early settlm.- **1091**

SHIPHERD,
Esq. Samuel T.- (also given as Shepherd) c. 1850, res. Ft. Miller, N. Y.; informs
Dr. Fitch concerning the encampment of Burgoyne's army here after it left Ft.
Edward- **800**; as a child, res. Peterborough, N. H.; his family was a neighbor of
Capt. William Robb, who described to him the circumstances of Col. Baum's death
at Bennington- **801**
Zebulon R.- (1768- 1841) a leading citizen, N. Granville, N. Y.; freq. served w.
Peter Parker & Butler Beckwith on committees of the Presbyterian church here;
Hon. Nathaniel Hall & Hon. Wm. Henry Parker studied in his law office at var.
times; John C. Parker began his study of law w. him in Apr. 1798, & after
practicing in Hartford, entered into partnership w. him for 20 yrs., until Shipherd
rem. from town; see Vol. 4- **759s**

Shipherd & Parker- law firm, early 1800's, Granville, N. Y.; Hon. William H.
Parker 1st studied law here- **759**

SHIRREFF,
William- of Old Alvesford, Hants co., Great Britain; appts. Jacob Sebor, June 18, 1796, as his atty. to coll. debts & transact all of his affairs; recorded Feb. 9, 1802; refers Miscellanies, pgs. 31- 35- **880**

SHUMWAY,
Lovina- m. Nathan, s. Ephriam Warren, of Killingworth, Mass.- **1038**

SIBLEY,
Family- of Fair Haven, Vt.; daus. Aurilla, m. D. Nelson; & Arvilla, m. William King, both sons of Daniel & Ann (Glover) Barton- **1093**

SIGOURNEY,
Mrs. Lydia Howard Huntley- (1791- 1865) presumed by Dr. Fitch to be one of those individuals accountable for promoting the subj. of Mrs. (Harrison G.) Blake freezing on a mountaintop as a theme of poetry- **733**

SILL,
Richard- adm. to practice in Wash. co., Feb. 24, 1784- **878½**

SILLICK, see also, SELLECK,
Benjamin- had the foll. children- Rev. Bradley; James & Henry, who both res. Schenectady, N. Y.; & Benjamin, who res. & d. in Pennsylvania, leaving children there- **950**
Rev. Bradley- s. Benjamin; b. Aug. 1783, Danbury, Conn.; Methodist minister, res. 86th St., Yorkville, NYC; informs Dr. Fitch, Sept. 25, 1851, concerning the hist. & origins of the Sillick family; m. Polly, 2nd dau. Thomas Pattison, of Stillwater, N. Y.; children-
   1. Harriet, m. Peter Cannon Oakley
   2. Elizabeth, m. Abiather M. Osborn
   3. Elias Pattison, m. Ann Warren
   4. John Ashton, m. Esther Ann Halstead- **950**; c. 1812/3, res. Mechanicville, N. Y.; his wf. informs Dr. Fitch, on the above date, concerning the family hist. of John McNeil, of Stillwater- **951**; his wf. also gives an acct. of John Ashton, of Stillwater- **952**
Elias Pattison- (s. Rev. Bradley & Polly Pattison) businessman, Troy, N. Y., w. his uncle, & then on his own; m. Ann Warren, of Warrensburgh, N. Y.; "became involved in his circumstances, dissipated, & died", leaving one son; his Wid. superintends "the female part of the Troy House" (this may have been The Warren Free Institute, incorp. Mar. 19, 1846; see p. 561, French's Gazetteer); their son res. in Warrensburgh, w. one of his Warren family uncles- **950**
Family- had its origins from 2 bros., who emig. from England, & settl. Horseneck & Norwalk, Conn. (acc. Savage, David, soapboiler of Boston, had sons David, Jonathan; John, b. Apr. 21, 1643; & Nathaniel- David & Nathaniel settl. Boston;

John & Jonathan settl. Stamford; John's vessel was capt. by the French, May 1689, & he never returned, leaving sons David, b. Dec. 27, 1672; Nathaniel, b. Apr. 7, 1678; & John, b. June 7, 1681; it was perh. these 3 bros. who were being referred to in the acct.)- **950**

John Ashton- (s. Rev. Bradley & Polly Pattison) Methodist minister, Greenwich, Conn.; m. Esther Ann Halstead, of NYC; had 5 children- Mary Griffin; Elizabeth, dec'd.; Esther Halstead, Sarah Amelia, & John Pattison; foll. his father's death, he took up the family business, as a real estate agent, & res. 119 E. 86th St., Yorkville, NYC; on Mon., July 10, 1865, bef. 4:00 AM, he rose from bed & "(in a fit of insanity, it is supposed, he having been unwell some days)" hung himself w. a sashchord, from the bannisters of the stairs- **950**

Nathaniel- acc. Rev. Bradley Sillick, a son of the orig. emig. settler; children- Benjamin, Nathaniel, James, Lewis; & Lydia, m. Benjamin Lobdell- **950**

Surname- appears in var. forms- Selleck, Sellick, Silleck, Sillick- Dr. Fitch being uncert. in his recording of an "i" or "e" as the vowel for the 1st syllable- **950**

SIMONDS,

Col. Benjamin- of Williamstown, Mass.; Sept. 1776, commanded a Mass. brigade that marched to Fairfield, Conn.- **747**

SIMPSON,

Mary- m. James, s. Andrew & Nancy (Stewart) Lytle- **1069**

SINCLAIR,

Robert- plaintiff, May 19, 1774, vs. William Masser- **878**

SISSON,

Hiram- s. Ira; b. ca. 1829; res. a mi. E. of Buskirk's Bridge, White Creek, N. Y.; witn., People vs. Martin Wallace; he & his father were among those who went w. Dr. Morris to the scene of Barney McEntee's murder; he testif. that he had known Wallace for 4 yrs., but did not know the dec'd., Barney McEntee; he arr. at Pratt's store abt. 7:25 PM, on the night of the murder of McEntee, Feb. 16, 1858, & saw Wallace & the dec'd. there, along w. Edward Hays, Charles Allen, Charles Coit, Daniel Mosher, William I. Perry, Jr., & Morris Pratt, the store clerk; he noticed that McEntee was very much intoxicated, & sitting there by the stove "acting silly"; Hays went up to him & suggested he leave, & along w. Mosher & Wallace, he helped him out; as they were going out, McEntee claimed to want tobacco, & fell against the counter while going for it; it was then sd. by someone that he was in no condition to leave on such a cold night, but then it was sd. that Wallace, Mosher, & Hays were going along w. him; after ano. 30- 45 min., he also left, walking fast, needing to go abt. 70 rods to his father's house; when he came to the curve in the road, he found McEntee's body, & suppos. that he had fallen & passed out, but discovered that he was dead, & went home to tell his father what had happened; while in the house, he noticed it was 8:30 PM; he & his father went to the barn &

got a horse, which he rode bare- back, ¼- ½ mi. to John Larmon, who was not home, & then went ano. ½ mi. to Teunis Cronkhite's; he & Cronkhite returned to the murder scene w. a lantern, to view the body, & then alarm neighbors; they called on Elijah Chase, & then went to Buskirk's Bridge for Dr. Morris; returning to the scene, Andrew Houghton emptied the victim's pocket, & other evidence was coll.; he then went to get their cutter, & rem. the body to Buskirk's Bridge; the foll. day, he found a $10 bill from the Bank of Brattleboro at the murder scene; the remainder of his testim. concerns his whereabts. & who he saw betw. the time he left home & the time he arr. at Pratt's store- **1048s**
Ira- Corp., Co. A, 2nd N. Y., Northern Black Horse, Cav., 1861- 2- **1080**

SIYFIELD,
John- oath of alleg.; Co. D, 22nd N. Y. Inf.- **(L)- 1074**

SKELLIE,
William- Co. I, 123rd NYSV; d. Nov. 3, 1862, at abt. 24 yrs. (see § 2106; Vol. 4)- **1098**

SKELN,
____- appears, prob. erroneously, as the name of the commander of an expedition to Bennington; prob. intended as Skene- **768**

SKENE,
Maj. Andrew P.- (1753- 1826) s. Col. Philip; he & his father forfeited Lots 39 & 47, Artillery Patent, sold Oct. 12, 1784- **(L)- 875**; plaintiff, Jan. 16, 1775, vs. Jeremiah Burrows- **878**; acc. Sabine, was taken prisoner on Lake Champlain early in the Rev. war, & confined in Conn.; no acct. of either his father, or him, having accompanied Burgoyne's army- **957**
Col. Philip- (1725- 1810) (as Maj.) a letter of Sir William Johnson, Nov. 25, 1769, to Gov. Colden, notes that he has taken the rank of Col. over a militia regt. formed abt. Ft. Edward, South Bay, & its environs w/o prior notice to him- **735**; several biog. items concerning him forwarded, c. 1848, to Rev. L. Kellogg, of Whitehall, N. Y., from Chauncey K. Williams, of Williams College, "from a Manuscript Memorial in the State Paper Office, London"- appt. Gov. of Ticonderoga & Crown Point, having lands & resid. at S. extreme of Lake Champlain; empowered to raise a regt. in America, he was taken into custody, June 1775, at Philadelphia, on this basis; had been an Ensign at Cathagena (1741, Cartagena, Columbia) & Porto Bello (1739, Portobelo, Panama) under Gen. Wentworth; served at Flanders (Ont., Canada) & was Lt. at battle of Culloden (1746); served under Sir Jeffrey Amherst in Canada; 1773, appt. to run a line betw. Canada & the British colonies, & superintend settlm. of uninhabited border country; also, from Sparks, Life & Writings of Washington, v. iii, p. 523, a letter of Gen. Washington to Gen. Howe, proposing the exchange of "Gov. Skene" for Mrs. James Lovell & family; Gen. Howe's reply, dated Boston, 2 Feb. 1776, notes his intention in that direction until

the recent disclosure of a prohibited correspondence by Mr. Lovell, preventing the exchange- **760**; appears as "Skeln" in orig. text, & acc. Richard Powell, was commander of an expedition to Bennington, & not Col. Baum- **768**; by report of Capt. John Lawrence to N. Y. Provincial Congress, Oct. 12, 1775, the current impression in England is that the latest American news might be of Maj. Skene's hanging- **783**; delegations from var. townships of the region ordered by Proclamation of Gen. Burgoyne, July 10, 1777, to convene at Castleton, Vt., 10:00 AM, Wed., July 15th, where Col. Skene will give instructions for further encouragement of those complying w. his prev. 'manifesto' & advise others on conditions under which 'the persons & properties of the disobedient may yet be spared'- **795**; Gouverneur Morris reports, July 21, 1777, that he is courting the inhabitants of the Grants 'w. golden offers', gaining many to his alliance & compelling others to submission; he 'is at hand to flatter them w. being a separate Province, & what will weigh more, to give them assurances of being confirmed in their titles, however acquired'- **796**; (Gov.) one of his servants appl. to Albany Comm. of Correspondence (n. d.) for a pass to go to Conn., & suspected of carrying letters detrimental to the American cause, he was searched; a letter for Skene was discovered, opened & inspected, & the servant then ordered to pass- **830**; acc. Peter Yates, June 14, 1775, he was sd. to have spoken self importantly of himself on his arrival in Philadelphia, due to his being appt. commander at Ticonderoga, etc., '& appeared much disconcerted on his being told this important post was already occ. by a Provincial Commander on a diff. establishment'; & he was sent off under guard to Lancaster, Pa.- **833**; along w. his s. Maj. Andrew P., forfeited Lots 39 & 47, Artillery Patent, sold Oct. 12, 1784- **(L)-875**; informs the N. Y. Council, Oct. 21, 1772, that Jehiel Hawley & James Breakenridge have been appt. agents to go to England & seek compensation for the Grants people- **907**; acc. Judge Blanchard, the "current report", c. 1851, was that he had rec'd. £ 50,000 from the British govt. for his lossess during the Rev. war- **916**; his practice of enforcing the laws, & the character of the inhabitants within his township referred to by J. Griffiths, Dec. 20, 1766, in a letter to Wm. Smith, Esq.- 'they are at their protector's commands, ready to say or swear to anything in order to carry on & accomplish his revengeful designs'- **929**; he was conveyed from Hartford, Conn., Oct. 1776, to a British ship of war in the Hudson, to be exchanged for James Lovell, it not being known that Lovell was already at liberty; & he. d. 1810, in England; refers Sabine's Lives of the American Loyalists- **957**; brief ment.- **998**; same material as § 760, except that his service w. Gen. Amherst is given as 6 yrs.; refers to Manuscript Memorial, State Paper Office, London; his title as Gov. of Ticonderoga & Crown Point signifies a position as their Superintendent only; although sometimes called Gov. Skene, the title made him appear more important than he had any claim to be- **1059**

Skenesborough (Whitehall, N. Y.)- several militia alarms ordered to scout there, as early as 1775, but most reports of the enemy's approach, or presence, proved to be false- 701; Oct. 1782, a party of 8 tories & British soldiers, imprisoned at Bennington, Vt., for the attempted abduction of Esq. Bleecker, were brought here for exchange & confined at the guard house, abt. 2 mi. from the landing; Col. Walbridge's regt. was stat. here at that time- 747; c. 1781, Col. Walbridge's regt., prob. consisting of 4 companies, was stat. here & acted as freq. scouts of Lake Champlain & the surrounding region- 749; the American army left here for Canada, & a battle at Three Rivers, Apr./ May 1776- 750; spring- fall 1778, Indians & tories freq. plundered homes of the inhabitants; the militia stat. at Maj. Skene's stone house, & at the landing, were in a state of constant alarm & freq. called out, & were again in constant alarm, throughout 1779; in Mar. (prob. 1780, no yr. being given w. the month), Indians & tories attacked Skene's stone house, burning it, & capt. all the guards; Mr. & Mrs. McCall were murdered at this time; see Vol. 1- 751; a small schooner (prob. Col. Skene's) was capt. here by Capt. Jonathan Brown & Capt. Oswald, & arr. at Crown Point, May 19, 1775, joining the force here commanded by Col. Benedict Arnold- 775; petitn. presented (n. d., prob. c. 1773) to have the Charlotte co. seat establ. here, as the most convenient & populous place other than New Perth (Salem, N. Y.), having 71 families & 379 inhabitants; a petitn. was also signed by the inhabitants of New Perth in support of the measure; refers Doc. Hist., iv, p. 818- 913; conditions & practices within the township illust. by a letter of complaint, Dec. 20, 1766, from J. Griffiths, Justice of Peace, Kingsbury, N. Y., noting Col. Skene's dominance within the region-

'not choosing to have a magistrate so nr. but such as will wink at the villany of those settl. on his lands, who are mostly the offscourings of the earth- they are at their protector's commands... I was obliged to take up one of his settlers for felony, some for debt, some I had bound over for several misdemeanors, others of his servants I fined for travelling through this township on the Lord's Day. In deed I row against wind & tide.

'The sd. Skene keeps his servants to work on the Lord's Day; allows his negroes to work for one of his tenants every Sunday, in order to get small necessaries'.- 929; Mr. Arnold, of Socialborough, Vt., was once sent here w. his teams (n. d.) to deliver supplies to American troops- 968; Burgoyne's Indian forces were not here when the expedition 1st arr. in early July 1777; during the army's occ., the settlers fled, leaving their houses empty; other families, from further S., seeking protection from Burgoyne, occ. their vacant houses, but as they were not crowded (as was the case later, at Ft. Edward) there were no sicknesses or deaths; the army's tents were pitched here, & they trained daily; the settlers' cattle ranged at large, the fields of grain here were all trampled down & destroyed; acc. Mrs. MacIntyre, no relicts of boats that had been burned along the lake shore were there when her parent's family was sheltering there; the English army departed 1st, foll. by the Hessians passing through, & all the troops were gone in 5 wks.- 998; among those taken from here (prob. Mar. 1780) & carried to Quebec, was William Gray, who later became prominent among the St. Regis Indians as an interpreter, or agent, in their treaties- **1015**

SKIDMORE,
William- s. Jeremiah; coal merch., NYC; m. June 5, 1847, Charlotte Harvey, dau. Dr. Alfred & Elizabeth (Martin) Freeman; children-
  1. Alfred Freeman, b. Mar. 4, 1848; unm.
  2. Jeremiah Skidmore, b. May 31, 1851; d. Sept. 6, 1873- **730**

SKINNER,
Austin- res. abt. 1 mi. from the falls, on the road to Crown Point, Ticonderoga, N. Y.; m. Lydia Almira, dau. Newell & Charity (Blackman) Angel; 2 daus.; his wf.'s grdm., Wid. Triphena (Martin) Angel, res. w. them- **848**
James R.- Corp., Co. A, 2nd N. Y., Northern Black Horse, Cav., 1861- 2- **1080**
Roger, Esq.- (1773- 1825) res. Sandy Hill, N. Y.; appt. U. S. Dist. Atty., Mar. 3, 1815, for the N. district of N. Y.- **711**; defeated Asa Fitch, Sr., in the U. S. Congressional election, 1810- **799**

SLAYTON,
_____- res. Harmony, N. Y.; m. Harriet, dau. Edmund Henry & Hepzibah (Buel) Wells; "& has children"- **839**

SLOAN,
Hugh- m. Ester, dau. James Harsha, the emig.- **973**

SLOCUM,
James B.- Co. A, 2nd N. Y., Northern Black Horse, Cav., 1861- 2- **1080**

SLOSSON,
Amos A.- (Slossen) kept store at Wait's Corners, White Creek, N. Y.; he testif. that Martin Wallace had a running acct. w. him, pd. mostly by Marvin Wallis; this acct. continued up to Feb. 5, 1858; when he refused to let Wallace's wf. have some fish, & asked for cash; he now owed $6 on the acct., & was last asked for money on the acct. in Dec. 1857- **1048s**
Capt.- commander of a Conn. militia co., called out Jan. 1776, to guard lines nr. NYC- **753**

SMALL,
Capt. John- advised by N. Y. Council, Oct. 22, 1765, that a reserve be made from lands in his & Mr. Napier's Patents for lands actually possessed & improved by Jacob Marsh & his associates- **894**
Mr.- c. 1854/5, res. Cambridge, N. Y.; perh. Irish Catholic; when Patrick Walls' health began to deteriorate, Bridget Dwyer (who was nursing him) came to him, &

it was suspected, contacted Priest Quigley through his auspices, so that last rites might be given to Walls- **1058**

Robert- (or Smalls; 1839- 1915; 44th, 45th, 47- 49th Congress, 1875- 79, 1882- 83, 1884- 87) ment. as an heroic individual who (n. d.) 'delivered up' a steamer (the *Planter*, May 13, 1862) to Union forces during the Civil War- **799**

SMALLEY,

Elijah- res. Washington, Conn.; rem. Norwich, & then, New Concord, Vt.; enl. Capt. James Hatch's co., Maj. Horsington's regt., Green Mtn. rangers, prob. May/ June 1777; his s. Reubin replaced him in this service- **756**

Reuben- of Whitehall, N. Y.; s. Elijah; b. Mar. 26, 1762, Washington, Conn.; res. Norwich & New Concord, Vt., foll. by Albany co., N. Y.; foll. the Rev. war, he res. for 6 yrs., Stephentown, Rens. co., N. Y., & 3 yrs., Cornwall, Conn.; he afterw. res. until 1817, in Northumberland, Saratoga co., N. Y.; replaced his father in service, Capt. Hatch's co., Maj. Horsington's regt., Green Mtn. rangers; marched to Royalton, Vt., & built a picket fort there, remained until June 1777, & then marched to the Onion river, foll. by Mt. Independence; after a few days, retreated to Castleton, & then to Bennington, Vt.; he was placed in guard of baggage there & did not participate in the battle of Bennington; his co. was sent home for 5- 6 wks., & then called out to Stillwater, N. Y., w. Capt. Hatch's co., in Col. Bailey's regt.; they arr. on the E. side of the Hudson at the time of the battle (prob. the 2nd battle, Oct. 7th) but did not cross until after the battle, & he was at Burgoyne's surrender; he returned home, & his co. disbanded in Nov.; Apr. 1780, he res. 3 mi. from Albany, N. Y., & 12 mi. from the Hudson; vol. for Capt. Miller's co., Col. Farnsworth's regt., & was marched from Albany to Schoharie; he was stat. there, scouting through the season, & disch. Christmas day, foll. 8 mos. service; Apr. 1781, vol. for 9 mos., Capt. James Harrison's co., Col. Willet's regt., & marched to the Schoharie middle fort, & remained until July; he was then detailed, along w. 30 other men, under Lt. Thomas Skinner, to Woodstock, N. Y., on Catskill creek; returned to Schoharie in Oct., & the town was burnt 2 wks. later (Schoharie was actually burnt Oct. 16, 1780); he defended the fort & pursued the enemy to Ft. Plain, on the Mohawk river (Dr. Fitch notes that Col. Brown fell into an ambush at Stone Arabia during this pursuit, & was killed w. abt. 30 other men); his co. learned that the enemy had fled down Lake Oneida; they returned to bury Col. Brown, & he acted as one of the bearers at his funeral; he was then marched to Schenectady, N. Y., & was disch. Dec. 26th- **756**

SMART,

James- res. Lot 178, Salem, N. Y., purch. from Robert Chapman- **1090**

William H.- oath of alleg.; Co. D, 22nd N. Y. Inf.- **(L)- 1074**

SMITH,

____- preceded Mr. Duryea as minister in the area surrounding Schuylerville, N. Y.; he afterw. became either the President of, or a Professor, at Princeton University- **804**

____- res. nr. James More, S. part of Salem, N. Y.; a Roman Catholic, m. the sist. of Richard & William Hoy; "The folks used to wonder how Miss Hoy ever came to do such an awful thing as to marry a Catholic"; their sons were excellent marksmen, & once after the Rev. war, they were hunting somewhere down Lake Champlain; it was reported that they way laid & killed an Indian, robbing his cabin of a large & valuable quantity of furs, bringing the plunder home using the Indian's hand- sled- **1000**

Almira- m. Col. John Williams, as his 2nd wf.- **1045**

D.- oath of alleg.; Co. D, 22nd N. Y. Inf.- **(L)**- **1074**

Elizabeth- m. Morgan Lewis, s. Walter & Sarah (Turner) Martin- **1046**

Hon. Ezra- m. Maria, dau. Dr. Philip Smith; port collector, Plattsburgh, N. Y., but keeps his farm at Tyashoke, & will prob. return there; by "the current report", Maj. Bliss, the son- in- law of the late President, Gen. Taylor, is his natural son- **845**

Lt. Henry P.- Co. D, 93rd N. Y. Inf.- **1090b**

Howell- res. S. 5th St., Williamsburg, N. Y.; m. dau. Mrs. Marcia R. Fitch- **799**

James- oath of alleg.; Co. D, 22nd N. Y. Inf.- **(L)**- **1074**

James- Co. A, 2nd N. Y., Northern Black Horse, Cav., 1861- 2- **1080**

John- oath of alleg.; Co. D, 22nd N. Y. Inf.- **(L)**- **1074**

Joseph- m. Rebecca, dau. Thomas & Abigail (Dutton) Parker- **759s**

Justin A.- witn., Dec. 1, 1858, for the certif. of the execution of Martin Wallace- **1050s**

Patrick, Esq.- (1747- 1814) an ordinance advised by N. Y. Council, Sept. 8, 1773, to establ. Charlotte co. courts, to be held on 3rd Tues., May & Oct., at his house, nr. Ft. Edward, N. Y.- **910**

Dr. Philip- res. Easton, N. Y.; Dr. Asa Fitch, Sr., studied medicine w. him during 1795- **799**; of Tyashoke, N. Y.; naturalized in 1768, only s. Thomas, & cousin of Dr. Sanford Smith; children-

   1. Maria, youngest dau., m. Hon. Ezra Smith

   2. Harriet, eldest dau., unm.; deformed by rickets; she was left $10,000.00 by her father, & kept it better than any of his other heirs

   3. Philip. "at the west", somewhere betw. Rochester & Syracuse, N. Y.

   4. Platt; at one time, he possessed great influ., & had the turnpike laid out over Oak Hill, "a route that has astonished everybody, from that time to this", the route going E. of there being incomparably better;"this act is always thought of in connection w. his name; it will cause him to be remembered (unfavorably) longer than any act in his life", it having greatly enhanced his property value at the expense of a more suitable route- **845**; when he 1st arr. here, c. 1795, he boarded at Benson's Tavern, Easton, N. Y.- **861**

Platt- s. Dr. Philip; m. Maria, dau. Hon. Gerrit Wendell; forwarding merch., Michigan, on the canal there somewhere- **845**

Dr. Sandford- of New England; physician, scttl. E. of Post corners, White Creek, N. Y.; he afterw. purch. the Colvin place; 4 children- Dr. James W.; Keziah, & ano. dau., who m. Dr. John Thompson; Lawrence, res. Chatauqua co., N. Y.; he "was a quick, active, vivacious man, but unfortunately, inclined to dissipation"; a corner of one of his fields was flooded by the raising of a mill dam, & being one of the leading spirits in "the war" against the dam, he arr. one evening at Daniel Wells', "pretty well stimulated", & demanded to know Wells' intentions concerning the dam, insisting that it be opened that very night; being "as deliberate & slow in moving in any matter as the Dr. was hasty & precipitate", Wells informed him that it was a matter of too great a consequence for a decision on the spur of the moment; "much excited", Dr. Smith stated that he would immed. "go forthwith & commence a suit", & then turning, mistakenly opened the cellar door & tumbled headlong to the bottom of the stairs; coming out, he remarked, 'Neighbor Wells, I haven't taken any of your pork; good night', & returned home, somewhat sobered by the incident; he signed the call, 1785, to bring Rev. L. Mitchell to Salem, N. Y.; Dr. Fitch specul. on whether or not he studied medicine w. Dr. Williams; abt. 1814, he sold his place to the Wilcox family, rem. west & d. there- **844**

Solomon- res. Hartford, N. Y.; m. Jane, dau. William & Jane (Lytle) Russell- **737**

Solomon- c. 1798, res. N. of the Matthews family & below Ft. Miller, N. Y.; a school house & 1 or 2 small houses were loc. above him, & his home is presently (1850) occ. by the Bragg family- **804**

Strobridge- Surgeon, 93rd N. Y. Inf.- **1090b**

Rev. Theophilus- b. Feb. 17, 1800, Halifax, Vt.; grad. Yale, 1824; Yale tutor, 1826- 28; ord. pastor, New Canaan, Conn., Aug. 31, 1831, belonging to the Fairfield West Consociation, a connection he continued in until he d. Aug. 29, 1853, while passing in a steamboat on Lake George, returning from a journey undertaken to benefit his health- **1008**

Thomas- acc. Judge Gibson, res. & d. nr. Buskirk's Bridge, N. Y.; Dr. Philip Smith was his only son- **845**

Thomas- Co. A, 2nd N. Y., Northern Black Horse, Cav., 1861- 2- **1080**

Timothy- Salem, N. Y.; "July 4th, 24th yr. of Independence" (1799), he & Caleb Fisher were "killed by the bursting of a gun disch. by Nathaniel Starns- w/o malice"- Hamilton McCollister, Coroner; see Holidays, Vol. 1- **(L)- 876**

William- he was among some whigs from Sodom (Shushan, N. Y.) who, along w. 'Mad' More, drove off the cows of "black Dunk" Campbell, Aug. 1777; when lots were drawn, he obt. one, & returned it to the Campbells the foll. day, unwilling to take milk from motherless children (Campbell's wf. d. while the family was in Burgoyne's camp at Ft. Edward, in the early part of Aug.); acc. Dr. Fitch, the return prob. occurred foll. Burgoyne's surrender, when the whigs would feel more at liberty to amend for losses incurred by their tory neighbors- **1063**

Hon. William- "dec'd."; his devisees, July 5, 1773, own Lot 70, Kingsbury, N. Y., bounded S. by Lot 55, owned by Daniel Jones- **938**

William, Esq.- (or William II; 1728- 1793) c. 1771, Atty. Gen., Province of N. Y.- **902**; a letter to him, Dec. 20, 1766, from J. Griffiths, Justice of Peace, Kingsbury,

N. Y., complains of Philip Skene's manner of traducing him to the Gov.- 'not choosing to have a magistrate so nr. but such as will wink at the villany of those settl. on his lands, who are mostly the offscourings of the earth...'; see Skenesborough, N. Y.- **929**; s. William, the elder; b. June 25, 1728; m. Janet, dau. Alderman James Livingston; grad. Yale, 1745; appt. N. Y. Council, 1759; Trustee, Dr. John Rogers' Presbyterian church, NYC; appt. Chief Justice of N. Y., he espoused the royal cause during the Rev. war & was appt. Chief Justice of Canada, 1786, serving in that capacity until he d. Dec. 3, 1793; author, Hist. of the Province of N. Y., from its Discovery, to the Year 1736; see Vol. 1- **961**

William- (1697- 1769; N. Y. Council, 1753- 67) the elder; from Newport Pagnel, England; arr. NYC, 1715, & attached himself to the Presbyterian church here, at its org., 1716, or shortly thereafter; appt. member, His Majesty's Council, & Judge of the Court of the King's Bench; founder, College of N. J. (Princeton); d. Nov. 22, 1769, at 73- **961**

SMYTH,
George- deed witn., Dec. 14, 1775, Michael Hoffnagle to Robert Gorden; & Jan. 2, 1776, Archibald Campbell, Esq., to Benjamin Griffin- **(L)- 936**

Dr. George- elected June 29, 1775, as an additional Charlotte co. delegate to N. Y. Provincial Congress- **780**

Patt- (1747- 1814) c. 1770's, clerk, Charlotte/ Wash. co., N. Y.; deed witn., Nov. 26, 1773, Daniel Jones to John Jones; Dec. 14, 1775, Michael Hoffnagle to Robert Gorden; & Jan. 2, 1776, Archibald Campbell, Esq., to Benjamin Griffin; see also, Smith, Patrick- **(L)- 936**

William- deed acknowl. bef. him, June 13, 1774; Francis Panton to Michael Hoffnagle- **(L)- 936**

SNELL,
Robert- plaintiff, in separate cases, May 19, 1774, vs. John Kenney, & vs. Jonathan Baker; & Oct. 19, 1774, vs. Asahel Jacques & Phineas Gage- **878**

SNYDER,
John- Co. A, 2nd N. Y., Northern Black Horse, Cav., 1861- 2- **1080**

Socialborough, Vt.- (Rutland, Vt.) loc. Charlotte co., N. Y.; one of its bounds was a line of trees marked by Archibald Campbell, 1767, as a boundary for Clarendon, a township erected under the govt. of N. H., called Durham, & now Clarendon, Vt.; Lot No. 1 began on the E. side of Otter creek, adjoin. S. bounds of the township; its description, given in chains & links- N- 18 ch. & 10 l.; W- 65 ch. & 50 l. to Otter creek, & thence along the stream as it winds & turns, to a line of trees marked by Archibald Campbell, & thence along the S. bounds of the township S86°E67.39 to place of beginning; contains 100 acres, w. allowances; abt. 12 acres of the lot already improved by Daniel Marsh bef. its survey, 1771; Lot No. 26 adjoins S. bounds of tract, beginning at a stake on the corner of Lot No. 1, its description not elaborated; contains 200 acres, w. allowances- **745**; petitn. of proprietors & others, Apr. 8, 1772, recommending loc. of Charlotte co. Court House here- **904**; SE lots of town contained 100 acres ea.; their plan shown by Dr. Fitch's sketch, w. Otter creek running N- S on their W. side, & N. line of Durham (Clarendon, Vt.) as its S. line; Lots 1- 5, beginning S. to N., & marked, beginning last N. in Durham, w. Silas Whitney; 1- Daniel Marsh; 2- Benjamin, or Asa, Foster; 3- Oliver Arnold; 4- Jacob Marsh; & 5- Amos Marsh; orig. sketch by John L. Marsh, acc. Dr. Fitch, "corresponds w. & helps to explain the items from Deac. Brayton's deeds" (§ 745); farms presently (1852) much altered from orig., though many present lines are the same as those orig. run & marked by N. Y. surveyors & proprietors, showing more traces of their lines than any of those run by N. H. surveyors; 1st settlers, mostly from Mansfield, Conn., or Mass.; they orig. purch. titles of Lydius, & then repurch. from N. Y. proprietors; to avoid all dispute, they also purch. title from N. H., paying 3 times for their land "& still were not allowed to enjoy them in peace"; see Vermonters- **967**; despite having titles from both govts., its settlers were still not left in peace, "& the only conceivable reason why they were not, is that Allen or some of his personal friends wished to obt. the lands... & in order hereto, were determined to harass, & annoy & maltreat the settlers, & thus induce them to forsake that part of the country"; they were 1st accused of being in N. Y.'s interest, & later of being tories, even as Allen's party was in correspondence w. & prepared to join the British; some examples of their maltreatment given; see Marsh, Daniel; & Arnold, Mr.- **968**

Society for Suppression of Vice & Immorality- a convention for its formation called, June 7, 1815, Hartford, N. Y.; chairman, Dr. Proudfit, & elected as President- Rev. Dr. Alex. Proudfit; Vice President- Rev. John Dunlap; Secretary-Hon. Z. R. Shipherd; Treasurer- Martin Lee, Esq.; convention resolved, Dec. 26, 1816, to enforce immorality laws by prosecuting all those traveling on the Sabbath, & the sale of liquor on that day; a comm. of 3 appt. for ea. town, to carry out enforcements; Salem- Wm. Williams, David D. Gray, Abraham Savage; Hebron-Daniel McDonald, Wm. McClellan, David Guthrie; Cambridge- John McLean, N. S. Prince, John Hill- **713**

SONGS, of the Revolution- a Tory song, recoll., c. 1852, by Mrs. Daniel (Catharine McDougall) Livingston, pert. to the battle of Bunker Hill, sung "Hundreds of times, as my father held me on his knee"; only 3 verses recoll.- "The 17th, by break of day/ The Yankees did surprise us,/ With their strong works they had thrown up/ To burn the town & drive us./ But soon there was an order came-/ An order to defeat them:/ The rebels spread themselves like men/ And we thought we never could defeat them./ ... Whilst some lie bleeding on the ground,/ And others fast are running/ O'er hills, o'er dales, o'er mountains high,/ Crying "There's Howe a coming!"- **980**; Whig songs- "Granny O'Wale", noted as one of the most popular; Peggy Bowman, who used to spin flax for Moses Martin, Sr., was particularly encouraged by him to sing this song, among the others popular at the time- **856**; of several, "American Taxation" noted as one still in print, c. 1850; ano. longer & unnamed song, w. the foll. opening lines- "Hark, Hark, the sound of war is heard/ And you must all attend/ Take up your arms & go w. speed/ Your counrty to defend,/ Husbands must leave their loving wives,/ And sprightly youths attend/ Leave their sweethearts & risk their lives/ Their country to defend"; but "Granny O'Wale" was "the greatest favorite" among whigs in Salem, N. Y.; its lyrics recoll. by Wid. Angel, in the version Betsey Taylor used to sing, incl. 44 lines of verse, recorded by Dr. Fitch, & concluding- "You need not pretend to frighten my sons,/ In Lexington's battle they made your men run/ They're men of experience in every degree/ And will turn your great ships in their helms- a- lee/ I have thousands of sons in America born/ And to yield to be slaves they do hold it a scorn/ They are men of experience in every respect/ And they never will yield to your cursed Tea Act"- **857**; a stanza from a very long song, recalled by Capt. Daniel McDonald- "Gen. Burgoyne from Canada set sail/ With 10,000 regulars he thought would never fail/ With Indians & Canadians & tories as we've heerd/ In place of better shipping through Lake Champlain they steered"- **923**

SOULE,
Benjamin- m. Sarah, dau. Alexander Standish- **757**
Esq. Timothy- of Dutchess co., N. Y.; dau. Elizabeth, m. Paul, s. David & ____ (Allen) Cornell; see Vol. 4- **806**

S. Argyle, N. Y.- c. 1789, Roger Reid moved here, when the area was then a wilderness, his neighbors being- E- Bain family; S- McNeil family; SW- Neal Gillespie; c. 1850, a store kept here by Aaron McCall- **802**

SOUTH CAROLINA- Charleston- 759s, 799, 990, 1075b; Cowpens- 1010

SOUTH DAKOTA- as Dakota Territory- Farm Island, Ft. Randall, Ft. Sally, Indian Agency, Indian Station, James river, & Vermillion- all 1089

The SOUTHWEST- Gila river- 971; Red River (Region)- 841; (Expediton)- 1072; Santa Fe (Trail)- 971

SOUTHWICK,
James M.- 2nd Lt., Co. A, 93rd N. Y. Inf.- **1090b**

SPAIN- 949b; Corrona- 990; Salmanca- 990; the Pyrennes- 990

SPARBURN,
Thomas- c. 1773, Justice of Peace,Charlotte co., N Y.- **911**

SPARKS,
Jared- (Mr.) (1789- 1866) see Vol. 4; an acct. of Jane McCrea's capt., given to him by Samuel Standish, at Granville, N. Y., appears within the text of his Life of Arnold; Standish later notes that Sparks' version was incorrect in claiming that the Indians had wnd. him bef. he was capt. by them- **757**

SPEARS,
Lydia- of New Berlin, N. Y.; m. Silas, s. Silas & Zerniah (Martin) Conkey- **730**

SPENCER,
_____ - c. 1852, res. on the 'South flats', Clarendon, Vt.; "was a very smart man, w. abilities giving promise of his becoming highly respectable in society. He was elected to represent the town in the legislature, & when in attendence thereon at Montpelier, to the astonishment of everybody, stole a sum of money from one of his fellow members, Daniel Marsh of Hinesburgh. He was arrested, & prob. intentionally on the part of the officers who had him in charge, he was allowed to escape, & fled from the country."- **965**
Andrew- defendant, May 19, 1774, in a case brought by John Js. Bleecker- **878**
Benjamin- acknowl. warrantee deed, Nov. 20, 1772, from Jacob Marsh to Thomas Brayton, for Lot No. 5, Socialborough, Vt.; witn., Mar. 25, 1773, along w. Thomas Greene, to quit claim of Edward Arnold to Thomas Brayton, for Lot No. 5, Socialborough- **745**; one of the charges brought by the Bennington mob against Benjamin Hough, Jan. 30, 1775, was that Hough had complained to the N. Y. govt. concerning injuries made by them to Spencer & others- **881**; June 11, 1773, mortgaged 100 acres in Durham (Clarendon, Vt.) to secure £ 941, & 1,000 acres in several other shares gr. by N. Y. govt. to himself & others- **938**; one of the 1st settlers, Clarendon, Vt.; was Justice of Peace under N. Y. authority; acc. John L. Marsh, c. 1852, several Spencers who res. in this vicinity are prob. desc. of him- **965**
Benjamin- defendant, May 19, 1774, in a case brought by John Thurman, Jr., & Jan. 16, 1775, in a case brought by John Munro, Esq.- **878**
Dr. D. Carlton- (Dr. D. C.) of Cambridge, N. Y; Assist. Surgeon, 44th N. Y. Inf.; a letter posted by him from Wash., D. C., publ., Dec. 5, 1862, *Wash. Co. Post*, "narrates the marching of the Regt., Nov. 5th from Rock's Ferry, 3 ms. to Snicker's Gap- Next day through Snickersville, Philamont, over Beaver Creek & Goose Creek, 12ms. to Middlebury, & 3 ms. beyond.- Next day to White Plains, Thoroughfare, & thence towards New Baltimore"- **1095**
Family- c. 1852, res. nr. Clarendon, Vt.; perh. desc. of Benjamin, "But they have all been in humble circumstances, & some of them, tho' of fair abilities, have appeared to have a hereditary disposition (if it may be called so) to dishonesty- for they are inclined to practice it, at times when they seemed to have no motive to excuse the act"- **965**
Jeremiah- defendant, May 19, 1774, in a case brought by John Js. Bleecker- **878**

Lt. John- commanded a co., July- Dec. 1781, in Col. Willet's regt., which successfully engaged the British at W. Canada creek- **748**

SPIKE,
Ethan- prob. fictitious; a sketch of his experiences as a juryman, contrib. to the *Portland Transcript,* & reprinted, c. Feb. 1862, prob. *Salem Press*; the article, an incomplete one, entitled 'A Down- East Juryman', appears on the reverse side of a clipping pert. to the 93rd N. Y. Inf.; although apparently of humorous intent, given the audacity of its sentiments, the contents reflects var. noxious, racist, & prejudicial sentiments of the time period; see Negroes; & Newspapers- **1090frag**

SPOONER,
Paul- (Dr. Paul; 1746- 1789) seated June 21, 1775, as Cumberland co. delegate, N. Y. Provincial Congress- **777**

SPRAGUE,
David- of Cambridge, N. Y.; for £ 242, Mar. 15, 1784, deeds Lot 60, Kingsbury, N. Y., to Asa Flint- **(L)- 936**
Joseph- Co. A, 2nd N. Y., Northern Black Horse, Cav., 1861- 2- **1080**
Judge- c. 1852, res. Brandon, Vt.; dau. Eliza, m. Rodney V., s. Daniel & Mary (White) Marsh- **962**

SPROAL,
Maj.- c. 1825, erected a frame house in Ft. Miller, N. Y., where the Potter family res. in 1798- **804**

SPROULL,
John- m. Elizabeth, youngest dau. Henry Cuyler, Esq.; his wf. d. May 14, 1823, at 37 yrs., 10 mos., & 17 ds., Ft. Miller, N. Y.- **(L)- 932**

SQUIRES,
Gideon- res. Granville, N. Y.; rec'd. recommendation, Jan. 25, 1776, as 1st Lt., Charlotte co. militia- **784**

STACKHOUSE,
J.- clothier; prob. res. Cambridge, N. Y.; an unattrib. newspaper article notes the restocking of his store, opp. Fenton's Hotel, w. a newer & better assortment of items- **1028**

STAFFORD,
John- of Harwich, Vt.; for $38.00, Jan. 29, 1784, quit claim a tract in Danby, Vt., to Thomas Brayton; tract orig. owned by Nehemiah Reynolds, its boundary beginning on NW corner of Lot No. 53; refers p. 211, Book of Deeds, Danby, Vt.- **745**

Thomas- witn., Aug. 9, 1774, along w. Philip Nichols, to deed transfer from Jacob Marsh to Amariah How; Clarendon, Charlotte co., N. Y.- **745**

STALKER,

Rev. Duncan- of Argyle, N. Y.; d. ca. 1851, & left his s. James to be raised by Deac. Abraham Johnston, of W. Hebron, N. Y.- **1081**

James- oath of alleg.; Co. D, 22nd N. Y. Inf.- **(L)- 1074**; s. Rev. Duncan; b. Sept. 1840; enl. 22nd N. Y. Inf.; d. abt. Jan. 18, 1862, Columbian hospital, Wash., D. C.; bur. Jan. 23rd, gr. 11, soldier's plot, Evergreen Cemetery, Salem, N. Y.- **1081**

STANDISH,

____- c. 1752, res. Norwich, Conn.; he & ____ Branch given £ 130 security by Dr. Peletiah Fitch, for debts incurred by his bro. Asa- **838**

Alexander- s. Capt. Miles; freem. 1648; res."Captain's hill", Duxbury, Mass.; m. 1. Sarah, dau. Hon. John Alden; 2. Desire Doter (Dotey, Dote, or Doten, dau. Edward, of the *Mayflower*, acc. Savage) wid. William Sherman & Isreal Holms (Holmes); children, by 1st wf.- Miles, Ebenezer; Lorah, m. Abraham Sampson; Lydia, m. Isaac Sampson; Mercy, m. Ebb (Caleb) Sampson; Sarah, m. Benjamin Soule; & Elizabeth, m. Samuel Delano; by 2nd wf.- Thomas, Ichabod, & Desire, b. 1689; he d. 1702, & his wf. Desire, d. 1723, Marshfield, Mass.- **757**

Ens. Josiah- s. Capt. Miles; res. E. Bridgewater, Mass.; m. 1. abt. 1654, Mary, dau. Dinby (Dingley, acc. Savage) of Marshfield, Mass.; & she d. the same yr (but, acc. Savage, 'was bur. 1 July 1665... had sev. ch. by her & also by sec. w. Sarah'); m. 2. Sarah, dau. Samuel Allen of Braintree, Mass.; rem. Duxbury, Mass., & was Capt., Selectm., Deputy, & one of the council of war; abt. 1686, rem. Norwich, Conn.; children- Miles, Josiah, "& others" ('... Samuel, Isreal, Mary, Lois, Mehitable, Martha, & Mercy', acc. Savage); his desc. also res. in N. Y., Samuel being a name given for several generations- **757**

Capt. Miles- of the *Mayflower*, 1620; res. Plymouth, Mass., until 1630, & rem. Duxbury, Mass.; m. 1. Rose ____, who d. spring 1621; 2. Barbara ____, who survived him; children- Alexander, Miles, Josiah, Charles; Lora, who d. bef. him; & John; he res. at the foot of "Captain's Hill", which was named for him, & d. 1656, at 62; his genealogy & that of his children taken by Dr. Fitch as notes from the Hist. of Bridgewater, Mass.- **757**

Miles, Jr.- s. Capt. Miles; m. Sarah, dau. John Winslow; went to Boston, Mass., & d. there, 1666; his wf. m. 2, 1669, Tobias Payne; & 3. Richard Middlecot- **757**

Samuel- "believed to have been the 3rd s. of Josiah Standish, last above ment."; his genealogy taken as "a verbal statement rec'd. from Samuel Standish,Granville, Aug. 16, 1850", by Dr. Fitch; b. in the Preston part of Norwich, Conn.; m. Deborah Gates (b. Feb. 22, 1684, prob. Stow, Mass., dau. Thomas & Elizabeth (Freeman) Gates, who rem. 1703, Norwich, Conn., acc. Savage); his eldest s. Samuel, b. Dec. 1, 1713, Preston, Conn.- **757**

Samuel, 2nd- (s. Samuel & Deborah Gates) b. Dec. 1, 1713, Preston, Conn.; m. Abigail Backus; refers § 242; see Vol. 1; eldest s. Samuel, b. May 8, 1753, Norwich, Conn.; & he d. abt. 1799- **757**

Samuel, 3rd- b. May 4, 1754, Norwich, Conn.; res. Granville, N. Y.; contents of his Rev. war pens. appl., May 8, 1832; c. 1776, res. Stockbridge, Mass., & vol. for Capt. Hewin's militia co. when tories disturbed & broke up sittings of the Comm. of Safety, New Canaan, N. Y.; 28 days service; enl. Sept. 1776, as 2 months' man, Capt. Hewin's co., later commanded by Lt. Hart, & afterw. by Lt. Colt; officers in his brigade were Col. Simonds, Maj. Rossiter, & Gen. Benjamin Lincoln; marched to Fairfiled, Conn., & 2 days later marched via Horseneck to NYC, meeting the retreating army; began building a fort at Valentine hill, but then retreated further N. & participated in battle of White Plains; marched & encamped at North Castle until disch., late Nov. 1776; his militia co. called out, 1777, in response to Burgoyne's invasion; abt. July 8, marched to Ft. Ann, N. Y., via Richmond, Hancock, & Williamstown, Mass., then to Pownal & Bennington, Vt., & finally, to Ft. Miller, Ft. Edward, & then Ft. Ann; joined Capt. Rowley's co., which was called along w. ano. to capt. a scow lying in Wood creek w. 2 field pieces on it; met the enemy- British, tories, & Indians, while proceeding towards the creek, & drove them up Battle hill; went to the rear of the hill w. Capt. Rowley & others, & attacked them from ano. position, driving the enemy from the ground & capt. the British Capt. Montgomery; retreated to Ft. Ann, & the entire army retreated towards Ft. Edward nr. nightfall; the foll. morning, arr. at Ft. Edward, foll. a skirmish w. tories & Indians at Sandy Hill; was called upon to relieve the guard on the hill above Ft. Edward, & witn. an Indian skirmish & capt. of Jane McCrea; capt. here as well, he was later interviewed by Gen. Simon Frazier & then sent to Ft. Ticonderoga w. other prisoners, where he escaped w. 3 other prisoners to Arlington, Vt.; when 1st enl., he res. W. Stockbridge, Mass., & since the Rev. war, at Granville, N. Y.; c. 1782, he was res. Bennington, Vt., when a party of 4 tories & 4 British soldiers came out of Canada & attempted to abduct Esq. Bleecker, who was capt. at his oat farm in Pittstown, N. Y., along w. his hired man & a negro; shortly afterw., the enemy party was capt., & he was appt. Sgt. of a 16 man guard that held the 8 kidnappers in a schoolhouse until they were sent in Oct. to Skenesborough, for exchange; refers Kettell's American Poetry, v. 1, p. 212, & Stone's Life of Brant, ii, p. 178- **747**; (s. Samuel, 2nd, & Abigail Backus) b. May 8, 1753, Norwich, Conn.; m. Lois Curtis, prob. in Pawlet, Vt.; during the Rev. war, he rem. Bennington, Vt.; served, 1777, & rec'd. a pension of less than $40.00 per annum; an eyewitn. to Jane McCrea's murder; while res. in Granville, N. Y., he gave a statement, found in Spark's Life of Arnold, that he later claimed was altered by the author, erroneously stating that he was wnd. when capt. by the Indians at the time that they took Jane McCrea; imprisoned at Ticonderoga, foll. his escape, he cut across country from Kingsbury, N. Y., to Arlington, Vt., sleeping overnight in the woods bef. deeming it safe to make his presence known; Esq. Parker vouches for the reliability of his claims, having known him "long & well"; in commenting further upon his character & the habit of other Rev. war veterans, Parker states that he would drink, & when "exhilerated" by liquor, would use profane language & prob. paint & adorn his stories, but was not a man of character to utter "anything that was a sheer fabrication"; d. Mar. 8, 1841, & bur. W. of N. Granville, N. Y.; the bur. grd. loc. a mi. W., on the edge of the Ft. Ann town line- **757**

Samuel, 4th- (Samuel, Jr., s. Samuel & Lois Curtis) their only s., b. Feb. 26, 1786, abt. 4 months after the family settl. in Granville, N. Y.; m. Elvira, dau. Jacob Allen; no sons, one or more daus.- **757**; his wf. Elvira, dau. Jacob & Lucy (Howard) Allen, expostulates that her family origins were prob. connected w. that of Samuel Allen of Braintree, Mass., an ancestor of her husb.- **758**

STARK,

Anna- (Starks) wf. Isreal; d. Apr. 28, 1802, at 38- **(L)- 772**

Gen. John- (1728- 1822) the detachm. under Col. Breyman arr. at the Bennington battlesite at the point when Col. Baum was defeated, forming a 2nd battle w. Stark- **728**; instead of coming along the Bennington highway & attacking the tory breastworks 1st, as Col. Baum anticipated, he kept his force on the N. side of the Walloomsac river, wholly out of sight & reach of Baum's cannon, & foll. up the hollow where the brook runs until he came directly upon the Hessian breastwork w. all of his force- **762**; his army encamped in the Henry family's orchard prior to the Bennington battle, abt. 2 mi. above Esq. Barnet's brick house, & 3½ mi. W. of the Bennington Court House; he reportedly found fault w. Col. Warner for not arr. at the battlefield sooner- **764**; Capt. Wm. Robb, of Petersborough, N. H., was a private in his regt. at Bennington- **801**; immed. prior to the Bennington battle, he & several officers stopped to obt. a draught of milk & water at Mr. Munro's, a loyalist house; when it was discovered that Munro was not there, one of his officers inquired of his whereabts., & when his wf. was unable to say, the officer drew his sword, endeavoring to intimidate her; on hearing the commotion, Gen. Stark severely reproved the officer's behavior, & the offender went out of the house much abashed- **953**; marched from Bennington, Aug. 14, 1777, proposing to attack Col. Baum the foll. morning, but the attack was prevented until Aug. 16th, by the heavy rains of the 15th- **1072**

STARKWEATHER,

_____- m. dau. _____ & Matilda (Martin) Brackett; they res. out W.- **730**

_____- m. Abby, dau. Jerry & Matilda (Cheney) Brockett- **1038**

Infant- Jan. 13, 1800; strangled by Comfort Starkweather, its mother? late of Skenesborough, N. Y.; John Perigo, Coroner- **(L)- 876**

STARR,

Comfort- of "Dembury" (Danbury, Conn.); his heirs, John & Daniel Starr, & Thomas & Henuriah Hill, transfer, Jan. 17, 1767, an undivided parcel of Kingsbury, N. Y., to James, John, & Amos McKenney- **(L)- 936**

STEARNS,
James- (s. Livy & Eliza Wells) kept the Stearns Hotel, Troy, N. Y., foll. his father-
839
Livy- hotelkeeper, Troy, N. Y.; "& too great a patron of his own bar, which
shortened his life"; m. Eliza, dau. James & Clarinda (Griffin) Wells; children-
James, Mary, Helen, & one other- **839**
Nathaniel- (Starns) he disch. a gun "w/o malice", killing Caleb Fisher & Timothy
Smith, July 4, 1799, Salem, N. Y; Hamilton McCollister, Coroner; see Holidays,
Vol. 1- **(L)- 876**
Seth- of Granville, N. Y.; juror, Oct. 1- 7, 1858, People vs. Martin Wallace- **1048s**

STEELE,
Alexander- (s. Deac. John & Eleanor Webster) res. Essex co., N. Y.; m. Betsey,
dau. Alexander & Sarah (McCoy) McNish- **1047**
Daniel- (s. Deac. John & Eleanor Webster) m. Nancy, dau. Maj. Lytle- **1047**
Col. John- (s. Deac. John & Eleanor Webster) teamster, res. on his father's farm,
Salem, N. Y.; he later sold the farm (1850's) to Hon. Bernard Blair; m. Ann
Kimberly; no children; his wf. d. 1872- **1047**
Deac. John- res. N. part of Salem, N. Y.; his farm orig. belonged to ____ Gibson,
the tory, was confiscated, & purch. by Judge Webster, bef. Deac. Steele occ. it;
m. 1. Mary, dau. David Tomb; she d. w/o issue; 2. Eleanor, dau. Judge Alexander
Webster, of Hebron; children-
1. Alexander, m. Betsey McNish
2. Polly, m. Daniel McFarland
3. Thomas, m. Sally McNish
4. James, unm., d. 1816, of consumption
5. Jane, m. ____ Wilson
6. Col. John, m. Ann Kimberly
7. Daniel, m. Nancy Lytle
8. Helen, m. Andrew Lytle
9. Margaret, m. John Doig; he was a carpenter & mill wright, "made the window
sashes, pew doors & c. of the White Church"- **1047**
Thomas- (s. Deac. John & Eleanor Webster) res. Salem, N. Y.; m. Sally, dau.
Alexander & Sarah (McCoy) McNish; they "have children, Z. R. Pike Steele the
only boy"; his wf. d. June 4, 1865, at 78; & he d. Apr. 26, 1865, at 74- **1047**

STEVENS,
Harvey- m. Sarah, dau. Silas & Zerniah (Martin) Conkey; he d., leaving 3 children
at Martinsburgh, N. Y.- Julia, m. Henry W. Hunt; Allen, m. Mary Burt; Mary, m.
Harrison Barnes; & Marcellus, d. Nov. 1848- **730**
John- res. Lysander, N. Y.; m. Hannah, dau. Paul & Elizabeth (Soule) Cornell-
806
John- Co. A, 2nd N. Y., Northern Black Horse, Cav., 1861- 2- **1080**

Simon- of Charlestown, N. H.; member, Gen. Assembly of the Province of N. H.; his deposition, sworn Mar. 2, 1771, states that Gov. Wentworth had often spoken w. him abt. annexing the Grants, w. the belief that it could easily be done- **896**

STEVENSON,
Benjamin- Deputy Surveyor of N. Y.; he was surveying along the Onion river w. John Brandon & John Dunbar, Sept. 29, 1772, when Remember Baker, Ira Allen, & 5 others came upon them, taking their property & effects, & throwing Dunbar into a fire- **306**
Family- res. on the Merrill farm, N. of Salem, N. Y., & afterw., for 1- 2 yrs. in the village, next to David Rumsey; rem. Steuben co., N. Y.; their s. John B., res. Wheeler, N. Y.- **1078**
James- Preceptor, Salem Academy; ments. s. James, Jr.- **721**; c. 1817- 19, Preceptor, Salem Academy- **1053**
James, Jr.- s. James; June 6, 1814, joined w. Dodd & Rumsey, in partnership at *The Northern Post,* & continued there w. Dodd foll. Rumsey's departure (abt. Jan. 1, 1815), or until nr. Dodd's death (Oct. 1834)- **721**; printer; some local publications noting his partnership w. Henry Dodd, dated 1818 & 1825; see Publications- **1082**
Deac. James B.- c. 1861, res. Salem, N. Y.; see Vol. 3- **1078**
John B.- res. Wheeler, N. Y.; visits Dr. Fitch, Dec. 24, 1861, along w. his cousin, Deac. James B. Stevenson, & informs concerning David Rumsey's printing business- **1078**
Joseph- res. N. of Salem, N. Y., during the Rev. war; John Todd res. next above him- **744**
R. M.- witn., Dec. 1, 1858, for the certif. of the execution of Martin Wallace- **1050s**

STEWART,
_____ - res. along Black creek, nr. Fitch's Point, Salem, N. Y.; see Vol. 1; acc. Wid. Angel, his house was orig. occ. by a Gillis family- **865**
Capt.- Aug. 1782, commanded a co., Col. Walbridge's regt. of Vt. State troops; stat. Arlington, Vt., his co. marched toWhitehall, N. Y., & reportedly was the only co. stat. there at the time- **752**
Esq.- c. 1850, occ. a house at Ft. Miller, N. Y., that orig. belonged to Noah Payne- **804**
Lt. Daniel- c. 1779, along w. Lts. Fuller, Boggs, & Gould, one of the alternating commanders of militia guards & scouts at Skenesborough (Whitehall, N. Y.)- **751**
David- plaintiff, May 19, 1774, vs. Neal Shaw- **878**
David G.- Co. A, 2nd N. Y., Northern Black Horse, Cav., 1861- 2- **1080**
George- operated a distillery (n. d.) in the Greenwich part of Argyle Patent- **873**
James- c. 1786, either he, or James Armstrong, was Capt. of the Salem militia, when it was ordered out to quell the tax rebellion in Granville, N. Y.- **701**
James- plaintiff, Nov. 3, 1784, vs. Robert Cochran- **878½**
James- deed witn., May 6, 1775, Francis Panton to Michael Hoffnagle- **(L)- 936**

Deac. Joseph- prob. res. Ft. Miller, N. Y.; dau. m. James, s. Elijah & Martha (McAllister) Mack- **734**

Lt.- c. 1781, officer, along w. Lt. Jonathan Wright, Capt. Parmlee Allen's co., Col. Walbridge's regt.- **754**

Lt.- c. 1777, officer, Capt. Eaton's light- horse co., prob. of Windham co., Conn.; he was detailed to remain at Bennington, Vt., w. part of his co., to act as scout & for sending expresses- **763**

Nancy- c. 1750's, m. Andrew Lytle, prob. Monaghan, N. Ireland- **1069**

Robert- m. Jane, dau. James & Rebecca (Lytle) Mills, as her 1st husb.- **737**

STILES,

Beriah- politically a Buck- tail, succeeded James B. Gibson, Esq. (n. d.), as editor, the *Washington Register-* **721**

J.- res. Granville, N. Y.; the Washington Benevolent Society's commemoration of Washington's birthday occurred at his house, Feb. 23, 1816; see Holidays- **723**

Ransom- of Argyle, N. Y.; m. Hannah, dau. Dr. Andrew & Mary (Lytle) Proudfit- **1069**

STIRLING,

Lord, William Alexander- (1726- 1783) late fall 1781, a packet was sent by him to the British commander at Crown Point, announcing the surrender of Cornwallis- **750**; s. James Alexander; his sist. Mary, m. Peter Van Brugh Livingston- **961**

STOCKINGS,

Capt. John- purch. Lot No. 1, Turner's Patent, Aug. 16, 11th yr. of Independence (1786) from Joseph McCracken & John Williams- **(L)- 936**; (Capt.) res. Granville, N. Y.; his lands form the N. bounds of an acre of Morrison's Patent, sold Aug. 6, 1785, by Daniel H. White to Capt. Thomas Converse; for £ 13, purch. Lot No. 1, Morrison's Patent, containing 23¾ acres- **(L)- 936b**

STOCKWELL,

Capt. Levi- c. 1779, commanded a co. at Skenesborough, N. Y.- **750**; c. 1778, commanded a co.of 8 months' men stat. at Skenesborough; acc. Moses Harvey's Rev. war pens. appl., he was prev. a Lt. at Ft. Stanwix, or some other fort; acc. Dr. Fitch, he was the one who crept out of Ft. Stanwix to warn the whigs of the fort's investment; he later res. on the old turnpike, at Whitehall, on the road to Granville, N. Y.; refers Stone's Life of Brant, i, p. 254- **751**; Oct. 1779, his co. was the only one stat. at Whitehall, N. Y.- **754**

STODDARD,

Reuben- (or perh. William, who d. 1854, at 75; p. 245, Hollister's Pawlet; see Vol. 1) res. his life long, a mi. S. of Mark's corners, Vt., along the Indian river, in the NE part of Hebron, N. Y.; Dr. John Williams made arrangements w. him to board for a few days when he 1st arr. in the area, & had not decided to settle;

during a day of trout fishing, Dr. Williams lost his purse (compare w. § 915) containing all of his money; apprehensive abt. whether his host would believe his story, or suspect a subterfuge to avoid payment, he retraced his steps, to no avail; Stoddard assisted in a 2nd search, & the foll. day, a 3rd & final search was made; while in this process, Stoddard discovered the tassel of the purse protruding above the mud in the margin of the stream, the weight of the purse having sunk it into the slime; he waited for Williams to come within sight of his discovery & then attempted to alarm him w. fears that he intended to filch the purse, as he "in great hurry crowded the purse into his pocket, & took to his heels, as if to run away w. the recovered treasure"; after a lengthy race over the terrain, "he gave over", & Williams came up w. him, receiving the purse; not knowing whether it had been pilfered or not, Williams counted it, & finding all the money there, loosened the strings & instructed Stoddard to take whatever he pleased for his time in the search, & his honesty; Stoddard refused any recompense, & when they arr. at his home, Williams opened his trunk & gave him a pr. of English vest patterns, promising that if he should settle in the region, he would provide all his family's medical needs w/o charge; Dr. Williams faithfully kept to his promise for the remainder of his life; being of humble means & w. a family, Stoddard could easily have sunk the purse & return later to retrieve it, however, his honesty lead Dr. Williams to decide to settle in the region- **924**

STONE,
Abner- along w. Alexander McNish, Overseer of the Poor, Salem, N. Y.; Sept. 26, 1815, they offered a $30.00 reward concerning a Mrs. Bealy, who had abandoned a newborn child in town- **718**; Sheriff, Wash. co.; once while riding on horseback, he struck a blow to the animal w. his rawhide, & by some mishap, hit himself across the thigh, "the stroke was so severe- the leg swelled & [illeg.] was very painful, & finally spasms similar to lock- jaw came on"; while physicians were at a loss to determine the cause, Dr. Williams was called to him immed. upon his return from the current Congressional session; after examining the case, the rawhide, & all the attending circumstances, he concluded that rawhide or some extraneous substance had been imbedded in Stone's flesh by the blow; to the objections of the other physicians, he cut into the wnd., & at length, rem. a piece of rawhide that had been festering there- **915**
Thomas- plaintiff, Oct. 19, 1774, vs. Jonathan Baker- **878**

The Stone Paper Mill- loc. E. of the Bennington battlefield, along the Walloomsac river, Rens. co., N. Y.; owned, c. 1853, by Mr. Orr; the grave of Col. Baum & several of the mortally wnd. from the battle were bur. nr. its site, "abt. 30 or 40 ft. W. of the W. end of sd. papermill"- **1022**

STORRS,
Mehitabel- m. Nathaniel Hall- **759s**

STOUT,
Joseph- c. 1813, he & Wm. McKellip were engaged as carpenters for erecting Fitch's Woolen Factory- **799**

STREET,
Alfred Billings- (1811- 1881) res. Albany, N. Y.; 'the poet', & keeper of the State Library (dir., 1848- 62); m. dau. Smith & Sarah (Fitch) Weed- **799**

STRINGHAM,
Joseph- along w. John Williams, & Samuel & Wm. McKinly, Feb.27, 1787, purch. for £ 2,750, Lot No. 23, Skenesborough, N. Y., containing 500 acres- **(L)- 875**

STRONG,
Capt. Thomas J.- of Sandy Hill, N. Y.; May 25, 1861, commanded Co. H, 22nd N. Y. Inf.- **(L)- 1074**
Mr.- R. R. conductor; he narrowly escaped mortal injury, Jan. 3, 1854, when a wheel flange broke as the 9:00 AM train was nearing the Hoosic bridge, nr. Schaghticoke, N. Y.; however, although no passengers were injured, his brakeman was killed instantly- **1021**

STROW,
George B.- Deputy Clerk, Wash. Co.; witn., Dec. 1, 1858, for the certif. of the execution of Martin Wallace- **1050s**

STUART,
George- of NYC; 'a disbanded soldier having served in North America during the late war & last belonging to the 78th Regt. of Foot'; along w. John McDonald, ano. disbanded soldier of the same regt., gr. 100 acres by Patent, loc. on E. side of the Hudson river, Albany co., beginning at the SW corner of land surveyed for Angus McDugald; the part vested in McDugald assumed by Stuart in deed; w. wf. Elizabeth, conveys his gr., May 8, 1766, to William Malcom, for £ 15; recorded May 24, 1775, bef. John H. Cruger- **(L)- 936**

STURGIS,
Gershom- of Albany, N. Y.; now dec'd. (prob. 1850); m. Elizabeth, dau. Andrew & Elizabeth (Fitch) Rowland; no children; his wf. was one of Dr. Fitch's informants concerning the Fitch ancestry- **799**

SULLIVAN,
Gen. John- (1740- 1795) officer witn. during Apr. 1776- Feb. 1777 service of Ebenezer Farnsworth, acc. his Rev. war pens. appl.- **750**

SUNDERLAND,
Peleg- res. Charlotte co., N. Y.; a member of the Bennington mob, he approached Benjamin Hough, Jan. 26, 1775, w. a hatchet in his hand, & made him a prisoner of the mob- **881**

SWAIN,
James- Queensbury, N. Y.; Feb. 13, 1788, frozen to death; Peter B. Tearse, Coroner- **(L)- 876**
William C.- 2nd Lt., Co. B, 93rd N. Y. Inf.- **1090b**

Swanzey vs. Byfield- court case, 1732, prob. Suffolk co., Mass.; Hon. Thomas Fitch, a Justice of the Court of Common Pleas, unable to preside over the issue due to lameness w. gout; refers Washburn's Judicial Hist. of Mass., p. 336- **799**

SWART,
Dirck- res. Stillwater, N. Y.; oneof the Albany co. delegates, N. Y. Provincial Congress; gr. leave of absence, May 30, 1775, to superintend rem. of cannon fron Ft. Ticonderoga to head of Lake George- **773**; his appt. noted again- **774**; allotted £ 200 from Treasury of the colony of N. Y., & £ 700 from the loan officers of Albany co., the Provincial Congress pledging themselves for their several portions of their sums- **776**; owned the foll. parcels of Schuyler's Patent- Lot No. 1- 8acres; & 2 acres, 2 roods, & 24 perches; Lot No. 5- 321 perches; Lot No. 6- 1 rood, 6 perches; & 20 acres, 1 rood, & 16 perches; all purch. by William Duer, Esq., & mortgaged by him, Feb. 14, 1769- **935**

SWEENEY,
Edward- Co. A, 2nd N. Y., Northern Black Horse, Cav., 1861- 2- **1080**

SWEET,
Almon- res. SE part of Salem, N. Y.; his s. Henry G., d. Harper's Ferry,Va.- **1098**
Henry G.- refers § 1133; bur. gr. 18, soldier's plot, Evergreen Cemetery, Salem, N. Y.- **1081**; s. Almon; Co. H, 123rd NYSV; d. abt. Dec. 30, 1862, in hospital, Harper's Ferry, Va.- **1098**
John C.- res. N. Hoosick, N. Y.; Barney McEntee res. w. him, & he testif. that he pd. $50 to McEntee 3 or 4 wks. bef. he was murdered, in money partly from the Adams bank, & partly from the Cambridge Valley bank; he also loaned McEntee the gloves he was wearing when he left his home, Feb. 16, 1858, the day of the murder- **1048s**

SWITZER,
Godliel- British Commissary, Ft. Ticonderoga; presented petitn. to Albany Comm. of Correspondence, July 9, 1775, representing himself in that capacity in the King's service; since the taking of the fortress, he has been sent to Albany, & 'is in a suffering condition w. his family, & is willing to serve his country'; comm.

resolved that they had no post or office to bestow to 'put him in any way of getting his bread', & recommended he go to NYC, furnishing him w. provisions out of the provincial stores; see Swisher, Vol. 1- **817**

SWITZERLAND- La Tour- 1045; Zurich- 1075b

SWORDS,
Lt.- along w. Capt. McAlpin & John Munro, an order, June 4, 1776, directs their removal to ano. place of confinement 'prepared for them in the fort' (prob. at Albany, N. Y.)- **889**

SYLVESTER,
Peter- (Silvester) corroborates Dr. John Williams' nomin. as surgeon for Col. Van Schaik's regt., pointing out his ignorance of any other arrangement w. regard to his replacement by Stephen McCrey, until Dr. Williams' Aug. 10, 1777 letter on the matter- **790**
Resetta- m. Dr. Samuel Curtis, s. Luther & Martha (Curtis) Parker- **759s**

T

TAGGERT,
David- m. Sarah, dau. Aaron & Olive (Harding) Martin- **1040**

TALLER,
Family- 2 bros., who occ. the place at Fitch's Point, Salem, N. Y., orig. belonging to Timothy Titus; their bro.- in- law, Thomas Williams, res. w. them; the bros. rem. Half Moon, N. Y., & operated a tavern there- **803**; from Stillwater, N. Y.; bros. Reuben & Swarrass; their sist. prob. m. Samuel Williams, the schoolteacher; they returned to Stillwater, & their place was later occ. by Reuben Cheney- **859**

TALLMADGE,
_____- c. 1817, attended Salem Academy, boarding at Rev. Dr. Proudfit's- **1053**
David- res. N. of Greenwich, N. Y.; shortly bef. New Year's, c. 1854/5, he discovered Patrick Walls "ere conscoiusness had fully returned, trying to raise himself up by a tree" foll. an accident that he had while chopping wood for Archibald Hay- **1058**
Mr.- offered a voluntary toast, w. classical allusions, at a public banquet given to honor Commodore Thomas Macdonough, Nov. 29, 1814, Salem, N. Y., referring to "The British fleet on L. Champlain- I who once was great as Caesar, Am now reduced to Nebuchadnezer"- **709**

TANNER,
John- char. witn., Samuel Standish's Rev. war pens. appl.- **747**; b. July 16, 1760, Exeter, R. I.; abstr. of his Rev. war pens. appl., sworn July 16, 1832; served 6 wks., Sept. 1776, as substitute, guarding the coast; enl. Oct. 1779, Lanesborough, Mass., for 1 month, Capt. Barn's co.; enl. forepart of May 1781, Granville, N. Y., for 9 mos., under Lt. Jonathan Wright, Capt. Parmlee Allen's co., Col. Walbridge's militia regt.; stat. Skenesborough (Whitehall, N. Y.) & freq. sent out on scouts of the region, some portions constantly employed abt. Lake Champlain; served 6 mos., then dismissed in the forepart of Nov.; refers p. 222, Duer's Life of Stirling; no witns. offered to prove his service- **749**

TARBELL,
Fanny- m. Pennel, s. Nathan & Lovinia (Shumway) Cheney- **1038**

Taxes- 1816- Wash. co. total- $27,955.56; of this total, $16,052.65 was to defray war exspenses; portions also given for var. towns- **725**

TAYLOR,

_____- m. dau. Jonathan & Sarah (Saltonstall) Fitch- **799**
_____- m. David Hann, s. William & Mary (Hanna) Lytle- **1069**
Wid. Betsey- her version of the lyrics to "Granny O'Wale", a whig song of the Rev. war, recoll. by Wid. Angel- **857**; m. _____, s. William Taylor; her history of 'old Mrs. Tosh', who developed a reputation as a witch, believed by Dr. Fitch to be more clearly remembered than Wid. Angel's recoll.- **871**; an heir of Peletiah Fitch; relates data concerning his bro. James- **1004**; worked for Deac. Daniel McNitt & his father at the time of the War of 1812; she recoll. how the events of this war revivied memories of the Rev. war among the older inhabitants- **1018**; she occ. a chamber in Dr. Fitch's house, July 11, 1860, when earthquake tremors were felt by guests & family members- **1075**
Duncan- his house (§ 132) was the 1st place where "Abe, the negro" (Abraham Kilmer) brought news of his discovery of the Allen Massacre; see Vol. 1- **983**
John- along w. Stephen Lush & John Williams, May 25, 1785, purch. the foll. forfeited lands, Skenesborough (Whitehall, N. Y.)- for £ 155- Lots 15- 18, containing 1,615 acres; for £ 277- Lots 30, 32, & 46, containing 1,218½ acres- **(L)- 875**
Lansing G.- c. 1798, Ephriam Crocker's bro. res. along the Hudson, just S. of Moses kill, where Taylor has "lately built" (1850) a mansion- **804**
William- res. E. Greenwich, N. Y.; early June 1814, he was crossing Angel's bridge w. his wf. & child, when both the bridge & child "were precipitated into the stream", after the parents had crossed; the "impetuosity" of the current & floating timber rendered recovery of the child impracticable, & the parents "beheld the little sufferer engulfed in the turbid wave"- **702**; his child's drowning noted again- **847**; a son, m. Betsey _____; his wf. was one of the attendants who dressed the body of old Mrs. Tosh for bur.; foll. these preparations, she was unable to spin on her wheel at night for several mos. w/o thinking that if she were to draw the thread further than the length of the wheel, then Mrs. Tosh, standing in the shadows, would catch & carry her away in death- **871**
Pres./ Gen. Zachary- (1784- 1850) a dau., m. Maj. Bliss, who was reportedly the natural s. Hon. Ezra Smith, of Plattsburgh, N. Y.- **845**

Teaching- c. 1820, avg. Wash. co. wage was $8- 10 per month- **1053**

TEARSE,
Peter B.- appl. for 40 guns, Aug. 9, 1775, as Capt. of a grenadier co. being raised in Albany, N. Y.; the Comm. granted a loan of that no.- **819**; recommended to Gen. Schuyler, prob. Feb. 1776, for position as Adjutant- **826**; res. Ft. Edward, N. Y.; m. grdau., Wid. McNeil; Sheriff, Wash. co., c. 1789; 2- 3 yrs. bef. he rem. Salem, N. Y., Anthony I. Blanchard "became an inmate" in his family, & observed that Terase "got into bad habits", which increased so much that he lost all of his property & rem., prob. to Albany, & perh. d. there- **914**; c. 1786, ordered out the "posse comitatis", to quell the tax revolt in Granville, N. Y.- **918**

TEFFT,
Betsey- m. Alphonso, s. Capt. Abner & Miriam (Martin) Dwelly- **731**
David- m. sist. Lyman Woodard; their s. Henry H., b. ca. 1823; purch. Lot 99,
Turner's Patent, the Deac. Abram Savage farm, from Newcomb Cleveland, c. 1836,
& res. there abt. 2 yrs.; he sold out, & took rooms w. Josephus Martin, at Fitch's
Point, then next rem. Battenville, foll. by Greenwich, N. Y.- **971**
Family- bros. David, & "Brint"; their old family homestead loc. at the lower end of
Battenville, Greenwich, N. Y.- **971**
Judge Henry- (s. David & ____ Woodard) b. ca. 1823; res. San Luis Obispo,
Calif.; studied law in Greenwich, N. Y., & shortly after adm. to the bar, emig.
Wisc.; 1840, went overland by Santa Fe, to Gila, & then to California; settl. San
Luis Obispo, 1849; member, Constitutional Convention, & elected Judge, 2nd
Judicial District; m. July 1850, "Senorita Eliza Josefa, eldest dau. of one of the
oldest & most respected American citizens of our state, Capt. Wm. G. Dana"; d. at
29 yrs.; news of his drowning arr. in NYC, Mar. 17, 1852, by the steamer *Ohio-*
971

TELFAIR,
Family- from N. Ireland; c. 1830, arr. Salem, N. Y., shortly bef. the birth of their s.
John; they res. on the upper part of the James McNitt farm, & c. 1848, rem.
Schuylerville, N. Y.; their son's body was discovered, acc. May 1, 1852 notice, at
Saw Mill Flat, Calif., "having been murdered, as was suppos., by a Mexican who
was seen in his company. He was suppos. to have had $1,200 or $1,400 w. him";
he had been in Calif. abt. 3 yrs., "having gone tither w. one of the 1st companies
from this district"- **972**

TELFORD,
____ - res. N. of Argyle corners, N. Y.; m. Jane, dau. David & ____ (Lowrie)
Dobbin- **732**

TEN EYCK,
____ - of Albany, N. Y.; heir of orig. patentee, Walloomsac Patent; his farm, which
incl. the Bennington battlesite, purch. c. Feb./ Mar. 1792, by Esq. Barnet- **763**

TENNESEE- Chattanooga- **1095**; Ft. Donelson- **1095**; Ft. Pillow- **799**; Nashville-
1095; Pittsburgh Landing, Shiloh- **1095**

THATCHER,
Josiah- of Norwalk, Conn.; m. Mary, dau. Gov. Thomas Fitch; 5 children- **799**

THOMAS,
Gen. David- (1762- 1831) his wf.'s sist. was Sarah Turner, a half sist. of Col. John
Williams- **730**; m. as his 2nd wf., Wid. ____, a sist. of Miss Hogeboom, of
Columbia co., N. Y.- **919**; m. Janett, dau. James Turner, his cousin; they had 7

children, the only child surviving to maturity was Jane, who m. George Vail, of Troy, N. Y.; his wf. d. Feb. 14, 1795, at 80- **1044**

Hiram- Co. A, 2nd N. Y., Northern Black Horse, Cav., 1861- 2- **1080**

Hiram L.- Co. E, 123rd NYSV; d. Nov. 30, 1862; see Vol. 4- **1098**

Susannah- of Brookfield, Mass.; m. Apr. 1, 1760, James, s. Alexander Turner; in Pelham, Mass.- **1044**

THOMPSON,

____- res. Moreau, N. Y.; children- Martin F.; dau., m. Dr. B. F. Cornells- **959**

____- m. Lucretia, dau. Reuben & Olive (Day) Cheney- **1038**

David- of Salem, N. Y.; called 'King David'; he was "dissolute"; m. Margaret, dau. William & Mary (Hanna) Lytle; children- Andrew I., Edward; Mary, m. Charles Getty; James, Jane, & Martha- **1069**

David N.- Co. A, 2nd N. Y., Northern Black Horse, Cav., 1861- 2- **1080**

Gen.- acc. his Rev. war pens. appl., an officer witn. by Ebenezer Farnsworth, during his Apr. 1776- Feb. 1777 services- **750**

I. W., Esq.- attributes the Quaker opposition to war, & the added taxes to defray the costs of the Rev. war, as contributing factors to the 1786 tax revolt in Granville, N. Y.- **921**

James- res. Fitch's Point, Salem, N. Y.; m. Axey Jordan, dau. Mrs. Seward, by her 1st husb.; they 1st res. nr. the Sewards, & then where Lyon lived, & then for several yrs. at Moffat's, where John McDonald now (1850) res.; they afterw. rem. Monkton, Vt., & then to Essex co., N. Y.; c. 1830, rem. Ohio, leaving 1 or 2 famil members in Essex co.; children- Samuel, James, John, Lydia, Rebecca, & Sarah, o Sally- **864**

James- d. Oct. 3, 1794, at 74- **(L)- 975**

Dr. John- res. Scipio, N. Y.; m. dau. Dr. Sanford Smith; began his practice in Cambridge, N. Y., c. 1813, abt. the same time as the spotted fever epidemic there- **844**

Judge John- member, Dr. Clark's colony; among those who settl. Stillwater, N. Y., instead of rem. to Salem; res. just S. of the village; c. 1852, his s. was "the recent Judge Thompson of Saratoga co."- **973**

Margaret- m. Abraham, s. James & Elizabeth (Lytle) Rowan- **737**

Martin F.- c. 1851, res. along W. side of the Hudson river, town of Moreau, N. Y.; while working w. his father (n. d.) on a highway above his dwelling place, some bones were discovered by them, abt. 3 ft. below the surface, & they unearthed an entire skeleton, lying w. its head pointing N.; acc. Jacob Bitely, the body discovered was prob. that of a teamster killed during an Indian ambush in the old French war; see Ft. Edward, N. Y.- **958**

THORN,

Jacob- res. Michigan; m. Lydia, dau. Ebenezer & Sarah (Hobby) Fitch; several children- **799**

THORNBURN,
Grant- called 'little Scotchy'; res. NYC; c. 1830's, operated a flower garden & seed store on the spot of the old Quaker church, Liberty St.; c. 1860's, his desc. opearate a similar business on John St., nr. Broadway- **1075b**

THORNTON,
William- of Washington, D. C.; rec'd. bequest from John Fitch, the steamboat inventor, in his Will, June 20, Prob. Aug. 14, 1798- **949b**

THURMAN,
John, Jr.- plaintiff, in separate cases, May 19, 1774, vs. Benjamin Spencer; vs. Isaac Hill; vs. Charles Button; vs. Micah Veal; & vs. Ephriam Mallory; pl. w. Jacob Van Voorhies, vs. Thomas Rowlee, Sr.; pl. w. Van Voorhies, as assignees of Philip P. Lansing, Oct. 19, 1774, vs. James Palmer & Robert Roset- **878**

TILLMAN,
John- recommended May 26, 1775, to serve as Lt. in a co. being raised by John Visscher- **832**

TINKEY,
_____- m. 1. _____ Beaty; 2. Miller Dobbin, as his 2nd wf.- **732**
Hannah- m. _____ Kilmer; during the Sun. night that the Argyle families had gathered at Neil Gillespie's (July 27, 1777) for safety foll. the Allen Massacre, she caught up a gun in her hand & leapt out the back window of Gillespie's house, wholly unconscious of her act; the perceived danger came from a violent fight breaking out among the settlers' dogs in the night stillness- it could not be determined whether or not the dogfight had anything to do w. an Indian assault or not- **983**
Henry- m. Elizabeth, dau. John & Betsey (Beaty) McDougall- **978**
Nancy- Argyle, N. Y.; Apr. 26, 1810, hung herself in upper loft of Henry Tinkey's house; William Stevenson, Coroner- **(L)- 876**

TIRRELL,
Josiah- defendant, May 19, 1774, in separate cases brought by Ebenezer Allen, Comfort Carpenter, & John Js. Bleecker- **878**

TITUS,
Timothy- res. Fitch's Point, Salem, N. Y., bef. Rev. war, & kept a blacksmith shop; his house afterw. occ. by _____ Taller & Thomas Williams, & c. 1850, occ. by James Harvey Fitch- **803**; res. in a log house nr. the dam; he & his wf. d. there; had sons Timothy, Bob, & Sam; his children rem. Rupert, Vt. area- **860**; his house was loc. S. of the Norton family, where the old bridge was, & was orig. occ. by Daniel Livingston- **867**

TODD,

_____- bro. John; next to John Cloughin, he was one of the worst tories in Salem, N. Y. during the Rev. war; he owned no farm, & had no fixed residence, & his name was not further recoll.- **744**

John- tory, res. Salem, N. Y.; he & John Cloughin stole John Lytle's yoke of oxen & drove them into Burgoyne's camp, later offering Lytle a receipt (which he refused) in order for him to obt. recompense- **739**; he res. N. of Salem village, next above Joseph Stevenson; his farm was "sequestrated" & purch. by old Deac. Matthew, although he was "by no means so active & rampant as his bro. was" in tory activities- **744**; he & _____ Fenton owned the lot orig. drawn by John McDougall, Argyle Patent; he moved onto the lot, but espoused the King's cause in the Rev. war & withdrew to Canada; foll. the peace, he returned & sold his lot, then rem. Bay of Quinte- **802**

TOMB,

_____- res. Salem, N. Y.; William McChesney accidentally killed, Dec. 1802, while returning home, drunk, from his still- **(L)**- **876**

Betsey- of Salem, N. Y.; m. Alexander, s. John & Betsey (Beaty) McDougall- **978**

David- an orig. founder, Assoc. Ref. Presbyterian church, Salem, N. Y.; was early elected an Elder, serving under Dr. Clark & his successor, Rev. James Proudfit; his s. Samuel was noted early as having 'powers above the ordinary grade' & was designed by his parents for the ministry- **810**

Mary- dau. David; m. Deac. John Steele, as his 1st wf.- **1047**

Rev. Samuel- appt. 1st Vice President of a public reception honoring Commodore Macdonough, Nov. 29, 1814, Salem, N. Y.; offered the prayer bef. his reception & toasted Gen. Macomb during the ceremonies- **709**; 4th s. David; exhibited early signs of precociousness & was destined by his parents for an educ. for the clergy; by his own narrative concerning his 1st religious impressions, notes his conversion at age 16, by public profession of faith, & his union w. Rev. James Proudfit's church; studied languages w. Mr. Watson, in Salem, & was then sent to Dr. Wilson's 'celebrated institution' in N. J.; returned to Salem abt. 1787, & was under direction of Rev. Proudfit; licensed 1789, by Assoc. Ref. Presbytery of N. Y.- **810**; rec'd. repeated calls to settle churches in Hebron, Argyle, & Cambridge, N. Y., but declined, & was settl., as pastor, Newmarket, N. H., by Presbytery of Londonderry, 1791; after several yrs., resigned & was settl. at Newbury, Mass., & continued there until 1806; installed Feb. 19, 1806, Gen. Assembly Presbyterian church, Salem, N. Y.; 2 religious revivals, or awakenings, occurred during his ministry, in 1824 & 1831; from the latter period, the increased pressures of his public duty & advanced age lead to his physical decline; d. Mar. 29, 1832, at 66, in the 43rd yr. of his ministry- **811**; his home constructed (n. d.) w. the assistance of Richard Gibson- **1073**

TOOHEY,

Dennis- Co. A, 2nd N. Y., Northern Black Horse, Cav., 1861- 2- **1080**

TORIES-

Bennington, battle of- their breastworks, drawn by Dr. Fitch on a plan of the battlesite, indicate its loc. in the SE corner of the ground, E. of the road along the Walloomsac river that intersects w. the Walloomsac- Bennington road- **761**; their breastworks fashioned from fence rails, laid up in 2 parallel tiers, w. flax stooks harvested from the surrounding field filling the interstices; was attacked from the rear & to the E., so that Col. Baum's cannon could not play upon the assault w/o killing tories as well; graves- loc. somewhat downwards from the front of their position; acc. Austin Wells, a log hut & small outdoor cellar were nr. the breastworks; at the time, the house was gone, & the slabs of the earth- covered cellar were rotted;"into this cellar hole those who were killed of the tories, at the breast work, were thrown, in a promiscuous heap, & the dirt thrown over them"; a total of 17 dead were bur. here- **762**; soil here & SE of their defense was peaty, interlaid w. hard pan, & produced large crops of wheat, corn, "& c.", but became exhausted & stiff by 1850- **763**;

E. Greenwich, N. Y.- possibly in retaliation for burning of the Salem church, a school house was burnt here, spring 1778, by area whigs; some sawmills, or at least those sawmills belonging to "Mad" More at Sodom (Shushan, N. Y.) were burnt in return for this, & also, the burning of "black" Duncan Campbell's house- **1064**;

New Canaan, N. Y.- sittings of the Comm. of Safety were being broken up & disturbed by them, c. 1776, & a request was sent to the militia of adjoin. Stockbridge, Mass. to assist in their capt.; a no. were capt. in Apr., & sentenced to imprisonment in Albany, N. Y.- **747**;

Pittstown, N. Y.- mid- June 1782; a troop consisting of 4 tories & 4 British soldiers came down from Canada & abducted Esq. Bleecker, his hired man, & a negro, at an oat farm owned by Bleecker; they began to head for the Green Mtns., but were discovered the next morning & an alarm was raised, which capt. them in the woods; a guard of 16 men was raised by Col. Robinson & the abductors were confined to a school house until they were sent to Skenesborough (Whitehall, N. Y.) in Oct., for exchange- **747**;

Refugees, foll. Rev. war- the current (1851) report has been that those who lost their property adhering to Britain in the Rev. war had, in many instances, more than the amt. made up by the English govt.; loyalists would claim loss of a cert. amt. & the govt., w/o means of verification, would allow the claim; many who were "attainted & exiled" afterw. returned & res. in N. Y. foll. the Legislature's act of amnesty- **916**;

Salem, N. Y.- late Aug. 1777; a party of more than a dozen, possibly Dr. Adams' scout party from Arlington, Vt., secreting themselves in some bushes nr. John Lytle's, rushed & seized a Hessian soldier who was inquiring of Susan & Rebecca Lytle abt. the route to Bennington, Vt.; Judge Hopkins, of Rupert, Vt., a well known whig, had been seized in the road by them earlier, & the Hessian was pinioned & added to their prisoner train as a deserter; the 2 girls were brought along as "traitors" for attempting to show the road to the Hessian; they were marched as far as David Russell's, Hebron, N. Y., when Wm. McNish, ano. tory, met them & convinced the band that the girls would be missed & presumed killed by the Indians; they were released into his custody w. the proviso that they would be held intil after sundown, enabling the company to make an effective escape- **740**; Alexander Wright "pilfered sheep from his neighbors flocks, till he coll. a large flock", which he then drove through Argyle to Burgoyne's camp, getting pd. for them in silver- **977**; the War of 1812 revived the earlier memories of the older residents, & old Capt. McNitt spoke continually abt. killing tories, until one day, c. 1814, he started out on his own "to take a co. of tories to Nova Scotia"- **1018**;

   W. Hebron, N. Y.- c. 1777, a party capt. Isaac & William Lytle, who were working in the area, & took them as prisoners into the British camp at Ft. Edward- **742**

Tory Songs, of the Rev. war- recoll., c. 1852, by Mrs. Daniel (Catharine McDougall) Livingston, pert. to the battle of Bunker Hill, sung "Hundreds of times, as my father held me on his knee"; only 3 verses recoll.- "The 17th, by break of day/ The Yankees did surprise us,/ With their strong works they had thrown up/ To burn the town & drive us./ But soon there was an order came-/ An order to defeat them:/ The rebels spread themselves like men/ And we thought we never could defeat them./ ... Whilst some lie bleeding on the ground,/ And others fast are running/ O'er hills, o'er dales, o'er mountains high,/ Crying "There's Howe a coming!"- **980**

TOSH, see also, McINTOSH,
William- res. Salem, N. Y.; his family, along w. David Hanna's, was part of the Jackson party foll. the Allen massacre- **701**; from Scotland, or Ireland; res. Lot No. 64, Argyle Patent (loc. E. Greenwich, N. Y.); m. Jennett ____; (who d. Nov. 19, 1801; § 474; Vol. 1) their house was loc.abt. ½ mi. over the hill from James Cherry; his wf. "was an active & very inquisitive woman- would work all night, & run abt. all day to gather the news"; in this respect, her accuracy in narrating the events & remarks of her neighbors lead them to suspect her of being a witch; see Witchcraft, Witches- **871**; m. 2nd, Betty Hoy, "a much less profitable & tidy wf."; her sist. Sally came to live w. them & the 2 of them made his life anything but pleasant, neglecting him shamefully in his last sickness; he purch. Pine Lot No. 20, nr. Fitch's Point, & prob. d. there; his 2nd wf. perh. m. ____ McMillan, of Argyle, N. Y.- **872**

TOWN,
Edward- oath of alleg.; Co. D, 22nd N. Y. Inf.- **(L)- 1074**
Salem, D. D.- (1799- 1864) was once Preceptor, Granville Academy, prior 1820; see Vol. 4- **759s**

TOWNLEY,
Wid. Mary- of NYC; m. Apr. 18, 1803, Gen. John Williams; she d. Aug. 19, 1819, at 50; see Vol. 4- **1044**

TRACY,
Jonathan- c. 1755, res. Norwich, Conn.; credited by Dr. Peletiah Fitch for work at his bro. Elisha's- **838**

TRANSPORTATION-
Bridges- Angel's bridge- built, c. 1790- 1800's, by Augustus Angel, & constructed above the dam at E. Greenwich, N. Y.- **847**;
Fonda' bridge- loc. 2 mi. above Eagle Bridge, on the old Albany- Bennington road that ran along the valley of the Hoosick river- **766**;
Ft. Miller- loc. 2 mi. above Saratoga (Schuylerville, N. Y.) nr. McNeil's ferry; the 1st bridge built across the Hudson from town of Northumberland, & wasn't built until after the turnpike co. had rec'd. a charter to build its road- **804**;
Red bridge- loc. Salem, N. Y., crossing the Battenkill into town of Jackson, nr. Fitch's Point- **732**; c. 1853, Lyman Jayner res. nr. here- **1005**;
Russell's- (c. 1858?) perh. loc. nr. Salem, N. Y.; brief ment.- **1034**;
Walloomsac- c. 1850; a covered bridge, constructed S. of the heights where the Bennington battle was fought, nr. Nathaniel Barnet, Esq.'s house; c.1777, a bridge was then loc. there, but rotted down, & for many yrs. after, a ford was there instead- **762**;
Roads- Albany- Bennington- the old road passed through Walloomsac & Sancoick, & down the valley of the Hoosick river, crossing the river at "Fonda's bridge", 2 mi. above where the Eagle bridge now (1850) stands- **766**;
Conditons- c. 1771, betw. Salem & Hebron, N. Y., were not open clear through; "indeed much of the way there was scarcely any road"- **997**;
Northern turnpike- through Cambridge, N. Y., it was laid out over Oak Hill, due to the influ. of Dr. Philip Smith, of Tyashoke, N. Y., rather than foll. a more suitable route to the E. of there- **845**;
Traveling time- c. 1774, acc.Wid. Angel, a journey from Stillwater to Fitch's Point, Salem, N. Y., took 2 days by oxcart; her father, Moses Martin, Sr., had to stop occasionally & cut the road in places- **852**;
Stage line- from Whitehall to Albany, N. Y., June 29, 1815; its schedule departs Whitehall on Mon.- Wed.- Fri. morning, returning on the foll. day- **719**;
Steamboat- Nov. 1815, the *Phenix*, a new boat, & the only one then on Lake Champlain, scheduled to leave Whitehall on Wednesdays, & St. John's, Canada, on every Sat. morning- **719**;
Trains- Troy & Rutland R. R.; its tracks were inaccurately depicted on an 1853 map of Wash.co., crossing very diff. from representations given; these variances noted from S. to N. in 5 figures sketched by Dr. Fitch, beginning on Hoosick river at the Rens. co. line as the track enters Wash. co. above Eagle Bridge, & the mouth of the Owl kill, showing & describing crossings as they should be; names of a no.

of inhabitants res. along the way; loc. of depots for Troy & Rutland, & Troy & Boston R. R. noted; fig. 1- Owl kill; fig. 2- Batten kill; figs. 3 & 4- White (Ondawa) creek; fig. 5- Indian river- **1003**; excavations for Troy & Boston R. R., Rens. co., pass through a deep cut E. of N. Hoosick, N. Y., beyond Webster' Tavern; a skeleton unearthed nr. E. end of these excavations, towards the base of the hill, & N. of the present (1853) course of the rail line, abt. 25 rods E. of Reubin Clark's farm, & abt. on the old line of the Hoosick & Walloomsac Patents; the opening of this line of R. R. celebrated, Aug. 16, 1851?, on the anniversary of the battle of Bennington; Mr. ____, who runs the factory here (woolen factory, N. Hoosick) was the leading man in organizing the festivities- **1007**;

Train derailments- R. R. collision of Western Pacific noted, Nov. 14, 1869, loc. not given- **799**; a 25 car freight train, Dec. 2 or 3, 1853, at Whitehall, N. Y., ran over a cow, derailing the engine & several cars; 'The engineer was killed & 2 cars full of hogs pitched into the canal'; refers *N. Y. Weekly Times*; the derailment occurred on Fri. evening, & not Sat., acc. *Whitehall Chronicle*; it was a horse on the track,"or rather, fallen in the bridge timbers";William McMillin (McMullen) was the engineer who was killed; the bridge was totally destroyed & the loss to the R. R. was $6- 8,000; the "engine, tender, 2 freight cars, precipitated into the canal, & 20 live hogs drowned"- **1017**; Jan. 3, 1854, "The morning down train" (9:00 AM), at Schaghticoke, N. Y., lost a flange "off the forward truck wheel" while approaching the Hoosick bridge at 30 mph, & the forward trucks became detached its single passenger car had "every seat filled w. 2 passengers & 10 or 15 more standing in the aisle"; its conductor, Mr. Strong, narrowly escaped injury, & the brakeman, Cornelius Chambers, was killed instantly; that afternoon, a carpenter repairing the bridge fell 30- 40 ft. unto the ice below, & d. from his injuries 1 or 2 days later- **1021**; Jan. 25, 1862, Shaftsbury, Vt.; a passenger car of the Western Vt R. R. was blown off a high enbankment by a heavy gust of wind, & rolled over 2- 3 times during its 25 ft. descent, killing 2 persons, one instantly, & the other soon after- **1087**;

Wagons- 1st one in Hebron & Salem, N. Y., was owned by ____ Brinkerhoef, 1788, who kept store a mi. above Bedlam (W. Hebron, N. Y.); ano. wagon, obt. by William Lytle, 1789, was long recognized as the 1st in Salem; "folks were afraid to ride in it- having only been used to carts bef." (this material conflicts w. earlier data, see § 150; Vol. 1)- **738**

TRICKETT,

Thomas- of Chambly, Montreal district, Province of Quebec, Canada; late Qtr. Master, his Majesty's 44th Regt. of Foot; w. wf. Margaret, Sept. 30, 1773, conveys to Peter Van Brugh Livingston & Francis Groome, for £ 150, a tract of land loc. in Albany, now Charlotte co., gr. to him Sept. 7, 1771, 'on the E. side of the waters running from Wood creek into Lake Champlain', beginning at the SW corner of L George McDougall; its description, given in chains & links, an "L" shaped tract, containing 2,000 acres; bordered N. by lots of Lt. George McDougall, & of James

Winterbottom & 9 other private soldiers; bordered E. by _____ Ludlow; & bordered
W. by Lt. John Hay- **(L)**- **936**

TRICKEY,
Hannah- m. 1. Peter Mallory; 2. Daniel Munroe- **812**

TRIPOLI- 1056

Troy, N. Y.- c. 1851, the Eaton family cemetery, loc. ½ mi. E. of the Sloop lock,
beside the tracks of the Troy & Greenfield R. R.- **954**; c. Nov. 1862, began issuing
25¢ & 50¢ bills, called shinplaster, as the availability of silver change decreased;
see Shinplasters, Vol. 3; & Currency, Vols. 2 & 3- **1099**

TRUMBULL,
Gov. Jonathan- (1710- 1785; Gov., 1769- 1776) of Conn.; Col. Benedict Arnold
writes to him from Crown Point, May 23, 1775, concerning his capt. of a British
sloop at St. John's, & other events; Arnold describes his inability to obt. gunpowder
from Albany, N. Y., despite repeated requests, seeking 4- 500 lbs., & suggesting
the need for at least 1,500 men from his colony for defense of Crown Point &
Ticonderoga- **774**; requests for aid sent to him, July 27, 1777, by N. Y. Council of
Safety, noting the current state of the countryside's occupation by the British- **797**

TRUMAN,
Clark- m. Sarah, dau. Sarah Latham; title to lands in Sag Harbor, N. Y., orig. part
of Samuel Burrow's estate, & prob. derived from him & his wf.- **1100**

TRYON,
Gov. William- (1729- 1788; Gov., 1771- 74; 1775- 76) of N. Y.; sends a lengthy
letter to Lord Dartmouth, July 1, 1773, in reply to his plans for settling & adjusting
the dispute w. N. H. over the Grants lands- **913**

Tryon co., N. Y.- its militia org. Aug. 22, 1775, along w. Albany co.'s, as one
brigade- **782**; numerous letters from here, noted by Dr. Fitch, within Proceedings
of the Albany Comm. of Correspondence, 1775- **818**

TUCKER,
Joseph- res. Fitch's Point, Salem, N. Y.; m. Lizzie, dau. Ezra Turner; the story that
he was whipped for his wf.'s crime (Vol. 1) "is true to its very letter", acc. Wid.
Angel, who relates that St. John Honeywood had hung some bacon to smoke in the
larger chimney of his neighbor, James Farrar, & one night, Mrs. Tucker "mounted"
the house & stole one of the pieces, which was fully proven; as no jail then existed,
& whipping was then the only punishment, the sentence was levied on her husb.,
she being so nr. the time of her confinement; the reasoning was that her husb.
"ought to have provided for his wf.'s wants & longings, w/o leaving her to

temptation", & since, "in the eye both of the law & gospel, they were one flesh, sentence was given that the husb. be tied to the whipping post & receive the lashes"; it was carried out so, maintaining the sovereignty of the law; he afterw. res. for several yrs. where the Dillon family currently (1850) res. & finally rem. Essex co., N. Y.- **863**; the Christie family later occ. the house from which his wf. stole Honeywood's bacon- **867**

TURKEY- **709**; Constantinople- **962, 1087**

TURNER,
_____ - when Dr. Williams 1st arr. in Salem, N. Y., he was keeping a public house nr. where the village was later loc.- **915**
Abraham- bro. Ezra; res. across Black creek from his bro., in the area of Fitch's Point, Salem, N. Y.; his s. Abraham, a physician, res. Ohio- **863**
Abraham- s. Abraham; res. Ohio; his dau. m. John Barnet, as his 2nd wf.- **863**
Alexander- ments. s. James & Alexander, Jr., who were orig. settlers of Turner's Patent (Salem, N. Y.), but their father never came here to settle- **1034**; ments. s. Reuben- **1044**; m. Mary Conkey, acc. V. R., Worcester, & Pelham, Mass.- **1085b**; ments. all 3 of the abovement. sons- **1086**
Alexander- (s. James & Susannah Thomas) b. 1766, Salem, N. Y.; m. Sarah McCrea; children- John, m. Betsey Huggins; Susan & Catharine, both unm.; Mary, m. _____ Hitchcock; & Stephen; rem., Feb. 1800, Lisbon, N. Y., & was Supervisor, & Co. Judge, until he d. 1806; refers Hough's History- **1044**
Deac. Alexander, Jr.- became Capt. of 1st Salem militia co. foll.Charles Hutchinson- **729**; proprietor, Turner's Patent, & Elder, Salem Presbyterian church, from its org. until Apr. 1802, when he rem. Kortright, N. Y.; his orig. house site comprises the SW corner of Evergreen Cemetery- **1034**; (s. Alexander & Mary Conkey)- **1085b**; was militia Capt. foll. Rev. war; among his children- William, Archibald, James Alexander; Polly (Mary), m. Matthew McWhorter; Sally, & Esther; when in advanced yrs., rem. W. or SW, but, acc. this acct., not to Kortright, as prev. noted; he discovered a variety of religious sentiments in his new loc., & was inspired to write a manuscript giving the grounds of his own beliefs, consulting Dr. Proudfit for his opinion on the correctness of his positions- **1086**
Chester- (s. James & Matilda Safford) res. Sandgate, Vt.; m. Maria Jocelyn; 3 children- Anna, Harriet, & Edward- **1098**
Ezra- he res. along Black creek, nr. Fitch's Point, Salem, N. Y., opp. the present (1850) home of Joseph Coon; dau. Lizzie, m. Joseph Tucker- **863**
Family- res. Fitch's Point, Salem, N. Y.; bros. Abraham & Ezra, res. opp. ea. other on Black creek; they later rem. Monkton, Vt., & afterw. Ohio- **863**
Gideon S.- (s. James & Matilda Safford) res. a mi. S. of the Notch, Sandgate, Vt.; m. Eliza, dau. Zaccheus Atwood; children- Ann- Eliza, Susanna, Maria, & James- **1090**
James- orig. settler, Salem, N. Y.; c. 1767, his was one of only 2 houses in the settlm., loc. on the site of the Coffee House (Union Hall)- **738**; his administrators,

John & Susanna Williams, were plaintiffs, Nov. 3, 1784, vs. Elizabeth & Martha McCrea- **878½**; s. Alexander, Sr.- **1034**; b. Dec. 2, 1735, Worcester, Mass.; res. Pelham, Mass.; m. Apr. 1, 1760, Susannah Thomas, of Brookfield, in Pelham; children-

1. Janett, b. 1764; m. David Thomas
2. Alexander, b. 1766, Salem, N. Y.; he was the 1st settler's child b. in town; m. Sarah McCrea
3. Sarah, b. Apr. 11, 1770; m. Walter Martin
4. James William, m. Elenour Hunsden; & he d. Feb. 15, 1773, at 38; his wf. m. 2nd, Gen. John Williams, & she d. Dec. 30, 1799, at 57- **1044**

James William- (s. James & Susannah Thomas) m. Elenour Hunsden; children-

1. James, b. Nov. 16, 1791; m. ____ Safford
2. Susan, m. ____ Hunsden, a cousin
3. Eliza, m. Rev. John Savage, D. D.
4. Jane
5. Eleanor- **1044**; (s. Alexander & Mary Conkey)- **1086**; res. Lot 178, known as the Smart farm, Salem, N. Y.; ano. acct. of their children gives the foll. var.-

James, m. Matilda Safford; William, d. unm., abt. 1836, Jamesville, Wisc.; Jane, m. ____ Platt; & Eleanor, prob. d. y.; his wid. m. Robert Chapman- **1090**

James, 3rd- (s. James William & Elenour Hunsden) m. Matilda, dau. Gideon Safford; 7 children-

1. William, m. Jane Vanderpool
2. Gideon S., m. Eliza Atwood
3. James, m. Ursula Vanderpool
4. Eleanor, m. Albert Hanson
5. Lucy M., m. Gideon Safford
6. Chester, m. Maria Jocelyn
7. Elizabeth, m. William White; his wf. d. Aug. 2, 1871, Sandgate, Vt.- **1090**

James, 4th- (s. James & Matilda Safford) res. New Baltimore, N. Y.; m. Ursula Vanderpool, niece of his bro. William's wf.; 3 children- Emma, Ida, & Catherine- **1090**

Reubin- (s. Alexander & Mary Conkey) m. Jane, dau. Robert & Margaret Armstrong- **1083**; res. Lot No. 55, N. of Salem, N. Y., & W. behind the brick house built by ____ Porter; rem., 1801, to St. Lawrence co., along w. the Armstrong families; his orig. lot sold, by Daniel Hill, c. 1861/2, to Abner Hill; d. July 1833, at 92; refers Hough's History of St. Lawrence co.- **1085**; s. Alexander & Mary Conkey- **1086**

Sarah- of Salem, N. Y.; sist. of Mrs. Gen. David Thomas, & half- sist. of Col. John Williams; m. Walter, s. Col. Adam & Abigail (Cheney) Martin; d. Aug. 4, 1815, leaving 9 children- **730**; her marriage noted again- **1039**

William- (s. James & Matilda Safford) res. a mi. N. of the Notch, Sandgate, Vt.; m. Jane Vanderpool; children- Joseph, Elizabeth- Matilda, William- James, Andrew, Cornelia- Jane, Ellen- Maria, & Virginia- **1090**

Turner's Patent- (Salem, N. Y.) had 25 orig. patentees, incl. Alexander Turner, Jr.; see Vol. 4- **1034**

TUTTLE,
_____- Cambridge, N. Y.; passing to Troy, Nov. 21, 1800, fell from his wagon & its wheel passed over & crushed his head; James Gilmore, Coroner- **(L)- 876**
Stephen- plaintiff, May 19, 1774, vs. John Cook- **878**

22nd N. Y. Infantry- (Second Northern N. Y.) newspaper article, May 25, 1861, notes the combining of several volunteer companies, taken from Camp Brintnall & Albany, N. Y., to Camp Rathbone, Troy, N. Y., to comprise this regt.; the nr. completion of the co. numbers indicates its impending mustering in to service; lists Co. Capts., & towns of origin, & a list of 78 members from Co. D, who took the oath of allegiance-
A- Capt. Yates, Waterford; B- Capt. Boynton, Whitehall; C- Capt. Peabody, Keesville; D- Capt. Milliman, Cambridge; E- Capt. Clendon, Glens Falls; F- Capt. Holden, Glens Falls; G- Capt. McCoy, Ft. Edward; H- Capt. Strong, Sandy Hill; I- Capt. Ormsby, Schroon Lake; J- Capt. Cadwell, Moriah- **(L)- 1074**; recruited in Wash. & Warren counties, Col. Walter Phelps, Jr., & Maj. McKie, commanding, 1861- **1080**; at 2nd Bull Run, "was in a most exposed position, on the last day of the fight, stood its ground w. the utmost coolness & resolution, & was terribly cut to pieces"; 2/3rds of its officers killed or severely wnd.; Maj. McKie was the only officer to escape unscathed; 2nd Lt. Wm. T. Beattie & 1st Lt. Duncan Lendrum killed on the field; Capt. H. S. Milliman later d. of wnds.; a record of officer field promotions or replacements, & deaths of var. soldiers foll. their return from service also ment.- **1195b**

TYLER,
Sarah- m. Charles Pinkney, s. Stephen & Jane (Martin) Leonard- **1046**

U

U. E. Loyalist List- (United Empire) this list entitled refugees from the Rev. war to land grants of 200 acres, in Canada; see Mosher's Diary, Vol. 4; Jan. 1, 1853, acc. John Munroe, of Michigan, several U. S. families, incl. the surnames Jones, Jessup, & Covill, were on this list, & res. in the same neighborh. in Canada (perh. in Ontario) as the Munroe family; see Vol. 1- **991**

UNDERHILL,
Amos- he & Henry Franklin owned Lot 15, Kingsbury, N. Y., acc. Nov. 26, 1773 deed description; see Vol. 1- **(L)- 936**

Union Village, N. Y.- orig. called Whipple City, & in modern times, Greenwich, N. Y.- **862**

UNITED STATES- ment. as Republic of Washington- **1027**; Congress- rec'd. pay increase, 1816, from $6.00 per day to $1,500.00 per yr., for 90 days service; their travel expenses, $12.00 for every 120 mi. travel in going to & returning from the Capital; vote of Wash. co. area representatives- Adgate, nay; Savage, aye- **725**; Public Debt, Nov. 1854; acc. to a partial newspaper article, the debt was $45 million- **1028**

UTAH- Salt Lake City- 730

UTTER,
Benjamin D.- char. witn., Rev. war pens. appl., Samuel Standish, of Granville, N. Y.- **747**
Dr. Benjamin- of Granville, N. Y.; m. Mary, dau. Jacob, Jr. & Lucy (Howard) Allen- **758**

V

VAIL,
Aaron- (b. Oct. 24, 1796, L'Orient, France; d. Nov. 4, 1878; arr. U. S., 1815; legation to London, 1831- 2, 1836) U. S. consul; dau. Eliza rec'd. a bequest from John Fitch, the steamboat inventor, in his Will, June 20; Prob. Aug. 14, 1798- **949b**
George- merch., Troy, N. Y.; m. Jane, dau. David & Janett (Turner) Thomas; 5 children- David Thomas, Jane, George Henry, Sarah, & Martha; his wf. d. 1866- **1044**

Valley Forge, Pennsylvania- among soldiers stat. in winter quarters here were Lt. Derick Lane, & his bro. Aaron, who were later merchs., Troy, N. Y.; & Moses Scott, later a merch., Waterford, N. Y.; the state of the hospital there was in such need that the Lane bros., on receiving fresh shirts from their mother, gave them up, saving only the ruffles to pin on their cuffs, to give the appearance that they were properly attired; Moses Scott recoll. that w. the advent of spring, the soldiers gathered the brakes as they started up in the woods & fields, boiling them as greens, it not being known until then that they were not poison, & used them as a welcome relief from their salt meat diets- **1036**

VAN BUREN,
Pres. Martin- (1780- 1862) Wid. Angel notes that the 1st child of Mott & Betsey (Newell) Van Buerin had the same given name- **849**
Mott- (Van Buerin) kept the ferry (n. d.) at Easton, N. Y.; m. Betsey, dau. John Newell of Sturbridge, Mass.; their 1st child was named Martin- **849**; (Van Bearin) same material, res. Stillwater, N. Y.- **1037**

VAN BENSCHOTEN,
Rev. Mr. Elias- b. Oct. 26, 1738; A. B., 1768; licensed to preach, 1773; settl. Shaticoke (Schaghticoke, N. Y.) & afterw. Minisink, N. Y., or N. J.; 3rd minister settl. minister N. of Albany in N. Y. State, & 1st install. at Schaghticoke; d. Jan. 10, 1815; bur. New Brunswick, N. J., at the old Dutch church; Dr. Fitch recoll. some incidents in the life "of this old Dutch Dominie", after discovering his gravesite, Sept. 24, 1851; see Church/ Clergy, & Vol. 1- **953b**; same incidents given, dated Sept. 23rd, w. Van Bunschoten as spelling variation- **954**

VAN BUSKIRK,
_____- acc. testim. during the trial of Martin Wallace, Oct. 1- 7, 1858, Wallace claimed that he intended to look at house owned by him, to rent or purch., on Feb. 16, 1858, the day that Barney McEntee was murdered- **1048s**

VANCE,

James- (s. Robert & Susan Lytle) res. Hebron, N. Y., w. his father; m. Jane Hanna- **737**

John- (s. Robert & Susan Lytle) res. Wallingford, Vt.; m. Abigail Kelley- **737**

Robert- of Drumgenny, Co. Monaghan, Ireland; b. ca. 1763; emig. 1788, & arr. in NYC, July 4th; m. Susan, dau. John & Eleanor (Lowrie) Lytle; res. Hebron, N. Y., on a farm ½ mi. E. of Judge William Porter; children-

 1. Elizabeth, m. John Shaw

 2. Robert, m. Jerusha Wheaton

 3. William, m. Jane McCleary

 4. Maria Lytle, d. unm.

 5. John, m. Abigail Kelley

 6. James, m. Jane Hanna

 7. Sophia Lytle, unm., res. w. her parents- **737**; his wf. Susan, gives witn. accts. § 737- 743; acc. Dr. Fitch, the deserter capt. in Salem, N. Y. by her acct. § 740, was the same person as the deserter executed at Ft. Miller, N. Y., by Mrs. Bain's acct.; see Hundertmark, George- **976**

Robert, Jr.- (s. Robert & Susan Lytle) res. Frankfort, N. Y.; m. Jerusha Wheaton, of Hebron, N. Y.- **737**

William- (s. Robert & Susan Lytle) m. Jane McCleary; he d. W. Troy, N. Y., leaving 2 children- **737**

VAN CORTLANDT,

Elizabeth- (Van Courtland) of NYC; was an aunt of Henry Cuyler, Jr.- **934**

James- his deposition, Mar. 4, 1771, that he was a member of the posse arresting Robinson, Ashley, & 2 others, bringing them to Albany jail; notes that they were never indicted, gave bail, or were ever brought to trial; Dr. Fitch notes that the remainder of his deposition coincides 'mostly' w. Sheriff Schuyler's letters- **897**

VAN CUYLER, see also, CUYLER, or KUYLER/ KYLER,

Family- prob. came here bef. the Rev. war, & settl. nr. Walloomsac Patent- **806**

Van Cuyler's Patent- also known as Lake's Patent; its boundary adjoin. Walloomsac Patent- **806**

VANDENBURGH,

Family- c. 1798, operated the sawmills on the W. side of the Hudson, at the upper & lower falls, Ft. Miller, N. Y.- **804**

VANDERPOOL,

Jane- of Greene co., N. Y.; m. William, s. James & Matilda (Safford) Turner- **1090**

Ursula- neice of Jane; m. James Turner, bro. of her aunt's husb.- **1090**

VANDERVOORT,
Peter- merch., NYC; w. wf. Sarah, rec'd. Lots 25, 47, 87, & 92, Kingsbury, N. Y., from Ebenezer & Benjamin Silye (Seelye); on May 11, 1773, conveyed the same lots to Albert Baker, for £ 300; recorded Feb. 1, 1774; refers p. 1, Liber A, Book of Deeds, Wash. co.- **(L)- 936**

VAN DUZEN,
Martha- m. Duncan, s. Duncan & Isabel (Duncan) MacIntyre- **999**

VAN DYCK,
Col.- commandant at Ft. George, July 1777; he abandoned & put the fort to flames, July 16th, foll. the capt. of 2 wagons nr. here by Burgoyne's Indian scouts on the prev. day- **794**

VAN ESS/ VANESS,
Family- their old homestead loc. 2 mi. from Walloomsac, N.Y., & abt. a mi. from Fonda's bridge, on the old Albany- Bennington road; c. 1850, owned by David Chase Goodwin- **766**; an old Dutch church & bur. grd., filled w. graves of the earliest inhabitants, loc. below N. Hoosick, in the vicinity of their house, but long demolished & plowed over- **(L)- 772**

VAN INGEN,
James- m. 1. ____; 2. Elizabeth Schuyler, who d. July 17, 1803, at 69- **(L)- 932**

VAN KIRK,
Norman- of Greenwich, N. Y.; juror, Oct. 1- 7, 1858, People vs. Martin Wallace- **1048s**

VAN NORDER,
Daniel- Co. A, 2nd N. Y., Northern Black Horse, Cav., 1861- 2- **1080**

VAN RENSSELAER,
Gen. Henry Killian- (Col. Rensselaer; 1743- 1816) officer witn. by Samuel Standish, acc. his Rev. war pens. appl.; notes his being wnd. at the battle of Ft. Ann, July 1777- **747**; he was sent out to pursue the British after they had been twice repulsed at Ft. Ann, & fell in w. their 9th Regt.; a severe conflict ensued, w. 12 Americans killed on the field & many wnd., incl. him; see Vol. 1- **792**
John- member, Hoosick Comm. of Correspondence; he & Daniel B. Bratt were among the 3 who interviewed Esq. Munro in late Aug. 1775, at the request of the Albany Comm. of Correspondence- **822**
Killian K.- adm. to practice law in Wash. co., Nov.3, 1784- **878½**

Van Rensselaer's mills- or Rensselaer's mills; c. 1777, loc. on the Little White creek, Sancoick, N. Y., some 50 rods above its entrance into the Walloomsac river; the creek "runs through a deep rock- bound chasm; across which chasm the bridge here is thrown"; (figures prominently in events immed. leading up to the battle of Bennington; a skirmish occurred nr. the bridge, as it was being torn up to prevent the progress of Col. Baum's cannon; see Vol. 1); c.1853, Elisha Brownell's grist & sawmill loc. in essentially the same spot- **1006**

VAN SCHAIK,
Family- their family bur. grd. loc. Court St., Albany, N. Y.- **(L)- 932**
Col. Gose- (1736- 1789) officers accepting commissions in his regt., 1775- Capts.- Daniel Mills, Joseph McCracken; 1st Lts.- Andrew Trink, Charles Graham, Moses Martin; 2nd Lts.- Guy Young, John Barns; by Feb. 29, 1776, nearly 3companies of his regt. complete, one stat. at Ft. George & ano. at Ticonderoga, ready to move as soon as others can be sent to garrison these posts- **784**; N. Y. Provincial Congress appt. John Williams as surgeon of this regt.; Aug. 1775, Williams discovers that he has been superceded in that capacity by Stephen McCrey- **790**; an order sent to him, concurrent w. a request, June 4, 1776, to Albany Comm. of Correspondence, for rem. of Capt. McAlpin, Lt. Swords, & John Munro, to ano. place of confinement- **889**; d. July 4, 1789, at 53; rem. from family bur. grd., Court St., Albany, N. Y., Dec. 1, 1808- **(L)- 932**
Susan- m. George B., s. Thomas & Elizabeth (Cramer) Whiteside- **805**
Lt. William H.- (Van Schaak) Co. G, 93rd N. Y. Inf.- **1090b**

Van Schaik's Island- loc. in Hudson river, below Stillwater, N. Y.; at the time of the battle of Bennington, the American army was encamped here, & left shortly after Gen. Gates assumed command; a riff of rocks on its E. shore afforded a safe passageway across from the island to the opp. riverbank; see Vol. 4- **763**

VAN TUYL,
Andrew- purch. orig. site of McNeil's ferry, on W. side of Hudson, after turnpike co. had constructed the Ft. Miller bridge- **804**
Maj.- res. Cambridge, N. Y.; a Miss Baker, apparently a member of his familiy, commited suicide in her chambers at the family home, spring 1815- **712**; m. _____ Berry?; acc. Dr. Fitch, she was perh. a relative of Lewis & Thomas Berry- **839**

VAN VALKENBURGH,
Sarah- m. Asa, s. Moses, Sr. & Lydia (More) Martin; her adopted dau. Jane Pike, rec'd. their home & lot foll. Sarah's death, June 23, 1864- **731**

VAN VECHTEN,
Cornelius- res. White Creek, N. Y.; he & his s. Henry testif. concerning Martin Wallace's pay during Wallace's murder trial, Cornelius noting that Henry pd. him $9 in the forepart of Aug. 1857, for pulling flax, & ano. $5 after Aug. 20th; his s. Henry was called by the def. on the 5th day of the trial, & testif. that he knew Wallace for abt. a yr. & had never heard anything bad abt. him until after the murder; on cross- exam, he sd. he knew Benjamin Baker, who worked w. Wallace in the flax- mill, but he had never heard prev. to the murder that Wallace had ever carried a pistol in order to shoot Baker- **1048s**
Col. Cornelius- (Van Veghten) d. Oct. 31, 1813, at 78 yrs., 8 mos., & 22 ds.- **(L)- 932**

VAN VOORHIES,
Jacob- plaintiff, May 19, 1774, along w. John Thurman, Jr., vs. Thomas Rowlee, Jr.; assignee of Philip P. Lansing, Oct. 19, 1774, along w. John Thurman, Jr., vs. John Palmer & Robert Roset- **878**

VANVURY,
Cornelius- res. Hoosick, N. Y.; June 1802, he shot John Viele, of Cambridge, & Viele d. the foll. day- **(L)-876**

VEAL,
Micah- defendant, May 19,1774, in a case brought by John Js. Bleecker- **878**

VEGETATION, Terrain- 761- 762b, 924, 983, 989
Argyle, N. Y., 1777- the little broad valley along Still (Dead) creek (loc. in the NW area of the Patent) consisted of swampy ground, w. "a dense grove of towering hemlocks which occ. this dell, [&] shut out every ray of light"- **983**;
Bennington battleground- hand sketch showing heights w. enclosed Hessian fort on W. side of Walloomsac river, & road from Walloomsac running along S. edge of heights; a ridge line traced below S. side of road to Bennington, & continuing over course of Walloomsac stream, w. tory breastworks indicated in SE portion of area- **761**; hill of hardpan or clay, in SE port. of ground, cleared to raise flax, c. 1777; tory breastworks loc. here, an abrupt rise of slate rock, nearly a precipice, 60 or 100 ft. above W. side of Walloomsac river as it turns, & N. of the road; Col. Baum's cannon loc. here- **762**; description of the "heights" where Hessian works were consrtucted - a gentle ascent, ledgy in many places, but w. only a slight cover of soil over principally slate rock; "many hummocks & irregularities, adapting it well for defense, esp. when covered w. forest trees"; summit rose to 500 ft. above river, & 140 rods to ½ mi. from bridge; loc. less than ½ mi. from S. line of Wash.co. & over a mi. from Vt. line; the summit contained a small level spot abt. 12 rods long & abt. a 3rd as wide; the hill, covered w. forest then, cut away to throw up breastworks, & a single oak tree left standing in its center, perh. to suspend their colors."it being nearly impossible to dig a hole here to plant a flag-

staff"; summit runs NW- SE direction, descending on all sides, w. slighter descent on NW; a ridge here, continues abt. ¾ mi. bef. shooting up to a higher point, called Cobble Hill, where the line betw. Wash. & Rens. counties runs; area was entirely cleared foll. Rev. war, & has a grove of 2nd growth trees on it since 1822; river flats were all cleared, c. 1777, & in places, the clearing reached up into the hills- **762b**; on abt. W. line of Walloomsac Patent, a ledge of rocks crosses the valley from hill on its N. & towards river, forming a ridge some 10 ft. above the plain, w. some brooks & slight ravines on its E. side; Col. Breyman's reinforcements arr. on the flats beyond these ravines in the afternoon of the battle; his forces advanced abt. a mi. past this ridge to a spot where the road ascends from the flats, bef. being driven back by Col. Warner- **766**;

Lake George, c. 1755- poetic description of the setting for the battle of Lake George, given by Mary M. Chase, in her poem, "The Bloody Morning Scout"- **989**;

Plattsburgh, N. Y., c. 1814- N. of the Saranac river, the country had been cleared of its orig. timber (pine) & a 2nd growth "had started up thick, & some 20 or 30 ft. in height, which was every where crossed by wood- roads- rendering it impossible w/o a guide to go through it"; it was not possiblbe for the British forces to determine their loc. until they had been lead off amid the bushes on the 5 mi. road to the American stores, & they were then able to glimpse the lake, discovering that their pursuit in this direction had rendered their efforts fruitless- **1055**;

Salem, N. Y.- an erroneous report of its burning, Oct. 17, 1780, noted by Gen. Schuyler; Gov. Clinton reports to Gen. Washington that 'the smoke was discoverable from the heights nr. his [Schuyler's] house'; acc. Dr. Fitch, Schuyler prob. saw "the smoke of some clearing in this direction, that was seen in Schuylerville", indicating the extensive & common technique of deforestation used during the early settlm. period- **1066**

VERMONT- 734s, 786, 812, 815, 816, 903, 915, 921, 966, 967, 970, 990, 998, 1027; controversy, disturbances- 971; naming of- 793, 796, 799, 1052, 1081, 1087; as New Vermont- 789, 796;

   Counties- Addison- 966; Bennington- 1022; Franklin- 759s; Rutland- 745, 936;

   Cities & Towns- Arlington- 731, 733, 740, 747, 752, 755, 757, 773, 805, 881, 893, 912, 1050s; Bennington- 708, 728, 731, 739, 744, 747, 750, 751, 759s, 783, 794, 801, 804, 821, 822, 831, 843, 847, 849, 853, 881, 893, 894, 899, 902, 908, 924, 926, 953, 1006, 1007, 1016, 1022, 1027, 1049, 1062, 1069, 1072; Benson- 847, 996; Brandon- 815, 962; Brattleboro- 1048s; Burlington- 708, 727, 755- 757, 761- 768, 770, 771, 968b, 1052;

   Castleton- 728, 730, 731, 738b, 750, 752, 754, 756, 795, 813, 1052; Clarendon- 745, 746, 759, 759s, 813, 855, 962, 963, 965, 966, 969; South flats- 965; Coos- 912; Coventry (Dorset)- 964;

   Danby- 745, 746, 893; Danville- 799; Dorset- 773, 781b, 962, 964; Draper- 893; Durham (Clarendon)- 745, 746, 881, 938, 967, 969, 970;

   Fair Haven- 723, 813, 1093; Fowlis (Albany co., N. Y.)- 898; 990; Guilford- 799;

Halifax- 838, 1008; Hartford- 968b; Harwich- 745; Highgate- 855; Hinesburgh-
965; Hubbardton- 750, 752, 795; Hyde Park- 799, 838, 947; Hydeville- 730; Isle of
La Motte- 799; Kent hollow- 1003; Leicester- 962, 966; Londonderry- 734; Lower
Arlington- 812;
    Manchester- 728, 733, 738b, 750, 773, 779, 794, 893, 907, 964, 1072; Mark's
corners- 728, 924, 1003; Marlboro- 733, 777; Middlebury- 759s, 1081; Monkton-
849, 863; Montpelier- 965, 1052;
    Newbury- 780; New Concord- 756; New Haven- 847, 848, 867; North Clarendon-
962; Norwich- 756; Orwell- 804;
    Pawlet- 727, 728, 750, 763, 773, 795, 936, 939, 962; Algiers- 727,728; Pownal-
744, 747, 881, 893, 894, 928; Poultney- 752, 799, 813, 1003, 1005; Princeton
(Manchester)- 896, 899, 900;
    Randolph- 968b; Royalton- 756; Rupert- 740, 773, 860, 915, 1003, 1081;
Rutland- 745, 795, 815, 962, 966, 970, 1003;
    St. Albans- 759s; Sandgate- the Notch- 1090; Shaftsbury- 754, 765, 766, 807,
849, 893, 894, 912, 1002, 1037, 1087; hollow- 766; Shoreham- 859, 1090;
Shrewsbury- 962; Socialborough (Rutland)- 745, 904, 967, 968; Stratton- 733;
Sunderland- 746, 764,881, 893; Swanton- 962, 966;
    Thetford- 772; Tinmouth- 759s, 795;
    Wallingford- 737, 962; Wells- 752, 773, 795; W. Haven- 996; W. Poultney- 806;
W. Rupert- 1003; W. Rutland- 966; Weybridge- 963; Willsborough- 750;
Windham- 734; Windsor- 928; Woodstock- 962;
    Regions & Features- East Bay, Lake Champlain- 754, 936; E. Green Mtn.- 747;
Green Mtns.- 733, 747, 756, 778, 781b, 782, 786, 789, 896; Mack's leg- 734; Mt.
Anthony- as old Mt. Antoine- 1027; Mt. Independence- 748, 750, 756; rivers &
streams- Gillinus creek- 750; Indian- 728, 924; Mill creek- 745; Onion- 756, 906,
917; Otter creek- 745, 756; Pawlet- 876; Poultney- 936; Roaring brook- 733;
Stratton Mtn.- 733;
    Institutions- Circuit court, Cumberland co.- 838; Committees of Safety-
Bennington- 783; Manchester- 794; Convention- 786, 789, 793;
    Military units, Civil War- 5th Inf.- 1081

VERMONTERS- Thomas Brayton & Benjamin Hough, both of Clarendon, then
Charlotte co., N. Y., were driven from Vt. by Ethan Allen & others; Brayton
finally settl. Little White Creek, N. Y., until the controversy was settl.; both
Brayton & Hough had been sentenced by Ethan Allen, Seth Warner, Robert
Cockran, P. Sunderland, James Mead, Gideon Warner, & Jesse Sawyer, to 200
lashes; Hough was capt. while his wf. was away on a journey, & taken to
Sunderland, Vt., where he was tried & rec'd. his lashes; after receiving his
sentence, he sent word to Brayton, the paper stained w. blood from his wnds.,
warning him of the impending enforcement of the sentence upon him; he was then
banished forever from the Grants, & went to the Gov., either in Albany or NYC, to
inform him of the situation; he then went to Ft. Edward, & requested that he might
be allowed to return to his house & retrieve his wf. & child; the outcome of this
request not indicated; a mob, apparently lead by Seth Warner & incl. Remember

Baker, later confronted Thomas Brayton at his house; Brayton bargained w. Warner for the right to settle on his land, arguing his willingness to settle any questions concerning title or other problems by an arbitrary body of peers; agreeing on the fairness of the request, Warner was asked to draw up an agreem., & on completing the document, it was discovered that it had been drawn up for the very person that had been sentenced by them; despite the mob's feelings at this disclosure, Warner was so pleased w. the ruse, that he agreed to Brayton's protection by the document's conditions; c. 1777, Brayton was held for 3- 4 wks., but became "so burthensome [sic] on their hands" that his captors released him, & it was eventually determined he should also be banished from the Grants; his father, Gideon, who had already rem. from Durham (Clarendon, Vt.) to Little White Creek, N. Y., obt. an ox cart to move his son's family, then numbering abt. 7 children, their beds, & some furniture, but was forced to leave behind a horse, a large stock of cattle, & the bulk of their belongings, w/o recompense; c. 1774, Hough appl. to Gov. Colden for a gr. of land, saying he had lost an arm in the service of his country, & was little better than a cripple, & also laid a memorial w. N. Y. authorities concerning the ill treatment given to him & Brayton by the Vermonters- **746**; Wm. Marsh & Samuel Rose, members of Manchester Comm. of Safety, correspond on June 28, 1775, that men from var. parts of Charlotte co., & some of Albany co., have assembled into a mob resolving to stop the courts at Ft. Edward, N. Y.; upon hearing that Capt. Motte's co. had been detained to protect the bench, & that Remember Baker & Robt. Cockran were also there, 'all w. intent to protect the court', they desisted in their design & elected a person to present their concerns to the Continental Congress that rem. the cannon from Ticonderoga was laying the country open to the enemy- **779**; election of officers for the Green Mtn. regt., July 27, 1775, Dorset, Vt.; a list given on July 31st, by Gen. Schuyler, in a letter to N. Y. Provincial Congress- **781b**; the controversy betw. Allen & Warner over election of officers noted by Gen. Schuyler, Aug. 19th, as a potential cause for recruitment to suffer in the Green Mtn. regt., Gen. Schuyler stating that he cannot resolve the question as 'the peculiar situation of these people & the controversy they have had w. this Colony or w. gentlemen in it, renders that matter [officers] too delicate for me to determine'; despite the situation, N. Y. Prov. Congress appt. Lt. Col. Seth Warner & Maj. Samuel Safford as the regt.'s duly elected officers on Sept. 1st- **782**; inquiring abt. the status of their reports, N. Y. Comm. of Safety appt. a comm., Jan. 18, 1777, to go to both Cumberland & Gloucester counties, observing that 'numbers of disaffected persons in Albany & Charlotte co., called Green Mtn. boys, w. divers persons of Cumberland & Gloucester, have industriously made use of every equipment to induce the inhabitants to disavow the authority of N. Y. & form a new & separate state- saying the land belonged 1st to N. H. & N. Y. got them to that state in a fraudulent & unjust manner'; Comm. further observes that 'their customs & manners are diff. from those of N. Y.' & that the Prov. Congress favors their separation by directing the Vt. regt. to be independent of N. Y. forces; report of Mr. Duane, Mar. 1, 1777, notes that only 20 of the expected 80 members attended their mock Convention, &

that most of the inhabitants in the 2 counties remain loyal in their allegiance to the
N. Y. govt.- **786**; Charlotte co. Comm. informs the N. Y. Comm., June 25, 1777,
that the Sheriff has repaired to the E. part of the co. to post notices of election 'but
was told by the people they would tear them down', so no election was held in that
part of the district- **787**; a pamphlet being circulated within the Grants, enclosed in
a June 23rd correspondence of John Williams to John McKesson, Esq., seen as a
response to some of N. Y.'s recent proceedings; also reported from Williams that a
recent meeting was held in the Grants to choose Deputies to sit in Congress, '& the
Convention declared the Grants to be an independent State, called by the name of
New Vermont'; ano. meeting soon to be held for choosing delegates to Continental
Congress; refers p. 578, Corespondence of Provincial Congress- **789**; James Duane,
N. Y. delegate, Continental Congress, informs N. Y. Council of Safety, July10,
1777, of arr. in Philadelphia of June 30th issue, *Connecticut Courant*, which incl.
a declaration from the part of N. Y. 'which is attempted to be wrested out of our
jurisdiction, & which is dubbed the state of Vermont, a name hatched for it in
Philadelphia'; the recent effort, acc. Duane, was evidently engineered by Dr.
Young, '& too probably of some others of more consequence & that his letters have
pushed the people to this last extremity'; along w. the declaration, a list of a no. of
complaints against N. Y. appears, apparently to bolster the cause in the public eye;
'such a train of falsehoods & misrepresentations does but little credit to this mock
Convention, which will prob. proceed to elect Delegates for Congress, & once more
press for their admission'; by Duane's further acct., the venture was not expected to
meet w. Congressional favor, as he ments. that one printer of their productions has
come to the delegates of N. Y. w. the suggestion of printing the June 30th
resolution of Congress either prior to, or foll. the Vt. notice; refers p. 1000, Journal
of Council of Safety; see Duane, James, & N. Y.- Committee of Safety- **793**;
Gouverneur Morris & Abram Yates, Jr., sent as comm. by N. Y. Comm. of safety,
to the army's HQ at Ft. Edward, N. Y.; Morris' correspondence, July 21, 1777,
observes the situation regarding Grants inhabitants, 1st congratulating the Prov.
Congress on the good sense of their recent resolutions 'relative to our north eastern
counrty' & then observing that Col. Skene has been courting the region into the
British cause w. 'golden offers'; Col. Warner identified as a leader of those who
have not yet succumbed as yet, but who 'should he be disgusted, depend upon it he
will draw after him... a very large train' into the other camp, as 'very many of those
villains only want a New England reason, or if you like the expression better, a
plausible pretext, to desert the American States, New Vermont among the rest';
Morris warns further that the movement for a separate govt. in the Grants, at this
juncture, is a 'mere feather' & that in our present dealings, we should take care not
to throw them to the enemy, where they might receive what they want now as a
temporary measure to ensure the success of the enemy's ultimate designs-**796**;
Convention, May 9- 15, 1781, at Cambridge, N. Y., proposing the union of Wash.
co., N. Y., w. the state of Vt.; 6 articles agreed upon, & 2 articles proposed by the
Vt. Legislature also agreed to; the 1st article defines the boundary of the district in
question as beginning N. of a line extended from the N. line of Mass. to the

Hudson river, & S. of 45° latitude; see Washington Co.- **816**; members of the mob confronting Samuel Gardenier, of Walloomsac Patent, abt. Aug. 1, 1771, described as 11 men 'disguised in blankets like Indians, others w. handkerchiefs & others w. Women's caps on their heads, some w. black working frocks, some armed w. sickles & others w. clubs & one w. a pistol'; on their return a fortnight later, the rioters arr. "some disfigured in black, others w. wigs & horsetails, & women's caps; armed w. guns, swords, pistols & clubs, to the no.of abt. 100 persons"; see Grants, N. H. Controversy- **902**; Remember Baker, Ira Allen, & 5 others came upon Benjamin Stevenson, John Brandon, & John Dunbar while they were surveying upon the Onion river, Sept. 29, 1772, & w/o provocation, took away their property & effects, & 'threw Dunbar bound, into a fire, burned him & otherwise beat & abused him in a cruel manner'; a reward of £ 100 recommended by N. Y. authorities for their capture- **906**; at a meeting in Manchester, Vt., Oct. 1772, Jehiel Hawley & James Breakenridge appt. agents, to go to England seeking compensations for those settl. in the Grants- **907**; many of those engaged in the controversy w. N. Y. "were more highly excited & warmed upon the subj. than they were upon the subj. of our national independence", along w. some found on the N.Y. side of the line- **917**; concerning Ethan Allen, his men & his activities, John L. Marsh comments- "It will not do for us Vermonters to say anything against him, unless we wish to incur a storm of popular odium. But it is more probable that he & his party, were as great land- sharks as the country ever saw. For it does appear as though the motive that laid at the foundation of their proceedings, could have been in part set forth in the public accts.; harassing them in every way, in order to induce them to quit the country"; in the Rev. war, they went on w. impunity, & were "the veriest 'cow- boys' in the country"; during the whole, or nearly all of the Rev. war, "they were prepared to be patriots or loyalists, & come under a republic or a monarchy, as their own self- interest might require"- **967**; the state of affairs concerning contested lands claimed by neighbors illustrated by the conditions betw. Daniel Marsh of Socialborough (Rutland) & Silas Whitney of Durham (Clarendon) foll. the Rev. war; where dominion over the contested lands was concerned, the litigants would continue, side by side, "perfectly understanding that when one got such an advantage over the other, there was no course whatever but for him to submit to it, & retaliate, in some analogous way to balance the acct."; acc. Dr. Fitch, this practice prob. existed during the period when the courts were prohibited from entertaining cases where land titles occurred & continued until 'the quieting act' was passed, 1785; refers p. 405, Slade's Vt. State Papers- **970**

VERNOR,
John- recommended for appt. as Qtr. Master, Oct. 3, 1775, Saratoga District militia- **823**; was appt. Adjutant, Col. John McCrea's regt., foll. Archibald McNeal's refusal of the appt.- **827**

VIELE,
Jesse- m. Sarah, dau. Ebenezer & Sally (Hobby) Fitch of Saratoga (Schuylerville, N. Y.); they rem. Wayne co., N. Y., where several of their children now reside- **799**
John- of Cambridge, N. Y.; shot in the side, June 20, 1802, by Cornelius Vanvury of Hoosic, & d. the foll. day; murder inquest held at the house of John Bratt; Barnabus Smith, Coroner- **(L)- 876**

VIRGINIA- 962, 1056, 1093;
  Cities & Towns- Alexandria- 706, 949b, 1081; Arlington Heights- 1098; Dumfries- 1098; Fairfax Station- 1098; Harper's Ferry- 1081, 1098; Pleasant Valley- 1098; Providence Church- 1095; Richmond- 799, 1095; Stafford Court House- 1098; Warrenton- 1094; Yorktown- 1081, 1094;
  Features- Cedar creek- 799; Loudon valley- 1098; Manasas (Bull Run)- 1095b; rivers-Potomac- 1081, 1097, 1098; Rappahannock- 1098; Shenandoah valley- 799, 1098; the Wilderness- 1081

VISSCHER/ VISSHER,
Capt. John- c. 1775, commanded a co. of N. Y. recruits, Albany co., w. Lt. Joseph Fitch as one of the co.'s officers- **799**; 'he was prob. from up Mohawk river'; appeared May 26, 1775, bef. Albany Comm. of Correspondence, offering to raise a co., & was recommended John Tillman & Joseph Fitch as Lts.; it was directed that his co. consist of 100 men, & that upon completion, the co. immed. go to Ticonderoga- **832**
Matthew- adm. to practice, Oct. 19, 1773, Charlotte co., N. Y.- **878**

Von Willebrand's disease- probable incidence of it described in connection w. old Mrs. Tosh, of E. Greenwich, N. Y., who was subj. to freq. nosebleeds; prob. because this condition had not been identified & named, Dr. Fitch queries whether or not her nosebleeds may have been symptomatic of an erratic menstruation; her death occurred one night when she had been taken sick w. bleeding from her nose & mouth so violently that it could not be stopped by usual remedies- **871**

VOORHEES,
Capt. George M.- Co. D, 93rd N. Y. Inf.- **1090b**

VOSS,
Peter- (Vaſs) in an undated letter to N. Y. Council, Sheriff Harmanus Schuyler notes that he & Bastian Deal were forcibly turned out of possession of lands within the Province of N. Y. that had been held by them for up to 30 yrs., under the pretence that the land was loc. in a gr. of N. H.- **885**; his ejection from his land prob. occurred July 30, 1764- **892**

VROOMAN,
Family- (or Frooman) c. 1777, res. on the S. side of the Hoosick river; a no. of families, prob. from the Salem area, quartered in a barn opp. them during "the Retreat"- **744**

W

WAGER,
Robert C.- Co. A, 2nd N. Y., Northern Black Horse, Cav., 1861- 2- **1080**

Wagons- c. 1781, the only one known in Hebron & Salem, N. Y., was owned by Brinkerhoef, who kept a store in the Bedlam (w. Hebron); in 1789, Wm. Lytle acquired one, which was the 1st in Salem; (compare w. Wagons, Vol. 1)- **738**

WAIT,
Alexander Dallas- (A. Dallas) Co. Judge, Oct. 1- 7, 1858, People vs. Martin Wallace- **1048s**; ment. in warrant of authority for the execution of Martin Wallace- **1050s**
Maj.- abt. Jan. 1778, his co. sent from Pawlet, Vt., to Mt. Independence, & then went to Gillinus creek, nr. Willsborough, Vt.; along the course of their movements, the co. coll. a no. of horses, & abt. 40 British & tory prisoners, bef. returning to Pawlet- **750**
Mr.- res. Walloomsac, N. Y.; Aug. 3, 1775, a meeting of the Cambridge, Hoosick, & Bennington Comm. of Safety was held at his resid.- **783**
Elder William- c. 1786, settl.Cambridge, N. Y., in the area that later bore the name Wait's corners- **987**
Zera- 8th s., Elder William; res. Wait's corners, Cambridge, N. Y., for nearly 70 yrs.; d. Oct. 7, 1852, at 82- **987**

WALBRATH,
Emma- of Chittenango, N. Y.; m. Nov. 28, 1866, B. Dwight Fitch, of Brooklyn, N. Y.- **799**

WALBRIDGE,
Col.- (Lt. Col. Ebenezer; 1738- 1819) Oct. 1782, his militia co. stat. Skenesborough (Whitehall, N. Y.)- **747**; 1781, his regt. stat. as scouts in the vicinity of Lake Champlain & Skenesborough, prob. in 4 companies- **749**; Aug.- Nov. 1782, a co. from his regt. of Vt. state troops was reportedly the only co. then stat. at Whitehall- **752**; acc. Thomas Griffith's Rev. war pens. appl., other officers in his regt., May- Nov. 1781, incl. Capt. Pratt, & Lts. Cook & Parker- **754**

WALDO,
Capt.- July 1779, commanded Shaftesbury, Vt. militia co. incl. in Col. Walbridge's regt.- **754**

WALKER,

Daniel- called 'little Walker' by Ethan Allen; he was one of Benjamin Hough's constables; Jan. 1775, Ethan Allen was overheard to have sd. that the Bennington mob would capt. him & Thomas Braten (Brayton) if they might be found above ground- **881**; bro. of Lewis; noted here that he prob. was never capt. by the Bennington mob- **966**

Daniel- m. Jane, dau. John & Betsey (Beaty) McDougall; his wf. d. 1838, E. Greenwich, N. Y.- **978**

Emmet- res. (n. d.) Greenwich, N. Y.- **04a**

Family- 2 bros., Daniel, 'little Walker'; & Lewis- **966**

Family- c. 1853, loc. along the Battenkill & the tracks of the Troy & Rutland R. R., nr. Salem, N. Y.- **1003**

George- m. Eleanor, dau. Deac. Samuel & Sarah (McNaughton) Dobbin; c. 1850, they res. E. Greenwich, N. Y., w. Thomas Cherry- **732**

James O.- s. Lewis; res. Swanton, Vt.; m. 1. dau. Gov. Olin, of Vt.; 2. Eunice, dau. Daniel & Phebe (Rice) Marsh; no children by 1st wf. survived to maturity; 3 children by 2nd wf.- Henry Olin, Daniel Marsh, & Juliett- **962**

Lt. John C.- of 26th Inf.; held a "rendezvous" for recruiting a rifleman regt., Aug. 29, 1814, at Well's Hotel, Union Village (Greenwich, N. Y.)- **705**

Lewis- bro. of Daniel; his s. James O., m. Eunice, dau. Daniel & Phebe (Rice) Marsh- **966**

Phineas- of Woodstock, Conn.; m. Lucy, dau. Jacob, Jr. & Mary (Corbin) Allen- **758**

William- m. Mary, dau. Aaron, Jr. & Artemisia (Lynn) Martin, as her 2nd husb.- **731**

WALLACE,

Martin- b. ca. 1823/4, Connaught, Ireland; res. White Creek, N. Y., occ. as a laborer on var. farms; he res. w. Michael Bradey, & on Feb. 16, 1858, they set out in the morning for Eagle Bridge, & went into Reynold's Tavern, where they met Barney McEntee, a stranger to both of them; after sharing a drink, Bradey left, & he & McEntee went off together towards Buskirk's Bridge, & arr. at Joice's store bef. noon; while there, he claimed to be interested in looking at a house, while McEntee sd. he was going on to Schaghticoke, to look for a dog; when it was his turn to treat at drinks, Wallace informed McEntee that he had no money, & McEntee showed him his wallet, w. over $100 in it, & they continued to drink together; testim. at his trial sd. that Wallace left either at 3 or 4:00 PM, & returned at dusk, asking McEntee to leave w. him; intoxicated & reluctant to go w. Wallace, he was eventually persuaded by the storekeeper, & they were last seen at Jesse Pratt's store, where he was again persuaded to leave w. Wallace, who offered to take him home w. him, or put him up at the tavern; McEntee was later found dead along the highway, betw. 8:00- 8:30 PM, & Wallace was suspected; at abt. midnight, he was reached at Bradey's home, searched & arrested; he was tired for McEntee's murder, Oct. 1- 7, 1858, found guilty of the murder foll. an hr.'s

deliberation, & sentenced to be executed on Dec. 1st; see People vs. Martin Wallace- **1048s**; b. July 18, 1836, youngest s. William; emig. from Co. Galway on the ship *Ashburton*, & arr. NYC, Sept. 1851 (the ship, *Ashburnton*, of Liverpool, John McWilliam, master, arr. Sept. 25th, NYC, w. 418 passengers); after a month, he rem. Hoosick, N. Y., where he res. w. his bro.; m. _____; a dau., b. May 1858; his execution, Wed., Dec. 1, 1858, was attended by 80 persons, incl. the Sheriffs, & Sheriffs- elect of Albany, Renseselaer, & Warren counties; on the occasion, "a suffic. no. of assistants were appt. to form a guard upon ea. side of the path from the Court- house door to the building for the execution"; the no. of other persons outside the scene of the execution as spectators was substantial, despite the coldness of the night & morning, w. persons coming from 30- 40 mi. distant, some under the rumor that the execution was to be public; to preserve order during the day, 4 companies of militia attended, & occ. the sidewalk along the front of the Court- house, & fences around the yard in its rear; the village of Salem was thronged w. spectators, some positioning themselves in trees or on housetops, in attempts to glimpse the scene of the execution; on the Sun. prior to the execution, Wallace attempted to break jail, & was afterw. confined in a cell "shackled by a fetter locked around his left ancle [sic], & connected by a chain 6 ft. in length to a staple in the floor beside his bed", & kept under constant guard; at 12:05 PM, the drop was sprung, & he hung for 5 min. bef. external appearance of life ceased, & his pulse stopped after 12 min.; at 12:42 PM, his body was lowered into the coffin, & he was taken to the Catholic Cemetery, N. White Creek, N. Y., for burial- **1050s**
Theodore S.- Assist. Surgeon, 93rd N. Y. Inf.- **1090b**
William- of Loughrea, Co. Galway, Ireland; had 3 daus. & 2 sons; his youngest s. Martin, b. July 18, 1836; he d. Jan./ Feb. 1837, & his wid. m. shortly thereafter; all but oneof his children emig. to America; c. 1851, his oldest s. res. Hoosick, N. Y., & at that time, his bro. Martin came to res. w. him- **1050s**
William Hugh- res. NYC; he & John Reid, along w. Atty. Gen. Smith, referred to by the Gov. when John Munro petitn. for an appt. as High Sheriff of Albany, Sept. 20, 1771- **902**

WALLER,
_____- of Union Village (Greenwich, N. Y.); c. 1861, Adjutant, 7th Illinois Inf.- **1080**

WALLIS,
George- called by the Dist. Atty., at the close of Martin Wallace's trial, to testif. that Wallace's character prev. to Barney McEntee's murder was not good- **1048s**
Joseph- called by the Dist. Atty., at the close of Martin Wallace's trial, to testif. that he had known Wallace for 2 yrs., had worked in the flax- mill nr. him, & heard that his general moral character was not good; on cross- exam, he could not give a specific name, but sd. he heard of his reputation generally, from other workers at the mill- **1048s**

Marvin- res. White Creek, N. Y., until May 2, 1858, when he rem. Shaftsbury, Vt.; flax mill owner; employed Martin Wallace during the months bef. the murder of Barney McEntee, & testif. to the type of currency that he pd. to Wallace, at one time a $10 bill from the Union Bank of Troy, & ano. time, a bill he obt. from David Kirk, of Troy, N. Y.; other currency found in Wallace's coat was not his, although Col. Crocker attempted to sway his testim. on whether he was mistaken abt. the form of currency he pd. Wallace; prior to the murder, Wallace came to him to borrow $10 or $15 to pay on some accts. he owed- **1048s**

Walloomsac, N. Y.- c. 1777, was apparently a precinct of the town of Cambridge; refers p. 71, Corey's Gazetteer of Wash. Co.- **762b**

Walloomsac Patent- one of the orig. patentees was named Ten Eyck- **763**; its W. line was abt. 20 rods W. of Reubin Clark's house- **765**; its boundary adjoin. Van Cuyler's (Lake's) Patent; several Quaker families settl. in this neighborh. bef. Rev. war & held meetings; their meeting- house was later erected in 1801; see Vol. 4; Baptist & Methodist meeting- houses were erected soon after that date; refers p. 132, Corey's Gazetteer- **806**

Walloomsac river- c. 1850, Dr. Fitch notes its width is 1/3rd larger than the width of the Hoosick river at the point where the 2 converge- **764**

WALLS,
Patrick- Irish laborer; c. 1851/2, arr. in Archibald Hay's neighborh., betw. Cossayuna & Greenwich, N. Y.; he was a pivotal figure in a controversy betw. Hay & Priest Quigley; professing not to be Catholic, he explained that he had a Protestant father & Catholic mother, & had attended both types of meetings, his bros. adopting their father's faith, & his sists. adopting their mother's faith; since he had arr. in America, he had only attended Catholic services twice; shortly after the fall election, he began chopping wood for Archibald Hay, & injured himself the Thurs. bef. New Year's, 1854/5, when "in falling a tree, a sapling bending & flying back struck him over his right eye, knocking him senseless"; he was discovered in this state by David Tallmadge & taken to the Hay's house, where a sick bed was made for him, & spent abt. 11- 13 wks. in recuperation; during the course of his recovery, Bridget Dwyer volunteered to nurse him, but after 4 wks. of steady improvement, his condition turned for the worse; at that time, she spent abt. a fortnight in Cambridge, & it was presumed that she contacted Priet Quigley while there; abt. a wk. after her return, Quigley arr., w/o disclosing his intention to perform the sacraments, an action that Hay had expressly voiced his opposition to within his own house; when it became apparent that this was the priest's intentions, a tremendous confrontation occurred betw. Quigley & Hay, marking the differences & prejudices in perspective betw. the Catholic & Protestant inhabitants of the area during that period; Walls, who had only seen the priest once bef., & then, not to speak to, became caught up in the controversy; feeling that he had been treated

well in his time of need, he appeared indiff. to Quigley's purpose, whom he felt had badly misused the Hay family; foll. Quigley's departure, the "constant string of Catholics" who had been coming to Hay's house to visit Walls, stopped, apparently by the priest's influ. over his flock; although still in feeble, condition, Walls left Hay's house on May 2nd, & began work as a gardener for Thurston Wilcox- **1058**

WALWORTH,
Benjamin, Esq.- d. Feb. 26, 1812, at 65- **(L)- 772**
Judge- c. 1825, presided over Wash. co. Court, during the trial of William Gordon for the killing of George Coggshall- **808**
Reuben Hyde- (Chancellor Walworth) (1788- 1867; Master in Chancery, circuit judge, 1811; 7th Congress, 1821- 23; N. Y. 4th Judicial Dist., 1823- 28; Chancellor of N. Y., 1828- 48; author, Hyde Genealogy) compared the legal stature of Hon. Jeremiah Mason to that of Webster & Choate- **759s**

WAPTHORP,
Hon. Charles- plaintiff, May 19, 1774, vs. Samuel Buel- **878**

WARD,
Benjamin- of Black Creek district (Hebron, N. Y.); for 10 shillings, Jan. 10, 1786, purch. land from Luther Clough- **(L)- 936**
Hosea- of Hartford, N. Y.; Oct. 12, 1802, cut his throat w. a razor; Alex. McNish, Coroner- **(L)- 876**
John- res. Canada; m. Catharine Reid, wid. John Munro, Esq., as her 2nd husb.; their dau. Sarah, m. Cruth Patterson- **812**
Pat- acc. testim., Martin Wallace had res. w. him prior to res. w. Michael Bradey, & he had turned him out for carrying a pistol; it was also sd. that Wallace had once attempted to trip & rob him- **1048s**

WARFORD,
Charles- res. Salem, N. Y.; his loc. orig. occ. by John Livingston- **1084**

WARNER,
Col. Seth- (1743- 1784) a letter of Judge C. K. Williams erroneously suggests he res. Greenwich, N. Y.; c. 1770's, he was apparently leader of a mob that confronted Thomas Brayton at his house in Clarendon, Vt., then Charlotte co., N. Y.; when Brayton bargained w. him for the right to remain in the grants, he agreed that the conditions were fair & reasonable, but when he filled out the agreem., it was discovered that Brayton had prev. rec'd. a sentence of 200 lashes (prob. if found in the grants); the mob., which incl. Remember Baker, became vociferous abt. pronouncing sentence upon him, but Warner was pleased by Brayton's ruse, & assented that he deserved their protection instead, & left him unmolested- **746**; ment. in Rev. war pens. appl. of Ebenzer Farnsworth as an officer witn. during his July 1777- Jan. 1778 period of service- **750**; officer witn., Rev. war pens. appl.

Joseph Crippen- **755**; did not participate in the 1st part of the battle of Bennington; either Maj. Samuel Safford, of his regt.; or Maj. Gilbert Bradley, one of Gen. Stark's officers, used to note that Gen. Stark found fault w. him when he 1st arr. on the field for not getting there sooner; on saying that his men were so fatigued & overcome by heat that they were unable to fight any longer & beat Col. Breyman back, Col. Warner was heard to say in reply- 'By the Lord! old John [sic] Warner has now come here to fight & if your men are too hot to go at it, get them out of the way & give me a chance'- **764**; his fresh troops met Col Breyman's forces abt. halfway betw. the point where his advance began & the loc. of Esq. Barnet's house, where the road leaves the river flats & ascends a hill; Warner's forces "capt. some of his advance parties, & opposed his further advance w. such spirit, that he was eventually compelled to retire"- **766**; he & Ethan Allen adm. to an audience w. N. Y. Provincial Congress, July 4, 1775, & a regt. of Green Mtn. boys was afterw. ordered to be raised distinct & independent from N. Y. troops, & £ 30 advanced to them by Gen. Schuyler's recommendation- **778**; elected to his rank in the Green Mtn. regt. by 41 to 5 vote, July 27, 1775- **781b**; arr. in Albany, N. Y., Aug. 23, 1775, to obt. clothing & c. for the men of his regt., who would not take the field w/o money for blankets & arms; Gen. Schuyler advanced £ 500 to him, & noted that the controversy betw. him & Ethan Allen over officers had been carried to such lengths that it served to frustrate recruiting within the regt.; Sept. 1st- N. Y. Provincial Congress appts. him to the rank he had prev. been elected to- **782**; directed by Gen. Schuyler to send his recruits to Ticonderoga as soon as they enl., Jan.- Mar. 1777; but by latest returns, only 24 men have come, despite his having recruited in Albany & other places, 'as well as his own beat'- **786**; July 1777, ordred by Gen. Schuyler to advance as nr. to the enemy w. the small forces he has in order to bring off cattle & carriages nr. them; part of Mass. militia & all of N. H militia ordered by Schuyler to join him at Manchester, Vt., July 17th- **794**; Gouverneur Morris observes, July 21, 1777, that he is a leader among the Grants inhabitants who, if 'should he be disgusted' (by the dealings of the N. Y. govt. w. the Grants inhabitants) 'will draw after him... a very large train' of converts to the British cause, based upon offers made to them via Col. Skene- **796**; he & Ethan Allen were principal leaders of the Bennington mob- **881**; a monument erected to him in his native place, Roxbury, Conn.; its cornerstone laid Dec. 23, 1858, when Judge Charles B. Phelps eulogized his memory; Phelps took ill & d. immed. afterw.; refers Dec. 24, 1858, semi- wkly. *N. Y.Times*; a subsequent newspaper notes that Judge Phelps had been ill prior to giving his address & that the event of his death was not as apocryphal as it appears to be- **1052**; only 120? men from his regt. turned out Aug. 14, 1777, & marched from Manchester to Bennington, Vt., to join Gen. Stark's forces; they became so wet during the march, that they excused themselves from the morning battle until they were able to dry themselves- **1072** *Solomon*-res. Jackson, N. Y.; his farm was occ. by John Younglove foll. the Rev. war- **843**

WAR OF 1812- reported June 23, 1814, that abt. 200 British prisoners of war passed through Salem, N. Y., "a few days since", from Greenbush, N. Y., to Canada; such large exchanges noted by the local press as an abandonment by the respective govts. of the "retaliation system"- **703**; due to the "alarming situation of our northern frontier" & rapid advance of the British army, the Salem militia assembled & departed the morning of Sept. 8th, by orders rec'd. from Gen. DeRidder, Sept. 6, 1814; they were instructed to rendezvous w. other units at Ft. Miller, N. Y., & proceed northward; the local press declared that the "zeal & alacrity w. which they turn out are evincive of true patriotism", & that 'our enemies will find that the disgusting transactions at Washington & Alexandria can never be performed w. the towns & villages in this state"- **706**; a letter from a militia member, dated Sept. 13, 1814, Burlington, Vt., note that the invading British army encamped at 3:00 AM, on the day prev. to the arrival of the Salem militia, which was the foll. morning; the naval engagem. on Lake Champlain commenced a little after sunrise, on Sun. (Sept. 11th)- **708**; the sloops *President, Montgomery, Preble, Chubb, & Finch*,10 gunboats, & boats & cutters, comprising the Lake Champlain squadron, slated to be sold June 28, 1815, at Whitehall, N. Y., by order of Sec. of the Navy- **715**; an article, Nov. 2, 1815, notes that cannon taken from British ships capt. at Plattsburgh by Commodore Macdonough were landed at Whitehall, N. Y., to be deposited w. their carriages & implements in a building being erected there for that purpose; their high quality remarked upon; a strong fortification planned by the British for construction on Isle- Aux- Noix, & several sloops engaged for transporting stone as soon as the lake opens in the spring- **719**; Wash. co. allotted $16,052.65 as its port. of a tax, 1816, to defray war expenses- **725**; boats & other properties of the Onondaga Salt Works confiscated for use by U. S. govt. to such an extent, that the works were abandoned until after restoration of peace- **1004**; a British co. at St. Regis, surprised & capt., fall 1812, by William Gray, who lead a party through the woods at French Mills to capt. them; considered a dangerous partisan, Gray was surprised & capt., Dec. 1813, & confined at Quebec, dying in prison, Apr. or May 1814- **1015**; acc. Betsey Taylor, Salem, N. Y., "In the time of the late war, the early recoll. of all the old people were revived, & they were continually talking over the incidents of the Revolution"; old Capt. (Alexander) McNitt's memories were stirred to such a degree that he continually spoke of killing tories, & one morning, prepared himself to escort a party of tories to Nova Scotia, bef. family members were able to stop him- **1018**; a no. of sailors killed during the battle of Plattsburgh were bur. at Burlington, Vt., in a spot nr. Ethan Allen's bur. site- **1052**; the land fighting at the battle of Plattsburgh consisted of only a slight skirmish at the river ford, 2 mi. up the Saranac from the village; Gen. Macomb posted a militia force here todefend the ford, w. orders to retreat to a quantity of stores loc. 5 mi. S. of there, & defend them, or if unable, to destroy them; Gov. Provost's army occ. the N. side of the Saranac in the village, opp. 3 or 4 small American forts; on the morning of the naval battle (Sept. 11, 1814), Provost sent a detachm. to engage the militia, suspecting that they would retreat to the forts, & he might fire upon both simult.; however, the detachm., in close pursuit of the militia, was unable to discern their loc. until drawn abt. 4mi. away from their anticipated loc., & toward the American stores; at this point, they were able to get a glimpse of the lake, & obt. news of their fleet's surrender; Provost, searching for signs of the militia & his pursuing detachm., observed the same event, recalled his troops, & decamped that same evening- **1055**; during the naval port. of the battle, when the British fleet was drawing itself up, one of the American vessels broke ranks & ran towards shore, to get under protection of the guns of the fort, presuming the others would foll. him; however, no other vessel stirred, & when halfway to shore, the vessel cast anchor & remained idle throughout the entire battle; Macdonough's flagship, the *Saratoga*, used up all its guns facing the enemy, & then a ketch was sent out to perform the perilous task of turning its opp. side to face the enemy; as it came abt., the *Saratoga* "disch. a whole broadside, well aimed, into her antagonist- carrying her masts by the board- & speedily ending the fight"- **1056**

WARREN,
_____- miller; dau. Minerva, m. Williams Blanchard- **1045**
Ann- of Warrensburgh, N. Y.; m. Elias Pattison, s. Rev. Bradley & Polly (Pattison) Sillick; his wid. superintends "the female part of the Troy House" (prob. The Warren Free Institute, incorp. 1846)- **950**
Ephriam- of Killingworth, Mass.; had 3 children- Ebenezer, Ephriam; & Abigail, m. Joseph Cheney- **1083**
Lyman J.- 2nd Lt., Co. E, 93rd N. Y. Inf.- **1090b**
Minerva- m.Williams, s. Hon. Anthony I. & Maria (Williams) Blanchard- **1045**
Palmira- m. George Newell, s. Newell & Charity (Blackman) Angel- **848**

Warren Co., N. Y.- (org. 1813, from Wash. co.) incl. w. Wash. co., 1814, as a district within the 37th session, N. Y. Legislature- **992**; c. 1861, the 22nd N. Y. Inf. was recruited here & in Wash. co.- **1080**; recruits from Glens Falls, N. Y., comprise Cos. E & F, 22nd N. Y. Inf.- **(L)- 1074**

WASHBURN,
Dr.- foll. his whipping by the Bennington mob, Jan. 30, 1775, Benjamin Hough was given over to his care- **881**
Milo E.- 2nd Lt., Co. C, 93rd N. Y. Inf.- **1090b**
Miss- res. Clear Creek, Iowa; gave an address, Nov. 2,1861, to the soldiers of Cos. A- C, 14th Iowa Inf., during their encampment here while on their march to Ft. Randall, Dakota Territory- **1089**

WASHINGTON,
Gen./ Pres. George- (1732- 1799) his memory toasted at a public banquet given in honor of Commodore Macdonough, Nov. 29, 1814, Salem, N. Y.- "We sigh while we ment. the name, as it gives us the melancholly [sic] recoll. of more auspicious days. Is there no Elisha to snatch as it falls, the mantle of this political Elijah?";

the only toast of the evening made while standing, foll. by the "Death March"- **709**; description of a celebration given in observance of his birthday, Feb. 23, 1816, Granville, N. Y.- **723**; (Gen.) officer witn. during Sept.- Nov. 1776 service of Samuel Standish, acc. his Rev. war pension appl.- **747**; his letter to Gen. Sir Wm. Howe at Boston, Jan. 30, 1776, offers the exchange of "Gov. Skene" for Mr. James Lovell; Gen. Howe notes in reply that an exchange may have been accomplished, except for the recent discovery of a prohibited correspondence by Mr. Lovell- **760**; letter to him from Gen. Schuyler, July 17, 1777, at Ft. Edward, identifies the block house at Ft. Ann as the advance post of Burgoyne's expedition; notes the abandoning of Ft. George on the prev. day, & among other details of events surrounding Ft. Edward, observes that 'so much toryism prevails among people, on what are commonly called the N. H. Grants, & amongst those that res. in the townships bordering them; that I should not be much surprised if Gen. B. should attempt to march as far as Bennington in order to procure cattle & carriages'- **794**; Morris & Yates report, July 23, 1777, that if he might 'spare' 1,500 good troops, along w. other proposed actions, it might be possible to halt Burgoyne's advance- **797**; an editor, perh. in Philadelphia, reportedly spoke of his death as being "of no more consequence than the death of a dog", an observation that, acc. Dr. Fitch, may be attrib. to "The infidel philosophy of France... rampant among the warm democrats at that day"; (this same sentiment was criticized in the July 26, 1804, *Northen Centinel*, examined by Dr. Fitch, & noting the death of Alexander Hamilton, where the same issue was alluded to in the *Centinel* while criticizing rival paper, the *Washington Register*, for its treatment of the Burr- Hamilton affair; see § 532;Vol. 1)- **919**; Gen. Schuyler assoc. w. him in the Continental Congress, 1775, to establ. governing rules & regulations of the Continental Army; Nov. 1779, Gen. Schuyler appt. by the Congress to confer w. him on the state of the Southern Dept.- **920**; brief ment.- **1036**; letter to him from Gov. Clinton, Oct. 18, 1780, giving an erroneous notice from Gen. Schuyler that the settlm. of White Creek (Salem, N. Y.) had been burnt; refers p. 121, v. iii, Spark's Letters to Washington- **1066**; when appt. Commander in Chief, a declaration was drawn up by the Continental Congress, giving the causes & necessity for their taking up arms, which was widely publ. when he assumed command at Boston; widely circulated at home & abroad, it acknowl. numerous instances of Divine favor & Providence permitting them to be called into the conflict of the Rev. war when grown to their present strength- **1072b**

Washington Benevolent Society- of Granville, N. Y.; description of their celebration of Washington's birthday, Feb. 23, 1816; ceremonies began at 10:00 AM, from the house of J. Stiles, w. announcement of the arr. of their associates from Fair Haven, Vt., bringing a frigate dubbed the *"Saratoga"*, & "drawn by 8 horses, completely equipped, officered & manned"; its arr. was accomp. by an artillery salute; banners described incl. an ensign- 'Washington: born Feb. 22d 1732'; a burgee upon the mainmast- 'Macdonough: the Hero of Lake Champlain'; & a jack upon the mainmast- 'The glorious 11th Sept. 1814'; when the display "anchored", her crew disembarked, formed within a procession, & proceeded to the Congregational church for an oration delivered by Robert Wilkinson, Esq., & then returned to their host's, partaking of dinner & drinking 14 regular & many voluntary toasts- **723**

Washington County Agricultural Society- Dr. Asa Fitch, Sr., elected its President, 1820- **799**; Sept. 1862, "the ground which is now being fenced & pitted up" for its Fair, Salem, N. Y., design. as Camp Washington, site for the org. of the 123rd NYSV- **1097**

Washington County Bible Society- its 1st organizational meeting held at the White Church, Salem, N. Y.; its "semi- centennial anniversary" held in the same loc., & under similar circumstances- "our country is now engaged in grappling w. the great rebellion; 600,000 men were in the field last spring & now 600,000 more are called for"; the anniversary held Sept. 4, 1862, while volunteers have been assembling for over 2 wks., to form the county's regt., the 123rd NYSV Inf.; Gen. Pope's defeat at 2nd Bull Run & the 1st official news of area dead from the 22nd N. Y. Inf. arr. amidst their convention; "the subj. so engrossed the public mind that everything else ceases to attract interest"; however, despite, or perh., because of the activity & general gloom arising from Pope's defeat, the meeting was well attended by the public; the meeting convened at 11:00 AM, by Vice President, Rev. Henry Gordon, as Rev. J. B. Scouller had retired to Philadelphia, in poor health; the assembly adjourned at 5:00 PM; its morning business consisted of the election of Rev. A. B. Lambert as its President, & the request of Dr. James Savage for his replacement as Secretary; Corresponding Secretary, Rev. E. H. Newton, delivered the annual report, incl. biog. sketches of the 4 dec'd. Presidents of the Society, & its prominent founders, incl. Dr. Nathaniel S. Prime; Rev. Gordon addressed the Soc., referring to the assembled soldiers nearby & the "vices that will beset them in camp"; during the afternoon session, Rev. E. H. Newton spoke of the 1st settlm. of Salem, a century earlier, from part of the Londonderry colony, at abt. the same time as Rev. James Proudfit was sent to America as a Presbyterian missionary, w. ment. of their influ. in relation to the creation of the Soc., & their desc.; Dr. Lambert spoke of Deac. McMurray, the sole survivor of the orig. meeting; Mr. Welsh, a converted Catholic, & agent of the Protestant Union, gave an address on the opposition of Catholic priests to general access to the Bible, giving numerous examples; Rev. Mr. Proudfit conveyed numerous anecdotes of his experiences in ministering to the spiritual needs of soldiers in camp, & the vices intrinsic to camp life; one additional speaker, not heard or recorded by Dr. Fitch, who had been in attendance during the entire proceedings- **1097**

Washington County Medical Society- convened July 4, 1815, at the Hotel, Salem, N. Y., & elected as officers, President- Dr. Asa Fitch, Sr.; Vice President- Jonathan Dorr; Treasurer- Asahel Morris; Secretary- A. McAllister; Censors- Abram Allen, Zebulon Reed, & John Thompson- **717**; org. 1807, w. Dr. Asa Fitch, Sr., as its 1st

Vice President; other offices held by him in the society incl. President- 15 yrs., 1st elected July 1812, & resigning the post Feb. 26, 1834; Vice President- 5 yrs.; Treasurer- 5 yrs.- **799**

WASHINGTON COUNTY, N. Y.- its union w. state of Vt. proposed at a Convention convened May 9, 1781, Cambridge, N. Y.; delegates from towns of Hoosick, Schaghticoke, Cambridge, Saratoga, Upper White Creek, Black Creek (Hebron), Granville, Skenesborough (Whitehall), Kingsbury, Ft. Edward, & Little Hoosick drafted 6 articles defining terms of union & appended 2 articles proposed by Vt. Legislature-

1. boundary of annexed district defined as N. of a line extended from N. line of Mass. to Hudson river, & S. of 45° latitude 'as comprehended in the late jurisdictional claim by the legislature of the State of Vt. be considered as part of the state & the inhabitants as free citizens';

2. that Vt. exert its military forces to the defense of the district's inhabitants 'against any Insurrection, Invasion, or Incursion whatsoever, but esp. against the common enemy';

3. that the legislature appl. to Congress for admission to the Union as soon as warranted;

4. that as people within the claim 'have been called upon & pd. a considerable part of the Continental taxes into the Treasury of N. Y.', that they should have that amt. credited should Vt. be required to pay their port. to Congress- agreed, provided services of Vt. in present war be incl.; agreed, provided expenses of sd. District in present war also be incl.;

5. that all actions pending within the claim be transferred in the situation they were, at the time of the Union, into courts erected under Vt. authority w/o costs beyond those ordinarily under N. Y. jurisdiction;

6. change of jurisdiction not to affect or alienate private private properties; the proposals by Vt. Legislature, agreed upon-

A. the Independence of Vt. to be held sacred, w. no member of the Legislature giving their vote or otherwise endeavoring to obt. an act or resolution that shall endanger its existence, independence, or well being by referring its independence to "arbitrament" of any power;

B. whenever Union occurs w. the American states & a dispute arises w. this state & any of the United States respecting boundary lines, the legislature will submit the dispute to Congress or such other tribunal as mutually agreed for settling the dispute; agreed to by the Convention & Comm., May 15, 1781; Moses Robinson, Comm. chairman; Jonas Fay, Clerk; John Rodgers, Convention chairman- **816**; its 1st brick houses, constructed 1787, prob. by the same person, for Edmund Wells, of Cambridge, & Noah Payne, Sr., of Ft. Miller, N. Y.- **840**; prev. to construction of the Co. Jail, when the co. was too poor to provide one, or to maintain anyone in confinement, it was deemed best to either whip or place an offender in the pillory for a short time & then let them go- **868**; John Telfair, b. ca. 1830, Salem,

N. Y.,"having gone tither w. one of the 1st companies from this district", arr. in California, c. 1849- **972**; listing of its State Assembly members, 1777- 1857, excluding 1779- 81, where records are either missing or not extant; 1st noted foll. 7th Assembly session, 1784, as a representative district; incl. w. Clinton co. foll. the 15th, 1792, session; incl. alone w. 28th, 1804, session; incl. w.Warren co. foll. 37th, 1814, session; incl. alone again, w. 44th, 1823, session- **992**; Wash. co. map, publ. 1853, by Scott & Smith, Philadelphia, Pa.; inaccuracies in depicting tracks of the Troy & Rutland R. R. noted & corrected by Dr. Fitch; see Transportation- **1003**; the no. of electoral districts per town, 1854, noted as-

1- Cambridge, Dresden, Hampton, Hartford, Jackson, & Putnam;
2- Argyle, Easton, Ft. Edward, Granville, Hebron, Kingsbury, Salem,White Creek, & Whitehall;
3- Greenwich; 4- Ft. Ann- **1028**; Capital Punishment- by 1858, there had been only 4 instances within the bounds of the co., "once under the military & thrice under the civil jurisdiction"; the 1st instance was a Hessian deserter (see Hundertmark, George; Vol. 1) from Burgoyne's army, who was caught by a tory scout party on the outskirts of Salem, nr. Creighton hill, on the road to Shushan, N. Y.; he was pinioned, & returned to Burgoyne's camp at Ft. Miller, where he was confined to the Duer Mansion, until he was executed in the meadow behind the mansion & bur. there; the civil instances were- Benjamin Holmes, Mar. 28, 1800, after being postponed twice; Thomas Qua, Aug. 12, 1808; & Martin Wallace, Dec. 1, 1858; all of these occurred in Salem, N. Y., the 1st at the site where the Catholic church stood in 1858; the 2nd, at Gallow's hill, on the N. end of the village; & the last, at a building & scaffold especially constructed nr. the Court House; refers Dec. 1, 1858, *Salem Press*- **1050s**; foll. units recruited here, c. 1861- 22nd & 93rd N. Y. Inf.; Co. A, 2nd N. Y. Cav., recruited from Salem, N. Y.; Sept. 1862- 123rd NYSV- **1080**; May 25, 1861, units to comprise 22nd N. Y. Inf. ordered to Camp Rathbone, Troy, N. Y.; Co. B- Whitehall; Co. D- Cambridge; Co. G- Ft. Edward; Co. H- Sandy Hill- **(L)**- **1074**; the co. quota for the current call of troops, Sept. 1862, amts. to some 1,400 men; less than 1,000 currently raised in volunteers; amt. of co. enl. bounty- $50, w. $25- 50 sometimes pd. by towns; for some 2 wks. prior to Sept. 4th, the 123rd NYSV, the Wash. co. regt., has been forming at Camp Washington, Salem, N. Y.- **1097**; loc. of troops, 123rd NYSV Inf.- Co. E- Hebron & Hartford; Co. H- Salem; Co. I- Cambridge & S. Easton; for complete list, & additional recruitment records, see Vol. 4- **1098**

Washington County, N. Y., Courts- (see also, Charlotte co., N. Y., Courts) held in 3 terms per yr., at Salem, N. Y., until 1787; refers Laws of N. Y., i., 307; its Feb. term held at Adiel Sherwood's, Ft. Edward, N. Y., refers Laws, i, 461, until an act passed Feb. 10, 1797; refers Laws, iii, 217; the last term at Adiel Sherwood's held Feb. 1797; Judges instructed that courts held 2nd Tues. of Feb. may adjourn to meet that day, or the next, at Mary Dean's, Kingsbury, N. Y., where all future Feb. courts were to be held, 1st convening in Feb. 1798; sessions held at Sandy Hill,

N. Y., Dec. 1811 & Jan. 14, 1812; see Criminal Offenders- **874**; 6 cases taken from records by Dr. Fitch, prob. to illustrate the severity of punishments; Oct. 1780- State of N. Y. vs. Thomas Beaty, Jr.; the same, vs. Alex. McNess- "the like" in all things; refers § 258, Vol. 1; Jan. 8, 1789- People vs. Edmund Hunt, bef. Judge Hobart, in Supreme Court; People vs. Squire Haskins- "The like Judgement in all things"; Jan. 7, 1789- People vs. John Wiser Wheeler; People vs. Thomas Burrell; see Criminal Offenders- **877**

Washington County, N. Y., Deeds- coll. of early entries, from Liber A, Book of Deeds, recorded during the period when Patt Smyth & John McCrea were clerks, ranging in date from 1766- 1792, w. principle no. of entries being the period bef. the Rev. war, foll. by 1780's- **(L)- 936**; a 2nd series of entries, some repeating the earlier series, taken from John McCrea's "parchment bound book", primarily from the 1780's- **(L)- 936b**

WASHINGTON, D. C.- 706, 709, 949b, 1056, 1080, 1081, 1097, 1098; as Washington City- 974; the capitol, Capitol Hill- 1098; Columbian Hospital- 1081; Ft. Washington- 974

WATER, bodies of, in N. Y. & vicinity-
Oceans & Seas- Atlantic- 759s, 809, 883, 1069;
Bays & Estuaries- East bay- 936; Long Island Sound- 940, 955; Mill Bay- 1020; NYC Harbor- 1070; South Bay- 894;
Lakes & Ponds- Champlain- 709, 715, 719, 723, 731, 749, 750, 774, 787, 814, 844, 880, 894, 911, 923, 936, 957, 998, 1000, 1052, 1059, 1070, 1093; as Lake St. Sacrement- 1013; Cossayuna- as McDougall's- 1093; as McNab's- 732, 847; Eire- 709, 730, 733; George- 747, 759s, 750, 753, 754, 773, 799, 931, 989, 1008, 1016; Hedges- as Big Pond- 732; Jackson Ponds- 739, 853; Oneida- 756; Ontario- 709; Seneca- 806; Summit- 732;
Rivers & Streams- Allegheny- 949; Battenkill- 701, 702, 732, 738, 738b, 852, 854, 855, 867, 876, 985, 1003, 1057, 1060, 1063, 1064, 1098; mouth of- 804; Beaver brook- 1047b; Beaver dam creek- 1095; Black creek- 730, 732, 855, 860, 863, 865, 873;
Camden creek- 738b; Catskill creek- 756; Cossayuna creek- 847; Fish creek- 799; Genesee- 759s; Gilliland's creek- 788; Gillinus creek- 750; Goose creek- 1095; Granville (Metowee)- 998, 1003;
Halfway brook- 837; Hoosick- 744, 764, 766, 839, 953b, 1003, 1021, 1048s; Hudson- 747, 756, 763, 800, 804, 816, 837, 852, 876, 894, 902, 930, 935, 936, 949b, 956, 959, 1072; as North river- 730, 731; Indian river- 728, 924, 1003; Little White creek- 746, 807, 1006; mouth of- 1006; Livingston's brook 1064;
Mill creek (Rutland co., Vt.)- 745; Mohawk- 748, 756, 788, 832, 989; Moses kill- 797, 804, 876, 1070, 1077; Niagara- 812; Onion river- 756; Otter creek- 745, 756, 789; Otter creek falls- 822; Owl kill- 739, 844, 1003, 1027; mouth of- 1003; Podunk brook- 837;

Reid's mineral spring- 802, 1081; St. Lawrence- 750, 812, 1054; Saranac- 1055;
Still (or Dead) creek- 983; Susquehanna- 930; Three rivers- 750; Trout brook- 738;
  Walloomsac- 761, 762, 764, 766, 767, 1006, 1007, 1022; W. Canada creek- 748;
White creek- 730, 732, 1003, 1006, 1098; White (Ondawa) creek- 860, 864, 867,
1003, 1073; Wood creek- 794, 928, 936, 1000;
  Canals- Champlain- 746, 800, 804, 1067, 1070; Eire- 730

WATERBURY,
Col. David- (Gen.; 1722- 1801) his regt., Jan. 1776, incl. Capt. Bradley's co., was
marched from Stamford, Conn., to NYC- **752**

WATERHOUSE,
Samuel- res. Pawlet, Vt.; 50 acres, Skene's Patent, "that takes in East bay & on
'Poultney river so called' ", conveyed May 12, 1783, to Jedidiah Humstead- **(L)-
936**

WATERS,
John- of Johnstown, N. Y.; m. Maria, dau. Willard Cheney & Mary (Faxon)
Conkey; they res. Trenton, N. Y.; children-
  1. Van Rensselaer, Baptist minister; m. Belinda Burr, & now res. Turin, N. Y.
  2. Mary Ann, d. June 10, 1829, at 22
  3. Charles George- d. Mar. 23, 1835, at 15 yrs., 7 mos., & 14 ds.
  4. Sophia, m. Lyman Pitcher
  5. John, m. & res. Trenton, N. Y.
  6. George, res. Trenton, N. Y.
  7. Marvin, d. May 6, 1813, at 2 yrs., 9 mos., & 6 ds.; other children d. y.- **730**
Mary Ann- (dau. John & Maria Conkey) d. June 10, 1829, when riding home from
school on horseback; "a hurricane prostrated a tree, which struck the horse, whose
head struck her side, & she d. within an hr."- **730**

WATKINS,
Asa B.- s. Seneca; b. ca. 1833, Salem, N. Y.; enl. summer 1861, 103rd Ohio Inf.;
d. Dec. 26, 1862, of fever, Frankfort, Ky.- **1095**
David- presented certif. to N. Y. Prov. Congress, July 18, 1775, noting his election,
along w. George Smyth & Archibald Campbell, Esq., as additional Congressional
delegates from Charlotte co.- **780**; he was the only Charlotte co. delegate present at
the close of the Congress, Sept. 2, 1775, & for most of the forepart of that session-
782; resumed his seat, Sept. 17th, & served until session close, Oct. 3, 1775- **783**
Seneca- of Salem, N. Y.; c. 1857, rem. Independence, Ohio; ments. sons Asa B., &
James, who enl. 103rd Ohio Inf.- **1095**

WATSON,

Mr.- 'an accomplished scholar from Scotland', he was the 1st to open a school for classical learning in the vicinity of Salem, N. Y.; one of his earliest students was Rev. Samuel Tomb; see Vol. 1- **810**

William- res. nr. Milliman's corners, Salem, N. Y.; m. Lydia, dau. Aaron & Elizabeth (Fitch) Martin, as her 2nd husb.; rem. LaCrosse, Wisc., & d. there; ments. only s. Martin- **731**

WATTS,

James- (Watt; 1736- 1819) of England; the idea of steam powered navigation 1st occurred to John Fitch while he was on the banks of the Ohio, & began musing abt. Watt's steam engine (however, the prev. acct., § 949, states that the initial idea occurred to Fitch in 1785, when he was unaware of the existence of a steam engine)- **949b**

James- (Watt) oath of alleg.; Co. D, 22nd N. Y. Inf.- **(L) 1074**

John- of NYC; lands of Wm. Duer, Esq., mortgaged to him Sept. 22, 1774, to secure payment on or bef. Sept. 7, 1775; see Duer, William, Esq.- **935**

WAYNE,

Gen. Anthony- (1745- 1796) (as Col.) commanded at Ticonderoga, Feb. 1777; delivered disch. to Ebenezer Farnsworth for his term of service there- **750**; 'Mad' Anthony; an anecdote from James McDonald, who served under him; at one point (n. d.) the butcher came to Wayne & reported that they were entirely out of meat, & he was instructed 'to kill & dress one of the best conditioned horses in the camp'; the butcher slaughtered McDonald's horse, & when McDonald returned from a 'scouring excursion', he drew his sword, determined to avenge his horse's death; the butcher took shelter in Wayne's tent, & the Gen. barred McDonald's way through its door, asking what he wanted, & telling him to put up his sword & leave; when McDonald would not yield, Gen. Wayne knocked him down, & the soldier went to his tent & wept over the demise of his horse- **1010**

WEATHER-

Earthquake- July 11, 1860; on a still, sultry night, abt. 9:15 PM, 3 persons, ea. in seaparate rooms of Dr. Fitch's house, noted tremors or aftershocks, attrib. them to an impending thunderstorm or other weather phenomena; Dr. Fitch notes that July 13th newspapers report an earthquake in Canada, felt at Montreal, Cobourg, Prescott, & Ottawa City, "so violent as to shake bricks from many of the chimneys"; notes of his observations forwarded to Smithsonian Institute- **1075**;

"Freshet"- June 9, 1814; the "impetuosity" of the current created in the Battenkill was so strong that it pulled down Angel's bridge at E. Greenwich, N. Y., carrying away one of William Taylor's children- **702**;

Frost Heaves- Feb. 6, 1855; cert. shocks & shakings of the ground nr. Fitch's Point & E. Greenwich, N. Y., presumed to be an earthquake, & occurring in other parts of the country, "accomp. w. fissures in the earth, 2 or 3 inches wide & several rods in length"; except for drifts nr. the fences, the ground was bare of snow; "from a spell of mild weather, it became intensely cold w. a violent N. wind- the thermometer late in the night being down to 24 & 26 below zero"; Dr. Fitch compares Peter Reid's temperatures w. that of his own, which read -14° at 7:00 AM the foll. morning; the intensity of shocks noted as strong enough to rattle dishes & shake houses & beds; cracks in the road & earth noted the foll. day nr. Fitch's Point & E. Greenwich; "This is no doubt all owing to the surface of the earth becoming suddenly frozen & contracted, & 'hide- bound' as the saying is, to such a degree that it cracked, & caused the shaking of the buildings in this manner"- **1026**;

Hurricanes- c. 1790's, nr. Salem, N. Y.; acc. Capt. Daniel McDonald, blew down all the trees on a small piece of land owned by ____ Bell, which he was then employed to help clear- **927**; June 10, 1829; prob. Oneida co., N. Y.; its effects contrib. to the death of Mary Ann, dau. John & Maria (Conkey) Waters- **730**;

Lightning- Aug. 13 & 14, 1853; several barns struck & totally consumed by lightning strikes in Dresden, N. Y., & Benson & West Haven, Vt.; other instances of lightning noted at abt. the same time by Dr. Fitch, nr. Salem, & at Fitch's Point; abt. 10:00 PM on Thurs., Aug. 11, 1853, lighning struck 3 pine trees in the W. corner of the pine grove of Wm. Fitch's heirs; the 3rd tree, standing abt. a rod apart from the 2 others, was split apart along its entire length, w. the top falling to the ground; on the others, the lightning ran down one side, splitting the bark & plowing a groove in the trees; "At the root of one of these, the earth was torn up, where the fluid entered the ground"; 3 other incidents recoll. betw. 1848- 1866, by Dr. Fitch, who also notes that abt. 1856, it "struck a stake of the rail fence" in the center of the flat on the line from his office to the house of Earl P. Wright- **996**;

Salem, N. Y.- var. entries discovered by Dr. Fitch "In a Bible in Alva Wright's seat in the Ass. Ref. Presbyt. church, Salem..."

June 16, 1816- "snowed all day";

Aug. 13, 1825- "terrible thunderstorm, which continued all night";

Dec. 13, 1825- "remarkably cold day";

June 2, or 9, 1833- a remarkably cold day; some snow fell";

May 15, 1835- "severe snow storm & wind all day"- **1047b**;

Wash. Co. & vicinity, Aug. 15, 1777- notes as "an unusually rainy day over Wash. co. & the adj. districts"; the importance of its effects over var. aspects of the operations of Col. Baum's expedition & Gen. Burgoyne's campaign ment. as giving a cert. Providential guidance to the outcome- **1072**

WEBB,

Abel S.- of Cambridge, N. Y.; juror, Oct. 1- 7, 1858, People vs. Martin Wallace; see Vol. 4- **1048s**

David- res. & d. Salem, N. Y.; c. 1767, he & James Turner had the only houses in Turner's Patent; ments. sons John, m. ____ Hutchison; & David, m. ____ McKellip; his desc. no longer res. here- **738**; his orig. homesite now (1850) occ. by the Rich family; "He was a drinking, horse- jockeying man, of no repute in town- & was supposed to be a Roman Catholic"; his political persuasion during the Rev.

war was uncert.; although prob. from New England, it was thought that he didn't care abt. the issue- **744**

William- res. Salem, N. Y.; a span of his horses went wild (n. d.) & dragged John Gerrold to his death- **734**

WEBSTER,

Col. Alexander- of Hebron, N. Y.; commanded militia co., Charlotte co., N. Y., 1782- **754**; clerk, Charlotte co. Comm. of Safety, 1776; recommended by his Comm. for appt. as Major, Charlotte co. militia- **784**; (Maj.) chosen along w. Col. Williams & Maj. Malcom to either individually, or as a group, be delegates from Charlotte co. to the 3rd Provincial Congress; certif. dated May 1, 1776, presented by him in Congress, May 14th, at the beginning of session; attended theProvincial Convention, July 9th, along w. Duer & Williams- **785**; along w. John Williams & Ebenezer Clark, inquired July 25, 1777, concerning the validity of the recent Charlotte co. election, as it was held only in the E. portion of the co.; foll. the state ruling on the inquiry, he was returned to the Congress as a Senator for the Eastern District- **787**; Commissioner of Forfeitures for the Eastern District, in a listing given for lands registered under an act May 12, 1784, for sale of confiscated & forfeited estates foll. Rev. war- **(L)- 875**; (Judge) was Commissioner for selling confiscated lands; Gen. John Williams was his intimate friend, & "did as he desired" concerning the lands in question, prob. serving as clerk to the commissioner, keeping acct. of the sales; Williams would have acted in Webster's place, except that he desired to purch. lands- **915**; deed witn., Gile Wilson to James Wilson- **(L)- 936**; witn., May 9, 1786, for security on Edward Savage as loan officer- **(L)- 936b**; brief ment.- **998**; dau. Eleanor, m. Deac. John Steele, as his 2nd wf.; purch. the confiscated farm of ____ Gibson, the tory, Salem, N. Y., which was later occ. by his son- in- law- **1047**

Sen. Daniel- (1782- 1852) brief ment.- **759s**; his funeral, Oct. 29, 1852; bur. old Marshfield, Mass. bur. grd., loc. abt. ½ mi. from his mansion- **988**

George- attests that Wm. Hoy's cellar hole was not the one built on by Colin McFarland, as Hoy's was loc. a little S. of McFarland's home- **873**

George- perh. surveyor, Lot 23, Hutton's Bush (Putnam, N. Y.)- **1092**

John- Co. A, 2nd N. Y., Northern Black Horse, Cav., 1861- 2- **1080**

WEED,

Smith- (1833- ?: N. Y. Assembly, 1865- 67, 71, 73, 74) of Albany, N. Y.; m. Sarah, dau. Ebenezer & Lydia (Mills) Fitch; their only dau. m. Alfred B. Street- **799**

WEEKS,

Ephriam T.- 2nd Lt., Co. H, 93rd N. Y. Inf.- **1090b**

WELCH,
Dennis- Co. A, 2nd N. Y., Northern Black Horse, Cav., 1861- 2- **1080**
Joseph- res. Salem, N. Y.; two Indians, fleeing the battle of Bennington, & making
their way to Skenesborough & Canada, approached his house, caught & killed a
sheep nr. his doorway; w. the knife in their bloody hands, they "boldly &
unceremoniously" entered the house, & his wf. presumed their knife was next
intended for her; they soon commenced helping themselves to "trifling things" that
they wanted, finally taking a double blanket; in a more composed state, Mrs.
Welch attempted to substitute a single blanket for the more valued one, but her
husb., fearing that they might be piqued & resent the change cried out,"Oh, Bessy
dear, gie the honest men the other", thus defusing a potentially bloody outcome &
disguising his true opinion of the circumstances- **741**; the three Indians who killed
his sheep were refugees from the Bennington battlefield; they entered the house
"(Crying broat! broat! & pointing to their mouth)"; Mrs. Welch recounts that she
prayed for death 1st, not wanting to see her own children slaughtered, as "the
family was excessively frightened, expecting they would all be murdered" (the
Allen family having been massacred less than a month bef., in Argyle)- **926**; at the
time that John McDonald res. w. him, he was using Dr.Clark's old log meeting
house as a barn- **1001**
Lucy- m. James, s. Duncan & Isabel (Duncan) MacIntyre- **999**

WELLINGTON,
Duke of- (Arthur Wellesley, 1769- 1852) the 42nd Royal Highland regt. was
reportedly in engagements in & nr. the Pyrennes, which terminated his campaign
in Spain- **990**

WELLS,
Austin- informed Esq. Barnet concerning the no. & loc. of tory dead bur. foll. battl
of Bennington; notes a tory gravesite nr. their breastworks & bur. of 30 others in 2
potato holes found betw. Walloomsac river & Esq. Barnet's house- **762**; acc. Sidne
Wells, Joseph Wells was in Cambridge, N. Y. earlier than the date stated by his
uncle Austin- **842**
Austin Henry- (s. Samuel & Loive Scott) clerk, Gould's Law bookstore, Albany,
N. Y.; m. _____ Mitchell; one child- **839**
Capt.- appeared bef. Albany Comm. of Correspondence, July 13, 1775, informing
the comm. that he had raised a co. of 25 men, incl. officers, at the request of Col.
Benedict Arnold, & on basis of an encouragement he had found in a cpopy of a
letter sent to John Knickerbocker by the Comm.; his co. marched to Ticonderoga &
served one day short of a month, in part certif. by Cambridge Comm., July 12th; h
requested pay for services & stated the willingness of his co. to march when called
upon; Albany Comm. resolved not to pay, but recommended to N. Y. Provincial
Congress for payment upon authenticated muster roll, indicating names & lengths
of service of co. members; Comm. also noted that appt. of officers to the Battalion
had been completed & no position was presently available for him- **818**

Col.- officer witn. by Ebenezer Farnsworth during his July 1777- Jan. 1778 service, acc. his Rev. war pension appl.- **750**

Daniel- a dau. m. 1. Esq. Raleigh; 2. Paul Cornell- **806**; s. Edmund, Sr.; children-

1. Daniel Lothrup, eldest, m. _____ Parks

2. Mary, m. Esq. Saunders

3. John; enl. in the army, was stat. up Red river, & d. unm., somewhere in the SW

4. Abigail, m. 1. Esq. Raleigh; 2. Paul Cornell

5. Elizabeth, res. Cambridge, N. Y.; unm.

6. James, m. _____ Scott

7. Laura, d. unm., summer 1849, Cambridge, N. Y.

8. Leonard, m. _____ Allen, of White Creek, N. Y.

9. Hamilton

10. Hannah, m. 1. Moses Younglove; 2. _____ Cobb

11. Elijah, d. Dec. 23, 1874, at 76, Buffalo, N. Y.; 'only survivng bro. of the late Leonard Wells'- **841**; he & other family members constructed a large gristmill on the Owl kill at the site of Morrison's old mill; neglecting to reserve enough land along the stream to accomodate the flow after it was dammed, flooding occurred on some of the lots they had sold to their neighbors, causing an uproar, & "war" against the dam- **844**

Daniel Lothrup- s. Daniel; res. Mattewan, N. Y.; m. _____ Parks; children- John Jay, Paul, Mary, & others- **841**

Edmund- (Sr.) § 254; Vol. 1; his bro. Joseph (§ 840) arr. in Cambridge, N. Y. at abt. the same time as the 1st settlers, & his s. Edmund, Jr., arr. in town shortly afterw., & bargained w. his uncle Joseph for the log house he had built, & occ. it until 1787, when his brick house was built- **840**

Edmund- (s. Edmund Henry & Hepzibah Buel) wagonmaker; res. Harmony, N. Y.; children- Henry, d. Quincy, Illinois; John, Harriet, George, Amy, & 1 or 2 more children- **842**

Edmund- s. Joseph, Jr.; d. 1840, Cambridge, N. Y., leaving 2 or 3 children- **842**

Edmund, Jr.- (s. Edmund; § 254; Vol. 1) m. Wealthy Ann Goodrich; children-

1. Edmund Henry, m. Hepzubah Buel

2. Elizabeth, m. Lewis Berry

3. Jamese, m. Clarinda Griffith

4. William, m. Wealthy Gilbert

5. Samuel, m. 1. Miriam Henry; 2. Olive Scott

6. Sidney, m. 1. Sylvia Fairchild; 2. Hannah Merriam

7. Solomon, m. Mary Ann Dunlap- **839**; his wf. was a noted cook of that day, especially w. the children, "they commonly receiving when happening there on an errand, a cake or crullie so delicious as to excite their surprise that they never had had anything at home or elsewhere, that tasted half as good"; he arr. in Cambridge after his uncle Joseph, bargained w. him for his log house, & occ. it until his brick house was completed in 1787, prob. by the same mason who built Noah Payne's brick house at Ft. Miller; thinking that he would keep up the custom of his native

state, he planned a sumptuous Thanksgiving Day dinner, c. autumn 1775, to "give his Scotch & Irish friends & neighbors some acquaintance w. the good old customs of Conn."; the guests came from quite some distance in the sparsely settl. district, & when seated, a whig & a tory were seated opp. ea. other, w. the main course providing a "secure barrier to preventing any clashing betw. them"; however, peace did not prevail, & the 2 diners had soon adjourned from the meal to contend the issue in Wells' yard, circled by the other guests; see Holidays- **840**

Edmund Henry- (eldest s. Edmund, Jr., & Wealthy Ann Goodrich) res. Cambridge, N. Y.; m. Hepzibah, dau. Ichabod Buel; children-

1. Edmund, m. dau. John Cooper
2. Wealthy, m. Samuel, s. John Cooper
3. James
4. Pamilla, m. _____ Dickison
5. Elizabeth, m. _____ Curtis
6. Sidney
7. Solomon
8. Harriet, m. _____ Slayton, res. Harmony, N. Y.; he was one of the 1st victims of 'the epidemic' (spotted fever) & prob. d. 1813- **839**

Hamilton- s. Daniel; printer, & now (1850) Inspector, Sing Sing state prison; m. in NYC, & has one child living- **841**

Helen- (dau. Solomon & Mary Ann Dunlap) a missionary of the American Board, d. Cape Palmas, Africa (Liberia) some 15 yrs. ago (c. 1835)- **839**

Henry Martyn- s. Sidney; daguerrotypist; res. New Haven, Conn., & m. there, _____ Bartholomew, summer 1849- **839**

Horace- (s. James & Clarinda Griffin) m. _____, in Syracuse, N. Y., & now (1850) res. Binghamton, N. Y.- **839**

James- s. Daniel; printer; m. _____ Scott; d. Rochester, N. Y., w/o children- **841**

James- (s. Edmund Henry & Hepzibah Buel) shoemaker; rem. Harmony, N. Y., & d. there, leaving 2 or 3 children- **839**

James- (s. Edmund, Jr., & Wealthy Ann Goodrich) merch., Galesville, N. Y., foll. by Union Village (Greenwich, N. Y.); m. Clarinda Griffin; he d. ca. 1820, leaving 4 children-

1. Frances, m. _____ Lockwood
2. Eliza, m. Livy Stearns
3. James Howard, m. _____ Follet
4. Horace- **839**

James Horace- s. Sidney; daguerrotypist; res. New Haven, Conn., in the same business as his bro. Henry M.; unm.- **839**

James Howard- (s. James & Clarinda Griffin) was once a broker, Troy, N. Y.; m. _____ Follet, of Pittstown, N. Y.; one child- **839**

John- res. nr. Center Falls, & at ano. time, at Fitch's Point, Salem, N. Y.; m. Harriet, dau. Moses, Jr., & Eunice (Clark) Martin; rem. Wisc. 3 yrs. ago (prob. 1847); "He is the lasiest [sic] man living, it used to be sd., & she a great sloven & slut, yet some of their children seem smart"- **731**

Rev. John D.- (s. Solomon & Mary Ann Dunlap) pastor, c. 1850, Presbyterian church, Williamsburgh, N. Y.; m. May 1, 1849, Jessie, dau. Daniel Henderson; one child- **839**

Joseph- bro. Edmund, Sr.; arr. Cambridge, N. Y., at the time of its 1st settlm. & built a log house betw. his present (1850) house & the mill W. of it, where the road ran prev. to the turnpike; his neph. Edmund, Jr., arr. in town soon afterw., bargained for his uncle's house, & occ. it until 1787; the house was demolished betw. 1800- 1810- **840**; was in Cambridge earlier than stated by Austin Wells, & so well known as to be one of the 1st committemen chosen at the outbreak of the Rev. war (§ 831), indicating that he was settl. & well establ. by Jan. 1775; children-

   1. Shaler, prob. eldest, d. Castile, N. Y.

   2. Joseph, res. & d. on his father's Cambridge place

   3. Azzan, "died in the western country"

   4. Timothy

   5. Elizabeth, m. Benjamin Fenton; he had other children, but not recoll. by witn. acct.; he rem. ¾ mi. W. over the hill from his orig. homesite after his neph. purch. it, & res. & d. there at an advanced age- **842**

Joseph- dau. Jane, m. James, s. Ebenezer & Betsey (Williams) Proudfit- **1045**

Joseph, Jr.- s. Joseph; res. & d.on his father's place, Cambridge, N. Y.; had a large family-

   1. Abiah, m. Edmund Austin

   2. Harriet, m. Edward Long

   3. Joseph, res. Denmark, N. Y.

   4. Edmund, d. ca. 1840, Cambridge, N. Y.

   5. David, res. Cambridge, N. Y.; a laborer, dissipated in his habits; he had 2 or 3 more children, names not recoll.- **842**

Joseph, 3rd- s. Joseph, Jr.; res. Denmark, N. Y.; he took sick while on business in Philadelphia 2 months ago (prob. Nov. 1849) & d. Lancaster, Pa.- **842**

"Landlord"- his dau. m. Hamilton, s. Anthony I. & ____ (Williams) Blanchard- **914**

Leonard- s. Daniel; merch., Justice of Peace, & Postmaster, Cambridge, N. Y.; he was also once Sheriff, Wash. co.; m. ____ Allen, of Little White Creek, N. Y.; ments. dau. Caroline, & s. George, described as "very bad"; & he d. Oct. 30, 1865- **841**; acted for the prosecution in Squire Dyer's examination of witns. connected w. the murder, Feb. 16, 1858, of Barney McEntee- **1048s**

Lewis Berry- (s. Samuel & Miriam Henry) res. Cambridge, N. Y.; m. ____ Burt, of Northumberland, N. Y.; has 2 children, & presently (1850) res. in California- **839**

P.- cashier, Bank of Brattleboro, Vt., as printed on a $10 note, Oct. 1, 1852, from sd. bank, that found found at the scene of Barney McEntee's murder- **1048s**

Samuel- (s. Edmund, Jr., & Wealthy Ann Goodrich) farmer, res. Cambridge, N. Y., adjoin. his other bros.; m. 1. Miriam, dau. Joseph Henry; 2. Olive Scott; children, 2 by 1st wf. & 4 by 2nd wf.-

   1. Lewis Berry, m. ____ Burt

   2. Margaret, m. ____ Howden

3. Austin Henry, m. ____ Mitchell

4. James, res. at home

5. Miriam, m. ____ Livingston

6. Solomon, d. 1848- **839**

Shaler- s. Joseph; res. & d. Castile, N. Y.; those children recoll.-

1. Timothy, res. Illinois

2. Ann, res. & m. in Castile, N. Y.

3. Mercy, m. Daniel Herrington; rem. Michigan

4. dau., m. Gideon Austin, of Castile, N. Y.

5. Nathaniel- **842**

Sidney- (s. Edmund Henry & Hepzibah Buel) res. 1st w. his uncle Sidney, & then w. his bro. Edmund, in Chatauqua co., N. Y., & then Albany, N. Y.; he recently (c. 1850) d. in California, leaving 2 children in Albany- **839**

Sidney- (s. Edmund, Jr., & Wealthy Ann Goodrich) informs Dr. Fitch on the Wells family hist.; m. 1. Sylvia, dau. Jesse Fairchild; 2. Hannah Merriam, of New Haven, Conn.; they "have lost several children, minors. Four living, viz."-

1. Mary, m. 1. ____ Baker; 2. ____ Clement

2. Jesse Fairchild, res. Troy, N. Y., unm.

3. Henry Martyn, m. ____ Bartholomew

4. James Horace, unm.- **839**

Solomon- (s. Edmund, Jr., & Wealthy Ann Goodrich) silversmith; m. Mary Ann, dau. Rev. John Dunlap; d. Whitestown, N. Y., leaving 2 children- Helen, & Rev. John D.- **839**

Solomon- (s. Edmund Henry & Hepzibah Buel) rem. Chatauqua co., N. Y., & then to Mauk Chunk, Pa., where he was m. & in trade for several yrs.; rem. Quincy, Illinois, & d. there of fever, leaving 3 or 4 children- **839**

Timothy- s. Joseph, Jr.; carpenter, killed during a barn raising at Edmund Wells, Jr.'s, leaving wf. & s. Timothy S., who now (1850) res. Illinois- **839**

William- (s. Edmund, Jr., & Wealthy Ann Goodrich) farmer, res. N. of his bro. Sidney, Cambridge, N. Y.; m. Wealthy Gilbert; he d. 1829, leaving 3 children-

1. Millicent, m. Leonard Johnson

2. William, res. Reynoldsburgh, Ohio; 2 children

3. Mary Ann, m. ____ Robertson- **839**

WELSH,

Mr.- an agent of the Protestant Union; gave an address, Sept. 4, 1862, at the annual meeting of the Wash. Co. Bible Soc.; a converted Catholic, the subj. of his lecture concerned the opposition of Catholic priests to Bible study by the general population, "giving the children in its stead, this rag (holding up a scapulary to view) telling them it would save them from drowning & would protect a soldier from being shot, & c."; acc. Dr. Fitch, his address was replete w. an hr. of such examples- **1097**

WELSH- 849

WENDELL,
Hon. Gilbert- dau. Maria, m. Platt, s. Dr. Philip Smith- **845**
John H.- adm. to practice, Oct. 19, 17773, Charlotte co., N. Y.- **878**

WENTWORTH,
Gen.- Maj. Philip Skene served as an Ensign w. him, at Porto Bello (Panama)-
1059
Gov. Benning- (1696- 1770; Gov., 1741- 1767); his commiss. gr. July 3rd, in the
15th yr. of his Majesty's reign (George II, 1741) at Whitehall, London, England,
giving the boundaries of his Province; see New Hampshire- **883**; at a meeting of
N. Y. Council, Dec. 6, 1753, his remarks & observations in his Mar. 23, 1750/1
letter to the Board of Trade, proposing the division line betw. N. Y. & N. H., read
& approved within N. Y. Council; & the Gov. advised to transmit the same"to the
Right Honorable the Lords Commissioners for Trade & Plantations"- **884**; from the
contents of his letter to Gov. Colden, Jan. 20, 1764, Dr. Fitch notes that by his
(Fitch's) definition of 'good faith', Gov. Wentworth's transactions w. N. Y. "greatly
violated 'good faith' " (a sentiment he would prob. apply to his successor as well)-
887; his fees secured by reserving to himself 500 acres within ea. township, while
other reservations of particular lots were made in the names of N. H. Council
members & other public officials (a practice continued by his successor & neph.,
Gov. John Wentworth)- **894**; his letter to Board of Trade, c. 1752, reportedly
indicated gross ignorance or a willful falsity in representing N. Y.'s boundaries;
also noted by N. Y. Council's report, delivered June 6, 1753, that a promised copy
of Gov. Wentworth's letter to England had not been rec'd. by them prior to its
delivery to the Board- **928**
Gov. John- (1737- 1820; Gov., 1767- 1775); the position of cert. people known as
the Green Mtn. boys, in regards to the Grants, was that he 'withdrew his
pretensions to these lands, fearing the seat of govt. of N. H. would be moved to the
interior', & that N. Y. had obt. the lands in question by a 'fraudulent & unjust
manner'- **786**; his arr. in office, acc. Ebenezer Cole, reserved hope for annexation
of the Grants lands to N. H.; petitns. to the King, for that end, were sd. to have
been circulated on his advice- **896**; w. reference to revoking the order suspending
the iss. of grants, & restoring the peace along the border of N. Y. Province, Lord
Dunmore, in a letter to Lord Hillsborough, May 9, 1771, encloses a petitn., by over
450 inhabitants, requesting a continuance under N. Y. govt.; he also encloses ano.
petitn. sent by Gov. Wentworth, signed by abt. 200 people, & requesting
continuance under N. H., 'but how these names were obt. your Lordship will easily
be able to conceive by looking into the diff. papers I have sent by this packet'- **898**;
chartered Windsor, Vt., 1761; writes to Gov. Colden, Aug. 17, 1764, that when a
Deputy Sheriff (prob. Samuel Ashley; § 892) was executing a legal precept, several
Pownal inhabitants were set upon by the Albany Sheriff (Harmanus Schuyler) &
more than 30 armed men on horseback, carrying 4 of them (prob. Robinson,
Ashley, Charles, & Horsfort) to jail; he states his desire to see their release, "as it

would be an act of cruelty to punish individuals for disputes betw. the two govts. & c."- **928**

M. H.- (prob. Mark Hunking; 1709- 1785) of Boston, Mass.; a shareholder, c. 1761, on the charter of Windsor, Vt.- **928**

Samuel- of Boston, Mass.; a shareholder, c. 1761, on the charter of Windsor, Vt.- **928**

WERMALL,
Desire- ment. as a grdau. Desire Doter (Doty)- **757**

WEST,
_____- m. Alpheus, s. Joseph Cheney, Jr.- **1038**
Richard- of Salem, N. Y.; Co. H, 123rd NYSV; d. Dec. 13, 1862, a suicide- **1098**
Susanna- m. David, s. David Mason, of Norwich, Conn.- **759s**
Thomas- Co. A, 2nd N. Y., Northern Black Horse, Cav., 1861- 2- **1080**

W. Hebron, N. Y.- orig. called Bedlam- **737**

Westmoreland, N. Y.- c. 1795, was only a wilderness, when a no. of families- Simpson Cowden, Peleg Havens, Phineas Bell, Rodrick Morrison, Amos Potter, & _____ Bessey, rem. there from Cambridge, N. Y., & were counted among its 1st settlers- **846**

WESTON,
Desire- ment. as a dau. Desire Doter (Doty)- **757**
Rev. S. H., D. D.- (Sullivan Hardy; 1816- 1887) officiated at the marriage ceremony, May 29, 1864, of Henry B. Hyde & Annie Fitch, Trinity chapel, NYC- **799**

WETMORE,
Sgt. George- promoted 2nd Lt., 22nd N. Y. Inf., Sept. 3, 1862, replacing Benjamin F. Wickham- **1095b**

WHALEY,
Family- or Wheldon; res. Union Village (Greenwich, N. Y.); acc. Wid. Angel, the mother was caring for a 3 or 4 yr. old niece, who was addicted to bed- wetting; at length, she became so enraged w. the child that, in an attempt to break her of the habit, she tied the child bef. the fire to dry her clothes; the heat was so great, that it blistered most of the child's skin, & she was burned so badly that she d. within a few days; arresting & trying the victim's aunt for murder was talked of, but the matter was dropped, due to the expense of the Holmes case & his recent execution (Benjamin Holmes, arrested Feb. 1798, sentenced June 1799, & executed Mar. 28, 1800; see Vol. 1) & the fact that the only evidence against her was the victim; recoll. of either surname uncert.- **862**

WHEAT,
Richard-he was one of 16 guards raised at Bennington, Vt., mid- June 1782, by Col. Robinson, to guard the would- be abductors of Esq. Bleecker- **747**

WHEATON,
George- res. Edinburgh, N. Y.; m. Hannah Amanda, dau. David Hanna & ____ (Taylor) Lytle- **1069**
Jerusha- of Hebron, N. Y.; m. Robert, Jr., s. Robert & Susan (Lytle) Vance- **737**

WHEDON,
Daniel- purch. 73 acre tract, May 13, 1785, from Jedidiah Darrow- **(L)- 936**; his tract purch. for £ 80- **(L)- 936b**

WHEELER,
____ - m. Mary Ann Eddy; his wf. m. 2nd, Hon. William Henry, s. Peter & Esther (Clark) Parker, as his 2nd wf.- **759s**
Alonzo- oath of alleg.; Co. D, 22nd N. Y. Inf.- **(L) 1074**
Charles A.- lawyer, res. Whitehall, N. Y.; c. 1810's, Hon. Wm. H. Parker 1st began practicing law in partnership w. him- **759**; same information- **759s**
Ephriam- of White Creek (Salem, N. Y.); Apr. 15, 1782, conveys to Phineas Bennet, Lots 282, 283, & part of 281, Turner's Patent, for £ 220; Jan. 10, 1785, part of Lot 281, formerly sold by the proprietors to Thomas McCrea, conveyed by Wheeler to Phineas Benet- **(L) 936**
Jemima- m. Joseph, s. William & Jane (Lytle) Russell- **737**
John Wiser- convicted Jan. 7, 1789, for knowingly & feloniously passing a counterfeit bill of credit; sentenced to be branded on his left cheek w. the letter"C" by a red hot iron & then confined to life imprisonment, w. hard labor, at the bridewell of NYC- **877**
Judge- prob. of Whitehall, N. Y., perh. Cahrles A. (above); c. 1836, he joined in business ventures w. Melancton Blin & Edward W. Parker- **759s**
Paul- dau. Sarah, m. John, s. Daniel & Polly (Steele) McFarland- **1047**

WHICKER,
Rev. Mr.- (or Whitcher, Benjamin W.) Episcopal minister, res. Saratoga Springs, N. Y.; m. Miriam (Frances Miriam, 1814- 1852), dau. Lewis Berry; 2 children; his wf. d. 1850?; "she wrote much for the Magazines" (principally *Neal's Saturday Gazette, & Lady's Literary Museum*), & a port. of her writings were publ. in "Widow Bedott"- **839**

WHIGS-
E. Greenwich, N. Y.- the schoolhouse standing on the hill above Esq.
McDougall's was set on fire & burnt one night in the spring foll. Burgoyne's
surrender; the children's books were all burned, but the vandalism that caused
much talk & consternation among the Argyle tories was that over 30 Bibles were
incl. among the ruined volumes; a few days afterw., "black" Duncan Campbell's
log house on the Battenkill was fired at night; it was known to have been set, as the
fire began on the opp. end from the fireplace; in retaliation, some sawmills were
burnt, thus ending the outrages, ea. party seeing how the reprisals could continue
endlessly- **1064**;
   Fitch's Point, Salem, N. Y.- foll. the Rev. war, some of the more violent Salem
whigs, incl. prob. the Carswells & McNishes, heard that James Campbell had
returned from Canada & was visiting his father, "white" Duncan; they decided to
go tar & feather him, & arr. at Capt. Martin's tavern for a drink prior to their
errand; disclosing their intent, Capt. Martin kept them entertained while he
conveyed this information to the Campbell's, thus allowing James to escape &
preventing the incident- **1065**;
   Salem, N. Y.- during the last yrs. of the Rev. war, to pay 3 & 6 months men for
guarding the frontier, "they would take cattle & sheep from the Argyle folks",
making themselves rich in this way, as no restitution was made- **977**; when "black"
Duncan Campbell's family went to Burgoyne's camp in Ft. Edward for protection,
Aug. 1777, the whigs tore down his fences, letting his cattle into his grain field &
nearly destroying it; after the family's return, 'Mad' More & others from Sodom
(Shushan, N. Y.) came & drove off his cows, casting lots for them; one of them
was returned the foll. day by Bill Smith, but More wintered over the other 3, losing
them during the spring thaw, when they drowned by falling through the ice on te
Battenkill- **1063**; on hearing that Gibson, the tory, had returned after some
absence, the sons of Capt. McCracken, 2 of the Hopkinses, & others of their
neighborh., 6 in all, came to Gibson's house one evening & fired a volley through
his door; he & his wf. afterw. fled to Canada, & their lot was confiscated & purch.
by Capt. McCracken- **1073**

Whigs, Songs of the Revolution- "Granny O'Wale", noted as one of the most
popular; Peggy Bowman, who used to spin flax for Moses Martin, Sr., was
particularly encouraged by him to sing this song, among the others popular at the
time- **856**; of several, "American Taxation" noted as one still in print, c. 1850; ano.
longer & unnamed song, w. the foll. opening lines- "Hark, Hark, the sound of war
is heard/ And you must all attend/ Take up your arms & go w. speed/ Your counrty
to defend,/ Husbands must leave their loving wives,/ And sprightly youths attend/
Leave their sweethearts & risk their lives/ Their country to defend"; but "Granny
O'Wale" was "the greatest favorite" among whigs in Salem, N. Y.; its lyrics recoll.
by Wid. Angel, in the version Betsey Taylor used to sing, incl. 44 lines of verse,
recorded by Dr. Fitch, & concluding- "You need not pretend to frighten my sons,/
In Lexington's battle they made your men run/ They're men of experience in every

degree/ And will turn your great ships in their helms- a- lee/ I have thousands of sons in America born/ And to yield to be slaves they do hold it a scorn/ They are men of experience in every respect/ And they never will yield to your cursed Tea Act"- **857**; a stanza from a very long song, recalled by Capt. Daniel McDonald- "Gen. Burgoyne from Canada set sail/ With 10,000 regulars he thought would never fail/ With Indians & Canadians & tories as we've heerd/ In place of better shipping through Lake Champlain they steered"- **923**

Whipple City, N. Y.- orig. name given Union Village, later Greenwich, N. Y.- **862**

WHITCOMB,
Oliver- of Salem, N. Y.; juror, Oct. 1- 7, 1858, People vs. Martin Wallace- **1048s**

WHITE,
Andrew- of Danby, Vt.; deeded Nov. 21, 1786, to Thomas Brayton, of "Herwich", Vt., a 600 acre lot in Danby, orig. owned by Benjamin Palmer; refers Danby, Vt. Deeds, p. 88- **745**
Daniel H.- of Granville, N. Y.; sold 1 acre, Morrison's Patent, Aug. 6, 1785, to Capt. Thomas Converse- **(L)- 936**; same material- **(L)- 936b**
Dr.- of Hebron, N. Y.; he substituted for Dr. Morris as one of the physicians attending the execution of Martin Wallace, Dec. 1, 1858- **1050s**
Family- res. Shrewsbury, Vt.; a dau. m. Gurley Marsh, & ano. dau., Mary, m. his bro. Daniel- **962**
James- of Hebron, N. Y.; m. Nancy, dau. Duncan & Isabel (Duncan) MacIntyre; his wf. d. w/o issue- **999**
Rev. M.- of Hebron, N. Y.; assisted Rev. Lambert, Jan. 23, 1862, at the funeral of James G. Stalker- **1081**
William- res. N. part of Salem, N. Y.; m. Elizabeth, dau. James & Matilda (Safford) Turner; no children- **1090**

Whitehall, N. Y.- Nov. 1815, the British cannon capt. at Plattsburgh by Commodore Macdonough were conveyed here for storage, w. their carriages & implements, in a building then under construction for that purpose- **719**; a R. R. accident, Dec. 2 or 3, 1853, given in 2 reports; the derailing a 25 car freight, "the engine, tender, & 2 freight cars, precipitated into the canal, & 20 live hogs drowned"; the bridge was totally destroyed & the engineer killed; see McMullen, William; & Transportation- **1017**; the Myers block burned, Mon. morning, Jan. 30, 1854, causing injury to other buildings & $20,000.00 losses in property, incl. J. R. Broughton, druggist; J. Dahn, tobacconist; & J. M. Myers, merch.- **1023**

The White House- "well known of old", stood ½ mi. W. of Hoosic corners (prob. E. Hoosick, N. Y.), on the present (1850) "MacAdamized" turnpike from Troy, N. Y., to Bennington, Vt.; purch. by Col. John P. Fistus (old 'Festus') foll. his retirement from service after the old French war; this house became the HQ for all the loyalists in the Hoosick vicinity when the Rev. war broke out; bef. the battle of Bennington, a party of 15 British soldiers was sent in advance of Col. Baum's expedition & came here to request Col. Fister enl. recruits in the royalist cause; they were instructed to go wherever he directed them in pursuit of volunteers, & they were then to rendezvous at his house, & proceed into Col. Baum's camp- **768**

White Plains, battle of- Oct. 28, 1776; in Sept., a Mass. brigade commanded by Gen. Benjamin Lincoln marched to Fairfield, Conn., & then to NYC, & 2 days later, via Horseneck, meeting the American retreat; construction of a fort was begun at Valentine's hill, foll. by further retreat to White Plains; his brigade arr. Sun. morning, & the battle occurred the foll. day, Lincoln's brigade suffering little, while Col. Brooks' co. experienced severe losses; Col. Glover commanded an artillery force, & other officers present were Col. How, Gen. Putnam, & Gen. McDougall; after the battle, Gen. Lincoln's forces were marched several mi. N. to North Castle, where they encamped- **747**; Capt. George King's militia co., of Barrington, Mass., Gen. Fellow's regt., was sent to Dutchess, & then to Westchester co., & then stat. at Valentine's hill; the co. afterw. participated in the battle- **755**

WHITESIDE,
Edward- (s. Phineas & Ann Cooper) m. Ann French; children-
  1. Henry, m. Margaret Whiteside
  2. Edward, m. Salina Sexton- **805**
George B.- (s. Thomas & Elizabeth Cramer) m. Susan Van Schaik; no children- **805**
Henry- (s. Edward & Ann French) m. Margaret Whiteside; 3 children- Emily, Edward, & Albert; & he d. Sept. 20, 1877, at 80- **805**
James- (s. William & Louis Freeman) m. Sophia Glover; 2 daus.- Maria- Louisa & Catharine; he d. & his wf. m. 2. Rev. Peter Gordon- **805**
John- (s. Phineas & Ann Cooper) m. Margaret, dau. Thomas Robertson; children-
  1. Eliza, d. at 18 yrs.
  2. Phineas, m. Abby Hunt
  3. Thomas I., m. Sophia Moers
  4. Ann R., m. Robert McMurray
  5. Robertson, m. Maria Pendergrass
  6. Catharine, m. John McKie- **805**
John- (s. William & Louis Freeman) physician, res. & d. Milford, N. Y.; m. Hannah- Alvira Goodrich; had 9 children- Flora, Phrocena, Adelaide, Pomcyn, Minerva, Alvira, Duherst, Harriet, & Jacqueline- **805**
John- (s. Thomas & Elizabeth Cramer) res. Galway, N. Y.; m. Maria Mairs; children- Thomas, Mairs, George, Laura, & Montgomery- **805**
Margaret- m. Henry, s. Edward & Ann (French) Whiteside- **805**
Oliver- (s. Phineas & Ann Cooper) b. ca. 1765, Cambridge, N. Y., abt. 2 months after the family had settl. on their land here; all of his other siblings were b. in

Pennsylvania; m. Susan Pendergrass; had 2 children- Martha, m. William Crafts;
Ann, m. Hon. John Beardsell- **805**

Peter- (s. William & Louis Freeman) m. Miss Hawley, of Arlington, Vt.; children-
Chloe- Ann, Ovid, & Ezra- **805**

Peter- (s. Phineas & Ann Cooper) m. Ann, dau. Thomas Robertson; had 3
children-

1. Neal, d. at 24 yrs.
2. Catharine, m. George McKie
3. Sophia, m. George McKie, as his 2nd wf.- **805**

Phineas- b. Co. Tyrone, Ireland; pursued a preparatory course for the ministry (in
the Cameronian church, acc. Deac. John McMurray) & emig. Lancaster, Pa.; he
res. there for many yrs., taught school, & was ord. an Elder; refers p. 111, Corey's
Gazetteer; m. Ann Cooper; 6 of their 7 children were b. in Pennsylvania, & their
youngest child was b. ca. 1765, abt. 2 months after the family arr. in Cambridge,
N. Y.; children-

1. John, m. Margaret Robertson
2. William, m. Louis Freeman
3. Peter, m. Ann Robertson
4. Thomas, m. Elizabeth Cramer
5. Ann, m. John Cochran
6. Edward, m. Ann French
7. Oliver, b. 1765, Cambridge, N. Y.; m. Susan Pendergrass; he rem. to this area,
1764, & made extensive explorations into Saratoga & Wash. co. to select a
dwelling spot; returned S., & brought his family up the foll. yr., leaving them at
Winnie's, in Schaghticoke, until he came to his lot & built a cabin; his deed for Lot
No. 83, May 9, 1775, from Richard Nichols Colden, of NYC, had a perpetual rent
of £ 29 16s annually for 596 acres- **805**

Phineas- (s. John & Margaret Robertson) m. Abby Hunt; children- Laura, Eliza,
Edward, Margaret, & Catharine- **805**

Robertson- (s. John & Margaret Robertson) settl. Mayville, N. Y.; m. Maria
Pendergrass; had sons William & Martin- **805**

Thomas- (s. Phineas & Ann Cooper) m. Elizabeth, dau. Conrad Cramer, Sr.;
10 children-

1. Margaret, m. Rev. George Mairs, Sr.
2. Ann, unm.
3. Mary, m. Jeremiah Platt
4. Eliza, d. 1832
5. Sarah, d. y.
6. John, m. Maria Mairs
7. Phineas, m. Clarrissa Goss
8. Thomas C., m. Margaret Proudfit
9. Jane, dec'd.
10. George B., m. Susan Van Schaik- **805**

Thomas C.- (s. Thomas & Elizabeth Cramer) res. Cambridge, N. Y.; m. Margaret Proudfit, of Argyle, N. Y.; no children; he & his sist. Ann, inform Dr. Fitch regarding the family genealogy- **805**; m. Margaret, dau. Dr. Andrew & Mary (Lytle) Proudfit- **1069**

Thomas I.- (s. John & Margaret Robertson) m. Sophia, dau. Judge Moers, of Champlain, N. Y.; children- Martha, John, Margaret, & Alexander- **805**

William- (s. Phineas & Ann Cooper) m. Louis Freeman; 6 children, only 2 still living in 1850-

    1. Peter, m. _____ Hawley, of Arlington, Vt.

    2. James, m. Sophia Glover

    3. Phebe, m. Dr. Bryant, of Fairfield, N. Y.

    4. William, unm.

    5. John, m. Hannah- Alvira Goodrich

    6. Oliver, d. at 15 yrs.- **805**

WHITFIELD,

Rev. George- (Whitefield; 1715- 1770) rem. (n. d.) Philadelphia, Pa., from Savannah, Ga., along w. the Moravian settlm., & later served w. Rev. Abraham Bininger as a missionary to the Indians- **1075b**

Rev. Henry- (1597- c. 1657) of Guilford, Conn.; dau. Abigail, m. Rev. James Fitch as his 1st wf.- **799**; some acct. of him was given in Mather's Magnalia (*Magnalis Christi Americana; or the Ecclesiastical Hist. of N. E., 1702*)- **834**

WHITLOCK,

_____- res. Galway, N. Y.; m. Matilda, dau. _____ & Matilda (Martin) Brackett- **730**; his wf., dau. Jerry & Matilda (Cheney) Brockett- **1038**

WHITMAN,

Dr.- "or some such name"; c. 1798, res. nr. mouth of the Battenkill, or "somewhere in that neighborh."; he was one "quite celebrated for his professional skill, & also for his awful wickedness, lawlessness, intemperance, lust, & debauchery"; later rem. Orwell, Vt., & became a Methodist,"wholly reformed in his character"- **804**

WHITNEY,

Benjamin- s. Silas, Sr.; m. dau. _____ Emmons, a tavernkeeper, Clarendon, Vt.; rem. Glens Falls, N. Y., & res. there a long time, leaving a large family, some of whom were active businessmen there; ments. sons Porter, Emmons, Jedidiah, & Silas- **969**

Dr. Moses- d. June 17, 1814, at 40, Palatine, N. Y., & rem. for bur. by his request to Hoosick, N. Y.- **(L)**- **772**

Oliver- s. Silas, Sr.; merch., nr. Clarendon, Vt.; "was noted for his tricks, & wit, & jugglery; he would often spend an evening at the tavern, w. the neighbors gathered around him, all telling stories, drinking & enjoying themselves; & he would always contrive some trick, upon some one of the company, by which to make him pay the bill, & thus get out of it himself"- **969**

Porter- (s. Benjamin & ____ Emmons) c. 1852, an agent of the express line betw. Troy & NYC- **969**

Silas- blacksmith; res. S. of Daniel Marsh, Durham (Clarendon, Vt.); "very strenuous in religious matters at the very time he was doing acts the most widely rem. from such a character"; his family members were noted as "peculiarly sharp & witty"; ments. sons Oliver, Benjamin, David, & Solomon- **969**; for some yrs., a strip of land lying betw. him & Daniel Marsh, & prob. abt. 50 rods wide, was claimed & occ. by both of them; a house on this disputed land was occ. by a tenant of Daniel Marsh, & Whitney was always sore abt. this, as it made it easier for him to be ousted from the claim; one Sun., he strove to get possession by force, & after finishing his breakfast pudding, he went to the tenant house "& w/o ceremony put the occupant & his furniture out of doors" (a similar incident lead to the arrest of Rogers the Squatter, at Fitch's Point; see Livingston, Archibald; & Rogers, the Squatter,Vol. 1); the tenant sent word to Marsh, & he arr. to find Whitney "inside, w. the door fastened, & an axe in hand, threatening to knock grdf.'s brains out if he burst in the door"; at that point, Marsh went around the house, opened a window, & jumped in; by their mutual understanding, ea. then had a right to take in whatever they pleased, & Marsh reinstated his tenants, the Green family; not having anything of his own by which to jointly hold possession w. Green, Whitney gave up the contest; the disputed land was managed similarly- a cert. field was sown to rye, both commencing to plow it simult. from opp. ends, sowing & harvesting it together, cutting the grain & putting the bundles in stooks, equally dividing it; but at night, Whitney came w. a team & drew off all of the grain to his barn & so it became all his, as understood betw. the two; "In this singular way did they live, side by side, several yrs., perfectly understanding that when one got such an advantage over the other, there was no course whatever but for him to submit to it, & retaliate in some analogous way to balance the acct."; Dr. Fitch notes that this situation was referred to, p. 499, Slade's Vt. State Papers; he was noted for being much in the law, contesting "energetically & strenuously", but once decided, regarded things to be fully & completely ended in a matter, & would at once be as friendly & amicable to his opponent as though nothing had occurred; he once sued his son- in- law, Emmons, the tavernkeeper, on a charge amounting to flagrant dishonesty on Emmons' part, & was "insensible" to any pleas to kinship ties that Emmons plied upon him, but returned to normal relations once a decision had been given- **970**

Silas, Jr.- s. Silas; merch.; m. ____ Wilson- **969**

WIBIRD,
John, Esq.- m. Elizabeth, dau. Rev. Jabez & Elizabeth (Appleton) Fitch; their s. was Rev. Anthony, of Quincy, Mass.- **835**

WICKHAM,
Benjamin E.- 2nd Lt., 22nd N. Y. Inf.; promoted to 1st Lt., Sept. 3 1862, replacing Daniel Bungey- **1095b**

WICKS,
____ - c. 1790's, foll. ____ Mayhew, at Wm. Duer's store, Ft. Miller, N. Y., leaving in 1797- **1032**

Wickwive, or Wickwire, House- constructed c. 1787, & loc. on the turnpike, N. of Lansingburgh, N. Y.; recently (1850) pulled down; see Brick Houses- **840**

WIGGINS,
James- Co. A, 2nd N. Y., Northern Black Horse, Cav., 1861- 2- **1080**

WIGRAM,
John- surveyor; along w. Wm. Cockburn, in 1771, laid out the lots in the S. part of Socialborough township, Charlotte, N. Y. (Rutland, Vt.); Lots 1 & 26 described; an affidavit signed by him, 1782, attesting to their descriptions, but w/o witns.- **745**

WILCOX,
Family- from R. I., foll. Rev. war; res. Cambridge, or White Creek, N. Y.; currently (1850) res. in the old Colvin place, purch. abt. 1814, from Dr. Sanford Smith- **844**
George?- res. abt. 2 mi. W. of Granville, on the road to Hartford, in Hebron, N. Y.; was prob. one of Daniel Shays' men driven from Mass. foll. his revolt; he was confined in jail on a sentence of death, & his wf., being abt. the same size, passed his guards & went into his cell, quickly changing clothes w. him; he repassed the guards w/o notice, & when the switch was discovered, the officers insisted to her that she must be hung instead; knowing enough of the law to realize she was in no danger, she resisted & defied their intimidations; acc. Dr. Fitch, he was prob. one of six men sentenced to death in Berkshire co., all of who contrived to escape; refers p. 140, Hist. of Berkshire co.; part of his farm later comprised the farm of Esq. Pember- **921**
Hazard- an active 'Yorker', became a tory during the 1st yr. of the Rev. war; when some neighbors attempted to break into his house & arrest him, he struck one named Perry w. a heavy piece of wood, killing him; he then fled & never returned; refers Bennington article, Thompson's Gazetteer of Vt.; this was perh. 'the alarming affair that lately happened in this place' referred to by the Comm. of Safety meeting, Aug. 3, 1775, at Sancoick, N. Y.; see also, N. Y. Provincial Congress, Sept. 14, 1775- **783**; resolved by Albany Comm., Apr. 30, 1776, that he enter into bond w. sufficient security 'for his good behavior during the present contest' & not depart from the district he res. in until given permission by the Comm. of his district- **830**; his story not recoll. by Sidney Wells- **844**

Thurston- prob. res. betw. Cossayuna & Greenwich, N. Y.; May 1854/5, Patrick Walls was engaged by him as a gardener, foll. his recuperation at Archibald Hay's home- **1058**

WILDER,
John- quit claim by Jacob Marsh, Dec. 2, 1773, to Thomas Brayton, for Wilder's right of 100 acres in Socialborough, Charlotte co., N. Y. (Rutland, Vt.)- **745**

WILDLIFE- 762, 863, 881, 924, 925, 945, 989

WILKINSON,
Robert, Esq.- delivered an oration, Feb. 23, 1816, at the Congregational church, Granville, N. Y., in observance of Washington's birthday- **723**

WILLARD,
Dr.- res. Pawlet, Vt.; m. Nancy, dau. Ephriam Fitch; "moved to the west", & settl. Rochester, N. Y.; c. 1852, res. Browhelm, Ohio- **727**
Mrs. Emma Hart- (1787- 1870; founder, Troy Female Seminary, 1821) her "seminary" (now The Emma Willard School) loc. Troy, N. Y.; Mr. Ingalls obt. the services of Miss L. Philips, one of her graduates, as an assistant at the Union Village Academy, Greenwich, N. Y.- **732**
Jonathan- defendant, Oct. 19, 1774, in a case brought by John Munro- **878**

WILLET,
Col. Marinus- (1740- 1830; Lt. Col., 3rd N. Y.; Mayor, NYC, 1807- 11) companies of his regt. engaged the British at W. Canada creek, July 1781- 747; c. 1781, commanded N. Y. militia regt.- **756**; c. 1780, Robert Ayres, & 4 other apprentices of ____ Dickinson, of Stillwater, N. Y., enl. in Willet's regt. to escape the harsh treatment of their master- **1054**

WILLEY,
George- town clerk, Putnam, N. Y., serving 11 yrs. from its organization, 1806; mortgages Feb. 24, 1804, to William Cockburn, of Kingston, N. Y., Lot 23, Hutton's Bush, Westfield, N. Y., containing 149¾ acres, for $393.50; its description incl., in chains & links; refers Wash. Co. Deeds, Liber E, p. 14- **1092**

WILLIAMS,
Brig. Gen. Alpheus Starkey- (1810- 1878) brief ment.; Sept. 1862, his division incl. in Gen. Banks' corps- **1098**
Judge Chauncey K.- res. Rutland, Vt.; his letter to Deac. William Brayton, "dated Feb. & Mar. 1850", relates cert. information concerning the ejection of Thomas Brayton & Benjamin Hough from Vt. by Ethan Allen's forces; he further states no knowl. of Sunderland or Sawyer, & supposes the Warner in question to be Col. Warner, of Greenwiich, N. Y.; Dr. Fitch notes the mistake, w. a query that he

supposes that (Robert) Cockran prob. res. in Ft. Edward, foll. the events ment.; see
N. H./ Grants Controversy; & Vermonters- **746**; of Williams College, 1848, when
he sent a letter to Rev. L. Kellogg, of Whitehall, N. Y., containing several items of
biog. material on Maj. Philip Skene- **759**

Col.- (perh. Dr./ Gen. John?) his militia regt. marched to Ft. Ticonderoga, c. 1777,
& was among those retreating w. the army to Castleton, Vt., when the fort was
evac., & continued retreating w. the army to Ft. Ann, & finally arr. at Ft. Edward,
abt. mid- July- **750**

Delia- m. Alexander, s. Ebenezer & Betsey (Williams) Proudfit- **1045**

Rev. Eleazer- s. Thomas (DeRougers); he & his bro. John were educ. at
Longmeadow, Mass.; he became an Episcopal clergym. & missionary, spending
several yrs. at Green Bay, Wisc., foll. by St. Regis, N. Y.; referred to as the
informant for all the material concerning the McCrea massacre, as found in
Hough's Hist., his observations on the murder obt. from a Winnebago chief at
Green Bay, who claimed involvement- **1016**

Elisha- his property was cited, Nov. 20, 1772, as the N. boundary of Lot No. 5,
Socialborough, Charlotte co., N. Y. (Rutland, Vt.)- **745**

Col. Ephriam- (1714- 1755) he & King Hendrick, the Mohawk chief, were killed
during an ambuscade known as the Bloody Morning Scout (Sept. 8, 1755), during
the battle of Lake George- **989**

Frank- on the dayof the Coroner's Inquest, Feb. 17, 1858, into the death of Barney
McEntee, he went in search of the red flannel wrist linings from McEntee's gloves,
& found several small pieces in the middle of the road, 15 or 20 rods from Ira
Sisson's house, White Creek, N. Y.- **1048s**

Jaben- of Granville, N. Y.; Nov. 10, 1783, conveyed Lot 9, Daniel Fisher's tract, to
Nathaniel Draper- **(L)- 936**

John- s. Thomas (DeRougers); he & his bro. Eleazer were educ. at Longmeadow,
Mass.; while their father was neutral during the War of 1812, he & his bro. took
opp. sides (although who was aligned w. which side, was not disclosed here)- **1016**

John- (s. Col. John & Ann Roy) m. Harriet Martin, of Avon, N. Y.; children- John
M., Fanny H., & Harriet M. (his mother's surname given as Wray, Vol. 4)- **1045**

Col. John- (Maj.) was Marshall of the Day, Nov. 29, 1814, at a public dinner held
in Salem, N. Y., honoring Commodore Macdonough- **709**; his half sist. was Sarah
Turner, wf. Walter Martin- **730**; (s. Dr./ Gen. John & Susannah Thomas) m. 1.
Ann, dau. Esq. W. Roy (see Wray; Vol. 4); 2. Almira Smith; 3. Fanny Hunt;
children, all by 1st wf.-

1. Mary, m. George W. Bethune

2. John, m. Harriet Martin- **1045**; Aug. 26, 1831, mortgage of Lot 23, Hutton's
Bush, Westfield, N. Y., assigned to him by Alexander Cockburn, surviving
administrator of William Cockburn; spring 1862, its sale advertised by Williams'
executors, for $855.59, then claimed due- **1092**

Dr./ Gen. John- (1753- 1806; N. Y. Prov. Congress, 1775- 77; Senate, 1777- 78;
Assembly, 1781- 82; Regents, 1784; 4th- 5th Congress, 1795- 99) (as Gen.) purch.
orig. Turner's Patent lot owned by Hamilton McCollister, from Ebenezer Clark-

744; (Gen.) selected along w. William Marsh, as Charlotte co. delegates to N. Y. Provincial Congress; seated May 24, 1775- 773; (Gen.) appt. by Provincial Congress, June 14, 1775, as part of a comm. to investigate the conduct of Wm. Duer, Esq.; June 15th, became sole Charlotte co. delegate to Provincial Congress foll. gr. of a leave of absence to Wm. Marsh; gr. leave to go home, June 23rd, & left June 26th- 777; by order, June 30, 1775, was appt. surgeon, Green Mtn. regt., to be effective foll. examination of a 3 man board; at the time of the exam, he was absent- 778; additional Charlotte co. delegates were elected, June 29, 1775, to serve w. him, or in his absence, in N. Y. Provincial Congress- 780; represented Charlotte co., July 26, 1775, when Prov. Congress resumed- 781; he & Alex. Campbell appt. Charlotte co. delegates, Jan. 25, 1776, to Prov. Congress; seated Feb. 13th, he attended through the session, which closed Mar. 16th; rec'd. recommendation for appt. as Col., 1st battalion, Charlotte co. militia, by Comm. of Safety; appt. to rank, Feb. 19th; he appl. on the same day, & obt. blank commissions for 3 minuteman companies for the co.- 784; chairman, Charlotte co. Comm. of Safety; appt. along w. Majors Webster & Malcom as Charlotte co. delegates to 3rd Prov. Congress; attended Prov. Convention, July 9, 1776, along w. Wm. Duer & Alex. Webster- 785; inquires, along w. other members of Charlotte co. Comm., July 25, 1777, regarding validity of recent co. elections, if held only in part of district; later returned as Senator, E. district of Charlotte co.; appt. by Prov. Convention, May 8, 1777, as (Assist.) Judge in co.- 787; sends letter to John McKesson, Esq., of Provincial Congress, June 23, 1777, from New Perth (Salem, N. Y.), concerning pamphlets lately circulated in the Grants in response to recent proceedings in N. Y.; also gives Charlotte co. results for election of Gov. & Lt. Gov.; makes request on behalf of Capt. Martin concerning procurement of Lot No. 68, Argyle Patent; & gives news obt. at Otter creek from Canadians there, w. regard to conditions in Canada, & the ill use of its inhabitants by the few British there- 789; his letter from Albany, N. Y., Aug. 10, 1775, states that he arr. here to confer w. Col. Van Schaik on new medicines to be obt. for the battalion, when he discovered, to his surprise, that Stephen McCrey (McCrea) had been appt. surgeon in his place; expresses his lack of understanding over the 'partiality' of his replacement, giving an acct. of his prev. training- attending St. Thomas' hospital, London, for a yr., & being 1st Mate on a Man- of- War; his skill & practice, particularly in surgery, having the wnd. at Ticonderoga referred to him by surgeons there; his surprise concurred in by Gen. Montgomery & Col. Van Schaik, as members of battalion are chiefly familiar to him in his private practice; gives note of his willingness to take a qualifying exam, even if necessitating a trip to NYC, noting that Albany doctors have refused to examine him unless appt. to do so; remarks that he has 'amputating & all kinds of instruments for a campaign', & has already planned his business acc. to the earlier notice of his appt.; refers p. 62, Correspondence of Provincial Congress- 790; as he signed the same minister's call, c. 1785, as Dr. Sanford Smith, Dr. Fitch specul. whether or not they may have studied together at one time- 844; purch. the foll. forfeited lands- Dec. 12, 1784, Artillery Patent, Lot 80, containing 242 acres, for £ 320; in Skenesborough, N. Y.,

Dec. 7, 1784- Lots 1- 4, 9, 19- 21, 25, 26, 28, 29, 34, & 33 & 36, w. respective acreages of 100, 115, 138, 149, 209, 276, 288, 288, 171, 314, 269, 216, & 400, & the last 2 lots containing 500 acres ea.; w. the foll. respective prices, in £- 76, 185, 322, 380, 101, 40, 41, 41, 376, 200, 440, 130, 180, & the last two lots at the combined price of £ 130; also in Skenesborough, Feb. 27, 1787- Lot 24, containing 171 acres, for £ 376; & Lot 29, containing 108 acres, for £ 5 8s; purch. along w. John Taylor & Stephen Lush, May 25, 1785, Skenesborough Lots 15- 18, containing 1,615 acres, for £ 155; & Lots 30, 32, & 46, containing 1,218½ acres, for £ 277; also, along w. Joseph Stringham, & Samuel & William McKinly, Feb. 27, 1787, Skenesborough Lot 23, containing 500 acres, for £ 2,750- **(L)- 875**; plaintiff, Nov. 3, 1784, vs. Robert Cochran, Esq.- **878**; w. wf. Susanna, admin. of James Turner, Nov. 3, 1784, vs. Elizabeth & Martha McCrea- **878½**; appl. to Board, Albany Comm., June 13, 1776, for a dozen lbs. of powder & a proportion o ball, for Charlotte co.- **890**; (Gen.) a dau. m. Anthony I. Blanchard- **914**; although an acute & skillful physician, acc. Judge Blanchard, his medical skills were chiefly derived from experience, personal judgment, & observation, as his educ. was quite limited; member, U. S. Congress (4th & 5th sessions, 1795- 99); nr. the end of one session, Abner Stone, then Wash. co. Sheriff, became infected w. a lock jaw- like ailment, & a message was left for him to attend to him immed. upon his return from the session; after examining the case & attending circumstances, he suggeste a fragm. of material had been imbedded in Stone's leg, a theory concurred in by th Sheriff, but objected to by other attendant physicians; Stone allowed him to cut open the wnd., & at length, he rem. a piece of rawhide, leading to the patient's rapid recovery; his selection of Salem as a home, was prob. the mere accident of "an adventurer in search of some spot to make his fortune"; only 2 or 3 physicians res. in the area at the time, & they sought to discredit his reputation; see Salem, N. Y.; he went "up into the edge of Vt.", toward Rupert, when he 1st arr. here & lost his purse, w. 50 gold guineas in it; he supposed a search for it in the muddy road was in vain, but a few days later, a man arr. w. his purse, w/o a single piece missing from the purse, "although the finder appeared to be in humble circumstances that would tempt him strongly to abstract some of it" (compare w. § 671, Vol. 1; & § 924); his fortune acq. by purch. of confiscated lands foll. the Rev war; he would have been Commissioner for their sale, except that he desired to purch. lands; see Webster, Alexander; "w. sensible men, made no pretensions to ledgerdemain [sic]- but some of his tricks w. the vulgar, made them firmly believe he could swallow log fence", an idea he fostered prob. to give stronger faith & confidence in him- **915**; while NYS Senator, 1791, he & Asa Adgate were referre to by Gen. Schuyler as politicians of the time who seem to have assisted Aaron Burr in his intrigues leading to Schuyler's defeat in his re- election bid as U. S. Senator- **920**; on his arr. here, he 1st res. along the Indian river, bef. he settl. in Salem; when he was deciding on whether to locate here, he arranged to stay w. Reuben Stoddard, & availed himself of some trout fishing; he became so excited w the sport & his luck, that he scarcely observed the distance he had wandered, & discovered on his return that he had lost his purse of 30 gold guinea pieces, all he possessed to make a beginning in the world; he retraced his steps w/o discovering the purse, & made additional searches w. his host bef. it was loc.; Dr. Fitch notes this incident as pivotal in Williams' decision to remain in the area; see Stoddard, Reuben- **924**; Salem Comm. of Safety met at his house- **925**; Mar. 7, 1785, sold Lot No. 264, Turner's Patent, toWilliam Henderson, for £ 250; he & Joseph Caldwell provide bail, Oct. 20, 1785, for Edward Savage's bond as loan officer; along w. Joseph McCracken, purch. Lot 1, Morrison's Patent, from Comm. of Sequestration, & deeded same, Aug. 16, 1787, to John Stockings; along w. McCracken, conveys other lots in Morrison's Patent to Asaph Cook & David Curtis; deed, Dec. 16, 1791, Dr. Peletiah Fitch to James Tomb, acknowl. bef. him & recorded, July 26, 1792- **(L)- 936**; along w. Edward Savage & Joseph Calwell, May 9, 1786, provide security for Savage as loan officer, in putting out £ 200,000 in bills of credit; c. 1782, Lot 8, Morrison's Patent, conveyed by Williams & McCracken to Asaph Cook, for £ 20; & Lots 9 & 12, of same patent, conveyed to Daniel Curtis, for £ 7 4s 2d- **(L)- 936b**; (Gen.) could not be confided in "for strict honesty & integrity", acc. Judge John Savage; during the Rev. war, he was guilty of an act rare for a public man in those days, but common since- he held an office in which he was responsible for paying the troops for their services, & he added imaginary names to the list, pocketing the extra money; this fact, acc. Judge Savage, was fully proved against him when he was a NYS Senator, & he was expelled, as shown in their journal; but he was so popular among the people, that he was immed. re- elected & seated, as his supporters "imputed this expulsion to the malice of his political & personal enemies"- **995**; (Gen.) his eldest dau. m. Anthony I. Blanchard, Sr.- **1012**; (Gen.) dau. Susan, m. Alexander Proudfit, D. D.- **1019**; m. 1. Susannah Thomas, wid. James Turner; 2. Apr. 18, 1803, Wid. Mary Townley, of NYC; his 1st wf. d. Dec. 30, 1799, at 57; & his 2nd wf. d. Aug. 19, 1819, at 50, w/o issue; & he d. July 22, 1806, at 53 yrs., 10 mos.- **1044**; children by Gen. John & Wid. Susannah (Thomas) Turner-

1. Maria, m. Hon. Anthony I. Blanchard
2. Susannah, m. Alexander Proudfit, D. D.
3. Betsey, m. Ebenezer Proudfit
4. Col. John, m. 1. Ann Roy (see Wray, Vol. 4); 2. Almira Smith; 3. Fanny Hunt- **1045**; brief. ment.- **1049**

Samuel- Dutch?; once taught school in a house nr. Daniel Livingston's, Fitch's Point, Salem, N. Y.; was prob. a bro.- in- law of the Taller family, as he res. w. them- **859**

Thomas- m. _____ Taller; he occ. Timothy Titus' place at Fitch's Point, along w. his bro.- in- law; both later rem. Half Moon, N. Y., & kept a tavern there- **803**

Thomas- (s. _____ & Mary DeRougers) b. abt. 1758/9, Caughnawaga, N. Y.; his grdm. was Eunice, dau. Rev. John, taken captive at Deerifeld, Mass., 1704; his mother d. when he was an inf., & he was raised by his aunt Catharine; in 1772, his adoptive parents were induced by Rev. Levi Frisbee, under the auspices of Rev. Dr. Wheelock, to send him to Dartmouth, but sickness prevented him; his adoptive father took him 'on hunting rambles, to Crown Point, Lake George, & the vicinity of Ft. Edward'; in 1777, he was made a chief, & gradually acq. the esteem of British officers; called upon w. others of his tribe to join w. Burgoyne's expedition, his feelings had begun to be enl. on the American side, & he went more in hopes of sparing bloodshed, than promoting the British cause; after joining the expedition at Cumberland Head (Plattsburgh, N. Y.), he was later directed to pursue the Provincial retreat from Ticonderoga; but, on pretense of falling on their flanks, 'he is sd. to have purposely led his party by a too circuitous route to effect their object'; he was also sent against Bennington, but did little for the services he was engaged in, almost coming into confrontation w. some of the British officers of the expedition; it was sd. that he was solicited to bring Jane McCrea into Burgoyne's camp, but refused, & foll. Burgoyne's rebuke of the Indians after her massacre, reportedly left the British camp & returned home; visited his New England relatives, 1782, & repeatedly afterw.; neutral during the War of 1812, his sons John & Eleazer took opp. sides; he d. Aug. 16, 1849, in his native village; refers pgs. 200- 203, Hough's Hist.- **1016**

William- "(Maj. Williams so styled) (of Marlborough)" was seated June 21, 1775, as Cumberland co. delegate, N. Y. Provincial Congress- **777**

Williams College- opened Oct. 1791, as Williamstown Free School, Rev. Ebenezer Fitch, D. D., its Principal; it 'became so prosperous it was charted as a college, & he its President from 1794 till 1815'; refers pgs. 167- 170, Hist. of Berkshire Co.- **799**

Williamstown, Mass.- foll. the evac. of Salem, N. Y., Aug. 1777, Robert Getty brought his family to the S. part of the town for safety; squads & companies passed through here, on their way to the battle of Bennington- **744**

WILLOUGHBY,
Samuel- constable, Albany co., N. Y.; affidavits by him, sent by John Munro, May 30, 1771, to Goldbrow Banyer; testif. that he was overtaken on the highway, May 16th, by Thomas French, Charles Bullen, & Martin Powel, of Princetown (Manchester, Vt.), along w. a no. of other rioters, all armed w. clubs; French then laid hold of him, & w. a club raised over his head, threatened his life unless he carry off the writ of ejectment that he had earlier served on his wf. during his absence; on his refusal, Bullen approached & laid it (the club?) on his arm & obliged that he bring off the writ or his life would be in danger; further, that on the night of May 23rd, he lodged at Samuel Safford's house while on his way to Bennington serve some Executions; at abt. 9 or 10:00 PM, the house was alarmed by gun firing, & in the morning, he discovered the barn door to be open, & his horse shot dead; John Munro notes that the felon who shot Willoughby's horse, in his confession, implicated 2 others in the act, who prob. will not be caught- **899**

WILSON,

____- m. Lavina, dau. Lemuel Dwelly, in Canandaigua co., N. Y.- **731**

____- m. Silas Whitney, Jr., of Durham (Clarendon, Vt.); her family was identified as one of those then (1852) holding conventions to make arrangements for obt. an immense fortune they believed that they were entitled to in England- **969**

____- res. Hebron, N. Y.; m. Jane, dau. Deac. John & Eleanor (Webster) Steele- **1047**

____- c. 1859, res. Albany, N. Y.; a distant relation of Nathan W. Wilson; attended Salem Academy, 1817- 19, boarding w. Dr. Proudfit's family; m. 1. ____, sist. Daniel Dickinson; 2. ____; reports that Mr. Shepherd, a waiter in David Russell's family, was consumed by fire (n. d.) when his breath ignited; c. 1819, he taught school for sevearl yrs. in Northumberland, N. Y., & was foll. there by Silas Wright; he later taught in Canada, & Albany, & "is now peddling books in a small way, around the public houses in Albany"- **1053**

Benjamin- res. W. Hebron, N. Y.; niece Eliza, m. James, s. James & Lydia (Martin) McNitt- **731**

Charles W.- oath of alleg.; Co. D, 22nd N. Y. Inf.- **(L)**- **1074**

Dr.- c. 1780's, superintended a 'celebrated institution' of academic studies in N. J., that was once attended by Rev. Samuel Tomb (prob. Dr. Peter, 1746- 1825; see Vol. 1)- **810**

Gile- of Black Creek (Hebron, N. Y.); Aug. 14, 1786, deeds Lot 35, Scott & Kemp's Patent, to James Wilson- **(L)**- **936**

James- res. Black Creek (Hebron, N. Y.); rec'd. recommendation, Jan. 25, 1776, for appt. as 2nd Lt., Charlotte co. militia- **784**

James- Lot 35, Scott & Kemp's Patent, deeded to him, Aug. 14, 1786, by Gile Wilson- **(L)**- **936**

Jane- m. William, s. John & Eleanor (Lowrie) Lytle- **737**

Lucius E.- (L. B.) oath of alleg.; Co. D, 22nd N. Y. Inf.- **(L)**- **1074**; Lt., Co. D, 22nd N. Y. Inf.; promoted, Sept. 11, 1862, foll. the death of Capt. H. S. Milliman- **1095b**

N. Albert- (s. Nathan W. & ____ McCracken) b. Salem, N. Y.; member, 44th N. Y. Inf. (Ellsworth Regt.); d. Oct. 1861, Wash., D. C.; bur. Dec. 10th, gr. 2, soldier's plot, Evergreen Cemetery, Salem, N. Y.; "He was the 1st martyr from this town, who perished in this wicked war"; slightly unwell from the affect of measles bef. leaving Albany, he was unfit to proceed from Wash., D. C.; resolutely determined to continue, pneumonia afterw. set in- **1081**

Nathan- (1759- 1834; Sheriff, Wash. Co., 1802- 06; 10th Congress, 1808, 1809) defeated Dr. Asa Fitch, Sr., in U. S. Congresional election, 1808- **799**

Nathan W.- prob. res. Salem, N. Y. (see Vol. 4); noted by Dr. Fitch that his family was distantly related to ____ Wilson, of Albany, N. Y.- **1053**; m. ____ McCracken; his s. N. Albert, was the 1st Salem death in the Civil War- **1081**

Nathaniel White- (s. Samuel & Mary Lytle) m. Matta, or Martha, Qua; several children- **1069**

Samuel- res. onthe W. line w. Hebron, Argyle, N. Y.; m. Nancy, dau. William & Mary (Hanna) Lytle; 2 children- Nathaniel White, m. Matta Qua; & Maria H.- **1069**

WINCHESTER,
Capt.- Aug.- Dec. 1777, commanded a port. of Capt. Stockwell's co., left at Bennington, Vt., to guard the wnd. & sick prisoners from the battle there, while the remainder of his co. went to Stillwater, N. Y.- **751**

Windsor, Vt.- c. 1761, chartered by Gov. John Wentworth of N. H., & incl. M. H. & Samuel Wentworth as shareholders- **928**

WING,
David- his affidavit, June 21, 1771, states that he was commanded to assist Samuel Pease, constable, in arresting Thomas French of Princetown, on May 21st, for rioting; on their arr. in that town, they were met by a no. of rioters armed w. clubs, & two w. guns; when coming to French's house, they found it surrounded by men, vowing against the constable & his party- **900**
Harvey S., Sr.- c. 1827/8, purch. Peter Parker's farm, in the NE part of Hartford, 3 mi. from N. Granville, N. Y.; c. 1874, his s. Harvey S., Jr., occ. the farm- **759s**

WINNIE,
Family- c. 1765, res. Schaghticoke, N. Y.; Phineas Whiteside left his family w. them while he constructed his family's cabin in Cambridge- **805**

WINSLOW,
Family- gave Plymouth Colony & Mass. "several governors & sturdy patriots"; their family tomb loc. Marshfield, Mass.- **988**
Hon. Isaac, Esq.- d. Dec. 14, 1738, at 67; bur. Marshfield, Mass.- **988**
John- dau. Sarah, m. 1. Miles Standish, Jr.; 2. Tobias Payne, in 1669; & 3. Richard Middlecot- **757**
Hon. John, Esq.- d. Apr. 17, 1774, at 72; bur. Marshfield, Mass.- **988**
Hon. Josiah- (b. ca. 1629- 1680; Assist. Gov., Mass., 1657- 73; Gov. of New Plymouth, 1673- 80); d. Dec. 18, 1630, at 73; bur. Marshfield, Mass. (his death date apparently miscopied from record)- **988**
Capt. Nathaniel- d. Dec. 1, 1719, at 81; bur. Marshfield, Mass.- **988**

WINTERBOTTOM,
James- gr. to him & 9 other private soldiers forms part of the N. boundary of a gr., Sept. 7, 1771, to Thomas Trickett, loc. on E. side of Wood creek as it enters into Lake Champlain- **(L)- 936**

WISCONSIN- 766, 1005, 1041;

  Counties- Columbia- 1005; Dade- 848; Lake- 731; Rochester- 1090;

  Cities & Towns- Fall River- 1005; Fond du Lac- 730, 731; Green Bay- 1016;
Jamesville- 1090; Kenosha- 730, 1038; La Crosse- 731; Milwaukee- 731, 940,
1005, 1069; Port Jackson- 1069;

  Rosendale- 759s; Sun Prarie- 848; Waukesha- 1044, 1086, 1090; Wilburn- 731

WITCHCRAFT, Witches- a horse purch. by Moses Martin, Sr., eventually
developed an ailment resembling blind staggers, & at length "was seen to be
walking upon the top of a log fence, & actually walked thus, a dist. of abt. 20
rods"; from the unusual performance, the residents of Fitch's Pont "{very sagely}
concluded on all hands that he was bewitched- for belief in witches was almost
universal at that time"- **870**; old Mrs. Tosh, c. 1800, res. E. Greenwich, N. Y.;
from her active & inquisitive nature in gathering the news in her neighborh. &
knowing all that was going on, "narrating time & place & persons present, so
correctly, when it was inexplicable how she got her information, she came to be
universally regarded as a witch"; she was subj. to freq. nosebleeds, & one night,
began to bleed profusely from the nose & mouth; not being able to staunch the flow
in any usual way, her husb. went to their neighbor, Mrs. Cherry, for help,
exclaiming 'Jennie is deeing'; but she was dead bef. they returned to the house (d.
Nov. 19, 1802; see Vol. 1), "which presented an awful spectacle; the floor & bed
being covered w. blood"; on this same night, a cat was discovered, either in the
cellar of Alexander Livingston, or James Shaw, acc. witns., "lapping the cream
from off the milk- as the cream had freq. been taken from the milk bef." (a similar
incident ment. earlier, § 59; see Witchcraft, Vol. 1); as it ran out of the cellar, the
cat was struck across the nose, causing the blood to spurt from the nose & mouth,
& it became the current report in the area that Mrs. Tosh had transformed herself
into a cat to lick the cream & had thus been killed, bef. returning to her human
form; for a more plausible explanation, see Von Willebrand's disease- **871**; c. 1780,
during an attempt to capt. John Younglove, of Cambridge, N. Y., the party's escape
route lead across the Battenkill & past John McNeil's, in E. Greenwich; their
guide, Neal Gillespie, warned that McNeil's dog would bark; but Myers, the party's
leader, sd. it would not, & when this actually occurred, it was thought at the time
that Myers "had some charm or spell which he drew over the dog, that kept him
quiet"- **985**; it was the "current report" in all of Argyle that Jane McCrea's ghost
appeared every night to her lover, David Jones; while in Canada, her bro., Col.
John, inquired of Jones upon this point & hedeclared it not to be so, saying that he
had only seen her in his imagination- **1061**; 'Castle Bininger', the homestead of
Abraham Bininger, Sr., loc. Camden valley, Salem, N. Y., was sd. to be haunted
w. ghosts, one of the rumors being that his son, Isaac, had murdered a man there
who had a quantity of money- **1076**

WOLCOTT,
Family- operated factories at Whitestown, N. Y., but closed them down prior 1853-
839

WOLFE,
C. M.- (Wolf) oath of alleg.; Co. D, 22nd N. Y. Inf.- **(L)- 1074**
Gen. James- (1727- 1759) the 42nd regt. of Highlanders was present w. him at the taking of Quebec, & incl. John Munro, Esq., of Shaftsbury hollow, Vt., among its troops- **812**

WOOD,
Isaac- was prominent among Quaker families who settl. Walloomsac Patent bef. the Rev. war; ments. a grds., John- **806**
Capt. John- chairman, Aug. 7, 1775, of Comm. of Safety meeting held at John Rensselaer's, Sancoick, N. Y.- **783**
Myron- Co. A, 2nd N. Y., Northern Black Horse, Cav., 1861- 2- **1080**

WOODALL,
Jonas- May 9, 1786, purch. Lots 30 & 31, Scott & Kemp's Patent, ea. containing 238 acres, from Samuel McWhorter, of Hebron, N. Y.- **(L)- 396**; above ment. lots purch. from McWhorter for £ 340- **(L)- 936b**

WOODARD,
Daniel- res. upper part, Munro's meadows, Hebron, N. Y.; m. Miriam, dau. James & Lydia (Martin) McNitt; foll. her father's death, they owned & occ. the old family homestead; afew yrs. bef. he d., her father had built a fine new dwelling on the farm- **731**
Lyman- c. 1800's, res. Battenville, N. Y.; a sist. m. David Tefft- **971**

WOODBRIDGE,
Col.- July 1777, commanded a Mass. regt. sent to Bennington, Vt., & from there, to Stillwater, N. Y.- **751**

WOODHULL,
Gen. Nathaniel- (1722- 1776; member N. Y. Provincial Assembly, 1768- 75) Col. Philip Schuyler co- operated w. him, George Clinton, & other patriots in the N. Y. Assembly 'in their struggle for the rights of the colonies against the British govt.'- **920**

WOODWARD,
Lucy- m. Thomas, s. Andrew & Elizabeth (Fitch) Rowland- **799**

WOODWORTH,
Ephriam- res. Northumberland, N. Y.; m. anner (Hannah?), dau. Ephriam? More-
850

WOORSTEN,
Gen.- prob. Col. Thaddeus Cook's regt. of his brigade was stat., Oct. 1776, at the
"saw pits", Rye, N. Y.- **752**

WRIGHT,
Abraham- s. Job, & his 1st wf.; kept Wright's ferry, nr. Stillwater, N. Y.- **850**
Alexander- tory; res. Salem, N. Y.; he "pilfered sheep from his neighbors flocks,
till he coll. a large flock" & then drove it to Burgoyne's camp at Ft. Edward, where
he was pd. for it in silver; foll. Burgoyne's surrender, a suit was commenced
against him by Capt. Barns, & he was freq. over to Neal Gillespie's to find out
what points Gillespie might be willing to swear to in court; however, he was unable
to get Gillespie to swear to all he wanted, the situation being different, from
Gillespie's perspective, "from what it was to tell 'a smooth lie' to keep himself out
of prison"; the outcome of his case not disclosed; he later rem. to Canada; a dau.
m. Andrew Martin, & he would often send her money; on visits, he would remark
on the difference betw. the currencies, it being 'all jaws (joes) & half jaws' in
Canada; acc. Dr. Fitch, he prob. returned & was bur. here (§ 98; Vol. 1)- **977**
Alva- blacksmith & horse doctor; res. next E. of Beaver brook, on S. side of West
St., Salem, N. Y.; the Bible, loc. in his pew of the Assoc. Ref. Presbyt. church,
contained several memoranda concerning weather events betw. 1806 & 1835,
copied by Dr. Fitch; see Weather; ments. s. John, & a dau., m. Henry Clark; & he
d. Jan. 4, 1867, at 61- **1047b**; same material; d. June 4, 1864, at 61- **1047½b**
Daniel- acc. Nov. 26, 1773 deed description, his assigns own Lot 29, Kingsbury,
N. Y.- **(L)- 936**
Earl P.- c. 1856, res. on the flats, prob. E. of Fitch's Point, Salem, N. Y., in abt. a
direct line from Dr. Fitch's office- **996**
Eleanor- m. William, s. James & Elizabeth (Lytle) Rowan, as his 1st wf.- **737**
Esther- m. Timothy, s. Timothy & Esther (Platt) Fitch- **799**
Family- those connected w. the Martin & Angel families res. W. of Easton, N. Y.,
along the Hudson river- **861**
Job- m. 1. ____; a son, Abraham; 2. Anna, dau. Ephriam? More; a son, John- **850**
John- Co. A, 2nd N. Y., Northern Black Horse, Cav., 1861- 2- **1080**
Lt. Jonathan- c. 1781, officer, Capt. Parmlee Allen's co., Col. Walbridge's militia
regt.- **749**; ment. again as officer, same unit, 1781, along w. Lt. Stewart- **754**
Joseph- blacksmith; m. Lucinda C. Martin, as her 3rd husb.- **730**
Lockland- res. Cambridge, N. Y.; was a neighbor of Sidney Wells, & related to
Wells a no. of incidents connected w. his parents' house that he recoll. from his
childhood days- **840**; (Lauchlin) d. Jan. 9, 1854, at 80, Cambridge, N. Y.; he had
res. on the same farm for 80 yrs., leaving a wf. & 9 children; 'what is very
remarkable, his own death is the 1st that ever occurred in the family'; he & his wf.

entered the Presbyterian church abt. 50 yrs. ago, & their children range in age from the oldest, at abt. 60 yrs., to the youngest, at nearly 40 yrs. of age- **1024**

Morgan- c. Mar. 1854/5, he & Nathaniel Carswell were standing in a roadway N. of Greenwich, N. Y., when they were accosted by Priest Quigley, who described to them the affair that he had just been involved in w. Archibald Hay, but discovered that his own behavior in the matter was met w/o favor, or sympathy, from their prespectives- **1058**

Moses- d. June 8, 1848, at 75- **(L)**- **772**

Reuben- of Stillwater, N. Y.; m. Phebe, dau. Ephriam? More; unrelated to either Abraham, or Job Wright; had son Silas, & other children- **850**

Hon. Silas- (1795- 1847; N. Y. Senate, 1823- 27; Comptroller, 1829- 33; 20th Congress, 1827- 29) c. 1819, taught school in the district adjoin. Northumberland, N. Y., & then foll. ____ Wilson (n. d.) at Northumberland- **1053**

Susan- m. John, s. Hon. Anthony I. & Maria (Williams) Blanchard- **1045**

Y

YATES,
Abraham- (Abram, Jr., 1724- 1796; Albany Comm. of Correspondence, 1774- 76;
Pres., N. Y. Prov. Congress, 1775- 76; Senate, 1777; Cont. Congress, 1788- 90;
Mayor, Albany, 1790- 96) June 14, 1775, appt. by N. Y. Provincial Congress as
comm. member to investigate conduct of William Duer, Esq.- 777; he &
Gouverneur Morris appt. as a comm. to go to Gen. Schuyler's HQ at Ft. Edward,
N. Y., to observe the current situation in that area, July 1777- 796; he & Morris
report from Moses creek (kill), July 23, 1777, describing Gen. Schuyler's retreat to
this area, & the daily departure of militia from the army's ranks, & possible
countermeasures that might serve to halt the progress of Burgoyne's expedition-
797
Capt. Jacob L.- of Waterford, N. Y.; May 25, 1861, commanded Co. A, 22nd
N. Y. Inf.- **(L)- 1074**
Peter- (Peter Waldron; 1747- 1826; Comm. of Correspondence, 1775; N. Y.
Regents, 1784; Assdembly, 1784, 1785; Cont. Congress, 1785- 87) corresponds
from NYC, June 14, 1775, to Albany Comm., concerning the arr. of Maj. Philip
Skene in Philadelphia, & his subsequent arrest & rem. to Lancaster, Pa.; see
Skene, Col. Philip, Vols. 1 & 4- **833**; (P. W.) atty. for Thomas Stone, Oct. 19,
1773, vs. Jonathan Baker; motions made on his behalf by Mr. Roorback, Charlotte
co. Court- **878**
Robert, Esq.- prob. Sheriff, Albany co.; "audibly read" a writ of ejection at James
Breckenridge's door, Aug. 1771, so that it was clear that those within had been
reasoned w. & distinctly told what the consequences would be should they remain-
903

YEMMONDS,
Elizabeth- m. William Marsh, some time after 1676, prob. within the vicinity of
Stonington, Conn.- **962**

YOUNG,
Capt.- accomp. Commodore Macdonough (prob. as his aide) to a public reception
held in Salem, N. Y., on Nov. 29, 1814, honoring Macdonough for his victory at
Plattsburgh; he was toasted on this occasion by Hon. John Savage, & in turn,
toasted the citizens of Salem- **709**
Lt. Joseph L.- Co. K, 93rd N. Y. Inf.- **1090b**
Dr. Thomas- (1732- 1777) James Duane noted July 10, 1777, at the Continental
Congress in Philadelphia, that he might be the probable architect of the current
effort to have 'our north eastern country' admitted into Congress as the State of
Vermont- **797**

YOUNGLOVE,

Family- from N. J.; bros. John & Joseph, both members, Cambridge Comm. of Safety; they res. White Creek, N. Y., during the Rev. war- **843**

Hon. John- (Col.) rem. Jackson, N. Y. foll. the Rev. war, & afterw., S. of the Cambridge bur. grd.; children-

   1. dau., m. ____ Cown, of Union Village (Greenwich, N. Y.)

   2. dau., m. 1. ____ Haynes; 2. perh. ____ Breckenridge, of Bennington, Vt.

   3. Moses, merch., Union Village, where he d.; refers Stone's Life of Brant,
      v. 1, Appendix 14, which prob. referred to an uncle of the same name

   4. Lewis, res. & d. Union Village

   5. Lucas, rem. Trenton, N. Y., & d. there ca. 1847/8; his wf. Martha d. Nov. 29, 1810, at 63; & he d. Feb. 3, 1821, at 77- **843**; presented a complaint, May 23, 1776, to Albany Comm. of Correspondence, saying that Peter Miller of Cambridge had declared an oath obliging his service in the king's troops- **888**; the party that attacked him during the Rev. war (§ 250) was lead by a man named Myers, who had a grudge against him & had come down from Canada to take him prisoner & burn his house; this raiding party's escape through Argyle was guided by Neal Gillespie; his wf. later recoll. that her wardrobe had been rifled through during the attack, & her chemise was the best garment left to her by the intruders; see Vol. 1- **985**

Joseph- bro. Hon. John; rem. Trenton, N. Y. after the Rev. war; a dau. m. William McCracken; he d. Mar. 30, 1810, at 68- **843**

Moses- m. Hannah, dau. Daniel Wells, as her 1st husb.; 2 children- Moses; & Ann Eliza, who m. Chauncey Ransom; & she afterw. m. ____ Cobb- **841**

Moses, Jr.- (s. Moses & Hannah Wells) c. 1850, res. Cleveland, Ohio- **841**

Made in the USA
Las Vegas, NV
25 February 2021